Microcomputers for Twenty-First Century Educators

Microcomputers for Twenty-First Century Educators

Third Edition

James Lockard

Peter D. Abrams

Wesley A. Many

Northern Illinois University

HarperCollins*CollegePublishers*

Sponsoring Editor: Christopher Jennison
Project Coordination and Text Design: Ruttle, Shaw & Wetherill, Inc.
Cover Designer: Molly Heron
Cover Illustrator: David Tillinghast
Production Manager: Hilda Koparanian
Compositor: BookMasters, Inc.
Printer and Binder: Malloy Lithography, Inc.
Cover Printer: Malloy Lithography, Inc.

Microcomputers for Twenty-First Century Educators, Third Edition
Copyright © 1994 by James Lockard, Peter D. Abrams, and Wesley A. Many

Library of Congress Cataloging-in-Publication Data

Lockard, James.
    Microcomputers for twenty-first century educators / James Lockard,
Peter D. Abrams, Wesley A. Many.—3rd ed.
        p.   cm.
    Rev. ed. of: Microcomputers for educators. 2nd ed. 1990.
    Includes bibliographical references and index.
    ISBN 0-673-52216-4
        1. Computer-assisted instruction—United States.
2. Microcomputers—United States. I. Abrams, Peter D. II. Many,
Wesley A. III. Lockard, James. Microcomputers for educators.
IV. Title.
LB1028.5.L58 1993
371.3'34'0973—dc20   93-5898
                                                      CIP

93 94 95 96 9 8 7 6 5 4 3 2 1

For Kathy, Barb, and Peg

Brief Contents

Contents

Preface

Microcomputers for Twenty-First Century Educators is based on our belief that computers are an inescapable part of education for, and in, the twenty-first century, both in the United States and worldwide. Computers are no panacea for the ills of education, but they can improve teaching and learning, if used appropriately. The challenge is to employ these extremely powerful tools to their greatest advantage. To do so, students and teachers alike must become *computer competent*. Computer competent means being able to take full advantage of the technology to enhance and expand learning opportunities, teaching methods, and ultimately, daily living. To develop computer competence takes time, more time than a single course experience. This book provides a foundation for personal growth toward a high level of computer competence.

Few developments in human history have had an impact on individuals and society comparable to that of computers and related technologies. Approaching the twenty-first century, the computer is our basic tool, our hammer, our pencil, our printing press, our rocket, our servant. It is what we make of it. Educators must help focus and guide the impact of computer technology, or we surely will be swept along in directions not of our own choosing.

Who Is This Book For?

This book is for any educator, or potential educator, seeking to become computer competent, ready to provide leadership in educational institutions of the twenty-first century. It evolved from our own experiences teaching an introductory instructional computing course, one which we created in the early 1980s. It serves both pre-service and in-service teachers, as well as many others from disciplines throughout our university, even from computer science. The course enrolls both upper division undergraduates and graduate students. We have attempted to write on a level appropriate to the former, yet suitable to the latter.

What Is the Premise of the Book?

We believe that software tools such as word processing are the cornerstone of computing in education. Following in importance is the computer as a tutor, a direct giver of instruction. The creation of software, historically treated as "programming," and once the primary element of instructional computing, now clearly takes third place, but may be re-emerging somewhat based on exciting new tools such as *HyperCard* and *Linkway Live!* In addition, specific concepts and issues related to educational computing and its implementation are important to any "computer educator." This book provides solid coverage of all these areas. Furthermore, because no one computer type now dominates education, we do not emphasize one over the others, making the book usable with whatever hardware is available. It is also software independent, focusing on principles and concepts, not the details of any specific program.

How Is the Book Organized?

We have organized the book into six parts and a total of 21 chapters. Chapter 1 puts microcomputers into perspective with a brief history of computers and computing, then an overview of hardware and software, including terminology fundamental to computing. Part 2 offers extensive treatment of the computer as a tool, both personally and practically in education. Chapter 2 focuses on written communication through word processing; Chapter 3 addresses information management with databases; and Chapter 4 looks at spreadsheets for working with numbers. In Chapter 5, attention turns to graphics software and numerous types of support tools that can make teaching easier and more effective. Chapter 6 examines integrated software that offers most major tools in a single, easy-to-use package, while Chapter 7 looks at desktop publishing and Chapter 8 presents computer networking and telecommunications.

Part 3 turns to the computer as tutor, as a teaching tool, treating computer-assisted instruction (Chapter 9), interactive multimedia (Chapter 10), courseware evaluation (Chapter 11), computer-managed instruction (Chapter 12), and computer (artificial) intelligence (Chapter 13). Part 4 offers a conceptual introduction to programming concepts (Chaper 14), Logo (Chapter 15), common languages such as BASIC (Chapter 16), and coverage of authoring and hypermedia tools, including HyperCard and Linkway (Chapter 17).

To round out consideration of using computers in education, Part 5 addresses the concepts of computer literacy, integration, and competence in Chapter 18. Chapter 19 presents concrete suggestions for successful implementation of educational computing, while Chapter 20 looks at issues and implications such as computer viruses and equity. Part 6 concludes the book with thoughts on the future of computer technology and its educational applications.

In addition, a detailed appendix cross-references software mentioned in the text and its producers or distributors, lists sources of CD-ROMs and laser discs, and provides contact information on major telecommunications/information services such as CompuServe. To assist with tight budgets, there is a listing of educational software discounters and sources of shareware and public domain software. The Appendix also lists selected suppliers of integrated learning systems and adaptive devices for special needs populations. Finally, professional organizations and publications of special interest to computing educators are listed. Concluding the book is an extensive glossary, including terms italicized in the text, and a comprehensive index.

What's New in This Edition?

The third edition of this book is not a cosmetic revision, but rather reflects the comprehensive updating essential to any book in a volatile field. All chapters have been revised, most of them extensively. New in this edition are complete chapters on desktop publishing, networking and telecommunications, interactive multimedia (hypermedia), and computer intelligence. Because of the decreased emphasis on computer languages and programming, Part 4 has been shortened significantly in this edition. We have retained and revised chapters on the practical aspects of putting computers to work in our schools to reflect current themes and issues.

How to Use This Book

Beginning with the first edition, our goal has been to provide a truly comprehensive resource on educational computing. In so doing, we have written a book that includes far more material than most one-term courses can possibly cover, as well as topics that are not included in every course which this book may serve. Throughout, we have tried to maintain maximum independence among our chapters, allowing you to select chapters best suited to your needs. Use only those chapters that are appropriate to your focus and time frame. (We do not cover all chapters in our own course, either!) We believe this flexibility, combined with machine-independence, makes this book one of the most broadly-suitable text resources on the market today.

We also acknowledge that some chapters are more difficult for novice computer educators than others. For example, networking and telecommunications concepts, interactive multimedia, and artificial intelligence are all aspects of contemporary educational computing that are apt to be totally new to many readers. However difficult, they represent key aspects of future computer use. We have presented them as simply as we knew how.

We strongly suggest that you use this book to support a hands-on approach to learning. Like bicycle riding, educational computing must be a practical, hands-on activity—not one about which you merely read, think, and discuss, important as those activities are. Whether you use an Apple II, an MS-DOS computer, or a Macintosh is irrelevant. That you use a computer, and *use it a lot*, is critical. Many lab manuals are available that integrate well with this work. Select one appropriate to your hardware and software. Personally, we use Microsoft *Works* and a companion "how-to" manual. Chapters from this book are assigned for reading prior to each unit in the course, with limited time spent in lecture/discussion and as much as possible spent hands-on in the computer lab.

We encourage instructors using this book to obtain our Instructor's Manual from HarperCollins. It contains last minute updates, teaching tips, test items, and transparency masters.

Acknowledgments

As with previous editions, we are indebted to our users worldwide who have made this book successful. We have worked hard to be current, accurate, and comprehensive, but accept responsibility for any errors that may have escaped our notice. The suggestions we received from our own students, current users of the book, and our reviewers contributed greatly to the major changes that permeate this edition. We extend a special thank you to the following colleagues who critically reviewed the second edition and recommended improvements, then assessed our efforts to meet their challenges in the revised manuscript draft: Marilyn D. Ward, Western Illinois University; Lorana A. Jinkerson, Eastern Michigan University; Debra A. Mathinos, Bucknell University; Helen Taylor, California State University; David F. Salisbury, Florida State University; William J. Hunter, The University of Calgary; and Terry Brink, Lock Haven University.

This edition would have been impossible without the advice, encouragement, and guidance of many individuals. At HarperCollins, we gratefully acknowledge the ongoing support of Chris Jennison, Sponsoring Editor, College Division, and Shadla Grooms, Assistant Editor, and look forward to future projects. At Ruttle, Shaw & Wetherill, Inc., we have appreciated the assistance and cooperation of Tom Conville. We also extend our thanks to Barry Stark and George Tarbay of Northern Illinois University for their photographic contributions.

Last, but far from least, we express our continuing gratitude to our families for their support and understanding. They bore the impact of the time demands that all authors face.

You, the users of this book, are essential to future editions. We welcome your comments, questions, and suggestions at any time. Address your correspondence to:

Jim Lockard
College of Education—LEPS
Northern Illinois University
DeKalb, IL 60115
Bitnet: P60JAL1@NIU
Internet: P60JAL1@MVS.CSO.NIU.EDU

J.L.
P.D.A.
W.A.M.

Microcomputers for Twenty-First Century Educators

Part 1

Getting
Started

Objectives

After completing this chapter, you will be familiar with:

The state of computers in education in the
   United States.
Basic terms and concepts, such as data, RAM, ROM,
   stored program control, microcomputer, main-
   frame, CPU, hardware and software.
The contributions to the development of computing
   of such major figures as Blaise Pascal, Charles
   Babbage and Ada Lovelace, Hermann Hollerith,
   and John Von Neumann.
The four generations of mainframe computers and
   their underlying technologies.
The basic components of a computer system.
A variety of input, output, and storage devices.
The important characteristics of monitors and
   printers.
The concept of programs and their importance.
The functions of operating systems.

Chapter 1

Microcomputer Systems in Perspective

The late 1970s brought a powerful new tool to educators—the personal computer (PC) or microcomputer. How to achieve the enormous potential of the microcomputer was not, however, obvious. Microcomputers were fundamentally different from earlier educational technologies. Learning to use a microcomputer was far more demanding than, say, an overhead or slide projector. Appropriate uses in education also were not intuitive. Few educators were prepared to adopt microcomputers immediately. The need for pre-service and in-service teacher education in computer applications grew through the 1980s and continues in the mid-1990s. That need is the reason for this book's existence. It will provide you with a comprehensive introduction to educational computing.

This chapter begins with an overview of the state of computers in U.S. schools. Next comes a short history of computer development, followed by basic concepts of microcomputer technology and terminology. A conceptual introduction to software concludes the chapter.

The State of Computers in Education

Very early in the microcomputer era, many observers predicted a rapid expansion of computer use in K–12 education that would sweep teachers along with it and send on to higher education students who were already comfortable computer users, individuals who had experienced what computers in education can do. This has happened to a lesser extent than predicted. In the mid-1990s, the need for introductory courses on computers in education remains strong, and is even growing.

Did something go wrong in the "computer revolution"? Is the microcomputer just a fad, as some have maintained all along? The answer is neither. Rather, projections of the speed with which change would occur were naive. Kozma and Johnston (1991) noted that the steam engine took 150 years to achieve a pervasive impact on society. The computer in just 50 years has had such an impact on business, but education lags behind. Borrell (1992) termed the U.S. record of implementation of computers in our schools "a growing national embarrassment" and compared it to the savings and loan industry scandal of the early 1990s. Neither teacher preparation nor in-service education has risen fully to the microcomputer challenge.

Statistics on computers in American education seem to show progress. The number of computers in schools increased 600 percent from 1983–84 to 1991–92, and the average number of students per computer nationwide fell from 125 to 19 (Kinnaman, 1992). This total number of computers, however, was about 2.5 million at a time when the U.S. teacher population totaled 3 million—less than one computer per teacher! Furthermore, many of the computers were already too old and underpowered to support contemporary software and hardware options. When Borrell and the editors of *MacWorld* looked beyond the statistics, they found "(a)ntiquated computers; unused computers; computers used for games and not for teaching; schools and teachers unprepared to use computers that they own; mismanaged or misdirected policies; and unknown hundreds of millions of dollars spent over the last decade for little return" (Borrell, 1992, p. 25).

Yet, this is rarely a matter of choice or conscious decision. The question is not *whether* to use computers, but rather how *best* to use them. Educators are not resisting computer technology; rather they are overwhelmed by it. Many are still in a position of having had computers thrust upon them, with little or no assistance in learning to use them. Pre-service teachers still may graduate with little or no exposure to role models who teach with computer technology. Few teachers ever will make effective use of computers in their teaching, unless they first become proficient computer users on a personal level. This requires ready access to computers, time, training, and support on a level that few educational institutions yet provide (Branscum, 1992).

Access to computers in K–12 schools continues to improve steadily amidst interesting changes. The Apple II, which defined educational computing in the 1980s, is being supplanted by far more powerful Macintosh and MS-DOS (IBM-compatible) computers. Mathis (1992) reported that Sunburst, one of the largest educational software companies, no longer develops new software for the Apple II. Apple Computer's total dominance of the school market has declined as the Apple II has been phased out. According to the most recent national data (*Technology & Learning,* 1993), 44 percent of the computers in schools still were Apple IIs, but 34 percent were MS-DOS systems, and 17 percent were Macintosh. Such trends support the authors' decision not to link this book to a particular type of computer. The principles of educational computing exist independently of the specific computer available. Ideally, teachers should have some level of familiarity with Apple II, Macintosh, and MS-DOS computers.

However much educator access to computers has increased, in-service computer education is spotty at best. Our experience suggests that many schools adopted a quick-fix approach. When the first computers were purchased, most schools provided limited in-service training. But just as computers themselves are often seen as one-time investments, so too was teacher training. Schools, of all organizations, have not recognized the need for on-going learning! Practicing teachers need support and regular opportunities to enhance their computer skills.

Pre-service teacher education often appears to be too little, too late. Many colleges and universities lack current hardware and software, and the time that has been made available in the curriculum for computer education is woefully inadequate. For maximum impact, teacher education students must become fluent computer users very early in their college education, then work with the technologies of learning in every phase of their teacher preparation. Technology should be integrated throughout their education courses.

Much attention in recent years has focused on concepts of school "restructuring." There is a growing belief that systemic change must occur (see, for example, Moursund [Aug/Sept 1991; Nov 1991]). As Brady (1992) and Longworth (1992) both document, if we cannot make the necessary changes within our schools, perhaps they will be replaced by private, profit-making schools as envisioned in Chris Whittle's Edison Project. Borrell (1992) laid the problem out bluntly: A recent study by the World Economic Forum placed the U.S. fifth among the world's economies, in part because of our education-base problems. We spend the most dollars per student on earth, but are only 11th as a share of GNP. Borrell fears that "America will march into the future without adequate planning, effective implementation, or a national agenda, while other countries such as Japan and France implement well-coordinated policies. . . . If computers are not successfully and widely integrated into primary and secondary education, our society will stratify into those with the knowledge to succeed and those who cannot" (p. 30).

Perhaps the foregoing discussion seems to be a pessimistic introduction to this book. We, the authors, do not intend it that way at all. Indeed, the challenges are enormous, but we face them with great optimism. We believe the computer is an inescapable component of the changes now facing education in the United States, indeed throughout much of the world. *You* can contribute to the necessary changes in education. Join us now on a journey through the challenging world of microcomputers in education!

Early Data Processing Devices

Today's microcomputers are the culmination of a long search for better and more efficient ways of getting things done (Figure 1.1). Humans have always sought

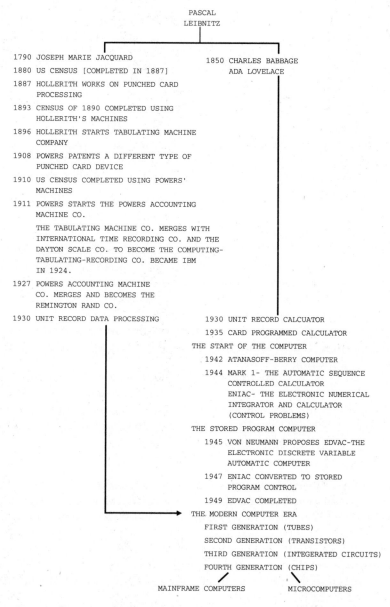

Figure 1.1. Computer history outline, showing two lines of development.

more efficient ways of meeting challenges. Just as we have created machines to ease our physical labors, we have also searched for ways to make mental work easier. The resulting tools are called *data processing machines.*

Data are meaningful pieces of information. Examples of data are names, numbers, addresses, ages, and similar descriptive information about individuals. *Processing* is doing something with data. Examples of simple *data processing* are alphabetizing names, ordering addresses, or calculating the average age of a group of people. While all these processing tasks can be performed manually, as either the amount of data or the complexity of the processing increases, a more efficient way of performing such tasks is not only desirable but often necessary—thus the need for data processing machines.

The Abacus

The abacus was invented and used by the Chinese centuries ago to speed up simple mathematical calculations. By moving little beads on wires, the process of addition and subtraction is facilitated. The abacus is probably the oldest data processing device.

The First Machines

Around 1650, the French mathematician and philosopher Blaise Pascal constructed the tooth-and-gear adding machine, which consisted of a series of interlocking wheels with ten teeth around their outside rims. When one wheel made a complete revolution, its gearing caused the next wheel to turn a single notch. The teeth on each wheel represented the digits 0 through 9. As each wheel was turned forward to represent the numbers to be summed, this device served as a mechanical adding machine. If one turned the wheels in the reverse direction, it served as a mechanical subtracting machine.

Twenty years later, Gottfried Leibnitz enhanced Pascal's device, giving it the ability to multiply and divide. Thus, by the end of the seventeenth century, a machine existed that could perform mechanically the basic operations of mathematics. The concept behind Pascal's machine remained the basis for the adding machines and calculators of the early twentieth century.

Automated Manufacturing and Jacquard

The next developmental step for data processing machines stems from the work of Joseph Marie Jacquard in 1790. Realizing the repetitive and time-consuming nature of hand weaving cloth, Jacquard designed and constructed an automated loom. This loom was controlled by a series of cards with holes punched into them. A single card directed the automated loom in constructing one row of the fabric. A set of such cards then directed construction of a series of rows of the fabric, eventually resulting in the desired pattern.

There were many advantages to such a process. First, the procedure was automatic. Once the cards had been prepared, they controlled the loom in making the desired fabric. Second, when a given fabric had been completed, the cards could be reinserted into the loom and used again to make an identical fabric. Third, by changing some of the cards, the operator of the loom could make material with variations in the original pattern. Fourth, an entirely new deck of punched cards could be inserted and used to create a totally different patterned cloth on the same machine.

Jacquard's concept, the use of a series of cards punched with holes that could be processed by machine, established one of the two paths that data processing machines would follow in the next 150 years. The other path developed from the ideas of Charles Babbage.

The Analytical Engine, Babbage, and Lady Ada

About the middle of the nineteenth century, an Englishman named Charles Babbage approached the processing of data from a different perspective. Living in the midst of the Industrial Revolution and aware of advances being made in motors and related devices, Babbage proposed a new concept for a processing machine. His machine would be capable of accepting a large amount of information. Once this information was stored internally, the machine would perform all the desired processing and output the results. Jacquard's processing was accomplished in small steps, each controlled by a punched card. Babbage's processing was to be accomplished only after all information was presented to the system.

Babbage called his machine the Analytical Engine, and while he drew plans for it, the engine never became fully operational. The concept was sound, but the technology of his time was inadequate for its implementation. About 100 years later, with much greater mechanical sophistication and the use of electricity, Babbage's concept served as the starting point in the development of modern data processing devices. It is for this reason that Babbage is often referred to as the "father of modern data processing."

Babbage was assisted in his work by Ada Lovelace, who was a gifted mathematician and the daughter of the poet Lord Byron. In fact, much of what is known about the Analytical Engine's programming potential comes from an article written by Lady Ada in which she presented a fascinating analysis of the machine and Babbage's ideas. Her contributions to the development of computing were acknowledged when a computer language—*Ada*—was named in her honor.

Two Lines of Development

Unit Record Data Processing

The next advance occurred in the United States in the late 1800s and returned to the concepts of Jacquard. With the beginning of the great immigration period in the United States, the taking of the census every ten years became an increasingly difficult task. Officials noted that the 1880 census had taken nearly seven years to complete and projected that the 1890 census would require over ten years to complete if performed in the same manner. Clearly, something had to be done!

The Census Bureau hired Hermann Hollerith to develop procedures for speeding up the processing of census data. To perform many of the data processing tasks, Hollerith designed a series of machines. They used a card punched with holes to represent the census information of one person. Other cards were punched to represent the census information of other people, one card per person. These cards became known as *unit records*, because they contained the record of one person or unit. A group of these unit records was referred to as a *file*.

Hollerith's machines processed these cards automatically and completed the necessary census tasks faster and more efficiently than by hand. The machine that prepared the punched cards eventually became known as the keypunch. Examples of other machines that Hollerith produced were the reproducer (which made copies of cards), the sorter (which rearranged cards in a file), and the tabulator (which counted the data on cards in files).

Commercial Applications

Using his unit record processing machines, Hollerith was able to complete the 1890 census in approximately three years rather than the previously estimated ten years. This procedure for processing data clearly worked. In fact, it worked so well that in 1896 Hollerith left the Census Bureau and founded the Hollerith Tabulating Machine Company. Hollerith reasoned that if such machines could process census data efficiently, they would also find applicability in the general business community.

During the early part of this century, the Census Bureau discontinued using the Hollerith machines and hired another engineer, James Powers, to develop other ways to process census data. By 1910, Powers developed and put into use a series of machines that, while functioning on concepts similar to Hollerith's, were different enough to qualify for patents. The 1910 census was run using these machines and was completed efficiently and speedily. Powers also saw the benefit of these machines for the business community and in 1911 founded the Powers Accounting Machine Company.

The history of data processing for a good part of this century is the history of these two companies. In 1911, the Hollerith Tabulating Machine Company merged with the International Time Recording Company and the Dayton Scale Company to become the Computing-Tabulating-Recording Company. In 1924, its name was changed to International Business Machines (IBM) to reflect the worldwide market served by the company.

The Powers Accounting Machine Company merged with several office supply companies to become the Remington Rand Company. Through mergers, the Remington Rand Company became Sperry Rand and then, Unisys.

The similar machines that these two companies produced served the data processing needs of the business community for many years. Their machines were continually upgraded to reflect technological advances and finally became the full-fledged unit record data processing equipment that was available into the 1960s.

While unit record processing met the needs of the business community, it did not serve the somewhat different needs of the scientific community. In an over-simplified comparison, business often requires relatively straightforward and non-complex processing of a large amount of individual data (such as payroll or billing), while scientific needs often focus on complex processing of a relatively small amount of data (as in statistics or engineering). There were many attempts to modify unit record machines to meet the demands of the scientific community. Examples include the upgraded unit record calculator and the card programmed calculator. Neither was completely successful. A scientific data processing machine had to be conceptualized differently from business data processing machines.

The Start of the Computer

Machines suited to scientific applications began to appear in the mid-1930s. They were developed from the concepts of Babbage's Analytical Engine rather than from the concepts of Jacquard's automatic loom. The first electronic digital computer was designed and built by John Atanasoff and Clifford Berry at Iowa State College in 1942. In 1944, with funding from IBM, engineers and scientists at Harvard University designed and built the Mark I (The Automatic Sequence Controlled Calculator). These machines worked on the principle of data being input into a central processing unit, where all processing was sequentially controlled until completed. The results were then output to the user. With the harnessing of electricity into vacuum tubes and electrical circuits, such a machine not only could be built, but worked as Babbage had predicted. For example, the Mark I could complete in approximately two minutes what had previously required over twenty hours of manual processing. Clearly, these were the types of machines that the scientific community needed.

About the same time, the University of Pennsylvania was also developing and building a data processing machine following Babbage's ideas and geared to scientific processing. This machine was called the ENIAC (the Electronic Numerical Integrator and Calculator). It also worked successfully. Scientific data processing machines were becoming a reality.

The Control Problem

These early machines also had problems, the most serious of which was control. Setting data processing machines up to perform a specific job often required many hours of actual rewiring. Once rewired, the machines could perform quickly and accurately, but after completing a specific task, extensive rewiring was again necessary to perform a different processing task. Researchers had demonstrated that machines could be built that were capable of doing scientific processing. What was needed was a method of efficiently controlling them.

The Stored Program Computer

The control problem was addressed eventually by a mathematician and physicist named John Von Neumann. In 1945, Von Neumann published an article proposing a solution and outlining a machine that incorporated his new control concepts. This machine he called the EDVAC (the Electronic Discrete Variable

Automatic Computer). The age of the unit record machine was ending; the age of the computer was about to begin.

Von Neumann's concept was termed *stored program control.* The idea was to build control capabilities into the machine and not view control as something external to the processing unit. The internal control unit would understand and use an instruction to direct the rest of the system to perform a desired operation. A series of instructions would make up a program that, when entered into the system, would be executed one instruction at a time to perform a complex processing task. Such computer systems were known as stored program computer systems to differentiate them from earlier machines.

Work was begun on Von Neumann's EDVAC. While this machine was being built, the ENIAC at the University of Pennsylvania was converted to stored program control. In 1947, the redesigned ENIAC became one of the first functioning stored program computer systems. By 1950, the EDVAC was completed, as were other stored program computers.

As the new computers were being developed, two fundamentally different approaches were proposed. Alan Turing and other British scientists argued that computers should be multipurpose. The multipurpose computer's instruction set would be based on *formal logic* and use *logical operators* such as "AND," "OR," and "NOT" to manipulate symbolic material, even ordinary language. Operators for arithmetic would be derived from the logical operators.

American scientists, on the other hand, argued for computers that were based on mathematics. The fundamental instruction set for this type of computer would use numerical operators such as +, -, <. Such a computer would be less complex and, therefore, less expensive to build. It would better serve what was then thought to be the primary function of computers, namely, the processing of numerical data.

The American approach won out and serves as one of the conceptual bases of contemporary computers. There has always remained, however, a core of logic-based computer scientists. Recently, research in artificial intelligence has led to a resurgence of interest in logic-based computers.

The Modern Computer Era

Although the paths from Jacquard and Babbage existed in parallel for many years, they converged in the modern computer era, which is identified by four generations of technology.

First Generation: Tubes

While a few stored program computers existed before 1950, they were still not widely available to the general scientific community. At that time, however, the Remington Rand Corporation hired some of the personnel who had worked on the ENIAC computer at the University of Pennsylvania. In 1951, Remington Rand introduced the first commercially available computer system, the UNIVAC I. The

IBM 650 soon followed. Thus, by the middle 1950s, both of the large unit record machine companies also built and distributed stored program computers.

The computers of this period are called the first generation of modern computer systems. They were constructed using vacuum tubes, were very large and relatively expensive, and were prone to break down, often from their own heat. But they did perform as indicated and started to gain acceptance in the scientific community and at least some notice from the business world.

Second Generation: Transistors

The mid-1950s saw development of the transistor, which made vacuum tubes obsolete. Tubes were replaced with transistors that were cheaper, faster, more reliable, and easier to incorporate into complex electrical circuits. As a result, computers were re-engineered using transistors. Remington Rand introduced the UNIVAC 1102 while IBM introduced a series of machines (the IBM 1620 and 7090 for small- and large-scale scientific processing and the IBM 1401 and 7070 to meet small- and large-scale business data processing needs). All of these machines were faster and more complex than previous machines. At the same time, costs were held down by advances in technology. These computers, along with those of new companies in this period, are called the second generation of computer systems.

The introduction of business-oriented computers marked a significant change in direction. While first-generation computers were oriented toward scientific processing, computer manufacturers soon realized that their machines could also perform the functions of unit record equipment more quickly, more efficiently, and at lower cost. These new computers eventually took over all of the business data processing that had been performed for over fifty years by unit record machines.

Third Generation: Integrated Circuits

The early 1960s saw the development of solid logic technology and solid-state integrated circuits (ICs), which allowed many single-function electronic components of a computer to be combined into one device. Computers were redesigned to take advantage of these advances in technology and the third generation of computers was born.

Similar to the advances of the second generation, third-generation machines were more complex and faster, while their costs were not appreciably increased. Because of greater capabilities, the distinction between business and scientific computers slowly disappeared. There was simply a range of small to large computers that could perform business or scientific processing with equal ease. Computers had become an integral part of both the business and scientific communities.

Fourth Generation: Microelectronics

The early 1970s saw another technological leap, the introduction of the *microprocessor*, a tiny device that combined the functions of numerous integrated circuits on a single chip. The fourth generation of computers was upon us. Again machines were redesigned to make use of new technology and became even faster and more complex at stable cost.

The Microcomputer

While computers were becoming increasingly complex, several individuals conceived of using microprocessors to build small, personal computers (PCs) for individual use. The first of these machines appeared in the mid-1970s. They became known as *microcomputers* to differentiate them from the much larger computers, which became known as *mainframe* computers.

The next few years brought innovation in the continual development and improvement of the microprocessors used in all types of computers. Both mainframe and microcomputers have continued to increase in power and capability. One can view mainframe computers as large systems serving multiple users and the complex needs of science and industry. Microcomputers can be considered personal systems serving the more modest needs of individual users.

Real Computer Power

The microcomputers of today should not be thought of as toys or scaled-down mainframe computers with limited power and applicability. In the early years, typical first- and second-generation mainframe computers cost over $250,000, and in terms of their processing capabilities, they were worth it. Today, an individual can buy a more powerful microcomputer system for 1 percent of that price or less. Such has been the technological advancement and improvement in computer engineering.

New Applications

Microcomputers are capable of doing more than just many of the same things that mainframe computers can. Many applications have been developed for microcomputers that are either inefficient or impractical on a mainframe, yet are extremely useful. Examples include word processing, spreadsheet management, and computer-based learning, applications that are more individual in nature and thus better suited to microcomputers than to mainframes.

New Users

Low-cost, remarkable processing power, and new applications have seen the movement of computers and computer power into areas with little or no prior access to computer capabilities. Such areas include K–12 education, small businesses, and the home. The microcomputer is already performing tasks that only a few years ago were not even thought of as potential applications for computers.

Microcomputers have extended computing power to a much wider audience than mainframe computers. Mainframe use had been limited to those who had access to such large computers. This excluded a great majority of individuals who, therefore, could not take advantage of the computer to satisfy their individual data processing needs. Microcomputers have changed this and have made computer power accessible to nearly everyone.

This book will introduce you to this type of widely available computer, the microcomputer. You will explore what it is, how it can be controlled, specific applications to education, and some of the implications as it finds its way more and more into our daily lives.

Hardware: The Physical System

Although the word *computer* implies a single machine, a computer is really a system of interconnected components, not just one piece of equipment. These components are collectively referred to as hardware. Figure 1.2 illustrates the basic hardware components of a microcomputer system. The primary component is the *central processing unit* (CPU), which includes the control unit and the arithmetic/logic unit circuits. In addition, the CPU contains circuits that connect to other internal and external units (memory, input devices, output devices, and storage devices). Let's consider these types of mechanical/electrical devices individually as they apply to a microcomputer system.

Central Processing Unit

The CPU is the key component, the "brain" of the system. This is where most of the work of the system actually takes place. The CPU of a microcomputer is a microprocessor that consists of two principal parts, the *control unit* and the *arithmetic/logic unit* (ALU).

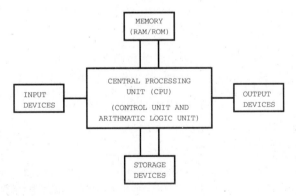

Figure 1.2 Components of a microcomputer system.

Control Unit

Because a microcomputer system consists of many components, something has to assure that they work together properly. The control unit of the CPU is the manager of all the other pieces of the system. It can be likened to a police officer directing traffic.

Arithmetic/Logic Unit

The power of a computer rests ultimately on its ability to perform arithmetic and logical operations. Microcomputer arithmetic is carried out in a series of steps by circuitry within the ALU. Arithmetic processing speeds can often be greatly increased by the addition of a special math chip that performs arithmetic operations directly rather than as a series of steps. Such chips are called *math coprocessors* because they add to the basic math capabilities of the CPU.

The logic circuitry of the ALU handles the decision-making capabilites of the microcomputer. The seemingly complex functioning of a microcomputer system is actually just the combination of many simple logic steps into a lengthly sequence.

Memory

In order to do anything, the CPU must have data to process. Memory consists of microchips that accept data from external sources, retain data for some time, route data to and accept data from the CPU, and, finally, provide processing results to the user through external devices. Memory has a capacity; that is, chips can accept and retain only a certain amount of data. The basic unit of memory capacity is termed a *byte*, the space required to hold one character. Because a computer must be able to hold and manipulate thousands of characters at once, RAM size is often specified as a number followed by the letter K, the scientific symbol for 1000. A microcomputer has two types of memory: RAM and ROM.

Random Access Memory

Random access memory (*RAM*) is a series of chips that can accept, retain, and have their data erased when it is no longer needed. A simple analogy for RAM is safety deposit boxes into which you can place items for storage until retrieved. RAM is termed *volatile* because all data in RAM are erased and lost when the computer is turned off.

RAM is very important in any microcomputer system. The amount needed depends upon the programs the computer is to run. Common memory sizes are 128K for some of the computers still used in schools up through many megabytes (1 megabyte or 1MB = 1 million bytes or 1000K). RAM can be increased in most computer systems by the addition of more chips.

Read Only Memory

The second type of memory in a microcomputer system is read only memory (*ROM*). ROM chips are programmed during manufacturing to contain information that the computer needs to function properly. ROM contains data that cannot be

Figure 1.3 Graphics pads are used widely in art and design.

erased, altered, or expanded by the user. It is termed *nonvolatile* because the data are retained regardless of whether the computer is turned on or off.

Input Devices

The CPU of a microcomputer system is capable of performing a wide variety of tasks, but for most things to occur, it must be given data. Data enter into the system through input devices. Most systems include one primary input device, a keyboard, and often a mouse. Various other input devices also are available.

Keyboard

A computer keyboard resembles a typewriter, often with the addition of a calculator-like set of numeric keys, directional arrow keys for movement about the screen, and other special-purpose keys.

Mouse

A mouse is a hand-sized device with buttons that the user moves around on a flat surface to move a corresponding marker (such as an arrow) on the video screen. The user can then select the screen area as input to the computer by simply pressing a button on the mouse. Variations of the mouse are available. The most common is a trackball, which is sort of an inverted mouse where the user rotates a small ball to move the on-screen marker. The mouse device has become an integral component of most computer systems today.

Other Input Devices

A *joystick* is a small box with a movable stick and one or two buttons. Moving the stick moves a marker on the screen, and pressing a button sends signals to the system. It is most often used to play games on the computer.

A *graphics pad* (Figure 1.3) is a board that the user touches and draws upon to communicate patterns to the computer system. These pads have gained wide popularity in art and computer-aided design (CAD).

A *light pen* resembles a ball-point pen attached to the computer by a wire. The user selects choices displayed on the screen simply by touching the pen to the item.

In some systems, a *touch screen* allows the user to input information by simply touching a special video screen with a finger or other pointer. This is much like a light pen, only simpler.

To use a *mark sense scanner,* the user uses regular pencils to fill in special spaces on preprinted forms. The scanner then senses these markings and transmits the information to the microcomputer. The most common use of these devices is to "read" test answer sheets, a function of growing interest to schools implementing competency-based educational programs.

An *optical scanner* is capable of "reading" typed or printed pages, including graphic images, into the computer system. *Optical character recognition* (OCR) software then converts the scanned image into normal text, just as if you actually had typed the material. This eliminates the need to retype existing material. Hand-held scanners are moved physically across the material. More sophisticated page scanners "read" a whole page of material at a time. Both black and white and color scanners are widely available.

One major area of continuing research and development is in *voice recognition*, which has special benefits for the handicapped. The ability to speak to a computer to control it promises to affect all computer users dramatically.

Output Devices

When the computer has performed its tasks, the results of processing must be conveyed back to the user. Information from the CPU is converted into an understandable form through output devices. The primary output devices are video monitors and printers.

Monitors

The most common way to receive information from a computer system is through a monitor. A monitor displays text and graphics on a screen that resembles a television set. Commonly referred to as a screen, tube, or CRT (cathode ray tube), monitors vary considerably in their characteristics: monochrome or color image, resolution, and size. Color and resolution are controlled by the type of video circuitry in the computer. Of course, the monitor itself must match the characteristics of that circuitry.

Monitors differ much like black-and-white and color televisions. Monochrome monitor display images in shades of only one color (e.g., black and grays against a white background). Color monitors display multiple colors and are more popular.

Resolution determines the clarity of the text or graphic image on the screen. The higher the resolution, the sharper or clearer the image. Higher resolution also permits the computer to display more information simultaneously on the screen, whether graphics or text, by reducing the size of all image elements. High resolution monitors provide increased readability and allow for more visually realistic graphic displays, but they do have a higher selling price.

Monitor sizes vary from 9-inch screens up through 25-inch or larger screens for classroom use. For effective use by groups of more than four or five, the video output of a computer should be connected to a video projector to display images on a large screen. A computer can also be connected to a liquid crystal display (LCD) viewer or panel that is placed on an overhead projector and focused on a large screen. LCD panels are especially cost effective and easy to use.

Printers

Printers produce paper output or *hardcopy*. Although the layout may differ, the contents of the hardcopy duplicate what could be viewed on the monitor and may be saved for use after the computer is turned off. Printers common to microcomputer systems differ from one another in print method, speed, range of capabilities, print quality, and interface method.

Three quite different methods of printing are widely used. *Dot matrix* printers use small "pins" to strike the paper through a ribbon. The dot pattern created gives them their name. Such printers tend to be relatively inexpensive, are reasonably fast, and are the only printers that can print on multipart forms. *Ink jet* printers form characters by spraying droplets of ink onto the paper. Ink jet printers tend to be slower, cannot print on multiforms, and cost somewhat more. Some operate on batteries for use with battery-powered *notebook computers.*

Becoming increasingly popular as prices fall are *laser printers,* which operate on the principle of photocopy machines. While more expensive than most other printers, their flexibility, print quality, and speed make laser printers desirable in most situations. They are rapidly becoming the norm.

Printers differ greatly in speed. The speed of a printer usually is measured by the number of characters per second (CPS) that it can produce. Dot matrix printers offer speeds of 100 to 300 CPS or more. The speed of ink jet printers varies widely, from 10 to over 100 CPS. Laser printers produce a full page at a time, so the CPS measurement is not used. These are the fastest printers available, commonly printing 4 to 20 pages per minute.

Print capabilities vary among printers in several ways. Most printers can print both text and graphics. While dot matrix printers (especially 24-pin printers) can produce respectable graphic pages, ink jet printers do an even better job of this.

Laser graphics printing is especially sophisticated and produces almost publishing grade graphics.

Through the use of colored ribbons or special ink cartridges, it is possible for some printers to print in a color other than the usual black, or even in multiple colors. Color laser printers are also available, but they are very expensive.

Most printers allow changes in the shape, size, and form of typefaces. This can be accomplished on many printers by printer control settings or through special print routines, insertable cartridges, fonts built into more sophisticated software, or the circuitry built into laser printers (making the printer almost a computer itself and allowing for nearly unlimited print capabilities).

Because dot matrix printers form characters out of dots, they tend to produce the lowest quality output. Advances in their technology, including more pins in the print head and multiple passes across a line, allow the more sophisticated dot matrix printers to produce some relatively high quality output, although at reduced speed. Ink jet printers, because of the darkness of the dots they produce, can print with still higher quality. Laser printers offer the finest print quality available, almost identical to professional typesetting.

The interface method between the computer and the printer is sometimes an important consideration. There are two basic ways that a computer can communicate with the printer: *serial* (one signal at a time) or *parallel* (multiple signals at a time). The computer, the connecting cable, and the printer must all use the same method. The parallel interface is easier to connect correctly and is faster. It is the most common printer interface method.

With appropriate additional hardware, one printer may be shared by many microcomputers, providing maximum economy in labs or offices. Often the cost of a laser printer may be justified if it is *networked* to several computers, thus avoiding the purchase of additional individual printers.

Other Output Devices

In addition to monitors and printers, the computer can output information as drawings or as speech. *Plotters* produce output by controlling pens that draw on paper. A single plotter contains many different colors of pens, thus allowing creation of sophisticated graphs, charts, and maps. Only a laser printer can equal the graphic quality of a plotter. *Voice synthesizers* convert output to ordinary speech that is intelligible to almost anyone. This is of special significance to visually impaired users.

Storage Devices

Storage devices are another vital component of a microcomputer system. They are awkward to classify because they function as memory and also as input and output devices. Floppy disks, hard disks, and optical drives compose this category.

A storage device is always accessible to the CPU. The CPU may send data to the device to store. The device can read stored data and send it to the CPU. In this way, storage devices serve both input and output functions. Furthermore, the data stored externally remain until explicitly erased. This constitutes an auxiliary memory whose capacity is typically far greater than the RAM size of the computer. These capabilities make some combination of storage devices indispensable for microcomputer systems.

Floppy Disk Drives

Disk drives use either a 3.5" flexible ("floppy") diskette in a hard plastic case to store information or a 5.25" diskette. Either size may be double density (DD) or high density (HD). The data storage capacity of a 3.5" double density diskette is 720K (MS-DOS) to 800K (Apple), while high density diskettes hold 1440K or 1.44MB. The storage capacity of a 5.25" double density diskette is 360K; a high density diskette can contain 1.2MB of data. Some IBM computers use diskettes with storage capacity of 2.88MB. Multiple disk drives can be used on a system, further increasing total storage capacity.

When a diskette is full or its files are no longer needed, it can be removed from the drive, saved, and replaced with another diskette. When the data are needed again, the diskette is inserted back into the drive to make its contents accessible. Diskettes also can be erased and reused.

Hard Disk Drives

Most microcomputers today are equipped with hard disk drives. A hard disk drive's rigid recording surfaces are permanently sealed inside a container and cannot be removed. Hard disk drives can store very large quantities of data, from around 40MB to over 1000MB (1 billion characters or 1 *gigabyte* = 1GB). Such drives also greatly increase the performance capabilities of microcomputers beyond what is possible with only floppy disks. They eliminate diskette handling, store and retrieve data much faster, and can handle much larger programs and data sets. Because software is distributed primarily on floppy disks, microcomputers normally need at least one floppy drive in addition to one or more hard disks.

In an educational lab setting, one hard disk drive may serve many microcomputers in a cost-effective network. In a network, individual computers do not need to have hard disks because they all can access a central hard disk. With proper planning and foresight, an educational lab with the proper mix of hardware can maximize individual user capabilities at the minimum overall cost.

Optical Disc Drives

Optical discs provide an extremely high volume of storage. The most common type is the *CD-ROM* or compact disc-read only memory, which is quite similar to an audio CD. CD-ROMs now provide a means of inexpensively distributing large volumes of data, such as electronic encyclopedias. Their capacity is about 550MB per disc. Educational applications of CD-ROMs are increasing very rapidly and will be discussed more in later chapters.

CD-ROM drives can only read prerecorded discs. Less common types of optical drives can both read and write data, but typically the discs can not be erased and reused. They are called *WORM* (write once read many) drives.

Other Storage Devices

In addition to the devices just described, there are still others that can provide storage for microcomputer system. A *Bernoulli drive* uses a flexible diskette in a removable rigid case with capacities similar to modest-sized hard drives. Some notebook computers feature *removable* hard-disk units. *Tape drives* (or tape "streamers") are high-speed precision cassette units. They use tapes that are similar in principle to those for audio equipment. Tape drives can read and write data at high speeds. They are used as backups for hard disk drives; that is, data from a hard disk are copied to a tape that is stored. If problems occur with the hard disk drive, the data can be recovered from the backup tape.

Modems

A modem (*mo*dulator *dem*odulator) is a device that allows one computer to communicate with another through phone lines. In this way, a modem provides for both input and output, much like storage devices.

The single most important characteristic of modems is their speed or *baud rate*; that is, how fast they transmit data through the lines. Common modem speeds are 2400 baud (about 240 characters per second), 9600 baud, and 14.4K baud. Many modems include send and receive FAX capabilities as well! Although more costly to purchase, a higher speed modem may pay for itself in reduced telephone costs by transmitting and receiving data more quickly. Modems have increased in importance as educators have developed telecommunications applications, a subject which you will learn about in Chapter 8.

Software: Making the System Work

The physical elements of a computer system are actually isolated components. While connected, they do not work as an integrated unit unless directed to do so by the control section of the CPU. The obvious question then is, how do you control the control section?

Programs

Getting a microcomputer system to perform a desired task is a matter of giving to the CPU individual instructions concerning what should be done. The control section then directs and coordinates the rest of the system in executing the instructions. A *program* is a series of instructions designed to cause the system to perform a logical sequence of steps that will produce the desired result. The process of writing these instructions is called *programming*. Even if you do no programming personally, programming is still vital. Without programs, a microcomputer can do little more than decorate your desk.

The programs that cause a computer system to perform desired tasks are called *software* to distinguish them from the physical components of the computer system, or *hardware*. Programs come from two basic sources: They can be written by a user or they can be purchased (Figure 1.4). We will look at both ways of obtaining computer programs, but not just yet. You first need to understand how to get the computer system "up and running" before you can be concerned with programs of direct interest to educators.

Operating Systems

Before a computer system can perform tasks it must be prepared to accept and execute instructions. Initial preparation of the system is the task of a very special program called an *operating system*. An operating system is supplied with the computer or purchased for it. The control section of the CPU uses the operating system both to set itself up and to get information on how to perform various system-related tasks.

The operating system is supplied to the user on one or more diskettes. On a floppy disk system, the programs needed to get the system started are read from a system diskette when the computer is turned on. This is called *booting* the system. On a hard disk system, the programs on the system disks are copied onto the hard disk and then read from it when the system is booted.

Figure 1.4   Microcomputer software.

Operating systems differ greatly among makes, and sometimes models, of computers. Several operating systems are in common use. The Apple II series uses either DOS 3.3 or PRODOS. Many IBM-PCs use PC-DOS and most compatibles use the very similar, generic MS-DOS. All of these are text-based operating systems; they respond primarily to typed commands. OS/2 for IBM-PCs and compatibles and the Macintosh operating system (Fig. 1.5) feature *graphical user interfaces* (GUIs). They use graphics or *icons* to represent items stored on storage devices. The user "points" to an icon or menu with a mouse and clicks to select a program, data file, or operation. Microsoft *Windows* adds a similar visual interface to MS-DOS. Finally, some microcomputers use UNIX, an operating system developed for mainframe computers.

Many incompatibilities exist among operating systems and computer types, but the trend for the future is toward increased compatibility, which will benefit all users. The current lack of standardization is a major contributor to incompatibility among computers. Our discussion of operating system functions is therefore general. You will gain a basic understanding of the principles from this presentation. Mastering the essential parts of the particular operating system for a specific microcomputer should not be too difficult.

There are two general categories of tasks that an operating system performs: system operation tasks and system utility tasks.

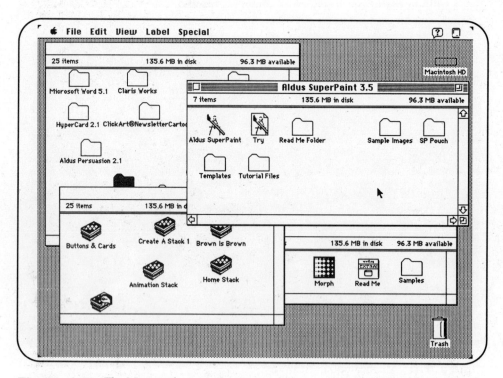

Figure 1.5 The Macintosh operating system features a graphical user interface.

System Operation Tasks

System operation tasks are those that guide the most basic functioning of the computer. They occur through the operating system as needed, without direct requests from the user. Three examples illustrate the concept.

- *Screen Control.* The system must be able to place characters on the video screen.
- *Keyboard input.* The system must be able to accept and interpret input from the keyboard.
- *Interfacing.* The system must be able to control its various components and allow them to communicate with each other.

System Utility Tasks

System utility tasks are functions that are often needed in the course of normal system use. These tasks are performed at the specific request of the user. The four most basic system utility tasks illustrate the concept.

- *Directory.* The system lists the contents of a disk on the screen or printer.
- *Format.* The system prepares a disk to accept information.
- *Copy.* The system makes duplicate copies of programs or entire diskettes.
- *Erase.* The system erases data from a disk.

Other operating system functions in both categories are too numerous to cover here. Users can refer to the operating system manuals to become familiar with those most commonly needed. Starting up the system and performing various necessary tasks are important functions of any operating system. Without them, a computer could not function and run the various programs that direct it to perform an almost unlimited variety of tasks.

Summary

The human search for easier ways to accomplish necessary tasks has produced many useful devices. Efforts to assist with mental tasks began with the abacus. Pascal and Leibnitz produced the first mechanical calculating devices in the seventeenth century. In the nineteenth century, the automation of weaving looms by Jacquard established one of two paths that led to the modern computer era. The other path stemmed from Babbage, who conceptualized the Analytical Engine.

Jacquard's concepts for automated looms guided the development of unit record data processing, which progressed rapidly from the work of Hollerith and Powers for the U.S. Census Bureau. From their government experience, both went on to form private firms that are known today as IBM and Unisys, respectively.

Unit record data processing satisfied the needs of business, but was less appropriate for scientific needs. Scientific requirements led to the development of the stored program computer, an outgrowth of the work of Babbage. The paths from Jacquard and Babbage converged at the start of the modern computer era in the 1950s.

The modern era is divided into generations of computers based upon the underlying technology. The first generation relied on vacuum tubes. Transistors marked the second generation. In the third generation, solid-state technology and integrated circuits were the key features. Microelectronics, specifically the chip and microprocessors, created the fourth generation.

These four generations bring developments to our focal point, the microcomputer. Microcomputers have placed computing power into the hands of millions, who before the late 1970s could never have dreamed of it. In addition, significant new applications have become available that hold special interest for educators.

A computer system consists of several physical components called hardware. The basic elements of a system are a CPU, memory, input and output devices, and storage devices. The CPU handles such critical aspects of the system's operation as arithmetic, logic, and control. The RAM and ROM are other critical components of the computer system. Input and output devices are essential to communication between the user and the computer. They exist in many different forms. In addition, to be useful, most systems require storage devices, which also provide essential input and output capabilities.

Making all the system components function as a unit is a control task. The heart of control is a series of instructions to the system called a program, or software. One highly specialized program essential to any computer is the operating system. Major functions of an operating system include system operation tasks of which the user is largely unaware and system utility tasks that are at the user's direct command. There is a need for standardization of operating systems across manufacturers to ease the problems of incompatibility among computer makes and models.

Chapter 1 Activities   Any two

1. Using whatever computer system is available, identify the input and output devices.
2. Read any available article about microchips. If possible, physically examine a RAM or ROM chip and try to imagine its actual operation.
3. If alternate input devices are unavailable in your school, go to a computer store and request a demonstration of as many as possible. How do they differ? Which appeals most to you? Why?
4. Compare sample output from dot matrix, ink jet, and laser printers, as well as a plotter. Discuss the merits and applications of each, keeping their relative costs in mind.
5. What types of monitors and printers are available in your school? If they are not ideal, what should you have access to? Why?
6. Make a side-by-side visual comparison of different monitor types. How noticeable are the differences? How significant are they?

7. If you have access to computers using different operating systems, try to familiarize yourself with their differences. Make a wall chart for the computer area that lists system utility tasks and the corresponding command or procedure for each system.

Bibliography

Borrell, J. "America's Shame: How We've Abandoned Our Children's Future." *MacWorld,* September 1992, pp. 25–30.

Brady, H. "Who Will Rebuild America's Schools?" *Technology & Learning,* September 1992, *13*(1), pp. 52–57.

Branscum, D. "Educators Need Support to Make Computing Meaningful." *MacWorld,* September 1992, pp. 83–88.

Capron, H. L. *Computers: Tools for an Information Age.* Menlo Park, CA: Benjamin/Cummings, 1987.

Galloway, J. P. "Misconceptions of Computing Concepts among Preservice Teachers." *Journal of Research on Computing in Education,* Summer 1990, 22(4),pp. 413-430.

Hayes, J. "Computers as Catfish." *Educational IRM Quarterly,* Spring 1992, *1*(3), pp. 29–31.

Kinnaman, D. E. "Newsline: 2.5 Million Strong—And Growing." *Technology & Learning,* September 1992, *13*(1), p. 67.

Kozma, R. B. and Johnston J. "The Technological Revolution Comes to the Classroom." *Change,* January/February 1991, *23*(1), 10–23.

Longworth, R. C. "Corporate Schools: Cure for Despair?" *Chicago Tribune,* 31 May 1992, Section 1, p. 7.

Maddux, C. D. "Educational Computing: Liabilities, Assets, Potential." *Computers in the Schools,* 1990, *7*(4), pp. 93–103.

Magel, M. "Getting Familiar with MacMultimedia." *AV Video,* July 1992, *14*(7), pp. 84–90.

Mathis, J. "New Software Releases." *The Computing Teacher,* March 1992, *19*(6), pp. 50–51.

Moursund D. "Restructuring Education for the Information Age." *The Computing Teacher,* August/September 1991, *19*(1), p. 4.

Moursund, D. "Buying into the Future." *The Computing Teacher,* August/September 1992, *20*(1), p. 6.

Moursund, D. "Restructuring Education Part 3: What is the Information Age?" *The Computing Teacher,* November 1991, *19*(3), p. 4.

Niemiec, R. P. and Walberg, H. J. "From Teaching Machines to Microcomputers: Some Milestones in the History of Computer-based Instruction." *Journal of Research on Computing in Education,* Spring 1989, *21*(3), pp. 263–276.

Piller, C. "Separate Realities. The Creation of the Technological Underclass in America's Public Schools." *MacWorld,* September 1992, pp. 218–231.

Reiss, L. and Dolan, E. G. *Using Computers: Managing Change.* Cincinnati, OH: South-Western Publishing, 1989.

Rohm, C. E. T., Jr., and Stewart, W. T., Jr. *Essentials of Information Systems.* Santa Cruz, CA: Mitchell Publishing, 1988.

Schnake, M. A. *The World of Computers and Data Processing.* St. Paul, MN; West Publishing, 1985.

Shelly, G. B. and Cashman, T. J. *Computer Fundamentals with Application Software.* Boston, MA: Boyd and Fraser, 1986.

Technology & Learning. "Update: The Latest Technology Trends in the Schools," February 1993, *13*(5), pp. 28–32.

Willis, J. *Peanut Butter and Jelly Guide to Computers.* Beaverton, OR: Dilithium Press, 1984.

Willis, J. and Danley, W. *Nailing Jelly to a Tree.* Blue Ridge Summit, PA: TAB Books, 1982.

Part 2
The Computer as Tool

Objectives

After completing this chapter, you will be able to:

Explain the basic concepts of word processing.

List and explain the basic functions of a word processor.

Discuss at least three additional functions of most word processors. Explain why they would or would not be useful to you.

Define the term prewriting and explain how software can contribute to this aspect of writing.

Discuss the functions, potential usefulness, and limitations of spelling, grammar, and style aids.

Take a position for or against the process approach to writing instruction.

Define keyboarding and explain some of the problems related to teaching keyboarding skills.

Discuss the outcomes of using word processors as indicated by the research, including why the results are mixed.

Differentiate editing from revision and defend the significance of each.

Discuss the role of the teacher in implementing word processing in the curriculum.

Discuss several considerations in teaching students to use a specific word processor.

Develop lesson plans that implement word processing in your area(s) of the curriculum.

Analyze the role of word processing in the curriculum.

Chapter 2

Word Processing: Managing Text

Have you ever finished writing a term paper or composition, only to find that you have misspelled or omitted a word or phrase? Unfortunately, this error may have forced you to retype the entire paper (or at least large segments of it) wasting time and effort—to say nothing of causing you frustration. Just think how great it would be if any writing could be revised by redoing only those parts that needed changing? Think of the time and effort that could be saved—not to mention the disposition of the writer. If that sounds good to you, then you are ready for word processing!

Among the potential uses of computers in the classroom, word processing probably has aroused the greatest interest. A bibliography of word processing-related articles in magazines and journals of just the past few years would fill pages. Each advance in technology has brought new potentials and problems of application for the educator. Yet many teachers, for all the excitement, are still uncertain of what may be achieved or how to proceed. This chapter provides information that will reduce this uncertainty.

An Overview of Word Processing

To introduce word processing, we will first define it, then explain its basic concepts. Finally, we discuss who uses word processing and how its use has grown.

Definitions

Early computers were valued for their "number crunching" abilities, and, even today, many people think of computers primarily as numeric devices. The more useful applications for teachers and general users, however, are related to text manipulation—the control of words by the computer. The earliest efforts along this line were text editors, which were crude word manipulators with limited capabilities to ease the mechanical burdens of writing. They did, however, whet the appetite of early users for more powerful ways to control text.

The advanced application of computers for text manipulation is the word processor. As used in this chapter, a *word processor* is (1) a computer program for writing, editing, revising, formatting, and printing text, or (2) a computer that runs such software. Here, the term *word processing* means using a word processor (Figure 2.1).

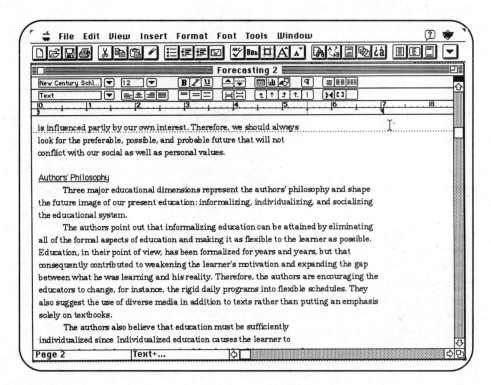

Figure 2.1. Word processing on a microcomputer.

Basic Concepts of Word Processing

Let's compare word processing to its predecessor, typing.

Improvements over Typing

A word processor takes away most of the mechanical problems associated with typing. Mistakes are corrected on the screen. Errors in the final printed copy should be a thing of the past. More complicated editing, such as repositioning words or blocks of text, is a matter of a few keystrokes. The days of laboriously retyping an entire document because of a spelling error or changed organization are gone. Once typed, anything that is correct need never be retyped. Any and all changes can be accomplished with relative speed and ease.

Some things that were never feasible with a typewriter have become commonplace. Boldface printing and aligned right margins (called *right justification*) are examples of these advances. Superscript and subscript elements require no more than a mouse click or a special command typed before the desired characters. Short lines of text can be centered on the page with a keystroke or click, eliminating counting of characters to determine the number of spaces to indent. Block indentation of paragraphs is equally simple.

Control over Page Layout

Word processing differs from conventional typing in another important way. Much of the typical typing effort focused on how to achieve the desired page format. Typists had to control margins manually and be alert continually to the approaching end of a line to decide whether to hyphenate a word or move to the next line on the page. A later decision to use double spacing or change margins meant retyping the entire document. Footnotes, footers, headings, and page numbering all required much thought and planning.

These mechanical matters are now left for the word processor to handle. Even when entering text, the ENTER key on the computer's keyboard serves only to signal the end of a paragraph or a line that must stand alone. There is no need to watch for the "end" of a line. The word processor manages all such concerns. The writer can focus on ideas, organization, and style. Mechanics, once a primary concern, are strictly secondary and readily altered.

Who Uses Word Processing?

Professional Users

Professional writers adopted word processing very quickly. It is likely that more microcomputers have been sold strictly for use as word processors than for any other purpose, including game playing. Journalists have all but switched completely to word processors. The steno pools filled with typewriters in business offices have virtually disappeared and have been replaced by word processing centers. Thus, word processing has significantly affected our communication efforts.

Casual Users

What about the rest of us, the nonprofessional writers? The steady decline in the price of microcomputers and the great improvements in word processing software have made this a tool for the masses. The level of sophistication available to the home user today rivals that of the most expensive systems used in industry. But sophistication has a price, that is, complexity of operation. Many word processors simply cannot be used on a once-a-month basis. The user actions necessary to make them perform are too numerous and difficult to remember without a lot of practice. Only through regular use do the procedures become automatic responses. For some people, then, there is a need for less complex approaches to word processing.

School Users

As the value of word processing became apparent, educators began to consider its application to writing in the schools. The same complexity affecting the casual user also made early word processing programs unsuitable for the classroom. Furthermore, educators wanted to extend the benefits of word processing to younger users. For them, however, a word processor with a densely printed multipage "Quick Reference" summary card showing the large number of commands available was unacceptable and unnecessary.

Fortunately, software such as *AppleWorks, Bank Street Writer,* and *Magic Slate* appeared. Such programs were inexpensive compared with professional word processing software. They proved to be versatile and, above all, easy to use. These attributes undoubtedly contributed to increased use of word processing by significant numbers of adults as well as children and students. Word processing programs have been improved and enhanced continually so that they are now even more versatile and capable of achieving a greater number of tasks that make writing efforts—particularly those related to editing and revising—even easier.

The Technical Side of Word Processing

All word processors share certain basic features, and most provide a range of additional functions. In addition, other common, useful writing aids that are available with word processors provide assistance with prewriting, outlining, spelling, grammar, and vocabulary.

Word Processor Functions

Basic Editing Functions

Much like automobiles, word processing programs come in different sizes. Some are large and very powerful, while others are smaller with somewhat limited power. Regardless of their size, all word processors offer the same basic functions (Figure 2.2).

ERASE	PERMITS DELETION OF UNWANTED TEXT AND "CLOSES" THE GAPS.
INSERT	PERMITS ADDITION OF TYPED MATERIAL WHEREVER NEEDED BY "OPENING" SPACE IN THE DOCUMENT FOR IT.
MARGINS	NEW MARGINS MAY BE SET AND THE DOCUMENT REFORMATTED TO FIT THEM WITHOUT RETYPING.
MOVE/COPY	RELOCATES/DUPLICATES TEXT WITHIN A DOCUMENT
REPLACE	AFTER LOCATING DESIRED TEXT, CHANGES IT TO WHATEVER IS SPECIFIED.
SEARCH	LOCATES A SPECIFIED WORD, PHRASE, OR GROUP OF CHARACTERS WITHIN A DOCUMENT.
WORD WRAP	AUTOMATICALLY MOVES A WORD TOO LONG FOR THE CURRENT LINE TO THE NEXT LINE OF THE SCREEN OR PAGE. ELIMINATES USER ATTENTION TO THE RIGHT MARGIN.

Figure 2.2. Basic editing functions of word processors.

Word wrap or *wrap around* allows you to type text without attention to the end of each line. When your typing reaches the end of a line and the final word will not fit within the margin, word wrap automatically moves it to the next line, enabling you to continue with text entry. You press the ENTER key only when you wish to begin a new paragraph or to move down to a new line prior to reaching the right margin.

With the *insert* function, space is created automatically. New material may be added anywhere in the document without retyping what follows.

The *erase* or *delete* function removes unwanted letters, words, phrases, sentences, paragraphs, and even more. Usually, the cursor is used to mark the beginning and end of the unwanted text. When you give the delete command, the unwanted text is immediately removed and the remaining text appropriately rearranged so that the layout remains correct.

The *search* and *replace* functions search the document for a specific character, word, or phrase and allow this specific text to be replaced with another. Perhaps you mis-used or misspelled a word. Assume you used the word *principle* when, in fact, the word should have been *principal*. By using search and replace, each occurrence of the incorrect word *principle* can be located and replaced by the correct word *principal*.

With the *move* function, a portion of the text is transferred from one location to another. Typically, you mark the beginning and end of the text block to be moved, then position the cursor at the desired new location for the text. When you give the correct command, the block is moved. All text material is rearranged automatically, so that proper spacing and page format are maintained.

Figure 2.3 shows how basic editing functions may be selected from a menu in one word processor.

Additional Functions

In addition to basic functions, word processors provide such capabilities as centering text, underlining, page numbering, and printing boldface characters. Other features produce variations in the document that are similar to typeset material.

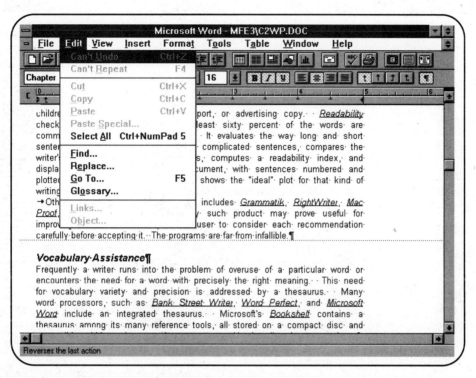

Figure 2.3. Basic word processing functions are available from a menu.

These include right justification of margins, proportional spacing of characters, and changing the number of characters per inch (called *pitch*.) All graphical word processors, such as those for Macintosh and *Windows,* allow you to select from a range of fonts and character sizes in order to vary headings or just as an aesthetic choice. Character-based software such as *WordStar 6.0* and *WordPerfect 5.1* also offer some font variations. Many contemporary word processors permit you to insert graphic images into your documents. The availability of fonts and graphics within a word processor has begun to blur the lines between word processing and desktop publishing (which is discussed in Chapter 7). Some additional word processor functions are outlined in Figure 2.4.

Note that some of the added features shown in the figure are dependent on the printer's capability as well as the word processor's. Not all printers can support all the possible functions, even if the word processing software offers them. Your choice of a printer may depend on your need for these features.

Writing Aids

In addition to the word processing functions that are so helpful in easing the writing process, several types of applications have been developed to assist with prewriting, outlining, spelling, grammar, and vocabulary.

BOLD	EMPHASIZES SPECIFIED TEXT IN THE PRINTOUT BY DARKENING AND SLIGHTLY ENLARGING EACH CHARACTER
CENTERING	AUTOMATICALLY POSITIONS TEXT AT CENTER OF A LINE, E.G., TITLES OR HEADINGS
CHAIN PRINTING	PRINTS TWO OR MORE SEPARATE DOCUMENT FILES AS ONE TO OVERCOME SIZE LIMITATIONS ON INDIVIDUAL FILES
FONTS/GRAPHICS	ALLOWS VARIETY IN TEXT APPEARANCE AS WELL AS INSERTING IMAGES INTO A DOCUMENT
JUSTIFICATION	PRODUCES AN EVEN RIGHT MARGIN BY ADDING SPACES BETWEEN LETTERS OR WORDS TO RESEMBLE TYPESETTING
MERGE PRINTING	CREATES PERSONALIZED DOCUMENTS BY INSERTING NAME, ADDRESS, OR OTHER MATERIAL INTO A BASIC "TEMPLATE," E.G., FORM LETTERS AND LEGAL DOCUMENTS
PAGE NUMBERING	AUTOMATICALLY NUMBERS PAGES OFTEN WITH CONTROL OVER WHERE ON THE PAGE, E.G., LOWER RIGHT OR TOP CENTER, AND WHETHER ROMAN OR ARABIC

Figure 2.4. Selected additional functions of word processors.

Prewriting

Considerable recent interest has been focused on the process of writing, which is discussed more fully later in this chapter. The first step is prewriting, which has generating ideas as its focus. Prewriting software is intended to help with that most difficult phase in writing, getting started.

One program aimed at helping students get started in the writing process is *Writer's Helper* from Conduit. Among the features of this software are user-modifiable prewriting and revision activities. The prewriting phase—helping the student to formulate a topic and organize facts and ideas—includes several helpful activities. "Idea Wheels" assists the writer by suggesting subjects and verbs. "Audience" asks the student questions that help to identify the readers for whom the writing is intended. "Organize" includes an outliner that helps students structure their writing ideas. *Let's Write*, a software system designed to let you teach writing like writers really write, includes *Writer's Helper* among its five software packages, along with the excellent journal *The Writing Notebook*.

Another example is *College Application Essay Writer*, a word processor from Scholastic. The "Getting Ideas" feature encourages brainstorming, but also has an "Idea Bank" of possible topics, words, and phrases. "Organizing Your Essay" guides the outlining phase. Best of all, it is inexpensive.

Hartley's *The Poet's Journal* is an 11-disk set with lesson plans, black line masters, and worksheets. Lessons encourage students to brainstorm, prewrite and analyze their work, and create poems. Forms include haiku, echoes, and limericks with guided use of alliteration, rhyme, rhythm, and onomatopoeia.

Prewriting packages such as these can be invaluable in moving the student past the stage of staring at a blank sheet of paper with pencil poised, unable to proceed because idea blockage prevents any meaningful writing activity.

Outlining

Outlining has become an integral feature of some word processors (Figure 2.5). You can begin to write by creating a multi-level outline, then fill in the subordinate text under each heading. The software helps maintain proper indentation to indicate outline levels. It allows you at any point to display the outline in whatever de-

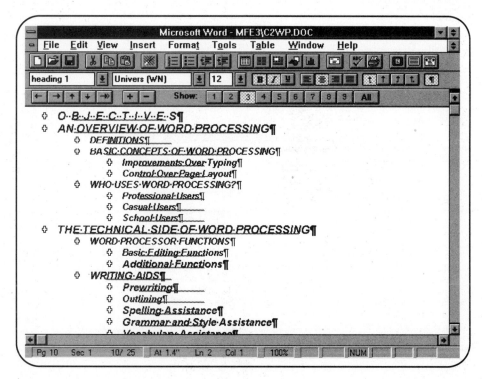

Figure 2.5. Outline mode of a word processor.

tail you wish, from only the main headings to all levels and their associated text. You can switch between levels of detail to get a broader or more detailed view of your work. Zeitz, Horney, and Anderson-Inman (1992) discuss applications of outlining software.

Spelling Assistance

The spelling checker (Figure 2.6) has become such an indispensable word processing aid that it is now part of virtually all word processors. Simply defined, a spelling checker is a program that compares all words in your document to those in a dictionary stored in the computer. Words that do not match those in the dictionary are then displayed as questionable. The time taken to check the spelling of words in the text is a fraction of the time required by the traditional proofreading method, as well as being more accurate.

Note that all words that do not match words in the electronic dictionary are questioned. When a spelling checker presents such a word, you may correct or ignore it, depending on whether it is actually misspelled or is simply not found in the electronic dictionary. Most spelling checkers permit you to add new words to the dictionary, if desired. Most programs even suggest alternatives for the suspect word. If the correct spelling is listed, a simple keystroke or click corrects the error. In short, a spelling checker is not a complete substitute for spelling knowledge, but rather a valuable helper.

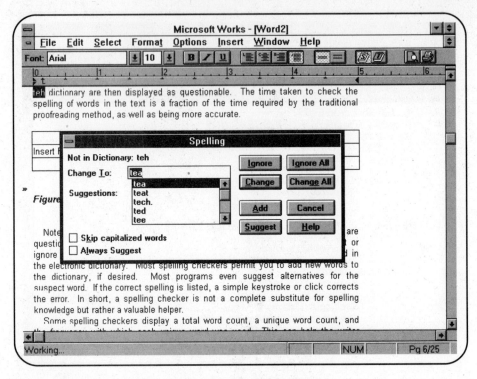

Figure 2.6. This spelling checker suggests corrections.

Some spelling checkers display a total word count, a unique word count, and the frequency with which each unique word was used. This can help the writer by pointing out possible overuse of certain terms. Spelling aids cannot, however, tell what you *meant* to write. If you type "there" instead of "their" or "contact" for "contract," a spelling checker will not find the errors because each "error" is listed in its dictionary.

Grammar and Style Assistance

Proofreading software (also called grammar checkers) is available to work with many common word processors and has become a built-in feature of more advanced word processors (Figure 2.7). These programs check documents for possible errors in grammar, punctuation, style, sentence and paragraph construction, usage, and so on, varied as appropriate to the type of writing or intended audience. Analysis is based on the conventions of language usage, specialized dictionaries of troublesome words, and complete phrases. Like spelling checkers, such programs have definite limitations. They tend to emphasize simple mechanical errors and miss many common writing problems. They are, however, much improved today from the early versions that acknowledged only basic business writing style. A grammar checker can be of value to any writer.

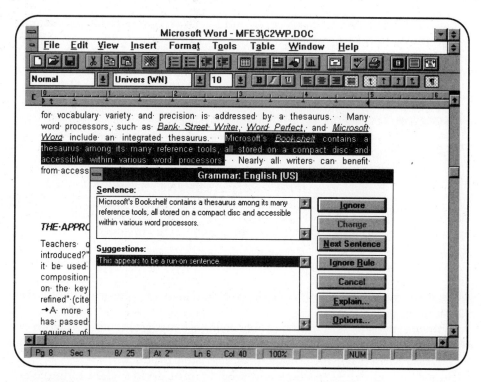

Figure 2.7. Output of a grammar and style-assistance program.

One program called *Readability* was designed to accommodate the varied styles required for different audiences and purposes. It can analyze writing as appropriate for a newspaper article, novel, magazine feature story, children's story or book, technical report, or advertising copy. *Readability* checks the text to ensure that at least 60 percent of the words are commonly used in American English. It evaluates the way long and short sentences have been mixed, identifies complicated sentences, compares the writer's style to that of other writers, computes a readability index, and displays a diagram of the entire document, with sentences numbered and plotted on a chart. The display also shows the "ideal" plot for that kind of writing for purposes of comparison.

Other popular software of this type includes *Grammatik, RightWriter, Mac Proof,* and *Sensible Grammar.* Any such product may prove useful for improving written text; all require the user to consider each recommendation carefully before accepting it. The programs are far from infallible.

Vocabulary Assistance

Frequently, a writer runs into the problem of overuse of a particular word or encounters the need for a word with precisely the right meaning. This need for vocabulary variety and precision is addressed by a thesaurus. Many word processors, such as *Bank Street Writer, WordPerfect,* and *Microsoft Word* include an integrated thesaurus. Microsoft's *Bookshelf* contains a thesaurus among its many reference tools, all stored on a compact disc and accessible within various word processors. Nearly all writers can benefit from access to an electronic thesaurus.

Issues in Word Processing

The Appropriate Age to Begin

Teachers often ask, "At what grade level should word processing be introduced?" Proponents of word processing for students tend to argue that it be used early in their schooling. Donald Graves, a prominent figure in composition theory, has stated, "[O]ne can imagine starting kids off writing on the keyboard and saving handwriting until motor skills are more highly refined" (cited in Green, 1984, p. 22).

A more acceptable view for many may be to wait until writing instruction has passed the point of sheer mechanics and at least a short paragraph is required of students from time to time. This timing differentiates the physical act of writing from writing as a visual representation of thoughts or writing as "art."

Another view is to start a little sooner than just suggested, because word processing may enable more significant writing activities at an early age by removing the physical barriers between thoughts and a visible product.

Ultimately, individual teachers and schools must decide when to implement word processing, taking into account not only appropriateness for the students but also the school's ability to provide sufficient computer access (Hunter, Benedict, and Bilan, 1989). Regardless of when it is introduced, word processing should support, enhance, and extend the curriculum, and should not become an isolated computer activity.

Keyboarding

Keyboarding means learning to use your fingers correctly on the keyboard for rapid text entry, free from the formatting concerns of pre-computer typing. Keyboarding is basic to most uses of the computer, not just word processing. Persons doing word processing, however, clearly benefit particularly from sound keyboarding skills. A related concern is that students may find it extremely difficult ever to learn to use the keyboard correctly if they do not learn keyboarding before they become hunt-and-peck typists (Ubelacker, 1992).

Many writers and advocates of word processing in the schools now presume the need for keyboarding instruction. The issue again is timing. For the youngest students, you must seriously consider keyboarding from the standpoint of both need and physical ability. There is general agreement that children are ready by grade 4 for keyboarding instruction. Hunter and colleagues (1989) concluded that keyboarding instruction should begin a few weeks prior to the introduction of word processing instruction. Once instruction has begun, they suggest that, in the absence of norms for keyboarding achievement, the most basic expectation should be typing at a speed at least equal to the student's handwriting speed. This assures that the potential to benefit from word processing exists.

A related issue is, who should teach keyboarding to children? Although business education teachers claim special expertise, Hunter and colleagues (1989) argue persuasively that elementary teachers are more appropriate, provided they are willing to learn how to teach keyboarding. In one study, just one day of instruction proved sufficient for teachers who already knew how to type, while non-typists needed three weeks of instruction.

Another approach to keyboarding instruction is to let the computer teach the student. Myers and Spindler-Virgin (1989) reported that keyboarding programs worked well for them at the fourth-grade level. In our own experience, *Mavis Beacon Teaches Typing* has been particularly impressive. This software keeps track of student strengths and weaknesses, then alters the lessons accordingly, much as a skilled teacher would.

Even when it is started with young users, effective keyboarding instruction is time-consuming and requires a high level of monitoring. Often, teachers must provide extrinsic motivation for children who are unable to foresee the eventual payoff. Collis (1988) reported on research showing that fourth-grade children improved their speed and accuracy significantly during 8 weeks of keyboarding instruction, but had reverted to preinstruction levels 8 weeks after instruction. This underscores the importance of continued practice to maintain skill levels, which will occur naturally if keyboarding and word processing instruction are linked properly.

The Process Approach to Writing

For word processing to have maximum value in composition, a particular view of instruction called the *process approach* to writing is recommended. Historically, writing has been viewed as product-oriented. The finished document was the crucial element, and most of the emphasis was placed on mechanics (Schiffman, 1986). In the 1990s, this view largely has given way to process-oriented writing instruction, which stresses the steps and processes over the finished product.

In an effort to synthesize many models of the writing process, Hunter and Begoray (1990) produced a four part framework. Writers first *generate* ideas, whether from memory, external resources, or original research. Next they *organize* the ideas, for example, by sorting and sequencing notecards or creating an outline. *Composing* translates the organized ideas into sentences and paragraphs. *Revision* seeks to improve the composition and may occur repeatedly until the writer is satisfied. Beaver (1992) included a publishing step in which the writing is shared with others.

Much of the interest in word processing has centered on its ability to facilitate the revision step. Hunter and Begoray (1990) note that comparatively little attention has been given to the role of word processing in the other stages. With appropriate instruction, word processing can be an integral part of each step in the writing process. The process approach to writing matches well with the power of a word processor to help produce an initial draft quickly, then facilitate mechanical editing and substantive revision, before producing a polished printed copy (see Boone, 1991). A computer, however, is not essential to this approach. Rather, the role of the teacher in guiding the development of writing skills and strategies is the essential feature, as noted in the following discussion of research on word processing.

Research on Learning with Word Processing

What is it that has caused countless computer-phobic teachers at all levels to suppress their high-tech anxieties and plunge into classroom word processing? Clearly, the answer must be a belief that word processing will allow their students to develop writing skills more quickly or to a higher level. Let's look at what educational researchers and users of word processing have reported.

Effects on Quantity and Quality

Anecdotal and research-based reports on the relationship between word processing and the quantity and quality of student writing have for the past decade been inconclusive, even contradictory. Owston, Murphy, and Wideman (1991) found in a middle-school study that word-processed essays scored significantly higher for writing achievement than those composed traditionally but typed by the researchers before evaluation. The researchers attributed part of the difference to better spelling in the word-processed essays, although they did not indicate whether spelling checkers were used. Word-processed papers were also significantly longer, which again may have contributed to better scores. Levin, Boruta, and Vasconcellos (1983), O'Brien (1984), Feldman (1984), Zurn (1987), Morton (1988), Schramm (1989), Montague (1990), Dudley-Marling and Oppenheimer (1990), and Weisberg (1992) all provide evidence that word processing leads to improvements in the quality or quantity of material.

Grejda and Hannafin (1991), however, studied fifth graders and found that those who used a word processor performed less well than the others on editing tests. Borgh and Dickson (1992) found many interesting effects in a study using a word processor that gave spoken feedback, but gains in the quantity and quality of students' writing were not among them. Levin, Riel, Rowe, and Boruta (1984) and Daiute (1985) found that students actually wrote less with a word processor. Roblyer (1988) concluded that word processing did not appear to improve writing quality. Schramm (1989) analyzed twelve studies, of which three reported no differences in quality, and one reported a negative effect for the word processing group.

One possible explanation for some of these discrepancies is the difficulty of quantifying the assessment of writing. Although most newer studies report using an holistic approach to judging quality, significant subjectivity persists in the end. Other problems with the research are discussed in the conclusion of this chapter.

Editing/Revision

Traditionally, teachers of writing have invested much time in commenting on student papers, with the goal of helping students to develop their writing skills. However, the next assignment given to the students will involve a different topic and different circumstances. It is doubtful whether or not the red marks on one assignment have any impact on current work. The real need in learning to write is to revise and polish each assignment through several iterations, based on suggestions and rethinking. Few teachers have been willing to require such revision because of the arduous and frustrating nature of the task without a computer.

Ease of text editing (small, mechanical details) and revising (making structural changes) is one of the most obvious benefits of using a computer to write. According to Grejda and Hannafin (1991, p. 89), "Improving the revising skills of young writers . . . is widely regarded as integral to all process writing approaches. . . . Yet, revision is among the least researched, least understood, and, usually, least taught aspects of the writing process. . . ." Noting the mixed results of past research, they investigated "the effects of word processing and requisite instruction on the mechanical and structural revisions of fifth graders." They found that their word-processing subjects performed the least well of all! They attribute this to insufficient time for the students to learn to use the computer comfortably and to a need for better teaching methods, two critical flaws in much research.

In Dudley-Marling and Oppenheimer's study (1990), students made changes in their initial text primarily at the word level, which the researchers considered editing, not revision. During direct observation, the researchers never once saw a student actually move text around, despite the ease with which it can be done. In fact, students simply ignored suggestions from the teacher that involved restructuring their work. This study offers evidence of the critical role that the teacher must play. According to the researchers, "it is much more likely that student revision will be affected by such factors as topic choice, ownership (determined often by the teacher's style), audience, purpose, and instruction than the mere presence of microcomputers" (p. 41).

Earlier studies by Levin, Boruta, and Vasconcellos (1983), Collier (1983), Harris (1985), and Haas (1988) all found that revision was generally superficial, regardless of whether the authors were children or faculty members. Wolf (1985) reported that although young writers lacked any sense of the totality of their work, and could therefore only edit, revision skills improved substantially with age.

The findings of Owston, Murphy, and Wideman (1991) are especially interesting because their study involved a larger number of subjects than most, and all subjects were already experienced with computers, a situation that addressed the "comfort" factor. Although the overall findings were favorable to word processing, student revision from draft to final copy did not vary significantly between word-processing and handwriting conditions. Kurth (1987) reported similar results.

Finding an Audience

Many writers experience difficulty in identifying an audience for their work. Writing is such an abstract process that they cannot relate their ideas to a specific audience and have trouble with their approach to these ill-defined recipients of their work. Composing on the computer appears to provide an audience with which students can carry on a "conversation." Dudley-Marling and Oppenheimer (1990, p. 38) have stated that "in the absence of communicative intent there is little motivation for students to revise their work."

In addition, students view the computer as extremely unintelligent, requiring a much more thorough explanation of their ideas than their teacher demands (Loheyde, 1984). Of course, the "author's chair" concept of process writing, in which writers sit before their peers and read their work aloud, also provides a concrete audience (Montague, 1990). Publishing student work (Beaver, 1992) also contributes to a sense of audience.

Effects on Attitudes

The favorable impact of word processing on writers' attitudes is much clearer (Roblyer, 1988; Montague, 1990; Owston, Murphy, and Wideman, 1991; Weisberg, 1992). Schramm (1989) reviewed six studies that compared changes in student attitudes toward writing after using word processing with those of students using traditional writing methods. Five of the six studies reported positive effects, while one study stated that the changes were negative. If one subscribes to the belief that students will perform better if they enjoy their task, then it seems reasonable to assume a relationship between student attitude and writing quality. Schramm found such a positive relationship in those studies that assessed the effects of word processing on quality of writing in addition to attitude change.

Owston et al. (1990) studied students who had had considerable computer experience and found very negative attitudes toward revision or making any significant changes to handwritten work. They frequently termed paragraph rewriting a "waste of time." The ease of revision in word processing does not appear to overcome this attitude, or perhaps even contributes to it, because these subjects were experienced word-processing users. In conclusion, the authors call for more research on the process of writing as well as its products to gain insight into the benefits of computer-based writing.

Teaching/Learning Requirements

Some issues raised by research concern the teaching and learning environment. Just how should you teach students to use a word processor?

Reed (1990) studied English education undergraduate majors in an 11-week course focused on computers and writing. Some had had no computer experience, others had prior word-processing experience, and a third group had both word-processing and programming experience. In the pre-test, students were asked to list potential uses of computers. At the post-test, the list increased by 52 percent

and the focus of the uses shifted from isolated skills development or drill and practice to uses that support the writing process. Attention shifted from the education
students themselves to concerns about their future students, and ideas for "doing
things better" began to surface. "The prospective teachers evidently began to view
computers as a system participant that could contribute significantly to providing
their prospective student writers with an instructional framework for breaking a
writing task into prewriting, writing, and revising stages." In other words, you
must learn to use a word processor well yourself before you will see its instructional value. This is your first task as a teacher.

Blau and Campbell (1991) concluded that their study did not show any gain in
the areas of writing skills or attitudes from using computers. They did note, however, that comfort with computers seemed to be a significant factor that they had
not addressed. They suggested that comfort be a focus of any computer writing
program. Further, they asserted that it may be inappropriate merely to substitute
the computer for the typewriter, as they did. Instead, teaching methods need to be
changed in order to work toward the desired effect. The direct instructional focus
needs to be on the revision possibilities that the computer enables and the new possibilities created by composing at the computer, rather than first handwriting, then
word processing. Similarly, Dudley-Marling and Oppenheimer (1990) noted that
word processing does not necessarily affect what teachers teach, which is the key
to the problem. They strongly urged an over emphasis on teaching learners the desired writing and revision strategies.

Grejda and Hannafin (1991) concluded that present methods of introducing
word processing (and computer use in general) are flawed. Competence with
the hardware and software is a critical factor, they believe, in obtaining meaningful gains from computer use. "While it is clear that word processing has significant
potential to improve young writers' compositions, it is equally clear that methods
that optimize both the technological and human aspects of writing have yet to
be developed."

Conclusion

On the surface, the research evidence fails to support unambiguously the value
of word processing and may seem disappointing. Yet virtually anyone who has
learned to use a word processor knows intuitively that it is somehow better. After
examining the available research literature, Hunter, Jardine, Rilstone, and Weisgerber (1990) concluded that there were many problems with the studies. "Much
of the research was based on samples of university students, nearly all of it relied
on comparisons of students who chose to use word processors (as opposed to using random assignment), few of the studies made any effort either to teach students
the use of word processors or to ascertain their levels of word processing expertise,
and none of the studies made any reference to systematic instruction in the writing process or in revision strategies" (p. 45). They further noted that only one study
involved rigid time limits, and it showed marked differences in quality, favoring
word processing. From this, they suggested that the lack of clear gains for word

processing may result partially from open-ended time frames in which students reach a personal "level of acceptable performance," regardless of writing method. What is not known is how time varies in attaining this level, or how to get students to raise their own personal level to new heights—interesting questions indeed.

It is apparent that, in and of itself, word processing does not improve writing skill. Writers still have to understand the need for and practice the art of editing and revising. Most research studies have paid little or no attention to the role of the teacher in stimulating and demanding the editing and revision that can improve writing. If revision remains a once-over-lightly activity, contrary to the intent of the process approach, there is little reason to expect students to show great benefit from word processing. Conversely, supporting fully the process approach with the power of a word processor may be the optimal combination of techniques.

Classroom Applications of Word Processing

The following applications, including many experiences and ideas of classroom teachers, represent but a few possible uses of a word processor for school-age students. The creative mind of the teacher and the desire to apply word-processing techniques in the classroom will increase and immeasurably enhance this necessarily limited list of possible activities.

Teaching Word Processing

There are many fine resources expressly for teaching specific word processors, many of which are listed in the bibliography for this chapter. Space permits only a few general suggestions here. If at all possible, demonstrate your points to your students by using an LCD panel or video projector connected to your computer before they attempt to perform the same operations.

How Much to Teach

Most word processors have such a wealth of features that even experienced users may not know or use them all. When working with any but the simplest word processors, teach only the really fundamental things initially, such as loading and saving files, rudimentary editing, and printing. Don't overwhelm your students; they'll learn more as needed.

Cursor Movement

Maneuvering within a document is a critical function. Most word processors have several different ways to move the cursor to a desired location: by clicking the mouse, using the cursor movement (arrow) keys on the keyboard, using function keys, and so forth. Be certain that students master the appropriate techniques for moving about a document quickly, rather than relying entirely on the cursor keys or scroll bars, which tend to be relatively slow.

Editing

To develop proficiency in editing with a word processor, prepare sample documents and give them to students on disks. Provide final printouts, as well as drafts, to read for content and organization. Leave wide margins to facilitate editing. This technique can be used effectively to stress the finalizing aspects of writing, rather than the initial creating, as well as the mechanics of editing. It's a good way to approach word selection and overuse of subject–verb word order, especially when the same pronoun begins each sentence, as is often the case in young children's writing.

Revising

The mechanical aspect of effective revision is the ability to move blocks of text around within a document. A "scrambled" file on disk, with accompanying printout and, typically, a correct copy, can provide basic practice in moving blocks. Beaver (1992) suggests using familiar content that has a definite sequence. Correcting the order will also reinforce the content while teaching about the word processor.

Locating Words in a Document

A word processor can be used as a crude data storage system. This offers a perfect excuse for mastering the SEARCH function, which can locate a particular piece of information in the file. Students might enter their own personal list of bothersome spelling words, adding and deleting as their spelling improves and new lessons are begun. Name and address files, lists of belongings, and catalogs of collections all offer potential subjects for this use of a word processor.

Students also can use their word processor as a tool for elementary analysis of writing. Provide a document on disk and guide student analysis with questions. How often does the word *honor* appear in a political speech? In what context(s)? How often does the pronoun *I* appear in student writing? How does the author use some specific word?

Teaching Sequencing

Explicit lessons on sequencing are common at various grade levels. Schipper (1991) types stories that students are reading in such a way that they can be cut into strips. Cooperative learning groups then each receive a set of strips to sequence, which creates the base for later, oral discussion of the story. Schipper also recommends this technique for larger content units, putting the major ideas or events on strips to sequence.

For seventh- and eighth-graders, Scotchmoor (1984) gave students a disk copy of a scrambled, unfamiliar story of 15 to 20 sentences. Students used their computers to sequence the scrambled sentences as they deemed logical. Scotchmoor then read her original version and allowed students to share theirs, many of which were quite different. Students later wrote and scrambled stories to challenge their friends.

Topic Identification

A major problem for writers is topic selection. Graves (1982) and many others have stressed the need for allowing students to select their own topics. Teacher-assigned topics often lack relevance and interest; it is better to help the student identify topics of personal significance.

At the very beginning of the term, have students prepare a list of possible theme topics. This will require prompting in most cases. Try to provide broad guidelines that afford flexibility. Here are some ideas that you can expand upon and adapt to various grade levels:

PEOPLE	THE FUTURE
The persons(s) I most admire	Careers I am considering
My most unusual relatives	Places I want to visit

FOODS	ACTIVITIES
Foods that I love to eat	Jobs I have to do around the house
Foods that I can't stand	My favorite television show
Foods that I'd like to try	The best book that I've ever read

Letter Writing

Despite the impact of the telephone, letter writing can still generate interest when it serves a real purpose. Where would FAX be without letters (and other documents) to send? In one school in San Francisco, students write to penpals who work at a local bank, exchanging their letters by FAX (Piller, 1992). Piller reports high motivation because the audience is real and students want to please their penpals. Beaver (1992) suggests requesting research materials from organizations, such as tourism bureaus, or preparing invitations to school events as ideal situations for teaching students how to merge form letters and database addresses, a process called *mail merge* or *merge print*.

Prompted Writing

Prompted writing guides the learner's writing with questions and instructions placed in a file by the teacher. The student loads the file, then composes a document by responding to the prompts. *FrEdWriter* includes provision for creating prompts that the student cannot erase. Rodrigues (1986) has explained how to do this with almost any word processor.

Beaver (1992) extended the idea of prompted writing to have students submit their draft documents only on disk. The teacher then adds comments right into the file, using a different font to make the "mark ups" stand out. Students can then revise the work, erasing the comments before printing. Beaver also noted that many worksheet activities can become computer-based. When students are to choose among alternatives, type the worksheet with the alternatives included. Students then edit the file, deleting the incorrect choices. This can be especially good for integrating word processing into many content areas. Here are two examples:

1. The twin's teacher *was/were* happy with *they're/their* science project.
2. *Chicago/Springfield* is the capitol of *Iowa/Illinois*.

Brainstorming

The principle of brainstorming is to generate and record ideas as rapidly as possible, without concern for typical issues of order, practicality, or viability. One member of each work group should act as recorder, typing all ideas directly into a word-processor file. The ideas then can be printed for discussion, with the list ready for modification on screen (Beaver, 1992; Schipper, 1991).

Writing for Beginners

Piller (1992) describes how kindergartners can dictate stories to older students who word process and edit them. The older student gets extra practice with the computer, gains editing skills, and learns how to interview someone as the story develops. The younger child gets a start on reading by watching the words appear on the screen, then seeing them printed on paper.

KidWriter exemplifies software designed to make writing more appealing in the early grades. First, the child creates a colorful picture by selecting from many background scenes and over 100 "clip art" graphics. Then the child can add text to the picture and write a story about it in the lower part of the screen, adding pages and illustrations as needed. Printouts include the pictures, in color with the right printer (Figure 2.8). This is not a word processor, so features are very limited, but the motivational value is high. *Explore-A-Story PLUS* and *Story Tailor* are other products with similar uses.

Group Projects

Computers can increase socialization through collaborative or cooperative learning projects (Montague, 1990; Collis, 1988). Montague specifically recommends daily writing activities with maximum peer interaction at all stages of the writing process. If you have students routinely proofread one another's work, both the writer and the proofreader will benefit.

Beaver (1992) suggests giving students a topic and time to brainstorm ideas. Ideally, the students would be in a computer lab, and each would begin to draft a document at the computer. After perhaps 15 minutes, direct students to finish their current sentence, then move to a different computer to read what others have already written and continue the story from there. If you have only one or a few computers, students can still rotate to the computer and continue whatever others have begun. You could also assign parts of a class story for independent development, then retrieve them in sequence into a larger file.

A class book based on student research is another good group project. Give each student a specific research assignment to complete, including doing the final

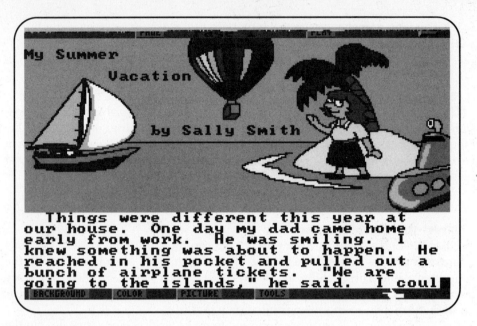

Figure 2.8. First page of an illustrated story from *KidWriter*.

write-up on a word processor. Combine all the reports in an appropriate order to create a class reference work.

Word Processing with a Single Classroom Computer

Obviously, word processing is well suited to schools with computer lab facilities that are adequate to accommodate many users simultaneously. This does not mean, however, that nothing can be accomplished with only one or a few computers.

While word-processing software greatly facilitates editing and revising, both tasks can be completed by hand. You can use a single computer with a projection system to display a sample paragraph or document, solicit ideas to improve its writing, and make the changes as the group observes (Beaver, 1992). This may be more effective than normal paper-based approaches. Montague (1990) recommends using one computer to demonstrate the processes of planning, drafting, and revising, by typing as students offer suggestions. Again, a projection system makes this feasible for groups of more than just a few. Montague also suggests handwritten initial drafts as a way to work around limited numbers of computers.

Weisberg (1992) describes in some detail how she used word processing with second graders in a one-computer classroom. Assignments included letters, narratives, and other creative writing. A year-long project involved kids taking a stuffed elephant, named Toby, home for the night or weekend, then writing about the experience on the next school day. The computer was in use all day in Weisberg's class, as students left the regular instruction to take their turns. Individual projects required from six days to one month to complete. Weisberg had been reluctant to try such projects with her class, but reported that it was exciting for everyone and very productive. Students preferred using the computer and their writing became more "lucid, creative, and interesting."

Writing across the Curriculum

Writing skills are critical to success in life for most individuals. These skills develop slowly and must be nurtured constantly. To teach writing skills in only one curriculum area is to deny their importance. Once students begin to write with a word processor, they should use it ideally for *all* writing assignments. This will contribute to maintenance of keyboarding skills, as well as extend the potential benefits of "electronic composing" to all writing endeavors.

For specific assistance in implementing word processing in your school, refer to the chapter bibliography, notably Boone (1991), Franklin (1991; 1990), Costanzo (1989), Howie (1989), Collis (1988), and Turner and Land (1988). Anyone seriously interested in writing with word processors should subscribe to the outstanding journal, *The Writing Notebook*. See the Appendix for the address.

Summary

Word processing has significantly changed the writing process. If not yet obsolete, the typewriter will soon become a curiosity. Word processing has greatly diminished the tedium of mechanical editing and has provided complete flexibility in reorganizing thoughts by moving and changing text. Revision need no longer be as difficult as previously.

Most word-processing software provides the same basic functions. Differences occur in such areas as control of fonts, handling of footers and headers, and integrated features such as dictionaries. To further enhance writing, electronic assistance is available for prewriting, outlining, spelling and style proofing, and even word selection with a thesaurus.

There are many benefits to writing with a word processor. The quantity and quality of writing may increase, attitudes toward writing may improve, writer's block may disappear, and even reading skills may improve. Few of these improvements, however, will occur effortlessly. Skillful instruction in composition remains essential. Unresolved are such issues as *when* word processing and keyboarding should be introduced. There is also much evidence that stimulating students to revise their work, so necessary to improved writing, is a difficult task. Those who use a word processor know from experience what a marvel it is. How *best* to bring its potential to our students is not yet clear.

Chapter 2 Activities

1. Learn to use any available word processor. Note that some have their own online tutorials for self-instruction.
2. Using the word-processing program that you have learned, write a letter to the publisher of the software, indicting what features you like about the program and what features you do not like. If appropriate, suggest improvements for the program.
3. Explore the availability of various writing aids in your setting. Read their manuals and determine their appropriateness for your use.
4. Using your word-processing program, enter the following lines as given
   All the king's horses
   Humpty Dumpty had a great fall.
   Couldn't put Humpty together again.
   And all the king's men
   Humpty Dumpty sat on a wall.
   Once entered, use the MOVE function to arrange the rhyme as it should correctly appear.

5. Use your word processor to complete this story.
   Bill and Mary watched intently as the bright light in the sky grew closer and closer. Suddenly . . .
6. Below is presented a definition of the term *word processor*. Notice that it is brief—too brief. Using your word processor, add to the definition to make it more meaningful: word processor—a program for writing and editing . . .
7. How would word processing benefit you as a teacher? List several applications in which you might use word processing in your work.
8. Investigate the keyboarding issue as well as available keyboarding/typing tutorial software. Explain your position related to teaching keyboarding skills.
9. Outline a research project to investigate some aspect of word processing's effect on writing skills.
10. Develop a lesson plan that implements word processing in your area(s) of the curriculum.
11. Write a position paper on the role of word processing in the curriculum. Be sure to address several content areas.
12. Select at least two classroom applications from among those discussed, and develop lesson plans that implement them.

Bibliography

Balajthy, E. "Keyboarding, Language Arts, and the Elementary School Child." *The Computing Teacher*, February 1988, 15(1), pp. 40–43.

Balajthy, E. *Microcomputers in Reading and Language Arts*. Englewood Cliffs, NJ: Prentice-Hall, 1986.

Beaver, J. F. "Making Word Problems Relevant to Your Students." *The Computing Teacher*, November 1991, *19*(3), pp. 50–51.

Beaver. J. F. "Using Computer Power to Improve Your Teaching." *The Computing Teacher*, February 1992, *19*(5), pp. 5–9.

Blau, S. R. and Campbell, P. B. "To Nibble or To Byte: The Impact of Computers on the Skills and Attitudes of First-Year College Writing Students." *Computers in the Schools*, 1991, *8*(4), pp. 147–157.

Bolter, J. D. *Writing Space. The Computer, Hypertext, and the History of Writing.* Hillsdale, NJ: Lawrence Erlbaum Associates, Inc., 1990.

Boone, R. *Teaching Process Writing with Computers.* Eugene, OR: ISTE, 1991.

Borgh, K. and Dickson, W. P. "The Effects on Children's Writing of Adding Speech Synthesis to a Word Processor." *Journal of Research on Computing in Education,* Summer 1992, *24*(4), pp. 533–544.

Britton, B. W. and Glynn, S. M. *Computer Writing Environments. Theory, Research, and Design.* Hillsdale, NJ: Lawrence Erlbaum Associates, Inc., 1989.

Bruce, B. C. and Rubin, A. *Electronic Quills. A Situated Evaluation of Using Computers for Writing in Classrooms.* Hillsdale, NJ: Lawrence Erlbaum Associates, Inc., 1992.

Collier, R. M. "The Word Processor and Revision Strategies." *College Composition and Communication,* 1983, *34*(2), pp. 149–155.

Collis, B. *Computers, Curriculum, and Whole-Class Instruction.* Belmont, CA: Wadsworth, 1988.

Costanzo, W. V. *The Electronic Text: Learning to Write, Read and Reason with Computers.* Englewood Cliffs, NJ: Educational Technology Publications, 1989.

Daiute, C. *Writing and Computers.* Reading, MA: Addison-Wesley, 1985.

Dickens, P. A. "*Success with Writing* and the Concept Formation Model." *The Computing Teacher,* December/January 1991–92, *19*(4), pp. 27–29.

Dudley-Marling, C. and Oppenheimer, J. "The Introduction of Word Processing Into a Grade 7/8 Writing Program." *Journal of Research on Computing in Education,* Fall 1990, *23*(1), pp. 28–44.

Dykes, D. *An Easy Course in Using WordPerfect.* Eugene, OR: International Society for Technology in Education, 1991.

Feldman, P. R. "Personal Computers in a Writing Course." *Perspectives in Computing,* Spring 1984, pp. 4–9.

Finkel, L., McManus, W., and Zeitz, L. *Microsoft Works Through Applications.* Gilroy, CA: Computer Literacy Press, 1991.

Franklin, S., ed. *Making the Literature, Writing, Word Processing Connection: The Best of the Writing Notebook* (Vol. 1). Eugene, OR: Creative Word Processing in the Classroom, 1990.

Franklin, S., ed. *Writing & Technology: Ideas That WORK!—The Best of the Writing Notebook,* (Vol. 2). Eugene, OR: Creative Word Processing in the Classroom, 1991.

Graves, D. H. *Writing: Teacher and Children at Work.* Exeter, NH Heinemann Educational Books, Inc., 1982.

Graves, D. and Hansen, J. "The Author's Chair." *Language Arts,* 1983, *60*, pp. 176–183.

Green, J. "Computers, Kids, and Writing: An Interview with Donald Graves." *Classroom Computer Learning,* March 1984, pp. 20–28.

Grejda, G. F. and Hannafin, M. J. "The Influence of Word Processing on the Revisions of Fifth Graders." *Computers in the Schools,* 1991, *8*(4), pp. 89–102.

Haas, C. "How Word Processing Affects Planning in Writing: The Impact of Technology." Reported in Collis, B. "Research Windows." *The Computing Teacher,* October 1988, p. 7.

Hall, J. M. and Yoder, S. *Beyond Word Processing in Microsoft Word 5.0.* Eugene, OR: International Society for Technology in Education, 1992.

Hamrell, D. K. "Macro Mischief II." *The Computing Teacher*, October 1991, *19*(2), pp. 22–27.

Harris, J. "Student Writers and Word Processing: A Preliminary Evaluation." *College Composition and Communication*, 1985, *36*(3), pp. 323–330.

Hawischer, G. E. and Selfe, C. L., Eds. *Critical Perspectives on Computers and Composition Instruction.* New York: Teachers College Press, 1989.

Heim, M. *Electric Language: A Philosophical Study of Word Processing.* New Haven, CT: Yale University Press, 1987.

Herron, J. "Computer Writing Labs: A New Vision for Elementary Writing." *The Writing Notebook*, January/February 1992, *9*(3), pp. 31–33.

Hooper, S. and Hannafin, M. "The Effects of Group Composition on Achievement, Interaction, and Learning Efficiency During Computer-based Cooperative Learning."*ETR&D*, 1991, *39*(3), pp. 27–40.

Hoot, J. L. and Silvern, S. B., eds. *Writing with Computers in the Early Grades.* New York: Teachers College Press, 1988.

Howie, S. H. *Reading, Writing, and Computers: Planning for Integration.* Needham Heights, MA: Allyn & Bacon, Longwood Division, 1989.

Hunter, W. J. "The Absence of Research in Writing and Technology: What Questions Should We Be Asking?" *The Writing Notebook*, January/February 1992, *9*(3), pp. 34–35.

Hunter, W.J. "Cooperative Group Writing." *The Writing Notebook*, April/May 1992, *9*(4), pp.40–41.

Hunter, W. J. and Begoray, J. "A Framework for Writing Process Activities." *The Writing Notebook*, January/February 1990, *7*(3), pp. 40–42.

Hunter, W. J., Benedict, G., and Bilan, B. "On a Need-to-Know Basis: Keyboarding Instruction for Elementary Students." *The Writing Notebook*, November/December 1989, *7*(2), pp. 23–25.

Hunter, W. J., Jardine, G., Rilstone, P., and Weisgerber, R. "The Effects of Using Word Processors: A Hard Look at the Research." *The Writing Notebook*, September/October 1990, *8*(1), pp. 42–46.

Kurth, R. J. "Using Word Processing to Enhance Revision Strategies During Student Writing Activities." *Educational Technology*, January 1987, pp. 13–19.

Levin, J. A., Boruta, M. J., and Vasconcellos, M. T. "Microcomputer-Based Environments for Writing: A Writer's Assistant." In Wilkinson, A. C., ed. *Classroom Computers and Cognitive Science.* New York: Academic Press, 1983, pp. 219–232.

Levin, J. A., Riel, M., Rowe, R. D., and Boruta, M. J. "Muktuk Meets Jacuzzi: Computer Networks and Elementary School Writers." In Freeman, S. W., ed. *The Acquisition of Written Language: Revision and Response.* Hillsdale, NJ: Ablex, 1984.

Loheyde, K. M. J. "Computer Use in the Teaching of Composition: Considerations for Teachers of Writing." *Computers in the Schools*, Summer 1984, pp. 81–86.

Luehrmann, A. and Peckham, H. *Hands-On AppleWorks.* Gilroy, CA: Computer Literacy Press. Multiple versions of varying dates.

Luehrmann, A. and Peckham, H. *Hands-On ClarisWorks.* Gilroy, CA: Computer Literacy Press, 1992.

Male, M. "Cooperative Learning, Computers, and Writing: Maximizing Instructional Power." *The Writing Notebook*, April/May 1992, *9*(4), pp. 21–22.

Marcus, S. "Machinery for the Muse: Computers and Poetry." *The Computing Teacher*, November 1991, *19*(3), pp. 40–43.

McCurry, N. and McCurry, A. "Writing Assessment for the 21st Century." *The Computing Teacher*, April 1992, *19*(7), pp. 35–37.

Miller, M. J. "The Good Word." *PC Magazine*, 13 October 1992, pp. 85–86.

Montague, M. "Computers and Writing Process Instruction." *Computers in the Schools*, 1990, *7*(3), pp. 5–20.

Morton, L. L. "Word Processing and the Editing–Revising Process." *Computers in the Schools*, 1988, *5*(1/2), pp. 165–178.

Morton, L. L. and Thibodeau, B. D. "Lab-Based Word Processing for the Learning-Disabled." *Computers in the Schools*, 1991, *8*(1/2/3), pp. 225–228.

Myers, S. and Spindler-Virgin, R. "Time to Teach Keyboarding?" *The Writing Notebook*, November/December 1989, *7*(2), pp. 26–27.

Nathan, R. "Throw the Gimmicks Out with the Trash—Please, Pretty Please!: Rewriting with Computers." *The Writing Notebook*, September/October 1990, *8*(1), pp. 26–28.

O'Brien, P. "Using Microcomputers in the Writing Class" *The Computing Teacher*, May 1984, pp. 20–21.

Owston R. D., Murphy, S., and Wideman, H. H. "On and Off Computer Writing of Eighth Grade Students Experienced in Word Processing." *Computers in the Schools*, 1991, *8*(4), pp. 67–87.

Piller, C. "Separate Realities." *MacWorld*, September 1992, pp. 218–230.

Pon, K. "Process Writing in the One-Computer Classroom." *The Computing Teacher*, March 1988, pp. 33–37.

Porter, B. "In Between Trapezes: Living Gracefully Between *OLD* and *NEW*." *The Writing Notebook*, January/February 1992, *9*(3), pp. 10–12.

Presley, B. and Freitas, W. *An Introduction To Computing Using Microsoft Works*. Pennington, NJ: Lawrenceville Press, 1989

Reed, W. M. "The Effectiveness of Composing Process Software: An Analysis of *Writers' Helper*." *Computers in the Schools*, 1989, *6*(1/2), pp. 67–82.

Reed, W. M. "The Effect of Computer-and-Writing Instruction on Prospective English Teachers' Attitudes Toward and Perceived Uses of Computers in Writing Instruction." *Journal of Research on Computing in Education*, Fall 1990, *23*(1), pp. 3–27.

Roblyer, M. D. "The Effectiveness of Microcomputers in Education: A Review of the Research from 1980–1987." *T.H.E. Journal*, September 1988, pp. 85–89.

Rodrigues, R. J. "Creating Writing Lessons with a Word Processor." *The Computing Teacher*, February 1986, pp. 41–43.

Rodrigues, D. and Rodrigues, R. J. *Teaching Writing with a Word Processor, Grades 7–13*. Urbana, IL: National Council of Teachers of English, 1986.

Rossa, D. "Computers in Literature." *The Computing Teacher*, August/September 1992, *20*(1), pp. 16–18.

Schiffman, S. S. "Productivity Tools for the Classroom." *The Computing Teacher*, May 1986, pp. 27–31.

Schipper, D. "Practical Ideas: Literature, Computers, and Students with Special Needs." *The Computing Teacher*, October 1991, *19*(2), pp. 33–37.

Schramm, R. M. "The Effects of Using Word Processing Equipment in Writing Instruction: A Meta-Analysis." Unpublished doctoral dissertation, Northern Illinois University, 1989.

Scotchmoor, J. "Order out of Chaos." *Classroom Computer Learning*, March 1984, p. 69.

Smith, R. A. and Sutherland, S. "Marrying the Process of Writing with Your Computer." *The Computing Teacher*, November 1991, *19*(3), pp. 29–30.

Sunstein, B. S. "The Personal Portfolio: Redefining Literacy, Rethinking Assessment, Re-examining Evaluation." *The Writing Notebook*, April/May 1992, *9*(4), pp. 36–39.

Theisen, E. "Writing in Concert: A New Generation of Networked Software." *The Writing Notebook*, April/May 1992, *9*(4), pp. 33–34; 43.

Tracey, R. "A Caveat about Writing Process/Word Processor Environments." *The Writing Notebook*, November/December 1989, *7*(2), pp. 8–11.

Turner, S. and Land, M. *Tools for Schools*. Belmont, CA: Wadsworth, 1988.

Ubelacker, S. "Keyboarding: The Universal Curriculum Tool for Children." *Proceedings of the 9th International Conference on Technology and Education*. Austin, TX: University of Texas, 1992, pp. 808–810.

Waetjen, M. and Bellisimo, Y. "Down from the Ivory Tower." *The Computing Teacher*, March 1992, *19*(6), pp. 16–18.

Weisberg, L. "Beyond Drill & Practice in a One-Computer Classroom." *The Computing Teacher*, August/September 1992, *20*(1), pp. 27–28.

Wolf, D. P. "Flexible Texts: Computer Editing in the Study of Writing." In Klein, E. L. *New Directions in Child Development, No. 28*. San Francisco: Jossey-Bass, 1985, pp. 37–53.

Wresch, W. *A Practical Guide to Computer Uses in the English/Language Arts Classroom*. Englewood Cliffs, NJ: Prentice-Hall, 1987.

Zeitz, L., Horney, M., and Anderson-Inman, L. "Empowering Students With Flexible Text." *The Computing Teacher*, May 1992, *19*(8), pp. 16–20.

Zurn, M. R. *A Comparison of Kindergartners' Handwritten and Word Processor-Generated Writing*. Unpublished doctoral dissertation, Georgia State University, Atlanta, 1987.

After you have completed this chapter, you will be able to:

Explain why information management has become a serious issue.
Give several examples of data management tasks relevant to teachers and discuss them in terms of appropriate use of the technology.
Discuss benefits of electronic data management over manual systems.
Define the terms field, record, file, and database and identify each in a structure diagram.
Explain the differences between a database-management system (DBMS) and a filing system.
List and explain the basic functions of a data manager.
Discuss key considerations in selecting a data manager.
Explain the significance of fields in terms of how many you should use in setting up a database and their storage capacity.
Discuss the significance of student use and creation of databases.
Define teaching and learning with databases in terms of three sequential stages.
Discuss the unique nature of databases on compact and laser discs.
State and defend a position on database use in education based on current research findings.
Develop lesson plans that include database applications.

Chapter 3

Databases: Managing Information

This chapter presents the computer as a highly sophisticated tool for data storage and retrieval. You will consider society's growing problems in information management and ways in which computers are assisting with the task. After examining concepts of electronic data storage, you will learn ways to apply computerized data management in your teaching, especially how students may enhance their learning through databases. In addition, you will consider what current research shows about databases and learning.

Challenges of the Information Age

The Trouble with Information

Among all of the human faculties, none is more impressive, or at times exasperating, than our memories. Everyone has many thousands of individual bits and pieces of information stored away in memory. We manage remarkable tasks of retrieving this information, associating it correctly with other items, and even combining pieces into new relationships. Regardless of whether one understands the neurological aspects of the mind, it is truly an amazing thing.

For all of its marvels, the human mind is also quite fallible. Just as we achieve great feats of remembering, we also commit great blunders of forgetting. The written word is clearly important as a means of transferring knowledge and information across time and space, but for us individually and daily, it is also an essential aid to our fragile memories.

As more and more written information has come into existence, problems of storage and retrieval have led to all manner of new devices—drawers in which to place papers, file folders and cabinets, and Rolodex cards and containers, to name a few. Today we are swimming in a sea of paper, and new industries have sprung up to try to handle it.

However, our advances have been less than perfect. How irritating it is to be able to store that valuable document safely in the file cabinet, only to discover later that the labeling on the folder has slipped your mind! "I know it's here, Ruth, but I can't seem to put my hands on it just now. I'll call you back when it turns up." There goes another valuable hour spent searching through file cabinet drawers.

The Need for Data Management

Data are the raw ingredients of the Information Age. Examples of "raw" data are words and numbers. Such data generally have limited usefulness until they have been processed in some way that adds meaning to them. Processed data may be termed information. For example, the raw data of a national census are just words and numbers, but they become information when they are organized into a report or a chart with labels that explain and clarify their meaning. Schools and teachers devote much attention to dissemination of information.

However, in the Information Age, it is inadequate merely to disseminate information. As Naisbitt pointed out in *Megatrends* (1982, p. 24), "We are drowning in information but starved for knowledge." When we analyze and synthesize information to gain insight or form judgments, that information becomes knowledge. Glenn (1990, p. 215) quotes a sixth-grade teacher: "I am no longer a provider and controller of information. I must teach these students the skills they need to use information. I have to rethink how and what I teach." Today's educators must guide students in the quest for knowledge. The computer's ability to manipulate the raw ingredients called data may contribute significantly to attaining this goal.

Let's consider briefly a data-management problem related to the life of a teacher. Libraries are among our most hallowed repositories of knowledge. In medieval times, keeping track of the collection was no great intellectual challenge. Today, the library of one million or more volumes is relatively common, to say nothing of nonbook materials. The task of finding what you need is hardly trivial. For the librarian, tracking what is in the collection, on loan, on order, lost, strayed, or stolen is formidable.

Considering only your need for books, you have long depended on the card catalog as your road map to the collection. For many, even most, purposes it is quite adequate. But consider its limitations. Books are categorized in three ways: author, title, and subject. This necessitates three different cards for each book, differing primarily in the order in which the information is recorded on each. Typically, the three cards are housed in at least two distinct sections of the card catalog, if not three. Thus, adding a new book to the collection means preparing three cards, *and* placing each one in the *correct* place alphabetically in the *correct drawer* of the card catalog. Hardly an impossible task for a human, but somewhat inefficient and clearly open to error.

Benefits of Electronic Data Management

Although we describe the benefits of electronic data management in terms of our card catalog example, the principles are broadly applicable.

A Single Data Set

From the paper-conservation viewpoint, or simply as a labor-saving aid, the use of a computer to replace the physical card catalog is a natural idea. What may be overlooked are other benefits of computerization. Not only are cards unnecessary, there is also no need for three versions of the same information. The computer stores only one copy of the book information and can easily retrieve that data based on a user-specified criterion. You need only go to the nearest terminal and enter a request.

More Information

Unlike the card catalog, the computer may also tell you whether the book is currently on loan, saving a futile search of the shelves. Some systems also can search for materials in many libraries across the region or nation, a feature not available with physical card catalogs. Interlibrary loans are encouraged and facilitated by such a system. Finally, in many cases the computer can print the results of the search, eliminating the need to copy down call numbers by hand before going to the stacks again, an operation open to possible error.

Greater Manipulation Potential

Reports on the status of the collection or items on loan can be produced easily. Need an alphabetical list of all titles in the collection? A modest request for the computer, a nearly impossible task otherwise. A list of all authors represented? Readily available! The library's one set of data on the collection can be rearranged at will with no disruption of service to the patron. In addition, book orders can be tracked and new acquisitions made available to users much more quickly by transferring on-order data electronically to circulation records. Small wonder that libraries ranging from the Library of Congress to modest school libraries depend on computers.

Easier Access to Data

There is another even less obvious benefit to a computerized card catalog, to stay with our example. When searching for materials manually, certain types of requests require sifting through the available data to find just what you are seeking. For instance, suppose you wanted to find all books by Stephen King that have a copyright date no older than 1990. You would go to the author section of the catalog, find the Stephen King entries, then read each one to determine which are of interest. Not impossible, but a needless chore. Computerized data can be retrieved readily based on a *combination* of criteria, such as "Stephen King" and "1990 or newer."

In a file cabinet, each item placed in a folder can be stored under only one heading. Locating the material later depends on your recall of the chosen heading or folder label. The ability to do so quickly and accurately is a hallmark of an outstanding secretary in most offices; the boss could never manage alone! Yet deciding on that heading initially is often difficult, because few materials worth filing fit only one possibility. The computer solves this problem by providing the equivalent of multiple headings or labels per item.

Enhanced Human Capacity

Computerized data storage and retrieval are big business and growing in importance. Starting with the capabilities of the human mind, the computer may be seen as a logical, valuable extension of our native abilities. It is not a replacement for mental ability, but rather an aid, much as other tools aid us in everyday living. Computers are not a crutch, as some contend, but merely the latest in an evolutionary chain of tools stretching back to the first stone ax. The major task for early humans was mastery of the environment. Many writers have concluded that our largest tasks in the Information Age relate to data management and manipulation. The computer is a key to our ability to turn data into information and knowledge.

Data Management in Education

Educational administrators have used computers to manage their data for many years. Applications range from scheduling, budgeting, and grade reporting to attendance records and bus routing. But as a teacher, your concern is with your own more direct data-management needs and problems. Some of these are obvious. Most teachers maintain various types of student records, including grade books. Other forms of student records include anecdotal information for reports to parents, mandated records on exceptional children, and team data in athletics.

What can you add to the list? Think of what is or could be in your file cabinet or desk drawers. Could a computer perhaps help you manage better? Think also of how student learning might be enhanced with databases, a topic that you'll look at in considerable detail in this chapter.

The Issue of Appropriateness

Just because a computer can do something does not mean it is the best or even a better way of doing it. Many early home computer owners were attracted to the idea of storing recipes on their new gadget, only to realize that it really didn't work well unless they intended to place the computer in the kitchen for use while cooking. Personal mailing lists can be computerized, but there is little gain over an address book, unless the list is long and a printer and blank mailing labels are always at hand. Creating a computer file of phone numbers may sound good, but chances are you can look up what you need in a telephone directory more quickly than you can turn on your computer, load and run the software, enter your request, and obtain the response. These are examples of where human judgement must determine appropriate use of the computer's capabilities.

The Technical Side of Data Management

Data File Concepts

Before turning to educational data mangement applications, let's look at the technical aspects of data storge and retrieval. Manual filing systems offer useful analogies.

Suppose that the data you wish to manage are all the things pertaining to your students. You would probably store these materials in a filing cabinet drawer. The electronic analog is called a *file*. A file is all of the information about some (typically) large class of data. Files have names and are stored by name on your diskette or hard disk.

Would you just toss your student data into a file drawer? Of course not, because that would make retrieval virtually impossible. Instead you organize it in some way, such as putting all the data about a single student into a file folder. The electronic analog of the folder is called a *record*. Many student records consist of special paper forms that have been completed with the appropriate personal data. Forms are designed to store various data items that pertain to a specific case, one record. The space for an individual item of data, such as first name or phone number, is called a *field*. A field is the smallest meaningful unit of data in a record. Just as you complete a paper form by filling in blanks with items of data, you also enter data into an electronic record one field at a time. When you look at your disk directory, you see only file names. The fields and records are stored in the files.

Figure 3.1 illustrates electronic file concepts, while Figure 3.2 shows one record from a specific file. Can you identify the file and individual field names, as well as the actual data? Figure 3.3 is a very small illustration of a file with sample entries in each field of several records.

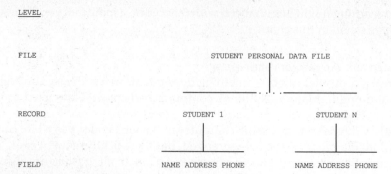

Figure 3.1. Student personal data file structure.

Database Concepts

Although the term *database* is often applied to data management applications on microcomputers, the term refers more properly to a collection of related files, as illustrated in Figure 3.4. Such databases can become very complex. They are usually created and manipulated using software called a *database-management system (DBMS).*

One problem that arises in large applications is *data redundancy.* Consider the central office in a school. Several different files may be needed for each student,

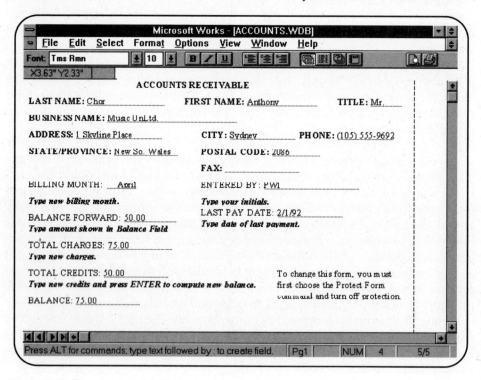

Figure 3.2. A *Microsoft Works* database record.

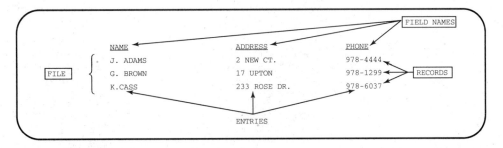

Figure 3.3 Student personal data file, sample contents.

such as basic demographic data, transcript data, test scores, and so forth. Suppose each were a separate electronic file. How much information would you have to duplicate in each file to be sure that the contents are meaningful and can be correctly identified? Often, the answer is, considerable. Such redundancy wastes time and storage.

The *relational* DBMS was created to minimize this problem. It links separate files or even entire databases through a common "key" field in the records, for example, student ID number or social security number. Data can be retrieved from any file by identifying the desired record's key field data. Software products such as *dBase* and *Paradox* provide this type of data management. Most classroom-level applications involve only individual files and do not require this much power (or complexity).

Data Management Software

Nearly all classroom data management needs are modest enough not to need true database software, but use instead much simpler, single-file software, more properly termed a *filing system*. However, we accept common usage and will call these products *data managers* and their files either *databases* or *data files.*

Common needs have led producers to create highly specialized data-management software for single purposes. Examples include mailing list managers,

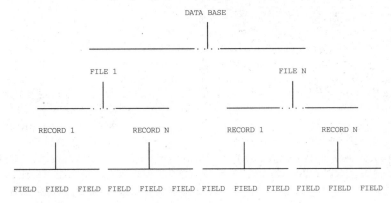

Figure 3.4 Generalized database structure.

electronic grade books, and test construction software. These are treated in Chapter 5.

Just as word-processing software serves a very general purpose, managing and manipulating words, there are also many common general-purpose data managers such as *AppleWorks, Bank Street School Filer, Claris Works, FrEdBase,* and *Microsoft Works.* All of these products have their own operating structure and procedures that are designed to make them easy enough for anyone, including children, to use. You can use any such product to create a specific application to meet your needs.

Many spreadsheet programs, which you will meet in the next chapter, also offer modest database capabilities. Furthermore, the Rolodex application of *Hyper-Card* and the card file application of *Microsoft Windows* are suitable for some kinds of data management. (See Chapter 10 for a fuller treatment of hypermedia software.) Depending on your needs, you might not even need to purchase a separate data manager.

Data Manager Functions

Regardless of the software you use for data management, certain basic functions are common, just as certain functions are common to word processors. Data are stored and retrieved in complete records, within which you can enter and modify individual data fields. The most basic functions of any data manager are:

1. Create new files
2. Add, change, or delete records (and, in many cases, fields)
3. Search for specific records
4. Sort (re-order) the records by the content of some field(s)
5. Print selected records or reports based on their contents

Figure 3.5 illustrates the functions of one data manager.

Selecting a Data Manager

It is beyond our scope and purpose to go into great detail about selecting data-management software. You should be aware, however, of some key considerations.

One major concern when selecting a data manager is the capacity of the software. Many systems have specific limits on the total data volume that they can accommodate. This may be a conscious decision by the developer to limit the software, or it may reflect hardware limitations. Some filing systems are RAM-based, meaning the program and all data must fit within the computer's RAM (random access memory) capacity. This allows very rapid manipulation of the data, but usually will provide the least storage capacity. Other systems are disk-based, typically limiting the file size to the storage capacity of the disk drive in use. Storage and retrieval are slower because of the frequent input/output operations involving the disk drive.

Beyond total storage capacity of the system, many systems place limits on the size of individual records or even fields within records. This is often expressed as

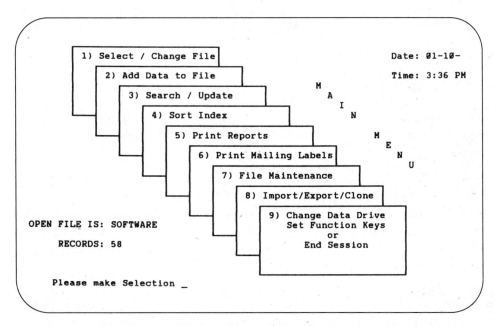

Figure 3.5 Main menu of a general purpose filing system

maximum bytes per record or *per field*. Thus, you must have a clear idea of the exact requirements of a given application before selecting filing software.

Filing systems vary widely in their ability to customize output to your needs, ranging from little more than displaying your data in the precise form in which you entered it to rearranging and manipulating it in almost any fashion. Many systems have no arithmetic capabilities, making them unsuitable for recording any numeric data from which even a simple sum might be required. Others even allow fields whose content is derived automatically from other fields. For example, if a record contained twelve fields, say, for number of books checked out each month, an average monthly circulation field could be calculated and filled in automatically.

Such factors will determine the suitability of a filing system for your needs. It should come as no surprise that the more flexible, versatile, and powerful a filing system, the more difficult it will be to master and use. When we turn to specific application suggestions, keep in mind the ramifications of these selection factors for ideas that appeal to you.

Setting Up Your Data File

To create a new file, you must first analyze the requirements of the application and determine what fields to include in each record. This task requires a thorough understanding of the system's capabilities and your desired output. For instance, if you need to be able to sort a file by zip code, then zip code will probably have to be a field of its own. If this will never matter, you could store in just one field both state and zip code or even more of the address. Similarly, if you anticipate the need for an alphabetical list of the names in the file, then you will probably require separate fields for first and last names. In general, use plenty of fields.

The order in which fields are arranged within the file may also be important. If the system can display the contents of records only in their physical order, then entering Doe before John would make it impossible to ever display John Doe, say, for a mailing label.

It may be necessary to specify the number of characters (bytes) allowed per field, either numerically or as visible space on the screen. Some systems store all of the space specified for a field, regardless of what is actually entered. Thus, the name Doe consumes as much memory as Schwartzendruber. In such cases, try to select the smallest practical size for a field. Other systems use little more storage than the actual entries require, so that you can afford to be generous in setting field sizes.

When setting field sizes, initially make the best guess possible, but later you may identify fields too small to hold some data items. Systems vary in the ease with which a field may be enlarged; in some cases, it is not even possible. Further, suppose you discover long after a file was created and all the data have been entered that you need to add a new field. Systems differ widely in how easily new fields may be added later, if at all.

It should be apparent that there are many pitfalls in learning to work with data files. Experience is clearly the best teacher, but the flexibility of the system you use makes a big difference as well. It is wise to create a file, using your best judgment and intuition, then enter only a few records before thoroughly testing your application. If you have made a major error that the system will not allow you to correct easily, at least you will not have invested a lot of data entry time before going back to replan and reimplement the file.

Hypermedia

Databases have been primarily means of organizing text. Their storage and retrieval methods are largely linear, that is, one piece of data follows another. You get to what you want by moving sequentially through all that precedes it, or by resorting to make access more direct.

But is that how your mind works? Hardly! You store far more than words in your memory. Did you ever say something such as, "Can you picture that?" You "hear" a familiar song whenever you think of it. Further, your retrieval processes are not linear, that is, you do not need to recall A before you can recall B. Your mind is a web of associations that are interrelated in a far more complex way than typical databases permit.

Hypermedia is a relatively new software type that can store and retrieve data nonlinearly, in ways that may more nearly resemble our minds. In fact, hypermedia software can store not only text, but also still images, sound, even movies! Look forward to all the details about hypermedia in Chapter 10.

Teaching with Data Managers

Now let's consider applications of data managers for you as a teacher and especially as learning tools for your students.

Teachers and Data Managers

Data managers can help you work smarter. Possibilities include computerizing any of the data that you now keep in file folders, on index cards, on a Rolodex, or in an address book. It requires some experience with databases to be able to judge the worthiness of computerizing any specific set of data. Honeyman (1985) described a project to cope with the reporting and recordkeeping requirements of federal law related to special education students. Computerization was a sound choice in the face of the massive requirements of such programs.

Perhaps you have difficulty recalling where you saw an article or other resources for class use. A personal annotated index to journals and other materials might be invaluable. If you work with student organizations, you may deal with mailing lists or membership rosters that are difficult to maintain manually. Slides, negatives, and prints for the newspaper or yearbook can be tracked with a database. The possibilities are endless; the specific applications of benefit to you may be unique.

The EPIE *Integrated Instructional Information Resource* is a group of databases designed to help educators identify and use all manner of educational materials. It is described further in Chapter 19.

Testing offers many possible applications, such as a data bank of test items to draw upon as needed. The *Test Center Database* provides access through an ERIC-based key word search to all tests and surveys available through the Northwest Regional Educational Laboratory Test Center (NWREL). "TESTNET," also from NWREL, links users via the Test Center Database to individuals who actually have used the test instruments identified. For details, contact NWREL Test Center, 101 S.W. Main St., Suite 600, Portland, OR 97204.

Students and Data Managers

Recall our earlier discussion of the distinction among data, information, and knowledge. Clearly, it is the analysis and synthesis, the internalization of information into knowledge, that is the goal of education. Geisert and Futrell (1990, p. 128) advocate data managers (and other software tools) as means for attaining objectives in the learning domains of verbal information and intellectual skills, and more importantly, enhancing development of cognitive strategies, "the skills that a student uses to govern his or her own learning, remembering, and thinking behaviors." This is the key to the lifelong learning that is critical to citizens of the twenty-first century. School must prepare students for this future.

Hunter (1985, p. 21) outlined several important skills that student users of databases and data managers develop:

1. Arranging information in more useful ways.
2. Organizing and sharing information.
3. Discovering commonalities and differences among groups or things.
4. Analyzing relationships.
5. Testing and refining hypotheses.
6. Looking for trends.

According to Collis (1988, pp. 17–60), the computer is an outstanding tool for developing skills to organize, display, summarize, extend, and evaluate information. Higher-order thinking skills clearly are required. In an Australian study, educators rated the potential of learning with databases one of the highest among current instructional technologies (Galbraith, Grice, Carss, Endean, and Warry, 1990). These educators believed that databases can enhance the quality of education beyond its present level and make possible new kinds of learning. They felt it would more severely detract from the quality of education if schools had to give up use of databases than to lose many other things.

A Three-Stage Learning Model

Let's look now at three basic stages in learning with databases, presented originally by Hunter (1985).

Learning about the Tool

As with any other software tool, users must first learn the basic concepts and operation of a data manager. Have students gather simple data on index cards, then use them as a manual database to learn basic terminology and simple search strategies Deming and Valeri-Gold (1990). This can also demonstrate how quickly a manual system becomes difficult to use.

Learning to use a computerized data manager should begin with existing data files (Simonson and Thompson, 1990). If the data are relevant to your instruction, this becomes far more than just an exercise in software mechanics. Initially, have students examine the structure of several files to internalize the concepts of fields, records, and files. Direct students to search a file for specific records. For example, if the database contains information about U.S. presidents, ask students to retrieve several specified presidents. Discuss what information is contained in each record, and try to elicit new higher-order questions to pursue.

Gradually extend the assignments to reach toward higher-level goals. Have students retrieve, and perhaps print, all records sharing a common field entry, say, all Democratic presidents. Examine these records for other commonalities. Suggest relationships that might be explored, perhaps party affiliation and serving only one term in office. An example of looking for trends might be to investigate the relationship between age at election and at death. Such ideas involve more complex search strategies, using multiple criteria. Search strategies are crucial when using large databases such as ERIC.

Once students begin work on a problem, consider stopping them after they have examined only some of the appropriate records. Ask what they think the answer to the question is, based on partial data. When their hypothesis has been formulated, guide continued database searching to test or perhaps modify the hypothesis. For example, White (1990) describes using a twentieth century database. After initial exploration, ask students to imagine a graph of the U.S. birthrate from 1900–1980. Have them sketch their guesses, then devise a search strategy to find the needed information, and finally graph it. Next, ask what might explain the trend shown. This yields a new hypothesis to investigate. Such an idea is suitable for small-group work, or in a large-group session, using a projection device to display the computer screen.

Many database activities require reorganizing the records for easier examination. Students may not recognize initially that an easy way to examine the pattern of age is to sort the file by age. Simply browsing through the sorted records may begin to reveal a pattern. You can encourage organizing and sharing information by assigning specific projects to individuals or groups of students, with guidelines for sharing their results with the class.

Students also should learn early to modify an existing database. Provide a small file (just a few records) that contains errors to correct. You may want to give specific instructions on what to find and change, or simply a printout of the records with the correct information. Provide the raw data for several new records to add to the database and instructions to delete certain records. Finally, pose several questions that students will be able to answer correctly *only* if their modifications to the file are correct.

Learning with the Tool

Once students understand the data management software, they can move to a second level of application, namely, extending existing databases or entering data into an empty template created by someone else (Hunter, 1985). The emphasis changes from the mechanics of a specific piece of software to the research required to locate data to be entered into a database. The tool itself loses prominence, but the structure for the data already exists. As Ryba and Anderson (1990) point out, an existing structure limits the research scope to what you, the teacher, find appropriate. Design time is not a factor, and students can move quickly into the actual research.

Your task as a teacher is to obtain or develop suitable databases for your subject areas. Perhaps you can meet your objectives with more advanced assignments by using one or more of the databases that you used to introduce students to the data-manager software. (Be sure to keep backup copies of any databases that you ask students to modify from their research so that you can reuse the original database with other students.)

At some point you will want empty templates that slowly evolve into useful databases as students complete their research and enter their data. See the Commercial Database Resources section of this chapter for information on some available database templates. Bright (1989) described a database activity based on a worksheet showing nine 4-sided plane geometric shapes. Students recorded in a database the ID number of each figure, the number of congruent sides, number of pairs of parallel sides, number of pairs of opposite congruent sides, number of right angles, and number of lines of symmetry. A Name field was left blank initially, to be completed from conclusions drawn after working with the database. Bright's article includes a lesson plan for the project and suggestions for assessing learning.

He also suggests many other math databases of a similar nature, including just numbers themselves. Such a database might have fields for prime number (Y/N), perfect square (Y/N), number of prime divisors, total number of divisors, list of prime divisors, and so on.

When students enter research data into a database, accuracy becomes an issue on two levels. First, the data found must be accurate. Second, entry into the database must be completed accurately. Beaver (1992) suggests that two separate groups be given responsibility for each section of the research. They should compare their findings and resolve differences before any data entry occurs, then crosscheck each other's work during data entry. Also have students do trial searches for which the answer is already known; this will help to validate the database.

Applying the Tool to New Tasks

The final application level is to plan, design, create, and use a totally original database (Hunter, 1985). According to Thomas (1988), such activities are significant because students learn that "the shape of the question is as important as the answer. . . . They learn to examine both questions and answers in light of their own biases and habits. . . . (T)hey learn that they can organize large amounts of data in a systematic fashion and derive meaning from it."

Salant (1990) stressed the need to develop research skills in high school. Databases offer one approach to teaching inquiry, information handling, and group-interaction skills. Creating a database puts students into an active role, determining what to collect and how to organize it for meaning.

Designing a new database is a stimulating process of decision making, according to Ryba and Anderson (1990). What fields are needed? Which potential records are worth including? How should the screen be laid out? What are the questions that we may want to try to answer using this database? The latter is critical in determining the fields of each record, which dictates the data one must collect. There are also many issues surrounding field entries. Suppose a field is labeled "size." What are the possible entries? For some situations, the answer may be numbers, as in clothing sizes. For others, gross categories may suffice: for example, small, medium, large. The authors noted the difficulty students had with a database on birds when it came to a field for color (not several fields for colors, as it perhaps should have been) and for sound made (how to describe a sound!). Ryba and Anderson's book is highly recommended to those seriously interested in databases in their classes.

Beaver (1992) suggests that students demonstrate their database projects to the class. Each student group should also prepare questions that other students can answer with each database. Let the groups explore each other's work to the extent that class time and hardware resources permit.

Riggs (1990) viewed database activities as ideal for developing integrative learning activities with social studies as the core. The article provides specific recommendations on ways to help children create and use a database, describes an example of a database project, and outlines various activities using it.

Although creating a database is widely viewed as the highest skill level, and best left until after other significant database experience, Unio (1991) reported considerable success with fifth graders who bypassed the lower levels of usage and created a new database as their initial experience.

Classroom Applications

Many teachers have developed methods of teaching with database technology, as well as exciting projects for their students. We can highlight only some examples, but urge you to read the entire reports on which they are based. Also, be alert for the very latest ideas as they appear in your professional reading.

Ryba and Anderson (1990) stress using computers to promote the development of effective learning and thinking skills. To do so, you as a teacher must learn the data-mangement software first. To teach with any software, the teacher plays five roles. The *planner* role consists of learning the software, exploring available files, and carefully linking the database activities to the curriculum. The *facilitator* role includes being competent enough with the software to troubleshoot for the students, posing questions to check understanding, and directing attention in the exercise. As *guide,* you use analogies and questioning strategies to direct learners toward higher-order thinking skills. The *manager* function includes preparing files, diskettes, and so forth, and assuring that the activity reaches closure. As *participant,* perhaps the largest challenge is to let the learners do it themselves, rather than intervening too strongly!

Ryba and Anderson (1990) offer countless constructive suggestions for the mechanics of teaching with databases. One particularly good idea is to have students develop goals and questions relevant to the database away from the computer. This prevents immediate keyboard activity to find a quick answer, which may bypass the more crucial deeper thought processes.

Specific activities suggested include "Simon Says" as a physical demonstration of search strategies; using a database of computer books to stimulate questions such as why all are so recent, why there have been so many in so few years, whether any subgroupings seem possible, and speculation about what types may next appear. In the case of an animals database, they report the outcome of asking whether all animals with kidneys also have a bladder. Learners first found that fish have no bladder and hypothesized that living in water made a bladder unnecessary. However, birds also lack bladders, the students found. This led to interesting speculation about why and whether there were any cross links (Ryba and Anderson, 1990).

A fifth-grade teacher (Goldberg 1992) in New York regularly vacationed at the beach. Each year, she gathered seashells for a science unit based on characteristics such as texture, color, size, and shape. Although the lesson was deemed successful, she and a colleague felt the students might gain even more with a database approach to recognizing patterns and relationships. The article describing this project includes much detail, ranging from lesson objectives to how the class was conducted, sample questions used to stimulate thought processes and samples from the database. Students gained experience in self-directed learning. They learned the limits of the database to provide answers to their questions and when to seek other resources. They also learned the meaning of a relationship among variables and how to identify when one exists.

Lai (1991) describes a database project in a girl's school in New Zealand. The goal was to enhance information-processing skills and metacognitive awareness, specifically including writing and testing hypotheses. Groups of two or three students (ages 10–13) each had a computer to work with over a seven-week period. The content was cultural differences between New Zealand and South America. The first activity implemented was to query the *One World* countries database, using a worksheet for guidance. Next, each group completed library research on a South American country of interest. In the third phase, the students created databases for the ten countries studied. Finally, students wrote stories based on their own and the commercial database's data.

A key part of the project was to pose questions (e.g., "Is there any relationship between population size and land size in this region?") and have students write a hypothesis concerning it. The database queries provided support for the hypotheses, or led to modifications that could be supported. Lai stressed that such activities should be student-centered, not computer-centered. Students need ample time to "ask questions, formulate and test hypotheses and make decisions" (p. 62).

Mernit (1991) describes how a Texas junior high teacher and her students developed their own database on influential Black Americans in observance of Black History Month. This database helped students appreciate Black history and strengthened critical thinking skills. A step-by-step plan for creating and using such a database is provided.

How about starting each school year with a survey of your students, including typical demographic items about family and most and least "favorites," ranging from food to sports to school subjects? (Beaver, 1992) Depending on your stage of working with the database manager, you could create the database yourself from the student information, then guide activities that use it. At higher levels, you might provide only the template as an electronic survey instrument for each student to complete, or you might challenge the students to devise the entire survey, thinking of the appropriate database structure from the very start, then designing and developing the complete file.

To apply the survey notion to mathematics, be sure that the data gathered include personal characteristics that involve measurement (Wiebe, 1990). Examples include hand span, ankle circumference, and length of pace. Other ideas from this author include a database inventory of math lab materials, and databases of items in commercial *Attribute Blocks* or *People Pieces*. With *People Pieces*, the solutions to problems posed for using the database can be verified concretely with the manipulatives. Wiebe also provided examples for extending many database activities.

Stearns (1992) was concerned that students with learning disabilities (LD) would be left behind as other students became involved in more active forms of learning aimed at higher-order thinking. She believes databases are especially well suited to this group of learners because they are open-ended tools that can be adapted flexibly to virtually any subject. Reporting on three different teachers' experiences, Stearns notes great success in all cases. Many LD students face difficulty separating vital from extraneous material. The outline form of a database helped them find main ideas. One teacher reported that the database research projects produced the best writing of the year. Another teacher found students who rarely would discuss their school activities at home suddenly taking their search printouts home and surprising parents with their questions. The third teacher allowed students to develop their own databases. As work progressed, many noticed common interests, and some voluntary joint projects resulted. The third teacher also found that student organizational skills and interests increased away from the computer, such as in their notebooks.

A Canadian fifth-grade project involved a community "census" (Unia, 1991). Students determined the questions they would ask, then interviewed residents of their community. Beyond the common activities, Unia tied the project to the previous national census, from which students found questions that they wished they had asked. To compare their findings to the national figures, they had to explore averages, proportions, and other mathematical concepts. They also investigated how individuals and organizations used databases (not just on computers!). Many students began their own personal databases after this experience.

Anderson (1989–1990) shares techniques used in the context of a sixth-grade science class to teach database structure and search strategies for science. The article includes templates and questions for class and element databases.

Thomas (1991) details a fascinating project involving a database derived from the 1835 census of the Cherokee nation. A major goal was to lead students into a more accurate understanding of the Cherokee themselves and of government policy toward Native Americans in the early 1800s.

The issue of "haves" and "have-nots" is hardly new, but Mittlefehldt (1991) developed a unique approach to it for his high school students. Using MECC's *Fifty States* and *World Community* databases, he first had students identify an underlying problem in a poor state or nation, for example, poverty in Haiti. Later, students used the database to propose a social, political, or economic solution to the problem, based on data about the rich states or nations. Several highly creative results are reported.

Beaver (1992) offers many suggestions for enhancing units in any discipline with database activities. He notes that typical text and table presentation of information often tends to obscure patterns as much as reveal them. Letting students discover trends or patterns themselves is likely to lead to longer-term retention than memorizing facts that are given.

Based on a project involving four teachers in Montana, Strickland and Hoffer (1990–1991) believe that higher-order thinking skills develop more efficiently when science inquiry and database techniques are combined. The problem posed was identification of pure substances. Students created a database of known substances and their seemingly relevant properties. Once the database was created, students received small quantities of unknown substances to identify. The researchers report many gains in higher-order thinking, such as efficient search strategies, as well as scientific concepts, such as the limited value of a single property in narrowing the list of possible solutions to the identification problem. They also report that lab time needed to identify the substances was cut in half.

Deming and Valeri-Gold (1990) discuss how databases can be used successfully in the language arts classroom. Among their suggested activities are monitoring grades, personal vocabulary and spelling lists, data for research projects, and data on books read.

A Redmond, Washington, sixth-grade project stressed the relationship between information access and analysis and the basic needs of a democratic society (Glenn, 1990). After studying the United States, students explored Europe in general, then chose one nation to study in depth, using print, video, and database resources. They prepared their findings by using a word processor, focusing on descriptive and explanatory generalizations about their nation and the world.

Kapisovsky (1990) focuses on the use of microcomputer-based laboratories in science and math instruction for elementary and secondary students. Data collection, storage, and display are discussed, and the use of databases to organize and manage information is described. Students also had the opportunity to exchange ideas with other students through telecommunications, a topic treated in Chapter 8.

If you happen to live near a cemetery, have students gather data from the headstones (Barbour, 1988). Depending on the age of the graves, you might guide students into discoveries about epidemics and war periods, as well as research into how longevity has varied by era. Do your data confirm for your area what other resources say about changes in longevity over time?

Lynch's (1988) sixth graders surveyed the residents of their community about attitudes toward their state's mandatory seat belt law. Students learned about social science procedures and practiced interviewing skills. They gathered and entered data, then manipulated it and graphed the results. This idea of "doing" social studies could be applied to countless topics.

Thomas (1988) carefully covers and illustrates the steps in designing a database, using an example based on prime-time television. For language arts classes, Collis (1988, pp. 99–102) suggests a poem database, containing keywords, time period when written, author, title, style, or format. When students learn to do research papers, they might develop jointly a bibliography of books or articles. Collis provides a lesson plan for this idea.

An unusually extensive project is reported by Modla (1988). An interdisciplinary Medieval life unit captivated social studies, language arts, and gifted classes. At the heart of the project was a *Bank Street Filer* database on life in the 1200s. Fields included home, clothing, food, and social status. Students also created their own files of fictional persons and places. Besides the database, the total plan encompassed thirty-one other software programs, including word processing and computer-assisted instruction.

Teaching Thinking Skills with Databases (Watson, 1991) was written for fourth grade through eighth grade classes. In fifteen carefully sequenced steps, it guides students from lower- to higher-order thinking skills. The book was field tested and contains scripted lesson plans, fourteen database files on disk, worksheets, and transparency masters. It is available in three editions: *Appleworks, MicroSoft Works,* and *FrEdBase.* Its low price includes an unlimited site license!

If you want a very complete treatment of databases, from planning and design through implementation, get a copy of *Introduction of Databases* (Townsend, 1992).

Commercial Database Resources

The initial stage of learning about databases requires existing files. Certainly, you can create them yourself and, over a period of time, accumulate files that students have created. There are commercial resources to consider, however, especially when the goal shifts from the mechanics of the data manager to learning from the content of the databases.

Sunburst Communications markets social studies databases that cover North America and the United States. Their science databases include animal life, astronomy, climate and weather, endangered species, minerals, space, and whales. All are for use with *Bank Street School Filer.* Scholastic offers ready-to-use files for various data managers in such areas as physical and life sciences; U.S. history and government; and world geography, economics, and cultures. The MECC *Dataquest* series includes *The Presidents, The Fifty States,* and *The World Community.* Data in *Hyper-Card* stack format can be purchased from the International Society for Technology in Education (e.g., *Presidents* and *World Data*) and the Hypermedia and Instructional Software Clearing House. The latter accepts stacks created by teachers for potential distribution to other users. Complete mailing addresses are in the appendix.

Sunburst's *Our Town* provides a template for recording data concerning your community, a high-interest research project. *Hometown: Local Area Studies* is similar in intent and includes survey forms and lesson plans to follow. *GeoWorld* has some initial data, but is intended for students to expand. Edwards, Bitter, and Hatfield (1990) discuss using templates developed with free, public domain software, rather than costly commercial products.

Compact and Laser Disc Databases

One problem with databases for microcomputers is data-storage capacity. Floppy disks are clearly very limited, as you learned in Chapter 1. Hard disks are a big step up, but even 100MB or 200MB can fill remarkably quickly. In contrast to these traditional magnetic media, optical disks offer very large amounts of storage, *as long as you do not need to change or update the data.*

With a capacity in the hundreds of megabytes, one CD-ROM can store more information than microcomputer users dared dream of a short time ago. When you purchase a CD-ROM, you typically also receive the retrieval software (the database manager) appropriate for the application. If this software is of high quality, you can find and retrieve any piece of information in the vast database on your CD-ROM in a few seconds at most.

CD-ROM technology holds enormous potential for educators. With such massive database capabilities, students can, perhaps for the first time, access primary source material, such as census data, quickly, easily and inexpensively. The challenge is to rethink our teaching strategies to incorporate the new possibilities, including databases that go far beyond just words and numbers.

Technically, there is no real limit to what can be stored on compact discs (CDs). Audio CDs are probably familiar to you. CD-ROMs are used to store digital files of all types: text, sound, computer graphics, photographic images, and even movies. Examples range from text-only, such as the *Library of the Future* series (hundreds of complete books on one CD) to full multimedia products such as National Geographic's *Mammals* and *The Presidents—It all Started with George,* the *Time Almanac,* and Microsoft's *BookShelf,* a vast collection of reference works, including an almanac, atlas, encyclopedia, dictionary, thesaurus, and books of famous quotations. The multimedia database is reality today (Figure 3.6).

Large-scale databases available on CD-ROM include *ERIC, Reader's Guide to Periodical Literature, Education Index,* and *Books in Print* (see Scott and Wolpert [1990]). Even the U.S. census data is available on CD. *Business Periodicals Ondisc* from University Microfilms International (UMI) may point the way of the future, because it contains not citations and abstracts, but the full text of articles. Combined with UMI's index and abstracts disc, it becomes possible to search for articles of interest, then retrieve, read, even print them, all right at your computer.

Figure 3.6. CD-ROM and laserdisc availability is increasing rapidly.

Of special interest to educators is the *First National Item Bank & Test Development System.* This CD-ROM contains thousands of validated test items, including graphics, linked to curricular objectives.

A helpful resource for those trying to keep up with the exploding world of CD-ROM is *CD-ROM Review* from IDG Communications (80 Elm Street, Peterborough, NH 03458; 603-924-9471). Meckler, publisher of *Multimedia Review,* also publishes *CD-ROMs in Print,* in both print and CD-ROM format.

The CD-ROM medium is digital. A single digital image can easily be several megabytes in size. For a limited number of images, this is fine, but for large numbers or motion segments, even CD-ROM storage capacity is inadequate. For total capacity and motion, the analog laser video disc remains the choice. Each 12-inch laser disc has a capacity of 30 minutes of motion video or 54,000 individual images, an enormous visual database. One disc can easily contain photos of the entire collection of the National Gallery of Art, or enough pictures to support an entire high school science curriculum, possibly replacing microscope or other slides. Many laser discs include both still and motion segments.

Optical storage technologies are already having a significant impact on education, further extending the range of resources that students can access in any classroom. They may well take us a step closer to ideal learning systems. As Gery (1989) explained, CD-ROM "permits random-access structure and inquiry-based learning," which computer-based learning has long promised but failed to deliver with its linear approach. Optical discs can provide a truly multimedia database. Computer-based learning " . . . automated the past. CD-ROM and related technologies redefine the future." The database becomes a unique, highly flexible learning tool. However, the sheer storage capacities involved magnify Naisbitt's concern about data. Teachers must strive to help students turn data and information into knowledge.

For more information about optical technologies, refer to D'Ignazio (1989–1990), Lambert and Ropiequet (1986), Ropiequet (1987), and especially Ambron and Hooper (1988). Beyond CD-ROM, Magel (1992), Bitter (1988) and *PC Magazine* (Staff, 1989) provide basic information about less common optical formats, including CD-V (V = video) and CD-I (I = interactive) that store full-photo-quality analog images and are more similar to laser video discs. The Kodak Photo-CD System will also find applications in education.

Research on Learning with Databases

Relatively little research has appeared to date concerning measurable impact of learning with databases, so one must be cautious about generalizations. Here are brief summaries of some published studies.

Kern (1990) trained students in database searching, using *Reader's Guide to Periodical Literature* on CD-ROM during the time they were assigned to the library to do research papers for English classes. All students were trained to use the print index, and one group was trained on the computer through group instruction, demonstration, observation, and a hands-on search. The results indicated that the database-search group outperformed the print-index group slightly in the number of articles found and that the electronic database was generally easy for the students to use. Nearly all students considered their searches successful, and they preferred the database-search method to using the print index.

Ehman, Glenn, Johnson and White (1992) undertook a highly detailed examination of eight social studies classrooms in which databases were used to teach problem solving. Their review of prior research on databases indicated that gains had been found related to higher-order thinking skills and problem solving, while no impact had been found on recall or lower-level knowledge acquisition. Researchers had also identified groups of two to four learners as effective. Ehman and associates worked with teachers who were relatively strong computer users and students who were already experienced with computers and databases. Each school had a computer lab. Thus, three of the most common concerns about computer studies (teacher and student knowledge and machine access) were addressed to start. Classes involved spanned grades 5 through 12 with ability levels from below average to high. The experimental treatment took ten class days. Several important findings were:

Problem solving occurs only when users are comfortable with the database tool. Too little time was spent on this preliminary step, to the detriment of outcomes.

Poorly chosen definitions of the fields in a database led to "almost comical" misunderstandings of some concepts. Field labels alone may not suffice to define a field.

Learners showed little analysis and planning, preferring to jump in and "wade about."

Large, highly detailed databases such as MECC's *GeoGraph* overwhelmed learners with information overload.

At least some students recognized that their database lacked critical information, necessitating a trip to the library. Ehman et al. cite this as evidence of higher-order thinking.

The most successful teachers were those who functioned as "metacognitive guides." They had a clear plan at the start, gave feedback and reinforcement all along, and used mini-debriefings regularly to identify progress and problems.

Time was a concern for all. Teaching with databases took more time than conventional instruction. With tight integration of the unit into the curriculum, however, there were fewer teacher concerns than where the unit was an "extra."

Structure in a database lesson is critical. The introduction to the lesson should stress the problem to be solved, not the computer. Clear expectations are vital, including intermediate milestones for students to attain. Teachers should model key problem-solving elements, and guide student practice. A daily 5-minute summary of where each group has been, its achievements, and next steps can be very useful. Be sure to allow for final, public sharing of results. Just as student knowledge of the software is important to good results, so too is some knowledge of the content. Where the content was new, less was achieved.

Small-group work is effective. Members challenge one another's thinking, clarify tasks, and develop more accurate generalizations.

Inquiry-based science teaching strives for higher-level goals than rote fact recall. Maor (1991) investigated both science understanding and the extent to which students' inquiry skills can be facilitated through the use of a computerized science database on birds of Antarctica and specially designed curriculum materials. Much attention was given in the program to developing both students' inquiry skills and their subject-matter knowledge. Grade 11 and 12 students' knowledge and skills development were assessed as they interacted with the computerized database and the curriculum materials. Overall, the mean score on the Inquiry Skills Test increased significantly, both on the total test and each of three subscales (analysis, interpretation, and application). Maor also found that students' ability to work with the software was dependent on their ability to envision the structure of the database. Time to attain this visualization varied widely, and those who were never able to do so also never progressed beyond simple interpretation-type questions. Like others, Maor noted the critical need to be able to manipulate the tool comfortably in order to make any skills gains. She also noted that a "constructivist" teacher (a facilitator) was far more effective than a "transmitter" teacher (a lecturer).

Collis (1990) summarized six database studies. One major concern was the difficulty that students have in formulating "good" questions to ask when interrogating a database. Many considered their task complete when the computer produced any kind of result, never stopping to analyze what they found for completeness, accuracy, adequacy, relevance, and so forth. In other words, the higher-order thinking skills did not develop automatically.

Gaffuri (1991) was concerned that third graders' vocabularies were too limited; their writing tended to be very repetitive and redundant. She developed a practicum to expand written vocabulary through training in using a database and brainstorming strategies. The students' goal was to collect personally unique, distinctive vocabulary words in their personal databases. Brainstorming generated specific words that might be used in lieu of general words (e.g., maple or oak for tree). Individual thesauri were written and published to demonstrate the results of collecting vocabulary and applying it to specific topics. Daily process writing became an integral part of the curriculum. Class time became an on-going procedure, consisting of reading, writing, editing, presenting, and rewriting. Collected data indicated the following: (1) brainstorming techniques are easily taught and help children organize for writing; (2) children can use a database for orderly collection of vocabulary; (3) children can write and publish their growing vocabulary studies in a more interesting manner; (4) all students gained confidence in their ability to write; and (5) writing became fun in an environment in which children succeeded.

Based on 665 subjects, White (1985) found that use of a database in social studies resulted in significantly higher performance on a test involving such tasks as evaluating the relevance of data to a problem, its sufficiency for reaching a conclusion, and ways to organize data to solve a problem more readily.

Rawitsch (1988) sought empirical evidence to support anecdotal claims that database use aids development of higher-order thinking skills. His study of 339 eighth graders examined their work styles and attitudes and had them perform exercises with both paper and computer databases. Rawitsch found that students solved more problems correctly when using the computer, but they took longer to do so. They preferred using the computer. Students with an unstructured work style were less efficient using the computer than those with a structured style. He also found evidence of transfer of learning to more life-like contexts. Rawitsch stressed that "problem solving with computer data base use . . . cannot effectively be learned as a one-time activity. . . . . " Rather, the skills should be taught and used repeatedly throughout the curriculum for maximum effect.

Rawitsch, Bart, and Earle (1988) examined how use of databases affected hypothetical–deductive and proportional reasoning. The study used *The Oregon Trail* simulation with part of the seventh-grade subjects, an *AppleWorks* database file with the others. The database group was further divided, with one subgroup receiving debriefing before the post-test, the other after. Although there were modest gains in the database groups, with the largest found on hypothetical–deductive reasoning in the group with debriefing after the post-test, they were not statistically significant. Actual computer time involved was only three successive days. The researchers believe this was insufficient to develop the anticipated changes. They also believe teacher behaviors played a role and require further study.

Although research evidence is limited, observation and anecdotal reports strongly suggest that databases have the potential to be an extremely powerful educational tool. Their optimal use must yet be determined.

Summary

Paralleling the explosive growth of raw data and information characteristic of the Information Age is the growth in problems of data management. However, existing microcomputers and inexpensive data-management software can ease some common burdens for the teacher. Current paper-and-pencil recordkeeping can be examined as a candidate for computerization. Just because data can be managed electronically, however, does not guarantee a better outcome. Before setting out to use a data manager, consider questions of appropriateness. Common sense comes before mere capability.

Of even greater potential are classroom uses of databases. Projects appropriate for students can be devised readily and may lead students to a clearer understanding of the place and significance of information in society. Students can experience first-hand the ramifications of their decisions about what information to store and how. Class or group research projects may become more exciting as all students benefit individually from the data gathered and entered by all. The massive storage capacity of CD-ROM and laser discs brings whole new possibilities to instruction. A CD of national census data, for instance, gives students access to primary data, something previously reserved for advanced graduate students. Class data files can support activities to develop problem-solving skills. All database projects should be designed carefully to require higher-order thinking skills to the greatest extent possible.

This chapter presented many concrete examples of database activities already used successfully by classroom teachers. You should find many ideas among them that you could modify to fit your own teaching situation. At this time, research on the demonstrable outcomes of learning with databases is scarce but generally encouraging. Of all the computer skills and knowledge that students gain in school, working with databases may be one of the most beneficial in terms of applications later in life.

Chapter 3 Activities

1. Take any common blank form used in your environment for recordkeeping and analyze it in database concepts. Write a brief explanation of it in terms of files, records, and fields.
2. Using the same form, jot down the fields that would be included in a computerized version and suggest the number of characters of space each would require in a computer file. Total the field requirements to determine the approximate size of one record.
3. List three or more data-management tasks of your own that you could consider for computerization. Are they appropriate for the computer? Why?
4. Select your most appropriate personal data management task. What sort of information would you need to retrieve from your system for it to help you? This is the information you would minimally put into your file or database. Can you think of additions that would give you potential for answering questions you currently cannot?
5. Explain how your selected application would be improved by using a computerized system. What would you lose in the process?
6. Examine software reviews or advertising literature for a variety of databases or filing systems. Compile a list of features allowing comparison of the systems. Which seems best to you, considering capabilities, ease of use, and cost?
7. Create a small database using any available data manager and one of your own application ideas. Just a few fields and records are necessary.
8. Explore any available CD-ROM or hypermedia database application.
9. Write a proposal to your principal (real or imagined) to request database software for your classroom. Include your best justification for the purchase, based on the most specific plans for its use that you can describe.
10. Design at least one lesson plan that includes database activities.

Bibliography

Ambron, S. and Hooper, K., eds. *CD ROM: Vol 3. Interactive Media.* Redmond, WA: Microsoft Press, 1988.

Anderson, C. L. "Strategies for Introducing Databasing into Science." *Journal of Computers in Mathematics and Science Teaching,* Winter 1989–1990, *9*(2), pp. 11–22.

Barbour, A. "A Cemetery Data Base Makes Math Come Alive." *Electronic Learning,* February 1988, pp. 12–13.

Beaver, J. F. "Using Computer Power to Improve Your Teaching." *The Computing Teacher,* February 1992, *19*(5), pp. 5–9.

Bitter, G. G. "CD-ROM Technology and the Classroom of the Future." *Computers in the Schools,* 1988, *5*(1/2), pp. 23–34.

Bright, G. W. "Data Bases in the Teaching of Elementary School Mathematics." *Arithmetic Teacher,* September 1989, *37*(1), pp. 38–42.

Collis, B. *Computers, Curriculum, and Whole-Class Instruction.* Belmont, CA: Wadsworth, 1988.

Collis, B. *The Best of Research Windows: Trends and Issues in Educational Computing.* Eugene, OR: International Society for Technology in Education, 1990. (ERIC document ED 323 993.)

Deming, M. P. and Valeri-Gold, M. "Databases: A Hidden Treasure for Language-Arts Instruction" (Computers in the Classroom). *English Journal,* February 1990, *79*(2), pp. 69–70.

D'Ignazio, F. "Through the Looking Glass: The Multiple Layers of Multimedia." *The Computing Teacher,* December–January 1989–1990, *17*(4), pp. 25–31.

Edwards, N. T., Bitter, G. G., and Hatfield, M. M. "Database and Spreadsheet Templates with Public Domain Software." *Arithmetic Teacher,* April 1990, *37*(8), pp. 52–55.

Ehman, L., Glenn, A., Johnson, V., and White, C. "Using Computer Databases in Student Problem Solving: A Study of Eight Social Studies Teachers' Classrooms." *Theory and Research in Social Education,* Spring 1992, *20*(2), pp. 179–206.

Gaffuri, A. *Expanding Third Graders' Vocabulary Using a Data Base, Individual Thesauri and Brainstorming Strategies.* Ed.D. Practicum I Report, Early and Middle Childhood Program, Nova University, 1991. (ERIC Document ED 331 035.)

Galbraith, P. L., Grice, R. D., Carss, M. C., Endean, L., and Warry, M. "Instructional Technology: Whither Its Future?" *Educational Technology,* August 1990, *30*(8), pp. 18–25.

Geisert, P. G. and Futrell, M. K. *Teachers, Computers, and Curriculum.* Boston, MA: Allyn and Bacon, 1990.

Gery, G. J. "CD-ROM. The Medium Has a Message." *Training,* January 1989, pp. 45–51.

Glenn, A. D. "Democracy and Technology." *Social Studies,* September–October 1990, *81*(5), pp. 215–217.

Goldberg, K. P. "Database Programs and the Study of Seashells." *The Computing Teacher,* April 1992, *19*(7), pp. 32–34.

Honeyman, D. S. "Data Bases and Special Education ITEP Reports." *Electronic Learning,* March 1985, pp. 24, 26.

Hunter, B. *My Students Use Computers.* Reston, VA: Reston Publishing Company, 1983.

Hunter, B. "Problem Solving with Data Bases." *The Computing Teacher,* May 1985, pp. 20–27.

Jacobsen, F. F. "CD-ROM Encyclopedias: A Product in Evolution." *TechTrends,* 1991, *36*(6), pp. 47–49.

Kapisovsky, P. M. "Math and Science: Vitality Through Technology." *Media and Methods,* September–October 1990, *27*(1), pp. 59–61

Kern, J.F. *Using "Reader's Guide to Periodical Literature" on CD-Rom to Teach Database Searching to High School Students.* Ed.S. Practicum Report, Nova University, 1990. (ERIC Document ED 328 291.)

Lai, K-W. "Integrating Database Activities into a Primary School Curriculum: Instructional Procedures and Outcomes." *Computers in the Schools*, 1991, *8*(4), pp. 55–66.

Lambert, S. and Ropiequet, S., eds. *CD-ROM: Vol 1. The New Papyrus.* Redmond, WA: Microsoft Press, 1986.

Lynch, C. "The Andover Seat Belt Project." *The Computing Teacher*, February 1988, *15*(5), pp. 31–32.

Magel, M. "What's New and What's Next in Multimedia Delivery." *AV Video*, September 1992, *14*(9), pp. 90–97.

Maor, D. *Development of Student Inquiry Skills: A Constructivist Approach in a Computerized Classroom Environment.* Paper presented at the Annual Meeting of the National Association for Research in Science Teaching (Lake Geneva, WI, April 7–10, 1991). (ERIC Document ED 336 261.)

Mernit, S. "Black History Month—Let Your Database Set the Stage." *Instructor*, February 1991, *100*(6), pp. 109–110, 112.

Mittlefehldt, B. "Social Studies Problem Solving with Databases." *The Computing Teacher*, February 1991, *18*(5), pp. 54–55.

Modla, V. B. "Using Computers in 'Medieval Life'. " *Media and Methods,* January/February 1988, p. 18.

Naisbitt, J. *MegaTrends.* New York: Warner, 1982.

Rawitsch, D. "The Effects of Computer Use and Student Work Style on Database Analysis Activities in the Social Studies." In *Improving the Use of Technology in Schools: What Are We Learning. Research Bulletin #1.* St. Paul, MN: MECC/University of Minnesota Center for the Study of Educational Technology, November 1988, pp. 1–3.

Rawitsch, D., Bart, W. M., and Earle, J. F. "Using Computer Database Programs to Facilitate Higher-Order Thinking Skills." In *Improving the Use of Technology in Schools: What Are We Learning. Research Bulletin #1.* St. Paul, MN: MECC/University of Minnesota Center for the Study of Educational Technology, November 1988, pp. 7–9.

Riggs, H. N. "Computer Data Base Activities in Upper Elementary School Social Studies: A Stimulus for Curriculum Integration." *History and Social Science Teacher,* Spring 1990, *25*(3), pp. 145–150.

Ropiequet, S., ed. *CD ROM: Vol. 2. Optical Publishing.* Redmond, WA: Microsoft Press, 1987.

Ryba, K. and Anderson, B. *Learning with Computers: Effective Teaching Strategies.* Eugene, OR: International Society for Technology in Education, 1990. (ERIC Document ED 327 157.)

Salant, A. "A Fully Integrated Instructional Database: Promoting Student Research Skills." *Educational Technology,* April 1990, *30*(4), pp. 55–58.

Scott, R. N. and Wolpert, E. M. "ERIC and Other Educational Databases: An Overview for Users." *Educational Technology,* August 1990, *30*(8), pp. 26–32.

Simonson, M. R. and Thompson, A. *Educational Computing Foundations.* Columbus, OH: Merrill, 1990.

Staff. "Archives in Miniature." *PC Magazine,* 31 January 1989, pp. 185–200.

Stearns, P. H. "Preparing Students with Learning Disabilities for Information Age Success." *The Computing Teacher,* April 1992, *19*(7), pp. 28–30.

Strickland, A. W. and Hoffer, T. "Integrating Computer Databases with Laboratory Problems." *The Computing Teacher,* December–January, 1990–1991, *18*(6), pp. 30–32.

Thomas, R., "The Student-Designed Database." *The Computing Teacher,* February 1988, *15*(5), pp. 17–19.

Townsend, J. J. *Introduction to Databases.* Carmel, IN: Que Corporation, 1992.

Unia, S. "Exploring Information." *The Computing Teacher*, August–September 1991, *19*(1), pp. 33–34.

Watson, J. *Teaching Thinking Skills with Databases.* Eugene, OR: International Society for Technology in Education, 1991.

White, C. S. *The Impact of Structured Activities with a Computer-based File-Management Program on Selected Information Processing Skills.* Unpublished doctoral dissertation, Indiana University, 1985.

White, C. S. "Access to and Use of Databases in the Social Studies." *International Journal of Social Education*, Spring 1990, *5*(1), pp. 61–73.

Wiebe, J. H. "Teaching Mathematics with Technology: Data Base Programs in the Mathematics Classroom." *Arithmetic Teacher*, January 1990, *37*(5), pp. 38–40.

Objectives

After completing this chapter, you will be able to:

Briefly discuss the development of application software.

Discuss basic concepts of spreadsheets.

List and describe generic functional commands used to construct and manipulate a computer spreadsheet.

Explain the significance of spreadsheet templates.

Describe potential uses of "what if" applications.

List and evaluate several classroom uses of computer spreadsheets.

Detail at least one spreadsheet application that you would like to try or explain why you see no personal application for spreadsheets.

Develop lesson plans that include spreadsheet use.

Chapter 4

Spreadsheets: Managing Numbers

This chapter examines one of the pioneering types of application programs for the microcomputer, the electronic spreadsheet. This application is first placed in the context of application software, followed by an overview of what a spreadsheet is and what spreadsheet software can do. A sample computer spreadsheet is developed step by step. Applications of spreadsheets in education conclude this chapter.

Development of Application Software

Computers for Programmers

When microcomputers became generally available in the latter part of the 1970s, computer languages were the first software. These programs presented the user with a variety of programming approaches patterned after the languages then in use on mainframe computers. Users were obliged to plan and write their own application programs, a topic discussed in Part 4 of this book. At that time, microcomputer usage was viewed largely as a downward extension of mainframe computing, with expertise in programming and programming languages being essential for using the machine. This made it appear that considerable technical knowledge and experience also would be necessary for the average person to take advantage of rapidly developing microcomputer technology.

Computers for Nonprogrammers

Word-processing programs were the first major microcomputer software development to approach usage from a different perspective, that of the computer as a tool. *Tool* or *application* programs allowed users to perform desired tasks without doing the actual programming. Someone else had already created a general-purpose tool for a common need. By learning how to use a specific application program, anyone could benefit from a microcomputer without having to learn or even be familiar with a computer language. This simplified computer usage and made the microcomputer accessible to a wide variety of potential users. Rather than devoting weeks, months, or years to mastering programming skills, users could achieve useful results in a period of hours or, at most, days.

Visible Calculators

The introduction of the *VisiCalc* program in 1979 continued and accelerated the trend toward application software. The creators of *VisiCalc* recognized that many common tasks entail working with a calculator and a sheet of paper to record and organize information in a row-and-column format. This was especially true in the world of business finance: accounting ledgers, forecasting documents, and so on. Their new product was a *visible calculator*, and much more.

VisiCalc presented the user with a simple and direct way to construct and manipulate a computer work area of rows and columns called a *spreadsheet*. A wide variety of useful tasks could be performed with no knowledge of a complicated computer language. *VisiCalc* was an immediate success and ultimately became a bestseller for use in business, education, and the home. It helped to convince countless mainframe users that microcomputers were more than toys. It also created a whole new generation of first-time computer users.

More Powerful Spreadsheets

Today, spreadsheets are a major category of computer software, along with word-processing and data-management programs. Since the creation of *VisiCalc*, improved versions of spreadsheet programs have been introduced by a variety of companies. Each new version and upgrade has built upon previous spreadsheet developments and introduced a wider range of more powerful capabilities. These capabilities represent improvement in two directions. The first adds more features to the basic spreadsheet, turning it into a "power" spreadsheet of large size with a wide variety of commands and functions available. The second adds tools to the spreadsheet, turning it into some level of integrated program. The most common of such additions are the capability to produce graphs and charts directly from the data within a spreadsheet, as well as the capability to surround spreadsheet data with appropriate narrative to serve as introductions, headings, or explanations. There are even programs that integrate full-fledged generic applications, such as word processing, database management, and spreadsheets, within the same program. Such programs are discussed in Chapter 6. The basic "stand-alone" spreadsheet is the focus of this chapter.

The Technical Side of Spreadsheets

Fundamental Concepts

While most spreadsheet programs are similar in their underlying concept and use, there are numerous terminology and technical differences among them. What is presented here is a generic spreadsheet description; that is, the basic concepts that underlie most spreadsheets. There is enough commonality among all spreadsheet programs to allow a user with a conceptual understanding to adapt quickly to the specific characteristics of any particular one.

Electronic Paper

A spreadsheet (also called a *worksheet*) can be thought of as a large piece of paper where data can be stored in rows and columns, to be manipulated by the computer. While spreadsheet processing can be accomplished by hand, using a computer spreadsheet is considerably easier and faster in all but the simplest cases. Many tasks become feasible that simply would be too time consuming or complex for a manual worksheet.

Cells

Once a spreadsheet program has been started on a computer, the user views a nearly blank screen. A typical empty spreadsheet is illustrated in Figure 4.1. The workplace is divided into columns and rows. Columns traditionally have been designated by one or two letters (starting with A), and rows are generally identified by numbers (starting with 1). The intersection of a row or column is called a *cell*. A cell is typically referred to by its column and row designation (e.g., A1 or K25, which is its unique "address" within the total spreadsheet).

A cell may contain one of three types of entries:

1. Numbers or *values* (numeric data).
2. *Labels* (alphabetic or alphanumeric data).

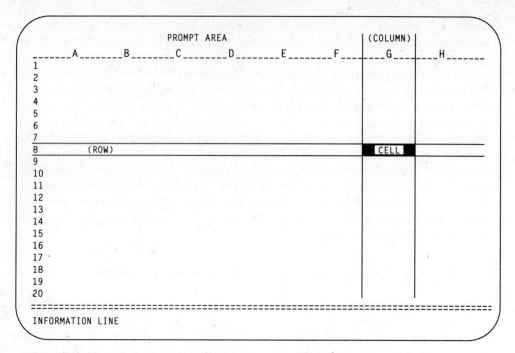

Figure 4.1. Typical spreadsheet form.

3. *Formulas* (expressions of calculations or relationships among cells). Pre-defined formulas are called *functions*.

Numbers and labels are displayed in the cell as entered. For a formula, the cell displays the result of the calculations.

Cell Pointer

When working within a spreadsheet, the *cell pointer* or cursor keeps you visually informed of your location within the spreadsheet. The cell pointer is a highlighted rectangle on the screen that identifies the current cell location. The cell pointer moves around the spreadsheet in response to the mouse, the cursor arrow keys, or special keyboard commands. In the cell currently shown by the cell pointer, you can make a new entry or edit an existing one.

Prompt Area

Often there are additional lines above or below the worksheet that are referred to as the *prompt area* (see Figure 4.1). The prompt area is used to show commands to alter or manipulate the spreadsheet and also to display the contents of the current cell. Formulas and functions are displayed in the prompt area only; the cell displays the result of the calculation. There also may be a line at the bottom that displays current information about the spreadsheet. Within a graphical operating environment, such as the Macintosh or *Windows*, pulldown menus and a button bar (a line of labeled buttons) provide information about the spreadsheet and simplify command identification. The important point is that information about the spreadsheet is easily identifiable, data entry is relatively obvious and simple, and command or procedure identification and use are readily available (Figure 4.2).

Automatic Updating

In a typical spreadsheet, many cells contain formulas that use the values contained in other cells. Much of the power of a spreadsheet stems from the *automatic updating* of the results of these formulas whenever the value in any related cell changes. For example, if cell B9 contained the price of a dozen eggs and cell D9 contained the formula B9/12, the value displayed in cell D9 would be the cost of one egg. If you changed the value in B9, the unit cost shown in cell D9 would change automatically. You could quickly compare the unit cost of various sizes of eggs by changing only B9.

The Window

Actually, only a portion of the complete spreadsheet can be seen at any time on the screen. As you move the cell pointer around the spreadsheet, previously hidden parts become visible and previously visible parts are hidden. The screen can

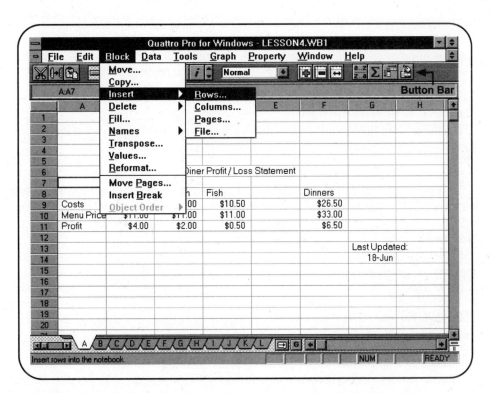

Figure 4.2. Pulldown menus and a button bar simplify spreadsheet use.

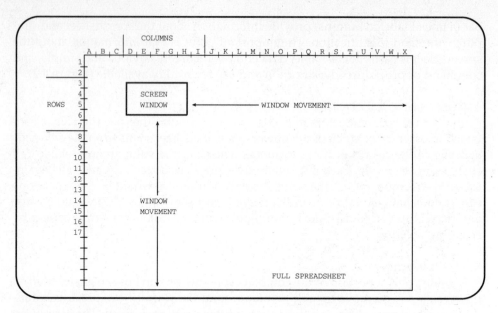

Figure 4.3. The spreadsheet window.

be thought of as a movable window or frame looking upon a much larger spreadsheet (Figure 4.3). While only a portion can be seen at one time, the entire spreadsheet is nonetheless still there and can be examined and manipulated by moving the cell pointer to change the location of the window on the spreadsheet.

Using a Spreadsheet

To understand how to use a spreadsheet, first recall the three types of entries that a cell may contain. They are numbers or values, labels, and formulas.

Entering Data

Two types of data can be entered into a spreadsheet. The most common is simple numeric information, placing a specific *number* or *value* in a cell. This is accomplished by moving the cell pointer to the appropriate cell and entering the required digits.

Alphabetic information, called *labels,* can also be entered into a cell in a similar manner. Labels make a worksheet easy to read and understand.

If the first character of a cell entry is a number, the program interprets the entry as a value; if the first character is not a number, the program interprets the entry as a label. Formula and function entries begin with special coding, such as + or − and @.

Generating Data from Relationships

Information in a cell can also be generated by *formulas* that cause a cell to display the result of a calculation. The calculation may involve the contents of other cells in the worksheet, or specific values and cell contents. For example, the formula +A1+B7 produces the SUM of the values in the indicated cells. The formula +3.1416*Q6*Q6 would yield the area of a circle, if cell Q6 contained the radius value. Remember, the cell contains a formula, which is displayed in the prompt area, but the worksheet shows the result of the specified calculation.

Analogous to formulas are built-in spreadsheet *functions*. Functions are special commands that allow you to achieve often complex processing without personally creating the necessary formulas. Some spreadsheet programs provide an extensive list of functions, including mathematical functions, trigonometric functions, statistical functions, and financial functions. Statistical functions useful to most educators include @SUM (add part of a row or column of numbers) and @AVERAGE (compute the average of part of a row or column of numbers).

Formulas and functions are powerful aspects of spreadsheets and will be used in the next section to create a practical example of spreadsheet use. They underlie the concept that the power of a spreadsheet stems from the user's ability to define *relationships* among the many values and cells. Because formulas and functions manipulate values from other cells, any change in those values automatically generates a corresponding change in the value displayed by the formula or function in its cell.

Spreadsheet Commands

Simple data entry and manipulation alone are inadequate to make a spreadsheet powerful and relatively easy to use. There are numerous commands at your disposal that perform manipulation and "housekeeping" tasks, offering enormous flexibility over paper methods of work. These commands may be displayed in the prompt area, in a menu, or on a button on the screen (see Figure 4.2). You select the command needed, supply any necessary information, and the computer executes the command on the spreadsheet.

Listed below are commonly encountered spreadsheet manipulation commands and brief descriptions of their use:

COPY	Duplicates the contents of one or more cells in another location on the spreadsheet.
DELETE	Removes either a column or a row from a worksheet. The remaining columns move to the left; the remaining rows move up to close the gaps.
ERASE	Deletes the contents of one or more cells.
FORMAT	Specifies how the information will be displayed within a cell (e.g., integer value, fixed decimal places, floating decimal point, flush at left edge of cell, centered within cell etc.).
INSERT	Inserts either a column or a row into a worksheet. The original columns move right and rows move down as necessary to accommodate the inserted columns or rows.
MOVE	Relocates the contents of one or more cells to another location on the spreadsheet.
WIDTH	Widens or narrows columns to meet display requirements.

These are commonly encountered spreadsheet housekeeping commands and brief descriptions of their use:

PRINT   Directs the system to produce a printed copy of the worksheet currently on the screen. Whereas the screen can display only as much of the worksheet as its window holds, a printout may contain the entire worksheet or any desired portion.

SAVE   Directs the system to save the current spreadsheet in a disk file for future use.

RETRIEVE   Causes the system to load the contents of a worksheet from a disk file and display them.

Many other commands are available within specific spreadsheet programs, but those just mentioned are the most basic types and are adequate to develop a concrete illustration in the next section.

Verification of Results

Depending on one's needs and skills in developing spreadsheet applications, the result can become very complex. Spreadsheets developed for projecting trends, for instance, may involve hundreds of cells with complex inter-relationships expressed in the formulas used. The possibility of errors in setting up the spreadsheet cannot be overlooked. It is vital to enter test data into any spreadsheet to verify against known results that the spreadsheet has been designed correctly. It is only too easy to believe that an answer produced by the computer is always correct.

An Example Spreadsheet: Class Recordkeeping

For a practical introduction to electronic spreadsheets in education, let's stay with the familiar and use a simple class recordkeeping or grade book example. This example addresses the need to keep data on the three quiz results of a group of students. Also desired are the sum of the three test scores for each student and the class average on each test.

Creating the Spreadsheet

While this simple example clearly could be done by hand, a computer spreadsheet offers a more flexible and efficient approach to this type of problem. A step-by-step guide to creating it follows, using our generic spreadsheet commands. The completed worksheet is shown in Figure 4.4.

1. Use the ERASE command to clear the entire worksheet area.
2. Widen column A and column E, using the WIDTH command to provide enough room for appropriate headings and data.

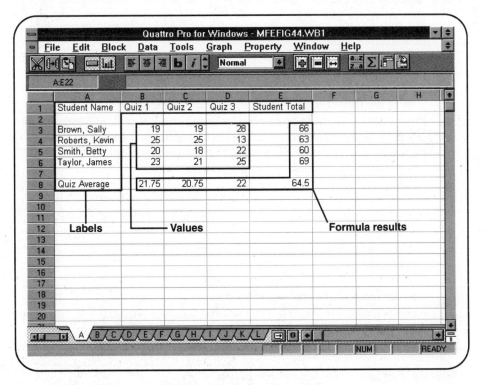

Figure 4.4. Example spreadsheet: class recordkeeping.

3. Enter the following headings into the spreadsheet at the specified locations:

COLUMN	ROW	ENTRY
A	1	Student Name
B	1	Quiz 1
C	1	Quiz 2
D	1	Quiz 3
E	1	Student Total

4. Skip row 2 (for visual clarity) and enter in each of the following rows a student's name, score 1, score 2, and score 3. In Figure 4.4, four students have been entered on the worksheet.
5. Skip another row for visual clarity and enter the label "Quiz Average" in column A row 8.
6. Use the @SUM function in column E row 3 to cause this cell to display the sum of the data in row 3, columns B, C, and D (i.e., the sum of the three test scores for this student). You have just established the first relationship among cells! You could, of course, have entered your own formula in cell E3, but functions are easier to use and more versatile.

7. For cells E4, E5, and E6, again use the @SUM function or comparable formulas. The simplest approach is to use the COPY command to duplicate the function or formula in E3. When the COPY command is used, any cell references are automatically changed to indicate the cells containing the appropriate data. The designated cells in column E would then display the sum of the three test scores for each of the students.

8. Enter either a formula or a function in column B row 8, indicating that this cell is to contain the average of all data in column B rows 3 through 6. Cell B8 would then display the average of the four student scores for test 1, a more complex relationship among cells.

9. Finally, use the COPY command to duplicate the function or formula in cell B8 into row 8 columns C, D, and E. As before, the COPY command automatically adjusts the cell references to reflect the appropriate data cells. The designated cells in row 8 would now contain the averages of the four student scores for each of the tests, as well as the average total score for all three tests.

10. The worksheet is now complete. Use the SAVE command to store a copy of this worksheet on the disk for future use.

11. If desired, use the PRINT command to obtain a hard copy of this spreadsheet.

Manipulating the Spreadsheet

The spreadsheet is basically complete at this point, much like a grade book at the end of a term. While useful as a recordkeeping tool, this is only the beginning of what can be done with this computer spreadsheet. The following is a partial list of additional possibilities that could be done within this illustration.

Changing Data

If you discovered that any of the data entries in this worksheet were incorrect, you only need to re-enter the correct data in the appropriate cell. With each new entry, the spreadsheet software would recalculate all affected cells automatically to reflect this data change. *Automatic recalculation* is one of the most powerful features of a spreadsheet program. Specifically, changing the score in cell B3 would also automatically alter the result in cells B8, E3, and E8 because each of these is based in part on the contents of B3. Figure 4.5 illustrates this process. In a manual system, you would have to recall which cells to change and, eraser in hand, make all adjustments yourself. Automatic recalculation becomes increasingly valuable as worksheet size and complexity grow.

Adding a Student

To add a student, use the INSERT command to open up a blank row at the desired location on the spreadsheet and enter the necessary data. Normally, this would be done so as to insert the student in the proper place alphabetically in the

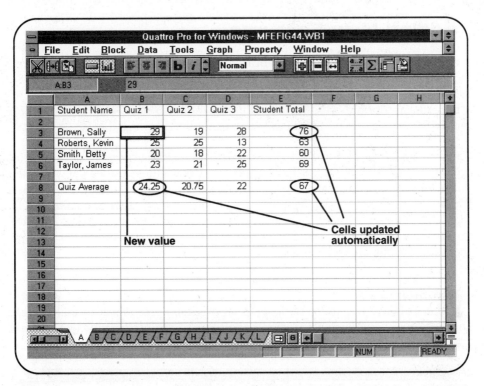

Figure 4.5. Automatic recalculation changed B8, E3, and E8 when B3 was changed.

list. Functions adjust automatically to include this new student. As scores are entered, the whole spreadsheet is recalculated to include the new data in the sum and average cells. Not only does this save you a lot of work, but your records are always in the correct order. Additions to a grade book normally must be made at the bottom of the list, which can be confusing.

Removing a Student

If a student who is already on the spreadsheet leaves the class, use the DELETE command to remove the row containing that student's data. Functions again adjust automatically to omit this student, and the whole spreadsheet is recalculated to exclude these data in the sum and average cells. This results in a set of records that is easier to read than the typical grade book with lines drawn through rows no longer needed.

Adding a Quiz

To add another quiz, use the INSERT command to open up a blank column at the desired location on the spreadsheet. Enter a heading in row 1, and enter the student data for this quiz. Functions will adjust automatically to include the new quiz. The sum and average cells are updated appropriately.

Adding New Features

Adding more features to this application is quite easy. Column F could become the student average. Row 10 might be test standard deviation or some other statistic. You need only determine and enter the formula or function once, then COPY it into all appropriate cells. The flexibility to establish new relationships among cells with very little extra work is a major attraction of spreadsheets.

Advanced Features of Spreadsheet Software

Most spreadsheet programs have additional capabilities besides the worksheet. The most common of these is *data charting* or *graphing* from within the worksheet. For example, in Figure 4.6, the student scores have been used to construct a bar chart that illustrates how the students have performed in class. Other advanced features include simple word-processing and database procedures, such as spell checking, sorting, and selecting.

Templates

It is not always necessary to develop an original spreadsheet to meet a need. There are books and journals articles that offer ready-to-use spreadsheet *templates*.

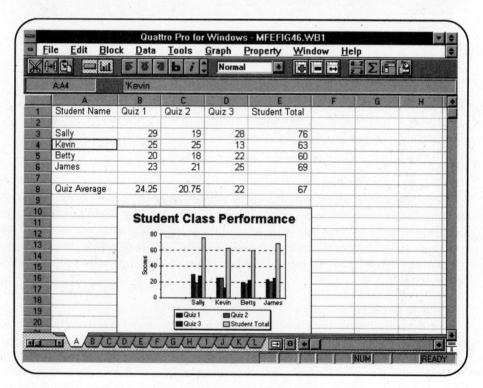

Figure 4.6. Bar chart constructed within the worksheet.

A template is simply a spreadsheet file (or the directions for creating one) with no data provided. First, you load the template from a disk file, then enter your own data into the appropriate cells. As data are entered, automatic recalculation occurs, and the appropriate results are displayed in cells containing formulas. When all data have been entered, the spreadsheet is saved onto the disk *using a new name* for the file. In this way, the template is available for further use.

By using templates, the person who despairs of being able to create an original application can still benefit from the power and versatility of a spreadsheet. Sticking with our example, a template for a grade book could be developed by one teacher and shared by any others interested in this approach to student recordkeeping.

Conclusion

It should be apparent that once a spreadsheet has been set up, it can be modified quickly and easily to change existing data, add new data, or delete data. Our example used only a small data set to illustrate some of the capabilities of a computer spreadsheet. Because some spreadsheets can have thousands of rows and hundreds of columns, it is possible to work with rather large data sets. The automatic adjustment of formulas and functions to reflect changes, as well as the automatic recalculation of all cells, makes a computer spreadsheet a powerful tool.

Categories of Spreadsheet Applications

For simplicity, possible uses for spreadsheets may be summarized under three headings: recordkeeping, complex calculation worksheets, and "what if" applications.

Recordkeeping

A computer spreadsheet might be used simply as a big scratchpad, a place to easily record information that is not manipulated. For example, a complete record of one's students, relatives, or business associates and any related data could be stored on a spreadsheet. Related data could be anything to which a user wished to have easy access. A spreadsheet can be used to manage a mailing list or telephone numbers, or to store other routine personal data. Room or department inventories could also be kept on a spreadsheet. The spreadsheet becomes a rudimentary database in such applications.

Advantages of using a spreadsheet in this manner include ease of changing data already on the sheet, easy of adding new data anywhere on the sheet, and ease of deleting unneeded data. Moving around to view data within this type of computer spreadsheet may be more efficient and easier than working with large amounts of paper. A very large amount of information can be stored on a single diskette, taking much less storage space than equivalent paper records. A hard copy of all or some of the spreadsheet can then be printed as needed. Even using a computer spreadsheet in this very simple manner can be advantageous, although it would hardly justify purchasing spreadsheet software. Such applications do not make use of the inherent power of a spreadsheet.

A computer spreadsheet becomes much more powerful as a "complex" record-keeping system. In addition to storing various amounts of information, simple calculations can be performed on the data. The student grade book illustration included two types of calculations: the sum of each student's scores and average of scores on each test. Many more calculations based upon the data in the spreadsheet could have been included.

Many educators find a spreadsheet grade book much easier, more flexible, and faster to use than special-purpose grade book programs that are described in Chapter 5. Inventory records may be more valuable if counts and/or sums of item values are added. In addition to performing the indicated calculations efficiently, the spreadsheet's ability to allow for data correction, addition, or deletion and the automatic recalculation of all formulas and functions after data changes have made this use of computer spreadsheets invaluable in a wide variety of diverse applications.

Complex Calculation Worksheets

Computer spreadsheets are not restricted just to simple recordkeeping. They were developed to speed up and ease many business applications that involve complex calculations. There are many specialized functions included in most spreadsheet programs that are useful in particular application areas. Of course, you could construct your own formulas or use those published in the general literature regarding spreadsheets.

An example is loan-amortization calculation. This involves specifying the amount of a loan, the interest rate, and the length of the loan. Based upon the entered value, a spreadsheet function or series of functions then calculates and displays the amount of each payment, the principal and interest component of each payment, and the remaining balance. In addition, other functions could produce the sum of all principal and interest payments to provide a clear picture of the total cost of a loan, as well as the monthly details. Such applications can be very useful when considering whether to borrow money, perhaps in a business math, economics, or family-living class.

"What If" Applications

Being able to answer "What if?" questions is another reason why spreadsheets were created and is a major factor in their popularity. Instead of looking at only one possibility you can have the computer calculate the results for different entered parameters.

From our loan example, you could direct the computer on the same spreadsheet to generate amortization data to answer many questions. What if the amount of the loan were increased or decreased? What if the interest rate were 2 percent higher or lower? What if the repayment period were extended or shortened? The results could be examined and compared and decisions made appropriately based upon this comparison.

There are two different methods for handling "what ifs." If the worksheet is not too large and the number of different parameters of interest is small, you can create multiple worksheets in one by using the COPY command to duplicate the first set of cells into unused areas of the sheet. For example, if the initial area used was cells A1 through G25, it could be duplicated from H1 through N25 or from A26 through G50.

In a more complex situation, "what if" questions are often explored interactively. Create a worksheet, enter one set of parameters, and print the results. Next, enter a new set of parameters and print the result. This is done as many times as necessary, after which the printouts are compared to see the effects of the changes. For a quick look at alternatives, the printouts may not be needed.

Even a spreadsheet grade book has "what if" uses. Suppose you have set up your worksheet to compute total scores and average marks. Your students know that their grades will be based on their final averages. With one test remaining, your worksheet shows each student's average to that point. If students ask what score they must achieve on the last test to earn a certain grade, you could very quickly enter any number of different scores for the final exam and watch the resulting average change. Many teachers regularly face such questions, but can give an answer only after finding time to do several sets of calculations. A spreadsheet offers almost instantaneous responses.

Can you think of other applications where this type of "what if" comparison would be important, even indispensable? Consider how often you must make decisions based on incomplete data. How could a spreadsheet help you weigh options?

Classroom Applications

The preceding section on application categories may have stimulated your thinking about potential uses for spreadsheets in your teaching. Other concrete examples should further help expand your thinking in an area admittedly foreign to many teachers.

Introducing Spreadsheet Use

The National Council of Teachers of Mathematics (1898; 1991) specifies that students should learn to use the computer to investigate and solve problems. Niess (1992) uses candy to introduce spreadsheets to her students. Each student gets a bag of M&Ms. The first task is to see what students know about them without looking (contents, descriptions, colors, etc.), including guesses as to total number, most common color, and so on. Next, the teacher demonstrates what is in one bag, then asks students to record estimates of what will be in their own bag on 3 by 5 cards. Students open their bag, count, and record. Niess then combines the data from the individual cards into a large, physical "spreadsheet" of cards on the floor. Students inspect the data to find the most reds, fewest yellows, or whatever. Spreadsheet terminology is introduced at this point. After a variety of activities, students construct a computer spreadsheet from their experience and graph the findings.

High School Mathematics

Bratton (1988) describes concrete ways to allow students to "do math" at a pre-calculus level using spreadsheets. Among the topics are the remainder theorem and synthetic division, graphing polynomial functions, and approximation of irrational roots.

Russell (1987) suggests ways of using spreadsheets to extend the normally limited treatment of probability, while Choate (1986) focuses on modeling and problem solving. For extensive applications in math, see Arganbright (1985).

Hypothesis Testing or What If . . . ?

You already have read about the power of spreadsheets to allow for hypothesis testing as you vary one or more values within your worksheet. Collis (1988) and Schiffman (1986) both discuss this approach to exploring personal finance issues, such as interest and loan amortization. Hoelscher (1986) describes how students may build new analytic skills by re-examining data from new perspectives. Karlin (1988) brought life to time and distance problems by using as a topic the running speed of dinosaurs. This example included "doing science" by starting with human movement, which was videotaped for analysis.

Budgets

Budgets are an obvious application of spreadsheet software. Beaver (1992) suggests beginning a budget activity by brainstorming common sources of income and typical spending categories. Settle on a common set, and then create a budget template or have students create their own. Have them track their personal budget over the school year or some significant time period and generate graphs that may demonstrate more clearly their patterns. Wilson (1985) described a challenging and usable budgeting experience with fifth graders. For older students, expand the activity to include monthly averages, quarterly figures, even income tax projections. Could you include projecting whether the student will have enough cash to pay anticipated prom expenses?

Sports Statistics

Students had little interest in spreadsheet applications (such as budgeting) until Miller (1988) turned to newspaper data on major sports teams. The activities described range from determining which team had the best record in various categories to predicting outcomes of future contests based on past performances. Beaver (1992) illustrates the same concept for baseball only. He also shows use of long labels to provide on-screen directions to users for entering data.

Anticipating Grades

Earlier in this chapter, you learned about the potential to use a spreadsheet to create a grade book that you could also use to project the effects of future test scores on final grades. Why not have students create their own personal grade book, with which they can track and project their grades at any time? The concept is identical to your own class record system, but students would record only their own data. Beaver (1992) suggests using this approach as well for high schoolers who wish to anticipate their grade point averages, whether to maintain sports eligibility or project college admission.

Tracking the Weather

The daily weather provides a ready source of data for ongoing science projects. Use a spreadsheet to store daily weather data (temperature at specified times, precipitation, barometer reading, wind conditions, etc.) Design the spreadsheet as a template for a specific time period, such as one month, and include provision for calculating appropriate averages and, perhaps, other statistics. Use the data to produce line or bar graphs and compare them to those published in most newspapers. Categorical data, such as type of cloud cover, can also be collected and used to generate pie or bar charts to illustrate weather patterns (Beaver, 1992).

The Magic Square

A magic square is a 3 cell by 3 cell grid. Each cell contains one of the digits from 1 to 9, without repetition. The challenge is to place the digits so that all row sums and column sums equal 15. Beaver (1992) demonstrates setting up this common puzzle, using a spreadsheet (Figure 4.7). Students use a discovery (i.e., trial and error) approach to find a solution. How many unique solutions can the class find?

Fundraisers, Grades 2 to High School

In one high school, students made personalized holiday greeting cards, using graphics software, then sold the cards as a fundraiser. Both a database and a spreadsheet tracked the entire project (Kneen, 1987).

Similarly, in Alaska, students and staff were involved in raising funds. A second-grade teacher created a simple worksheet and taught his students how to enter the figures that were reported by students from all classes (Sopp, 1985). These second graders managed the recordkeeping for the entire school!

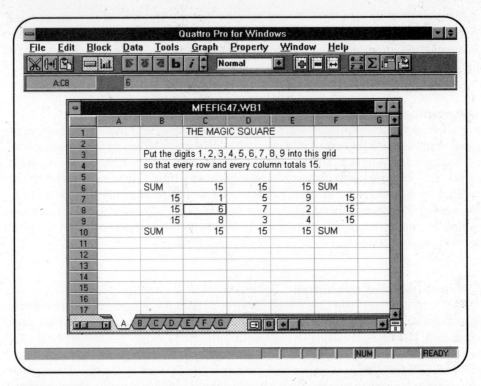

Figure 4.7. The Magic Square implemented with a spreadsheet (Beaver, 1922).

Class Surveys

Beaver (1992) suggests a simple template to facilitate compilation of class survey projects. Students replace simple categorical labels (topic 1, survey item 1, 2, etc.) with their own wording for each project. Other columns record the survey tallies. Results are easiest to understand when the data are presented in graph form. Beaver suggests having students select specific topics on which to survey one another, then using the final graphs for a bulletin board that profile the class. Extend the project across classes to generate discussions of similarities and differences, then perhaps to teachers, parents, or the community.

Fast Food Comparisons

Students are likely to view themselves as experts on local fast foods, but there is probably much that they still can learn. On a very simple level, students can research costs at various restaurants, enter the data into a spreadsheet, and produce a graph comparing the popular establishments (Blank, 1985). A more challenging and potentially valuable exercise would be to research the nutritional value of common fast-food meal combinations. A more complex spreadsheet could then reflect cost and health issues, possibly including daily dietary needs and recommended intake of fats, cholesterol, vitamins, and so forth.

Energy Usage

A spreadsheet could be devised to study energy usage. Students could inventory their home appliances and record their energy use in kilowatts per hour. After estimating hours of use for each appliance over some time period, an energy-consumption model could be developed.

Also in the area of energy, students might take measurements of their home, recording or calculating square footage of the residence and all windows and doors, as well as thickness of attic insulation. Based on published formulas, home heating and cooling requirements could be determined. The effects of increasing insulation could also be estimated.

Teaching Spreadsheets

One day, you may find yourself in a situation that requires you to teach others to use spreadsheets. Just as you were probably mystified by the concepts at first, so your students will be. An excellent introduction to spreadsheets is carefully laid out, complete with lesson plans, activities, and reproducible handouts, by Brown (1986–1987;1987). Lesson plans are also provided in Collis (1988) and Luehrmann (1986). Other sources of suggestions include Carey and Carey (1986) and Dyrli (1986).

Summary

Spreadsheets are a major form of application software, joining word processing and databases as productivity tools. They were developed to cope with often difficult and time-consuming financial calculations, but have found wide usage in other situations as well.

A spreadsheet is simply an arrangement of rows and columns in which data may be stored and manipulated. The intersection of a row and a column is termed a cell. Each cell may contain numeric or alphabetic data or a formula or function that establishes a mathematical relationship among cells. The latter is one key to the power of spreadsheets. Templates offer this power to users without the need to create original applications.

Spreadsheets quickly become larger than can be displayed on a computer screen at once. The screen then becomes a window or frame, which can be moved about on the spreadsheet as needed. Changing the value in any cell in the spreadsheet will automatically alter any other related cell. This is a major advantage of electronic spreadsheets over their manual counterparts. It opens the way to answering "what if?" questions to check the results of varying assumptions or projections.

Spreadsheets seem alien to teachers, who tend not to see applications for a "financial" tool. Yet there are many viable classroom applications of spreadsheets. Examples in this chapter presented uses across many subject fields and at various grade levels from elementary through high school. While it may require more effort for a teacher to become comfortable with a spreadsheet than with word processing or databases, the benefits are worth the effort. The potential of spreadsheets in education is limited only by the teacher's creativity.

Chapter 4 Activities

Use any available spreadsheet to carry out the following activities.

1. Compare the specific screen format of your spreadsheet to the general design in Figure 4.1. What are the differences? Determine the maximum size of a worksheet, that is, what is the maximum row and maximum column?
2. Make a list of the actual commands used with your spreadsheet in place of the generic commands described in this chapter. You may want to create a wall chart for your computer room.
3. Create a functional grade book similar to the illustration given.
4. Expand your basic grade book by determining what additional functions your spreadsheet offers and adding those that you consider potentially useful.
5. Develop a personal budget. You'll need both an income and an expenditure portion. Divide the expenses into major categories, such as housing, food, automotive, clothing, and so forth. Set up a "base" budget and leave space to record actual expenses for several months. Be sure to include cells that compare expenses to budget each month.
6. Develop a lesson plan for using a spreadsheet with your students.

Bibliography

Albrecht, B., and Firedrake, G. "Power Tools for Math and Science." *The Computing Teacher*, August/September 1992, 20(1), pp. 34–35.

Arad, O. S. "The Spreadsheet: Solving Word Problems." *The Computing Teacher*, December/January 1986–87, pp. 13–15, 45.

Arganbright, D. *Mathematical Applications of Electronic Spreadsheets*. New York: McGraw-Hill, 1985.

Beaver, J. "Using Computer Power to Improve Your Teaching Part II: Spreadsheets and Charting." *The Computing Teacher*, March 1992, 19(6), pp. 22–24.

Blank, D. E. "Stepping through Fast-Food Land: A Spreadsheet Tutorial." *The Computing Teacher*, June 1985, pp. 26–28.

Bratton, G. "Spreadsheets and Synthetic Division." *The Computing Teacher*, March 1988, pp. 38–40, 61.

Brown, J. M. "Spreadsheets in the Classroom." *The Computing Teacher*, December/January 1986–1987, pp. 8–12.

Brown, J. M. "Spreadsheets in the Classroom: Part II." *The Computing Teacher*, February 1987, pp. 9–12.

Caffarella, E. P. *Spreadsheets Go To School*. Reston, VA: Reston Publishing, 1985.

Carey, D., and Carey, R. "Make Spreadsheets Make Sense: A Model for Introduction." *The Computing Teacher*, February 1986, pp. 62–64.

Choate, J. "Using *VisiCalc* and *DYNAmo* to Make Models and Solve Problems in High School Math Classes." *Computers in the Schools*, Spring 1986, *3*(1), pp. 75–81.

Collis, B. *Computers, Curriculum, and Whole-Class Instruction*. Belmont, CA: Wadsworth, 1988.

Dribin, C. I. "Spreadsheets and Performance: A Guide for Student Presentations." *The Computing Teacher*, June 1985, pp. 22–25.

Dyrli, O. E. "Electronic Spreadsheets in the Curriculum." *Computers in the Schools*, Spring 1986, *3*(1), pp. 47–54.

Flake, J. L., McClintock, C. E., and Turner, S. V. *Fundamentals of Computer Education*. Belmont, CA: Wadsworth, 1985.

Hannah, L. "Social Studies, Spreadsheets and the Quality of Life." *The Computing Teacher*, December/January 1985–1986, pp. 13–17.

Hoelscher, K. "Computing and Information: Steering Student Learning." *Computers in the Schools*, 1986, *3*(1), pp. 23–34.

Karlin, M. "Beyond Distance = Rate · Time." *The Computing Teacher*, February 1988, pp. 20–23.

Kneen, T. J. "A Computerized Fund Raising Project." *The Computing Teacher*, May 1987. pp. 11–12, 56.

Luehrmann, A. "Spreadsheets: More Than Just Finance." *The Computing Teacher*, April 1986, pp. 24–28.

Miller, M. "Using NFL Statistics to Teach the Spreadsheet." *The Computing Teacher*, March 1988, pp. 45–47.

National Council of Teachers of Mathematics, Commission on Standards for School Mathematics. *Curriculum and Evaluation Standards for School Mathematics*. Reston, VA, 1989.

National Council of Teachers of Mathematics, Commission on Standards for School Mathematics. *Professional Standards for Teaching Mathematics*. Reston, VA, 1989.

Niess, M. L. "Mathematics and M&Ms." *The Computing Teacher*, August/September 1992, *20*(1), pp. 29–31.

Riedesel, C. A., and Clements, D. H. *Coping with Computers in the Elementary and Middle Schools*. Englewood Cliffs, NJ: Prentice-Hall, 1985.

Russell, J. C. "Probability Modeling with a Spreadsheet." *The Computing Teacher*, November 1987, pp. 58–60.

Schiffman, S. S. "Productivity Tools for the Classroom." *The Computing Teacher*, May 1986, pp. 27–31.

Schwinge, S. "Spreadsheets and Simulations." *The Science Teacher*, 1985, *52*(9), pp. 27–28.

Sopp, N. P. "Do You Really Need a Children's Data Base?" *The Computing Teacher*, November 1985, pp. 43–45.

Wilson, J. W. "*VisiCalc* in the Elementary School." *The Computing Teacher*, June 1985, pp. 29–30.

Wright, E. B., and Forcier, R. C. *The Computer: A Tool for the Teacher*, Belmont, CA: Wadsworth, 1985.

After completing this chapter, you will be able to:

Differentiate print from presentation graphics.

Describe varied applications of print graphics software that are applicable to your teaching situation.

State and defend a position for or against using presentation graphics.

Identify potential applications of draw and paint software.

Discuss uses of scanners and related software.

Explain possible applications of graphing in your field.

Give at least three examples of support tools and explain how each could be used in your teaching.

Describe several ideas for student use of support-tool software.

Chapter 5

Graphics and Support Tools: Making Teaching Easier

Preceding chapters have shown numerous ways for teachers and students to benefit from use of common, general-purpose computer applications. In this chapter, you will study more specialized software, which is of use in the classroom. The first topic is graphics, which includes print and presentation development tools, drawing software, scanning and image manipulation, and graphing programs. The second part of the chapter treats a range of specialized software that may be useful in specific areas of your teaching. No one teacher is apt to find all such programs useful, but all teachers will find something of value among the available resources. These programs provide means to accomplish common, even daily, tasks in less time. In many cases, teachers can produce results of which they could once only dream. None of these tools replaces the more general ones discussed previously; rather, they are important additions to a teacher's software collection.

Graphics

Although early microcomputers were limited to alphanumeric input and output, today they are part of the age of graphic communication. The Macintosh initiated a move toward graphical user interfaces (GUIs) to simplify human–computer interaction. Most personal computers (PCs) can now use GUIs. This section presents graphics software. Some packages are basic communications products that allow you to produce pages or screens of text and images. Others are artistic products, computerized drawing, and image-manipulation tools whose output is often incorporated into other packages to create a finished product. A final group consists of specialized tools for creating charts and graphics.

Print Graphics

Print graphics describes those ingenious, inexpensive products that allow you to create banners to festoon your room and bulletin boards; posters (single pages) to announce coming events and dates; signs to serve as certificates of recognition for some achievement; simple letterhead for your own personalized stationery; and greeting cards for all occasions. Since the original *Print Shop* program, competitors have appeared, including *PrintMaster, Print Magic,* and *SuperPrint.* The latter can produce wall-size calendars and graphics nearly six feet high. Figure 5.1 is typical of output for this software group.

Beyond such general-purpose graphics software, there are also many specialized products, such as *Certificate Maker* and *Calendar Creator.* General-purpose software offers a great range of output types in a single package. Specialized products generally have far more flexibility and variety in their one type of output. In other words, *Calendar Creator* can tailor a calendar more to your needs than can *Print Shop* (Mathis, 1991–1992).

Common to all such software is a choice of text fonts in different styles and sizes, border designs, and a selection of ready-to-use "clip art." The latter is a great benefit to those computer users who have limited artistic skill. Enhancements to the original concept have been minor, but new collections of art work appear regularly.

Applications

Beyond the obvious uses of these programs, educational applications abound. How many classroom posters, handouts, even worksheets might be done more attractively and more "professionally" using a graphics program? You can also make great transparency masters. Figure 5.1 is an example. If you use a video recorder to document class (or family) activities, try using your graphics software to create title boards to tape at the start of each new segment. Be sure to include the date, because it may be forgotten later.

School fundraisers have become a way of life, given stark budget realities. Graphics software offers a nearly limitless range of possibilities. School calendars, special stationery, note pads, custom certificates, menus for local restaurants are among the more obvious. Because many such ideas have little to do with the cur-

Figure 5.1. A poster or transparency master.

riculum, they may be more appropriate as projects for a school computer club. Students might also volunteer to produce saleable items after school for the local PTA/PTO. While commercialism should not mix with or influence the curriculum inappropriately, students can polish their computer skills with projects such as these. Isn't that more valuable than simply selling purchased candy or other items?

Many issues of *The Computing Teacher* journal include a feature called "Kids on Computers," which is devoted to creative uses of computer graphics. Figure 5.2 illustrates a variation on an animal riddle idea from the March 1988 issue. Using the greeting-card format, the cover gives clues to the graphic answer inside.

Many elementary language arts teachers seek to vary both reading and writing with an occasional *rebus*, a story in which small graphics replace some words in sentences. Your print graphics software may be suitable for creating a rebus.

One fall, third graders in Lana Sternberg's suburban Chicago class used *Print Shop Companion* to produce a calendar for the coming year. Each month's page fea-

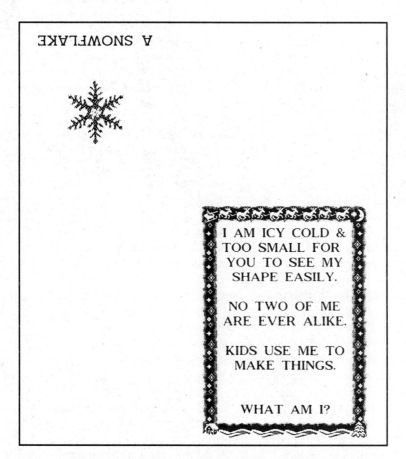

Figure 5.2. A single sheet of paper becomes a card when properly folded.

tured the best work from the class poetry unit, creating a special outlet for student writing (Sternberg, 1991).

Beaver (1992, February) suggests allowing students to create personal stationary (a common option in print packages) and to print enough copies to use for special events during the year, such as family invitations to the school play or open house.

Use *Certificates and More* to create bookmarks for a specific story that students are reading (Schipper, 1991). How about a bookmark contest? A sale to raise funds? Schipper also places student posters around school to promote books in a "Sell a Story" activity. She suggests using a graphics program to create faces for puppet shows (paste onto a paper bag, paper plate, sticks, etc.). To make mobiles, print two copies of an image and paste them together (or print double-sized to begin!), attach string, and hang. How about illustrating aspects of stories being read, to assure comprehension? Students can make picture strips to illustrate the introduction, body, and conclusion of a story, or its major events. Print them for sequencing practice. Make stationary and use it to write letters to story characters or authors (the card format works, too.) These ideas can integrate literature and letter writing. Schipper's final suggestion is to use a certificate program to create awards for characters (such as bravery, achievement, etc.) or official documents (birth certificate, driver's license, report cards, etc.). The possibilities are nearly endless.

Presentation Graphics (Desktop Presentations)

Presentation graphics software has many of the same preparation capabilities as print graphics: multiple fonts, clip art, even manipulation of image size or orientation. It produces individual "screens," however, that can be printed, but often are not. Rather, they are put together into "computer slide shows" for electronic delivery. For small groups, shows are viewed on a regular monitor. For larger settings, a video projector or liquid crystal display (LCD) panel is used.

Envision replacing all of your physical transparencies with graphics files. As necessary, you can quickly and easily update your images. Unlike plastic transparencies, which are usually monochrome, colors are basic design tools of presentation graphics. The software also provides transitions from one screen to the next that rival special effects seen in films and on television: wipes, fades, dissolves, checkerboard, starburst, and so on. Graphics shows are impressive, and development is easier than you may imagine.

Software for presentations varies considerably. Scholastic's *Slide Shop* for the Apple II offers basic capabilities. For DOS computers, products like *Storyboard Live!* and *Compel* feature a very wide range of color clip art, excellent transition effects, animation, direct import capabilities to accept content from other software, control of digitizing hardware, and run-time modules so that the computer used to deliver the presentation need not have the entire software product installed. The latter is not a trivial matter. Powerful packages such as these require many megabytes of hard disk space.

Aldus *Persuasion* and Microsoft *PowerPoint* have functionally equivalent versions for Macintosh and DOS computers. Both feature templates to speed the process of presentation development. Just add your text to professionally designed backgrounds. You can also enter notes along with each screen. Printout capabilities include full size for transparency masters and speaker's guides and audience handouts with small images of several screens per page, with or without your notes aligned alongside.

Presentation graphics add a whole new dimension to teaching if you take time to explore the possibilities and master a software product. You could bid farewell to chalk, transparencies, and other teaching tools. With battery-powered portable computers and lightweight LCD panels, you can even take your show on the road!

Applications

The most common application of presentation graphics is as an advanced electronic replacement for overhead transparencies to support presentations to your student group. Possibilities start with traditional lecture outlines, but consider the potential for prepared discussion questions, graphics to stimulate thinking (such as for a writing assignment), or any time a large, viewable image would be useful. You can also enter and display comments from class members, and then save the new screens for future use. Don't limit your imagination to the classroom, either. Presentations to the school board, for example, can carry greater impact when they show the preparation care and professionalism of computer-generated graphics. The many possible display effects can enhance the overall impact of the presentation and help to hold audience attention better than more traditional approaches.

Because the applications of presentation software are intentionally general, educators have shared few specific ideas in the literature. As one example, idioms are common in our language, and learning their nonliteral meaning is essential to their correct use. Lanman-Givens (1991) augmented a fourth-grade unit on idioms by having students illustrate their favorite idioms, using *Storyboard,* then share them with their classmates. The same lesson concept could be implemented with a print graphic program, provided that paper output was the goal. Projecting the student work may enhance the class interaction in a lesson such as this.

For tips on using a computer to deliver your presentation, see Ferrington and Loge (1992).

Drawing Programs

If you have an artistic bent or just can't find a suitable graphic in existing software, you may turn to a drawing package to create your own. Computer-based tools such as these have taken the art world by storm, creating whole new classes of artistic work and ways for artists to express themselves.

Among the first drawing programs were *Delta Drawing* for the Apple II, *MacDraw* and *MacPaint* (free with early Macintosh computers), and *Paintbrush* for DOS users. All have been upgraded and enhanced since their introduction, often making the early versions seem primitive. Still, they were adequate to stimulate a whole new use for a microcomputer.

As with most types of software, enhancements to drawing programs have greatly extended their sophistication, but at a price of increased complexity. At the same time, no software seems to be able to give drawing skills and talent to those not otherwise blessed with them. True, clip art gives us all a chance to incorporate much more imagery into our work than we otherwise would, but the nonartists among us are unlikely to become Michaelangelos, regardless of the tool that we use.

Because artistic skill and comprehension are still required when using a drawing package, bigger is not necessarily better. For the professional graphic artist, software such as Adobe *Illustrator,* Aldus *Freehand, CorelDraw,* or Micrografix *Designer* provide complete work environments. Far simpler products such as *Delta Drawing Today* (available in a Spanish version, too!), the most basic *PaintBrush,* the built-in Macintosh drawing tools that you can use in *HyperCard,* or the limited paint package in *IBM Linkway* succeed in offering more capabilities than most nonartists can use effectively, but with less complexity. Even a children's paint program such as *KidPix* (available for DOS and Apple) may serve your needs. Countless products fit between the extremes. Figure 5.3 is one example.

Applications

Because draw/paint software is by definition a generic tool, the applications are essentially unlimited. A few examples will illustrate.

These suggestions are from eighth graders who had used *KidPix* without knowing it was for "kids": have kids create personal name tags for field trips, "calling cards" for kids with businesses such as baby-sitting or yard work, personalized placemats for birthday parties (Nicholson, 1991).

Junior-high-age Native American students attended summer math camp at Oregon State University. One of their projects was to illustrate some of their native legends, using the drawing capabilities of *HyperCard* (Beekman, 1992).

Patricia Glieber teaches eighth grade in Milwaukee's only computer-specialty middle school. She teaches the use of *MacDraw Pro* by asking students to reproduce floor plans for new homes, based on model books provided by local builders. Four 45-minute periods are used to create and print the plans. Students

Figure 5.3. Sample image from *Windows Paintbrush*.

are assessed on their detail recognition, organizational skills, and creativity. The project introduces them to aspects of architecture, drafting, and graphic arts careers (Skwierawski, 1992).

In a New Jersey middle school, sixth graders combined a creative writing unit with art and journalism (Finlay 1990). Given the open-ended topic of imagination, what could you imagine? Students word processed their ideas, then added graphics created with *Dazzle Draw*. Completed stories were combined into a class booklet called "Imagination Stories."

Wiebe (1992) suggests using a drawing program to help students solve math problems involving logical and spatial relationships, which are notoriously difficult for many learners. He illustrates the potential with a problem of who lives in which house. The problem gives varying information, such as the house numbers, who lives where in respect to the others, and so forth. The visualization provided by creating a computer diagram of the known facts, plus the ability to move the graphics around until they fit in the desired relationships should aid comprehension.

Research

Freedman and Relan (1990) were concerned that many common uses of computers in schools "exclude and even delegitimize certain types of thinking, including . . . aesthetics." They turned to drawing software in an art education course to explore alternatives for working with a computer. As the course progressed, students grew artistically as they came to focus on formal and conceptual content of their images more than on the technical and manipulative concerns that dominated at the beginning. The researchers also found a marked shift from pre-planned activity (problem solving) to situated actions (problem posing), that is, spontaneous development or change facilitated by the flexible software. The computer became another sketchbook. Interaction was on a much higher level than in noncomputer drawing courses. Students assisted one another in mastering the software, in sharing techniques for using it, and in critiquing each other's achievements. Experimentation was much greater than typical, because changes to a drawing did not destroy the original version. The authors concluded that open-ended software, such as art packages, offers the breadth of application missing from typical "instructional" programs and, as such, is desirable.

Scanning and Image Manipulation

Scanners are computer peripherals that convert *existing* printed materials into computer graphics files. Hand scanners are inexpensive devices that the user rolls over the material to be scanned. Normally, you are limited to an image area just over 4 inches in width. To handle wider images, many software packages have the ability electronically to join two separate scans into a single file, aligning the two strips with reasonable accuracy. Page or flatbed scanners are similar to photocopiers. They are able to scan an entire sheet or page at one time. Both scanner types are available in black-and-white or color versions.

All scanner files are initially graphics files. If the original material was text, the scanned image file usually is processed next by *optical character recognition* (OCR) software, which tries to match graphic patterns to alphanumeric characters. You can then save the result as a word-processor document. It is beyond the scope of this text to discuss OCR further.

If the original material was not text, the scanned image can be manipulated with a variety of graphics software, ranging from simple drawing programs such as *PaintBrush* to highly sophisticated image-retouching software such as *PhotoStyler, PhotoFinish,* and *Picture Publisher.* The latter products have the power of photo re-touching to remove unwanted elements, add others, change colors, and so forth. With the right scanner and software, it is possible to begin with, say, a damaged photograph, scan it, retouch it, and then print it again in its original (or even en-hanced!) form.

Because of this potential to *create* images that never really existed, image ma-nipulation is open to a wide range of abuses. Students who learn to work with such software should discuss the related ethical issues.

Applications

A scanner with OCR software can be a lifesaver as well as a great work saver. Suppose you are just moving into the use of a computer for routine teacher duties, such as preparing tests. You already have old tests from previous years and dread

Figure 5.4.   Page and hand scanners are invaluable tools.

the thought of retyping them into the computer. Your paper copies can become computer files in very little time with a scanner. Suppose you already had computer files, but your diskette suddenly goes bad. Again, scan your paper copy of the documents to re-create the files. You might even scan sections of a document to print out double- or triple-spaced for students to edit or comment on, say, in a writing course.

One of the most common applications of scanners is to create computer images to use in documents, computer-based presentations, and even new computer software. There long has been a market for clip art for educators who lack the time or skill to draw their own images. Today, there are vast clip-art libraries on the market, already in computer graphics format. If you still have printed books or folders of clip art, you can scan those images for use in your next newsletter or whatever you wish to illustrate.

Beyond commercial clip art, scanning is simply today's means of extending the range of available images. Perhaps you have students with artistic skill. Scan their work for their (or your) use. How many different print materials cross your desk weekly that contain images you might use? No doubt, many of them began as clip art, which you might want to "recycle."

Just as legal issues surround use of photocopiers, there are similar issues with scanners. A scanner gives you the potential to copy virtually any flat image, which immediately suggests many popular sources, such as comic strips, newspaper ads, magazine images, and so on. You should be aware that comic strips, in particular, are copyrighted images. Whether they may be scanned legally and used for your educational purposes seems to fall under the murky "fair use" concept. Just as educators have long appropriated materials from a wide range of sources (not always legally), the same is occurring now with scanners. We can only alert you to an issue that has yet to be resolved clearly.

In Phoenix, high school students went to an elementary school to interview first-grade students (Braden, 1992). The project was to make a personal book for the interview subject. From the interview, students created storyboards, using graphics software. Eventually, they completed entire pages of the story they were telling and added text. They also scanned photos of the first graders and added them to the finished books, which they then printed. Most of these first graders had few books of their own. Their teachers reported that they carried their personal books around until the school year ended.

The range of applications for scanners is virtually endless. Whenever you have a need for an image or have text material in print that you would like to have in a computer file, turn to your scanner for help.

Charting and Graphing Software

You know the value of seeing information presented graphically, yet how many teachers ever attempt to produce graphs for their classes? A major deterrent is the time it takes to produce a good graph by hand, not a lack of appropriate uses for graphs. Today, creating graphs is simple, and you probably already have the necessary tools. Most spreadsheet software can turn numbers instantly into different kinds of graphs. You can also create graphs using most drawing packages, though it will be up to you to draw the graph to look as it should.

There are also specialized powerful graphing programs such as *MagnaCharta, Imaginator 3-D,* and *Microsoft Chart. Graph-in-the-Box Executive* captures text and data directly from the screens of other programs! The data can be manipulated, displayed, and printed in any of fifteen different chart types, even with 3-dimensional effects. Beyond basic data graphing, there are unique programs for graphing mathematical functions and equations, such as *Visualizing Algebra: The Function Analyzer, Graph Wiz,* and *Graphical Analysis.* Where there's a need, there's no good excuse to avoid graphing.

Applications

To introduce students to charting software, begin by asking them to interpret available graphs, such as those found in the newspaper (Beaver, March 1992). Next, move to graphs that you have produced based on class projects to bring greater interest to the lesson. Ask students to complete several graphing activities manually. This should be a good lead-in to the advantages of using software.

How much are we influenced by numbers alone? Suppose a student were to be graded based on five separate assessments, each with a maximum value of 100. Further assume that the student's five scores were 85, 94, 92, 86, and 90. What impression do you obtain from just the values? Now look at Figure 5.5. Does it appear that this student performs erratically? It does to many observers. Next examine Figure 5.6. The data are unchanged, but the vertical axis divisions have been altered. How does this affect your impression of this student? What could you (and your students!) learn about data representation from this exercise?

How might students learn the effects of extreme values in a set of data? It's particularly easy if you are using a spreadsheet to generate graphs. A single row or column of a few numbers is sufficient to generate a graph. Begin with a data set that lacks extremes and graph it as a line or bar chart. Then modify the data, re-

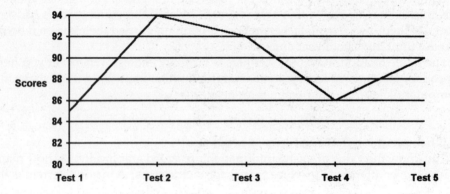

Figure 5.5. Student performance using small vertical axis divisions.

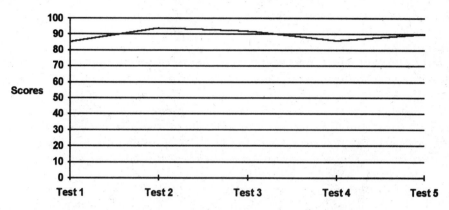

Figure 5.6. Student performance using larger vertical axis divisions.

placing one or more values with numbers well above or below the rest. Re-graph (some software will even allow you to keep several graphs on screen at once to compare!) and guide a discussion of the results. This works particularly well when you can project the computer image in your classroom, so that students instantly see what happens as you vary some values. Of course, it also works well in a lab. Lacking either, you can create and print the graphs, then distribute them only as needed for your lesson plan.

Many student projects could benefit from the inclusion of graphs. How about having students track their performance (in class, athletically, or whatever) over some period? If there is a class fundraising project, track sales or income over time with graphs. What might students in social studies learn by graphing stock market activity? How about trends in voting patterns over some period? Population trends, inflation, unemployment, the national debt—all offer significant learning potential with graphing. Even if similar graphs are already available in newspapers, students will profit from collecting raw data and developing a representation of it.

In geography, reading, using, and drawing maps are common topics. Many software products offer maps to study or even to use as clip art. A special program called *MapView3D* lets the user draw contours, lakes, rivers, and so on quite easily, and then it translates them into 3-dimensional maps automatically. Use it to develop students' deeper understanding of topography.

Because it is inescapable, weather is an ideal topic for graphing. You can integrate it into science activities at any grade level. Beaver (1992, March) views this as an ideal way for students to learn more deeply about weather phenomena by means of observation, rather than memorizing data. He suggests having students gather daily data, including temperature and barometric pressure at specific times, rainfall, and wind velocity. Use these as appropriate to your lesson plans to generate line or bar charts. By displaying rainfall and barometer readings on a single chart, students can discover the relationships between pressure changes and weather conditions. Also, have students record nonquantitative data such as cloud cover and type, which can be turned into pie charts showing patterns over a period of time. Consider having students track available weather information for cities from diverse parts of the world to compare climates and spark interest in other nations.

Niess (1992) provides great detail on a weather project designed for mathematics instruction. Students use technology to analyze and interpret U.S. Weather Service data. Among the unique aspects of Niess's project is analysis of wind direction and frequency. She shows how the data can be manipulated in a spreadsheet and ultimately turned into a *wind rose*, a graph that plots number of days of wind from each compass direction over a certain period. Niess demonstrates clearly a wide range of investigations of weather based on graphing and interpretation.

Science students might track and graph personal dietary information, weight and height changes, or any data gathered from experiments, for example.

A final note of caution. In one study (Machmias and Linn, 1987), researchers found that eighth graders accepted graphs generated from data collected by the computer, even when they should have spotted obvious problems such as scaling that failed to show all the data or results that had to stem from errors in equipment usage. Computer-generated graphs simply were not questioned as they should have been. This study points out the need for explicit teaching of data interpretation (see also Huff, 1954).

Let's turn now from graphics to the topic of support tools.

Support Tools

Support tools is our term here for a wide range of special-purpose computer software that we present here in several categories. Most can assist you to do some task more quickly than by traditional means, possibly with greater variety than ever before. Support tools may relieve some of the burden of time-consuming, nonprofessional work that all teachers face. Many can also be used for student projects or activities.

Puzzle Generators

The most common types of teacher-created puzzles are word searches and crossword puzzles. Both can be done by hand, of course, but these are labor-intensive activities! Teachers can "work smart" with special programs to meet this need, devoting more effort to content and virtually none to layout and printing.

Word Searches

You can create a word search puzzle easily by following prompts from the program. First, of course, you must compile the list of words to be hidden in a rectangular grid of letters. The program may ask that you specify the dimensions of the puzzle in advance, or it may calculate what is necessary as you go. Because words may be positioned vertically, horizontally, diagonally, and going either forward or backward, it is necessary to first enter the entire list. The computer then arranges the words into the puzzle and fills the blank spaces with random letters.

The computer may have to cycle through your list of words more than once to find a suitable place for each entry. Sometimes, it may be impossible to include all words within the specified puzzle size. At that point, you have the option of increasing the dimensions or doing without the words that did not fit. Despite such minor problems, the entire process is much faster than manual puzzle creation.

The final printout will contain the puzzle and the list of words to be located within it. An answer key is provided, as Figure 5.7 shows. Word searches and activity sheets are the specialities of the program *Activitymakers*, which also produces cryptograms. *Magic MacSearch* creates word searches that are more than just a game. Students must answer a series of questions, then locate the one-word answers in the puzzle. The program prints the puzzle with clues, answer key, and sorted word list.

Crossword Puzzles

Word searches are generally used just for a change of pace. Crossword puzzles, on the other hand, can serve to reinforce learning by presenting content review in an entertaining, alternative format. Any fan of such puzzles already appreciates the difficulty involved in creating them. It's not hard to come up with words and clues, but fitting it all together and coordinating clues to puzzle locations is a real challenge.

A crossword-puzzle generator requires little more effort than a word-search program. Armed with your items and clues, let the machine prompt you for both. Again, sizing is often automatic but can usually be specified if there is a reason to do so. The final printout is achieved so easily as to be all but unbelievable to anyone who has ever made such a puzzle by hand (Figure 5.8). Of course, an answer key is also provided—not that you need one!

Crossword Magic not only does all of the above, but also shows you the puzzle on screen as it is being created. If you do not like its choice of location for a particular word, ask the computer to move it. Words that do not fit at the time of entry are retained and tried again as the puzzle grows. If no fit is ever found, leftover words can be saved for another puzzle, rejected entirely, or exchanged for new words. *Designer Puzzles* from MECC is another good product. Schipper (1991) suggests using literature names, titles, or vocabulary lists as content for crossword puzzles.

Student Applications

If you have access to puzzle-generating software, do not keep it to yourself. Have your students create puzzles to demonstrate their knowledge and challenge their classmates. Virtually any field of study and all but the lowest grade levels offer lots of material for such puzzles. With some creative guidance from the teacher, preparing a puzzle can be a meaningful learning experience. In fact, even the teacher may find a new challenge in student-created materials!

```
                    COMPUTER LANGUAGES

                 F  Y  F  E  S  L  F  W  Q  H
                 E  Y  T  R  C  O  O  A  D  A
                 G  D  U  I  R  Z  Y  G  S  M
                 R  I  S  T  L  L  I  L  L  M
                 F  A  R  O  A  Y  P  O  U  A
                 B  A  B  C  R  P  P  G  Z  S
                 N  O  S  P  M  S  I  O  J  I
                 C  A  G  V  I  U  B  L  M  Z
                 P  T  S  L  U  X  Y  P  O  T
                 U  T  M  R  U  P  Z  V  F  T
```

FIND THESE WORDS IN THE ABOVE PUZZLE:

ADA	ALGOL	BASIC	COBOL	FORTRAN
LISP	LOGO	PASCAL	PILOT	RPG

HERE IS THE ANSWER KEY:

```
                 .  .  .  .  .  L  F  .  .  .
                 .  .  .  .  C  O  O  A  D  A
                 .  .  .  I  R  .  .  G  .  .
                 .  .  S  T  L  L  .  .  L  .
                 .  A  R  O  A  .  .  O  .  A
                 B  A  B  C  R  P  P  G  .  .
                 N  O  S  P  .  S  I  O  .  .
                 C  A  G  .  I  .  .  L  .  .
                 P  .  .  L  .  .  .  .  O  .
                 .  .  .  .  .  .  .  .  .  T
```

FIND THESE WORDS IN THE ABOVE PUZZLE:

ADA	ALGOL	BASIC	COBOL	FORTRAN
LISP	LOGO	PASCAL	PILOT	RPG

Figure 5.7. A word search puzzle.

Test Generators

In Chapter 12, you will consider the potential of computer-administered tests. At this point it is appropriate to present software that you can use to create traditional paper-and-pencil tests with format flexibility and potentially significant time savings.

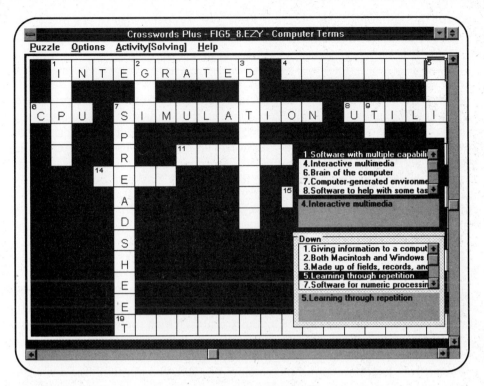

Figure 5.8. Review content with a crossword Puzzle.

Capabilities

Programs for creating paper tests generally accommodate such formats as multiple-choice, matching, true/false, and fill-in-the-blank. Some programs handle short-answer and essay exams, although a word processor may do just as well. Questions are typically entered into an item bank. They may be grouped as a specific test, by objective, by unit, or by subject. Let's look briefly at representative test-making software.

Quiz Writer Plus is an easy-to-use test generator for which databases of questions in popular subject areas are available. *Testmaker's* macros allow the user to write, edit, select, sort, save, number, and print tests of any size. Fill-in, multiple-choice, true/false, and matching tests are supported. *TestBank 4.0* can read and write word processor files; it permits item selection based on learning objectives or other criteria and even has tutoring on how to create good objective tests. *Test Quest* supports multiple-choice, true/false, completion, matching, and essay test formats. Answer sheets and keys are provided automatically. It offers random answer printouts, that is, varied test forms to befuddle roving eyes in crowded classrooms at test time. Purchase includes a building license covering all staff in one building. Furthermore, if you purchase the program personally, and your school later buys it, the producer will refund your full purchase price upon request. In addition to the program itself, the company also offers many data disks of questions that are potentially usable in high school science, English, and social studies classes.

Advantages

A significant advantage of a test-generating program is the ability to produce alternate forms of a test with little effort. Once an item bank of sufficient size exists, the computer easily could prepare a unique test for each student in the class, if desired. Even if this idea appeals to you, however, it is apt to be impractical unless you have access to a very fast printer. It is far more sensible and feasible to think in terms of a basic exam with alternate forms for each class section and for make-up or retesting purposes.

Programs of this type often allow you to select specific items from the pool, with the program performing only the clerical service of arranging everything on the page in an appropriate layout. Items in the bank can be deleted, modified, and added easily, with the current pool always available for the next exam on the subject.

Because the test-item bank is normally prepared with both questions and answers, most programs also provide a complete answer-key printout along with the test. This may be little more than a memory crutch, which some people need more than others. Consider the potential time savings of complete answer keys, however, when alternate forms of a test have been generated.

Even if you do not need multiple versions of a test, you may still find a test generator useful. The final printout will be free of typographical errors, if you proofed your items carefully when you created the item pool. The computer assists with matters of page layout, so that the test is well-formatted. You do the thinking; the computer handles the drudgery.

Worksheet Generators

There are many similarities between test generators and worksheet generators. In fact, for many purposes, there might be no need for separate software at all. There may be no major difference between the content of a unit exam and the practice items that one would give to students during the teaching of the unit. One area for which specialized programs are available is arithmetic practice work sheets. These amounts to little more than software that can generate an infinite variety of arithmetic problems within a specified range of parameters (times tables, single-digit factors, answers less than 100). Teachers have long typed out such practice sheets by hand. While such work presents no great intellectual challenge, the time can be spent better on other duties.

More than just a worksheet generator, Prentice-Hall's *Reading Strategy Series* enables teachers to create reading exercises that can be completed at the computer or printed for desk or homework. Text is created with a word processor. Cloze and fill-in formats are possible with the *Super Context* system, while *Super Skills* handles speed reading, scrambled letters, scramble words, and completion types. Although reading selection files are included, the teacher may input any content.

Readability Analysis

Teachers may be interested in the readability level of text for many reasons. Perhaps a student or group of students is having difficulty with assigned material. The cause could be that the reading level is too high. When selecting material for a class, you should determine the reading level as part of the assessment. Even materials that we develop for students ourselves should be analyzed to be sure they are appropriate.

Readability analysis is very straightforward and well suited to a computer. A typical program is *Readability Machine,* which requires the user to type in three pages of one hundred words each. The program analyzes word frequency, syllabication, long words, numbers of sentences, and so on. Eight different readability formulas are calculated. This is beneficial because each follows differing assumptions. Results can vary significantly. When finished, you can save and print both your text passages and the analysis scores!

Many word processors now provide at least some aspects of readability analysis, often automatically as part of spell checking. Other writing aids, such as *Grammatik, RightWriter,* and *Readability,* also analyze reading level among their numerous assessments.

Some teachers approach creative writing assignments for older students by having them write stories for others, usually younger children. This is an excellent opportunity for use of readability analysis to assure that the materials are suitable for their intended audience. Students develop beneficial insight into language use through such exercises.

Statistical Packages

Classroom use of statistical analysis is a highly individual matter. Teachers who have been exposed to such analysis often are enthusiastic about the potential benefit of calculating minimally the mean and standard deviation on their tests. Enthusiasm generally wanes in the face of hand calculation. You, of course, have long since realized that there must be programs to calculate all the common statistics that a classroom teacher could ever desire. You are correct again!

What less than ten years ago could be achieved only on a mainframe computer is now available in microcomputer statistics packages. With the right package, you can proceed from the simplest mean all the way to complex analysis of variance, multilinear regression, multiple and partial correlation, even factor and time series analysis. Microcomputer versions of the legendary *SPSS* and *SAS* mainframe programs are available. Both are extremely powerful and priced to match. *Mystat* is a scaled-down version of *Systat* and often has been given away as an introduction to microcomputer statistics software. Advanced spreadsheets offer built-in statistical functions that are adequate for many classroom needs. It is not our intent to suggest what statistical applications you should find beneficial. Rather, you should be aware that you can perform any analysis you may desire with your school's microcomputer.

Grade Books

Among the earliest of teacher-support programs to appear on the market was the grade book. Although similar to an actual grade book on the surface, any grade-book software worth considering will have far greater flexibility and capability.

Typically, you begin by entering student names and the number of values (assignments) to be entered per student. Good grade-book software then allows weighting of the individual assignments (e.g., tests are worth four times as much as quizzes) and provides alternate methods of dealing with missing values or late work. The weighting factors generally can be changed at any point, allowing great flexibility in overall grading with no modifications to the data.

Among representative products, *Grade Machine* (available for all three micro-computer platforms) features full-screen editing so that you work on a replica of a paper grade book. You are free to use your own grading scales and assignment weights and can customize reports as well. *J&S Gradebook* has a flexible spreadsheet format and on-line help. It handles virtually unlimited numbers of students and grades per class and will create customized progress reports. It can read and write data from other applications, too. *Gradebook Plus 6.0* includes a built-in word processor. It supports up to 60 grades for each of 45 students in 8 classes. You can preview reports before printing, add sound/comments, and sort by name, ID, or class standing. *Kalamazoo Teacher's Record Book* starts with the now common basic features and adds individual messages on student reports, as well as the ability to print graphs and charts, class or school calendars, even seating charts!

If some of the features that go well beyond a normal grade-book appeal to you then seek out the best grade-book software that you can find. On the other hand, if all you really want is an automatic calculator of final grades, which can also allow experimentation with weights, use a spreadsheet as your grade book, as described in Chapter 4.

Mailing List Managers

In most schools, major mailing lists are a problem for the central office, not for individual teachers. Some teachers, however, wish to keep a handy record of their students' addresses for their own purposes. A mailing list manager could be just right. Such a program typically would begin with a menu. For example:

1. Create a mailing list.
2. Add to an existing list.
3. Delete from an existing list.
4. Delete an entire list.
5. Print out a list.

Depending on your choice, the program then would prompt you for the information needed to perform the specified task. A good list manager should allow for varied processing of the information, such as producing the list on paper for proofing or on labels for easy mailing. You should also be able to specify whether output will be in alphabetic order, sorted by zip code, or as entered. Such a program is limited in potential, but will be simpler to use than a general-purpose data manager. For example, Spinnaker's *Address Book & Label Maker* is a low-cost special-purpose database manager tailored to mailing list and related needs. One basic function is simple data storage and manipulation to generate mailing labels. The database has unlimited record capacity and can sort by three different fields. It also features cross-referencing on up to twelve fields. Going beyond just mailing-list management, this product also can print directly onto computer Rolodex-style cards and in the format needed to insert new pages into popular daily planning books, such as Day-Timer.

A mailing list manager might be used with elementary students to reinforce learning regarding components of addresses and how envelopes are properly addressed. For young pupils just learning to remember their own address or writing for the first time, having them enter their personal information into such a program might offer useful practice. Older students involved in school organizations might benefit from access to such a program, using it for membership lists, mailing to past supporters of group activities, or comparable purposes.

Research Bibliographic Aids

Many databases do not support fields and records of sufficient size for academic researchers. *Notebook II* was designed to store and manipulate article abstracts, research and lab notes, then aid in compiling bibliographies and reading lists. A companion product, *Bibliography,* uses *Notebook II* database information to construct a bibliography from citations in manuscripts. Another companion imports data from on-line databases.

Form Tools

Many data-gathering and data-recording applications involve use of paper forms. Any educator has surely completed countless of them, by hand or with a typewriter. How do you suppose those forms were designed?

Traditionally, forms design was manual work. You would sketch out what you thought you wanted, then give it to a print shop to have it evaluated for feasibility, likely problems, or suggestions. Eventually, you would get a printed form.

Clever entrepreneurs have addressed the forms problem with software, such as *FormTool,* to create and print all manner of forms. You'll no longer need a professional print shop to prepare forms. This specialty software allows you to adjust type size to available space and provides easy-to-use tools for adding lines, boxes, and grids. Many generic graphics programs and even word processors have the fundamental capability to create forms, but only with far more work on your part.

Furthermore, a good form tool is also a data manager. It allows completion of forms on line, then stores them for later retrieval.

Whether the paperless office will ever exist is questionable. Form tools, however, seem to be a step in that direction with considerable promise.

A Caveat

Among the criticism commonly leveled at schools is that students spend too much time completing relatively trivial assignments, especially worksheets of all kinds, puzzles—some of the very things that the software presented in this chapter now makes easier than ever to create. Remember, anything you do with your students should have sound justification. Don't allow easy creation of varied yet simplistic materials to substitute for planning more intellectually challenging activities. Keep the curriculum foremost, and use graphics and support tools to reach for higher-level goals.

Summary

In this chapter you learned about applications software packages that are fun, powerful, practical, and useful across the curriculum. Print and presentation graphics, draw and paint programs, scanning and image-manipulation software, and charting and graphing software all offer new ways to communicate and new levels of sophistication in the outcome.

Beyond such major software categories, you also learned about some specialized tools that can make your life as a teacher easier. Whenever you want to create puzzles or tests, determine the readability level of some materials, perform statistical analysis on your class data, manage your grading more easily, or handle forms more readily, helpful tools are available. Most are also inexpensive and easy to use. Whenever the computer assists with a routine task, you reclaim time for other activities, especially direct contact with students. That's the greatest benefit of all.

Chapter 5 Activities

1. Create at least one product from each of the formats available with your print graphics program, for example, card, poster, or calender. Suggest several potential fundraisers using this package.
2. Experiment with any presentation graphics package. Create a slide show of at least five frames, using varied transition effects.
3. Learn to use any available draw or paint program.
4. Your budget can only stretch to purchase one graphics package. Would you choose print graphics, presentation graphics, or draw-and-paint software? What factors must you consider? Explain and justify your decision.

5. Experiment with any scanner to which you have access. Try both text and OCR, as well as graphics. See if you can use your scanned graphic in another program, such as your word-processor or a graphics package. Try to enhance it with your paint software.
6. Plan a lesson unit that involves graphs or charts, focusing on how appropriate software can enhance the lesson.
7. Which of the support tools presented in this chapter seem to have the most applicability to your needs? Explain your reasoning.

Bibliography

Beaver, J. "Using Computer Power to Improve Your Teaching." *The Computing Teacher*, February 1992, *19*(5), pp. 5–9.

Beaver, J. "Using Computer Power to Improve Your Teaching, Part II: Spreadsheets and Charting." *The Computing Teacher*, March 1992, *19*(6), pp. 22–24.

Beekman, G. "Recreating Native American Legends with HyperCard." (Kids on Computers). *The Computing Teacher*, February 1992, *19*(5), p. 31.

Braden, D. "Storyboards & More." (Kids on Computers.) *The Computing Teacher*, August/September 1992, *20*(1), p. 53.

Ferrington, G., and Loge, K. "Making Yourself Presentable." *The Computing Teacher*, February, 1992, *19*(5), pp. 23–25.

Finlay, G. "Imagination Stories." (Kids on Computers). *The Computing Teacher*, August/September 1990, *18*(1), p. 55.

Freedman, K., and Relan, A. "The Use of Applications Software in School: Paint System Image Development Processes as a Model for Situated Learning." *Journal of Research on Computing in Education*, Fall 1990, *23*(1), pp. 101–113.

Hubert, E., Winebrenner, J., and Qualkenbush, D. "Planning Your Print Shop Projects." *The Computing Teacher*, February 1987, pp. 18–20, 26.

Huff, D. *How to Lie with Statistics*. New York: Norton, 1954.

Johnson, J. "Graphing Packages for Mathematics Teachers: An Overview." *The Computing Teacher*, November 1988, pp. 50–53.

Kneen, T. J. "A Computerized Fund Raising Project." *The Computing Teacher*, May 1987, pp. 11–12, 56.

Kossey, J. A., and Dwyer, C. A. "Windows Presentation Software: An Overview and Comparison." *TechTrends*, 1991, *36*(6), pp. 13–16.

Lanman-Givens, B. "Idiom Graphics." (Kids on Computers.) *The Computing Teacher*, October 1991, *19*(2), p. 55.

Machmias, R., and Linn, M. C. "Evaluations of Science Laboratory Data: The Role of Computer-Presented Information." *Journal of Research in Science Teaching*, 1987, *24*(5), pp. 491–506.

Mathis, J. "Personal Tools for Administrators." *The Computing Teacher*, December/January 1991–1992, *19*(4), pp. 44–50.

Mathis, J. "Turning Data into Pictures: Part I." *The Computing Teacher*, October 1988, pp. 40–48.

Mathis, J. "Turning Data into Pictures: Part II." *The Computing Teacher*, November 1988, pp. 7–10, 56.

Mendrinos, R. "Computers as Curriculum Tools: Exceeding Expectations." *Media & Methods*, January/February 1988, pp. 14–18.

Nicholson, M. "KidPix." (Software Reviews.) *The Computing Teacher*, November 1991, *19*(3), pp. 45–47.

Schipper, D., "Practical Ideas: Literature, Computers, and Students with Special Needs." *The Computing Teacher*, October 1991, *19*(2), pp. 33–37.

Schrum, L., Carton, K., and Pinney, S. "Today's Tools." *The Computing Teacher*, May 1988, pp. 31–35.

Skwierawski, G. "Drafting in MacDraw." (Kids on Computers.) *The Computing Teacher*, May 1992, *19*(8), p. 28.

Sternberg, L. "Happy Holidays." (Kids on Computers.) *The Computing Teacher*, November 1991, *19*(3), p. 44.

Wiebe, J. "Word Processing, Desktop Publishing, and Graphics in the Mathematics Classroom." *The Computing Teacher*, February 1992, *19*(5), pp. 39–40.

Chapter 6

Integrated Software: Getting It All Together

In this chapter you will learn about software that integrates multiple major applications into a single product. After considering the need to exchange data among applications, you will learn why exchanges can be difficult. This leads to the primary chapter focus on the sophisticated software available today for full-range application integration. Next, a generic example of working with integrated software illustrates its potential. Advantages and disadvantages of such programs are presented. The chapter concludes with selected educational uses of integrated software.

The Rise of Integrated Software

Fundamental Data Processing Applications

The previous four chapters presented the most common general application areas for microcomputer software. These were word processing (using the microcomputer as a sophisticated typewriter), data management (using the microcomputer as a sophisticated file cabinet), spreadsheets (using the microcomputer as a sophisticated calculator), and specialized programs for graphics and teacher support.

While software is available to perform a wide variety of additional tasks, those applications represent the tools that are of general interest to a wide spectrum of users. In each of these areas, numerous software products are available that differ considerably in their scope and power, although designed to perform similar basic functions. Users must pick and choose among them in order to meet specific needs.

Approaches to Multiple Processing Needs

Consider now the situation in which a user wishes or needs to use the same data in two or more different applications. For example, you might have a spreadsheet file and need to perform data-management procedures on this file. There are five possible alternatives in such a situation.

Make Do

You could attempt to make do with any data-management procedures already contained within the spreadsheet program itself. Some contain simple routines, such as basic sorting, within their command options. Not all spreadsheet programs contain such commands, and even if a specific program does, the commands tend to be limited and do not perform more than a minimal function. Most spreadsheet programs are not very capable data managers.

Re-enter Data

The spreadsheet data could be re-entered as input into a data manager; that is, the data could be typed again as required by the data-management software. Although the data manager then could manipulate the data, there are at least two major problems with this approach.

First, someone has to input the data a second time. This is obviously a time-consuming and tedious task that does not take advantage of the fact that the data already exist in computer form, that is, as a spreadsheet file. The potential for typing errors during data entry exists as well.

Second, even if the data were entered a second time, after data-management processing was completed, it would not be possible to access the altered file directly from within the spreadsheet program. Rather, someone would again have to re-enter all the data manually into the spreadsheet software. Even for very small files, this would be a nuisance at best and on medium-sized to large files, it would be totally impractical.

Share the Data File

There is, though, a third possibility that can be used to solve this data-transfer problem: file sharing. Once a data set has been created, the same file serves as input to varied applications and can be processed appropriately within each. The terminology that is often used to describe this file sharing process is *exporting* or *importing* files between programs. This procedure overcomes the limitations of the first two alternatives and is a viable approach to multiple processing requirements.

With this approach, however, there are potential problems. File sharing requires that one program be able to access the files of another program. Unfortunately, there is little standardization of file structures on microcomputers. Many software packages use unique procedures in setting up their files. While this is understandable as an attempt to make files as efficient as possible within the context of a specific program, such files usually cannot be directly read and used by another program that employs a different file structure.

Many programs can both read and write files in ASCII or text formats, two generalized file structures useful for data exchange. The ASCII and text files are "flat" files of just alphanumeric characters. They do not include special codes that are stored when a file is saved in program-specific format, such as those that give formatting instructions to the printer (font, bold, underline, etc.). Thus, some information is "lost" when using ASCII or text files.

Transform the File

In order to overcome the problems of file sharing, special programs have been developed that can input a file of one type, modify it to conform to the parameters of another file structure, and then output this transformed file. The newly created file can then be used as input by the program that requires the different structure. The process can also be reversed. Files may be transformed even further for use in additional programs.

The difficulty is availability of such transformation programs. Some are provided as part of major application packages. Other transformation programs are available individually as stand-alone programs. While file transformations are available for popular programs, there are many situations involving more specialized programs where none exists, or if available, only limited types of file transformation are possible. Even if file-transfer programs are available to meet a specific need, some are relatively difficult to use.

Integrated Applications

While file transformation enables data sharing among programs, there is another approach to meeting this same need. It involves not two different programs using the same file, but one program performing many different operations on a single file.

This approach was pioneered in the early 1980s by the Lotus Development Corporation with the program *Lotus 1-2-3*. While basically a spreadsheet program, *Lotus 1-2-3* also has database-management and graphics capabilities. That is, this program functions as three programs (spreadsheet, data management, and graphics), all within the context of a single package, thus completely avoiding the problems of file transfer. None is necessary because only one program performs different applications on the same data and files.

This first "combination" program was soon followed by others that integrated two or more separate applications within the same package. Examples include *SuperCalc, Excel,* and *Quattro Pro* (spreadsheet, graphics, and database) and *Apple-Works* (word processor, database, spreadsheet). Other combination programs include even more applications within their integrated structure. Programs such as *Symphony, Framework,* Microsoft *Works* for both MS-DOS and Macintosh, and *ClarisWorks* offer five different applications within the same program structure: word processing, database, spreadsheet, graphics, and data communications. Figure 6.1 illustrates an integrated program.

Concepts of Integrated Software

Integrated software is any program that performs the functions of more than one specific application. While this definition would have sufficed a short time ago, many programs today perform more than one function, as discussed previously. For example, many spreadsheet programs have some graphics capability,

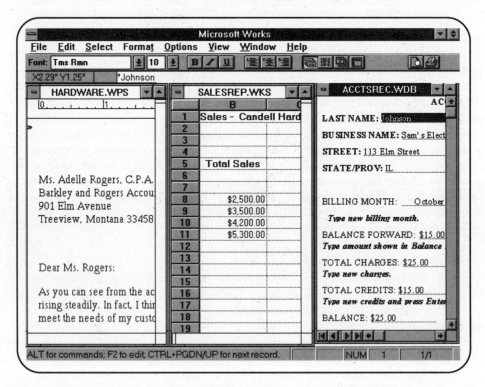

Figure 6.1. In Microsoft *Works,* all major modes can be used simultaneously.

many word-processing programs have some table or spreadsheet capability, and many data-management programs have some communication capabilities. Such multiple-application software is now common. What differentiates such software from what is called *integrated software* here is that integrated software attempts to perform *most* of the basic applications. That is, these programs usually have word-processing capabilities, database capabilities, and spreadsheet capabilities and many also have graphics and communications capabilities.

There seem to be two ways that integrated software can be constructed conceptually: the first uses windowing, and the second involves a common workspace.

Windowing

The windowing approach to integration allows the user to display different parts of the same workspace on the screen simultaneously, but in different modes. The user can then work within each of these mode windows. For example, the screen could be split in half horizontally. In the lower window, a spreadsheet could be displayed, while in the upper window, the user could work within the word-processing mode, typing a report based upon the spreadsheet data (Figure 6.2).

An interesting example of window use would be displaying a spreadsheet in one window, while a second window displays a graph of the spreadsheet data. By altering some figures on the spreadsheet, the user then could observe immediately the effect of this change on the graph.

This approach is similar to the use of windows on a Macintosh or in the *Windows* graphical user-interface mode of computer operation. However, in the *Windows* environment, it is possible, through a feature called *dynamic data exchange* (DDE), to have different programs operating in each window and to pass data between them.

Common Workspace

A common-workspace approach to integration allows different programs to share the same workspace. Thus, the user could have on one screen narrative text (e.g., a word processor), a table (e.g., a spreadsheet), and a chart (e.g., a graphing program). These all could be linked so that changes in one aspect of the information would affect other parts of the program: that is, data in the spreadsheet table could feed into the text and form the basis for the chart. The next section of this chapter illustrates working with this approach to integration.

Working with Integrated Software

Assume that you want to write a document that includes within the text a spreadsheet table and a graph derived from it. The following is a brief generic description of how this might be done with an integrated program.

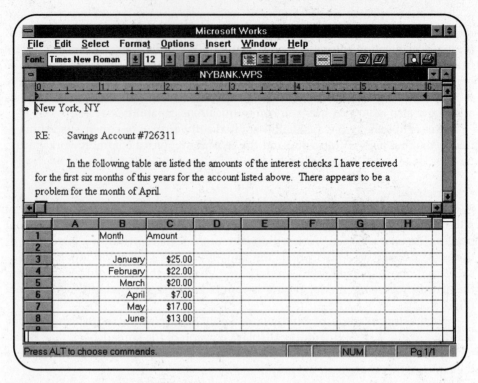

Figure 6.2. Different applications can operate in each window

1. Enter word-processing mode and type the text up to the beginning of the spreadsheet table. When you are in word-processing mode, the program allows you to perform the typical word-processing functions discussed in Chapter 2.
2. Switch to spreadsheet mode and enter the table data. In spreadsheet mode, you can perform common spreadsheet functions, as described in Chapter 4.
3. To continue with the text after the table, switch back to word-processing mode and continue entering text up to the location where the graph is to appear in the document.
4. Switch to graphics mode and direct the software to construct a graph from the data in the spreadsheet table. In graphics mode, the program performs many of the typical graphing functions illustrated in Chapter 5.
5. To continue with text after the graph, switch back to word-processing mode and enter text to the end of the report.
6. The document can now be printed, as illustrated in Figure 6.3.

This is not the end of what can be done with this document, using an integrated program. The data-management mode could manipulate the table to arrange the data in alternative ways. If the person who is to receive the document also has a

September 5

MEMORANDUM

To: All School Principals

From: Hershey M. Barr, Superintendent

Subject: *Annual All-Schools Fund Raiser*

Each year the four schools in our district compete to raise the funds for special purchases such as more computers. As the school year begins, I want to remind you of the results of last year's competition.

Here are the actual sales figures, expressed in boxes of 24 candy bars each.

	1st Qtr	2nd Qtr	3rd Qtr	4th Qtr
East	20	27	65	20
West	31	39	35	32
North	42	47	51	44
South	40	35	39	40

The same data in graph form are presented below. While North School sold the most candy overall, East had the highest sales in any one nine-week quarter, as noted by the arrow.

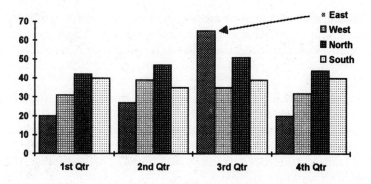

My challenge to each of you is to beat East's best effort of last year. Remember, my office will match the amount you raise in this way, thereby doubling the value of this activity.

Remember, candy is dandy!

Figure 6.3. The common workspace approach to integrated software.

microcomputer, instead of sending a printed copy, the communication mode could be used to send it over phone lines directly to the person's microcomputer for immediate access. The recipient would decide whether to print it or read it on the screen.

It should be obvious from these examples that an integrated program allows the user to perform quickly and easily various processing possibilities well beyond the scope of individual application programs. And these were only simple examples! With integrated software, you can perform a vast array of complex processing tasks on the same data without being limited to programs that can share files or having to rely on file transformation programs to act as a link between various application programs.

Assessing Integrated Software

Advantages

Following this brief overview of integrated software, let's consider several major advantages of such programs.

1. *No file transfer problems from one application to another.* All processing modes (spreadsheet, word processing, data management, graphics, and communications) can function on the same data and data file.
2. *One command structure that is reasonably similar among all applications.* Because integrated software is one program with different modes, the operating command structure tends to be similar across all modes. For instance, cursor movement and file saving or retrieving would use the same commands regardless of mode. Separate application programs often have considerably different command structures, which force the user to master many varied procedures. This is confusing and inefficient at best and counterproductive at worst. Using integrated software should be much easier.
3. *The integrative nature of a single multipurpose program.* With a true integrated package, the same data can be handled in many different ways within the workspace. As previously described, a set of data may be presented in a spreadsheet table and also be shown as a graph on the same screen. Adjustments to achieve the desired result are simple. This flexibility is seldom available with separate programs.
4. *An integrated program may be more cost effective.* When considering software costs, remember that an integrated package provides the functions of several stand-alone programs. Be sure to compare its cost to the total cost of multiple programs. Even if you do not foresee a need for all the functions of the integrated program, you still may save money compared to buying software for only the functions you truly want. Later, you may find the additional features useful as well.

Disadvantages

On the other hand, integrated software also has disadvantages that the potential user must consider.

1. *Less powerful or flexible than single-purpose application programs.* In the design of integrated software, some compromises are inevitable. While some modes of an integrated program may be as powerful as their single-application counterparts, this is usually not true of every mode. A single-purpose program may have more features or particular features that are lacking in the corresponding mode of the integrated program. Still, each mode of integrated software probably has all the functionality that the majority of users even actually use, even in the most complex, full-featured software.

2. *Difficulty of learning.* Integrated programs may seem difficult to learn because of their complexity. With so much capability comes a lot to master in order to take full advantage of the potential. This can be overwhelming, especially to beginners. Overall, there actually may be less to learn than with comparable separate packages, but it can look overwhelming when presented at once.

3. *Greater memory requirements.* Combining many functions into one package may increase computer memory requirements. This poses no problem for MS-DOS and Macintosh computers, but users may need to expand the random access memory (RAM) in an Apple IIe or IIgs.

4. *Difficulty in selection.* It may be difficult to find an integrated package that meets your specific needs. Often, products have modes of little interest to some users, but some also lack major functions that you may require. Furthermore, critical functions may lack specific capabilities of importance to you. Investigate carefully to be sure that the product that you are considering will be truly satisfactory.

If an integrated program approach is to be taken, the selection of the appropriate package involves many dimensions. All software programs have advantages and disadvantages. In selecting software, whether single-purpose applications or multipurpose, integrated software, these strengths and weaknesses as well as alternatives must be taken into consideration.

Classroom Applications of Integrated Software

Single-Mode Applications

Because an integrated program is essentially a single package made up of various modes, each concerned with the tasks of a single-purpose application program, many educational uses of integrated software parallel the uses of each mode. These have been treated in earlier chapters. Rather than reiterating ideas here, refer to the appropriate chapter for application ideas. While such uses do not take advantage of the unique potential of integrated software, cost-effectiveness may suggest use of an integrated package for nonintegrated purposes.

- Word processing. Refer to Chapter 2.
- Data management. Refer to Chapter 3.
- Spreadsheets. Refer to Chapter 4.
- Graphics. Refer to Chapter 5.

Integrated Applications and Resources

The following are some areas in which the unique strengths of an integrated program might be useful in an educational setting.

Administration

An integrated program might be useful for particular administrative applications. Setting up one big file (for instance, a class or school student list with appropriate data) and then processing this file in many different ways would allow an administrator to manage effectively many aspects of record reporting and to approach the task of achievement management in a more systematic fashion. Presentations to the school board or state agencies might well be more effective with greater use of graphic representations of data. Direct communication of data and reports to state officials is already possible in some states.

Science

Elementary school children can do field observations near their school (Strickland, 1987). Using integrated software, they record and analyze data on the flora and fauna with the database and spreadsheet, and complete integrated writing assignments with the word processor. Similar activities could be planned for many curriculum areas.

Commercially, *Weather and Science Lab* is a series of *Appleworks* database and spreadsheet files that contain real data from the National Oceanic and Atmospheric Administration. Guided use of the database files progresses from the simple (e.g. "When was it coldest?") to higher-order inquiries, such as "What would you have been wearing on this date?" From their observations, students generate hypotheses and test them by querying the files and graphing data. Nine weather experiments involve science concepts of increasing difficulty which demand increasingly sophisticated manipulations of the files. A side benefit of this package is that students gain a clear understanding of when a database or a spreadsheet is the appropriate tool to use. The concepts of this product could be adapted to other content areas or just to local data.

Social Studies

The Power of Nation States, about 167 nations of the modern world, includes two spreadsheets, three databases, lesson plans and handouts in both hardcopy and disk files, and more. This product was developed by three teachers, who then wrote about their experience to encourage others to follow their lead (Jagger, Layton, and Veeck, 1988). Users are encouraged to adapt everything to their unique needs.

Immigrant is a set of middle-school social studies materials produced at the Harvard Educational Technology Center (ETC, 337 Gutman Library, Harvard Graduate School of Education, Cambridge, MA 02138) to exploit the potential of integrated software. The subject is the wave of immigration in the 1840s. Immigrant families are selected from a database file containing the ship's passenger lists. Other files deal with employment and housing issues. The spreadsheet is used to explore income and expenses over a period of ten years. Instructions for working through the experiences are provided in word-processor files. Aside from the use of integrated software as a learning tool beyond its own merits, this is an excellent example of materials designed to promote group work among users. *Computers in the Schools* published extensive articles on experiences with *Immigrant* (1988, 5(1/2), pp. 179–211).

Elementary Education

A zoo can be a source of inspiration for many types of projects. Children might work with their teacher to design an animals database, then enter initial data from school reference materials. Data could then be extended, even modified, based on field observations at the zoo. Extended projects could include comparing animals sizes using a spreadsheet and writing stories about animals or from the point of view of a zoo animal. This idea originally appeared in the Winter 1989 issue of *DBKids*.

Resources

The popularity of integrated software among schools has led to development of many commercial resources for teachers. Although these materials are software specific, many of the ideas could be implemented with any integrated package. Some portions may also be useful ideas for single-purpose software. Here are some selected examples.

The International Society for Technology in Education (ISTE) markets *The Power of Nation States*, described previously. ISTE also publishes *AppleWorks for Educators, ClassWorks: AppleWorks for the Classroom, ClassWorks: Microsoft Works for the Classroom,* and *Microsoft Works for the Macintosh: A Workbook for Educators. Microsoft Works in Education* is a quarterly newsletter, also from ISTE. Computer Literacy Press offers *Hands-On AppleWorks, Hands-On ClarisWorks,* and *Microsoft Works through Applications.* The chapter bibliography includes more publications.

Works-in-a-Box from Microsoft (1-800-426-9400) is a complete kit for teachers who wish to teach Microsoft *Works* in the 7–12 curriculum. Both MS-DOS and Macintosh versions contain a teacher's edition of the respective student workbook, transparency and handout masters, and a data files diskette. Heizer Software offers templates and data files for *Excel* and Microsoft *Works* as well as a series of tutorials on getting the most from *Works. Inside Microsoft Works* is a monthly publication from the Cobb Group (P.O. Box 35160, Louisville, KY 40232-9719.)

Disks of user-developed *AppleWorks* files and templates are available from many sources. Quality may vary, but prices are low, and the inevitable treasures make it worth searching through some marginal items. Naturally, these do not offer the level of documentation support that accompanies commercial *AppleWorks* resources, but that's part of the price difference. Sources include:

CUE Softswap, Box 2087, Menlo Park, CA 94026.
Teachers Idea and Information Exchange, P.O. Box 6229, Lincoln, NE 68506.
Apple Library Users Group, 10381 Bandley Dr., Cupertino, CA 95014.
Resources for AppleWorks, Box 24146, Denver, CO 80224.
The AppleWorks User Group, c/o Computer C.A.C.H.E., P.O. Box 37313, Denver, CO 80237-7313.
National AppleWorks User Group, P.O. Box 87453, Canton, MI 48187.

Summary

Integrated programs are a relatively popular innovation in microcomputer software. They were developed to address two aspects of total software use. The first was the problem of using a single file as input/output for more than one program. The second was a desire for the convenience of a single program to perform the functions of many individual application programs.

There is no doubt that the first concern has been solved efficiently by integrated programs. Software to transform files for compatibility among different programs, however, also has been improved to the point that such an approach is less of a problem than in the past.

As for the second aim of integrated software, a single integrated program can indeed perform the functions of multiple individual applications programs. But functions within an integrated software system are seldom as comprehensive as the most common and popular of their single-application counterparts.

Because there are both advantages and disadvantages to the use of single-application software, as well as integrated software, it remains for the user to decide which approach to take when setting up a total application software environment. Many schools find integrated software to be an ideal choice.

Chapter 6 Activities

1. Use an integrated program to develop a report, using at least two different functions in your program.
2. Develop a lesson plan for your content area that uses at least two functions of an integrated program. You may wish to review application ideas presented in earlier chapters.

3. Integrated packages vary in the number of functions provided, and prices differ as well. Prepare a comparison report on at least three packages. Printed reviews, publisher's literature from a dealer, software manuals, or "How to Use XYZ" type books are possible resources.
4. If availability were equal, would you choose separate application programs or an integrated package for your personal use? For use with your students? Why?

References

Beaver, J. F. *Microsoft Works for Educators on the IBM PC and Compatibles.* Belmont, CA: Wadsworth, 1992.

Beaver, J. F. *Microsoft Works for Educators on the Macintosh.* Belmont, CA: Wadsworth, 1992.

Finkel, L., McManus, J., and Zeitz, L. *Microsoft Works Through Applications: IBM PC, version 2.0.* Gilroy, CA: Computer Literary Press, 1991.

Finkel, L., McManus, J., and Zeitz, L. *Microsoft Works Through Applications: Macintosh, version 3.0.* Gilroy, CA: Computer Literacy Press, 1992.

Jagger, A., Layton, T., and Veeck, B. "Making Sense of World Power." *The Computing Teacher,* June 1988, pp. 16–18.

Luehrmann, A., and Peckham, H. *Hands-On Appleworks.* Gilroy, CA: Computer Literacy Press, several editions, dates vary.

Mirecki, T. "Integrated Software Smooths Data Transfer." *PC Week,* 26 March 1990, pp. 65–67.

Pompili, T. "Spinnaker Gets Jump on Windows Integrated Package." *PC Week,* 13 May 1991, p. 29.

Rathje, L. *AppleWorks for Educators—A Beginning and Intermediate Workbook* (3.0 edition). Eugene, OR: International Society for Technology in Education, 1990.

Schroeder, E. "Integrated Packages Persevere in the `90s." *PC Week,* 11 February 1991, pp. 133–139.

Strickland, A. W. "*AppleWorks* Afield." *The Computing Teacher,* November 1987, pp. 9–11.

Thomas, R. *Classworks: AppleWorks for the Classroom,* 2nd ed. Eugene, OR: International Society for Technology in Education, 1989.

Thomas, R. *Classworks: Microsoft Works for the Classroom.* Eugene, OR: International Society for Technology in Education, 1991.

Wetzel, K. *Microsoft Works for the Macintosh: A Workbook for Educators.* Eugene, OR: International Society for Technology in Education, 1989.

Chapter 7

Desktop Publishing: Professional-Looking Print Materials

This chapter examines *desktop publishing,* a relatively recent addition to the list of applications that have already been presented in this section. Kearsley, Hunter, and Furlong (1992, p. 35) suggest that desktop publishing may be the second most popular use of computers in schools, after word processing. Desktop publishing can be considered an integrated or capstone type application, because the output of other microcomputer applications (such as a word processor, graphics package, database, or spreadsheet) often becomes the input to desktop publishing software.

This chapter first explores the nature of desktop publishing, then explains its basic technical aspects and requirements. Potential educational applications of desktop publishing round out the chapter.

The Nature of Desktop Publishing

Desktop publishing means producing with a personal computer print materials that closely resemble those produced by a professional printer and print shop. The essential element is *precise* control over placement of all materials on each page. The purpose of desktop publishing software, then, is to produce more sophisticated printed output than is typical of word processors or the types of print graphics software that you learned about in earlier chapters. You effectively become your own publisher, and your computer system becomes an electronic printing shop.

If you need to produce a sophisticated document, whether it has only one or many pages, you face limitations using the types of programs previously studied. You can produce an all-text report with any word-processing program or a spreadsheet layout with any spreadsheet software. To mix text with graphics in simple ways, a print graphics program may suffice. You can with today's more powerful word processors even combine text, spreadsheet data, and graphics into one document. But control over the final page layout remains limited.

To format documents in the most flexible ways or to bring the most varied document elements together into one sophisticated product is beyond the capabilities of typical single-purpose and most integrated software today. What is required is software of the type used by professionals that can take different types of input (text, spreadsheet, graphics, etc.) and bring them together, modify, and manipulate them to produce a final document that is similar in visual qualities and style to commercially published material. This is what a desktop publishing program is designed to do. Desktop publishing software is not necessarily effective for original creation of document components. Many products lack solid word-processing functionality, for example. Instead they combine and manipulate the basic output of other programs in ways that they themselves cannot, to eliminate physical "cut and paste."

Two relatively recent hardware developments have greatly increased the practicality and potential of desktop publishing. The first is the introduction of and now common availability of laser printers for very high-quality output. Dot matrix printers are incapable of near-professional quality output. The second development is the continual increase in the size and sharpness of monitor screens, so that very accurate, high-resolution representation of a document under development is now possible. This gives new meaning to *WYSIWYG* ("what you see is what you get"). Couple this improved resolution with larger screens that are capable of displaying a whole page (or even two pages!) full size on the screen at one time, and you have an application area that quickly has become invaluable for professionals in printing and publishing as well as a growing number of others who want to take control of their own publication needs. You, too, can say good-bye to plain, dull, mundane, typewriter-grade printed materials.

The Technical Side of Desktop Publishing

Desktop publishing programs have certain characteristics and capabilities that are relatively unique to this category of application software. While other programs may offer some of these capacities, only desktop publishing programs are written to provide most, if not all, of them and at a more sophisticated level that other software.

Page Setup

One unique and powerful feature of desktop publishing programs is that they allow you to design each page exactly as you wish. While typical word-processing programs provide some page-setup control, such as margins and tab stops, most lack the range of capabilities available with desktop publishing. Besides the one full-width column setup that you are familiar with from basic word processing, desktop publishing software allows you to set up the page easily for multiple columns, such as two columns for many books, three or four columns for newsletters, or still more if you wish. It is possible to mix the number of columns on a page so that, for example, a headline or title spans the page as one column, while the text beneath is arranged in two or more columns.

For even greater flexibility, desktop publishing software allows *frames* of various sizes and shapes to be placed on pages (Figure 7.1). Text in the same column or columns can be set up to flow around these frames. This type of frame-based page setup allows you to design a page or pages for the desired visual effect and to then place text, charts, diagrams, or photos into the frames and columns to build the type of document desired. This can be done either from within the desktop program itself, such as typing text directly into a frame, or by importing text, charts, graphs, or photos from files produced by other programs.

In addition to being able to work with the standard 8 ½" by 11" page, many desktop publishing programs enable you to work with custom-sized pages for specific purposes. For example, you might choose to work on an 8 ½" by 14" page to create a document to fold into a standard-sized tri-fold brochure. You could use a 5 ½" by 8 ½" page to create a small booklet. This page-size feature allows desktop publishing programs to produce a wide variety of documents to satisfy most needs.

Type Control

Another important capability of desktop publishing programs is their sophisticated ability to control the form of the character set that is used for various portions of the document. When someone talks about type forms, usually three characteristics of type are involved.

The first is *typeface*, or the actual shape of the letter that comprise the character set. Typefaces are usually classified into two broad categories: *serif* and *sans-serif*. Serif typefaces have small curves called serifs at the ends of the lines of each character. Such typefaces are often used for main body text, where the primary concern

FIGURE 7.1. Page setup based on frames.

is easy readability. Examples of serif typefaces are `Courier` and Times Roman. Sans-serif typefaces have a plainer appearance. Their lines are straight at the ends; they have no serifs. Such typefaces are used for emphasis such as in headings. **Helvetica** and **Univers** are examples.

The second characteristic of type is the actual *size* of the typeface. Size is measured in *points*, a point being 1/72 of an inch. Thus, a character in a typeface at 12 points is approximately 1/6 of an inch high and approximates the old standard pica type on a typewriter. Smaller point sizes (down to about 6 points) and are used for special purposes such as footnotes and the "fine print" in insurance policies, while larger point sizes up through 72 or even greater can be used for headings and titles.

The third type characteristic is *style* or typeface family. Style refers to variations created in the appearance of a character while keeping the same form and size of the typeface. Examples of different styles are **boldface**, *italic*, and ***bold italic*** type. Additional styles include light, condensed, and compressed. Different styles of the same typeface can be used sparingly for emphasis within a document.

Different typefaces with certain point ranges and styles are supplied along with many desktop publishing programs. Additional typefaces, point ranges, and styles may be purchased separately to increase the type control that you have with your desktop publishing software. Better still is the scalable font technology pioneered by Adobe as *Adobe PostScript* and further popularized by *TrueType* in *Windows 3.1.* Instead of storing in separate files an actual image of each size and type of character called a *bitmap, PostScript* and *TrueType* store a set of instructions for drawing the typeface, from which the computer can then render the size requested (Wood, 1992). This approach requires only one file for each typeface and yet provides a virtually unlimited range of sizes.

Graphics Control

Graphics control refers to the ability of desktop publishing software to import various types of graphics into a document. Graphics can be roughly classified into two groups: charts, graphs, and tables; or illustrations and photos.

Charts, Graphs, and Tables

Charts, graphs, and tables are usually produced with software specifically suited to such needs and output into files in a format that a specific desktop publishing program can read.

Examples of charts and graphs include histograms, pictograms, bar charts, line graphs, or pie graphs that spreadsheet programs and many of the graphics programs discussed and illustrated previously can produce. You might create various tables, using standard spreadsheet programs as well. These graphics then can be inserted into selected frames to become part of your new document. Needless to say, a single document may contain any combination of graphs, charts, and tables in addition to text.

If you need to make changes to any chart, graph, or table, you must return to the program that produced the graphic, make the necessary changes, resave the file, and again import the file into your desktop publishing document. Some desktop publishing programs allow you to create charts, graphs, or even spreadsheets within the program itself for direct insertion into frames. This feature can save steps, but like other integrated software, the power of built-in tools is seldom as great as that of separate specialized software.

Illustrations and Photos

Illustrations and photos are more complicated graphics than graphs, charts, and tables. They can add an extremely important dimension to a desktop-published document, further enhancing its professional appearance.

Illustrations are line drawings that are produced with drawing or paint programs discussed and illustrated in Chapter 5. Such programs can output these drawings to a file in various graphics formats that most desktop publishing programs can read and insert into selected frames. They become part of the new document.

If you lack artistic talent, desktop publishing and graphics programs often include files of drawings called *Clip Art,* from which you can select images to insert directly into your documents. Many books suitable for scanning, diskettes, and even CD-ROMs of clip art are available for purchase at reasonable prices. Clip art is very much a part of "real" printing and publication. Much of the artwork you see in newspapers and magazines is clip art, so why not use it in your own publications?

Working with photos in a document is even more interesting. Professional printers create a digital file of a photograph directly, using a special photographic origination procedure. For desktop publishing, you typically scan an existing photo into the computer, using a hand or page scanner or digitize directly from a video source, using a digitizing card in your computer. The resulting photo file can be read by most desktop publishing software to insert the image into the selected frame where it becomes part of the document. Once the image is within the frame, you have various capabilities to manipulate it. Generally, you can enlarge or reduce the image size to fit the frame or crop the image (i.e., move it around so that only a certain portion of the original photo appears in the frame). You may be able to enhance the image by lightening, darkening, or shading it for special effects.

Whether you create illustrations with a desktop publishing program's own tools or with an illustration program, use graphics included with your software, select an illustration from a library of clip art, or digitize an image, you can increase dramatically the professional look and functionality of the document in preparation.

Enhancement Tools

In addition to page setup control and managing text, graphs, charts, illustrations, and photos, desktop publishing software usually gives users a series of enhancement capabilities to put the finishing touches on their product. Some typical enhancement tools are discussed below.

Visual Cueing

Visual cueing means helping the reader distinguish elements of a document quickly and easily. Desktop publishing software enables you to place lines anywhere in the document, horizontally or vertically, to identify areas and to enhance the visual appearance of the document.

With desktop publishing, you can place various boxes or borders around frames containing different forms of data. This can highlight selected parts of the document and decrease the potential for confusion when you are reading a complex document. Within a frame, you often can apply a shading pattern as a background to the text, thereby creating attractive special effects.

Desktop publishing software also lets you quickly and easily caption the graphics you choose to incorporate.

Templates

A template is a file that contains instructions to the software about the page layout, typefaces, frames, and enhancements that are to be in effect for a given document. Many programs include a variety of professionally designed document templates. Of course, you can create your own as well. By using a template, you determine the appearance and design elements for a document before actually putting any data into it. When data are entered or imported, they will conform to the specifications of the template. This allows you to prepare the document efficiently and maintain consistency throughout without consciously formatting details. A template also provides for consistency in routine publications, such as a school newsletter. Once a format is determined and a template has been created, all issues will follow the format, even if different individuals work on the newsletter over time.

Marginalia

By *marginalia*, we mean those elements of a publication that appear in the margins of a page, including the margins themselves. The ability to handle page numbering consistently yet flexibly in multipage documents is a feature of desktop publishing software. Page-numbering schemes often vary according to common practice. Roman numerals are used frequently in the preliminary pages of a book, and Arabic numerals are used elsewhere. The first page of a section generally has no page number, while the page number appears bottom left on even-numbered pages and bottom right on odd-numbered pages. Odd and even page margins (facing pages) may differ to accommodate binding needs. Variations such as these are handled automatically by the program. The result is, again, a more professional-looking finished product. There are many additional such features in most desktop publishing programs. With these capabilities at your command as a desktop publisher, the type of final document that you put together should suit your purpose and reflect your imagination.

Requirements for Desktop Publishing

Before turning to classroom applications of desktop publishing, let's look at the three major requirements of desktop publishing: software, hardware, and graphic design skills.

Software

In our view, the minimum requirement for software to qualify as desktop publishing is its ability to handle multipage documents. This eliminates such popular software as *The Print Shop,* which you read about in Chapter 5 as "print graphics." Beyond that basic distinction, desktop publishing software comes in various "sizes," as do most major types of application software. One popular low-end choice is *Children's Writing and Publishing Center,* which is geared to elementary ages. There are also modest packages that generally are tailored to specific purposes such as simple newsletter production. *NewsMaster* and *NewsRoom* are examples. Such programs are relatively easy to learn to use, are inexpensive, and are somewhat limited in their capabilities. Still, they represent a step above simple word processors for producing anything beyond simple text documents. Full-feature word processors, however, such as Microsoft *Word* or *ClarisWorks* equal or exceed these products in capability, but may be less suitable for younger users.

At the opposite end of the range are professional-grade desktop publishing programs such as *PageMaker, Ventura Publisher, Interleaf,* and *Quark XPress.* With these products, you have virtually the same capabilities as a professional printer. In fact, these programs are now widely used by commercial printers, which is a tribute to their capabilities. To get the most complete range of features, you will likely have to pay several hundred dollars. In addition, the learning curve can be very steep. What you can learn to do quickly with one of these products may not be much better than you can do with a less expensive one.

In between the extremes are smaller-scale programs that offer excellent functionality for the most common needs, but not the full range of a *PageMaker.* Prices are more reasonable, and the learning curve is also more modest. Examples include Microsoft *Publisher* and *Publish-It!.* At least above the elementary-age level, these products offer a reasonable compromise for most school applications, where the need for all the bells and whistles is debatable, and the cost and learning curve of the major products can be overwhelming.

No matter which desktop publishing program you use, it will not be as simple as some of the other applications programs that you have been introduced to previously. They all require at least a moderate amount of preparation, study, and practice in order to produce the types of documents for which they are intended.

Hardware

The hardware requirements of many desktop publishing programs are greater than other programs that you may be using. Virtually all work best with a mouse, and most require it. High-resolution screens are highly desirable for all but the simplest packages. For serious users, a full-page or multipage monitor is essential. Because graphics require a lot of memory, increased RAM (random access memory) and a large amount of hard disk space are generally necessary. Finally, if you put so much effort into a professional product, the printed result must also be of higher quality than a dot matrix printer can provide. You will want at least an ink jet printer, but preferably a laser printer to produce the high-quality results that you see on your monitor.

Graphic Design Skills

Finally, the user of a desktop publishing program will need to learn at least basic graphic design skills, that is, the fundamentals of how to produce visually appealing documents. A desktop publishing program will give you the capabilities to produce such a document, but good design is far from automatic. What type of document will best meet your need? How should the document's elements be arranged on its pages? What typeface(s), styles, and sizes are best? How many and what type of illustrations do you need? Or should you use photos? Deciding about such issues requires knowledge of good graphic design. All too often, desktop-published documents show the technical excellence that the software assures, but they are neither visually appealing nor effective communicators because they have not been designed properly. Just as a word processor does not give you writing skills, neither does a desktop publishing package teach design. To get the most out of desktop publishing, you must not only learn *how* the software works, but also *what* to do with it. This can be fun and exciting, too, but it takes time and effort on the part of the user.

The chapter bibliography lists several good references on graphic design. We can highlight only a few very basic points, which may guide you away from some of the most common errors. See Rose (1988) for more detail.

- Select easy-to-read typefaces. Avoid 𝔒𝔩𝔡 𝔈𝔫𝔤𝔩𝔦𝔰𝔥, for example.
- Do not use too many typefaces on a page.
- Use type styles and size changes sparingly to maximize their effect.
- Use a serif typeface for body text; use sans-serif for titles and headings.
- Headings help to guide the reader.
- Lines and boxes create organization.
- Consider multiple columns. Short lines may be easier to read.
- Don't crowd! White (empty) space is a vital element of good design.
- Place captions below illustrations.
- Think visually! Become familiar with your clip art resources.

Classroom Applications

Many different types of desktop-published products support common classroom applications. Such products can be classified into three basic categories: single-page documents, basic multipage products, and large-scale multipage documents. Each category is illustrated next with potential classroom uses. Some are appropriate for you as a teacher, and others can be creative student projects.

Single-Page Products
The following are simple single-page documents that are easily produced using a desktop publishing program.

Flyers/Announcements
A flyer or announcement is a single-page document much like a poster. While such documents can be produced with some of the programs discussed and illustrated in Chapter 5, you will have more flexibility and greater overall capability when producing a flyer with a desktop publishing program. Besides the better text control, the more versatile incorporation of graphics into the flyer can make it more appealing. Figure 7.2 provides an example.

The classroom uses of desktop-published flyers are limited only by your imagination. Think of handouts for the class, for other students and classes, and even for parents, to name only a few. To help parents reinforce at home what is taught in school, the Oklahoma City public schools produce and distribute over 125,000

LEARNING

C E N T E R

Northern Illinois University   College of Education   August 25, 1993

TELEVISION TECHNOLOGY FOR CLASSROOM SUPPORT

NEW ADULT ESL LITERACY VIDEO SERIES...
SHARING WHAT WORKS

Sharing What Works is a series of videos for staff development documenting effective ELS and adult literacy programs and produced by the Center for Applied Linguistics (CAL)

with funding from the William and Flora Hewlett Foundation.
VTR #906 Introduction to the Series
VTR #907 The Invergarry Learning Center

VTR #908 ILGWU Worker-Family Education Program
VTR #909 The Arlington Education and Employment Program

A multimedia curriculum for kindergarten that offers a multisensory and interdisciplinary approach to science with connections to social studies, language arts, math and the arts.

KinderVentures,© from Optical Data™ uses videodiscs, hands-on activities, read-aloud stories, literature and manipulatives to introduce young children to the world of science. This program was developed in consultation with early childhood specialists, kindergarten teachers and young children.

VD 710 KinderVenture: On the Move
Adventures in transportation have children meeting new people and seeing new places as they learn about motion and forces and the environment.

Making Tracks - Looks at how people and animals travel by foot, where they go, how they get there and the tracks they leave behind.
All Aboard! - Investigates one of humankind's greatest inventions-the wheel-and highlights adventures on trains.
Splish, Splash - Investigates concepts of floating and sinking, moving in water and water safety.
Bon Voyage - Looks at ways boats

help people travel, with adventures to glaciers, wetlands and oceans.
Up and Away - Travels to great heights-by balloon!
Fly With Me - Looks at ways wings help people and animals fly, with adventures over volcanoes, fields and mountains.

FIGURE 7.2. A desktop-published flyer.

monthly calendars called family learning guides. Daily activities correlate with the curriculum to enhance school/home relationships (Kearsley et al., 1992).

Stationery

You could set up a template to produce desktop-published stationery or letterhead, which could then be used instead of costly commercially prepared letterhead. Wouldn't it be fun to have students compete to design class stationery?

Basic Multiple-Page Documents

Let's now consider a few examples of documents that exceed a single page.

Brochures

A brochure is usually a folded multipage document that presents something in some detail. Using enlarged page setup capabilities, (8 ½" by 14" or greater), text, and graphics, you can produce a completely professional-looking final document (Figure 7.3).

FIGURE 7.3. A desktop-published brochure.

If you teach social studies, you could have students prepare travel brochures for the areas they are studying. Any travel agent can provide samples as a starting point and might also be a source of maps or other illustrations. Your class could design and construct their own brochures to explain a unit of instruction (perhaps, mammals) or to provide a summary of topics in the course. Students would review the content and focus their thinking as they decide what needs to go into such documents.

Newsletters/Newspapers

This is one of the most common and useful school applications of desktop publishing. Anything from simple one-page newsletters to lengthy, complex, professional-looking newspapers with charts and photos can be created using most desktop publishing software. It takes considerable skill with the software to produce the best product, but the results can be worthwhile and rewarding (Figure 7.4).

While all-school newspapers or newsletters are fairly common, a class newsletter/newspaper could be an interesting project that involves more students, especially when tied to the language arts curriculum. Better yet, how could you integrate various parts of the curriculum into one project? One way is to have science reporters, current events columnists, arts critics, and so on. The possibilities are almost endless. Think of what fun it would be for the class to plan, write, design, construct, and publish their class news for other students and parents. Older students, especially, will appreciate the appearance of a desktop-published product and find the effort worthwhile.

Kearsley et al. (1992, p. 38) outline elements of successful school-newspaper production. Start by having students analyze the local paper. What are its sections? How is it laid out? Visit the newspaper office or arrange for an editor as a class guest. Student staff should have specific roles, such as writer, editor, photographer, advertising salesperson and so forth. Writers should prepare their "copy" with a word processor and submit the files to the editor. Advertising staff should sell and also create their ads. Final decisions on what to include and overall layout rest with the chief editor, while the detail work falls to the production staff.

A biology teacher in California was the first in his school to learn to use desktop publishing. He taught students to use the system to improve the student newspaper. Other faculty quickly saw applications in their areas and asked him to prepare materials for them. In the end, he produced his own course reader and lab manual, programs and posters for the athletic director and drama department, and a wide range of general school publications, including a *College Counseling Guide, Parent Guide,* and *Student Handbook* (Kearsley et al., 1992, p. 36).

Large-Scale Multiple-Page Documents

This last category includes multipage documents that are much larger in scope than those previously mentioned. While large-scale documents take time and effort to produce, generally they are not throwaways like a newspaper, so they are worth the extra effort.

THE

SMITH SCHOOL
FAMILY NEWS

Well, the new school year is off to a roaring start for all of us here at Smith School. Every fall at this time, we like to inform the parents and friends of Smith Students about all the latest happenings.

Kindergarten

The big news for our youngest pupils is the addition of ballet to our already long list of gym activities. Many parents have requested this move over the years, and we were fortunate to be able to hire a new kindergarten teacher, Sue Smith, who once danced with the Geoffrey. We know the boys will be especially excited by this development.

First Grade

The first graders will be busy little bees this year. We will be extending the range of activities for them in both math and science. Look for many requests from their teacher, Shirley Smith, for help with field trip transportation,

butterfly net repairs, etc. You intrepid ichthiologists may want to join the group on their visit to the Smith Shark Sanctuary.

Grade 2

We know there has been some controversy about our decision to add driver training to the second grade curriculum this year. However, our curriculum expert, Sheila Smith, insists that it is important to get an early start. We are grateful for the cooperation of Six Sox Over Smithville in allowing us access to their excellent bumper car facility for this new class. Transportation will be provided.

Third Grade ?

Due to unusual circumstances, the third grade has been cancelled.

Grade IV

In a move certain to provoke discussion for days to come, Principal S. Sophokles Smith has instituted a sweeping change in the writing curriculum for fourth grade. Word processors are forbidden and all students will learn quill-manship.

FIGURE 7.4. Try *NewsMaster* for your class or school newsletter.

Manuals

Teaching and training manuals are relatively easy to produce using desktop publishing programs. Once you have set up a form as a template (or have selected an existing template), you can produce training manuals quickly. If you include diagrams and photographs, you can produce a manual comparable to those that are professionally produced (Figure 7.5).

As another cross-curricular project, your class could produce instructional materials to be used by students the following year, for make-up or review, or perhaps for younger students. Besides textbook-like manuals, student workbooks could also be produced.

Booklets/Books

Finally, desktop publishing enables you and/or your students to produce booklets and books. One such possibility is the school yearbook. You might also collect your original handouts or lecture notes into your own book. Figure 7.6 illustrates such personal publishing.

Any class could write their own stories and publish them for other students and classes, perhaps even to sell as fundraisers. Student literary magazines are now widely produced in-house. Outstanding student work could be published for use in other classes. This would be an exciting and beneficial activity for the students

OBJECTIVE #9 - OPERATE THE CAMERA ZOOM CONTROL.

The camera's zoom lens allows you to "zoom" in/out for a closer/wider picture with motor drive, which is activated by the power zoom control. To operate the zoom feature, locate the zoom control (A) on the camera pistol grip of the camera. Press the "T" (tighten) section to zoom in, or press the "W" (widen) section to zoom out from a desired scene.

The camera also has a zoom speed control (B) which allows you to choose either faster or slower zooms.

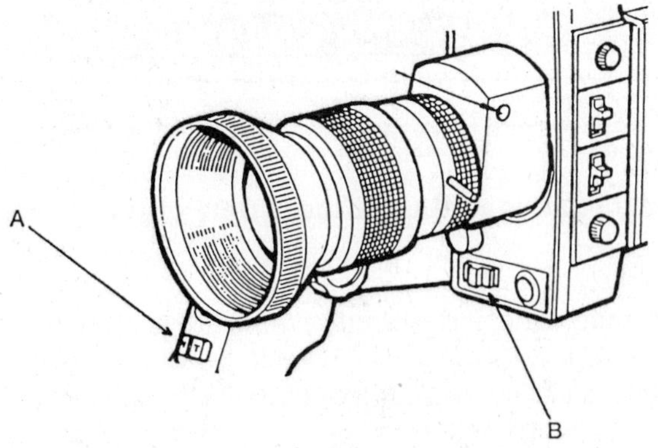

FIGURE 7.5. One page from a desktop-published manual.

A major feature of this redefined Enhanced-ACT scale is that subject-area score differences of four or more points for any student should be given serious consideration. Subject-area score differences of fewer than four points may simply represent chance variations.

ACT personnel report that the mean and median Composite scores of college-bound students in recent years have indeed been in the 19-21 range on this 1-36 scale.

Exhibit 7 shows score equivalences between the new Enhanced-ACT Composite Score and the SAT V+M score. These data should be useful to college-bound students, high school counselors, and Admissions Committees in colleges receiving one or the other of the two scores. (Please note that the ACT scores are for the new Enhanced ACT Assessment program in effect since 1989-90.)

EXHIBIT 7

ENHANCED ACT COMPOSITE SCORES AND THE SAT V+M:
SCALE SCORE EQUIVALENCES

ACT Composite	SAT V+M	ACT Composite	SAT V+M
36	1540-1600	23	940-970
35	1490-1530	22	890-930
34	1430-1480	21	850-880
33	1370-1420	20	800-840
32	1330-1360	19	740-790
31	1280-1320	18	700-730
30	1230-1270	17	640-690
29	1190-1220	16	600-630*
28	1140-1180	15	570-590*
27	1100-1130	14	530-560*
26	1060-1090	13	500-520*
25	1020-1050	12	470-490*
24	980-1010	11	UNDER 470*

* Data below ACT 17 are tenuous, based on small Ns.

These equivalence data are based on three studies conducted at Illinois universities, especially those of Langston (1987). All ACT data have been brought to the ACT-Enhanced scale.

The data in Exhibit 7 are *equi-percentile equivalences*, with no attempt to regress from one scale to the other. There would be little regression in either case, with correlations between the two sets of scores typically in the .80s.

FIGURE 7.6. A page from book that was written and self-published by a teacher.

preparing these materials as well as for the current or future students who would use them.

Kearsley et al. (1992) describe in some detail how New Jersey students write and publish their own magazine, *Newark InDepth*. Content ranges from historical stories to investigative reports and interviews with local politicians.

Families often take a variety of trips together. Students in an Indiana school used their own experiences on trips in the region to prepare a book called *Special Places In and Around Michiana*. They wrote descriptions and prepared illustrations for hundreds of places and events in northern Indiana and southern Michigan (Kearsley et al., 1992).

Whatever the publishing task, whether it is the work of a teacher or students, there is no reason now that locally produced materials should not look as good as professionally prepared materials. We've come a long way from the days of smudgy, purple dittos!

Desktop Publishing as Curriculum

As desktop publishing has grown in businesses of all kinds, demand for employees with desktop publishing skills has also developed. Vocational education programs are now adding training in desktop publishing to their offerings. Kearsley et al. (1992) report that students from such programs readily find employment.

Summary

This chapter has examined a very special type of application software, one that oftentimes uses the output from other application programs as input to produce a single document containing different types of information (text, graphs, illustrations, and photos) in a professional-looking publishable document. In many ways, desktop publishing software is like a capstone program, that is, integrating data from other programs into a final combined form. These types of programs, while more complicated and somewhat more difficult to learn and use than many of the applications programs that have already been examined, provide capabilities important in the professional world of microcomputer use, as well as offering many possibilities within the educational community. Many schools now publish materials in-house that only recently were produced commercially. Still more exciting are those publications that were never feasible before.

Chapter 7 Activities

1. Create a newsletter in two-column format to bring your family up to date on your activities. Illustrate it with appropriate clip art.
2. Produce a piece of classroom stationery.
3. Create a flyer or announcement for some class event.
4. Develop an educationally oriented brochure, perhaps for a local public service agency.
5. Prepare a class newsletter/newspaper.
6. Produce a short classroom manual.
7. Develop a lesson plan that incorporates desktop publishing into your curriculum area.

Bibliography

Black, R. *Roger Black's Desktop Design Power*. New York: Bantam, 1991.

Burns, D., Venit, S., and Hansen, R. *The Electronic Publisher*. New York: Brady, 1988.

Harris, R. *Understanding Desktop Publishing*. San Francisco, CA: Sybex, 1990.

Kearsley, G., Hunter, B., and Furlong, M. *We Teach with Technology*. Wilsonville, OR: Franklin, Beedle, & Associates, Inc., 1992.

McCarthy, R. "Stop the Presses! An Update on Desktop Publishing." *Electronic Learning*, June 1988, 7(6), pp. 24–30.

Parker, R. *Looking Good in Print: A Guide to Basic Design for Desktop Publishing*. Chapel Hill, NC: Ventana Press, 1988.

Pfeiffer, K. S. *Word for Windows Design Companion*. Chapel Hill, NC: Ventana Press, 1992.

Rose, S. Y. "A Desk Top Publishing Primer." *The Computing Teacher*, June 1988, 15(9), pp. 13–15.

Stanley, M. L. G. *Exploring Graphic Design*. Eugene, OR: ISTE, 1989.

Wood, F. W. "Font Technology." *Data Training*, May/June 1992, XI(4), pp. 32–33.

Objectives

After completing this chapter, you will be able to:

Explain the basic concept of a computer network.
Differentiate major types of networks from the most local to those with the broadest service area.
Sketch the most common local-area network configurations.
Identify and briefly describe several specific networks.
List and briefly describe several distinct advantages of telecommunications over other means of communication.
Discuss hardware and software requirements for telecommunications.
Evaluate the potential impact of digital systems such as ISDN.
Define BBS, e-mail, and CMC.
Assess the potential and the problems of using commercial information services to access data.
Describe several classroom applications of telecommunications. Develop a specific instructional unit that incorporates telecommunications.
Identify potential problems in implementing telecommunications and propose solutions to them.

Chapter 8

Networks and Telecommunications: Reaching Out into the World

For all its warmth and rich potential, the typical classroom is actually a relatively isolated place (Kearsley, Hunter, & Furlong, 1992). In many ways this isolation is beneficial, as it affords teachers a great deal of freedom to interact with their students as they deem best. The classroom walls help to close out the countless distractions around us. But isolation can also be undesirable. The classroom limits student and teacher access to others and to information resources beyond those physically housed in the room. How many teachers have so much as a telephone in their room?

More and more teachers are becoming aware of the vast resources that exist beyond their own rooms, schools, and even districts. Information abounds for those who know how to find and use it. Colleagues are available for advice, counsel, and sharing around the world, if you know how to connect to them.

This chapter introduces you to computer networks that enable broader communication links and to the specifics of telecommunications, another important tool for the educator in the Global Village of the twenty-first century.

Computer Networks

Until now, you have seen the microcomputer as a personal tool for a single user. In fact, the microcomputer liberated computing precisely because it was a personal tool, free of dependence on a mainframe computer. The microcomputer empowered the individual. Something was lost in the process, however, namely contact with others. A *computer network* is any of several distinct ways in which computers and their users are connected together so that information may be exchanged among them.

Workgroups

Imagine that you are part of a work team. One team task is to prepare a complex report jointly, say, a new curriculum for K–8 social studies. Each member has a specific assignment, but each piece of the report depends on other pieces. Team members work on their parts during planning periods scattered throughout the day, before or after school, or even at home. Group meetings occur only at critical points. Relatively few printouts are ever made. Yet each member has constant access to the latest draft of each part of the report, because the computers at which the team members work are interconnected as part of a workgroup (Figure 8.1).

A *workgroup* is a collection of microcomputers that are physically connected by cabling to enable individuals in the group to share files and peripheral hardware. Members of the workgroup decide which file directories on their computers are to be available to the other members of the group. (This might be just one common directory.) All other files remain private for the local user. Through workgroup software, each group member can then access whatever has been made "public" on each machine in the group. There is no central computer that all users share.

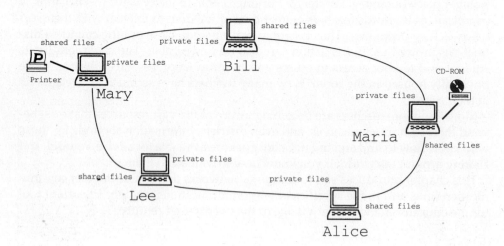

FIGURE 8.1. Five computers connected as a workgroup.

In our curriculum development example, teachers would be responsible always to leave a copy of the latest version of their individual work in a public directory, from which any other member could then retrieve, read, annotate, modify, and re-save it as needed. The advantages of such an arrangement over sharing printouts should be no mystery. If group members are diligent about maintaining their own parts of the document and placing them in the shared directory, all members will be up-to-date at all times. The group can function as a group without regard to individual work schedules. Face-to-face meetings, which can be so difficult to schedule, are minimized, and progress toward the common goal becomes faster.

Of course, specific hardware and software are required to create a workgroup. Microsoft's *Windows for Workgroups,* for example, comes in many packages, including any necessary hardware and makes sharing directories among the group just another "clickable" option. The software also provides electronic mail among members and an electronic appointment scheduler that can determine common free times among members and automatically schedule meetings that all can attend.

Local Area Networks

Roberts, Blakeslee, Brown, and Lenk (1990, p. 97) define *local area network* (LAN) simply as "computers tied together in a limited area such as a classroom, school building, or perhaps a college campus." According to Kearsley et al. (1992, p. 47), a LAN may "facilitate creative collaborations and new social organizations by helping teachers and students across subjects create work groups, share data, and collaborate with one another." While this may sound much the same as a workgroup, there are important distinctions.

First, a LAN has as a major purpose the sharing of common *hardware* resources. One of the major forces that led to creation of LANs was a need to justify the high cost of early laser printers, yet not force users to take files on diskette from their computer to the one that happened to have the laser printer attached. Each computer on a LAN can print directly to a single, shared printer. In addition, a LAN can link difference types of computers (e.g., Macintosh and MS-DOS).

Second, file sharing normally occurs not among the individual LAN computers directly, but between individual stations and a common master computer called the *file server* or simply, *server.* A server is dedicated to the management of the LAN. All communication occurs through the server. In a workgroup, all connected computers are essentially equal; there is no server.

Third, a LAN can store a master copy of a software application (like your word processor), and provide it upon request to any workstation on the LAN. The workstations do not need their own copy. In fact, they do not have to have disk drives of any kind. The server can provide all the necessary storage and operating capacity. This does not mean that you simply install one copy of whatever software you have on a server, and then all may use it. Most popular software packages also are sold in special network versions. These versions generally cost much more than a single copy of the same software, but far less than it would cost to buy enough copies for an entire lab, school, or district.

Many schools have installed LANs in their computer labs to simplify operations. There is no need for multiple sets of diskettes for students to use (or abuse). New software is installed on just the server, rather than on each computer in the lab. Updates of software are similarly handled on only one system, which means all computers on the LAN always have use of the exact same version of the software.

Fourth, there are three common physical configurations of the computers, peripherals, and cabling that constitute a LAN: *bus, ring,* and *star* (Figure 8.2). The ring is most similar to a workgroup arrangement.

The physical concerns of setting up a LAN are largely beyond the scope of this book. You only should be aware that each workstation requires some means to connect by cable to the network, typically through an add-in card. Although there are many different approaches to this, the most widely used is *Ethernet. Ethernet* is a networking standard that details hardware and software specifications that permit devices to communicate electronically at speeds up to 10 million data bits per second (Roberts, et al., 1990). Because *Ethernet* was adopted as a standard by the Institute of Electrical and Electronic Engineers (IEEE), virtually any computer, supercomputer to the most basic Macintosh or PC, can be connected to an *Ethernet* system.

While the advantages of a LAN are substantial, there is also a negative side. LANs have a reputation for being somewhat difficult to install, configure, and maintain. For MS-DOS systems, each computer must have a network card installed. Cables must be installed in one of the configurations to physically connect each workstation to the server. Each computer must have appropriate, compatible network software installed, such as *Netware* or Novell *LANtastic*. The server must be configured and dedicated to managing the LAN. Common wisdom is that organizations virtually must have a trained network manager to keep a LAN running.

More limited networks, such as *Windows for Workgroups* and the *LocalTalk/ AppleTalk* system, are comparatively easier to set up. *LocalTalk* has an inherent advantage because the networking capability is built into each Macintosh and many Macintosh peripherals. You only need to add appropriate cables and connectors. However, *LocalTalk* installations often are limited to peripheral sharing, primarily a common printer. File sharing requires Operating System 7 and increased RAM. While cheaper than *Ethernet,* the *LocalTalk* data transmission speed is much slower, only about 1/40 of the Ethernet speed (Kinnaman, 1991), which can limit its functionality.

Wide Area Networks

Although rare in education compared to LANs, you should also be aware that there are also *wide area networks* (WANs). A WAN is conceptually similar to a LAN, but the location of workstations on the network is much broader. Technically, a WAN could connect all the computers owned by your state government, regardless of where they are in the state. For a company, a WAN could be a worldwide network of in-house computers. Within a single school building, a LAN is appropriate. If the district consists of many buildings scattered over a community, a WAN can connect them to a common server, also called a *host*.

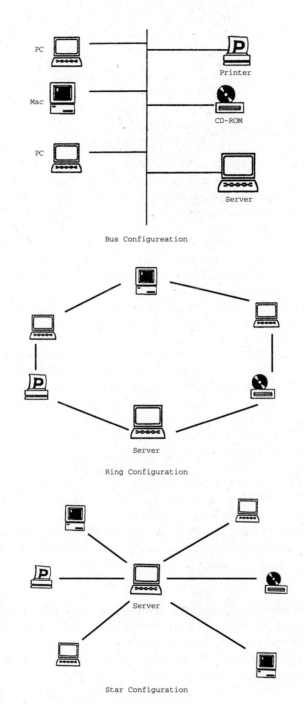

Bus Configureation

Ring Configuration

Star Configuration

FIGURE 8.2. Common LAN configurations.

Technically, a WAN differs in the method of connecting the workstations as well. Within a physical location, hard-wiring with cables is possible. To connect locations beyond your physical property, where cable installation is not feasible, dedicated telephone lines are leased from the local phone company.

Information Services

One fundamental aspect of workgroups, LANs, and WANs is that they are individually owned and operated by the user organization. Usage is normally restricted to members of the organization, such as employees, students, and so forth. Such networks are clearly limited in purpose and scope of use.

Yet another type of network is the *information service*, sometimes called an *information utility* or simply a *commercial network*. Such services operate on much the same principle as cable television. A company establishes the service, buys and installs the necessary hardware and software, and then sells access to its resources to subscribers. (Just how you make the connection to such a service is described under telecommunications later in this chapter.)

There are many information services available today, offering a diverse range of resources at widely varying prices. Among low-cost, general-purpose services, the most widely known are *CompuServe, Prodigy,* and *America On-Line* (Figure 8.3). Thousands of individuals turn daily to these services to obtain up-to-the-minute news or the latest stock market prices. (*Dow Jones News/Retrieval* is a service all its own, but many others also give access to market information.) You also can be your own travel agent, ordering tickets directly through the service. Information utilities provide direct access to almost unlimited data resources, resources contained in more than 1,400 publicly accessible databases. The information age puts the world's data at your fingertips and those of your students!

Specialized data needs are served by certain information services. *Accu-Weather* is limited to weather-related information. *NEXIS* is a full-text news service of Mead Data Central, which also offers specialized services to the legal profession with its *LEXIS* service and to the medical community with *MEDIS*. OCLC provides automated services to libraries, notably to speed and standardize cataloging of materials. DIALOG and BRS offer access to hundreds of databases, without all the other "electronic playground" aspects of, say, *CompuServe*.

Research Networks: The Internet and Others

The final type of computer network of which you should be aware is the *research network*. These networks exist primarily to allow easy communication among scientists, educators, and other researchers worldwide. The Internet is a huge network of interconnected computer networks spanning the globe for millions of users. Users include virtually all types of organizations, schools and institutions of higher education, research centers, military installations, commercial firms, and public service organizations.

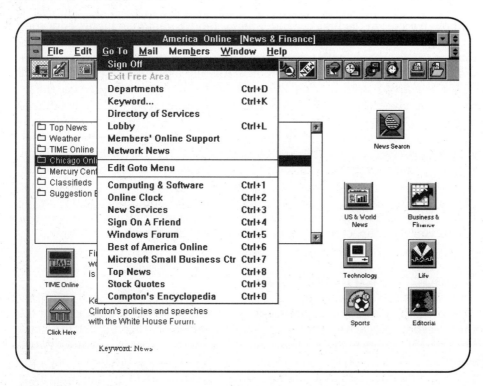

FIGURE 8.3. Vast resources are available through information services.

Wilson (1992, p. A24) described the Internet as "a way to move vast amounts of information—reports, pictures, graphs—almost instantaneously anywhere in the world." It has enabled users to create "workgroups" without regard for members' locations or time zones in the world. Internet also supports remote log-in, which means that from your own microcomputer, you can work on a distant computer as though you were on-site. Vast file resources are available on many computers for you to download to your own microcomputer. Regrettably, the Internet is not particularly user-friendly.

Specifically, for the academic community, there is BITNET (Because Its Time NETwork), which provides communication capabilities similar to the Internet, but with much more limited capacity to send more than text across the network and without remote log-in. Many universities are members of both networks, and users of either can communicate easily with each other.

Under development is the National Research and Education Network (NREN), defined in the federal High-Performance Computing Act of 1991 (P.L. 102-194) and intended to replace the Internet. Eventually NREN users will have access not only to indexes and abstracts but also to full-text books and journals through a system that is much easier to use than the Internet (Wilson, 1992).

Although access to the Internet and Bitnet is more common in higher education than in K–12 schools, the situation is changing rapidly. Many universities are providing access to schools with which they work. DeLoughry (1992) documented a rapid rise in demand for books to help new Internet users. Interest was sufficient for *The Computing Teacher* to begin in the fall of 1992 a series on how to use the Internet effectively (Harris, 1992). The series is a good primer for educators new to the network.

If you are seriously interested in computer networks, what they have to offer, and how they work, read *The Matrix* (Quarterman, 1990) or *The Whole Internet* (Krol, 1992), which are among the most comprehensive resources on the subject. The potential for learners is enormous, and accessibility is rapidly improving. Many current limits are disappearing in the face of new, wireless communication based on cellular phone technology (Arndt, 1990). With notebook computers and cellular modems you can connect with the world from virtually anywhere, any time.

Telecommunications

The foregoing discussion of networks attempted to focus on the nature of the communication that each enables, rather than the means of achieving it. It may have been apparent, however, that there are two very different types of networks. Workgroups and LANs involve machines that are directly connected by cabling. The WANs, information services, and research networks involve communication among systems that may be very far apart, even on opposite sides of the globe. Their interconnections depend on *telecommunications*, that is, connection by telephone lines. Because telecommunications need not involve a computer at the user's level, Kearsley et al. (1992) suggested the term *telecomputing* for what we are discussing. While the point is well taken, telecommunications is so commonly used to mean communication at a distance by computer that we consider either term acceptable.

The Nature of Telecommunications

The very nature of telecommunications is different from more common forms of communication. Perhaps most obviously, telecommunication is largely independent of distance. If you have access to Internet or Bitnet you can communicate just as readily with someone in Hong Kong as in Chicago, New York, or Podunk Center. Location is irrelevant as long as each party has access to the network.

Worldwide communication is a daily necessity for vast numbers of businesses, yet it poses serious problems because of changing time zones. Prime business hours in North America are late in the day for Europeans and in the middle of the night for much of Asia. This makes telephone calls problematic and may have contributed greatly to the rapid acceptance of FAX.

Telecomputing suffers from the same problem if the communication must be interactive, in "real time." Many communication needs, however, are more like mail that you want to reach its recipient as quickly as possible. The recipient can retrieve and read your communiqué at any convenient time. The reply may be sent in the middle of your night, but it will be waiting for you when you log on to your network the next day, or even days later. Just as the VCR's most important function for most owners is time shifting, making it possible to view programs on your schedule, not the broadcaster's, so telecomputing offers the same option. This fact alone makes possible communication among users that could hardly occur otherwise.

Telecommunications enables the rapid formation and dissolving of special interest groups to serve varied purposes. For example, groups come into being on Bitnet in response to world events, such as the Tienneman Square uprising, the Exxon Valdez disaster in Alaska, and the international humanitarian effort to aid the starving people of Somalia. Anyone who follows such situations can get current information that has not been filtered by the media.

Another intriguing aspect of telecommunications is that all participants are essentially on the same level. Because you interact with others through your computer screen, you never see the other individuals. Rather, you interact only on the level of the ideas expressed. Unless a discussion participant chooses to reveal any of the things that are immediately apparent in face-to-face conversation, such as age, gender, or ethnicity, you will not know these things, nor will you be influenced even subtly by them. Kearsley et al. (1992, p. 49) tell the wonderful story of a ten-year-old who engaged in a discussion of how to design a space station with a college student. The boy was delighted that an older person would interact with him as a peer, possibly because "he doesn't know I'm just a little boy!" Think about the possibility such "blind" communication offers as educators work toward greater understanding among diverse groups of people.

Finally, electronic communication occurs in digital format. You can retrieve, store, modify, and otherwise manipulate your messages, including files. Collaboration on writing projects can take the form of exchanging a copy of the master file. Each participant retrieves it, adds annotations, comments, and so forth, and returns it to the originator. The process repeats as needed. The potential for deeper learning is great.

The Technical Side of Telecommunications

If the potential that telecomputing offers has raised your interest, as we hope it has, then you need to know a few basic things about its technical side. We will deal only with remote access needs, not the technicalities of LANs or workgroups. (For detailed treatment of all aspects of telecommunications, see Dvorak and Anis [1990].)

Hardware

Whatever personal computer you currently have can take you into the world of telecomputing. The only hardware required to connect to other computers anywhere in the world is a modem and a phone line. Assuming you have a typical, single-line telephone, the cable that now leads from the wall to your phone is connected instead to the modem, and a new cable connects the modem to your telephone. A modem is required because the telephone is currently *analog,* while computers are *digital.* (Analog means the signal is in the form of waves, while a digital signal consists only of "off" or "on" states.) The modem converts between the two data formats (see Figure 8.4).

Software

By itself, a modem is just one more batch of chips and circuits. To use it, you need communications software, which is included with many modems. A modem is a serial device that can be connected to a computer in several ways, which affects the software. A Macintosh has two serial connections, one labeled for a printer, the other for a modem. Actually, these ports are relatively interchangeable. Macintosh modem software just needs to know which port is being used, normally a simple "click." With MS-DOS machines, as many as four serial ports are common, even more are possible. Switches on the modem determine which port will be used, and this must also be indicated to the communications software. Setting the port correctly is the most basic element of configuring communications software to your specific system.

Beyond the port, communications software involves communication parameters, file transfer protocols, and terminal emulations. *Communication parameters* are the *baud rate* (data transfer speed, typically 2400, 9600, or 14,400 bits per second), number of data bits (7 or 8), parity (even, odd, or none, which can detect transmission errors) and number of stop bits used to indicate the end of a piece of data (typically 1 or 2). For two computers to communicate, they must both operate on the same parameters. Currently, the most common parameters are given as 2400 8N1, meaning 2400 baud, 8 data bits, no parity, and one stop bit. Usually, the required parameters are given for any computer you might wish to call, or you can just assume 2400 8N1.

File transfer protocols are specifications for how two computers may exchange files accurately, including means to check for and correct errors in transmission. As

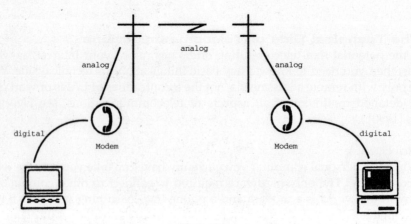

FIGURE 8.4. Telecommunications using modems.

with communication parameters, both computers must use the same protocol for successful transfers. Common protocols include XMODEM, ASCII, and KERMIT.

In any telecommunications connection, the host computer must know how to send data to the calling computer in a format that it can understand. Because the first remote connections to computers used dumb terminals with many differing characteristics, computers had to be able to work with many different terminal types. Microcomputers often must emulate some type of terminal to communicate with larger systems. Communications software provides some range of terminal emulations, most commonly terminals made by Digital (e.g., VT-100) and Televideo (e.g., TVI 950). The large system just needs to know which emulation you are using to respond properly (Figure 8.5).

The Future of Telecommunications: ISDN

As mentioned, telecommunications requires use of a modem to bridge between analog and digital data formats. However, work is well underway to solve this problem in a different way, based on a new standard called the Integrated Services Digital Network (ISDN). ISDN is an international communications network architecture and related standards for data exchange. All phone exchange systems will eventually conform to ISDN, as will LANs. ISDN makes it possible for "any digital data device to communicate with another by any available channel" (Roberts, et al., 1990, p. 191). Intelligence embedded in ISDN removes any need for concern

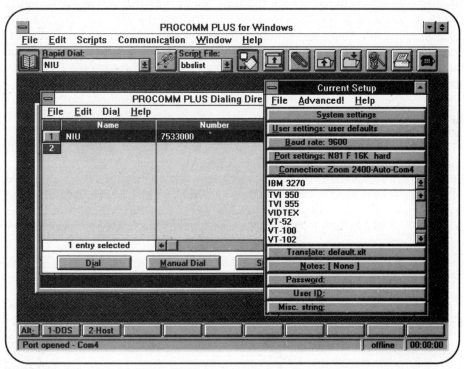

FIGURE 8.5. Communications software provides many terminal emulations.

about the hardware or software in use. Phones and modems will no longer be fundamentally different.

In addition, ISDN has much greater *bandwidth*, meaning it can carry more information concurrently (using fiber optics) than current systems. This makes it practical to move vast amounts of data quickly, data such as digital videos. Once ISDN (or its variants) is implemented widely, it will largely remove the current distinctions among communications methods. The era of an integrated communications system, in which voice, data, images, and even videos are simply varied data types, is upon us.

Costs

Anyone contemplating a move into telecommunications should clearly understand and prepare to handle the costs involved. Adding a modem (and communications software) to a computer is quite inexpensive, but using it can become costly. First, there is the telephone line itself. Most users simply split their regular phone line between the modem and telephone. If you can't tie up your line for the periods of time that you anticipate being on-line, start with the cost of installation and monthly service for a separate line. This aspect alone poses problems for many teachers, as few classrooms now include telephones.

Next come the telephone company charges for the time you are on the line. When local calls were still included in basic monthly phone bills, this was less of an issue, but as unit call pricing spreads across the country, lengthy local calls begin to affect the monthly bill. Of course, you may have no local computer to connect with, or local systems may only partially meet your needs. When you phone another computer outside the local calling area, you incur long-distance charges. Of course, school hours are also prime calling hours, with the highest long-distance rates.

Some information services provide "local access" phone numbers, but you actually may be connecting to the service through a switching network such as Telenet or Tymnet, the first commercial telecommunications networks (Roberts et al., 1990, p. 5). You may pay per-minute charges for this type of access. If so, it should still be substantially cheaper than regular long distance.

Finally, there are the costs for connecting to the other computer. While there are many free opportunities, information services charge either monthly, flat usage fees or by the hour. Hourly rates often vary depending on the time of the day when you call, the baud rate you use, and the exact database or other resource you access. Online, an hour passes quickly.

In sum, purchasing a modem is only the start, a necessary but not sufficient beginning. You also must anticipate and budget for usage costs from the start.

Common Telecommunications Applications

Conferencing

Although time shifting is a great advantage of telecommunications for many users, real-time interaction is also possible. *Computer conferencing* or "chat" mode is much like talking on the telephone, except that you "speak" with your keyboard and "listen" with your monitor. It can be as simple as calling on the phone. If your school has a LAN, it may support conferencing among the workstations.

Beyond a LAN, the major information services host conferences. CompuServe calls theirs *forums*. Education Forum features weekly opportunities to interact with guest "experts." You can be an active participant by submitting questions or an eavesdropper who merely reads the ongoing conversation.

Because this type of conferencing occurs in real time, you must be on-line all through it. A 60-minute conference means a minimum of 60 minutes of telephone costs. Conferencing can get expensive! To minimize costs, conferences typically are held evenings and weekends, when all related charges are lowest.

To learn more about computer conferencing and its potential to empower learners, see Waggoner (1992).

Discussion Groups (Lists)

One potential problem with networks such as Internet is that there are no directories of users, that is, nothing comparable to a phone book. How, then, do you contact others who may share your interests?

More and more educators are including their electronic addresses as part of their normal address information. You may acquire addresses from persons whom you meet at the professional conferences in your field. Typical electronic addresses consist of a user ID and a location ID, joined by @ (e.g., johndoe@niu.mvs.cso.edu).

Many educators break into electronic communications through the discussion groups called *lists* on Bitnet and Internet. A list exists when someone interested in a particular area of discussion, say *HyperCard*, establishes a central electronic address through which others may communicate. There is no cost to "subscribe" to a list, and lists of lists are readily available. Once you subscribe, you receive all the mail from all the other subscribers. For educators, Bitnet and Internet have become major means of gathering information and sharing ideas and research with colleagues everywhere.

Generally, lists are not interactive in real time. You decide what your level of participation will be. Kibitz, or get your own views in at every opportunity. Even if you only read initially, sooner or later someone will say something that you wish to know more about or pose a question that you can answer. You can then join the discussion, or if it is more appropriate, contact the person directly at his or her own electronic address. This becomes a whole new way to expand your professional contacts, even worldwide.

Electronic Mail

The previous discussion of lists begins to enter the world of electronic mail. Electronic mail, commonly called *e-mail*, is not limited to, but surely includes the type of communication that lists provide. E-mail is generally not in real time. Rather, you compose a message (memo, letter, report, first draft of a steamy new novel) with your word processor. Then you transmit the document as a file to someone else, using your LAN, an information service to which you both have access, or a network such a Bitnet or Internet. The network computer stores your message in the recipient's "mail box" until retrieved at that person's convenience.

Because e-mail is not real-time communication, it works equally well between any two points in the world, when recipients are vacationing, or when someone is simply too busy to attend to anything else immediately. It also avoids telephone tag. Once you experience e-mail, you are likely to be hooked forever. It is especially handy on LANs, where the server notifies you whether or not you have mail waiting whenever you log on. There also seems to be less justification for procrastinating over a reply when you can compose and send your response very easily immediately after reading a message.

Imagine the potential when ISDN affords you all of this with still pictures or video in living color!

Electronic Journals

So powerful is the potential and so appealing the immediacy of telecommunication that there are now many electronic journals—journals that exist only on the electronic networks. When authors complete an article, they submit it to the journal electronically. The editor shares it with reviewers electronically, who critique it electronically. If it is accepted, it becomes part of an issue of the journal, which is sent electronically to the subscriber list. Some journals distribute articles individually when they are ready rather than waiting to compile an issue. The whole process from time of submission may take only a few weeks, compared to the many months, or even a few years, that often are required to get an article in print in a paper journal. For individuals in fast-changing fields, the appeal is enormous. As Tennant (1992) notes, the very meaning of the term "journal" is undergoing change in the electronic age.

Remote Bulletin Board Systems

A *remote bulletin board system* (RBBS) is a publicly accessible host computer that stores messages, bulletins from the operator, and a wide range of computer software (Maddux et al., 1992, p. 124). The system operator is called the *sysop*. An RBBS offers private communication between any user and the sysop, but other messages generally are posted for anyone to read. Virtually all communities of any size have at least one RBBS, operating from someone's home or business, especially computer clubs and dealerships. Most are free except for any local phone charges, although some require a membership fee to gain access to all parts of the system. An RBBS offers one of the easiest and cheapest ways for teachers to introduce their students to telecommunications.

Often, an RBBS is created by someone with a particular interest. A common example is computerized "dungeons-and-dragons" type games. The RBBS will then have a special section for players and others interested in the theme. By connecting to such a system, you can make contact with others who share your interests. A bulletin board also can be an excellent source of advice on any problems you may be having with your own computer, software reviews by current users, and much more.

The possibilities are as endless as the physical bulletin boards you routinely see. Bulletin boards serve buyers and sellers, much like classified ads in the newspaper or garage sale notices. Nearly any RBBS will list the phone numbers for other boards in the area or of special interest.

The dominant function of many bulletin boards is to make available public-domain software and shareware that you can download (transfer) to your own computer. You'll learn more about this type of software in Chapter 19. For now, suffice it to say that an RBBS can be a gold mine of useful software, especially graphics files and utilities that are valuable but often are unavailable from commercial sources.

On-Line Information Access

In presenting information services, we noted that most provide their users with access to a wide range of electronic databases. Such access opens new potential for student (and teacher!) research. For years, there has been largely idle talk about the paperless society, where everything you write is electronically created, stored, delivered, and retrieved. One concrete example where some of this potential is being realized is on-line reference materials and other databases.

You may well realize that ever-increasing costs make it extremely difficult for libraries to maintain up-to-date collections. As a patron, your real concern is *access* to the information you need. Does it matter whether the library *owns* the material? As long as it is available, your need can be met.

The point is simply that print versions of reference materials are becoming obsolete. They are costly to produce and distribute, require space that most libraries need for other purposes, and always are somewhat out of date. Because such books are produced on computers today, their basic data already exist in electronic form. Why not distribute and share it in the same way? Updates and new information become available the instant they are entered into the database. You always have the very latest information.

For decades, students have learned to use library card catalogs and research tools such as the *Reader's Guide*. Today, from their own libraries and offices, Illinois students and educators can search the catalogs of hundreds of libraries that belong to the state network called *Illinet On-Line*. To locate the latest periodical literature they connect to the computer and use *Carl Uncover*, a comprehensive index to journals since 1988. The *ERIC* database is equally easy to access, as are various others.

Apart from ecological and logical arguments, electronic research tends to be faster and more efficient. Resources are all in a common location, not scattered across many large paper volumes organized by time period. Your search criteria can include multiple descriptors, which is not practical in manual searching. The speed of a search makes it feasible to refine the descriptors repeatedly until you get exactly what you need. Perhaps most importantly, your research is not limited to whatever subset of the world's knowledge your particular library happens to own. Truly, it is all at your disposal.

Of course, there is a down side to on-line research. Access charges can mount quickly, making a single search potentially very expensive. Also, many systems were designed originally for professional librarians, not lay users, and thus they can be difficult to learn to use efficiently.

Computer-Mediated Communication (Distance Learning)

Although *computer-mediated communication* (CMC) can be no more than a fancy term for the kind of routine exchanges that occur on discussion lists, e-mail systems, and bulletin boards, it is often used to mean something much more. As a form of electronic *distance learning,* CMC means situations in which learners need not (or cannot!) be together physically. The use of CMC appears to be a growing phenomenon in higher education, as institutions seek to extend their services to new segments of the population.

Imagine taking a course with few or no group meetings. Instead, your instructor arranges for you and all other students to have access to a network or bulletin board. To begin the course, the instructor sends the syllabus to you electronically along with any pertinent details of the course, how to use the system, and so on. Instead of group lectures and demonstrations, the instructor sends a common message (somewhat like a lecture) to all students that presents course content in some way and requests learner input into an electronic discussion. The teacher sends messages at certain intervals, say, every Monday. In between, class members read the instructor's message and append their responses to it, asking questions, contesting or analyzing points made, offering insights from experience or readings, and so forth. Students learn from and react to each other's comments, as well as the instructor's contributions. Anyone, including the instructor, may contribute at any time and as often as desired until the next part of the course takes the discussion in a new direction.

Sounds like fantasy? Something new? It's not. Batey and Cowell (1986) provided an overview of the concept some years ago. Alaska and Idaho began to explore the possibilities of reaching their small, scattered, rural populations this way in the late 1980s (Bruder, 1988). Another pioneer at Penn State delivered a speech course using CMC in 1988 (Staff, 1988). BESTNET (Bilingual English and Spanish Telecommunications Network) was started in 1985 to link institutions in the Southwestern United States and Mexico (BESTNET, 1992). Members have delivered courses in composition, anthropology, sociology, and psychology. Users claim students are more active learners; interaction among students increases; and skills in writing, editing, and logical reasoning improve.

Admittedly, CMC is not for every course in all fields of study. Can you picture laboratory science done by CMC? Still, limited research evidence suggests that electronic distance education is as effective as traditional instruction (e.g.,

DeLoughry, [1988]), at least for some types of learning and CMC may have particular appeal for adult education. Its inherent flexibility makes it well suited to the diverse schedules of working adults, who also need to keep up with the demands of their jobs. Therefore, CMC can support life-long learning.

Networks for Educators and Students

Before turning to specific telecommunications applications for educators, you should know also that there are varied special networks just for educators. You already read about Bitnet and the Educator's Forum on CompuServe. Next, we'll highlight several other unique systems. Contact information is in the appendix.

Probably the most famous educator's network is *FrEdMail*, the Free Educational Electronic Mail Network. *FrEdMail* is a network of daytime school bulletin boards that exchange data automatically at night when long-distance rates are lowest. The network seeks to encourage student writing. Past projects have included compiling an international cookbook and consumer product and price comparisons (Kurshan and Dawson, 1992).

Similar to FrEdMail is *FIDOnet*, "one of the largest grass-roots telecommunications networks in the country" (Roberts, et al., 1990, p. 197). Each local bulletin board acts as a distribution center, storing messages it receives and forwarding messages on to other boards. Overall, the system resembles a star LAN. According to Roberts et al., a message generally will appear at all sites in the country within two days of posting. FIDOnet can be an economical choice for educators, as many local bulletin boards operate nodes. The Physics Forum, for example, was created on FIDOnet to link physics teachers. Frequently, physic teachers feel isolated because most school systems employ only one teacher in this area, who must also teach other science classes. The forum grew to cover a much broader range of sciences than just physics (Roberts, et al., 1990).

The *AT&T Learning Network* is designed for grades 3–12. Schools that join the program receive communications software and curriculum guides that help establish common goals, then guide working toward them with peers around the world. Each class becomes part of a geographically diverse "learning circle" of about ten classes. Students may communicate in English, French, German, or Spanish, thus polishing language skills as well (Kurshan and Dawson, 1992). A high school class in Seattle was part of a learning circle that included two schools in Germany just when the Berlin Wall was dismantled. American students got firsthand, even eyewitness insight into a major historic event (Kearsley et al., 1992, p. 50).

National Geographic's *Kids Network* links elementary school children around the world in hands-on science and geography lessons. Students gather data locally, then share them with others over the network. Topics have included pets, acid rain, weather, water pollution, and recycling. Participants can also take part at no extra cost in the *Global Common Classroom* to exchange information with peers in Russia and other Eastern European nations (Kurshan and Dawson, 1992).

NASA Spacelink is an RBBS that provides current and historical information about NASA activities, as well as suggested science lesson plans and classroom activities. The only cost is a phone call to Alabama (205-895-0028, up to 2400 baud, 8N1). Spacelink also provides files that you can download for local use. Many schools use Spacelink in science classes.

Dialog's *Classmate CIP* (Classroom Instruction Program) is an information service specifically for users in education. Through *Classmate CIP*, your students can access U.S. census data, the complete text of over 50 popular magazines, a magazine index similar to *Reader's Guide*, an index of major U.S. newspapers, a daily index to over 2,000 news stories, full-text stories direct from major news wire services, historical research information on the United States, and encyclopedia-like articles on the world beginning in 1450, just to highlight a few options. *Classmate CIP* features access to over 60 popular Dialog databases especially appropriate in K–12 education through a simpler, more limited set of commands than full Dialog. There are also student workbooks and a teaching guide.

Finally, there is *SpecialNet*, devoted to assisting teachers and administrators in special education settings.

Practical Classroom Applications

Maddux et al. (1992, p. 317) believe that "telecommunications has a great, but nearly untapped educational potential." This is because most telecommunications projects in education are Type I applications (i.e., doing differently something we already do) rather than the more innovative, more powerful, more desirable Type II activities that enable work to occur that would be otherwise impossible. As an illustration of the potential, they suggest this scenario (p. 122):

> Sixth grade students are working on an acid rain research project with peers throughout the U.S. and around the world. Using telecommunications, they search libraries worldwide for reference material. Locally they gather pertinent data, which they compare with that of other participants via the electronic network. A joint report is prepared using group writing techniques on the network. The final version reaches all students electronically and each location downloads it and submits it to the local newspaper for publication.

The technology to realize that scenario exists today, but few educators are ready to make it happen. You could be among the first to do so. Let's look at what some educators have done.

In the province of Ontario, one school district is 100 miles wide. As of 1992, two elementary schools and one high school were connected on a WAN, with plans to link all 60 schools in the region (Carpenter, 1992). Among the applications is writing over the network, in which students in first, fifth, and sixth grades get peer feedback on their papers. High school students also review the work and learn mentoring skills. Teachers report that students are becoming better communicators because they are forced to write everything. The network also maintains a complete record of everything that transpires on it. In addition, teachers are developing a new math curriculum without the typical problems of travel and meeting times.

Piller (1992) described a computer magnet school in a low-income San Francisco neighborhood that obtained antiquated home banking terminals (300 baud modems) for $50. The school sent the modems home with kids. (The terminals plug into home TVs and the regular phone line.) Kids use them to talk on-line at night rather than watching TV. Students and parents also use the systems to talk to the teachers, opening communication lines. In one case, a semiliterate parent learned to write by watching a child work with the terminal.

Solomon (1989) claims that student writing benefits when shared with a broad, if unseen, audience. Stories may begin with one writer, then grow as others add their ideas from wherever they live. Tamashiro and Hoagland (1987) called this *chain writing*, and reported that students benefited from the risk-free self-expression. They could focus on the content of the story, not the teller. Elsewhere, a similar project across grades 3–6 produced a 21-page booklet of student work (Lake, 1988–89), while yet another focused on the geography and history of the area covered as students from two schools "biked" toward each other, "meeting" half way as their reports converged.

In New York City, students used the Board of Education network to learn about the Biosphere II project (Reissman, September 1992). They began with an on-line encyclopedia to research the scientific basics. Next they placed an open e-mail request for input on the bulletin board system, and then made direct contact with those who responded. Students appreciated the fast turnaround time for replies, noting that in the past, information requested by writing often had arrived after the assignment was finished, if at all. This immediacy and the currency of information were major advantages. Results appear to far exceed more typical student research projects.

Readers' Circles bring students together to share what they have read and to respond to what is shared. Typically, they are conducted face to face within a class. A sixth-grade teacher expanded the concept to include a second class. Students in each class wrote their summaries of and reactions to what they had read, using a word processor, and then shared the diskettes with the other class. Students read each other's files, added responses, and then returned them to the original group. After a successful year, the circle went on-line using an existing city-wide network and brought another class into the circle from a different part of New York. Students reportedly enjoy the experiences very much, and the teachers believe their writing has improved because they want everything just right before their peers read their work (Reissman, February 1992).

Campus 2000, Britain's educational network, is used by countries around the world. Through the state Department of Education, the Florida–England Connection Project took shape in the late 1980s. Teachers from eleven schools received training in curriculum development for an international telecommunications project. Outlines of instructional units were placed on the *Campus 2000* Noticeboard, inviting schools on the network to participate in joint studies. Units had to be instructionally significant, involve information extremely timely or not otherwise available, and not merely duplicate what might otherwise occur anyhow. Preliminary data indicate that students found the experiences positive and that their cultural awareness increased (Roblyer, 1992).

A middle-school teacher in British Columbia appealed to colleagues through AppleLink for mentors for his students (Kearsley et al., 1992, pp. 48–49.) An extensive exchange ensued in preparation for Earth Day. It culminated with the collected information being reported back to all participating schools on Earth Day, where students were waiting to prepare articles for their student newspapers, much like a wire service provides its information.

Many schools now have access to on-line searching for student research. In Silver Spring, Maryland, the media specialist works with teachers and students to develop basic searching skills (Kearsley et al., 1992, pp. 51–52). She also works with selected teachers to develop whole class projects and with individual students on special research tasks. Students learn to define a research question, identify the needed information, plan a search strategy, and then carry out their search. Worksheets structure the activities. The specialist also developed a teacher collaboration worksheet to plan projects and clarify her and the teacher's respective responsibilities. Science fair and special senior projects have been fruitful sources of valuable research topics.

Implementation

Before leaping into telecommunications, educators should consider the experience and advice of those who have already done so. Attractive as telecommunications is, there also are potential pitfalls.

Planning for Success

Based on experience, Schrum, Carlton, and Pinney (1988) offer some sound advice. First, tie any project to a specific curriculum need or opportunity. Don't telecompute just to be doing it. Second, for any potential project, telecommunications should promise to be more effective than any other possibility, that is, a Type II application. Third, if the project involves participants communicating among themselves, allow time for them to get acquainted. This is essential to meaningful communication. Fourth, be sure teachers are committed to the project and its use of telecommunications. Otherwise, the almost-inevitable problems that arise will overwhelm their determination.

Problems to Overcome

There are also administrative issues involved in telecommunications. Your school may not have a modem. Even if there is a modem, is there an accessible phone jack? Is there technical support and assistance available in the school or district? Scrogan (1987) claimed there are dozens of potential roadblocks, such as cost and potential abuse of a phone line. This article offers practical tips on meeting such challenges, as do Waggoner (1992) and Collis (1988). Kearsley et al. (1992) suggest seeking outside sponsors for telecommunications if the school cannot or will not bear the costs. They also warn of potential false starts, citing an example of one school's initial project involving computer penpals. Differing numbers of participants in the California and Alaska sites meant not all children got individual responses, and some received no response at all. Ultimately, the project became too frustrating to continue, because its worth was unclear. This is a good example of the points made by Maddux et al. and Schrum et al. about initial planning and worthwhile projects.

Role of a Coordinator

Clearly, any organization that installs a LAN should budget for a network coordinator/administrator. Despite improvements in the technology, it is still essential to have a designated and trained staff member to keep the network operating. If this step is ignored, a sizable investment may turn into a white elephant.

Alternatives to the Real Thing

Perhaps you believe in the concepts of telecommunications and that students should be exposed to them, but your institution simply cannot fund phone lines, modems, and other costs. Another possibility is to simulate the experiences. Various software products exist for this purpose. *Electronic Village* includes tutorials on telecommunications concepts, along with an RBBS simulator. *Electronic Mailbag* is an e-mail simulator for up to 100 learners. *Windows on Telecommunications* is a tutorial on concepts with a simulation of going on-line. *KidMail* is another e-mail simulator that encourages writing-skill development. *SimuComm* simulates both e-mail and an RBBS. It features a modifiable database for learning search strategies. *Modemless CMS* simulates an RBBS with two message boards, e-mail, a news and features display, and capability to conduct user polls.

Cautions

Maddux et al. (1992) express many concerns about what has passed for educational uses of telecommunications. They fear that a promising application is being diluted with trivial uses and excessive hype. They suggest that telecommunications is too often the same old thing in a new form, as exemplified even by the very terms we apply to it, such as "e-mail" and "bulletin boards."

They cite older literature that claimed electronic field trips would provide experiences comparable to the real thing. They question the usefulness of such innovations as electronic penpals as a contrived application that loses more than it adds. Even sharing writing with peers in distant places need not involve telecommunications; fax could serve equally well.

While not so harsh in our judgment as they are, we do agree that educators must look to applications that truly add a new dimension to learning. Locating and retrieving resource materials through the electronic networks that already exist is clearly what Maddux et al. envision as a Type II application, something previously impossible in our schools.

Still another issue of great importance is who has access to the vast resources available by telecommunications. According to Coates (1992, p. 1), "Work-a-day Americans have two choices in this age of laptop computer modems and mega-databases: Join the computer class or join the underclass. The underclass, of course, doesn't even have a modem to phone on. The computer class controls the world's modem-accessible databases." Coates quotes the claim of the president of a publishing company that 23 million Americans read below the sixth-grade level. What does a vast information resource mean to them? What is the effect of direct delivery of information into homes when one-quarter of homes below the poverty level lack telephones? Only 13 percent of homes have computers, and only 10 percent of them have modems. Among white children, 17 percent use computers at home; it's 6 percent among minorities. Coates concludes that "(r)ather than providing universal delivery, . . . technology could widen the gap between the information-rich and the information-poor" (p. 5). Educators must address this equity issue.

Summary

The usefulness of a computer often increases dramatically when it is part of a network. The ability to exchange information with other users, whether simply messages or major data files, without regard to location or time, can have a major impact on how individuals work and what they accomplish. Computer networks range from workgroups in which all linked computers are relatively close to one another to worldwide networks such as the Internet.

Some networks rely on direct wiring among nearby computers. Telecommunications allow computers far apart from each other to share information, whether from home to school or around the world. Telecommunications requires adding a modem and appropriate software to a computer system. The ISDN promises to enhance current capabilities by providing the necessary bandwidth to transmit vast volumes of information, such as is required for images and motion. With ISDN, telecommunications will join the multimedia age.

Among the many specific types of telecommunications opportunities, this chapter highlighted conferencing, discussion groups (lists), e-mail and electronic journals, remote bulletin board systems, on-line research, and computer-mediated communication. You also learned of some of the network systems developed specifically for educators and sampled a variety of classroom applications. Finally, the chapter presented issues related to successful implementation. The potential of connecting with colleagues and peers is alluring, but careful planning is essential to success.

Our own experiences suggest that relatively few educators yet realize the potential of computer networks and telecommunications. Used wisely and well, they could contribute significantly to transforming our educational system. *T.I.E.*

(Telecommunications in Education), published by the International Society for Technology in Education Special Interest Group for Telecommunications, is an excellent resource for telecomputing educators.

Chapter 8 Activities

1. Contact local public or educational libraries to learn whether their card catalogs are accessible by modem. If so, log on to one and explore its operation and resources.
2. Obtain an account for access to Internet, Bitnet, or whatever network your college or university supports. Learn to use the system and set up a group among your peers that will communicate regularly in this way.
3. Join a discussion group on one of the networks. Monitor the messages carefully for at least one month. When you are comfortable, join in the discussion. Keep a log of your interaction with the group. If you have access to Bitnet or Internet, a particularly good group to join is called EDTECH. You can join it by sending the following message to the address LISTSERV@MSU:

    ```
    SUB EDTECH your full name (e.g., SUB EDTECH John Doe)
    ```

    Your first reply will provide instructions on how to use the system.
4. Subscribe to an electronic journal. For example, send the message:

    ```
    SUB DISTED your full name
    ```

    to LISTSERV@UWAVM for the Online Chronicle of Distance Education and Communication.
5. Obtain a list of local bulletin boards. Add their numbers to the dialing directory of your communications software. Log on to as many as possible. Keep a log of their user requirements.
6. Download a file from a local BBS, such as a utility you might use.
7. Contact the SYSOP of a local BBS, using the BBS itself. Inquire about the operation of the system and how many users it has.
8. Use an appropriate on-line database to prepare a bibliography for your next class assignment. If you have no pending project, look up the topic of telecommunications in education.
9. Investigate several information services. Prepare a chart or report comparing offerings, including special services for education, and costs.
10. Kearsley et al. (1992) mention the concept of "virtual classrooms," but they do not explain the idea. What do you think it means? Is there any literature on the topic?

11. Prepare a position paper on the issue of access to information through telecommunications, specifically the potential for increased gaps between "haves" and "have-nots" and the proper role of schools in providing access.

12. Plan a unit for your students in which telecommunications plays a key role. Hypothesize that you are participating in Kids Network, for instance, or that your AT&T Learning Circle includes two schools in South America. Do not plan a unit *about* telecommunications, but rather one that makes effective Type II use of telecommunications.

Bibliography

Allen, A. A. and Mountain, L. "When Inner City Black Children Go Online at Home." *The Computing Teacher*, November 1992, *20*(3), pp. 35–37.

Arndt, M. "Radio Data Net Allows Laptops to Communicate." *Chicago Tribune*, 4 May 1990, Business Section, pp. 1, 4.

Batey, A. and Cowell, R. N. *Distance Education: An Overview*, Portland OR: Northwest Regional Educational Laboratory, 1986.

"BESTNET: New Ways of Learning Through Computer Networking." *EDU Magazine*, Winter 1992, pp. 21–25.

Bruder, I. "Electronic Learning's 8th Annual Survey of the States, 1988." *Electronic Learning*, October 1988, pp. 38–45.

Burrall, B. "Telecommunication = Motivation. (Social Studies. Computers in the Curriculum.)" *The Computing Teacher*, October 1992, *20*(2), pp. 27–28.

Carpenter, C. L. "Plugging into the Information Age." *The Computing Teacher*, April 1992, *19*(7), pp. 38–39.

Coates, J. "The Next Ruling Class." *Chicago Tribune*, August 7, 1992, Section 5, pp. 1, 5.

Collis, B. *Computers, Curriculum, and Whole-Class Instruction*. Belmont, CA: Wadsworth, 1988.

D'Amicantonio, J. "Using Online Services in the Junior High School." *The Computing Teacher*, October 1991, *19*(2), pp. 53–54.

Dede, C. J. "The Evolution of Distance Learning: Technology-Mediated Interactive Learning." *Journal of Research on Computing in Education*, Spring 1990, *22*(3), pp. 247–264.

DeLoughry, T. J. "Publishers Find a Hungry Audience for Books about the Internet." *Chronicle of Higher Education*, 16 December 1992, pp. A12, A15.

DeLoughry, T. J. "Remote Instruction Using Computers Found as Effective as Classroom Sessions." *Chronicle of Higher Education*, 20 April 1988, pp. A15, A21.

Dvorak, J. C. and Anis, N. *Dvorak's Guide to PC Telecommunications*. Berkeley, CA: Osborne McGraw-Hill, 1990.

Farley, L., Ed. *Library Resources on the Internet: Strategies for Selection and Use*. Chicago, IL: American Library Association, Reference and Adult Services Section, 1991.

Froman, A. D. "Electronic Baby Steps. (Language Arts. Computers in the Curriculum.)" *The Computing Teacher*, October 1992, *20*(2), pp. 24–26.

Greenberg, D. "Information Access: Our Elitist System Must Be Reformed." *Chronicle of Higher Education*, 23 October 1991, p. A48.

Guthrie, J. and Crane, B. "*Science*: Online Retrieval Adds Realism to Science Projects." *The Computing Teacher*, February 1992, *19*(5), pp. 32–34.

Harris, J. "Telnet Sessions on the Internet. (Mining the Internet)." *The Computing Teacher*, October 1992, *20*(2), pp. 40–43.

Harris, J. "Electronic Treasures by Electronic Mail." *The Computing Teacher*, August/September 1992, *20*(2), pp. 36–38.

Harris, J. and Anderson, S. "Cultivating Teacher Telecommunications Networks from the Grass Roots Up: The Electronic Academic Village at Virginia." *Computers in the Schools*, 1991, *8*(1/2/3), pp. 191–202.

Harris, J. and Grandgenett, N. "Writing Apprehension, Computer Anxiety, and Telecomputing: A Pilot Study." *Journal of Instructional Technology in Teacher Education*, 1992, *1*(1), pp. 115–125.

Hazari, S. I. "A LAN Primer." *The Computing Teacher*, November 1991, *19*(3), pp. 14–17.

Hezel, R. T. "Statewide Planning for Telecommunications in Education: Some Trends and Issues." *TechTrends*, 1991, *36*(5), pp. 17–20.

Holznagel, D. C. *Enhancing Instruction Through Telecommunications*. Portland, OR: Northwest Regional Educational Laboratory, 1991.

Hudspeth, D. "The Electronic Bulletin Board: Appropriate Technology." *Educational Technology*, July 1990, pp. 40–43.

Jenson, E. "At-Risk Students Online." *The Computing Teacher*, December/January 1991–1992, *19*(4), pp. 10–11.

Jost, K. L. "Computer Mediated Communication—An Overview." *Instructional Developments*, Spring 1990, *1*(1), pp. 15–22.

Kearsley, G., Hunter, B., and Furlong, M. *We Teach with Technology*, Wilsonville, OR: Franklin, Beedle & Associates, 1992.

Kehoe, B. P. *Zen and the Art of the Internet: A Beginner's Guide to the Internet*, 2nd ed. Englewood Cliffs, NJ: Prentice-Hall, 1993.

Kinnaman, D. E. "Networking—The Missing Piece in your Technology Plan?" *Technology & Learning*, November/December 1991, *12*(3), pp. 28–38.

Krol, E. *The Whole Internet: User's Guide & Catalog*. Sebastopol, CA: O'Reilly & Associates, Inc., 1992.

Kurshan, B. and Dawson, T. "The Global Classroom: Reaching Beyond the Walls of the School Building." *Technology & Learning*, January 1992, *12*(4), pp. 48–54.

Lake, D. "Two Projects That Worked: Using Telecommunications as a Resource in the Classroom." *The Computing Teacher*, December/January 1988–1989, *16*(4), pp. 17–19.

LaQuey, T. and Ryer, J. C. *The Internet Companion: A Beginner's Guide to Global Networking*. Reading, MA: Addison-Wesley, 1992.

Maddux, C. D., Johnson, D. L., and Willis, J. W. *Educational Computing. Learning with Tomorrow's Technologies*. Boston, MA: Allyn and Bacon, 1992.

Maule, R. W. "Online Multimedia for Education." *Journal of Educational Multimedia and Hypermedia*, 1992, *1*(2), pp. 169–177.

Marine, A., Ed. *Internet: Getting Started*. Englewood Cliffs, NY: Prentice-Hall, 1993.

Molettiere, R. "A Guide to Networking." *Media & Methods*, November/December 1991, *28*(2), pp. 40–43.

Moursund, D. "Restructuring Education, Part 3: What Is the Information Age?" *The Computing Teacher*, November 1991, *19*(3), p. 4.

Piller, C. "Separate Realities." *MacWorld*, September 1992, pp. 218–230.

Polly, J. A. "Surfing the Internet: An Introduction." *Wilson Library Bulletin*. 1992, *66*(10), pp. 38–42.

Quarterman, J. S. *The Matrix. Computer Networks and Conferencing Systems Worldwide*. Bedford, MA: Digital Press, 1990.

Reissman, R. "A Biosphere Research Expedition." *The Computing Teacher*, August/September 1992, *20*(1), pp. 32–33.

Reissman, R. *"Language Arts:* Creating a Readers' Circle Online." *The Computing Teacher*, February 1992, *19*(5), pp. 35–36.

Riedl, R. "CompuServe in the Classroom." *The Computing Teacher*, March 1986, *13*(6), pp. 62–64.

Riel, M. "Approaching the Study of Networks." *The Computing Teacher*, December/January 1991–1992, *19*(4), pp. 5–7, 52.

Roberts, N., Blakeslee, G., Brown, M., and Lenk, C. *Integrating Telecommunications into Education.* Englewood Cliffs, NJ: Prentice-Hall, 1990.

Roblyer, M. D. "Electronic Hands Across the Ocean: The Florida–England Connection." *The Computing Teacher*, February 1992, *19*(5), pp. 16–19.

Schilling, N. "Computer Networking for Native American Schools: A New Technology for the Bureau of Indian Affairs." *Computers in the Schools*, 1991 *8*(1/2/3), pp. 187–190.

Schrum, L., Carlton, K., and Pinney, S. "Today's Tools." *The Computing Teacher*, May 1988, *15*(8), pp. 31–35.

Scrogan, L. "Telecomputing: How to Overcome the Roadblocks." *Classroom Computer Learning*, February 1987, pp. 40–45.

Sloan, F. A. and Koohang, A. A. "The Local Area Network and the Cooperative Learning Principle." *Computers in the Schools*, 1991, *8*(1/2/3), pp. 207–210.

Slovacek, S. P. and Doyle-Nichols, A. R. "Enhancing Telecommunication in Teacher Education." *Journal of Research on Computing in Education*, Winter 1991, *24*(2), pp. 254–264.

Solomon, G. "A Writing Class Taps into a World of Knowledge." *Electronic Learning*, March 1989, pp. 16–17.

Staff. "For Professor at Penn State, Class Lectures Do Not Compute." *Chicago Tribune*, 20 March 1988, Section 1, p. 28.

Stall, K. and Lawson, V. "KidLink: Elementary Classroom Telecommunications." *The Computing Teacher*, October 1992, *19*(2), pp. 30–34.

Stanton, D. E. *Using Networked Information Resources: A Bibliography.* Perth, Western Australia: Author, 1992.

Tamashiro, R. and Hoagland, C. "Telecomputing a Chain Story." *The Computing Teacher*, April 1987, *14*(7), pp. 37–39.

Tennant, R. "Internet Basics." *ERIC DIGEST,* September 1992, ERIC Clearinghouse on Information Resources, EDO-IR-92-7.

Tennant, R., Ober, J., and Lipow, A. G. *Crossing the Internet Threshold: An Instructional Handbook.* Berkeley, CA: Library Solutions Press, 1993.

Turner, S. and Land, M. *Tools for Schools. Applications Software for the Classroom.* Belmont, CA: Wadsworth, 1988.

Waggoner, M. D., Ed. *Empowering Networks. Computer Conferencing in Education.* Englewood Cliffs, NJ: Educational Technology Publications, 1992.

Wilson, D. L. "Huge Computer Network Quickens Pace of Academic Exchange and Collaboration." *The Chronicle of Higher Education*, 30 September 1992, pp. A24–A26.

Part 3

The Computer as Tutor

Objectives

After completing this chapter, you will be able to:

Explain the nature of computer-assisted instruction (CAI) in terms of its three main characteristics.

Discuss the historical development of CAI.

Identify five major types of CAI, based on the traditional taxonomy.

Suggest appropriate applications of each type of software.

Explain the issues surrounding each of the five software types.

Discuss the basis for the Learner-Centered Taxonomy as an alternative to the traditional software classification scheme.

Describe the basic findings of research studies on the effects of CAI.

Analyze the merits of new directions in CAI research.

Chapter 9

Computer-Assisted Instruction Fundamentals

Microcomputers are just tools, but arguably the most versatile tools known to humans. Thus far, you have learned about their potential as a *personal productivity tool*: word processor, spreadsheet, database manager, graphics and support system, publishing center, and communications aid. This chapter introduces yet another major application area: the computer as an instructional tutor, a *tool for learning* specific things. You will study the nature and evolution of computer-assisted instruction, major types and primary characteristics of such software, their potential strengths and weaknesses, and research findings concerning the outcomes of computer-assisted instruction.

The Nature of Computer-Assisted Instruction

Computer-assisted instruction (CAI) is the most common term for the interaction of a learner with a computer in a direct instructional role. CAI software purports to teach some particular content in any of a variety of formats, with or even without any involvement of a human teacher. Much of CAI is "designed to make it easier, quicker, or otherwise more efficient to continue teaching the same things in the same ways we have always taught them" (Maddux, Johnson, and Willis, 1992, p. 23). Maddux et al. call these Type I applications, and are quick to point out that their definition is not at all an indictment of CAI, despite its tone. Rather, there is a clear potential role for CAI within the total scope of educational computing. They note that using a computer in such ways *exclusively* does not take adequate advantage of the technology. They, like we, believe that the software tools presented in Chapters 2–8 of this book should be the main focus of computing in schools, with CAI in a supporting role.

What, then, are the major characteristics of CAI?

Interaction

In typical classroom group instruction, it is difficult at best for a teacher to keep all learners actively engaged in the learning process. With CAI, learners interact directly and continually with the computer, responding to prompts and questions, receiving feedback to whatever they have done. The computer becomes a sort of private tutor. Computer-assisted instruction largely removes the potential for learners merely to observe without active participation.

Flexibility

Another appealing aspect of CAI is its flexibility to teach virtually anything from higher-order thought processes such as problem-solving skills to the relatively simple cognitive learning usually associated with stimulus–response theory. Teachers can use CAI for instruction that is integral to the on-going curriculum, to enrich or supplement basic instruction, or for remediation.

Meeting Student Needs

Interaction and flexibility are key elements of meeting the diverse learning needs of individual students. Not all students learn at the same rate or in the same way, yet typical classroom instruction does little to account for this reality. In fact, schools are ill-equipped to deal with individual differences. Children typically start school at about the same chronological age, advance one grade per year, use the same textbooks, do the same assignments, follow the same curriculum, and are expected to attain essentially the same standards. As you have experienced, one teacher with thirty students per class is unable to devote significant attention to just one student at a time. These conditions all *minimize* rather than capitalize on individual differences.

Teachers working one-to-one with a student adapt their instruction continuously based on the learner's responses, both in method and in content. Computer-assisted instruction also can provide instruction adapted to the current user of the software, which may vary greatly from the needs of the next user. As in one-to-one tutoring, CAI users can set their own pace through the material, taking as little or as much time as they need to achieve mastery. Based on student responses, the computer can make decisions to provide remediation or to advance the learner to new topics or more difficult material, much as a tutor might. In addition, most CAI attempts to appeal in some ways to varied learning modalities by offering text, graphics, and even sound.

Evolution of Computer-Assisted Instruction

Computer-assisted instruction has evolved over a period of more than 40 years. Let's briefly trace the major developments.

The Early Years

In 1950, scientists at the Massachusetts Institute of Technology designed the first CAI (a flight simulator for training combat pilots), using a mainframe computer. This led to CAI for staff development and training in many industries. In 1959, IBM adapted its staff-development CAI technology for use with schoolchildren. At about the same time, Florida State University developed and offered credit CAI courses in physics and statistics, and Dartmouth College researchers created the first simple CAI programming language (BASIC).

Researchers at the University of Illinois initiated the PLATO (Programmed Logic for Automatic Teaching Operations) project in 1960. The goal was to demonstrate the technical feasibility, manageability, and economic viability of an extensive computer-based education network. High cost proved a significant barrier to adoption by other educational institutions.

At Stanford University, Patrick Suppes and his team developed a small tutorial system in mathematics and language arts, primarily for disadvantaged elementary school students. Parallel to this, the Stanford Drill and Practice System was introduced. The fundamental assumption of this mainframe system was that the teacher would first present the basic concepts, then the computer would provide *intensive* drill and practice at a level of difficulty tailored to each learner.

Computer technology advanced steadily during the 1960s. The precursor to today's computer monitors was the cathode-ray tube, which IBM introduced in 1964, followed in 1966 by the first computer system designed expressly for CAI (the IBM 1500). Late in 1971, Intel Corporation introduced the "computer on a chip," the microprocessor technology that made possible low-cost, readily accessible microcomputers appropriate for instructional use.

Major Research and Development Efforts

Although early efforts led to much enthusiasm for the potential of CAI, cost was a serious deterrent to its application. Access to mainframe systems with terminals was limited. Educational software was scarce and often of questionable quality. These are typical problems with any new technology.

Based on what had been demonstrated, in 1971 the National Science Foundation invested $10 million in two CAI projects, the PLATO system described previously and TICCIT (Time-shared Interactive Computer Controlled Information Television). The aim of TICCIT was to demonstrate in community colleges that CAI could provide better instruction in mathematics and English at lower cost than traditional instruction could. TICCIT was based on an educational philosophy termed *Learner Controlled Instruction* (LCI), which stressed that students must be able to adapt the sequence of instruction to their own pace and learning style. A special keyboard made it easy to request additional examples, redisplay of rules, practice items, and so forth (Merrill, Schneider, and Fletcher, 1980).

Educational Testing Service evaluated both PLATO and TICCIT. In community colleges, PLATO lessons produced achievement gains in mathematics, chemistry, and biology. Teacher and student attitudes toward PLATO were positive. In grades 4, 5, and 6, PLATO math lessons also produced significant achievement gains and more positive attitudes toward the subject matter than among students in a traditional class. TICCIT also produced achievement gains among community college students in math and English, along with positive attitudes. See Steinberg (1991a) for more details.

Thus, by the mid-1970s evidence supported the instructional potential of CAI in different settings using different instructional models and differing hardware technologies. The major remaining barrier to broad CAI viability in education—economics—began to fall in 1977 with the successful introduction of microcomputers by Radio Shack (now Tandy), Commodore, and Apple Computer. Mass access to computers was becoming a reality.

A Taxonomy of CAI

Today a wide range of CAI is available, which has led to attempts to categorize and succinctly describe these software products. Certain labels are now common, including drill and practice, tutorials, simulations, games, and problem-solving software. Not everything fits neatly into such categories, however, nor do their definitions necessarily suffice to clarify their intent.

Drill and Practice

Drill and practice is the most common and best known form of instructional program. The name appropriately suggests its purpose—to help learners remember and use information they have *previously* been taught. Teachers assign students to use these programs for extensive repetitive work with selected skills or knowledge (Figure 9.1).

It would be erroneous to assume from this that drills apply only to lower-level tasks. While this is often true, drill and practice can also develop skills that are vital to more complex tasks. For instance, work on subword and word recognition is important in the development of reading comprehension. Even what appears to be routine practice on arithmetic facts can be essential preparation for coping with more difficult skills at a later time.

Types of Drill and Practice

The lowest level of sophistication in drill and practice resembles traditional flash cards or programmed instruction. Every user of the program receives a fixed number of problems. A student who has mastered the content must complete the same tasks as one who truly needs the additional work before moving ahead.

Slightly better is the program that uses an arbitrary mastery criterion, perhaps ten correct responses in a row. The best students should complete the program in just ten items, while a student needing more practice might require several times that number to achieve the criterion. Upon completion, the student is able to select the next level of drill.

The most highly adoptive program might assume "mastery" after relatively few responses and automatically increase the difficulty level, or even move on to the next topic, say, from addition to multiplication. If performance falters, the diffi-

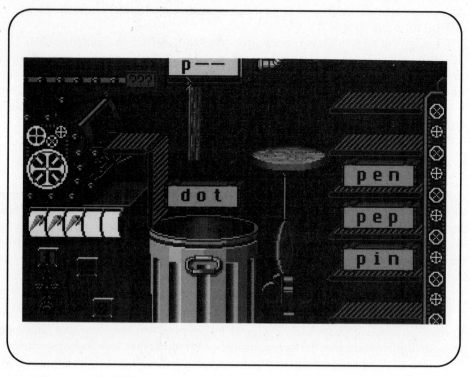

Figure 9.1. Drill and practice on initial letter recognition in *Reader Rabbit.*

culty is decreased or the student returns to the previous topic. Such continual adjustment seeks to assure mastery throughout, while neither boring the student with needless repetition nor causing frustration by demanding something beyond the student's capabilities.

Examples of Drill and Practice

A third-grade teacher noticed that several of her students were still having trouble with basic math skills. She selected *Mental Math Games, Series 1* to motivate and assist these students to master math operations and facts. Five separate games aim at speed and accuracy in all operations. In "Tip-A-Duck," problems appear on figures in a carnival shooting gallery. To move through "Maze," learners must solve problems that appear on arrows pointing in the direction they wish to move. The scope of work ranges from single-digit addition to three-digit division. This software received a 1992–1993 Award of Excellence in the November/December 1992 issue of *Technology & Learning*.

All Star Drill provides the context of a baseball game. You enter multiple-choice or open-ended questions for *any* content, or purchase question disks on states and capitals, world geography, health, or spelling. You can print the questions to aid in your class preparation or for students to use in studying. The teacher's guide contains many creative lesson plans.

The Drill and Practice Controversy

Drill-and-practice programs have attracted considerable criticism. Critics claim that they are often boring, very narrow in their pedagogical approach, drill all students the same way regardless of their ability or level of functioning, interfere with desired remembering, and often provide undesirable negative feedback.

Proponents argue that drill and practice already exists as flash cards and worksheets in most classrooms. Software motivates students better and can effectively reduce the tedium of learning many skills that require extensive practice for retention or speed. Because feedback is immediate and errors are not allowed to compound, CAI avoids a major weakness of traditional worksheets and other independent work forms with which a student may actually "master" incorrect material. Also, the computer can target practice where it is most needed without dwelling on what the learner has mastered, something difficult, at best, with traditional methods.

Drill and practice as an element of learning is hardly subject to debate. Much of the criticism of such CAI is attributable to poorly conceived and executed software, rather than computer-based drill and practice *per se*. Design flaws can lessen, even negate, the impact of a product that is sound in its basic concept, as Collis (1988, p. 70) reported concerning the widely used *Writing to Read* program. Still, useful drill-and-practice programs are available, and they may save teachers much time that would otherwise go into preparing and grading alternatives. Drill-and-practice CAI need not produce greater achievement than under traditional instruction to be valuable. If it is merely "as good," it can regain for the teacher time to use more profitably to work with students directly.

Characteristics of Better Drill and Practice

Viable drill-and-practice programs possess certain characteristics. Summarizing a variety of sources, these characteristics typically include:

- Clear educational purpose/goals.
- Information quantity appropriate to memory limits (e.g., no more than seven items/elements at once).
- Appropriate use of graphics, sound, and color.
- Use of appealing gaming elements to provide motivation.
- Inclusion of tutorial "help" options.
- Effective feedback for correct and incorrect responses.
- Control over the rate of presentation.
- Provision for reviewing directions or previous information.
- Random generation of items.
- Application of appropriate learning theory and pedagogy.
- Presentation of accurate content with correct language.
- Ability to stop at will and resume at the same point later.

For in-depth treatment of drill and practice, read Chapter 8 of Alessi and Trollip (1985).

Using Drill and Practice Software (Applicability in the Curriculum)

Drill-and-practice CAI is not equally common for all areas of the curriculum. Not every subject fits the appropriate uses of this CAI format, nor do teachers of all subjects use drill and practice of any kind uniformly. Much of the available software is for elementary-level arithmetic and language arts, or for adult remedial learning. Basic arithmetic facts, spelling, and punctuation are fundamental learning for all and involve the kinds of learning tasks appropriate to drill and practice.

Essentially, drill-and-practice activities present a stimulus to the student, elicit a response, and provide immediate reinforcement. One appropriate use of drill and practice programs is when the learning objectives relate to multiple discrimination learning. This type of learning involves, first, perceptually differentiating among events and, second, attaching the proper labels to each of them. Discrimination learning emphasizes the ability to distinguish among members of a set of stimuli and to make an appropriate response to each.

Paired associate tasks are also appropriate for drill and practice. In these tasks, the computer helps to create meaningful links between related items or ideas. Overlearning is the goal, to enable the student to perform a task automatically with very little mental activity. Examples of this type of desired overlearning are addition and multiplication facts, sight vocabulary words, and correct spelling of commonly used words.

Your task as a teacher is to *evaluate* any software personally prior to using it in the classroom to determine its potential role and value. (In Chapter 11, you will learn about evaluation techniques.) You must determine that the software is compatible with your curriculum, then plan your lessons so that students will have adequate preparation before using the software. Drill and practice should not introduce new materials, but rather provide needed work with already familiar content. This need not mean teaching as usual. Rather, you should incorporate CAI into your lesson plan from the beginning, omitting what you would otherwise do that the software can do for you, changing aspects that can be done differently because of what the software should help students achieve. The goal is to integrate the computer work into the lesson, not tack it on as an afterthought.

Beyond such integrated use, profitable ways to use drill and practice CAI include (1) to maintain a performance level previously reached, (2) to automatize skills, and (3) to review material prerequisite to a new lesson (Geisert and Futrell, 1990). How you implement drill-and-practice CAI is also important. Govier (1988) found that pairs or groups of students achieved more than individuals and that drill effectiveness was greatest early in its use, then declined with familiarity. As with any tool, drill-and-practice software must be used properly to help assure the desired outcome.

Tutorials

Tutorials are intended to introduce and present new, unfamiliar material to the student. As the name suggests, they are designed to tutor, or to instruct. They are often designed for stand-alone learning, for which other CAI forms are less likely to be suitable. Tutorials typically present content in chunks (Figure 9.2), then ask the learner questions to verify short-term learning. At various points in a lesson, including the end, larger units of content become the focus of the questioning. If the learner at any point fails to meet the program's criteria for achievement, the lesson may move to review and remediation before advancing to the next topic.

Types of Tutorials

There are two general types of tutorial CAI: *linear* and *branching*. Linear tutorials have a single path through the lesson for all students. Regardless of any performance differences, every learner must read and respond to the same content. The only aspect of individualization involved is that learners set their own pace through the lesson. All learners experience the same instruction, however, early tutorial CAI was mostly linear.

In branching tutorials, learners follow alternate paths through the lesson based upon their responses to questions. During a pre-test or at any point in the lesson, if the learner demonstrates mastery of the content, the lesson "branches" to the next topic or lesson. Some pattern of incorrect responses leads to remediation segments. It is always the learner's response that determines what happens next in the lesson. Branching tutorials are clearly more in line with sound learning theory.

Examples of Tutorials

Tool software, such as word processors, often includes on-line tutorials for new users to supplement the printed manuals, which many users never read anyhow.

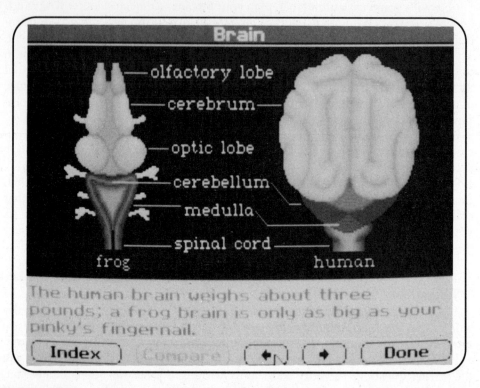

Figure 9.2. A biology tutorial is part of *Operation Frog*.

This is an ideal application for stand-alone CAI, because new users of complex software often have no access to other means of learning to use their new purchase. Do you know whether your word processor has a tutorial? If so, have you tried it?

Keyboarding and typing tutors are also common "self-help" software aimed at the individual user working independently to master a skill. Such software also illustrates the difficulty of using terms such as *tutorial,* because they are actually combinations. They clearly tutor the learner but also provide substantial drill and practice to help the learner achieve the automatic response patterns so essential to effective keyboard use.

Tutorials are also available for mainstream content areas. Each lesson in *Verb Usage* teaches one verb that is commonly misused. Students must choose its correct form to complete a sentence and can put each alternative into the sentence to "try it" before giving their final answer. *Understanding Multiplication* begins with dot counting and patterns followed by successive addition that leads to addition of patterns and, finally, multiplication.

The Tutorial Controversy

Critics of tutorial software contend that, as with drill and practice, many of the programs are poorly written and deal primarily with "trivial" concepts. Tutorials are regarded as nothing more than electronic page-turners that force the student into a limited range of possible responses, thus severely restricting meaningful exploration of the concept.

Advocates of tutorials, however, contend that in some cases tutorials might teach material even better than a teacher. Tutorials provide a one-to-one teaching situation and afford learners an opportunity to proceed with the learning task at their own rate. An additional benefit is that learners respond to *every* question—not just a very few—as is the case in typical classroom instruction.

As with drills, many of the concerns about tutorials are really about poor design. Tutorial CAI is widely used in adult-learning situations, such as training in business and industry. It is well accepted as efficient and effective. Within K–12 education, tutorials may offer make-up opportunities for students who are absent, an alternative approach to a topic for a student having difficulty, or a way to offer some instruction not possible otherwise. The quality of the software is, of course, critical, which underscores the need for evaluation prior to purchase and use.

Characteristics of Better Tutorials

You can find detailed treatment of tutorials in Chapter 7 of Alessi and Trollip (1985). In short, a solid tutorial should include the following:

- Acceptable instructional methodology/strategy.
- Valid pre-tests and post-tests.
- Internal questioning that measures progress toward criterion.
- Appropriate sequence and scope of content.
- High interest for the potential audience.
- Learner control over pacing.
- Ability to move backward for review.
- Automatic record-keeping so that the teacher can access class and individual performance data.

Using Tutorial CAI (Applicability in the Curriculum)

Tutorials exist for most areas of the curriculum and for content ranging from simple factual information to higher-order problem-solving processes. They have been particularly effective in science and foreign-language learning, as well as for learning to use other software. Based on a review of research (Roblyer, 1985), using CAI to *supplement* teaching should produce greater effects than replacing a teacher with CAI. Caution is in order when considering how to use a tutorial.

Assuming a sound rationale for using a tutorial, such as enrichment of the curriculum, your evaluation should include congruence of the program with the curriculum and completeness of topic treatment. As you plan a lesson for which a tutorial exists, determine exactly where and how you will incorporate it into the lesson, for example, to extend, to review, to remediate. Make it integral to the lesson from the start of your planning.

Simulations

A computer simulation is an interactive model of some "reality" such as an event, object, or phenomenon (Geisert and Futrell, 1990; Simonson and Thompson, 1990). Typically, simulations offer learners the opportunity to manipulate variables that affect the outcomes of the experience. Often learners read or view a scenario, analyze it, and make decisions based on the data. The simulated environment then changes, based on the student decision, creating a new situation with new decisions to make. This type of activity continues until some predetermined solution is obtained, the learner runs out of time or enthusiasm, or the number of inappropriate decisions terminates the activity.

Simulations are Type II applications, those that make possible new and better ways of teaching (Maddux et al., 1992). They offer some of the most exciting potential of CAI. No doubt, you see immediately that simulations are complex to design and create. Designers must anticipate all reasonable responses at each point and account for the effect of each on the model (Figure 9.3).

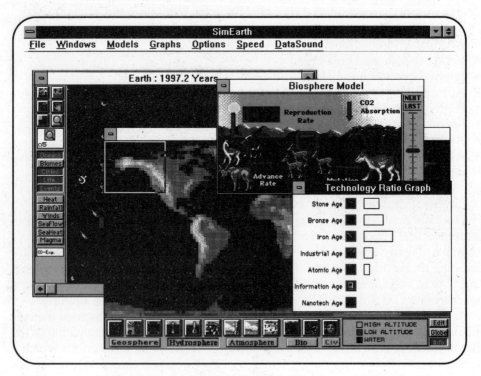

Figure 9.3. The user monitors and controls many factors in *Sim Earth*.

Types of Simulations

Alessi and Trollip (1985, pp. 162–167) distinguish four categories of simulations. While useful, the definitions are not mutually exclusive.

First, *physical simulations* relate to some physical object, which the student may "use" or learn about. Appropriate content for such a simulation ranges from aircraft instruments to experiments in the physical sciences and includes such subjects as the operation of micrometers in industrial education.

Second, *procedural simulations* "teach a sequence of actions that constitute a procedure." The situation presented is not an end in itself (e.g., learning about the instruments in an airplane cockpit), but rather a means for developing the skills and activities needed to function in the situation (e.g., flying the aircraft). This category also includes diagnostic simulations, such as those used in medical education.

Third, *situational simulations* place the learner in a role within the scenario presented. Rather than explicitly teaching rules or procedures, situational simulations follow discovery learning principles. The learner explores various responses to a situation and various roles through repetition of the simulation. Other roles in the scenario may be played by the computer or other students.

Fourth, in *process simulations*, the learner does not play a role, but rather is an external experimenter. Initial decisions are made regarding parameters for one cycle or trial, then the simulation progresses to conclusion without further learner intervention. It is the result of the process that is of primary interest. This form of simulation changes the rate at which the process might occur to one more suited to learning. In the case of economic forecasting or genetic experimentation, time is compressed. In the study of physical phenomena, time may be extended to permit thorough observation of the outcome.

Examples of Simulations

The Brøderbund *SIM* series has been a commercial success as well as popular among educators. In *SimCity*, you take charge of a growing, evolving city. You can design your own model or pick from real cities. You must deal with budget, traffic, population, pollution, disasters, industrial growth, and so forth (Jacobsen, 1992). *SimEarth* models our planet as a single interconnected organism. Everything you do affects the entire planet! If you'd rather be an ant out to conquer a suburban yard and house, try *SimAnt*, where you'll face such obstacles as rival ants, spiders, a dog, the lawnmower, water hoses, and, of course, human feet.

Decisions, Decisions is a social studies simulation series for grades 5–12. Individual titles are *Colonization, Revolutionary Wars, Immigration, Urbanization, Foreign Policy, Television, Prejudice, The Environment, Substance Abuse, Budget Process,* and *On the Campaign Trail '92.* As a specific case, in *Substance Abuse* a scenario involves seeing a friend buying drugs in school. As a teacher approaches, the friend flees, dropping the drugs at your feet. What would you do? The simulation provides a structured, nonthreatening situation in which learners can observe and practice positive actions in difficult circumstances. The hope is that they will internalize real-life skills. Similarly, *The Environment* requires students to think and act to balance the competing needs of the environment and area economics.

Science Literacy: The Lio Project seeks to develop process skills by allowing sixth- through ninth-graders to actually "do" science. A Lio is a one-cell organism that is of economic interest when productive. In a simulated lab, users must determine how to grow their randomly generated Lio to achieve maximum productivity. The task begins with the microscope, then proceeds to a database for research on similar organisms. Optimal conditions are hypothesized and then applied. Students observe results, modify hypotheses, and so on. This program was developed following the guidelines for science as process of the National Science Teachers Association and the American Association for the Advancement of Science.

The Simulation Controversy

Proponents see in simulation CAI much promise for teaching problem-solving and decision-making skills. Simulations allow students to explore environments that are too expensive, too dangerous, impractical by virtue of time or location requirements, or otherwise impossible to attempt in reality. In a simulation, students may safely make errors and explore complex problems without fear of being wrong. Good simulations are highly motivating because they present options that are thought-provoking and choices that are not easily made. They readily evoke higher-order thought processes such as reasoning and critical thinking.

Geisert and Futrell (1990, p. 96) claim there are indicators that simulations "not only effectively meet their stated instructional goals, but may well modify to advantage how students approach data and decision making." Critics note, however, that it is often difficult to assess just what truly has been learned. For example, one popular simulation for upper elementary grades is *Oregon Trail*. The program simulates a trip from the Midwest to Oregon in a covered wagon. The student makes decisions related to food, ammunition, medicine, clothing, travel, and safety that affect travelers' survival. As part of the simulation, it is sometimes necessary to hunt for food. The animated graphics are so appealing to children that they often hunt at every opportunity regardless of need. What, then, have they learned from the experience?

Another concern is content accuracy. How can you assess the apparent realism of a scenario? What about the accuracy of the model underlying the simulation? Complex mathematical relationships are often involved. Can you be certain of their validity? Teachers may need to help students deal with these issues. However, in terms of desirable learning outcomes, perhaps only the *process* of working through the problem is critical.

Characteristics of Better Simulations

Better simulations exhibit certain qualities or features. They should:

- Be engaging to gain and hold user attention.
- Permit continuation from any stopping point over multiple sessions.
- Allow attainment of meaningful goals within a reasonable time.
- Be realistic, or at least plausible.
- Have clearly defined learning goals that fit your curriculum.

- Be appropriately random and unpredictable.
- Include extensive support materials to guide integration into your lesson.
- Focus on significant content, not trivial details.

Using Simulations (Applicability in the Curriculum)

The availability of simulations across the curriculum varies. While there are few limits to what the creative software developer might conceive, the greatest concentration is found in the natural and social sciences. It is more difficult to conceive of scenarios and situations in which the content of mathematics or language arts lends itself to simulation activities.

For maximum effectiveness, simulations require careful background preparation of students. Seldom are simulations designed to support a discovery-learning approach; rather, the user must have mastered the content or procedural fundamentals to benefit from the simulation. Would you allow students to work in a chemistry lab with a discovery-learning approach?

Simulations are especially well suited to group work. The McGraw-Hill *Search* series and many products from Tom Snyder Productions were designed expressly for group use in a one-computer classroom. Others can be used readily in this way. Divide the class into teams that must reach consensus on each response. Establish specific tasks for team members to assume, such as recording decisions and their outcomes, researching the next decision, and so on. Class use of a simulation may be greatly enhanced with large-screen projection, so that students need not try to follow the activity on a small monitor. Both data projectors and LCD panels for the overhead projector are well within school budgets today. Woodward, Carnine, and Gersten (1988) offer insights from their research on effective implementation strategies for group simulations.

To help in determining what has been learned as a result of a simulation activity, it may prove extremely beneficial to have teacher-directed "debriefings" after completion of the simulation. The teacher can help the group to focus on the desired learning outcomes and determine what in the simulation "worked" and what did not. Other questions to pose include: What might have been the situation in real life? How might that have differed from the simulated experience?

Instructional Games

Instructional games present content in a game format. The content and the game are integrated and inseparable, in contrast to a game that is a reward for performance within another form of CAI (such as a drill). In the latter, the game may be unrelated to the content, serving solely a motivational purpose. Instructional games have been designed to help teach or reinforce a wide range of instructional objectives.

Game Characteristics

Instructional games typically are governed by a clear set of rules, are competitive, and have a winner and a loser at the end. They are designed to be entertaining and make use of the computer's color, sound, and graphics capabilities to capture and hold the student's interest.

In his study of children and their preferences regarding computer games, Malone (1981) reported three characteristics of intrinsically motivating environments: challenge, curiosity, and fantasy. In instructional games, there typically is a goal to achieve (challenge). The player anticipates what will happen (curiosity), but these anticipations are not always fulfilled because chance plays a role. Games rely heavily upon creative mental imagery on the part of the participant (fantasy).

Types of Instructional Games

Instructional games fall into one of two categories on each of two dimensions. First, they may be derived from games already well known in other formats, (e.g., hangman), or they may be new creations for the computer. The second dimension is the nature of the competition involved. In some games, individual players compete against themselves, a time limit, or the computer. In others, players compete against each other, or even as teams.

Examples of Instructional Games

Hangman is one of the most ubiquitous of paper-and-pencil games and has been adapted to the computer in a wide range of subjects. Content is integrated with the game in that the player must correctly guess a letter contained in the "secret" word or have a piece added to the "victim." Hangman games have been criticized for their inherently morbid theme.

What began as an intriguing geography game became an unprecedented media phenomenon. The *Carmen Sandiego* series challenges users to track the nefarious Carmen and her criminal gang, using reference tools to decipher clues. Individual geography games cover the United States, Europe, and the world. History becomes vital in *Where in America's Past is Carmen Sandiego*, as well as *Where in Time*. . . . Like the *SIM* series of simulations, these programs have been commercial successes and are sold in most computer stores that carry software. There is also a complete line of Carmen Sandiego merchandise (mugs, shirts, etc.) and even a television game show based on the concept. Kids may well know about Carmen without realizing that it all started with a computer game. Magee (1991) describes a teaching unit built around Carmen.

The Game Controversy

Proponents of instructional games stress that they provide yet another instructional strategy for the teacher that has been a proven motivator. They have the flexibility to be used effectively with simple drill-and-practice type activities or may be designed to foster higher-level cognitive processes such as analyzing relationships or synthesizing previous learning when faced with new situations. Such analysis and synthesis can greatly enhance retention of learning.

Opponents focus on the potential for abuse that exists when games are permitted in the classroom. While learning is the desired outcome, play may become the dominant goal for the student. This is especially true in situations where the game

The slave-based economy of the South provided agricultural products such as cotton, sugar and tobacco to northeastern states and Europe.

READ MORE

SOUTH

SEARCH   RECORDS   MAP   LAUNCH

1801 – 1825

Figure 9.4. United States history is the basis for a *Carmen Sandiego* Mystery.

is a reward, rather than the essence of the activity, although we do not classify such programs as instructional games. Clearly, any game should be carefully scrutinized for its likely educational value prior to using it in the classroom.

Problem Solving

Concern over student development of critical-thinking skills has led to the creation of many pieces of CAI that are designated as problem solving. There now appear to be two distinct types of software in this category.

Types of Problem-Solving Software

The first and oldest type of problem-solving CAI is based on the view that there are generic problem-solving skills that can be learned in one environment and then applied successfully in others. Examples include searching for patterns, alternate strategies, process-of-elimination, and trial-and-error. A second and more recently developed type is software that is itself a problem-solving tool focused on a specific domain and its unique requirements. Unlike the generic tool software you learned about previously in this book, tool CAI is designed to focus your attention and thinking on the skills, concepts, and procedures needed to solve specific types of problems, as well as providing support for the mechanics of each.

Examples of Problem-Solving Software

The Incredible Laboratory illustrates the generic-skills development approach. The learner creates monsters in a "science" lab, using such chemicals as alien oil, yellow rind, and blue goo. Each chemical produces a different part of the monster, but all go into a beaker at the same time, after which the monster appears. The problem is to determine which chemical produces which of six variations in each of five body parts. At higher levels of difficulty, the effects of a chemical change each time the program is run. The learner needs to use both trial-and-error and process-of-elimination skills to solve the problem. There is also a challenge mode in which players alternately add to the beaker chemicals that each hopes the other has not investigated. Three monsters appear, one of which is the product of the combined chemicals. The players must determine which monster they produced.

The tool type of problem-solving CAI is illustrated by *SemCalc*, the semantic calculator. Students use *SemCalc* as they work on story problems in mathematics. The concept is highly significant, because many students find word problems extremely difficult and never learn to solve them well. One common error is to focus on the numbers in the problem. *SemCalc* directs the user's attention to the referent, the unit to which the number refers, such as apples or pounds. The software prompts the user to enter numbers *and* referents. After the learner selects a com-

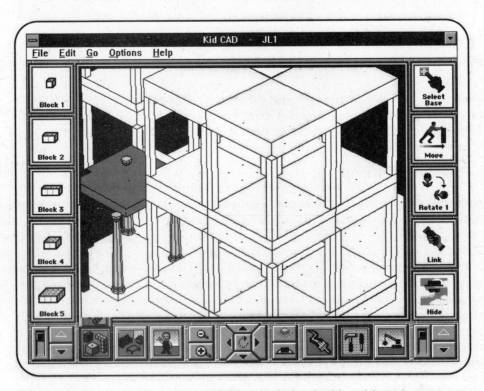

Figure 9.5. KidCAD challenges children to design, build, and furnish structures.

putation process, say, addition, the program guides consideration of whether the selected process will yield a result with a common referent. If not, it asks whether a conversion of units is possible. This goes beyond feet to inches to include, say, converting both apples and oranges to fruit!

Math Connections: Algebra II offers learners a wide array of tools and objects from which to build concrete representations of expressions, matrices, tables, graphs, even conic sections. Next students connect objects into networks to visualize and explore relationships. Free exploration is encouraged, and instant results promote experimentation. *Technology & Learning* magazine (November/December 1992) honored this product with a 1992–1993 Award of Excellence.

The Problem-Solving Controversy

Interest in helping students acquire and develop problem-solving skills is high among educators. Concern over actual student abilities in this area figures prominently in many critiques of American education and in the education reform movement. Advocates of problem-solving software assert that it contributes to enhancing student skills.

Critics question whether problem-solving software can deliver on its promise. The assumption that any skills developed will indeed transfer is open to question. Maddux et al. (1992, p. 37) suggest that automatic transfer is doubtful, but that there may be general groups of problem-solving skills for which proper teaching strategies can facilitate transfer across applications.

Using Problem-Solving Software (Applicability in the Curriculum)

Most of the problem-solving tool CAI available to date is for various aspects of mathematics. In addition to *SemCalc*, Sunburst offers packages for algebra (*The Function Supposer*, *The Function Analyzer*), geometry (*The Geometric Supposer* series), graphing (*Green Blobs and Graphing Equations*), even calculus (*A Graphic Approach to Calculus*). If any of these is appropriate to your teaching, your first and foremost task is to master use of the software yourself. Once you understand its operation and capabilities, you will have little difficulty finding applications to your teaching, whether for individual student use or to enhance group learning experiences.

With all previous types of CAI, curriculum fit is largely a conscious effort of the teacher to integrate software use into lesson plans. Generic problem-solving CAI is obviously not curriculum specific, making it difficult to determine where, when, and how to integrate it into lessons. We question the value of such software if it will be used only by an individual teacher. It appears that such software requires a commitment across grade levels and content areas to maximize its potential impact. General problem-solving skills do not develop quickly, nor are they limited to one field. To the extent that they can be taught at all, the task should be undertaken on a broad scale throughout the school district, at least K–8, if not K–12. A team of teachers should develop a scope and sequence for problem solving, then monitor and assist the classroom teachers who work with the software.

An Alternative Taxonomy

Thus far, our consideration of CAI has been guided by a traditional taxonomy of CAI formats. We noted at the outset that not all software was easy to classify. There are several reasons for the difficulty.

Consider a product called the *Math Shop* series. In the producer's advertising literature, you can find the following terms: problem-solving, beyond drill and practice, "real world" situations, and simulations. Assuming that each of those conjures up a particular expectation for you, how do you envision the entire product? Do you think it can really be all of the above?

Caputi (1991) was concerned with the labels so widely applied to CAI. Her experience convinced her that regardless of her own understanding of what, say, tutorial, meant, there was no assurance that software producers used the term in the same way. In fact, she found numerous examples of "mis-labeled" software, especially products that seemed to fit the drill and practice type, yet were labeled otherwise, possibly because of the negative connotation of the term *drill and practice*.

In addition, Caputi believed that existing CAI labels reflected the behaviorist origins of CAI at a time when cognitivism is gaining ground as the dominant view of learning. She set out to develop a new taxonomy for CAI, based not on the external form of the software, but rather the underlying instructional strategy; not the computer's activity, but the learner's. The result was the *Learner-Centered Taxonomy of Instructional Software*.

Briefly, the taxonomy classifies software according to the extent to which it supplants the learner's own mental processes (metacognition). The metacognition dimension of the taxonomy has three levels: program-initiated (the software is in control), guided (the software suggests, but does not require actions), and learner-initiated (the learner directs and controls the interaction). Each may be divided according to the primary cognitive processes involved: organizing (semantic encoding and elaboration), rehearsal (practice), or response organization (assessment). Finally, the focus of the content presentation may be topic-oriented, domain-oriented, or operation-oriented. Figure 9.6 illustrates this taxonomy.

The Learner-Centered Taxonomy is new and awaits further refinement. One problem is a lack of handy terms, such as tutorial or game, to apply to the 27 possible categories. The sheer number of categories is also daunting compared to the past. However, Caputi's arguments about the weaknesses of the traditional classification system are sound and the goal of providing an identification system upon which educators could better rely when selecting and evaluating CAI is laudable. Watch for further developments.

What the Research Shows

Computer-assisted instruction has been used for over 30 years. Although the emphasis in educational computing has shifted to application software tools, as presented in Part Two of this book, CAI remains popular among educators. The

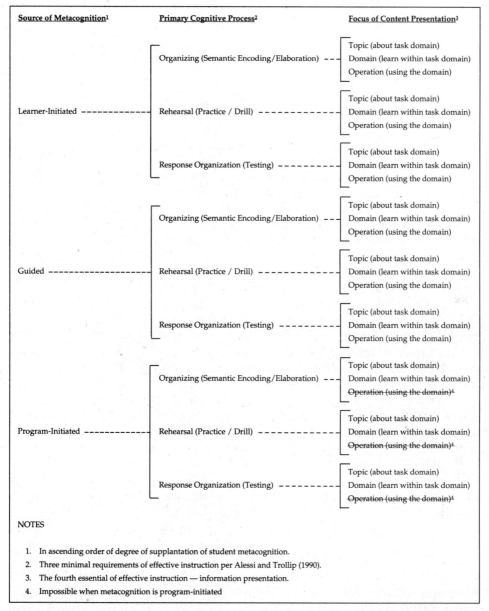

Source of Metacognition[1]	Primary Cognitive Process[2]	Focus of Content Presentation[3]
Learner-Initiated	Organizing (Semantic Encoding/Elaboration)	Topic (about task domain) Domain (learn within task domain) Operation (using the domain)
	Rehearsal (Practice / Drill)	Topic (about task domain) Domain (learn within task domain) Operation (using the domain)
	Response Organization (Testing)	Topic (about task domain) Domain (learn within task domain) Operation (using the domain)
Guided	Organizing (Semantic Encoding/Elaboration)	Topic (about task domain) Domain (learn within task domain) Operation (using the domain)
	Rehearsal (Practice / Drill)	Topic (about task domain) Domain (learn within task domain) Operation (using the domain)
	Response Organization (Testing)	Topic (about task domain) Domain (learn within task domain) Operation (using the domain)
Program-Initiated	Organizing (Semantic Encoding/Elaboration)	Topic (about task domain) Domain (learn within task domain) ~~Operation (using the domain)[4]~~
	Rehearsal (Practice / Drill)	Topic (about task domain) Domain (learn within task domain) ~~Operation (using the domain)[4]~~
	Response Organization (Testing)	Topic (about task domain) Domain (learn within task domain) ~~Operation (using the domain)[4]~~

NOTES

1. In ascending order of degree of supplantation of student metacognition.
2. Three minimal requirements of effective instruction per Alessi and Trollip (1990).
3. The fourth essential of effective instruction — information presentation.
4. Impossible when metacognition is program-initiated

Figure 9.6. The Learner-Centered Taxonomy of Instructional Software, based on Caputi (1991).

number of available CAI packages continues to grow, especially for Macintosh and MS-DOS computers as producers wind down their support of the Apple II (Kinnaman, 1991). Because CAI use is widespread, it is vital that you consider what researchers have learned about its impact. Consistent findings make some conclusions clear, but inconsistency is the hallmark of other aspects. An overview is presented below.

Subject-Matter Achievement

Numerous studies over many years have compared achievement scores of students using CAI to scores obtained in regular instruction. Typically, the results have shown that CAI produces greater achievement or shows no significant difference, meaning that it is at least equally effective (e.g., Alderman, 1979; Bracey, 1982; Burns and Bozeman, 1981; Fisher, 1983; Glenn, 1988; Goode, 1988; Krein and Maholm, 1990; Kulik, Bangert, and Williams, 1983; Magidson, 1978; Splittgerber, 1979; Swan, Guerrero, Mitrani, and Schoener, 1990).

In a 1985 overall assessment of the research, Roblyer (1985, p. 20) concluded that "computer-based instruction achieves consistently higher effects than other instructional treatments to which it is compared in experimental situations, but the effects usually range from small to moderate in magnitude." She further noted that the greatest effects appeared to occur at the elementary grade levels, with achievement decreasing as grade level increased. Finally, effects were not uniform across all curricular areas, with mathematics typically benefiting more and reading/language arts less. She did note, however, that newer studies seemed to be yielding greater effects and that much research remained to be done.

More recently, Roblyer, Castine, and King (1988) conducted a meta-analysis of studies dated from 1980 on. Of the content areas reviewed, CAI appeared to have the greatest effect in science. The authors noted, however, that this finding was based on only a few studies and must be interpreted cautiously. Consistent with previous findings, mathematics skill learning appeared to profit most from CAI, while reading skills continued to profit least. In the area of science, the authors reported that the most effective type of application was simulations for unstructured work. When CAI applications were used for drill in science, much lower effects were determined. In reading, tutorial applications achieved higher effects than any other software type, while all applications for mathematics were found to be about equally effective.

Learning Retention and Speed

In addition to positive achievement gains, Kulik et al. (1983) found that CAI improved retention of learning. They reported that four of five studies investigating retention over a period of from two to six months showed greater retention by those students who used CAI. These differences were not, however, large enough to be statistically significant. Robyler (1985, p. 24) concluded that "data lend little support to the belief that computer-based instruction enhances retention."

Computer-assisted instruction has often decreased the *time* that students require to learn material. Reports of the time saved range from 10 percent (Blaschke and Sweeney, 1977) to 25 percent (Krein and Maholm, 1990) to 40 percent (Fisher, 1983) to an incredible 88 percent (Lunetta, 1972). Dence (1980) also cited a variety of studies showing significant time savings to achieve the same level of mastery.

Attitudes

In addition to investigating the impact of CAI on cognitive growth, researchers have studied its impact on affective outcomes. Kulik et al. (1983) reviewed ten studies related to student attitudes toward the subject matter. In eight of these studies, students who used CAI had more positive attitudes toward the content than those in regular classes. However, the differences were statistically significant in only three cases. Kulik, Kulik, and Cohen (1980), Baer (1988), McLeod (1988), and Hatfield (1991) all reported positive affective value attributable to CAI.

Roblyer, Castine, and King (1988) also found generally positive attitudinal outcomes. They argued, however, that the attitudinal impact of CAI is greater toward the computer itself than toward learning the subject matter. In addition, they found little evidence that positive attitudes about computers contributed to better attitudes toward school and academic achievement.

Westrom and Shaban (1992) studied the intrinsic motivational effects of an instructional game compared to a noninstructional game. Although the motivation for the noninstructional game started out higher, it dropped significantly with experience, whereas that of the instructional game actually increased slightly. The researchers also found no gender differences, which supports the use of games to motivate all learners, contrary to some other gender studies. Westrom and Shaban suggest that CAI could be made more effective by greater attention to factors enhancing motivation.

Problem Solving

Dudley-Marling and Owston (1988) critically assessed the potential of CAI to teach general-thinking and problem-solving skills. The investigators wrote, "In the absence of any significant research literature evaluating the claims of the developers of problem-solving software, the CAI approach . . . can be evaluated only in terms of the general research and theory in problem solving. Based on this literature, it is highly unlikely that the use of CAI will lead to the development of generalizable problem-solving skills. . . . " They cautioned that this does not mean such software is useless, but rather that there are no simple solutions to developing higher-order skills. They did not test their views.

Funkhouser and Dennis (1992) studied the effects of software on the problem-solving skills of students in high school geometry and second-year algebra. They selected software from Sunburst (*Building Perspective* and *Blockers and Finders*) after extensive efforts to identify products that seemed most likely to produce the claimed effect. The control group had lab activities, the experimental group used the CAI. GPA was used as a covariate to control for base academic ability. On measures of problem-solving skills, the control group achieved significantly better results in solving word problems. When looking only at the geometry subgroup, the experimental group outperformed the control group on spatial ability. Both results were consistent with the skills most evident in the traditional instruction and software, respectively. The researchers also gathered term test data on all subjects, their regular tests that were written by the textbook publishers. The students who had used the CAI performed significantly better overall in their course than did the control-group students. Thus, time "taken" for problem solving actually enhanced the basic expected performance.

Duffield (1990) also assessed the outcomes of using popular software designated as problem solving, specifically Sunburst's *The King's Rule* and *Safari Search*. She concluded that the software was of limited value in developing problem-solving skills.

A meta-analysis of studies reporting cognitive performance (Liao, 1992) found that 23 of 31 studies favored the CAI group over a control group. Overall, "students who had CAI experiences scored about 18 percentile points higher on various cognitive ability tests than (students without CAI)." Of 29 variables examined, six contributed significantly to the outcome, showing that CAI had an impact beyond its specific content. Cognitive performance included such things as planning skills, reasoning, logical thinking, and transfer.

At-Risk Students

Ross, Smith, and Morrison (1991) studied at-risk seventh graders who had participated in grades 5 and 6 in intensive computer-based learning experiences in the Apple Classroom of Tomorrow (ACOT) program. Subjects were matched with others from the same elementary school who had not been part of ACOT. Treating the complex ACOT program as a whole, comparisons examined attitudes toward school, teacher evaluations, grades, computer skills, and standardized test scores. On the California Achievement Test, the ACOT group was significantly superior to the control group in mathematics, and the advantage in reading approached significance. Also, despite relatively little computer use in seventh grade, ACOT students seemed to retain their keyboarding skills. Less encouraging was the finding that, overall, ACOT students were indistinguishable from others in their school, when achievement was defined as the grades earned. There were also no attitudinal differences. The researchers concluded that the ACOT students remained at-risk in the seventh grade, as did the controls. In a potentially significant finding for all schools that use computers, they suggest that achievements during the ACOT period were rapidly lost by the lack of on-going computer use and access after the two year experiment. Continuity of experience appears to be critical, suggesting need for an articulated curriculum.

Problems with Traditional Research

One might expect some relatively definitive results from research on CAI, given more than 20 years of experience. This is not, however, exactly true. There are two major problems that trouble many who read existing research.

First, many CAI studies were conducted prior to the availability of microcomputers. While Roblyer (1985) maintained that the similarities in instructional features are great enough to dispel concern, many disagree. Surprisingly few *thorough* studies have been reported that are based on microcomputer environments.

Second is the question of thoroughness or, more broadly, methodology. Roblyer (1985, p. 22) wrote of two 1984 studies, "Descriptions of the study methods do not give sufficient information to determine if methodological flaws are present. And, perhaps because the reports themselves are so brief, the conclusions drawn by the researchers do not always seem supported by the results presented."

In their meta-analysis, Roblyer et al. (1988) reported that of some 200 studies initially reviewed for consideration, 38 studies and 44 dissertations were included in the analysis. The remainder were omitted because of insufficient data or methodological flaws. This is a serious indictment against the quality of research being performed. Our observation is that much of what passes for "research" in CAI is actually anecdotal reports of experiences that in no way resemble experimental research. Clearly, there is a need for more and better research into the outcomes of computer intervention in the instructional process.

New Research Directions

The results of relatively traditional investigations into the effects of CAI on student learning have been mixed in many aspects. Still, as you read previously, there is solid evidence that CAI can foster achievement gains and that it is at least as good as traditional instruction. CAI has a place in education alongside many other uses of the computer. The question is not whether to use computers in the schools, but how best to use them.

If you accept this as the starting point, then the direction of research must change. Important questions become: What are the most appropriate tactics/ strategies/approaches, and so forth, for which types of CAI users under what circumstances? Studies may then compare, say, alternate CAI conditions to see which is more effective, rather than comparing the computer to traditional teaching. Willis (1991) cogently discussed the "error" of the social-science research base, including the flaws of comparison studies. Salomon (Polin, 1992) suggested a need to direct research attention to patterns of groups and interactions, making the classroom the unit of analysis, not individuals and variables.

Polin (1991) provides a fascinating introduction to what could become another research base—the theories of the Russian scholar Vygotsky (1896–1934), which contradict Piaget's developmental concepts. After finding disappointing results in transfer from CAI to concrete tasks based on a fairly typical CAI simulation, Russian researchers tried a different approach that permitted learners to work with a faulty model that reflected the students' own ideas. Attempts to apply the faulty model led to failure, but in over 60 percent of the cases, students quickly self-corrected their concepts. Where investigations such as this may lead is unpredictable.

Some researchers suggest that it is time for an entire paradigm shift away from the objectivism of behavioral and cognitive psychology to constructivism. The latter holds that "knowing is a process of actively interpreting and constructing individual knowledge representations" (Jonassen, 1991, p. 5). This view partially may explain a shift in interest toward multimedia and hypermedia, which you will meet in the next chapter.

A Sampler of Studies

Traditional CAI research was based largely on media-comparison studies such as achievement gain, attitudes, and so forth for CAI versus standard classroom instruction. We can only give you a small taste of the newer research that accepts effectiveness of CAI as a starting point.

Dalton and Goodrum (1991) investigated the effects of three pre-testing strategies on learner motivation and achievement. Randomly assigned groups took either no pre-test, a full-length pre-test, or an adaptive pre-test that concluded as soon as it diagnosed nonmastery. Learners in the adaptive group scored significantly higher on the achievement post-test. The other two groups did not differ significantly. The full pre-test group showed significantly lower motivation than either of the other groups, which themselves did not differ significantly.

In a study of computer simulations, Gorrell (1992) analyzed changes in learners' responses to the classroom-management situations presented as they tried to improve their performance over multiple tries. While results were positive, Gorrell concluded that the primary learning gains were "best understood as being associated with increased practice rather than with the development of integrated schematic knowledge." In other words, evidence of higher-order thinking skills development was lacking.

In a study of a small group of at-risk urban minority high school students, Signer (1991) found achievement gains on re-tests as well as increased motivation, self-confidence, and self-discipline. Contrary to other studies of female self-confidence with computers, this study found its female subjects were highly confident of their abilities to use a computer.

Morrison, Ross, and Baldwin (1992) investigated two adaptive CAI strategies that might have beneficial effects on motivation and cognition. One was the amount of instructional support provided in a lesson, and the other was variable contexts so that the material might better relate to student backgrounds and interests. The researchers hypothesized that elementary-age children would benefit in achievement from context choices, but would lack ability to make effective use of control over instructional support. As expected, students able to control the level of instructional support performed least well on the post-test. The expected benefits of context choice did not materialize, however. Subjects varied their choice of context across lessons, rather than selecting those most relevant to them as had been expected. Although achievement gains did not result from the flexibility provided, subjects reported positive attitudes about the strategies.

Hooper and Hannafin (1991) studied the effects of student ability, learning accountability, and cooperative work on achievement, interaction, and instructional efficiency using CAI. They were concerned that, although highly adaptive software is clearly desirable, it is difficult to find because it is difficult and costly to create. The results of 185 studies on achievement under cooperative versus competitive conditions favored cooperation. The researchers assigned sixth grade and seventh grade students to heterogeneous or homogeneous pairs based on ability. The pairs were then designated as having either group or individual accountability for mastering the content. Results showed a significant positive correlation between cooperation and achievement for heterogeneous pairs. They also found that low-ability students interacted more in heterogeneous pairs, but did not actually learn more. Also of interest was the finding that students who collaborated on quizzes scored higher on the post-test than those who completed quizzes individually. The effect size was, however, rather small. In addition, the study found that high-ability student pairs learned most efficiently, while low-ability pairs were least efficient. In heterogeneous groups, the low-ability student benefited from, but slowed the progress of the high-ability student.

Hooper and Hannafin considered their study to be preliminary and did not offer specific suggestions of its practical ramifications, nor shall we attempt to do so. Our purpose in detailing this study is only to show you how very different current research directions are from those of a short time ago. If you wish to obtain and read other, newer studies, consider some of the following: Mattoon (1991); Morrison et al. (1992); Pridemore and Klein (1991), and Reglin (1990).

Summary

Computer-assisted instruction has existed for over three decades. Its potential has been the subject of much speculation and prediction from the beginning. Early laboratory studies were sufficiently encouraging to keep interest alive until the microcomputer made CAI economically viable to use with large numbers of students. Today, CAI is used to teach a wide range of skills and knowledge, from relatively simple stimulus–response learning to complex forms of problem solving. CAI offers a higher level of interaction than group instruction, is inherently flexible, and may better meet individual student needs.

Traditionally, CAI has been classified into the categories of drill-and-practice, tutorials, simulations, instructional games, and more recently, problem solving. Drill-and-practice software has been the most widely available and used. Now, quality simulations and problem-solving software are available in greater quantity and have been well received. They appear to use the power of the computer more effectively and often permit instruction that was previously impractical or impossible.

One major problem with our common labels for CAI is that there is no standard definition of each nor is there any standard for applying them to specific software products. Mislabeling is common and may lead to inappropriate purchases or even misuse of the product. The Learner-Centered Taxonomy of Instructional Software is an effort to classify CAI based on the learner's metacognitive processing, rather than the activity of the computer itself. It may offer a more useful way to look at CAI.

Research findings suggest that outcomes of CAI depend on many factors and have not been equal at all levels or in all fields, as was once widely hoped. Under the right circumstances, CAI has shown positive achievement gains, learning in shorter periods of time than traditional instruction, longer retention of content learned, and a more positive attitude on the part of the student toward the learning process. These results are encouraging and provide support for the use of CAI in our classrooms. Much research is still needed to learn how best to apply the computer to instruction.

Many of the research studies to date have been comparison studies, seeking to establish the value of CAI vis-à-vis traditional instructor-led classes. Newer studies assume that CAI is a viable learning medium and focus on alternative approaches or strategies. The goal is to investigate what approaches work best with which types of learners under what circumstances. Other new research directions rest on different theoretical bases such as the non-Piagetian psychology of Vygotsky and constructivism in lieu of behaviorism or cognitive psychology.

The best advice available to those who wish to use CAI in their classrooms is to be cautious about expectations. CAI is not an automatic route to learning; it is not a stand-alone resource. Rather, teachers must devise ways to carefully *integrate* CAI into instruction. Gray (1988) presented concrete ways to enhance learning from CAI. Of critical importance are "debriefing" strategies, including role playing, reaction papers, compare and contrast, visual summaries, panel discussions, software evaluation, and noncomputer simulation. All are means for integrating computers and instruction. Viewed in this way, as yet another learning tool, CAI can assume a vital role in our schools.

Chapter 9 Activities

1. For the grade level you teach or plan to teach, select *one* content area (e.g., social studies or science) and determine what CAI programs are available in your school. Review them with the intent of determining whether they are drill and practice, tutorials, simulations, games, or problem-solving programs.
2. Review the available drill and practice and tutorial programs, using the suggested characteristics of good software presented in this chapter. You may want to set up a data file for each program, including such information as name, appropriate grade level, and strengths and weaknesses of each program.
3. Examine the CAI material available in your school or school district and determine what unit(s) of your curriculum would be most appropriate for the material. You may want to add this information to the files suggested in item 2.

4. As you examine various CAI products, try to categorize them using the new Learner-Centered Taxonomy. Does this cause you to see their potential differently?

5. Actually try a CAI program with a group of your students. How did it work for the slow learner? How about the gifted child? Discuss the software with the children to determine their feelings about its use. What did *they* see as strengths and weaknesses?

6. Work your way through any available computer simulation. Can you place it into one of the four types presented? How would you rate the simulation for motivation? For entertainment? What would the student minimally have to know before use would be profitable? Design a lesson plan for using a simulation.

7. Examine any available CAI package that claims to teach problem-solving skills. Begin by carefully examining the accompanying documentation. Can you place it within the paradigm presented? Where might the package "fit" in the curriculum? Does the producer encourage use of the package alone, or is there evidence of concern for the total context of problem-solving instruction?

8. Read at least five CAI research articles published since 1990. Which of the new directions in research do they exemplify, or do they set other directions themselves? Can you find a traditional "comparison" study in the recent literature?

Bibliography

Alderman, D. I. "Evaluation of the TICCIT Computer-Assisted Instruction System in the Community College." *SIGCUE Bulletin*, 1979, *13*(3), pp. 5–17.

Alessi, S. M., and Trollip, S. R. *Computer-Based Instruction. Methods and Development*, 2nd ed. Englewood Cliffs, NJ: Prentice-Hall, 1990.

Baer, V. E. "Computers as Composition Tools: A Case Study." *Journal of Computer Based Instruction*, 1988, *15*(4), pp. 144–148.

Blaschke, C. L., and Sweeney, J. "Implementing Effective Educational Technology: Some Reflections." *Educational Technology*, January 1977, pp. 13–18.

Bracey, G. W. "Issues and Problems in Devising a Research Agenda for Special Education and Technology." Paper presented at Special Education Technology Research and Development Symposium. Sponsored by U.S. Department of Education, Washington, D.C., 1984.

Bracey, G. W. "What the Research Shows." *Electronic Learning*, November/December 1982, pp. 51–54.

Burns, P. K., and Bozeman, W. C. "Computer-Assisted Instruction and Mathematics Achievement: Is There a Relationship?" *Educational Technology*, January 1981, pp. 32–39.

Caputi, L. J. *A Taxonomy of Instructional Software for Nursing Education*. Unpublished doctoral dissertation, Northern Illinois University, 1991.

Collis, B. "Research Windows." *The Computing Teacher*, December/January 1987–1988, p. 6.

Colorado, R. "Computer-Assisted Instruction Research: A Critical Assessment." *Journal of Research on Computing in Education,* Spring 1988, *20*(3), pp. 226–233.

Dalton, D. W., and Goodrum, D. A. "The Effects of Computer-Based Pretesting Strategies on Learning and Continuing Motivation." *Journal of Research on Computing in Education,* Winter 1991, *24*(2), pp. 204–213.

Dence, M. "Toward Defining the Role of CAI: A Review." *Educational Technology,* November 1980, pp. 50–54.

Dudley-Marling, C., and Owston, R. D. "Using Microcomputers to Teach Problem Solving: A Critical Review." *Educational Technology,* July 1988, pp. 27–33.

Duffield, J. A. *Problem-Solving Software: What Does It Teach?* Paper presented at the Annual Meeting of the American Educational Research Association, Boston, MA, April 16, 1990. (ERIC document ED 329 239.)

Fish, M. C., and Feldmann, S. C. "Learning and Teaching in Microcomputer Classrooms: Reconsidering Assumptions." *Computers in the Schools,* 1990, *7*(3), pp. 87–96.

Fisher, G. "Where CAI Is Effective: A Summary of the Research." *Electronic Learning,* November/December 1983, pp. 82, 84.

Funkhouser, C., and Dennis, J. R. "The Effects of Problem-Solving Software on Problem-Solving Ability." *Journal of Research on Computing in Education,* Spring 1992, *24*(3), pp. 338–347.

Geisert, P., and Futrell, M. *Teachers, Computers, and Curriculum.* Boston: Allyn & Bacon, 1990.

Glenn, C. "Results of Using CAI to Improve Performance in Basic Skills Areas." *T.H.E. Journal,* June 1988, pp. 61–64.

Goode, M. "Testing CAI Courseware in Fifth- and Sixth-Grade Math." *T.H.E. Journal,* October 1988, pp. 97–100.

Gorrell, J. "Outcomes of Using Computer Simulations." *Journal of Research on Computing in Education,* Spring 1992, *24*(3), pp. 359–366.

Govier, H. "Microcomputers in Primary Education: A Survey of Recent Research." In Collis, B., "Research Windows." *The Computing Teacher,* December/January 1988–1989, p. 7.

Hatfield, M. M. "The Effect of Problem-Solving Software on Student's Beliefs About Mathematics: A Qualitative Study." *Computers in the Schools,* 1991, *8*(4), pp. 21–40.

Heck, R. H. "Secondary Science Teachers' Attitudes About Microcomputer-Based Laboratory Techniques: Instructional Uses and Needed Improvements." *Computers in the Schools,* 1990, *7*(3), pp. 71–86.

Hooper, S., and Hannafin, M. J. "The Effects of Group Composition on Achievement, Interaction, and Learning Efficiency During Computer-Based Cooperative Instruction." *Educational Technology Research & Development,* 1991, *39*(3), pp. 27–40.

Jacobsen, P. "Save the Cities! SimCity in Grades 2–5." *The Computing Teacher,* October 1992, *20*(2), pp. 14–15.

Johnson, T. R., and Geller, D. M. "Experimental Evidence on the Impacts of Computer-Assisted Instruction in the Job Corps Program." *Evaluation Review,* February, 1992, *16*(1), pp. 3–7.

Kinnaman, D. E. "Newsline." *Technology & Learning,* October 1991, *12*(2), p. 8.

Krein, T. J., and Maholm, T. R. "CBT Has the Edge in a Comparative Study." *Performance & Instruction,* August 1990, pp. 22–24.

Kulik, J. A., Bangert, R. L., and Williams, G. W. "Effects of Computer-Based Teaching on Secondary School Students." *Journal of Educational Psychology,* *75*(1), 1980, pp. 19–26.

Kulik, J. A., Kulik, C. C., and Cohen, P. A. "Effectiveness of Computer-Based College Teaching: A Meta-Analysis of Findings." *Review of Educational Research,* 1980, *50*(4), pp. 525–544.

Leeds, M., Davidson, R., and Gold, S. "Computer-Assisted Instruction and Developmental Studies: An Analysis of Student Performance." *Journal of Educational Technology Systems,* 1991–1992, *20*(1), pp. 73–79.

Liao, Y-K. "Effects of Computer-Assisted Instruction on Cognitive Outcomes: A Meta-Analysis." *Journal of Research on Computing in Education,* Spring 1992, *24*(3), pp. 367–380.

Lunetta, V. N. "The Design and Evaluation of a Series of Computer Simulated Experiments for Use in High School Physics." Dissertation, University of Connecticut, 1972. *Dissertation Abstracts International* 33:2785A.

Magee, D. "Carmen Sandiego & World GeoGraph: A Teaching Unit." *The Computing Teacher,* November 1991, *19*(3), pp. 31–32.

Maddux, C. D., Johnson, D. L., and Willis, J. W. *Educational Computing. Learning with Tomorrow's Technologies.* Boston, MA: Allyn & Bacon, 1992.

Magidson, E. M. "Trends in Computer-Assisted Instruction." *Educational Technology,* April 1978, pp. 5–63.

Malone, T. W. "Toward a Theory of Intrinsically Motivating Instruction." *Cognitive Science,* Vol. 4, 1981, pp. 333–369.

Mattoon, J. S., et al. "Learner Control Versus Computer Control in Instructional Simulation." Paper presented at the Annual Convention of the Association for Educational Communications and Technology, Orlando, FL, February 13–17, 1991. (ERIC document ED 334 995.)

McGinley, R. C. "Start Them Off With Games!" *The Computing Teacher,* November 1991, *19*(3), p. 49.

McLeod, D. B. "Affective Issues in Mathematics Problem Solving: Some Theoretical Considerations." *Journal for Research in Mathematics Education,* 1988, *19*(2), pp. 134–141.

Merrill, M. D., Schneider, E. W., and Fletcher, K. A. *TICCIT.* Englewood Cliffs, NJ: Educational Technology Publications, 1980.

Morrison, G. R., Ross, S. M., and Baldwin, W. "Learner Control of Context and Instructional Support in Learning Elementary School Mathematics." *Educational Technology Research & Development,* 1992, *40*(1), pp. 5–13.

Polin, L. "Looking for Love in All the Wrong Places. (Research Windows)." *The Computing Teacher,* October 1992, *20*(2), pp. 6–7.

Polin, L. "Vygotsky at the Computer: A Soviet View of 'Tools' for Learning. (Research Windows)." *The Computing Teacher,* August/September 1991, *19*(1), pp. 25–27.

Pridemore, D. R., and Klein, J. D. "Control of Feedback in Computer-Assisted Instruction." *Educational Technology Research & Development,* 1991, *39*(4), pp. 27–32.

Reglin, G. L. "The Effects of Individualized and Cooperative Computer Assisted Instruction on Mathematics Achievement and Mathematics Anxiety for Prospective Teachers." *Journal of Research on Computing in Education,* Summer 1990, *22*(4), pp. 404–412.

Roblyer, M. D. *Measuring the Impact of Computers in Instruction: A Non-Technical Review of Research for Educators.* Washington, DC: Association for Educational Data Systems, 1985.

Roblyer, M. D., Castine, W. H., and King, F. J. "Assessing the Impact of Computer Based Instruction: A Review of Recent Research." *Computers in the Schools,* 1988, *5*(3/4).

Ross, S. M., Smith, L. S., and Morrison, G. R. "The Longitudinal Influences of Computer-Intensive Learning Experiences on At-Risk Elementary Students." *Educational Technology Research & Development,* 1991, *39*(4), pp. 33–46.

Signer, B. R. "CAI and At-Risk Minority Urban High School Students." *Journal of Research on Computing in Education,* Winter 1991, *24*(2), pp. 189–203.

Simonson, M. R., and Thompson, A. *Educational Computing Foundations.* Columbus, OH: Merrill, 1990.

Splittgerber, F. L. "Computer Based Instruction: A Revolution in the Making?" *Educational Technology*, January 1979, pp. 20–26.

Steinberg, E. R. *Computer-Assisted Instruction. A Synthesis of Theory, Practice and Technology.* Hillsdale, NJ: Lawrence Erlbaum, 1991a.

Steinberg, E. R. *Teaching Computers to Teach*, 2nd ed. Hillsdale, NJ: Lawrence Erlbaum, 1991b.

Swan, K., Guerrero, F., Mitrani, M., and Schoener, J. "Honing in on the Target: Who Among the Educationally Disadvantaged Benefits Most From What CBI?" *Journal of Research on Computing in Education*, Summer 1990, 22(4), pp. 381–403.

Thompson, A., Simonson, M., and Hargrave, C. *Educational Technology: A Review of the Research.* Washington, DC: Association for Educational Communications and Technology, 1992.

Westrom, M., and Shaban, A. "Intrinsic Motivation in Microcomputer Games." *Journal of Research on Computing in Education*, Summer 1992, 24(4), pp. 433–445.

Willis, J. "Research and Instructional Technology: What We Have and What We Need." *Computers in the Schools*, 1991, 8(4), pp. 115–133.

Woodward, J., Carnine, D., and Gersten, R. "Teaching Problem Solving Through Computer Simulation." *American Educational Research Journal*, 1988, 25(1), pp. 72–86.

Yates, B. C., and Moursund, D. "The Computer and Problem Solving: How Theory Can Support Classroom Practice." *The Computing Teacher*, December/January 1988–1989, pp. 12–16.

Chapter 10

Interactive Multimedia: A New World of Educational Software

This chapter describes an exciting development in educational computing: interactive multimedia (IMM). Although the concepts are not difficult to understand, there is considerable confusion over terminology, which we attempt to clarify. You will consider several hardware technologies that contribute to IMM applications. A brief look at software for IMM may be useful as you consider your own potential applications. Finally, consider with us some classroom applications of this new tool and what limited research findings tell educators about it.

Interactive Multimedia Environments

To begin consideration of interactive multimedia, let's explore its concepts and terminology in some detail.

Limitations of Traditional Tools

From its beginning, computing has been largely sequential and linear. Computers carry out instructions one by one. Databases organize and store information in a largely linear fashion. Although books cannot restrict your approach to reading them, how often do you read a book other than linearly? Even if you take chapters out of sequence, do you also read pages or paragraphs out of sequence? Perhaps in reference works, but not generally.

Think of what it is like to look for information in encyclopedias and other reference works. What happens when your reading brings up a topic you'd like to pursue further? Assuming that the same book even contains this related topic, how easily can you find it? Linearity is limiting when compared to the way in which the human mind interconnects the contents of its knowledge store.

Have you ever struggled to read a text because you encountered words that you did not know? Did you immediately look them up in a glossary or dictionary? Was a dictionary even at hand? Might it have helped if you had heard the words pronounced? Have you ever tried to understand a procedure or process based on a verbal description of it, perhaps accompanied by diagrams with arrows showing the action?

If you can relate to any of these limitations of traditional communications media, you will welcome the wonders of hyper environments.

Hyper Origins

In 1945, Vannevar Bush, an electrical engineer and science advisor to President Franklin D. Roosevelt, described an integrated workstation that he called memex. Memex was "a hypothetical, mechanical device that predated computers and that would use state-of-the-art photographic technology to manipulate, display, and interconnect information on microfiche" (Locatis, Letourneau, and Banvard, 1989, pp. 66–67). Conceptually, memex would emulate the human mind, but it never existed. (For an informative discussion of the mental analog for computer software, see Nelson and Palumbo, 1992).

In the early 1960s, Douglas Engelbart adapted Bush's concept to the computer. His oNLine System (NLS) provided the means to organize and retrieve text, as well as electronic mail and a teleconferencing facility. At about the same time, Ted Nelson created a literary system called Xanadu that allowed complex derivations of new material from existing text. It could trace the development of ideas by recording linkages and information transfers, and provide royalty payments to the original creators (Locatis, et al., 1989). Nelson coined the term *hypertext* to describe his system.

Hyper What?

In this context, the term *hyper* means the potential to move about within an environment without linear, sequential restrictions. A hyper environment consists of information in *nodes,* such as pages, notecards, computer screens, or even individual objects on a screen. Nodes are interrelated through *links,* as Figure 10.1 illustrates. You move about through a web of information by using these links (Grabinger, Dunlap, and Jonassen, 1992).

Hypertext

If the information in nodes of a hyper environment is (predominantly) text, it is termed *hypertext.* Hypertext can be as simple as pages (or screens) of text, each of which is "linked" to one or more others. Nelson attempted to demonstrate this in print form with his book *Computer Lib/Dream Machines* (1987). The concept becomes more concrete when implemented on a computer. Imagine an electronic encyclopedia or other reference work. A simple mouse click on an unfamiliar word could take you to a glossary entry, which itself contains links back to your starting point and on to other related items. If you assume the existence of *all* appropriate linkages, you should readily see the potential and power of such a system. Text need no longer be constrained by its basic, linear form, as Figure 10.2 illustrates.

Multimedia

Multimedia simply means any system that unites two or more media into a single product or presentation. Perhaps the earliest multimedia system was the movie theater in which a pianist played appropriate music to augment silent movies.

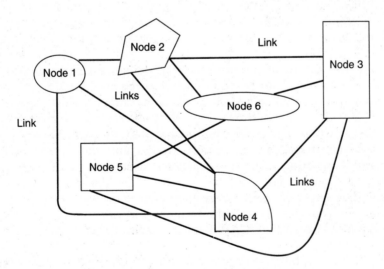

Figure 10.1. A hyper environment consists of interlinked nodes.

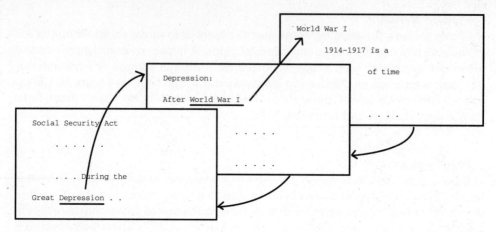

Figure 10.2. Concept of hypertext.

From this evolved the "talkie" and eventually television. Educators have long used sound filmstrips and slide-tape sets. All of these represent multimedia—materials that communicate through more than one sense.

What is *not* inherent in multimedia is the hyper element, or Bush's linkage concept. Multimedia can be just as linear as a book! Think about your experiences with filmstrips or slide sets. Have you ever seen either used in a nonlinear fashion? What happens if someone wants to see a previous frame or slide again? To back up (or jump ahead) requires going through the intervening frames, which may discourage users from doing so because it takes time and often disrupts the train of thought. Similarly, video and film are essentially linear. Their physical nature makes it difficult at best to locate particular segments. VCRs and film projectors are *not* random access devices. Furthermore, linkages imply interactivity between the user and the environment, which is also not inherent in multimedia (Blum, 1991; Magel, September 1992).

To clarify the nature of multimedia, consider an excellent product series: *The Voyage of the Mimi. Mimi* is based on a research expedition to study humpback whales. This multimedia package contains thirteen video segments that are adventures of the research party and thirteen documentary videos of visits to scientists at work. There are four independent software modules dealing with ecosystems, maps and navigation, whales and their environment, and the basics of computing. There are teacher and student guides, even a *Mimi* newsletter. (The popularity of the first *Voyage of the Mimi* led to production of two more.) The parts of this package are integrated by the way in which the teacher uses them. The computer is just one element and offers only rather standard computer-assisted instruction (CAI) that is related to the video lessons. There are no hyper elements.

Multimedia has become a buzzword for the 1990s, yet it is often used interchangeably with hypermedia. There is a distinction.

Hypermedia/Interactive Multimedia

Hypermedia is the integration of a computer and multimedia to produce the interactive, nonlinear hyper environment that is the current rage and seems certain to remain prominent. The nodes of a hypermedia environment contain some combination of text, graphics, sound, and video, which are interlinked and associated nonlinearly by the computer, as Bush envisioned. Imagine studying the Civil Rights Movement at your computer. As you read a basic article on the movement, you come to a reference to Martin Luther King's "I Have a Dream" speech. A mouse click brings up the text of the speech, with hypertext links to written explanations of specific words or context explanations. With another click you listen to Dr. King deliver the speech, or even see that event as a video plays on your screen! You are experiencing the power of hypermedia.

Commercially, many hypermedia products are labeled simply multimedia. For example, National Geographic calls its *Mammals* "a multimedia encyclopedia." In fact, it is a hypermedia encyclopedia. However, the term multimedia probably seems somehow more approachable, less "techie," and therefore more marketable. For now, there is no agreement upon the appropriate terminology for this type of learning material, no doubt because of its newness. In our view, hypermedia is the appropriate term, but we are also comfortable with *interactive multimedia* or IMM, which many writers use (e.g., Ambron and Hooper, 1988; Gill, 1992; Magel, September 1992). "Interactive multimedia" also can serve to differentiate such products from traditional television and other noninteractive, nonhyper environments.

Blum (1991) considers IMM to be the most exciting and creative interactive technology. Magel (September 1992, p. 97) reminds us that it is all rather new. "Interactive multimedia technology, the market's understanding of interactivity and multimedia and our understanding of the applications and design of effective interactive multimedia titles are all in their infancy." Yet the potential is so enormous that Moursund (1992) talks of IMM delivery systems as potential competitors for schools in the restructuring of education.

The Technologies of Interactive Multimedia

Beyond the basic definition of interactive multimedia, you should understand some of the technologies available, even needed, to create and support such a hypermedia environment (Figure 10.3). Currently, IMM systems must be assembled from various components, which we will describe. However, IBM announced in late 1992 that even its lowest-priced computers would incorporate at least basic multimedia components within two years (Scannell, 1992). Apple Computer also has moved in this direction.

Hardware

Let's look at four potential hardware technologies for an IMM system: compact discs, laserdiscs, *digital video interactive* (DVI) boards, and other digitizing boards.

Figure 10.3. Interactive multimedia components.

Because of their simplicity and familiarity, we will not discuss sound board or circuits, which are also parts of most systems.

Compact Disc

The audio compact disc is now a familiar medium, having led to the virtual demise of the LP record. The second most common CD format is CD-ROM, which was introduced in 1985. A CD-ROM stores data in a spiral track of digital pits that would be three miles long if unrolled. A CD can store any digital data—text, digital sound and graphics, even digital movies—with equal ease. Compact disc players use a laser beam to "read" the digital data. Because only a light beam contacts the disc, there is no wear and no loss of initial quality over time. Data can be accessed randomly, making possible highly interactive environments. Also, CD duplication is quick and easy, which helps to keep costs down (Magel, September 1992).

One CD-ROM can store about 650MB of data, equivalent to some 270,000 pages of text, 5000 Apple II 5.25" diskettes, 400 3.5" high-density diskettes, or seventeen 40MB hard disks! This is ideal for large databases, and because a duplicate disc costs about $1 to produce, initial production investments can be recouped quickly from savings on paper copies. Now, there is a major move to CD-based multimedia, which requires such large storage capacity. However, digital audio and video quickly can tax even CD-ROM capacity. If you are interested in how to produce a CD, see Rumfield (1991).

The CD-ROM is especially appealing for computer use because a CD player will fit in the same space as a floppy disk drive in most microcomputers, becoming just another drive on the system. The small discs are also easy to carry and store. On the less positive side, digital photographs and movies tend not to be as clear as analog media such as television. Stills tend to show some jaggedness or distortion and movies may be somewhat jerky, as if in slow motion. Some of these problems stem from the player hardware, not the discs, and are certain to be solved.

To use CD-ROM technology, your computer system must include a CD-ROM drive. Many Macintosh computers now come with internal CD drives. Increasingly, MS-DOS computers are being sold with the *MPC* (multimedia personal computer) designation. An MPC meets certain minimum specifications for the computer and includes a CD-ROM drive and a sound system (Salpeter, 1991). Otherwise, to upgrade any system, add a CD-ROM drive, an audio board, speakers, and software. Software is vital, because, unlike audio CD players, most CD-ROM players have few external controls. They are designed strictly for computer control.

Other CD formats also exist, though they have been slow to gain acceptance. The most prominent among them is *compact disc interactive* (CD-I). Although jointly introduced in 1985 by Philips and Sony, CD-I did not reach the consumer market until fall 1991. CD-I is a technical specification for storing text, data, animation, graphics, audio and video together on a compact disc and playing them back in synch on a standard television (Magel, September 1992). A CD-I system is self-contained, except for the TV receiver, and does not use an external computer as CD-ROM requires.

Standard audio CDs can hold about 75 minutes of music. CD-I audio can be true CD quality, but lower quality levels (e.g., LP, FM radio, telephone) make possible up to 19 hours of speech on one disc. Three quality levels of video range from slightly lower to higher than standard TV, including accommodation for eventual high-definition TV (HDTV). One CD-I disc can hold up to 7,000 high-resolution images, or 74 minutes of video with audio. Refer to Miller and Miller (1991) for full treatment of CD-I.

The CD-I has the backing of over 150 companies, including virtually all European and Japanese consumer electronics companies. The goal is standards that will make CD-I satisfactory for applications ranging from children's games to the most demanding industrial training. Both home and portable models exist, the latter with small built-in screens. There is even a boom-box style (Magel, September 1992). CD-I is still too new to assess from an educational perspective, but it appears to have considerable potential. Watch for developments.

What is the future of compact discs? MacKenzie (1992) clearly explains some of the problems and limitations of current CD technology. Ongoing CD directions include double-sided CDs, modifications to the laser angle and color, and increased data densities (Magel, September 1992). These changes should yield 180 minutes of motion video at double the current quality.

Laserdisc

Despite the appeal of CD-ROM, the laserdisc (or videodisc) remains the choice for the highest-quality randomly accessible motion video. Although the electronics of a videodisc player are similar to a CD player (i.e., a laser beam reads the disc), laserdiscs are analog, not digital. Image quality is better than VHS videotape. As audiophiles embraced the CD over tape and LPs, so movie connoisseurs favor laserdiscs over videocassettes. However, you cannot record your own laserdisc with inexpensive equipment. Original production can be costly, but duplicate discs cost little.

There are two distinct laserdisc formats: constant angular velocity (CAV) and constant linear velocity (CLV). Each side of a 12-inch CAV laserdisc can contain up to 54,000 individual photo-quality images. At normal playback speed of 30 frames per second, 54,000 frames provide 30 minutes of motion video. Laserdiscs have two or more audio channels to provide stereo sound, bilingual or multilingual narration, commentary on the video separate from the original sound track, or independent audio unrelated to the video. Many CAV laserdiscs contain a mix of single frames and motion segments. Because only a light beam touches the disc, single frames can be viewed for indefinite time periods with no quality loss or equipment damage, unlike videotape.

CLV discs are more like videotape in organization. They do not have individual frames, but rather, a stream of data marked with time codes. This difference essentially doubles the playing time for motion video to roughly one hour. While segments are still randomly accessible, still frames are not possible except with the most expensive laserdisc players, and there is less flexibility in sound tracks. The CLV format has made it possible to distribute inexpensive laserdisc versions of Hollywood motion pictures and popular TV series such as "National Geographic" and "NOVA."

In 1991, Texas became the first state to permit textbook funds to be spent on videodiscs as basic curriculum materials (Fritz, 1991, pp. 44–45). In the first year of this option, 65 percent of Texas elementary schools opted for videodiscs alone or in conjunction with texts. This suggests remarkable enthusiasm for the format, given its lack of familiarity among teachers.

Most videodisc players can be controlled by a computer. Videodiscs created expressly for education are being released regularly, many with controlling and supplementing software for easy access to their vast visual resources. When videodiscs are an essential element of a computer-based lesson, it is called *interactive video instruction* (IVI). Most IVI uses CAV laserdiscs for maximum flexibility. It often has multiple sound tracks to enhance the visual content or adapt it to a wider audience.

Digital Video Interactive

Yet another technology that seems likely to increase in popularity is digital video interactive (DVI). Unlike CDs and laserdiscs, DVI is not a visible hardware product. Rather, it is a multimedia encoding/decoding scheme built into special chips on circuit boards you install in your computer (Magel, September, 1992). Although still images are possible, DVI was designed to create, manipulate, store, and play digital motion video. You may purchase playback only boards or complete hardware to digitize your own video. The DVI boards connect to standard video sources, such as VCRs, and produce compressed digital video files with synchronized audio. The files are stored on a hard disk or, eventually, on CD-ROM.

According to Amthor (1992), DVI is to communication what word processing is to writing. Both involve "soft" documents that can be created quickly, edited at will, and shared over networks. With DVI, video can be cut and pasted, duplicated like any other file, even updated in pieces as needed at any time.

Analog video signals cannot be transmitted over digital networks, so traditional IVI requires a laserdisc player at each workstation (Amthor, 1992). With DVI, you can provide "interactive video" to all workstations on a network. In a technical first, the Jostens Learning Corporation worked with many vendors to combine several existing technologies to make networked digital multimedia a reality. The result is called Jostens Learning InterActive Media. Full-motion video and audio became accessible to all users on the network (Kinnaman, 1992).

Significantly, DVI technology is platform independent, meaning developers can produce the multimedia files once and use them for both MS-DOS and Macintosh products. IBM plans to put DVI on the motherboard of its microcomputers; eventually, DVI will be part of the central processing unit itself. With software that supports DVI, (e.g., *Multimedia Toolbook, Authorware Professional, LinkWay Live*, and *Harvard Graphics*) you can create final products that are essentially IVI without a laserdisc.

One key to DVI is image compression. Uncompressed, 30 seconds of video would require 600 MB of disk storage! Compression techniques reduce the size of files by storing only what has changed from one frame to the next. DVI supports two compression schemes. In your own computer, digitizing boards such as Intel's *ActionMedia II* produce adequate compression called real-time video (RTV) with near-VCR quality. *Production level video* (PLV) must be digitized by a lab and equals a VCR in quality with even greater compression. Neither yet rivals the video clarity of analog laserdiscs, but either is sufficient for most purposes. PLV can put up to 72 minutes of VCR-grade video on a single CD-ROM. A library of educational CDs in this format should develop soon.

For detailed information about DVI technology we suggest Luther (1991) and Bunsel and Morris (1992).

Digitizing Hardware

Images are a critical element of hypermedia, so producing them is a vital issue. Often what is desired is photographic level of realism, not just computer graphics. There are basically two ways to produce photo-quality images. The first is with a scanner, as discussed in Chapter 5. The other uses digitizing circuit boards installed in a computer. Such boards have video input jacks to connect to a video source, such as a laserdisc player, still video camera, or camcorder. DVI boards are one example, but with specific capabilities for digitizing real-time motion. Basic digitizing boards such as *Computer Eyes* and *VideoSpigot* produce either still images or less-than-real-time video in a relatively uncompressed file format. *Overlay cards* such as IBM's M-Motion Adapter display live digital video on a regular computer monitor. The card digitizes audio and video signals from a video source in real time and passes the running video on to the monitor. No files are created on the hard disk, so the original video source is always required. Single frames can be captured and saved to disk.

Your use of images need not be linked to your own artistic skill. Prices of digitizing boards are within reason for school budgets and offer many interesting application possibilities. If you can produce or find a suitable image in some video format, you can include it in your computer projects.

Software

Software is as essential as hardware to a computer-based interactive multi-hypermedia environment. Hypermedia software is typically also *object-oriented* software. Very simply, this means you create IMM software screen by screen, working directly on the screen. Each complete screen is made up of objects, most typically fields (for texts), pictures (for images, still or motion), and buttons to control action and provide the linkages among screens and objects within screens (Figure 10.4).

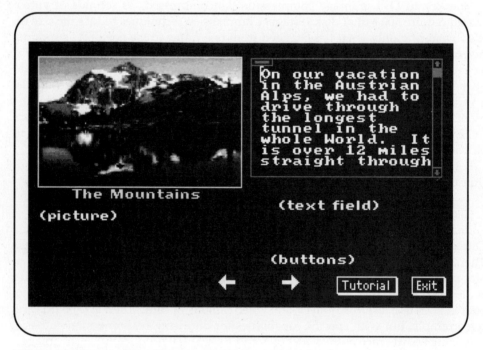

Figure 10.4. IMM screens consist of text fields, pictures, and/or buttons.

HyperCard

The first major software for hypermedia was *HyperCard* for the Macintosh, introduced in 1987. With *HyperCard*, a screen is called a *card*, and cards are organized into *stacks*. Potentially, any object on any card can be linked with a button to any other card in the same or any other stack. *HyperCard* has been promoted as an erector set, a type of software "Tinker toys." The idea is that it is simple enough for anyone to learn to use it to create applications easily. Many *HyperCard* stacks are available commercially and from vendors or bulletin boards as *public-domain* software (i.e., free) or *shareware* (i.e., try it free, pay the author if you continue to use it). *HyperCard* deserves much credit for triggering the explosive growth of hypermedia.

Beyond HyperCard

Because it was first on the market, *HyperCard* has become somewhat synonymous with hypertext or hypermedia. However, just as *Kleenex* is only one brand of facial tissue, *HyperCard* is only one software product. Most similar in concept and operation, but for MS-DOS computers, are *Linkway*, which is even simpler than *HyperCard*, and *ToolBook*, which runs only under Microsoft *Windows. Spinnaker Plus* is available for both Macintosh and Windows. Macintosh and Apple IIgs users can explore *HyperStudio*, while for the Apple II there is *TutorTech*. We'll look at the workings of some of these programs in more detail in Chapter 17 in the context of software authoring tools.

Adding Motion (*QuickTime*, and others)

Previously, you learned about hardware solutions to motion-video needs. You may realize that software solutions also exist. This is a fast-changing area of technology, but here's the situation as we write.

Once again, Apple has led the way in integrating motion video into software by adding an extension called *QuickTime* to the Macintosh operating system. *QuickTime* provides image compression and a control mechanism for external devices such as CD-ROM (Helsel, 1992). The MS-DOS options include Microsoft's *Audio Video Interleaved* (*AVI*), *QuickTime for Windows*, and IBM's *PhotoMotion* (Said, 1992; Salpeter, 1992; Streho, 1992). No special hardware is required to play videos in any of these formats, as they are simply digital files on the hard disk. (Of course, a digitizer was required to create the files. Also don't confuse these approaches with DVI, which requires hardware even for playback.)

While the advantages of a software-only approach to playback should be obvious, there are also some problems, regardless of platform. A major trade-off for the low cost of this approach is low-resolution video in small video windows, typically one sixteenth to one quarter of the full screen area. Video playback speed usually depends on the power of the computer (remember, this is a software-only solution), but typically is half of normal speed or less (Corcoran; 1992, Magel, September 1992). Digital video on a typical school computer is likely to be rather jerky.

Aside from the problems inherent in less-than-real-time video in small viewing windows at low resolution levels, the issue of video file size remains a serious concern. Quinlan and Borzo (1992) reported that *QuickTime* soon would reach a 25:1

compression ratio. That is still far too low to reduce files to a size that is truly reasonable for typical hard disk capacities, to say nothing of problems in distributing huge files. Compression is the major challenge on the road to "desktop video."

If you want to experiment with *QuickTime*, the *VideoSpigot* is among the least-expensive digitizing hardware available to support it. Much Macintosh software supports *QuickTime*, including *HyperCard*, Adobe *Premier* and MacroMedia's *Director*. The MS-DOS and Windows options include *Linkway, Linkway Live!, Compel*, and *Multimedia Toolbook*, which support digital movies, that can be created in ways that range from *ComputerEyes* hardware and software to files from AutoDesk *Animator* and *Delux Paint Animator*. Joining the digital revolution need not require a major investment.

Learning with Interactive Multimedia

You only need to scan the contents of computer and professional education publications, starting about 1991, to see the attention being given to interactive multimedia. Clearly, many educators are fascinated by its potential as a learning tool. Let's look at some possible applications.

Interactive Multimedia as an Access System

One popular application of IMM is to provide flexible, nonlinear access to large amounts of information stored on CD-ROM. *Compton's Interactive Encyclopedia*, Grolier's *New Multimedia Encyclopedia*, and Microsoft *ENCARTA* and *Bookshelf* are representative of the new generation of reference works. (Incidentally, *Bookshelf* was chosen one of the top six software products for 1992–1993 by *Technology & Learning*, November/December 1992.) These are multimedia resources, not just digitized text, complete with hyper links among articles that allow much more rapid location of related entries than do print encyclopedias. Further, users can copy information of interest directly from the CD into a word processor for report and other writing. Educators have yet to consider the learning ramifications of this capability. Melnick (1991) discusses effective use of electronic encyclopedias with children and offers considerable detail about *Compton's Encyclopedia*. Krushenisky (1993) reviews several CD encyclopedias.

The range of CD-ROM software is vast and rapidly growing. Among our favorites are two from National Geographic (see Figure 10.5). *Mammals* is a superb "multimedia encyclopedia" that covers an enormous range of mammals in considerable detail. Far more than just text, this product takes full advantage of its medium to offer color photos, sound clips, and color movie clips. *The Presidents: It All Started with George* is the most comprehensive CD database on the U.S. Presidency that we know of. As with *Mammals*, the text data are augmented with photos and movie clips. Your students can see and hear such dramatic figures as John F. Kennedy, Franklin D. Roosevelt, and other twentieth-century

Figure 10.5. Sample main entry from Mammals: A Multimedia Encyclopedia.

presidents. (Regrettably, there were no films in George Washington's day.) Both CDs have a game component to encourage exploration of the data in a *learning* mode, not just wandering.

Another interesting type of CD-ROM product is the children's storybook as pioneered by Discis. Typical is their *Tale of Benjamin Bunny.* This CD uses images taken directly from the original book—one picture and one page from the story per screen. Narrators read the story aloud, while the computer highlights the corresponding words in the text image. A child can "read" this story without adult assistance and in a straight, linear fashion. The child can also, however, click on any part of each picture. The computer will display the word for the item selected and also say the word. The user can listen to individual words in the story, look up a glossary definition, and get help in English or Spanish. Discis offers many popular children's stories in their series. One of the top six software excellence awards of 1992–1993 from *Technology & Learning* magazine went to a similar product from Brøderbund, *Just Grandma and Me.* It allows the user to select English, Spanish, or Japanese text and soundtracks.

In the appendix you will find many sources of CD-ROMs. Remember, too, that not all CD-ROMs are also hypermedia. Many are just massive data banks. Among the best resources for keeping up with the market is Meckler's *CD-ROMS in Print,* in either print or CD format. The 1993 issue covered some 3,000 CDs internationally. Meckler also publishes *CD-ROM Librarian*, which features reviews, news, and bibliographies.

Interactive Multimedia as a Presentation System

Suppose you have videodiscs that you would like to use with your entire class. Some discs aimed at education include a print index of all the material on the disc. Others include teaching guides that feature bar codes to control the laserdisc player and thus provide easy access to selected stills or motion segments. Lake (1992) provides a partial lesson plan on the artist VanGogh, using a laserdisc with a bar-code reader. Some users find bar-code readers difficult to manipulate accurately.

If there are no bar codes and no index, you need to view the disc and record the frame numbers of the stills and segments that you want to use. You then call up the images as needed using the remote control unit of the laserdisc player.

A more elegant approach is to let the computer control your laserdisc player. Hypermedia software typically includes the control capabilities to do this. Suppose you create a lesson outline by using text fields. For each point in the outline, add one or more buttons that access the appropriate frames from the videodisc. You won't need sheets with printed bar codes, and you won't have to fuss with the reader. Unlike using the remote control, you won't need a list of frame numbers to punch in when required. Rather, your outline serves to guide the class presentation and also to access the videodisc support with no bother. Further, because you are using hypermedia, you are free to click on the buttons in any (nonlinear!) order, so that the class need not follow the predetermined flow, yet the potential to do so remains. Of course, you could also create multiple levels of screens, so that one outline point button links to another screen with, perhaps, the next-deeper outline level or other related material. Hypermedia offers you complete flexibility to build and deliver your lesson as you see fit and as student interest and responses warrant.

Interactive Multimedia as a Student Tool

Throughout this book, we continually stress computer use by both teachers and students. When you understand hypermedia as a software tool kit, you'll want to make it available to students as well. Many teachers have done so to enthusiastic response from their students.

The first step in using hypermedia with students is to gain enough experience with it personally to be able to envision student uses that support the curriculum. We do not advocate using hypermedia simply for its own sake. Within the curriculum, you probably need a flexible project orientation in your teaching, one that goes beyond written assignments, drawing, physical model building, and other traditional learning projects. How might students demonstrate their learning by creating a hypermedia product?

High school physics teacher Clarence Bakken got information from a nearby amusement park about how their rides work. Students then did library research and field study on the rides. The "Great America Sampler" became an elaborate hypermedia project on the physics of amusement rides (Piller, 1992).

In addition to generic hypermedia software that students quickly can learn to use, there are specialized products such as *MediaText*. *MediaText* easily creates multimedia documents by enhancing word processor files with "media links." Media links are icons that embed in the original document other text files, graphics, sound, simple animations, or selections from laserdiscs and audio CDs. The manual includes practical suggestions for using *MediaText* in the curriculum. In bestowing one of its top six awards for software excellence on *MediaText*, *Technology & Learning* magazine (November/December 1992, p. 16) noted enthusiastically, "The program is not fancy or glitzy, just wonderfully usable." More software should deserve such praise!

Interactive Video Instruction

Interactive video instruction (IVI) is CAI that incorporates content from a laserdisc. You learned about laserdisc technology earlier in this chapter. Now let's look more closely at IVI itself.

All IVI is described by levels of interactivity. At level I, all of the instruction is contained on the laserdisc. Content is organized into "chapters," which users can access randomly with the player's remote control. Typically, a motion segment plays, and the disc halts automatically on a still image of a multiple-choice question. The user indicates answers by keying in the frame number specified for that choice, and the lesson continues at that point. Level I lessons are relatively unsophisticated, and they require only the most basic laserdisc player and a TV set. No computer is involved.

Level II IVI requires a special laserdisc player that contains its own microprocessor and RAM. A level-II disc contains a computer program as well as video and audio. The player loads the program into its RAM and controls the instruction by executing the program. Because the program is part of the disc, it cannot be modified.

Far more versatile is level III, in which a videodisc player is connected to and under the control of an external computer. Any type of CAI becomes IVI when video and sound are added elements of the lesson. With an overlay device, the video and the computer's output are displayed on the same monitor screen. Otherwise, the user must alternate between the computer monitor and a TV. Many level-III products also use alternative input devices, especially touch screens, to reduce or eliminate difficulty in using the system (Figure 10.6). See Phillipo (1988) for a full discussion of interactivity levels in IVI.

Although IVI is still far less common in schools than its potential value warrants, it is a growth area. More and more laserdiscs become available each year, many with IVI software included or optionally available. Perhaps the growing impact of IVI is indicated by the 1992–1993 software excellence awards from *Technology & Learning* magazine (November/December 1992, pp. 14–16). Of the top six awards, three went to interactive video products: *Science 2000; Columbus: Encounter, Dis-*

Figure 10.6. A touch-sensitive IVI system that displays video on the computer screen.

cover, and *Beyond;* and *Illuminated Books and Manuscripts.* The latter two are part of a major IBM multimedia product line called *Ultimedia.*

Classroom Applications

Falk and Carlson (1992) suggest interactive multimedia is the best "single set of technologies to promote among teachers to improve the way they educate students. . . . " How, then, do creative teachers actually use IMM products or tools with students?

Falk and Carlson offer an integrated model of how educators use hypermedia products (Figure 10.7). One dimension of the model is the method of use, either *model T* as a teaching tool (in the hands of the teacher) or *model L* as a learning tool (in the hands of the learner). Either may involve any of five different instructional styles. *Video-enhanced didactic presentations* use IMM materials to enhance the teacher's presentation (model T) or as tutorial CAI. *Exploration* models allow teacher or learner to move about freely through the content. *Structured observation* requires students to attend to specific things as they use the lesson or see it presented in a group setting. *Simulated personal interaction* is a hypermedia simulation in which the learner assumes a role and interacts with the media. *Assessment and*

Instructional Style

Method of Use	Video-Enhanced Didactic	Exploration	Structured Observation	Simulated Personal Interaction	Assessment & Focused Instruction
Model T					
Model L					

Figure 10.7. Hypermedia usage model (Falk and Carlson, 1992).

focused instruction involves testing the learners' knowledge and directing them to appropriate instruction or remediation.

San Francisco middle schools have used *GTV: A Geographic Perspective on American History* since May, 1990 (McDonnell, 1992). Teachers received four days of training, during which they learned to apply *GTV* to the social studies curriculum and align it with the state Social Studies Framework. At its simplest, teachers used video segments from *GTV* to introduce a new text chapter. Some selected still images to spark discussion prior to introducing a new topic or as prompts for writing assignments. As they become more comfortable with the product, teachers began to use the software tools in *GTV* to assemble their own "shows" such as for review prior to a test. That review appears to have enhanced test performance. Eventually, teachers began to let students use *GTV* for their own presentations to their classmates or within specific assignments. Some even output their show to videotape and added their own voice-over narration. Student projects are shared widely among district schools.

Holden created "The Aids Virus," a *HyperCard* stack for middle school children (Holden et al., 1992). The design expressly aims at cooperative learning, creating positive interdependence among the group members. At the same time, each individual is responsible for mastering the content. To achieve both goals, some questions require a single, group response whereas others expect individual input from each group member. A limited field test indicated that cooperative learning goals could be attained successfully with this software. The importance of the article is less the specific stack, or even the idea of developing your own software of this type, but rather the specific concepts of cooperative learning that are addressed. Although easier with this specially created software, the same goals could be reached with more typical software by using alternatives to what Holden built in. If you are excited by the idea of cooperative learning, be sure to read this short article.

Perhaps the largest collection of multimedia data available as a single product is the *Video Encyclopedia of the 20th Century*. There are many discs in the set, which costs about $10,000! Typically, users must look up the topic of interest in the printed index, locate and load the appropriate disc, and then access the segments. Educators in Fairfax Country, Virginia, have developed *Linkway* software to control a multidisc "jukebox" to make access much faster and easier (Fritz, 1991). The system allows students to create their own custom presentations drawing from the entire encyclopedia. Once completed, the system can save the presentation onto videotape and print out documentation relevant to the video segments used. (For those unable to afford the entire encyclopedia, Scholastic offers a single disc of excerpts called *History in Motion: Milestones of the 20th Century* for use with their *Point of View* software.)

Gerrish (1991) started an after-school club for kids in the 1970s. From a beginning in the performing arts, notably magic, activities grew into computer programming. Later incorporated as a nonprofit organization separate from schools, the Wiz Kids Inc. responded to a 1989 request from a software publisher for proposals to develop a multimedia-based core curriculum. Their *Fields of Learning (FOL)* proposal won the contract. The first module is life science, with others to follow in earth and physical science, and several areas of history. Wiz Kids involves many youths who might otherwise be active in gangs. We strongly recommend Gerrish's article as an example of what student involvement with the computer can achieve. This isn't exactly a "classroom application," but it is inspiring.

Native American students used *HyperCard* to create illustrated versions of their own legends. The project stimulated the students' understanding of their heritage while applying a new software tool (Beekman, 1992). Groups of three or four students researched traditional legends and developed storyboards as part of their communications class. They created their stacks in computer class. All stacks included original artwork; many featured animation and sound. Project leaders stressed not only the skills development, but also the sense of accomplishment and mastery, which was uncommon for many disadvantaged students. How could you apply this idea to any student group?

The Department of Classics at Harvard University noted the difficulty that many students face in understanding Greek literature without broad appreciation of Classical Age art, music, religion, geography, and so forth. This led to the *Perseus* project, in collaboration with several other institutions and with many corporate sponsors (Kearsley, 1992). Students can access original texts and translations of them, lexicons, drawings and video images of archaeological treasures, an atlas supplemented with modern satellite photos, site plans of major locations in classical Greece, using a flexible navigation system through it all. Similarly, the *Ulysses* project at IBM shows how something relatively dry and inaccessible to today's high school students (e.g., an ancient poem) can become exciting through hypermedia. You can read a segment, then view a dramatic reading by any of six professional actors. In some cases, you can even specify the mood the actor should use in the interpretation.

Concern over lack of interest in math and science among young women led to a project at George Washington University (Baxter and Heller, 1992). Over a period of 9 months, participants attended Saturday sessions during the school year and a 10-day residential program in the summer. Formal Saturday sessions developed participants' computer applications skills. Professional scientists made presentations to the girls in the afternoon. The summer focused on cooperative learning built around *HyperCard*. Teams worked together to create and present a science project. Each team had to research their topic and prepare an outline.

Next, they designed and created the presentation. After delivering the presentation, students revised it based on audience feedback. Anecdotal evidence suggests the program may meet its purposes of encouraging young women to consider careers in engineering.

The North Central Regional Education Laboratory has developed an interactive multimedia product to help teachers modify or refine their teaching approaches and develop alternative strategies (Duffy, 1992). *Strategic Teaching Frameworks (STF)* presents actual classroom video illustrating critical classroom skills with the teacher's own commentary and that of education experts on alternate sound tracks. *STF* is used in methods classes for group presentation or individual study and for inservice education. The product is aimed at educational change in support of school restructuring, not just content delivery, through an interactive "apprenticeship."

How might your expectations for student research change if students had ready access to a truly broad range of resources? *Facts on File News Digest CD-ROM 1980–1991* provides hypermedia access to the full text of every news article in the print version of *News Digest* for over a decade, more than 300 detailed maps, and a 12-year index. You can print all or part of an article, or export data to a word processor.

Trautman (1992) suggests that building a multimedia product is an active, creative effort to compose meaning, as are reading and writing. Every multimedia application has two operational modes: editing (creating or altering a product) and exploring (using, investigating). As editor, a teacher or student should progress through three distinct stages of creation. First, planning involves preparation to undertake the project and goal setting. Second, drafting is the design phase. Trautman suggests working on large posterboard with sticky notes to create and modify a diagram of how the product will work. Third, aligning is making the product fit the intended audience. As editor, you try to keep the audience in mind as you create the product. When a preliminary version is complete, you mentally shift to the explorer mode to look at it from the audience's perspective. Group critiques can be helpful. If pieces are out of alignment, revising allows creators to fix the problem. The main explorer function is monitoring, being alert at all times to the success of or need for the other processes. Figure 10.8 illustrates the model.

Issues in Interactive Multimedia

One major issue with interactive multimedia is the problem of *copyright*. The potential to digitize virtually anything and incorporate the digital result in a software product raises numerous concerns among copyright holders. While the legal issues are murky, it is at least clear that digitizing many materials for inclusion in new commercial products would deprive the copyright holder of justifiable income from the original, which is the essence of copyright protection. Yet the new medium offers potential access to materials that was previously inconceivable.

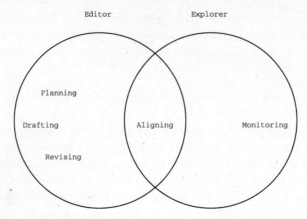

Figure 10.8. Model of hypermedia application development (based on Trautman, 1992).

Robert Stern of the Voyager Company, a major multimedia producer, has labeled outdated copyright laws as the single biggest barrier to good multimedia products (Greenberger, 1990). We hope that appropriate cooperative arrangements eventually will develop.

Can content be made *too easy?* Two early CD-ROMs presented the lives of Stravinsky and Beethoven and their music (Figure 10.9). With these products, it is possible to read a biography of the composer, view portraits and other illustrations, listen to the music, study the musical score, and even take a quiz on the content, all without leaving your computer. The creator of the CDs reported divergent reactions to the works. Music students and the general public liked them, but music professionals were disturbed that they were so attractive and easy to use that " . . . the technology diminishes the difficulty of the subject, and it becomes *too* accessible." He suggested such attitudes are a major reason for slow acceptance of IMM instructional materials (Greenberger, 1990).

There are several *operational issues* with hyper environments as well. Let's look at wandering, disorientation, cognitive overload, and use of one or two screens for IVI.

The term *wandering,* or "unmotivated rambling" (Hammond, 1989), refers to the ability of the user of hypermedia to meander aimlessly through the vast available resources, potentially gaining little or nothing beyond enjoyment. This becomes an issue when the product is used specifically for learning. Traditional CAI, as presented in the previous chapter, is generally designed to all but assure some type of learning will occur. Its control structures are notably absent from many hypermedia products, such as ABC News Interactive's products *The Election of 1988* and *Martin Luther King.* Learners have vast *potential* to learn, but must make a definite effort on their own to do so. How many learners in any given context are capable of profiting fully from the freedom hypermedia provides? Should the software include more traditional approaches (regular questions to answer, feedback and guidance, exit criteria, etc.), or is it the teacher's responsibility to prepare the learner for hypermedia and to set learning expectations outside of the software?

Figure 10.9.   IMM offers easy access to the life, times, and music of Beethoven.

Are such products equally beneficial to all types of learners? Only much further research will provide the answers.

Disorientation is another concern (Conklin, 1987; Stanton and Baber, 1992). When you have flexibility to move about in a hypermedia environment, you also have the potential to become "lost in hyperspace." As one idea leads to another and then another, you may no longer recall where your inquiry started, much less how to return to the screen from which the digression began. Good hypermedia products include maps of their organization that you can access at any time, clearly marked to show exactly where you currently are. Another approach is buttons that return you to some intermediate point, such as the menu level just above your current location. From there, you usually can re-establish your orientation. The magnitude of the problem and the difficulty in effectively managing it is proportional to the overall size of the environment. Displaying an understandable map of a large, complex system is itself difficult.

Because an interactive multimedia environment can—indeed, should be—rich in content, users may face *cognitive overload*, or a sense of inability to cope with and draw meaning from an overwhelming array of information (Stanton and Baber, 1992). This may lead to "flagging commitment" to pursue any goal (Heller, 1990). We have observed this phenomenon when students encounter *GTV: A Geographic Perspective on American History* with little guidance as to what they are supposed to do or learn. Do not expect students to know how to approach something so radically different as IMM.

The design of interactive video products begins with a determination that the finished product will use *separate video and computer monitors or only one* for both images. Thus far, most IVI products use two screens to minimize the user's hardware requirements. Any computer can be connected to and control a laserdisc player easily and inexpensively. In order to display both video and computer images on a single screen, the computer must have some type of overlay card or circuitry, of which there are many different, incompatible types. This discourages commercial development by limiting markets. However, single-screen IVI offers the great advantage that the image and related material from the computer can exist side by side. Thus, the computer is better able to amplify on the imagery, even to draw over it to call your attention to specific aspects of what you are seeing. This has always been possible with computer graphics but largely has been lost with IVI. If DVI technology becomes integrated into future central processing units, this issue will become moot. All such computers will be capable of showing video on their monitors.

Finally, Polin (1992) suggests that educators need to look carefully at the content and suitability of many of the videodiscs now on the market. Most books are new, carefully designed materials. In contrast, most videodiscs have been created from existing footage that the producer *"re-purposes."* While such video is not likely to be far off target, it may well not be suited ideally to a new purpose for which it was *not* intended.

What the Research Shows

Fewer research reports exist for interactive multimedia than for traditional CAI. A meta-analysis of 38 studies of IVI in higher education and training found that overall achievement improved compared to more traditional instruction by about 0.5 standard deviations. In military training, students who scored at the 50th percentile improved to the 65th; in higher education, they advanced to the 75th percentile (Fletcher, 1990). Fletcher also found a direct correlation between the level of interactivity and effectiveness. Another study of nineteen reports comparing achievement found three with negative findings. The others all found small positive differences or none at all (Stevens, Zech, and Katkanant, cited in Barba and Armstrong, 1992). This suggests that comparative studies of IMM may be no more productive than their predecessors regarding CAI. Students learn from IMM. The issue to research is maximizing the effect through instructional strategies and styles.

Barba and Armstrong (1992) believed general research missed such important issues as which types of students benefit more from various learning systems. They compared the effectiveness (i.e., achievement gains) from a *HyperCard* stack to those from the same stack enhanced with video from a laserdisc. They found no significant difference for the two treatments *per se,* but, as expected, there was a significant difference among low-, average-, and high-verbal-ability students. They also found a significant interaction between treatment and verbal ability. Students with low verbal ability benefited disproportionately from the IVI. High-verbal-ability students in the no-video treatment actually outperformed their counterparts in the IVI group, but the differences were not significant statistically.

Falk and Carlson (1991) studied multimedia applications in human service and teacher education. They concluded that use of multimedia can enhance learning on such measures as efficiency of learning, satisfaction with the instruction received, skills development, and content attainment.

Romance and Vitale (1991) used a carefully designed and tested commercial earth science IVI product with elementary education students. They reported substantial achievement gains on core science concepts from pre-test to post-test for their experimental group. They also found that the IVI students' attitudes toward teaching science became significantly more positive, while their confidence in their ability to deal with science content increased. Preliminary longitudinal results seem to indicate that these differences carry over into the field as the students graduate and assume teaching positions.

Carlson (1991) investigated variations in an IVI lesson. First, students used the lessons either individually or in small groups. Second, the style of the lesson presented was either deductive (concepts followed by examples) or inductive (examples led to generation of concepts). Third, learners either used a lesson style that matched their own learning style or not. The research measured content scores (achievement), observation skills scores, overall satisfaction, and attitude toward learner control. No significant differences existed among groups for achievement. When student and lesson learning style matched, scores on observation skill were significantly higher. Students in small groups were significantly more satisfied with the instruction overall, while those working individually perceived significantly greater control over the pace and sequence of instruction. Carlson suggests that designers should provide variations in their IVI lessons to maximize their effectiveness.

Do all users of hypermedia use its flexible movement potential essentially to the same degree? Beasley and Vila (1992) thought navigation might relate to scholastic aptitude or gender. They devised an instructional module on artificial intelligence, which also tracked each user's path through the nodes. They found a noticeable pattern; students with lower ACT English scores used a more exploratory or nonlinear approach to the content than did those of middle or higher ability. The differences were not significant, however, within normally accepted confidence ranges. The gender analysis showed significant differences, namely, that females followed a more linear path than males.

Enhanced motivation is commonly attributed to use of hypermedia. One explicit goal of the Texas Learning Technology Group's Physical Science program is to enhance student interest in elective high school chemistry and physics courses, although the design of the program was aimed solely at science content. Nearly half of the instructional program is provided by interactive videodisc. Coleman, Koballa, and Crawley (1992) set out to investigate the program's success on this one measure. They found no significant differences between classes using the IVI and those following traditional textbook instruction. The authors concluded that "carefully developed, stimulating programs" cannot be assumed to provide affective value. Rather, desired affective goals must be integral to the design of hypermedia products. They also noted that the IVI students liked the ease of making up missed lessons or reviewing what they had not understood, but they thought it was important to have a text to take home to study and were put off by IVI equipment problems.

Similarly, Janda (1992) conducted an experiment with college students in introductory American government courses. Students were in either traditional lecture/discussion sections, sections that briefly used a small CAI tutorial, and then concentrated on data-analysis software, or sections that used IVI. Janda anticipated no difference in achievement, so he investigated student perceptions of their knowledge, their interest in the subject, and their intent to take another course in the field. All groups showed significant gains in their perceptions of their knowledge but no difference among the groups emerged on any other measure.

Heller (1990) summarized the work of many researchers who explored aspects of hyper environments. Among the more interesting findings was that users who browsed through a hyper environment grossly overestimated the amount of the total system they had actually seen. Further, high school students tended to browse using simple techniques, rather than developing effective search strategies. In summarizing the research on discovery learning, Heller suggested that the inherent flexibility of a hyper environment may be inappropriate for children below junior high age. She also noted that research on hypermedia is comparatively scarce.

A group of researchers at the University of Nebraska-Omaha investigated the anticipated use of multimedia among pre-service teacher education students (Grandgenett et al., 1992). The subjects had enrolled in a course that focused on multimedia hardware and its use. The study found no relationship between students' perceived familiarity with the equipment and anticipated multimedia use. There was also no relationship to measured computer anxiety. Four learning styles were assessed. Students classified as "assimilators" were significantly less likely to project using multimedia than others. The study also found a significant relationship between anticipated use and gender (females indicated greater likelihood than males), as well as the students' certification category. The researchers concluded that pre-service training should focus initially on clearly viable applications, rather than the hardware mechanics of multimedia. It also should take into account applicability to the students' intended teaching area and probable lower interest among male students.

In sum, there is a need for much research concerning all the possible variations in learning materials that constitute interactive multimedia. A Delphi study among members of the Hyper/Multimedia Special Interest Group of the International Society for Technology in Education identified seven broad categories of needed research and multiple areas within each (Raker, 1992). Interactive multimedia (IMM) is relatively new to most teachers as a learning tool, and much remains to be learned about how to achieve its maximum potential.

Summary

In this chapter, you learned about the nature of what are called hyper environments. Linear computer applications seem very limited once you have experienced the flexibility and naturalness of hypermedia. There is tremendous intuitive appeal in the added sensory communication of computer-based multimedia. A critical element of worthwhile applications is interaction between user and computer. Hypermedia seems an appropriate term for this learning tool, but multimedia is already commonly used. We support *interactive* multimedia (IMM) to properly identify the key aspect.

Interactive multimedia draws on the hardware technologies of compact disc, laserdisc, DVI, and digitizing boards. Software products, such as *HyperCard*, *Linkway*, and *Toolbook*, provide software construction sets that are relatively easy to learn to use. Hardware and software technologies such as *QuickTime* add digital video to IMM, though with some clear limitations.

Interactive multimedia can provide easier access to vast multimedia resources. Teachers can use IMM tools to deliver more exciting presentations. Some of the most intriguing possibilities stem from students creating IMM projects as alternatives to traditional school assignments. Of course, there are areas of concern with this technology, as with all others. Copyright issues and acceptance by educators are common concerns. Operational issues include wandering through an IMM product, becoming disoriented, and dealing with cognitive overload. In interactive video applications there is also the issue of separate video and computer monitors versus one-screen systems.

Concerning the potential of IMM to enhance learning, limited research is encouraging, but there is still a need for much research to determine what strategies are most appropriate for which learners under what circumstances.

According to Gillette (1992, p. 27) " . . . [C]omputer multimedia form will come to be seen as one of the contributions and transformations of the computer revolution." Robert Abel, producer of *Columbus* for the IBM Ultimedia line, views multimedia as the next great computer hit after desktop publishing (Silverstone, 1992). No one expected individuals to do their own professional-level layout work some years ago, yet products like *PageMaker* made it possible. Abel believes user developed and published multimedia could be equally common before the turn of the century.

Perhaps the ultimate application of interactive multimedia is what is termed *virtual reality*, an interactive, computer-generated microworld. You'll learn about virtual reality in Chapter 21.

Chapter 10 Activities

1. Explore as many hypermedia products in as many formats as possible.
2. Create a poster or bulletin board that explains the differences among hypertext, multimedia, and hypermedia (or interactive multimedia.)

3. Try out several different types of CD-ROM products, from text-only to hypermedia. Compare those that have hypermedia access systems, such as an encyclopedia, with those that do not, such as the ERIC database.
4. Look at several different videodiscs and briefly note their potential applicability in your teaching. Experiment with the remote control and a bar-code reader. Which do you prefer? Why?
5. Critically study a computer-controlled laserdisc product such as the Voyager *Laserguide* to the National Gallery of Art videodisc. Compare this to what you could do with the same disc using either bar-codes or the remote control. What strengths and weaknesses do you find in the computer software?
6. Develop a group-based lesson plan that incorporates a videodisc.
7. Compare a videodisc-based lesson to one that uses *QuickTime* or another digital video format. What advantages and disadvantages do you see in each?
8. Experiment with any video and audio digitizing hardware that you have access to.
9. Learn to create a simple product using any hypermedia software. Develop a basic lesson outline for something you (could) teach with about four main points. Create and link support screens for each of the main points. The support screens may consist of further text or they may call up other resources.
10. Plan an assignment for your students that would encourage them to develop an IMM product in lieu of more traditional projects.
11. Read any current research literature on interactive multimedia that you can find.

Bibliography

Ambron, S., and Hooper, K., Eds. *CD ROM, Vol. 3. Interactive Media.* Redmond, WA: Microsoft Press, 1988.

Ambrose, D. W. "The Effects of Hypermedia on Learning: A Literature Review." *Educational Technology*, December 1991, *31*(12), pp. 51–55.

Arone, M. P., and Grabowski, B. L. "Effects on Children's Achievement and Curiosity of Variations in Learner Control over an Interactive Video Lesson." *Educational Technology Research & Development*, 1992, *40*(1), pp. 15–27.

Atkins, M., and Blisset, G. "Interactive Video and Cognitive Problem-Solving Skills." *Educational Technology*, January 1992, *32*(1), pp. 44–50.

Barba, R. H., and Armstrong, B. E. "The Effect of HyperCard and Interactive Video Instruction on Earth and Space Science Students' Achievement." *Journal of Educational Multimedia and Hypermedia*, 1992, *1*(3), pp. 323–330.

Baxter, T., and Heller, S. "Getting Closer to Science: Experiences Using HyperCard to Interest Young Minority Women in Science," *Journal of HyperMedia and MultiMedia Studies*, Fall 1992, *3*(1), pp. 8–11.

Beasley, R. E., and Vila, J. A. "The Identification of Navigation Patterns in a Multimedia Environment: A Case Study." *Journal of Educational Multimedia and Hypermedia*, 1992, *1*(2), pp. 209–222.

Beekman, G. "Recreating Native American Legends with *HyperCard.*" *The Computing Teacher,* February 1992, *19*(5), p. 31.

Blum, B. "Software That Can Sing and Dance. (Interactive Multimedia)." *CBT Directions,* October 1991, *IV*(10), pp. 9–10.

Brandt, R., Ed. "In Review." *Multimedia Review,* Summer 1992, *3*(2), pp. 64–74.

Braswell, R. "The Use of *HyperCard* and *Hypersound* to Design Interactive Videodisc Instructional Materials." *Computers in the Schools,* 1991, *8*(1/2/3), pp. 251–254.

Bunsel, M. J., and Morris, S. K. *Multimedia Applications Development Using DVI Technology.* Englewood Cliffs, NJ: Prentice-Hall, 1992.

Carlson, H. L. "Learning Styles and Program Design in Interactive Multimedia." *Educational Technology Research & Development,* 1991, *39*(3), pp. 41–48.

Cognition and Technology Group at Vanderbilt. "The Jasper Experiment: An Exploration of Issues in Learning and Instructional Design." *Educational Technology Research & Development,* 1992, *40*(1), pp. 65–80.

Coleman, D. C., Koballa, T. R., Jr., and Crawley, F. E. "TLTG Interactive Videodisc Physical Science Program: Interest Results of the 1988–89 Field Test." *Journal of Educational Multimedia and Hypermedia,* 1992, *1*(2), pp. 223–234.

Conklin, J. "Hypertext: An Introduction and Survey." *IEEE Computer,* 1987, *2*(9), pp. 17–41.

Corcoran, C. "AVI Video Module for PCs to Come from Microsoft." *InfoWorld,* 10 August 1992, pp. 1, 87.

de Felix, J. W., Johnson, R. T., and Schick, J. E. "Socio- and Psycholinguistic Considerations in Interactive Video Instruction for Limited English Proficient Students." *Computers in the Schools,* 1990, *7*(1/2), pp. 173–190.

Duffy, T. "Hypermedia for Educational Change. Strategic Teaching Frameworks." *TechTrends,* 1992, *37*(4), pp. 37.

Falk, D. R., and Carlson, H. L. "Learning to Teach with Multimedia." *T.H.E. Journal,* September 1992, *20*(2), pp. 96–100.

Falk, D. R., and Carlson, H. L. "Evaluating the Effectiveness of Multimedia Applications in Human Service and Teacher Education." *Multimedia Review,* 1991, *2*(3), pp. 12–17.

Fletcher, J. D. *Effectiveness and Cost of Interactive Videodisc Instruction in Defense Training and Education. IDA Report R2372.* Arlington, VA: Institute for Defense Analysis, July 1990.

Franchi, J. "CBT or IVD?—That's the Question." *TechTrends,* 1992, *37*(2), pp. 27–30.

Fritz, M. "Videodisc Update: The Power of Visual Learning." *Technology & Learning,* November/December 1991, *12*(3), pp. 39–50.

Gayeski, D. M. *Multimedia for Learning.* Englewood Cliffs, NJ: Educational Technology Publications, 1992.

Gerrish, J. "New Generation of `Wiz Kids' Develop Multimedia Curriculum." *T.H.E. Journal,* October 1991, *19*(3), pp. 93–95.

Gill, E. K. "High-Voltage PCs." *Presentation Products,* September 1992, *6*(9), pp. 24–30.

Gillette, J. E. "The New Language of Images: Observations on Computer Multimedia Form." *Multimedia Review,* Summer 1992, *3*(2), pp. 20–29.

Grabinger, R. S., Dunlap, J. C., and Jonassen, D. H. "Making Information Accessible—Part 1: Hypertext Links." *Performance & Instruction,* October 1992, *31*(9), pp. 36–39.

Grandgenett, N., Ziebarth, R., Koneck, J., Farnham, M. L., McQuillan, J., and Larson, B. "An Investigation of the Anticipated Use of Multimedia by Pre-service Teachers." *Journal of Educational Multimedia and Hypermedia,* 1992, *1*(1), pp. 91–101.

Greenberger, M., Ed. *On Multimedia: Technologies for the 21st Century.* Santa Monica, CA: The Voyager Company, 1990.

Hammond, N. "Hypermedia and Learning: Who Guides Whom?" In G. Goos and J. Hartmanis, Eds. *Lecture Notes in Computer Science: Computer Assisted Learning.* Berlin: Springer Verlag, 1989, pp. 167–181.

Hamrell, D. "Hypermacros III." *The Computing Teacher,* November 1991, *19*(3), pp. 23–28.

Heeter, C. "Dilemmas and Delights of *QuickTime* (Developer's' Dialogue)." *Journal of Educational Multimedia and Hypermedia,* 1992, *1*(3), pp. 377–382.

Heller, R. S. "The Role of Hypermedia in Education: A Look at the Research Issues." *Journal of Research on Computing in Education,* Summer 1990, *22*(4), pp. 431–441.

Helsel, S. K. "Interview: Vicki Vance of Apple Computer, Inc." *Multimedia Review,* Summer 1992, *3*(2), pp. 52–56.

Holder, S., and Daynes, R. *CD-I and Interactive Videodisc Technology.* Indianapolis: H. W. Sams, 1987.

Holden, M. C., Holcomb, C. M. and Wedman, J. F. "Designing HyperCard Stacks for Cooperative Learning." *The Computing Teacher,* February 1992, *19*(5), pp. 20–22.

Hopper, J. "Student-Directed Learning Using HyperCard." *Computers in the Schools,* 1990, *7*(4), pp. 83–98.

Iuppa, N. V., and Wade, M. *The Multimedia Adventure.* White Plains, NY: Knowledge Industries Publications Inc., 1992.

Jacobsen, F. F. "CD-ROM Encyclopedias: A Product in Evolution." *TechTrends,* 1991, *36*(6), pp. 47–49.

Jamsa, K. *Instant Multimedia for Windows 3.1.* Somerset, NJ: Wiley, 1992.

Janda, K. "Multimedia in Political Science: Sobering Lessons from a Teaching Experiment." *Journal of Educational Multimedia and Hypermedia,* 1992, *1*(3), pp. 341–354.

Jonassen, D. H. *Hypertext/Hypermedia.* Englewood Cliffs, NJ: Educational Technology Publications, 1989.

Kearsley, G., Ed. "Substance or Flash? (Multimedia Projects: Issues and Applications." *Journal of Educational Multimedia and Hypermedia,* 1992, *1*(2), pp. 251–253.

Kinnaman, D. E. "Jostens Launches Full-Motion Video on Networks." *Technology & Learning,* September 1992, *13*(1), pp. 35–36.

Krushenisky, C. "Lightening Your Load with Multimedia Encyclopedias." *PC Novice,* October 1993, *4*(10), pp. 62–65.

Lake, D. T. "ART: Technologies in the Curriculum." *The Computing Teacher,* March 1992, *19*(6), pp. 44–46.

Lanza, A. "Some Guidelines for the Design of Effective Hypercourses." *Educational Technology,* October 1991, *31*(10), pp. 18–22.

Levin, S. R. "The Effects of Interactive Video-Enhanced Earthquake Lessons on Achievement of Seventh Grade Earth Science Students." *Journal of Computer-Based Instruction,* Autumn 1991, *18*(4), pp. 125–129.

Litchfield, B. C., and Dempsey, J. V. "A Seven-Stage Quality Control Model for Interactive Video Projects." *Journal of Educational Technology Systems,* 1991–1992, *20*(2), pp. 129–141.

Locatis, C., Letourneau, G., and Banvard, R. "Hypermedia and Instruction." *ETR&D,* 1989, *37*(4), pp. 65–77.

Luther, A. C. *Digital Video in the PC Environment, Featuring DVI Technology,* 2nd ed. New York: McGraw-Hill, 1991.

MacKenzie, I. S. "Beating the Book: Megachallenges for CD-ROM and Hypertext." *Journal of Research on Computing in Education,* Summer 1992, 24(4), pp. 486–498.

Magel, M. "Getting Familiar with MacMultimedia." *AV Video,* July 1992, *14*(7), pp. 84–90.

Magel, M. "What's New and What's Next in Multimedia Delivery." *AV Video,* September 1992, *14*(9), pp. 90–97.

Martorella, P. H., Barton, D., and Steelman, J. "Training Teachers in Interactive Video Instructional Applications." *Computers in the Schools*, 1991, *8*(1/2/3), pp. 293–301.

McDonnell, M. E. "San Francisco GTV." *The Computing Teacher*, February 1992, *19*(5), pp. 37–38.

Melnick, S. A. "Electronic Encyclopedias on Compact Disk." *Reading Teacher*, February 1991, *44*(6), pp. 432–434.

Miller, E., and Miller, W. *Discovering CD-I.* White Plains, NY: Knowledge Industries Publications Inc., 1991.

Moursund, D. "Restructuring Education for the Information Age. Part 7: Competition." *The Computing Teacher*, April 1992, *19*(7), p. 4.

Nelson, T. *Computer Lib/Dream Machines.* Redmond, WA: Tempus Books (Microsoft Press), 1987.

Nelson, W. A., and Palumbo, D. B. "Learning, Instruction, and Hypermedia." *Journal of Educational Multimedia and Hypermedia*, 1992, *1*(2), pp. 287–299.

Phillipo, J. "Videodisc Players: A Multi-Purpose Audiovisual Tool." *Electronic Learning*, November/December 1988, pp. 50–52.

Piller, C. "Separate Realities." *MacWorld*, September 1992, pp. 218–230.

Polin, L. "Examining the Emperor's New Clothes: The Uses of Existing Video in Multimedia Packages." *The Computing Teacher*, March 1992, *19*(6), pp. 5–7.

Quinlan, T., and Borzo, J. "Apple Boosts Speed and Frame Size of *QuickTime.*" *InfoWorld*, 10 August 1992, pp. 1, 87.

Raker, E. J. "Research Issues in Educational Interactive Multimedia." *Journal of HyperMedia and MultiMedia Studies*, Fall 1992, *3*(1), pp. 4–6.

Reed, M. "Videodiscs Help American Indians Learn English and Study Heritage." *T.H.E. Journal*, October 1991, *19*(3), pp. 96–97.

Reisman, S. "Development Strategies for Interactive Videodisc Applications," *Interactive Learning International*, January–March 1992, *8*(1), pp. 55–62.

Romance, N. R., and Vitale, M. R. "Enhancement of Teacher Education and Practice in Elementary Science Through Applications of Videodisk Technology." *Computers in the Schools*, 1991, *8*(1/2/3), pp. 259–270.

Roselli, T. "Control of User Disorientation in Hypertext Systems." *Educational Technology*, December 1991, *31*(12), pp. 42–46.

Roth, C., and Hickman, T. "*QuickTime*: A Compression Technology with Expansive Educational Promise." *TechTrends*, 1992, *37*(4), pp. 26–27.

Rumfield, N. "Getting Started with CD-ROM." *TechTrends*, 1991, *36*(5), pp. 21–23.

Said, C. "*QuickTime* to Crack Windows." *MacWEEK*, 26 October 1992, *6*(38), pp. 1, 131.

Saldarini, R. A. "Multimedia: An Object and a Subject of Instruction." *Instruction Delivery Systems*, November/December 1991, *5*(6), pp. 16, 22–23.

Salem, J. "Did Pick Have This Much Fun?" *The Computing Teacher*, December/January, 1991–92, *19*(4), pp. 30–32.

Salpeter, J. "Breakthroughs in Digital Video." *Technology & Learning*, April 1992, *12*(7), pp. 66–74.

Salpeter, J. "The Multimedia PC." *Technology & Learning*, October 1991, *12*(2), pp. 10, 23–24.

Scannell, E. "IBM Will Use Multimedia in All Its Systems by 1994." *InfoWorld*, 12 October 1992, pp. 1, 151.

Schwier, R. A., and Misanchuk, E. R. *Interactive Multimedia Instruction.* Englewood Cliffs, NJ: Educational Technology Publications, 1992.

Silverstone, S. "Robert Abel Discovers a New World." *Publish*, March 1992, p. 108.

Smith, E. E. "Wait Time and Guidance in Interactive Videodisc Instruction." 1990. ERIC DOCUMENT ED 329 241.

Stack, J. P. "Interactive Video: The Barriers Have Fallen." *TechTrends*, 1990, *35*(2), pp. 38–40.

Stanton, N., and Baber, C. "An Investigation of Styles and Strategies in Self-Directed Learning." *Journal of Educational Multimedia and Hypermedia*, 1992, *1*(2), pp. 147–167.

Strehlo, K. "Video for Windows Will Grab Viewer's Attention. (First Looks)." *InfoWorld*, 9 November 1992, *14*(45), pp. 1, 129.

Stroot, S. A., Tannehill, D., and O'Sullivan, M. "Skill Analysis Utilizing Videodisc Technology." *Computers in the Schools*, 1991, *8*(1/2/3), pp. 271–291.

Trautman, P. "Reading, Writing, and Digitizing!" *The Computer Teacher*, April 1992, *19*(7), pp. 40–41.

van den Berg, S., and Watt, J. H. "Effects of Educational Setting on Student Responses to Structured Hypertext." *Journal of Computer-Based Instruction*, Fall 1991, *18*(4), pp. 118–124.

Wilson, C. "Interactive Videodisc (IVD) Training and Network Development for Middle School Mathematics Teachers." *Computers in the Schools*, 1991, *8*(1/2/3), pp. 303–306.

After completing this chapter you will be able to:

Discuss the issue of courseware quality and suggest possible reasons why complaints about quality have been so common.

Explain why educators need to evaluate courseware for classroom use and who should be involved.

Describe the three major components of courseware evaluation.

Explain the primary means of identifying courseware to evaluate.

Discuss the purpose of and procedures for hands-on evaluation by educators.

Assess the importance and viability of student field-testing of courseware.

Explain the significance of courseware's intended use as an element of evaluation.

Discuss the merits of learning theory as an element of evaluation.

Select five general instructional criteria that you believe are the most critical, and defend your choices.

Identify at least four CAI-specific evaluation criteria, and defend their importance.

Explain which usability criteria are most significant to you.

Devise one or more courseware evaluation forms incorporating your most vital criteria.

Assess the variations in evaluation criteria and procedures that might arise from different software formats, especially hypermedia and multimedia.

Chapter 11

Courseware Evaluation

The sheer number of software products on the market, the range of content they entail, the widely differing formats they employ, the cost involved in acquiring them for school use—these are the elements of a confusing situation for many educators. How can you know what is available, whether it is worth using, and how best to use it.

In this chapter you will consider selecting and evaluating *courseware* for your students. The term courseware acknowledges that many instructional programs consist of more than just a diskette or two. Software is the computer files on diskette; courseware includes support materials such as documentation, teacher guides, and student manuals, which are important components of the total package.

This chapter first considers the issue of courseware quality, which leads directly to the need for evaluation and our suggested approach to it. You will learn about specific evaluation criteria in several categories, including those applicable to all educational materials, those unique to the computer, and those that contribute to usability. You will also consider the creation and use of an evaluation form.

The Issue of Quality

The rapid acquisition of computers by schools is well known. Daily newspapers and weekly news periodicals regularly inform us of the latest figures on school computer purchases, figures that change so rapidly as to be outdated in any book. Suffice it to say that for several years now the number of computers in schools has about doubled annually.

Software: The Critical Element

Except for programming, which will be discussed in Part 4 of this book, hardware by itself is relatively useless—too large to make a good paperweight and too costly to serve as a boat anchor. A computer may make a nice conversation piece on someone's desk or in a classroom or learning center. Only with the addition of software does the hardware become truly useful (Figure 11.1).

If software rings "life" to a maze of electronics, then clearly that software is more critical than the hardware. The significance of hardware is its ability to run the soft-

Figure 11.1. Software brings "life" to a computer.

ware you need to perform a given task. Thus, it is vital to meeting your goals for your students to use the best possible software. Mediocre software (or worse!) only hides the computer's potential.

Quality Trails Quantity

Anyone following developments in the computer industry knows that improvements in hardware are an all-but-daily phenomenon. Regrettably, the same cannot be said of courseware. Virtually any gathering of educators with computer interests will at some point prompt discussion of the appalling quality of courseware on the market. This concern, which borders on a cry for help, is not a reflection of naivete on the part of educators with limited computer experience. Alfred Bork, a major early figure in educational computing, commented on the rapid increase in software *quantity*, but not *quality* (1984). He stated:

> We know how to produce decent computer-based learning material at the present time. But most of the available programs have not been produced by any careful process, and few have undergone careful evaluative study. Our increased capabilities in producing materials have largely gone unused (p. 93).

Remarkably, quality concerns remain strong today, many years after Bork's comment (e.g., Zane and Frazer, 1992).

Why Quality is Problematic

There appear to be several possible explanations for problems of courseware quality.

Lack of a Theoretical Base

The field of learning theory offers many views concerning how we learn. Yet little educational courseware appears to reflect an effort to apply *any* theory. Many courseware developers seem to require little more than a vague notion of content to begin production of a new package. Would it not be wiser to consider what we know about learning and include that in the design?

Technical Concerns Dominate

In the early days of educational software, errors in programming were common, even in commercial materials. Developers were still exploring the capabilities of the new microcomputers and lacked sophistication. Complaints of amateurish results were common. Today, this has changed dramatically. Most commercial materials are technically sound. Graphics are slick, sound may be varied, and concern for visual appearance is evident (Figure 11.2). Actual programming flaws are rare. In most cases, however, nothing resembling comparable attention to the methodology of the program exists. Jaeger (1988) and Trollip (1987) both addressed these concerns and offered evidence concerning the real value of popular "features." We

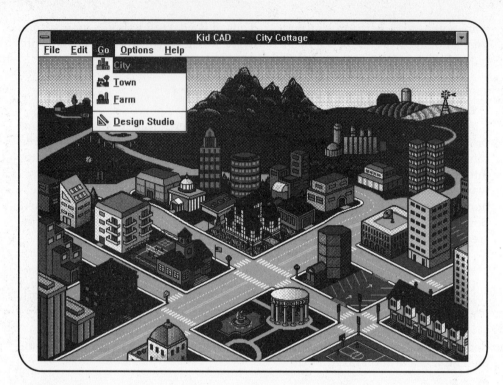

Figure 11.2. Technical quality runs high in current software.

have reached a level of technical excellence and continue to ignore educational soundness. One can only wonder whether experienced educators have played a role in developing many of the materials on the market.

Applying Old Models to a New Medium

Someone once observed that the railroads sealed their doom by failing to realize that their business was transportation, not trains. The history of motion pictures contains something of a parallel. Early film makers viewed the new medium as a means of recording stage plays for posterity. Only after considerable time did the adventurous begin to break out of old patterns and seek to determine the limits of the new medium itself.

This echoes the concern of Maddux, Johnson, and Willis (1992) that far too much computer use in schools is Type I, which is doing with a computer what educators and students have always done. Instead, educational computing takes on real value when it empowers students and teachers to do what they otherwise could not, that is, Type II applications. Much educational courseware is obviously Type I, notably drill and practice, many games, and tutorials. Simulations and the still-newer interactive multimedia and hypermedia products offer real promise of

Type II activities. Quality courseware must go beyond what other alternative learning approaches offer to create a niche of its own. That's not impossible, but it's not yet the norm.

Educators Have Not Demanded Quality

Courseware production and sales are big business. Success is measured in gross sales and net profits. With hardware springing up like mushrooms and software necessary to make it useful, there was an initial rush to get courseware on the market. In those early days, educators were too desperate for anything to use with their new tools to be fussy about quality. The new equipment dared not just sit there! Regrettably, the situation has changed less than you might expect.

The real meaning of quality is *student learning achievement.* We educators largely have failed to look at our results. In too many cases, we accept courseware based on its producer's claims of value. A catchy title, flashy graphics, and bold claims of applicability from kindergarten students through adults sell materials to uncritical consumers.

Indeed, software producers themselves appear to be little concerned about the effectiveness of their products. Have you ever seen a piece of instructional software that had field-test data? Zane and Frazer (1992) contacted thirty-four software producers whose products they were evaluating. Each was asked to provide "any evaluative data, research findings, or field-test results" in five areas, including documentation that students learn something from the software, evidence of generalization from the software to other contexts, and comparative data showing an advantage for the software over other independent learning materials, such as workbooks. Only fifteen companies responded at all. Nine just sent more literature. Six admitted having no data. The researchers state: "It should not be the responsibility of computer software users to conduct initial validation evaluations of the effectiveness of a software program" (p. 416). Not only should producers provided basic effectiveness checks, they also should determine the instructional characteristics (gender, achievement level, etc.) most relevant to success with or efficient use of their product.

The Need for Evaluation

Computers in the schools could ultimately join other technological devices in dusty storerooms if beneficial outcomes are not demonstrated. Courseware is a critical element in this, and a more serious approach to courseware selection will be required. Consider the elaborate efforts undertaken in most schools for textbook selection. It is common for teacher committees to devote much time and effort to assessing and comparing the latest offerings of publishers before adoption. Educational videos and other media under consideration for purchase are evaluated similarly. Snap decisions are unacceptable because too much is at stake. Does courseware deserve less attention?

Evaluating courseware is significantly different from examining other educational materials. Teachers involved in selecting textbooks and media tend to have years of experience teaching and learning from such materials. Few educators have such an experience base to draw on for courseware evaluation. We believe educators are well aware of the need to evaluate courseware. However, many are perplexed about procedures, so let's consider basic guidelines.

Who Should Evaluate Courseware?

There is no magic answer to the question of who should be involved in courseware evaluation. In most cases, the best approach is probably to begin in the same manner used to select textbooks. Clearly, the teacher(s) who will use the materials must be involved. If these individuals have no role in selection, the likelihood of their using the materials declines significantly.

Because of the technical aspects of courseware, it seems likely that the school's computer "expert" should also be involved. This may be a designated coordinator, a resource specialist, or even an administrator. It should be someone with a greater understanding of computer materials than a typical classroom user is apt to have or need. This person's role might be to conduct a workshop for the actual working committee on the process of courseware evaluation, rather than to be involved actively in the entire process.

If school policy includes administrators or parents in selection of other materials, the same should be true of computer materials. It may, in fact, be advantageous to include parents in the process. Even those who are highly and vocally committed to bringing computers into the schools may have little knowledge themselves of the whys and wherefores. We can ill afford a repeat of the "new math" situation of some years ago. That curriculum development failed in part because parents had not learned in such a manner in their school days and were unable to cope with what their children were doing. Parental support of computers in the schools is vital to the success of a program. Efforts to involve parents and inform them about these tools can only help.

Phases of Courseware Evaluation

There are three distinct phases to courseware evaluation: identifying products of interest, hands-on evaluation by educators, and student field-testing.

Identifying Courseware to Evaluate

To identify courseware of potential interest, you may simply look through catalogs or nearby stores, ask the advice of professional colleagues, or consult published reviews.

Catalogs and Dealers

The quickest way to get a lead on software is often to look through producers' and distributors' catalogs. If you know of a company that is well-regarded for courseware in your field of interest, be sure to get their latest literature. Otherwise, you will find listings of the products of many companies in catalogs from distributors, such as Education Resources (1-800-624-2926) and Queue (1-800-232-2224). The best catalogs include program descriptions, not just long listings of titles.

Most instructional software does not have the broad sales appeal that would place it on the shelves of a major software retailer, such as the Egghead chain. Some programs, however, do become popular well beyond schools. The *Carmen Sandiego* series, *Reader Rabbit,* and the *Oregon Trail* can be found in many retail stores. In addition, there are specialty firms that cater to the needs of educators for everything from bulletin-board materials to resource books and fancy chalk. Often, such companies operate both mail-order and retail-store businesses and include computer products in their lines. If you have access to such a store, by all means visit it.

Advice of Colleagues

Another way to identify potentially appropriate courseware is to ask colleagues in other buildings or districts what they are using and how satisfied they are with it. Do not rely on colleagues for much more than a pointer in the right direction though, because what works for them may not be right for you. The key element must be effectiveness in promoting learning, and that is related to curriculum. To what degree is your curriculum comparable to that of your colleague? Are your course objectives similar enough that you well might find the same courseware valuable? Does you colleague have any hard data on the value of the software? One of the most useful services your professional contacts can provide is to tell you which products to avoid, rather than which you surely will want.

Published Reviews

At one time, it took some effort to locate software reviews. Today, the professional journals and periodicals in most fields publish them, a reflection of the broad acceptance of computer-based learning. Start with the publications most relevant to your needs (e.g., *Arithmetic Teacher*) as any reviews that they publish will be for software in your broad area of interest. Computer-oriented educational publications such as *Electronic Learning, The Computing Teacher, Classroom Computer Learning,* and *Technology & Learning* all publish reviews of educational software in all content areas. Even consumer publications such as *PC Magazine* occasionally review educational products of particular note (e.g., *Carmen Sandiego* again!), but their real strength is thorough reviews and tests of hardware and general purpose tool software such as word processors and databases.

There are also many specialized resources to which educators can turn. *Only the Best* (Neill & Neill, 1993) is an annual guide to the most highly rated educational software for preschool through high school. Another well-regarded review source is MicroSIFT, a clearinghouse for courseware at the Northwest Regional Educational Laboratory. For current information on services and resources, including their Resources in Computer Education (RICE) database, contact the lab at 101 SW Main St., Ste 500, Portland, OR 97204.

TESS (*The Educational Software Selector*) is a product of the EPIE (Educational Products Information Exchange) Institute, whose *EPIEgram* is sometimes called the *Consumer Reports* for educational materials. Published biennially, *TESS* has four volumes, each covering different subject areas. The volumes contain brief program descriptions (including title, subject area, type, grade level, producer, required hardware, etc.) and also list published reviews and EPIE's own rating. The EPIE Institute also publishes *The Latest and Best of TESS*, which focuses on new releases. For more information about the work and services of EPIE, write to EPIE Institute, Box 839, Watermill, NY 11976. EPIE reviews are widely regarded as among the finest available.

The Florida Department of Education funds the @Micro evaluation project to acquire and evaluate 200 products each year (White and VanDeventer, 1991). Evaluators are subject-matter experts, who teach the content at a target level. Each uses the software with students in a class for 1 to 6 months. Evaluators are trained in the evaluation process developed for the project, which stresses open-ended responses, not the more limited, forced choice of most forms. Evaluators are also paid for their efforts. Dissemination is in print, on diskette as database files, and as a mainframe database accessible on the Florida Information Resources Network.

While reviews can be useful in identifying courseware for further evaluation, they are inadequate for making purchase decisions. One limitation is the objectivity of the reviews. You might want to look at several issues of the same review source, especially one that carries producer advertising, to see whether only positive reviews are published. If so, can you determine whether this is because it is the best use of limited space in the publication, or just that this source likes everything? Who wrote the review? What are that individual's qualifications? Was the software actually tested with students? Could the review reflect only the producer's advertising campaign? A related problem is the inevitable lag time between the release of new software and the appearance of reviews in any publications. Printed reviews seldom treat the very latest products.

Another limitation is the lack of accepted standards for reviews. Evaluation is not a science. For example, Jolicoeur and Berger (1986) found a low correlation between the overall ratings of two review services on the same eighty-two pieces of software. Most reviews are not based on actual student-performance achievement. Rather, they are one person's impression of the software and related materials. It is relatively rare to find a review based on actual classroom testing or the experiences of multiple users of the package. Zahner, Reiser, Dick, and Gill (1992) reported that software rated highly in *Only the Best* and *TESS* actually produced only modest learning gains when tested with students. Owston and Wideman (1987) found that trained evaluators rated software lower initially in about one third of the cases than they did after field-testing the same software. Thus, objective testing with students may suggest different conclusions than initial subjective assessment.

Borton and Rossett (1989) found a major discrepancy between factors highly valued by teachers and those valued by software evaluators. Evaluators tend to focus on pedagogical concerns, such as content presentation, integration into curriculum, and how well the software uses the computer's capabilities. Teachers tend to value freedom from bugs and other operating difficulties above all, followed by content accuracy. The researchers believe this reflects the view of most teachers that the computer is strictly peripheral, meant to stand alone as a supplement or for enrichment. If this is true, what then is the value of published reviews, because they may rest on factors other than those of most concern to teachers?

Hands-On Evaluation by Educators

Once you identify courseware of potential interest in your curriculum, you must actually try out the materials. There are several aspects to this.

Obtaining Courseware to Evaluate

You might be able to try out a product of interest in a local computer store, but that limits you to the relatively few titles they are likely to carry. Further, not all stores permit on-site trials.

Software producers develop products for only one reason—to earn a profit from sales. Copying computer diskettes, of course, is a simple task. The desire to protect their investments caused software producers to develop methods to make diskettes difficult or impossible to copy. Even so, software previews or return privileges were viewed as tantamount to giving away their software. Educators long had to buy to be able to try. Fortunately, most reputable software producers and distributors have recognized that software must "fit" to be of use and that a bad experience means a lost customer. Preview and return privileges are now the norm rather than a rarity. Educators must continue to insist on such access to courseware and refuse to buy what they have not seen in action. In turn, you must also scrupulously resist any temptation to duplicate software on loan or trial. (Software piracy is addressed in Chapter 20.)

Don't overlook the potential to review courseware yourself at a neighboring school where it is now used. A local community college, college, or university may have a courseware collection available to you. Some states support regional media or computer consortia with courseware collections for preview or loan. Become familiar with resources in your area.

Standardizing the Evaluation

Once you obtain courseware to evaluate, you'll probably want to follow some guidelines in conducting the evaluation. This is especially true when multiple reviewers examine the same product and must compile their results. Evaluation forms, discussed in more detail later, serve this purpose.

Conducting the Evaluation

While the only real test of courseware is in the hands of students, initially you or a teacher committee should evaluate courseware to determine that it even merits testing with students. This can be very time-consuming because of the number of criteria to consider and the fact that courseware is different from other educational materials. As previously mentioned, educators have a personal experience history with most other educational materials, which provides some basis for judgments. Relatively few have used much instructional software. Furthermore, you cannot skim courseware as you would a textbook; rather, you must work your way through the lesson as a student would. You also need to examine any accompanying student and teacher guides, workbooks, activity sheets, and so on. The software itself is the most time-consuming component, for which we recommend a three-step assessment.

First, go through the program as a high-achieving student might; that is, give relatively few incorrect responses along the way. This will demonstrate what the top students will experience and clearly show how the software treats correct responses. Keep track of how long it takes to complete the program in this way to approximate minimal student-usage time.

Second, complete the lesson again, but as a low-achieving student might. This will demonstrate how the program handles incorrect responses and the branching provided. How much remediation is provided to a user having difficulty? Does the program just display the same screen again, or are there different approaches to the same content? What is the nature of the on-line help, if there is any? Record the time you spend with the program in this manner, which will be much longer than in the first trial.

Third, execute the lesson again, testing its ability to handle totally inappropriate responses. For instance, if the desired answer is numeric, enter letters or symbols and vice versa. This must not cause the program to crash. What happens if you press just the "Enter" key instead of typing an answer? You should hear a beep or see a message to enter a valid response. This should never be accepted as a wrong answer. Can you find any "invisible" buttons that you can click to cause something unexpected to occur? It may seem trivial or absurd to test a program this way, but students delight in finding such "features" in software, which then detract from the learning experience. Good software can handle all accidental and malicious actions gracefully.

The next major section reviews specific evaluation considerations.

Student Field-Testing: The Real Test

Most discussions of courseware evaluation stop at the "expert" review stage just described, assuming that such a subjective process will indeed identify appropriate products to purchase and use. If the ultimate criterion of quality is student learning, however, then only actual use with students can demonstrate the value of a product.

Reiser and Dick (1990) proposed a model for software evaluation that rested primarily on student learning, not subjective judgments concerning content, accuracy, and so forth. After identifying software of interest, teachers or media specialists identify or develop instructional objectives appropriate to the software, then appropriate test items and attitude questions (to try to get at some of the more subtle effects). Students are pre-tested, and subjects selected from the top, middle, and bottom of pre-test results. Next comes a series of one-on-one evaluations, with the evaluator observing and interacting with individual student users. They are then tested and questioned about attitudes. This may lead to a conclusion that the software is usable, or may lead to further testing, possibly after changes in test or attitude items. The final phase is a small group of eight to twenty students using the software under "realistic" conditions (e.g., in the school lab with other students doing their work at the same time). There is an immediate post-test, then a retention test after 2 weeks. Reiser and Dick suggest that a valid measure of instructional effectiveness is average retention test score less average pre-test score. Needless to say, this is somewhat lower than it would be using the immediate post-test score.

In two pilot tests (see also Gill et al., 1992), this process proved impractical for teachers to use routinely, suggesting a need for a more efficient model if it is to be implemented on any scale. Zahner et al. (1992) reported on the simplified model, which replaces the one-on-one and the small-group evaluations with just three students (high, medium, and low prior learning) and the evaluator. The post-test is immediate, as is the attitude survey, and the retention test follows in 2 weeks. This change addresses many of the implementation concerns and reduces the time and number of students involved in the evaluation, but does it produce comparable results?

Two studies compared published ratings to ratings produced by the full model and the simplified model (Zahner et al., 1992). One used a tutorial selected from *Only the Best,* and the other used a tutorial that was highly rated in *TESS.* Use of tutorials made it easier to write objectives and test items and to determine appropriate duration for the treatment. In the first case, the simplified model led to a different conclusion than the full model; in the second, the results were comparable. The researchers concluded they have yet to find the ideal approach that is practical for the busy teacher, yet also accurate in its results. In neither case, however, did the software produce the high level of learning that one might expect from the glowing published evaluations.

Furthermore, Zahner et al. (1992) found that teachers do not necessarily judge the value of software on learning achievement. In one case, teachers accepted the program despite modest gains because they needed something, so it was better than nothing. In the other case, the teachers had disliked the software in their own initial review. The researchers believe they would have rejected it, even if it had produced substantial learning gains.

We strongly support student learning gains as the primary measure of worth in a software product. The process being developed by Reiser, Dick, and their colleagues is, perhaps, idealistic. It certainly would be desirable as an added component of or even a replacement for the current, subjective published reviews. It is obviously too demanding, however, for you or most teachers to even consider routinely for your own needs. Instead, we suggest a simpler approach that summarizes this section of the chapter.

First, identify candidate software. Review it to determine whether it seems suitable; if the software seems to have merit, try it out with your students. Measure what they have learned, both immediately and after some delay such as Reiser and Dick's 2-week period. Also check student reactions to it, as Reiser and Dick suggest. Then make your decision about purchasing and using the product. By carefully scheduling software for preview, you should be able to manage this approach without having to buy what may not meet your needs.

If you want further insight into student field-testing, read Dudley-Marling, Owston, and Searle (1988) and Callison and Haycock (1988).

Evaluation Considerations

Perhaps the day will come when educators can turn to a review service that bases its evaluations on student learning outcomes. Better yet, producers should be accountable for the results their software products. Evidence of effectiveness should be an expected part of each courseware produces. Realistically, however, review services find field-testing too difficult and costly (Sherry, 1987), and producers no doubt consider their current profit margins too slim to warrant testing as well. Therefore, we must rely on our own devices.

While traditional subjective evaluation has its flaws, many of the issues addressed by typical evaluations do have merit. They are not the final word on effectiveness, but neither should they be ignored. The following sections provide considerations for you to take into account in your own review phase or during student testing.

Intended Use

A major aspect of identifying potential software is its match to your need. While the same courseware may serve multiple goals, it may not be equally suited to all. Two teachers may evaluate the same courseware differently, based on their different goals. What are the objectives for this part of your curriculum? Do you want courseware to address all of them? Do you really want something to help with those aspects that cause students the most trouble? Perhaps you want a supplement for students who are ready for more than you can offer the entire class. In other words, you determine what needs to be learned and then seek appropriate courseware.

Obviously, a producer of courseware had some intended use in mind for the product, which may have led to specification of objectives for it. If so, consider them a guide to appropriate use of the software, but not a prescription that precludes other uses your creativity may suggest. Reiser and Dick (1990) include developing objectives for the courseware as part of their field-testing model. For evaluations that will be widely disseminated, this is appropriate, so that potential users can match their course objectives to those of the courseware. For an individual evaluator, however, the objectives for the curriculum take precedence. The software should fit the curriculum; its effectiveness should be judged by current student performance expectations, not something tailored just to the software, unless the software is so compelling that it warrants changing the curriculum.

Learning Theory

Theories of learning seek to explain how individuals learn or to identify factors that contribute to learning. You might evaluate courseware based on its inclusion of elements consistent with one or more learning theories. Jonassen (1988) provides a very detailed discussion of many theories and their application to courseware.

The Nine Events of Instruction

One of the better-known learning theories is the nine events of instruction (Gagné and Briggs, 1974). Figure 11.3 adapts the nine events into a flow chart, showing how a learner might progress through a lesson. Not all nine events will be found in every courseware product, nor must they be. Some may be left intentionally for the teacher to develop with students before or after the lesson. Keep the overall requirements of the lesson content and instructional format (e.g., drill, etc.) in mind when considering these criteria. Let's consider each briefly.

The first event is to *gain attention and provide motivation*. A common approach is the colorful, even animated graphics that appear at the start of most commercial courseware. Once student attention is gained, motivation is provided by various features. Having a *clear goal* to work toward is a sound motivator. Though not always appropriate, *competition* against the clock can be highly motivating. Look for a visual cue, such as a clock face, a digital display, or an hourglass slowly emptying. Many packages provide for competition against the computer or another student. Simple scorekeeping on the learner's performance provides competition with oneself or against a criterion. Finally, motivation is enhanced by *challenge,* but only if effort is required (not too easy) and the goal seems attainable (not too hard). Software may offer user-selectable difficulty levels or may adjust itself based on patterns of responses. If difficulty is self-selected, the user should be able to leave the current level for a less or more difficult one at any time.

Event two is to *present the objective.* A fundamental principle of performance objectives is that the learner must know what is expected and what the result of the lesson will be. The software may present the objectives, they may be in the student learning guide, or perhaps you will just present them to students verbally before they begin the lesson.

The third event is to *recall prerequisite knowledge.* New learning usually builds on existing knowledge. Learners should review whatever prior knowledge or skills are required to benefit from courseware. Again, this could be part of class activities before using the computer. If the computer provides this event, the software should direct the learner to earlier materials if the learner is not ready, or place the individual appropriately into the current lesson based on demonstrated mastery of components.

The lesson actually begins with the fourth event: *present the stimulus.* In a tutorial, the content will be new to the learner; in a drill, it will be familiar. A simulation

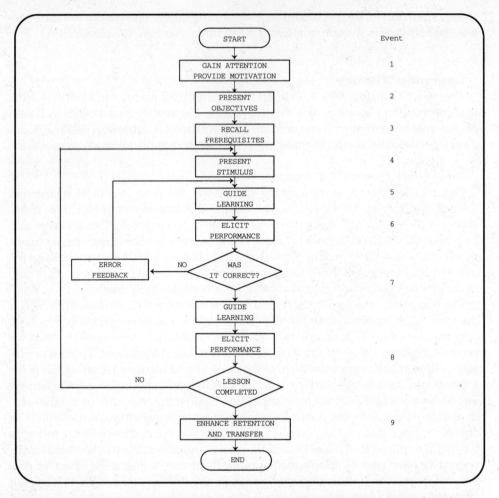

Figure 11.3. The nine events of instruction (based on Gagné and Briggs [1974].)

must present the scenario. All lesson types must establish and follow a strategy appropriate for the content.

Next the lesson should *guide the learning* (event five). Stimulus presentation alone is often inadequate. Guidance may take the form of examples to illustrate the rule or concept, questions to probe the learner's understanding, or hints or clues available on request or provided automatically at certain points in the lesson.

The key aspect of interactivity is the sixth event: *elicit performance*. Books are excellent conveyors of information, but they cannot demand activity. Courseware poses questions frequently to which the learner must respond. One great advantage of courseware is that every learner must respond to every question, in contrast to the occasional opportunity to respond in group instruction. The level of interactivity is a critical benefit of courseware.

Event seven acknowledges that following a performance, any form of instruction should *provide feedback*. A major problem of typical homework assignments is that the student may not learn of errors until the next school day or later. Courseware typically provides feedback to every question. You should consider carefully the quality of this feedback. Related to this is whether the learner is allowed multiple tries per question and, if so, whether the number permitted is appropriate. Courseware that traps the learner until a correct response is made is likely to destroy the motivation of a learner having difficulty with the lesson.

Though not an event in the model, *reinforcement* is closely related to feedback. Feedback entails knowing that a response was correct or incorrect, or its ramifications. Reinforcement takes two forms. One is to provide the correct answer for the learner. This should occur regardless of how the learner responded. Feedback and reinforcement often are combined in a form such as, "That's correct. A mammal nurses its young." The second form of reinforcement is to praise a job well done or encourage the learner to continue. Psychologists have studied various levels and schedules of reinforcement, but their findings generally seem to be ignored in courseware. Reinforcement tends either to be absent or it appears for every item.

The eighth event is to *assess performance*. Learners need to know their progress toward the criterion as they study a lesson. This provides a feeling of accomplishment and adds to motivation. For a timed lesson, a timer on screen may serve the purpose. A scoreboard showing number of correct responses also works. To stress achievement, it may be best to report only the number of correct responses and wait until a final summation to list the number of errors or percentage correct. Other methods that provide some assessment, but also encourage the learner, are special displays at specific points in the lesson such as halfway, a periodic report of the number of items completed, or a countdown toward the end. Many students are encouraged more by knowing only 2 items remain than that they have completed 98!

The ninth and final event is to *promote retention and transfer*. Neither should be assumed in any lesson. Instead, explicit provision should exist to enhance both. Within the lesson, this might be user-selectable enrichment activities after mastering basic content or the option to request further practice. Simulations and newer interactive multimedia courseware often provide for concurrent on-computer and off-computer activities, such as data-recording forms to help students organize data, analyze results, and determine appropriate actions for the next session at the computer. Hypermedia courseware often includes directions to jot down points using an on-line notepad, which can be saved or printed for further study. In addition, do not overlook the need to promote retention and transfer after the computer lesson. Many products contain suggested follow-up activities. Modify or add to the list as you deem appropriate. This is a vital element in integrating the computer into the curriculum, one often lacking in schools.

Specific Criteria

Beyond the general concerns of intended use and evidence of application of learning theory, a wide range of evaluation factors can and should be considered.

Bitter and Wighton (1987) described the criteria of one major evaluation group. There is no standard list of such factors, however, so we'll divide ours into three major categories: general instructional criteria, CAI-specific criteria, and usability.

General Instructional Criteria

This category covers broad concerns for *all* educational materials, whether print, traditional media, or computer format.

1. *Is the content accurate?* Obviously, errors in fact are unacceptable. Content accuracy, however, may be relative. For example, a simulation such as *SimEarth* or any of several based on elections may be difficult to assess in terms of accuracy. The purpose of such programs is less to convey content than to provoke analysis of the context presented, to raise questions for discussion, and to allow testing of strategies. Adherence to "reality" is not crucial to these goals. Likewise, a business simulation such as *Lemonade Stand* may not be "accurate" enough for older students, but will suffice as an introduction to business principles for young children. Accuracy depends on the learning objectives and student level in some cases.
2. *Is the instructional strategy sound? Appropriate? Creative?* Would you use such a strategy yourself? Does it clearly enhance the lesson?
3. *Is the material free of violent or aggressive behavior and all bias, including gender and race?* You might expect this to be a given in the 1990s, but in evaluating twelve career-oriented educational software packages, Benoit et al. (1991) found that gender fairness had not been achieved.
4. *Are the objectives clearly stated?* With courseware, often no objectives are specified, or they are general and low level, perhaps a result of claims that some packages fit users from preschool through adult!
5. *Are the objectives important to the curriculum?* If a courseware product does not fit the curriculum, does it offer so much that you should change the curriculum to fit it?
6. *Is the readability level appropriate for your audience?* Do not rely on the publisher's claims for audience suitability. Check readability yourself.
7. *Is the material free of grammatical errors, typos, and misspellings?* The infallible image of the computer might well reinforce language errors as correct usage.
8. *Are instructions clear and correct?* Users should never wonder what's next.
9. *Is the overall difficulty level appropriate for your learners?*
10. *Will the material help to motivate your students?*
11. *Does the package appear to offer good value for the price?* Important here may be the versatility of a given product. In how many different courses or grades could it be used? Will it fit only a brief period of instruction in one grade? Are there both remedial and enrichment applications that extend usability? A costly graphing program may find wider usage in mathematics than an inexpensive tutorial on a specific topic, for example. Price alone is an inadequate criterion.

CAI-Specific Criteria

The unique qualities of courseware require evaluation criteria that are not applicable to other educational materials.

1. *Does the package take advantage of the computer's capabilities?* What does it offer that students could not previously do (i.e., is this a type II application)? Litchfield (1992) stresses this factor especially in evaluating substitutes for science lab experiences.
2. *Is this a more effective or efficient approach to the content than any other?* Or is it really a case of print materials converted to the computer screen?
3. *Is the sequence of the presentation appropriate?* Is it compatible with your approach to the topic or are you willing to change? Remember, with a book or set of slides you can alter the sequence if you wish. There is usually less potential to do so with computer materials.
4. *Does the learner control the pace and/or sequence of the presentation?* Is there a menu of choices or does the computer adjust the sequence to fit user response patterns? Can the user back up in the program to review? Are displays changed by user action or are they timed? The programmer should not presume to know how long an individual needs to read any screen.
5. *What is the level of interaction?* How much must the student read before making a more meaningful response than pressing the space bar or just clicking the mouse to continue? Do not accept "electronic page turners."
6. *Can the student exit the program before the end is reached?* If so, are the directions for exiting clear and easy to remember? Better yet, are they given on the screen whenever it is possible to exit? Can the student later re-enter the program at the point of exit, or is it necessary to start all over again?
7. *Is the program designed for only one student at a time or does it encourage group activities?* Many persons are concerned that the computer could decrease student socialization, if all activities are individual. Could you use this program with only one computer for the group?
8. *If there are pre-tests and post-tests, do they appear to be valid?* Do all "tests" actually measure learner progress?
9. *Is feedback to responses appropriate?* Does it help the learner to understand the cause of an error or just say it was wrong? Feedback should never demean or belittle the user, regardless of the error.
10. *Is feedback effective?* Some programs provide more attractive feedback for wrong answers than correct ones, especially in graphics. This may encourage students to give wrong answers just to see what happens.
11. *Are graphics, if used, supportive of the learning process?* Or are they merely window dressing? Graphics, including animation, can readily enhance the appeal of a program, but they should also provide visual learning.
12. *If sound is used, does it serve a useful purpose?* Auditory cues when a user has made an error can be very helpful, but musical tunes can become a nuisance in a classroom or a lab. Can the sound be turned off?

13. *Do verbal responses require more than minimal typing?* If so, typing skill or spelling may be as much a key to success as knowledge or analytic thinking.

14. *Do all typed responses require pressing the "Enter" key?* If not, users can become confused. When is the "Enter" key needed, and when is it not? Why the distinction?

15. *Is the program "bombproof?"* Can the user give responses that cause the program to crash? Students will find such problems if you do not.

Usability Criteria

Various factors make one product easier to use than another. Consider usability from both the teacher's and the learner's perspective.

Teacher Concerns

1. *Can the program easily be integrated into your instruction?* What support materials are provided? How appropriate and useful do they appear to be? Are both teacher and student manuals available, if appropriate? Are there worksheets or study guides? Are suggested activities and references to related materials included? The more assistance provided, the easier the package will be to incorporate into instruction. That is the difference between courseware and just software. Figure 11.4 is an example.

2. *Is there a recordkeeping or management component?* If so, what does it provide, and how complex is it to use? Chapter 12 will examine the potentials and pitfalls of computer-managed instruction.

3. *Can the program be modified?* Most teachers lack the time and knowledge to tamper with a program and make major changes. However, drill programs become more versatile if the teacher is able to enter or change the content of the drill, altering, say, a weekly spelling list. This is usually achieved through a utility program provided with the package. If this option exists, how difficult is it to enter your material?

4. *How manageable is the program's flexibility?* This is an issue with interactive multimedia. How will you guide student usage for varying goals? How will you know what (or if) your students have learned?

Student Concerns

1. *Can the package be used with little or no teacher intervention?* Are all directions presented on screen or must the user keep a manual at hand for guidance? Manuals are not necessarily less effective, just more cumbersome. On the other hand, printed manuals allow skimming or bypassing information for quick access to what one is seeking. In classroom settings, wall charts of directions can also be very effective. Preparing them could be a worthwhile student project.

2. *How difficult is it for a student to get started on a lesson?* Some packages with management components require elaborate "log-on" procedures.

Figure 11.4. Educational courseware should include ample support material.

3. *Does the package require much disk handling or swapping?* Especially with younger students, it is desirable to avoid student contact with diskettes as much as possible. Networks and hard disks eliminate this potential problem.
4. *Is there provision for use of alternative input devices* such as light pens, joy sticks, or touch screens that could make the package more usable for special needs populations?
5. *Is there a "HELP" function available?* If so, what does it provide?

Evaluation of Specific CAI Types

Some authors suggest that the task of courseware evaluation differs significantly according to the type of CAI involved. For example, Bitter (1989) offers separate forms for evaluating software in four categories: drill and practice, tutorial, simulation and problem solving, and tool applications. While there is merit in this approach, we have tried to provide a comprehensive set of criteria, most but not all of which apply to all CAI forms. This avoids the redundancy inherent in approaches such as Bitter's.

Ultimately, the most important aids in evaluating courseware become your own personal experience in using CAI with your students and a broad understanding of factors that may contribute to effectiveness. There is a holistic element to evaluation that cannot be reflected in narrow prescriptions of absolutely mandatory evaluation components. Common sense, after all, has not been rendered obsolete by computer technology.

Creating and Using Evaluation Forms

Courseware evaluation is multifaceted and complex. The time required simply to review a package to decide whether to test it with students can be significant. Any evaluation approach may fail to reveal some aspects of a program, especially a simulation or today's complex hypermedia. The more sophisticated the courseware, the less certainty that you will ever see all of it. How can you at least get a handle on your task?

The most common answer is to use an evaluation form. Such a form will assure some level of attention to key factors, as well as a common base for all evaluations that you undertake. Evaluation forms abound in the literature, with new variations appearing regularly. Each form has its own predilections, revealing its creator's biases. Any one may or may not suit your needs.

The goal of an evaluation form is to organize the plethora of factors and concerns in some coherent and manageable way. Otherwise, the task quickly becomes overwhelming. At the same time, there is a tendency to view the result as some relatively simple, highly quantifiable, and totally accurate wonder. Just make checks where a quality is observed, leave blank all others, tally the checks, and violà: a good or bad product has been found. Would that it were so simple!

Creating an Evaluation Form

Recognizing the complexity of evaluation and the undeniable need to organize it, Figure 11.5 offers a sketchy evaluation instrument in comparison to most. Our experience is that the most useful form is one that includes the primary concerns of the evaluator, be that an individual or a team. Therefore, we recommend that anyone setting out to evaluate courseware begin by developing a personal, school, or district form for that purpose. The form should begin with basic descriptive information, followed by elements from each of the three broad categories. Exactly which elements are included will vary depending on your own needs and views, perhaps even the type of courseware. Thus, we offer only an outline and leave it to you, the user, to include as many elements as you choose from the suggestions in this chapter. Several factors make up the overall assessment.

Description
Most useful descriptive information comes directly from the resources you used to identify the package initially or from the product literature. The item CAI

COURSEWARE EVALUATION FORM

Date of Review_____   Name of Reviewer _____

DESCRIPTION

PACKAGE NAME:_____   CAI TYPE: _____
CURRICULUM AREA:_____   LEVEL CLAIMED:_____
PRODUCER:_____
BACKUP POLICY: _____
_____
COMPATIBILITY: _____
_____
AVAILABLE FROM (FULL ADDRESS): _____
COST: _____   REFERENCE SOURCE:_____

GENERAL INSTRUCTIONAL CRITERIA

CRITERION	RATING	X	WEIGHT	=	TOTAL PTS.
_____	_____	X	_____	=	_____
_____	_____	X	_____	=	_____
_____	_____	X	_____	=	_____

CAI SPECIFIC CRITERIA

CRITERION	RATING	X	WEIGHT	=	TOTAL PTS.
_____	_____	X	_____	=	_____
_____	_____	X	_____	=	_____
_____	_____	X	_____	=	_____

USABILITY CRITERIA

CRITERION	RATING	X	WEIGHT	=	TOTAL PTS.
_____	_____	X	_____	=	_____
_____	_____	X	_____	=	_____
_____	_____	X	_____	=	_____

GRAND TOTAL POINTS FOR THIS PACKAGE: _____

OVERALL ASSESSMENT

HOLISTIC REACTION TO THE PACKAGE: _____
_____
_____

INSTRUCTIONAL STRATEGY (from the Learner-Centered Taxonomy):
  Circle the appropriate item in each column.

Metacognition Source	Primary Cognitive Processes	Content Presentation
Program-Initiated	Organizing	Domain-Oriented
Guided	Rehearsal	Topic-Oriented
Learner-Initiated	Assessment (Response Organization)	Operation-Oriented

APPLICATION POTENTIAL (circle one):   Type II   Type I only

RECOMMENDATION:

_____   Excellent. Purchase without Field Test
_____   Good. Proceed with Field Test
_____   Fair. Marginal, Test Only If No Better Alternative
_____   Poor. Insufficient Merit to Field Test

FIELD-TEST DATA SUMMARY:

Figure 11.5.   Courseware evaluation form.

Type means the producer's claim that the package is a simulation, tutorial, or whatever. The producer's backup policy usually is explained in the documentation. It is critical to have a backup copy of any software, just as it is for your own personal files. You may be permitted to make such a copy, or you may have to order one. The worst situation of all is being allowed to request a backup only after your original fails.

One compatibility factor is whether the product is available for more than one type of computer. Even if your school has only one type, you may later change and want to acquire the same software for a different computer. Record the information for possible future use. Also note which models of a particular computer may be used, how much RAM is required, whether a hard disk is mandatory, and whether the product can be used on a network. Is the software offered on both 5.25" and 3.5" diskettes? Can it be installed on a hard disk? Is some other software required to use the product, such as a specific database or graphics package for which you are evaluating only data files? For *HyperCard* stacks, which version of *HyperCard* is required?

Finally, if you found a review of the product, note the source for future reference.

Category Criteria

Review the many criteria discussed previously in this chapter. Include as many in each of the three categories as you find important. Our skeletal form is not meant to suggest a specific number of criteria, but rather the flexibility to use as few or as many as you wish.

Adding a Rating Scale

Once you have chosen your criteria, you have the basis of a simple checklist evaluation form. What is the meaning, however, of a series of checks? We suggest quantifying your assessment by using some scale. You might rate each item as Outstanding, Acceptable, or Unacceptable, assigning 3, 2, or 1 points, respectively. Devise a scale that you like. The verbal meaning need not be identical for every item either, as long as the relative point values remain consistent. A sum of these values will quantify your assessment.

Adding Weights

Going a step further, it is unlikely that all chosen criteria are of equal importance to you. This suggests weighting each in some manner. In most cases, assigning a weight from 3 (most important) to 1 (least important) will probably suffice. Adding a numerical value to your rating categories and multiplying your assessment by the weight for that item yields a potential score of 9 (outstanding and most important) to 1 (unacceptable and least important). A final sum of these values would probably yield a more complete picture of the package's merits for your context.

Overall Assessment

After completing the first parts of the evaluation form, briefly write your overall reaction to the courseware. Think about the merits of the product by classifying its instructional strategy according to the learner-centered taxonomy that you learned about in Chapter 9. The source of metacognition is particularly important. Is the program controlling the learning (program-initiated), is the program guiding the learner (guided metacognition), or is the learner in control (learner-initiated)? Your final recommendation may be wholehearted endorsement without further ado, a decision to proceed with a student field-test to determine instructional effectiveness, or rejection of the product as unsuited to your needs and interests.

How you go about a field-test is at your discretion. Reiser and Dick's (1990) model is as good as any. The critical point is to measure in some viable way the learning gain derived from the software. You then may wish to record at least a summary of your field-test results right on your form to complete the record.

Using Your Form

In general, once you have created a form to your liking, applying it to any specific product should pose no problems. To guard against over-reliance on the quantifiable data, complete your narrative assessment and classification by the learner-centered taxonomy *before* you tally the rating numbers. Indicate whether the software clearly promotes a Type I or Type II experience. You may be willing to take more of a chance with Type II courseware than you can justify for Type I. Within each criteria category, do not reject a product based solely on concerns with one or a few items. Consider omissions or weaknesses in the total context of what the product provides and how well it fits your need. You should compare your holistic reaction to the "hard data" from the numbers and consider their respective merits. The more experience you develop in examining and actually using software with your students, the more valid your subjective view is apt to be. Still, it is the field-test data that should be the final determiner of whether to use a product widely with your students.

Other Approaches to Evaluation

If you wish to consider more prescriptive approaches to courseware evaluation, you can find ready-to-use forms in Brownell (1992, pp. 287–290), Maddux et al. (1992, pp. 305–307), Merrill, Hammons, Tolman, Christensen, Vincent, and Reynolds (1992, pp. 131–132), Simonson and Thompson (1990, pp. 268–269), and Geisert and Futrell (1990, p. 208), among many sources.

Beyond such general-purpose form approaches, Litchfield (1992) provides a specific form for evaluating inquiry-based science software and multimedia. Owston (1987) offers an extensive treatment of evaluation based on the York Educational Software Evaluation Scales (YESES). Majsterek (1990) provides a specific approach to evaluating IEP software for special education needs.

Finally, Zahner et al. (1992) speculate on the impact of current trends toward hypermedia and multimedia. Their initial work has focused on drills and tutorials, which are far simpler. If the learner is in an interactive microworld, which is learner controllable, how do you measure effectiveness? Are there measurable objectives?

Over what time period may it be reasonable to look for outcomes? How do you assess critical-thinking and problem-solving skills? Knussen (1991) and Tucker and Dempsey (1992) offer some possible approaches to complex assessment needs.

Summary

With appropriate and effective courseware, the computer can become an integral part of the learning process. It can assume a portion of the teaching responsibility, becoming a student's private tutor. In turn, this may free the teacher to spend more time with individual students. However, to achieve such a goal assumes the availability of excellent courseware.

The first step in courseware selection is identification of potentially useful products. Catalogs and dealers, colleagues, and published reviews are all useful at this stage. Next, you should do a hands-on evaluation of candidate courseware to determine whether it is worth testing with students. Much software is of little or no value, and you may be able to eliminate many packages through your own assessment. The ultimate value of instructional courseware, however, is the student learning that it develops. Evaluation of effectiveness requires student field-testing, something developers appear rarely to do.

During your own initial screening, as well as during field-testing, there are so many potential evaluation considerations that they appear impossible to manage. An evaluation form can help to assure that no vital point is overlooked and to standardize to some extent the work of multiple reviewers. It seems best that individuals, schools, or districts develop a form that addresses their own major concerns, rather than adopt one that seeks to serve all. If you alone are responsible for evaluating software, you will find that you can make holistic judgments more readily and comfortably as you gain experience, both in evaluation and in using courseware with students.

Despite all efforts to streamline the process, courseware evaluation, if done conscientiously, will always be a time-consuming task, much more so than teachers are accustomed to in selecting other materials. If the computer, however, is to live up to its potential as an aid to learning, this task cannot be ignored or minimized. The quality of materials and curriculum fit will determine whether the computer achieves its potential as an indispensable element in the educational process or joins earlier technological marvels in the school storeroom.

Chapter 11 Activities

1. Starting with the outline model of an evaluation form shown in Figure 11.5, complete the form by adding the criteria most important to you, your school, or district. (Expand the space devoted to categories as you wish.) Try to

balance a desire for thoroughness with concern for the time it will take to complete your instrument.

2. Compare your evaluation form with those of your colleagues. Discuss the reasons for selection of different elements to include.

3. In groups of at least three persons, try to create a common form acceptable to all, much as a school or district committee would. What did you have to give up from your list of important elements to reach consensus while avoiding a ten-page instrument? Did your negotiations cause you to rethink the merits of certain possible items?

4. Using your instrument, critically evaluate at least one courseware product in each of as many different categories (e.g., simulation) as you can.

5. Using your instrument, evaluate three or more courseware products intended for the same or similar instructional use. Does your "objective" assessment agree with your holistic view of these packages? If not, why? Does your form require modification?

6. Organize a project to contact producers of the software to which you have access to request student field-test data. Compare your results to those of Zane and Frazer (1992) reported earlier in this chapter. If you do get a positive response, look to Smith (1988) for guidance in evaluating claims.

7. Try to find several published reviews of a product to which you have access. Without first reading the reviews, conduct your own evaluation of the package. Compare your findings with the reviews. What does this tell you about relying on "professional" reviews?

8. Evaluate at least one courseware package solely on the basis of Gagné's events of instruction. From this theoretical perspective, does the package appear to be effective? If you could find no evidence of one or more events, is the omission justifiable in this case?

Bibliography

Bangert-Drowns, R. L., and Kozma, R. B. "Assessing the Design of Instructional Software." *Journal of Research on Computing in Education,* Spring 1989, *21*(3), pp. 241–256.

Barrett, A. J., et al. "Objectively Determining the Educational Potential of Computer and Video-Based Courseware; or, Producing Reliable Evaluations Despite the Dog and Pony Show." Paper presented at the 7th International Conference on Technology and Education (Brussels, Belgium, March 20–22, 1990). (ERIC Document ED 324 337.)

Benoit, S. S., et al. "Gender Fairness: Is It Prevalent in Career-Oriented Software?" *Delta Pi Epsilon Journal,* Summer 1991, *33*(2), pp. 106–116.

Best, A., Ed. *The 1990–91 Educational Software Preview Guide.* Menlo Park, CA: Educational Software Evaluation Consortium; and Eugene, OR: International Society for Technology in Education, 1991. (ERIC Document ED 338216. For the 1988–89 edition, see ED 313 011.)

Bitter, G. G. *Microcomputers in Education Today.* Watsonville, CA: Mitchell Publishing, 1989.

Bitter, G. G., and Wighton, D. "The Most Important Criteria Used by the Educational Software Evaluation Consortium." *The Computing Teacher,* March 1987, pp. 7–9.

Bork, A. "Education and Computers: The Situation Today and Some Possible Futures." *T.H.E. Journal,* October 1984, pp. 92–97.

Borsook, T. K., and Higginbotham-Wheat, N. "Interactivity: What Is It and What Can It Do for Computer-Based Instruction?" *Educational Technology,* October 1991, *31*(10), pp. 11–17.

Borton, W., and Rossett, A. "Educational Software and Published Reviews: Congruence of Teacher, Developer, and Evaluator Perceptions." *Education,* 1989, *109*(4), pp. 434–444.

Brownell, G. *Computers and Teaching,* 2nd ed. St. Paul, MN: West Publishing, 1992.

Callison, D., and Haycock, G. "A Methodology for Student Evaluation of Educational Microcomputer Software." *Educational Technology,* January 1988, pp. 25–32.

Charleston, G. M., et al. "A Project To Design an Evaluation of the Appropriateness and Effectiveness of Computer-Assisted Instructional Packages Used in the Remediation of Basic Skills." University Park, PA: Pennsylvania State University, Institute for the Study of Adult Literacy, 1989. (ERIC Document ED 321 088.)

Directory of Software Data Sources. Reston, VA: Council for Exceptional Children, 1990. (ERIC Document ED 339 160.)

Dudley-Marling, C., Owston, R. D., and Searle, D. "A Field-Testing Approach to Software Evaluation." *Computers in the Schools,* 1988, *5*(1/2), pp. 241–249.

Ely, D. P. "Portability: Cross-Cultural Educational Perspectives." *Journal of Research on Computing in Education,* Winter 1990, *23*(2), pp. 272–283.

EPIEgram: The Educational Consumers' Newsletter. Volume 17, Numbers 1–9, 1990–1991. Water Mill, NY: Educational Products Information Exchange Institute, 1991. (ERIC Document ED 340 354.)

Gagné, R. M., and Briggs, L. J. *Principles of Instructional Design.* New York: Holt, Rinehart, and Winston, 1974.

Geisert, P., and Futrell, M. *Teachers, Computers, and Curriculum.* Boston, MA: Allyn & Bacon, 1990.

Gill, B., Dick, W., Reiser, R., and Zahner, J. E. "A New Model for Evaluating Instructional Software." *Educational Technology,* March 1992, *32*(3), pp. 39–44.

Jaeger, M. "Zaps, Booms, and Whistles in Educational Software." *The Computing Teacher,* March 1988, pp. 20–22.

Jolicoeur, K., and Berger, D. E. "Implementing Educational Software and Evaluating Its Academic Effectiveness: Part I." *Educational Technology,* September 1988, *28*(9), pp. 7–13.

Jolicoeur, K., and Berger, D. E. "Implementing Educational Software and Evaluating Its Academic Effectiveness: Part II." *Educational Technology,* October 1988, *28*(9), pp. 13–19.

Jolicoeur, K., and Berger, D. E. "Do We Really Know What Makes Educational Software Effective? A Call for Empirical Research on Effectiveness." *Educational Technology,* December 1986, *26*(12), pp. 7–11.

Jonassen, D. H. *Instructional Designs for Microcomputer Courseware.* Hillsdale, NJ: Lawrence Erlbaum Associates, 1988.

Knussen, C., et al. "An Approach to the Evaluation of Hypermedia." *Computers and Education,* 1991, *17*(1), pp. 13–24.

Kozma, R. B., and Johnston, J. "The Technological Revolution Comes to the Classroom." *Change,* January 1991, *23*(1), pp. 10–23.

Litchfield, B. C. "Evaluation of Inquiry-based Science Software and Interactive Multimedia Programs." *The Computing Teacher,* March 1992, *19*(6), pp. 41–43.

McCormick, T. E., and McCoy, S. B. "Computer-Assisted Instruction and Multicultural Nonsexist Education: A Caveat for Those Who Select and Design Software." *Computers in the Schools,* 1990, *7*(4), pp. 105–124.

Maddux, C. D., Johnson, D. L., and Willis, J. W. *Educational Computing. Learning with Tomorrow's Technologies.* Boston, MA: Allyn & Bacon, 1992.

Majsterek, D. J., et al. "Computerized IEPs: Guidelines for Product Evaluation." *Journal of Special Education Technology,* Summer 1990, *10*(4) pp. 207–219.

Malouf, D. B., et al. "Integrating Computer Software into Effective Instruction." *Teaching Exceptional Children,* Spring 1991, *23*(3) pp. 54–56.

Merrill, P. F., Hammons, K., Tolman, M. N., Christensen, L., Vincent, B. R., and Reynolds, P. L. *Computers in Education,* 2nd ed. Boston, MA: Allyn & Bacon, 1992.

Moore, J. "Finding the Right Educational Software for Your Child." *Exceptional Parent,* October 1990, *20*(7), pp. 58–62.

Neill, S. B., and Neill, G. W. *Only the Best, 1993. The Annual Guide to Highest-Rated Educational Software/Multimedia for Preschool–Grade 12.* Carmichael, CA: Educational News Service, 1993. (1991 edition: ERIC Document ED 325 102. For the 1990 guide and a cumulative guide, see ED 316 209/210.)

Owston, R. D. *Software Evaluation. A Criterion-Based Approach.* Scarborough, Ontario: Prentice-Hall Canada Inc., 1987.

Owston, R. D., and Wideman, H. H. "The Value of Supplemental Panel Software Reviews with Field Observations." *Canadian Journal of Educational Communication,* 1987, *16,* pp. 295–308.

Preston, M. *Courseware Evaluation: A Review of Existing Services and Publications.* Calgary, Alberta: Canadian Centre for Learning Systems, 1987.

Reiser, R., and Dick, W. "Evaluating Instructional Software." *Educational Technology Research and Development,* 1990, *38*(3), pp. 43–50.

Sales, G. C. "Factors Influencing the Design, Development, and Implementation of Instructional Software." *Computers in the Schools,* 1990, *7*(4), pp. 135–148.

Sales, G. C., et al. "The Evolution of K–12 Instructional Software: An Analysis of Leading Microcomputer-Based Programs from 1981–1988." *Journal of Computer Based Instruction,* Spring 1991, *18*(2), pp. 41–47.

Schwarz, I., and Lewis, M. "Selecting Basic Concept Courseware for Preschools and Early Elementary Grades." *The Computing Teacher,* December/January 1991–1992, *19*(4), pp. 15–17.

Sherry, M. "EPIE Responds to Article on Software Evaluation." *Educational Technology,* April 1987, *27*(4), p. 53.

Simonson, M. R., and Thompson, A. *Educational Computing Foundations.* Columbus, OH: Merrill, 1990.

Sloane, H., Gordon, H. M., Gunn, C., and Mickelsen, V. G. *Evaluating Educational Software: A Guide for Teachers.* Englewood Cliffs, NJ: Prentice-Hall, 1989.

Smith, R. A. "Claims of Improved Academic Performance: The Questions You Should Ask." *The Computing Teacher,* May 1988, pp. 42–44, 61.

Software Evaluation: Criteria for Educational Computer Software Evaluation. Toronto: Council of Ministers of Education, Canada, 1985.

Trollip, S. "Four Computer Features to Avoid." *The Computing Teacher,* May 1987, pp. 33–35.

Tucker, S. A., and Dempsey, J. V. "Semiotic Criteria for Evaluating Instructional HyperMedia." Paper presented at the Annual Meeting of the American Educational Research Association (Chicago, IL, April 3–7, 1991). (ERIC Document ED 337155.)

Voogt, J. "Courseware Evaluation by Teachers: An Implementation Perspective." *Computers and Education,* 1990, *14*(4), pp. 299–307.

White, J. A. and VanDeventer, S. S. "A Successful Model for Software Evaluation." *Computers in the Schools,* 1991, *8*(1/2/3), pp. 323–326.

Zahner, J. E., Reiser, R. A., Dick, W., and Gill, B. "Evaluating Instructional Software: A Simplified Model." *Educational Technology Research and Development*, 1992, 40(3), pp. 55–62.

Zane, T., and Frazer, C. G. "The Extent to Which Software Developers Validate Their Claims." *Journal of Research on Computing in Education*, Spring 1992, 24(3), pp. 410–419.

Objectives

After studying this chapter, you will be able to:

Define computer-managed instruction (CMI) and explain its bases.

Describe several ways of facilitating classroom-management tasks with a computer.

Explain several roles of the computer in individualized instruction.

Assess uses of the computer in testing, including consideration of views of alternative assessment.

Explain the nature and scope of integrated learning systems(ILS).

Evaluate the advantages and disadvantages of integrated learning systems.

Criticize or defend CMI.

Chapter 12

Managing Learning: Computer-Managed Instruction

This chapter examines another facet of the computer as tutor: computer-managed instruction (CMI). The term CMI refers to software and systems that aid teachers in performance assessment and monitoring, evaluation, and recordkeeping. While superficially similar in some ways to support software presented in Chapter 5, the nature and scope of CMI is sufficiently different to warrant distinct treatment. Often CMI is intimately linked to computer-assisted instruction (CAI), such as in integrated learning systems (ILS). CMI can refer also to myriad central administration applications, such as budgeting, attendance, transcripts, and inventory, but these topics are beyond the scope of this book. See Visscher (1991) and Visscher and Spuck (1991) for more information.

An Overview of Computer-Managed Instruction

To introduce you to *computer-managed instruction (CMI)*, let's consider its bases: the teacher's role in management, the concepts of mastery learning and individualized instruction, as well as why the latter have had limited success.

The Teacher as Manager

When teachers prepare résumés of their professional experience, comparatively few identify management skills among their achievements. Yet many management activities are part of daily life in the classroom. Teachers organize and direct a complex array of activities, learning resources, and even auxiliary personnel, such as aides. There are countless records to keep: attendance, grades, text distribution, classroom inventory, and so forth. The end of a marking period brings with it the calculation of grades and preparation of grade reports. Parents may desire, or demand, more thorough information about their children's progress.

Teachers often complain about the proportion of their time that management activities consume. A microcomputer in the classroom can help the teacher dig out from under the paperwork avalanche and reclaim time for working with students. This is, after all, a teacher's primary function.

Using software to aid in classroom management is often referred to as CMI. The primary purpose of CMI is to help track and document student achievement. The forms that CMI takes are as diverse as the needs that led to creation of such software. Early efforts in this direction predate microcomputers by some years. They were an outgrowth of the concepts of mastery learning and individualized instruction.

Mastery Learning

Simply put, mastery learning contends that all students can achieve at a very high level under the right conditions. To implement mastery learning, the curriculum is defined as a series of objectives stated in observable, measurable form. Students progress to new objectives by demonstrating mastery of logically preceding ones. These concepts are fundamental to the teaching/learning models of Benjamin Bloom, Madeline Hunter, Ronald Edmonds, and the Outcomes-Based Education movement (Hall, 1988). The teacher must identify the proper starting point on the objectives continuum for each student, provide instruction appropriate to each student for each selected objective, and monitor performance. Teachers attempting to implement mastery learning quickly found themselves facing enormous management tasks.

Individualized Instruction

Implementation of mastery learning all but necessitates some form of individualization of instruction as well. Not all students will "master" the content in the same time, so a lock-step approach to instruction is inappropriate. Individualization acknowledges differences in learning needs and rates, and adds the idea that students have differing learning styles or modalities. The basis of mastery learning, as well as other effective learning experiences, is individualization.

Prescription of learning activities results from individual diagnosis of needs. As Becker (undated, p. 31) notes, "Research suggests that using tests to individualize instruction targeted to each student's identified skill deficiencies is a practice that has merit." The teacher now faces a group of students progressing at different rates through diverse sets of objectives using varied materials and forms of learning. Assuming a satisfactory method of handling diagnosis and prescription, the teacher must next find a way to gain time to work with students individually. See Szabo and Montgomerie (1992) for an excellent discussion of the foundations of CMI.

Problems in Implementation

Many efforts at individualization and mastery learning have foundered on problems of management. The Chicago Public Schools abandoned a mastery learning reading program after 4 years because it was "just so demanding" and the record-keeping was "overwhelming" (Banas, 1985). The teacher's role can decline quickly into that of a clerk just to deal with recordkeeping. In fact, neither concept has achieved broad implementation, largely because of management problems. This is where CMI comes in.

An Early CMI System: Project Plan

One early effort at CMI was Westinghouse Learning Corporation's Project PLAN. PLAN was conceptualized as a method of returning the teacher to the most productive role possible, largely small-group instruction and individual student assistance. A large computer at a remote location took over the tasks of assessment, progress monitoring, and prescription of student work.

Based on the data entered into the system, the computer selected objectives and prescribed learning activities for each student. Objectives were linked to a wide variety of textbook series and other learning resources. To end a "unit," students took a test using machine-readable answer sheets. Overnight, the computer evaluated tests, updated records, and determined the next day's assignments for each student. Each teacher received a daily printout on student achievement, progress through the specified objectives, and future lesson projections. Most student work was individualized, so class-preparation time was reduced significantly. Time became available for teachers to work directly with learners.

For some teachers, PLAN was a great success because it clearly provided for mastery learning, allowed individualization to work, and assumed most management tasks. For others, it also removed their sense of purpose and control. Some teachers felt like laborers, carrying out orders from the "great boss computer."

Project PLAN enabled schools to implement the concepts of individualized instruction, but ultimately it foundered on high costs, like most early computer projects. Schools were generally impressed by the achievement gains of their students under PLAN, but few could afford to use it.

Microcomputers and CMI

Some aspects of mainframe attempts at CMI, such as PLAN, reappeared with the spread of microcomputers in schools. Let's look at CMI as performance monitoring and analysis, and as a means of testing.

CMI as Performance Monitoring and Analysis

Microcomputers provided schools with inexpensive computer power to diagnose, deliver instruction (which PLAN never did), process learner responses, and analyze and store results. PLAN had been an external traffic manager for an individualized learning system, not an integrated part of it. When microcomputers made instruction delivery viable, it was natural to include a recordkeeping management component in CAI software.

A Typical CMI System

To use the CMI component of software, you usually must begin by establishing a class roster on the computer, following the guidance of on-screen menus. The sequence of events might be:

1. Load the software and access the management system.
2. Enter your name as the teacher.
3. Enter the name or other designation of the class.
4. Enter all student names.

From this class database, the software controls student access to lessons through log-on procedures. Any student not found on the roster for the requested class and teacher is denied use of the lessons. Students who successfully log on proceed through the lessons. The computer records their performance as they work. The teacher accesses the performance data at any convenient time, either on-screen or by requesting a printout.

Differences in Implementations

The CMI aspect of software has highly varied levels of sophistication. The information monitored and stored may be as minimal as total correct and incorrect responses or as complex as each individual response to all questions throughout every lesson. It may be possible to analyze student responses individually, for the entire class, or even across classes.

If the software involves multiple lessons, the teacher may need to assign a starting point for each student during setup. The program will then not require the student to repeat work already mastered and can remind students at each work session of what they have already completed. In some systems, the teacher may also specify the order in which the student is to receive the instruction, how long each student may spend on a given lesson, acceptable performance levels, minimum and maximum numbers of items to be presented, and other individual parameters.

The most sophisticated CMI pre-tests the student on the content of the lesson(s). From this diagnosis, the computer begins the instruction at the most appropriate point for that student. As the learner progresses, the computer monitors achievement and moves the student forward as rapidly as possible and backward whenever errors warrant. Such an approach is highly efficient; the student need never linger on previously mastered material, yet is never frustrated by material that is too advanced.

Benefits of Performance Monitoring

One common criticism of computer-based learning is that the teacher may have little sense of what a student has learned until the next oral or written exam. Unlike written homework, individual work at separate computers is difficult to monitor, and there is seldom any paper record of the student's work.

Even a simple scorekeeping approach to CMI can reduce this concern. Just a retrievable record of questions attempted and number correct, such as many programs provide on-screen for the learner, can help you to guide student study and reduce the need for some other forms of testing. In fact, evaluation may require less time overall because fewer questions, randomly selected by the computer, may provide performance data comparable to that of lengthier paper-and-pencil assessments in the past.

CMI as Test-Scoring and Testing

The term *computer-managed instruction (CMI)* is also applied to the use of the computer for testing, even apart from computer-based learning materials. Beyond our presentation, Baker (1990) summarizes trends and discusses the advantages and limitations of computer-based testing.

Automated Test Scoring

One form of CMI uses the computer only for test scoring by interfacing a microcomputer and an optical scanner that reads those ubiquitous answers sheets that you may mark only with a No. 2 pencil. The computer merely performs a clerical service and does not function as an integral part of the teaching/learning process. The scoring software determines just what information you get from such machine-scored tests, from just individual student scores to complex analyses of all tests scored in one batch.

Computer-Assisted Testing

The computer can create and give objective tests apart from CAI. With typical computer-assisted testing (CAT) software, you prepare a bank of test items for each objective and unit of instruction. Students take their tests at the computer when they are ready and get their score at the end. Each completes a different test because the computer selects items for each student at random from the item bank. Kingsbury (1990) describes use of the MicroCAT system in the Portland (Oregon) Public Schools.

With on-line testing, you do no scoring, and there is no need to prepare alternative forms of tests. Testing need not occur at only one time for the entire class. Students benefit from immediate feedback on their performance. The computer stores the records for you to retrieve and examine at your convenience. Such testing has great potential (Bugbee and Bernt, 1990), but Sarvela and Noonan (1988) raise issues about interpreting the results.

Adaptive testing seeks to determine the user's performance level by varying item difficulty according to patterns of correct and incorrect responses. A shorter test should provide the same assessment as a longer, traditional test. Educational Testing Service has moved into adaptive testing for the GRE and SAT exams (*Chicago Tribune*, 1992).

The Computerized Adaptive Testing System (CATSYS) can administer and score adaptive tests or conduct on-line computer simulation studies (de la Torre and Vispoel, 1991). The package incorporates several innovative features, including skip and review options, content balancing, item eligibility flagging, mastery testing, self-adapted testing, and listening items. An initial study found that examinees: (1) preferred CATSYS-produced tests to paper-and-pencil alternatives; (2) found CATSYS-produced tests clear and simple to take; and (3) appreciated the review, skip, and self-adaptive options.

TestBank 4.0 (from Microsystems Software) allows you to select test items by learning objective or other criteria. Its companion product, *Test and Tutor*, permits using the computer for essay exams by providing modest word-processing capabilities and secure storage of the student's answers. Former Secretary of Education Terrell Bell (1992) noted the growing application of computerized job simulations as a way to assess *performance* abilities, rather than just knowledge. For extensive treatment of alternative assessment concepts and the place of technologies within them, see Bruder (1993). There is a justifiable trend to augment objective testing with real-life measures, including performance assessments and portfolios. Because computers have become so integrated into daily life, their role in assessment will be fundamental, but that role may be very different from today's CMI.

Test Item Analysis

If you use objective tests and want to improve them over time, machine test scoring and on-line testing often provide for *item analysis*. This is a valuable procedure for determining which test items are sound and which should be improved or eliminated. The key is whether individual items measure the same thing as the total test.

A question that typically is answered correctly by students earning high total scores but is missed by those with low total scores contributes properly to the overall assessment. If the opposite is true, the item is not contributing to the overall assessment and should be revised or replaced. Item analysis also will reveal response patterns, such as showing that students rarely choose certain alternative answers. Such alternatives thus are ineffective and should be improved.

Integrated Learning Systems

The Rolls Royce of CMI is the *integrated learning system* (ILS). The term ILS reflects the total integration of CAI and management into a single system. Some ILSs can be installed on existing microcomputers, whereas others require their own hardware, sometimes even a minicomputer. Most operate as a local area network (LAN) (see Chapter 8). Computer Curriculum Corporation (CCC), Jostens Learning Corporation, and WICAT are among the best-known providers of ILSs. These and other selected vendors are listed in the appendix.

The traditional ILS is a complete computer-based learning system provided by a single vendor. Schools purchase (or lease) "turn-key" hardware and software for the total curriculum, which is carefully integrated from level to level. There is no need to shop around for other software with comparable curriculum goals. The quantity of software provided is enormous compared to what schools would buy as individual packages. Of course, there is a price for such a complete "learning solution." In late 1992, a basic ten-station system from Jostens, including hardware, cost about $70,000 for the first year, with optional service contracts for succeeding years. Jostens's *InterActiveMedia* is the first ILS to provide full-screen, full-motion video within its courseware (Tyre, 1992), but was still being tested and its cost was not set as we write. Despite the large costs in establishing an ILS in a school, there is increasing interest in ILSs (Butzin, 1992; Sherry, 1990). According to Trotter (1990), schools are investing about a half billion dollars per year in these systems.

Evaluation of ILSs

Because of the growing interest in ILSs and the lack of information about them, the EPIE Institute conducted a study (Sherry, 1990). Their report contends that such systems are not truly integrated, in that they do not extend beyond themselves to include "all of a school's educational resources and students' in-school learning experiences." Further, they may be described more accurately as *instructional* systems, because they are derived from earlier CAI efforts and lack "the level of learner-adaptiveness and artificial intelligence" required of a *learning* system. (Smith and Sclafani [1989] suggested the name integrated *teaching* systems, because the systems teach rather than learn!)

The EPIE Institute invested much time and effort in their evaluation. Trained evaluators examined the courseware and the CMI components. Schools using the eight systems reviewed were visited extensively; administrators, teachers, and students were interviewed. Missing from the report is any hard data on effectiveness, because there was little valid research available. However, interviewees overwhelmingly expressed great satisfaction with their ILSs. Teachers were highly positive, despite having far less training in working with the ILS than EPIE deemed necessary to exploit such a system. Few had any training in how to integrate the system into their own teaching. Still, teachers praised the systems for their individualization and the match of the computer's curriculum to the school's. Administrators shared those views, adding completeness of content, reporting capabilities, and ease of use. EPIE was particular impressed that 26 percent of the schools claimed to have restructured their curriculum to integrate the ILS.

The significance of courseware evaluation grows when a school contemplates an investment of the magnitude of an ILS. The DeKalb County (Georgia) schools decided to make such an investment over several years (Curlette, et al., 1991). Following a plan much like the evaluation system you studied in Chapter 11, educators first screened thirteen candidate systems, then selected three for field testing. When all three systems proved to meet county criteria for student achievement, teacher satisfaction using the system, and technical and administrative concerns, the final selection was based on cost.

May (1991) reported on elementary-school field trials of three major ILSs in reading/language arts and math. The trials assessed academic achievement improvements, implementation problems, day-to-day operations, correlations with instructional program and district goals, and staff and parent ratings. Both qualitative (classroom observations, implementation difficulties, and curriculum review) and quantitative measures were used. Test scores did not show major differences in achievement among the systems. Teachers, parents, and principals concurred that an ILS had positive effects on children's learning. The schools elected to continue with two of the three systems for a second year.

Project CHILD has been described as "a new twist on integrated learning systems" (Butzin, 1992). Basically, CHILD (Computers Helping Instruction and Learning Development) provides a level of computer integration into the curriculum similar to that of an ILS. Rather than creating vast numbers of new software products, however, as do ILS vendors, CHILD relies on carefully selected and aligned commercial software packages. Several different evaluation studies have established the effectiveness of Project CHILD.

An ILS is, of course, not a totally problem-free system. Although critical of the concept as "one of the newest educational computing fads," Johnson and Maddux (1991, p. 9) acknowledge that "such systems are neither good nor bad in themselves." One concern they express is that schools with an ILS may be limited in what additional software they can use with the system. Not all products are available for network use, and custom-fitting "foreign" software to the ILS management system may be difficult and/or costly. They further assert that a school will need an on-site network manager (an issue we raised in the discussion of networks). Additional problems cited are need for security on the server to guard against software erasure, system down-time when the server or software fails, and maintenance difficulties. These concerns really deal more with the LAN aspect of an ILS than the ILS concept.

Sherry (1990) provides this advice to potential ILS buyers:

1. Determine exactly what your goals are.
2. Get all the evaluation data possible, including EPIE's own report.
3. Seek out other schools that already use the system you like.
4. Involve as many people in the district as possible throughout the process. How you use whatever you have may be more important than the system itself.

The CEO of Jostens Learning Corporation has predicted that ILSs will disappear around the turn of the century, replaced by "mixed media basal" systems that integrate much more than just courseware (Hill, 1993). He views Jostens's *InterActiveMedia* as a prototype of such a new system. For further reading on ILSs, see *Educational Technology*, September 1992, which is devoted to the topic.

What the Research Shows

Szabo and Montgomerie (1992) focus their definition of CMI on the diagnosis and prescription aspects we have described, a definition well-suited to systems such as PLAN. They do allow, however, that the ideal may be a combination of their concept of CMI and CAI, much as an ILS provides.

Based on their narrower definition of CMI, Szabo and Montgomerie conducted an extensive review of the research literature, which merits some attention. They note that research on "pure" CMI is "thin," in part because much CAI includes elements of CMI, making it difficult to focus on only one or the other. From literature going back well into the 1970s, the researchers concluded that "CMI has been shown to be efficient, effective, and relatively easy to develop compared to other forms of mediated instruction" (pp. 128). CMI works well both for individual instructors and teams. Studies show it to be useful with existing courses and as a component of newly developed courses, for basic and supplemental instruction, and across many content areas. In short, the researchers make a solid case that CMI deserves more attention than it now receives.

As for ILSs, vendors trumpet achievement gains as a major selling point, often disregarding the fact that no software serves all learners equally well. Smith and Sclafani (1989) cited a New York City study that found that achievement in math and reading varied with the specific ILS, the student grade level, and the type of students. Within the same ILS, math and reading instruction were not necessarily equally effective. In certain subjects and with certain systems, some students actually learned less than under regular classroom instruction. They suggested requiring a money-back performance guarantee from the vendor!

Another study raises particular concern. Hativa (1988) studied 300 students who used the CCC mathematics curriculum. The researchers created paper-and-pencil tests clustered around the level indicated by the CMI, but with problems both above and below that level. Most of the subjects went further than their recommended level on the paper test—on average, over seven levels higher! Those classified as lowest-achieving based on their computer work averaged thirteen levels higher on paper than on computer. Possible reasons for the differences are carefully assessed, focusing on software design and instructional considerations. The point is that, even with extensively researched materials like CCC's, we seem not to have reached the desired level of sophistication in computer analysis of student achievement.

Other Concerns Regarding CMI

As with all aspects of computer-based learning, CMI raises certain concerns.

Complexity of Set-Up

The most common complaint about software with a full management component is difficulty in setting up the system for student use. Teachers must spend considerable time entering the student rosters, defining task sequences for each student, and so on. Do not be unrealistic in your expectations of what the computer should do on its own. Realize, too, that work you otherwise would complete over an extended period of time suddenly must be done all at once before students can use the programs. This also makes the task appear larger. Teacher aides can assist with the clerical aspects of CMI (Hall, 1988).

Software Quality

Many complaints about software quality actually concern the CAI aspects of products, especially ILSs, rather than the management software. Try to keep the two components separate. Concerns about CAI were presented in Chapters 9 and 11. As for the management component, you must assess whether the kinds of records and performance analyses provided are, indeed, what you need and want. If they are, then CMI may prove useful to you; otherwise, it probably will not.

You might find, for instance, that for your needs, the diagnosis and prescription capabilities of the software are too simplistic or needlessly complex. If you cannot retrieve the stored records in a useful format, the labor-saving potential of CMI declines. If you can achieve the same net results manually in equal or less time, CMI has little to offer you.

Cost

When CMI is simply a feature of a CAI package, it has no separate cost, so there is no issue. An ILS, however, can easily be expensive. To justify such expense requires a strong commitment to both CAI and the benefits expected from the CMI dimension. On a cost-per-hour of student-use basis, an ILS may well be the least expensive approach to computer-based learning. But schools without such a system are far less likely to even attempt such extensive computer use. Cost comparisons are, therefore, difficult to make. Szabo and Montgomerie (1992) contend that cost comparisons mislead because we lack a clear picture of what it costs to design, develop, and deliver conventional instruction—the obvious base of comparison.

Evaluating a CMI System

Assuming your school is considering a major CMI system, such as an ILS, you would, of course, evaluate the courseware components as you would any other instructional software (see Chapter 11), with special attention to the sequence throughout an entire curriculum area. What special additional criteria should you apply to evaluating candidate systems? Smith and Sclafani (1989) suggest several questions to consider.

- Did you clearly identify the problem that the system is to solve?
- What educational benefits are you expecting? What evidence demonstrates the system's ability to produce them?
- Do you understand the instructional theory underlying the system?
- Is the system completely self-contained ("closed") or can you use it to organize and manage varied resources, including what you already have ("open")? Hill (1993) reports a trend toward more open systems, such as Jostens's *InterActive-Media* and Curriculum Networking Specialist's *ClassWorks* II.
- Is the scope and sequence of available curricula adequate for your need?
- Is the system aimed at the students you most need to serve? Systems are not truly all-purpose.
- Is the management and reporting system adequate?
- Can you afford it?

For additional advice on system evaluation, see Hall (1988) and Curlette et al. (1991).

Summary

Teachers perform many management functions that the computer may support. The foundations of CMI are the concepts of mastery learning and individualized instruction, both difficult to implement without technological support. Project PLAN demonstrated the potential of CMI, but the microcomputer has permitted combining instruction and management in one system at reasonable cost.

CMI may be a part of computer-assisted learning, supporting instruction by monitoring and analyzing student performance. It may focus on testing, ranging from automated test scoring to adaptive testing and test improvement by means of item analysis. ILSs manage or even provide comprehensive curricula. Schools can obtain complete hardware and software systems from a single vendor.

As with most educational research, studies on CMI show mixed results. The management aspects of CMI appear to have definite merit. Total systems such as

ILSs may be oversold by their vendors, but they also provide value when used appropriately. Complexity, software quality, and cost are all concerns with CMI. Any school considering CMI or an ILS should evaluate candidate systems carefully before making a purchase. Given the substantial investment, try demanding a money-back performance guarantee.

Chapter 12 Activities

1. Examine any available software with a management component. What are its claimed capabilities and limitations? If possible, actually set up a hypothetical class using the software. How easy is it to do so? Does the benefit appear to justify the effort?
2. Visit a school using CMI or an ILS. Discuss with teachers, administrators, and students their experiences with the system.
3. Research the computer as an element of testing, particularly adaptive testing. Write a position paper based on your research.
4. Contact several ILS vendors and request their literature. (Some addresses are provided in the appendix.) Prepare a product comparison based on features. Which system do you find most appealing? Why?

Bibliography

Baker, F. B. "Some Issues in the Application of Microcomputerized Testing Packages." *Educational Measurement: Issues and Practice*, Summer 1990, *9*(2), pp. 18–19.

Banas, C. "Mastery Learning Demoted." *Chicago Tribune*, August 15, 1985.

Becker, H. J. *Microcomputers in the Classroom: Dreams and Realities*. Eugene, OR: International Council for Computers in Education, undated.

Bell, T. H. "On Education." *School and College*, August 1992, p. 6.

Bernt, F. M., Bugbee, A. C., Jr., and Arceo, R. D. "Factors Influencing Student Resistance to Computer Administered Testing." *Journal of Research on Computing in Education*, Spring 1990, *22*(3), pp. 265–275.

Bruder, I. "Integrated Learning Systems: An Overview of What's Available." *Electronic Learning*, November/December 1988, *8*(3), pp. 54–57.

Bruder, I. "Alternative Assessment. Putting Technology to the Test." *Electronic Learning*, January 1993, *12*(4), pp. 22–29.

Bugbee, A., Jr., and Bernt, F. M. "Testing by Computer: Findings in Six Years of Use 1982–1988." *Journal of Research on Computing in Education*, Fall 1990, *23*(1), pp. 87–100.

Butzin, S. "Project CHILD: A New Twist on Integrated Learning Systems." *T.H.E. Journal*, September 1992, *20*(2), pp. 90–95.

Chicago Tribune. "GRE College Test Shifting to Computer." 22 March 1992, Section 1, p. 25.

Curlette, W. L., et al. "An Evaluation Model To Select an Integrated Learning System in a Large, Suburban School District." Paper presented at the Annual Meeting of the American Educational Research Association. Chicago, IL, April 3–7, 1991. (ERIC Document ED 334 236.)

de-la-Torre, R., and Vispoel, W. P. "The Development and Evaluation of a Computerized Adaptive Testing System." Paper presented at the Annual Meeting of the National Council on Measurement in Education. Chicago, IL, April 4–6, 1991. (ERIC Document ED 338 711.)

Frisbie, A. G., Harless, R., and Brunson, G. "Computer Managed Instruction in a Large Undergraduate Teacher Education Course." *Computers in the Schools*, 1991, *8*(1/2/3), pp. 135–138.

Hall, M. "The Case for Computerized Instructional Management." *Educational Technology*, June 1988, pp. 34–37.

Hativa, N. "CAI Versus Paper and Pencil: Discrepancies in Students' Performance." *Instructional Science*, 1988, *17*, pp. 77–79.

Hill, M. "What's New in ILSes?" *Electronic Learning*, January 1993, *12*(4), p. 12.

Johnson, D. L., and Maddux, C. D. "The Birth and Nurturing of a New Discipline." *Computers in the Schools*, 1991, *8*(1/2/3), pp. 5–13.

Kingsbury, G. G. "Adapting Adaptive Testing: Using the MicroCAT Testing System in a Local School District." *Educational Measurement: Issues and Practice*, Summer 1990, *9*(2), pp. 3–6.

Mageau, T. "ILS: Its New Role in Schools." *Electronic Learning*, September 1990, *10*(1), pp. 22–32.

May, C. S. "Integrated Learning Systems: A School-Based Evaluation." Paper presented at the Annual Meeting of the American Educational Research Association. Chicago, IL, April 3–7, 1991. (ERIC Document ED 332 327.)

Sarvela, P. D., and Noonan, J. V. "Testing and Computer-Based Instruction: Psychometric Considerations." *Educational Technology*, May 1988, pp. 17–20.

Sherry, M. "An EPIE Institute Report: Integrated Instructional Systems." *T.H.E. Journal*, September 1990, *18*(2), pp. 86–89.

Smith, R. A., and Sclafani, S. "Integrated Teaching Systems: Guidelines for Evaluation." *The Computing Teacher*, November 1989, *17*(3), pp. 36–38.

Szabo, M., and Montgomerie, T. C. "Two Decades of Research on Computer-Managed Instruction." *Journal of Research on Computing in Education*, Fall 1992, *25*(1), pp. 113–133.

Trotter, A. "Computer Learning with Integrated Systems." *The Education Digest*, December 1990, pp. 28–32.

Tyre, T. "Jostens Learning's InterActiveMedia: The Ultimate ILS Delivers Networked Video." *T.H.E. Journal*, August 1992, *20*(1), pp. 14–15.

Visscher, A. J. "School Administrative Computing: A Framework for Analysis." *Journal of Research on Computing in Education*, Fall 1991, *24*(1), pp. 1–19.

Visscher, A. J., and Spuck, D. W. "Computer Assisted School Administration and Management: The State of the Art in Seven Nations." *Journal of Research on Computing in Education*, Fall 1991, *24*(1), pp. 146–168.

Objectives

After studying this chapter, you will be able to:

Discuss the nature of human and machine intelligence.

Name at least three areas of applied artificial intelligence.

Evaluate the potential benefits of natural language processing.

Define the concept of an expert system and give an example of one.

Explain briefly the components of an expert system.

Assess major criticisms of AI and expert systems.

List and briefly explain several educational applications of expert systems.

Distinguish a performance support system from other computer applications.

Compare and contrast CAI and ICAI.

Explain why working intelligent tutoring systems seem elusive.

Chapter 13

Computer Intelligence: Refined Roles for Computers in Education

To round out your consideration of the computer's potential as tutor—that is, as an integral part of instruction—join us for a tour into territory that may seem futuristic at first. We are referring to the realm of artificial intelligence (AI) and its applications. In Chapter 12, you learned about adaptive testing, and in Chapter 9, the concept of branching in CAI. Both involve some form of decision making by the computer. Just how far might this go? What are the possibilities for "intelligent" computers? Is there even such a thing as intelligence apart from that present in living organisms? If such questions interest you, read on!

Concepts of Artificial Intelligence

It seems appropriate to start this chapter with a conceptual discussion of human and machine intelligence.

Human Intelligence

No doubt, you consider yourself intelligent. In fact, you probably consider most, if not all, humans to be intelligent. You also may believe that other creatures, perhaps the family dog, possess intelligence. What, then, is this quality called intelligence?

Students to whom we have posed that question countless times have thoughtfully given numerous answers. The essential ingredients seem to center on aspects of consciousness such as the abilities to think, reason, and learn. Most students readily admit that individuals are endowed with varying amounts or levels of intelligence as it applies to different facets of life. Not everyone is equally "intelligent" in all subject matter or in all skill areas. That's why we turn to specialists as needed. Whatever it may be, intelligence is more than some simple attribute that can be reduced to a number such as an IQ.

Machine Intelligence

Machine, or artificial, intelligence (AI) is a specialty area of computer science concerned with creating machines capable of functions that, in humans, require consciousness or intelligence. Whether or not there *can* be machine intelligence is a hotly debated point, and we prefer to avoid that quagmire. Rather, we suggest that if intelligence can exist to varying degrees in living beings, machine intelligence need be no more than equivalent to its minimal form to exist. Even more significantly, if research and development in the name of AI produce useful results, does the theoretical debate matter? In other words, let's be reasonable and realistic in our expectations—perhaps even suspend disbelief—and we may be rewarded for our insight.

What might constitute an intelligent machine? We have suggested a minimal definition: a machine that can do something that parallels applying human intelligence on a minimal level. The classic test of machine intelligence was proposed in the 1940s by a British computer scientist named Turing. Turing's "test" had three components: a computer and two people. One of the people carries on two "conversations" via keyboard and monitor, one with the computer, the other with the second person. If, at the end, the tester cannot determine which correspondent was the computer, the computer has passed the test of intelligence. This seems to exceed our definition considerably, yet it is inadequate to demonstrate intelligence to some critics.

If you would like to know more about machine intelligence, see Cox (1992).

Applied Artificial Intelligence

Artificial intelligence (AI) is a highly theoretical field of study, but there have been many offshoots that may benefit us all (see Figure 13.1). From its early days, one major area of AI inquiry has been *game theory*. The goal is to create software that plays games at the level of a master player, most commonly chess. The complexities of chess make it an excellent choice for AI. Work on chess software continues to this day, some of which actually "learns" from its experience and becomes better over time (Geisert and Futrell, 1990). If you enjoy computer and video games, you may owe some of your pleasure to AI research.

Another common area of AI application is in *robotics*. Real robots lack the human-like appearance and qualities (called anthropomorphism) of those stars of science fiction from the films *2001: A Space Odyssey* or the *Star Wars* trilogy. Robots are an essential component of manufacturing technology today and also serve us in many other ways. Industrial robots are valued for their consistent and tireless performance as well as for their usefulness in conditions inhospitable to humans, such as high levels of radiation or lack of an atmosphere, notably in outer space. Robots that can manipulate objects and "see" production defects on an assembly line are the result of AI research.

Oral communication is one of the essential characteristics of fictional robots. They understand speech, even in multiple languages, and speak in return. The fascination of such devices is obvious, as are the practical applications. Even today's graphical user interfaces seem downright primitive compared to a computer that you control by voice command and that interacts with you using only everyday, oral language.

The reality is somewhat less in the AI subfield of *natural language processing (NLP)*. Scientists have long shared the dream of the fiction writers, but NLP is a particularly stubborn problem. Humans have no trouble understanding different voices, inflection variations, and even many mispronunciations. Machines with relatively limited language capabilities do exist, but they are poor embodi-

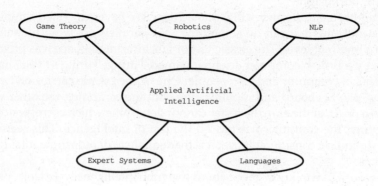

Figure 13.1. Applications of artificial intelligence.

ments of human communication. Casper, a Macintosh voice recognition system first demonstrated in 1992, is supposed to be able to recognize 100,000 words and different voices without training. More typically, voice recognition systems must be trained to a very limited vocabulary spoken by each voice to which they should respond. Voice recognition systems have little or no ability to go beyond some programmed response to whatever word(s) they have "understood." Real conversation, as in the Turing test, is more fantasy than reality. Germain (1992) provides a good overview of NLP, while Wetzel (1991) tries to envision the future of speech technology.

Beyond voice recognition, NLP includes synthetic speech (the other side of any conversation) and language understanding, such as the ability to summarize a scanned document or to translate automatically from one language to another. Science fiction leads reality in both areas.

Despite the limitations, NLP has contributed significantly to making the computer accessible to more people (Brownell, 1992). Kurzweil Applied Intelligence markets speech recognition products. Kurzweil Voice is a document-creation system for those unable to use their hands. Their Voice MED product line offers voice-driven medical reporting systems. Devices to aid the blind include the Xerox/Kurzweil Personal Reader that "reads" aloud from printed text using a synthesized voice.

AI has had an impact within computer science directly as well. Computer languages, briefly surveyed in Chapters 15–17, are mostly algorithmic in nature and based on mathematics. They serve procedural needs where solutions to problems can be specified as a precise sequence of steps that assure a correct solution. Such languages are not suited ideally to the problems of AI. Instead, logic-based languages such as LISP and PROLOG enable AI practitioners to pursue their goals much more efficiently. They are based on declarations of facts and rules that govern them. LOGO which you will study in Chapter 15, is widely used in education and is actually a variation of LISP. See Muir (1990) for some creative AI applications using LOGO.

The final major area of applied AI is expert systems, which merit more detailed coverage.

Expert Systems

Perhaps the most widely known and used application of AI is *expert systems*. An expert system is an AI program that performs a somewhat difficult task at the level of an expert. As examples, expert systems emulate the problem-solving methods of human experts to diagnose medical or automotive maladies, assess insurance risks and loan applications, prescribe an appropriate wine for your dinner, evaluate purchase versus lease of equipment by a business, or classify learning objectives according to Bloom's Taxonomy.

As humans often must do, an expert system can reach a conclusion even in the absence of complete data. The goal of conventional data processing, such as a spreadsheet application, is to produce the *correct answer* to a problem. Mistakes are unacceptable. This involves classical logic, in which the premises all are true or false. Expert systems use *fuzzy logic* to yield *usable answers*. Fuzzy logic attaches confidence factors to premises, rather like tomorrow's weather forecast or the responses Spock elicited from the computer system in television's "Star Trek." Like a meteorologist, an expert system may make errors. Like a colleague, an expert system also is able to explain the reasoning behind its conclusions.

A classic example is MYCIN, the first large expert system to perform at truly expert level. MYCIN's expertise concerns meningitis and bacteremia infections (Harmon and King, 1985, p. 15). Both are conditions that may be fatal and that require swift diagnosis and treatment. In fact, treatment must begin before conclusive diagnosis from tests is possible. The "knowledge base" of MYCIN pools the expertise of medical specialists to perform at par with the best of them.

A *knowledge base* consists of facts and rules defining their relationships. Driscoll et al. (1991) describe a system that automates text indexing. The knowledge base consists of insertion and deletion rules generated by experts. An expert system also requires information about the current "problem." If a system contains countless facts about illnesses, it becomes useful only when someone provides symptoms and other data for a real case. Expert systems are interactive and request needed information from the user. An *inference engine*, the logical component of the system, then reasons from the knowledge base and case information to a conclusion. (See Figure 13.2.)

Expert systems are currently in use in a large proportion of the major corporations throughout the world and in many smaller ones as well. Volvo uses a particular type of expert system called a *neural network* in quality control (Kestelyn, 1992). As the name implies, neural networks are patterned after the human brain. One system at Volvo "listens" to auto engine sounds and compares them to a fixed set of values, a task previously subject to much variability with human inspectors. Security experts for the 1992 Winter Olympics in Albertville, France, used *Ramses*, an expert system, to assess many extremely complex security vari-

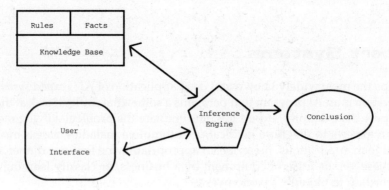

Figure 13.2. Components of an expert system.

ables (Kestelyn, 1992). Norway is considering using *Ramses* for the 1994 Winter Olympics as we write. Its underlying technology is contributing to a European Community project on managing environmental disasters. Feigenbaum, McCorduck, and Nii (1989) offer a fascinating look at selected applications, some of which you unknowingly may have had contact with. Certainly, you will relate to many of them. Like computers, expert systems are all around us, but usually we are unaware of them.

Expert Systems Controversies

Artificial intelligence (AI) and expert systems take computing into aspects of life normally reserved for belief systems. In turn, they have the potential to ignite veritable "holy wars." Joseph Weizenbaum of MIT created a computer psychologist dubbed *Eliza* to demonstrate what he perceived as the absurdity of AI. To his horror, when the system was demonstrated, many professional analysts were so impressed with its seemingly human capabilities that they wanted to buy it! Weizenbaum (1976) disputes the whole concept of AI because he believes intelligence derives from human experience and "no computer can be made to confront genuine human problems in human terms" (p. 223). Dreyfus and Dreyfus (1988) also attack AI as they seek to discount the concept of an expert system, based on their careful and precise definition of expertise. They conclude that such systems at best deserve to be labeled "competent." Such criticisms have led some educators (e.g., Maddux, Johnson, and Willis, 1992) to deny the potential value of AI to educators. We believe this is as extreme as the Polyanna-ish claims of the most fervent AI believers. Even a "competent" system may be valuable indeed.

While a huge system such as MYCIN may be entrusted with final decision-making authority, most expert systems must be viewed as aids to human decision makers. These systems often can reach a conclusion much more quickly than a human, they don't overlook factors of which they are aware, they reach consistent conclusions given comparable evidence, and they can be refined and improved by changing the knowledge base. But remember, expert systems are by definition capable of error. Perhaps some of the negative reactions to them stem from a fear that their limitations will be ignored.

Expert Systems in Education

Is there a place for expert systems technology in education? Like many other observers, we believe there is. Brownell (1992) envisioned computerized curriculum consultants. Van Horn (1991) suggested that expert systems in education might assist with solutions to such problems as diagnosing learning problems, handling classroom discipline, critiquing student writing, career counseling, or configuring a new computer network. Expert systems have assisted with student advising (Wehrs, 1992). Martindale and Hofmeister (1988) described "Written Language Consultant," designed to help teach mildly and moderately handicapped students to write business letters. Special education applications are particularly common, including broad decision support (Hofmeister, 1991) and classification of learning disabled (LD) students (Steele and Raab, 1991). Juell and Wesson (1988) discussed a system for diagnosing learning problems in mathematics.

Lockard and McHugh (1989) created a system to assist residence hall advisors to perform their duties within the requirements of a university's judicial system. Merrill and his associates (1990, 1987) want to enhance and speed up the process of instructional design, in part through expert system support. Systems also exist to help researchers select and apply the most appropriate statistics to their data. Further references of potential interest include Vitale and Romance (1991), McFarland and Parker (1990), Ragan and McFarland (1987), Poirot and Norris (1987), Lawler and Yazdani (1987), Brady (1986), and, especially, Romiszowski (1987).

Another promising application is to have students develop expert systems, which some educators see as a means of enhancing problem-solving skills and stimulating deeper learning within content domains (Valley, 1992; Knox-Quinn, 1988; Wideman and Owston, 1988; Trollip and Lippert, 1987). Jonassen ("A Conversation . . . ," 1992) stresses the significant intellectual benefit to those who build expert systems from the depth of knowledge processing required. So great is this benefit, in fact, that he contemplates a book called *Mind Tools for Schools*, "which basically says let's throw away all the computer assisted instruction and teach students how to use computer-based knowledge representation and construction tools" (p. 5).

There are many development tools called *expert system shells* that make student creation of expert systems conceptually and financially practical. Shells are easy to learn and to use. Popular computer publications review shell software periodically (e.g., Knox-Quinn, 1988; Rasmus, 1988) and are your best source of more information. Our students have had good experiences with *1st Class* and *VP-Expert*.

Performance Support Systems

Previously, we noted that the proper role of an expert system is to assist the person who ultimately must make the final decision. This role may lose value if the person needing the assistance must go to a particular computer that has the software to get help. Even if the person routinely works at a computer, the need to stop one process, execute another program, get its advice, and then return to the original task can be enough to doom the use of the expert system.

The term *performance support system (PSS)* is applied to one type of solution to such concerns. A typical PSS unites expert system technology with other software applications to which the system applies or with which it works. Carr (1992) defines a PSS to include expert systems, hypertext, online reference, databases, and related technologies "to provide support on the job, where they need it, when they need it, in the form most useful to them." He claims expert systems have not and will not reach the usage level that they could because they sound too exotic, lack obvious sponsors in most organizations, threaten by seeming to aim at the most interesting work of those they should help, and are too rigid. A PSS has few such liabilities.

Carr provides several easy-to-follow examples of a PSS, but none for education, so we'll improvise. Imagine the management features of an integrated learning system, all the daily software tools a teacher uses (word processing, etc.), a comprehensive classroom advisor that includes discipline, learning problems, and special needs populations, built-in telecommunications support—all in a unified, seamless, integrated system. Someday there may be such a PSS for twenty-first century educators. For more detailed information, see Gery (1991).

Intelligent CAI/Tutoring Systems

Many criticisms of CAI reflect a vision of courseware that is less directly descended from programmed instruction and behaviorism than is typical. Some critics see the power of the computer as a tutor as severely limited unless it can more closely emulate a human instructor.

Intelligent computer-assisted instruction (ICAI) is CAI that uses AI techniques to help the user learn more effectively and efficiently. Of several types of ICAI, *intelligent tutoring systems (ITS)* have the broadest potential. An ITS is complex CAI that engages the learner in a dialog to identify misconceptions about the content being learned and then remediates in an appropriate manner. Burns and Parlett (1991, p. 1) state, "In the 21st century, professional credibility will depend in part on how well educators have kept up with technology in general and the development and use of intelligent tutoring systems (ITS) in particular."

One type of ITS consists of modules (Lianjing and Taotao, 1991; Rambally, 1986). An expertise module contains the lesson content, that is, the system's knowledge. A tutor module contains a repertoire of instructional strategies for bringing the learner closer to the ideal, which is represented in the expertise module. A student module tracks performance, including types of errors and misconceptions (see Figure 13.3). In theory, an ITS knows what to teach, to whom, when, and how! It is not limited to sequences and responses programmed into it, but, rather, it dynamically tailors content and approach to each user. When the learner errs, rather than just repeating the same presentation as is typical of tutorials, an ITS would analyze the cause of the error and then remediate appropriately.

Practical applications that exemplify ICAI ideals are somewhat rare. Early systems (Rambally, 1986; Kearsley, 1987) included SCHOLAR, which taught South American geography, SOPHIE (for electronics troubleshooting), and BUGGY (for arithmetic). Knezek (1988) listed over twenty ICAI packages, but noted that most were not "fully functional." McArthur and Stasz (1990) detailed research and development work on an algebra tutor. McEneaney (1991) described a system to diagnose and remediate reading problems. MacKenzie (1990) assessed the extent to which intelligence exists in ITS and ICAI products. Yang (1987) offered a perspective on individualizing instruction using ICAI.

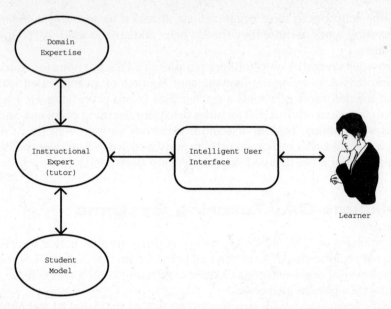

Figure 13.3. Anatomy of an intelligent tutoring system (adapted from Burns and Parlett, 1991).

One reason for the scarcity of products has been the substantial computer power required to operate a comprehensive ITS. As the hardware issue declines, a more significant problem remains: the very real limits of our understanding of human learning, which make the critical error assessment aspect difficult and imperfect. For example, enormous effort went into creating one system to teach algebra (Collis, 1987–1988), but in a study with ninth- and tenth-graders, it only anticipated thirty percent of the errors. In addition, development time for ICAI has been enormous, as much as 1000–2000 hours per hour of student lesson, or about ten times that of typical CAI.

In a vision of the future (Geisert and Futrell, 1990, pp. 316–317), a human welcomes new students to a school. Students next interact with a computer, communicating orally in natural English. The computer gathers the students' history and interests, determines and conducts appropriate diagnostic tests, and then assigns appropriate study units. The computer provides most lessons on facts and concepts, tailoring instruction precisely to the student's level, rate, and learning style. Periodic automatic drill and practice assures retention. Teachers no longer perform traditional duties. Their role instead is to help students with personal development, motivation, and thinking, problem-solving, and creative tasks. AI is fundamental to such a dream.

Software producers claim the existence of AI in products such as *RightWriter* (a document proofer/writing analyst/grammar checker) and the typing tutor *Mavis Beacon Teaches Typing*. You may well be impressed by the capabilities of products such as these. However, it is far from clear just when we may benefit from ICAI as it is ultimately envisioned—that is, as each learner's personal Socrates.

Summary

On the frontier of tutorial computer applications are those based on artificial intelligence (AI). AI is a field within computer science that seeks to endow computers with capabilities to function more like humans than is currently true. The model may well be the humanoid robots long popular in science fiction, though the physical resemblance to humans is the least significant characteristic. Of real importance is the computer's ability to communicate naturally, to reason, to make decisions, and to learn from its own experience.

Whatever the ideals of AI, the reality is far less than science fiction portrays. Practical applications exist in computer games, robotics, natural language processing (NLP), logic-basic computer languages, and, especially, expert systems. Natural language processing has incredible potential, but many problems remain in perfecting it.

Expert systems are the most promising area currently for education. An expert system is simply a program that performs some task on a level comparable to a human expert. Most are designed to function as a personal advisor to the individual making the final decision. Unlike other computer programs based on algorithmic thinking, expert systems use fuzzy logic to reach conclusions, even without all the desired data. Like humans, expert systems do make mistakes. There are many vocal critics of the very concept of AI and expert systems.

Useful educational applications include both ready-to-use advisors and student development of their own expert systems. Much like the argument for student creation of interactive multimedia projects, allowing students to create an expert system demands a different, perhaps more significant, type of cognitive activity than more typical class assignments. Parsaye and Chignell (1992) discuss systems that blend hypermedia, databases, and AI.

Where might AI lead? Performance support systems (PSSs) are now being created in industry to provide comprehensive tools for today's knowledge worker. Researchers have dreamed of and experimented with Intelligent CAI and Intelligent Tutoring Systems as ways to create vastly superior computer-based learning environments. The Institute for the Learning Sciences at Northwestern University was created in 1990 just for that purpose. Aspects of AI are also critical to the growing field of virtual reality, which you will encounter in Chapter 21 of this book. As a final example, Thomas Ray, a biology professor at the University of Delaware, has created a system that "approaches artificial life" (Wilson, 1991). Ray wanted to capture two aspects of life. Self-reproduction was trivial, as computer viruses already replicated themselves. Evolution by natural selection proved far trickier and required redesigning the computer itself. "(Tierra) allows a computer program that is capable only of reproducing itself to evolve into more sophisticated organisms."

The implications of this research are staggering. Educators for the twenty-first century must stay abreast of developments in AI.

Chapter 13 Activities

1. Read more about any aspect of artificial intelligence (AI) that particularly interests you.
2. Research and prepare a position paper on the potential application of expert systems technology to education or your specific level/area of teaching interest.
3. Watch for software product advertising that claims to incorporate AI. Try to assess the meaning of the claim, that is, in what way is AI present, if at all?
4. Try out any AI software to which you have access, ideally both an expert system and a product such as *Mavis Beacon Teaches Typing*.
5. Create a small-scale expert system.
6. Prepare a lesson plan in which your students would create an expert system.

Bibliography

Brady, H. "Artificial Intelligence: What's In It for Educators?" *Classroom Computer Learning*, January 1986, pp. 26–29.

Brownell, G. *Computers and Teaching*, 2nd ed. St. Paul, MN: West Publishing, 1992.

Burns, H., and Parlett, J. W. "The Evolution of Intelligent Tutoring Systems: Dimensions of Design." In Burns, H., Parlett, J. W., and Redfield, C. L., (Eds.). *Intelligent Tutoring Systems. Evolutions in Design*, pp. 1–11. Hillsdale, NJ: Lawrence Erlbaum Associates, 1991.

Burton, R., and Brown, J. "An Investigation of Computer Coaching for Informal Learning Activities." In Sleeman, D., and Brown, J. S. *Intelligent Tutoring Systems*. London: Academic Press, 1982.

Capell, P. S. "Planning Videodisc Production for an Intelligent Tutoring System." *TechTrends*, 1991, *36*(2), pp. 23–26, 37.

Carr, C. "Performance Support Systems: A New Horizon for Expert Systems." *AI Expert*, May 1992, *7*(5), pp. 44–49.

Collis, B. "Research Windows." *The Computing Teacher*, December/January 1987–1988, p. 6.

"A Conversation with David Jonassen." *Dialogue* (AECT's Division of Instructional Development newsletter), January 1992, *4*(1), pp. 1, 3–6.

Cox, E. "How a Machine Reasons: Part 1." *AI Expert*, August 1992, *7*(8), pp. 13–15.

Cox, E. "How a Machine Reasons: Part 2." *AI Expert*, September 1992, *7*(9), pp. 13–15.

Cox, E. "How a Machine Reasons: Part 3." *AI Expert*, October 1992, *7*(10), pp. 13–15.

Dreyfus, H. L., and Dreyfus, S. E. *Mind over Machine*. New York: The Free Press (Macmillan), 1986.

Driscoll, J. R., et al. "The Operation and Performance of an Artificially Intelligent Keywording System." *Information Processing and Management*, 1991, *27*(1), pp. 43–54.

Expert Systems and Intelligent Computer Aided Instruction. The Educational Technology Anthology Series. Volume Two. Englewood Cliffs, NJ: Educational Technology Publications, 1991.

Feigenbaum, E., McCorduck, P., and Nii, H. P. *The Rise of the Expert Company*. New York: Vintage Books, 1989.

Freedle, R. *Artificial Intelligence and the Future of Testing*. Hillsdale, NJ: Lawrence Erlbaum Associates, 1990.

Geisert, P., and Futrell, M. *Teachers, Computers, and Curriculum*. Boston: Allyn and Bacon, 1990.

Germain, E. "Introducing Natural Language Processing." *AI Expert*, August 1992, 7(8), pp. 30–35.

Gery, G. J. *Electronic Performance Support Systems*. Boston: Weingarten Publications, 1991.

Hajovy, H., and Christensen, D. L., "Intelligent Computer-Assisted Instruction: The Next Generation." *Educational Technology*, May 1987, 27(5), pp. 9–14.

Harmon, P., and King, D. *Expert Systems*. New York: Wiley, 1985.

Hofmeister, A. "Expert Systems and Decision Support in Special Education: Results and Promises." *Educational Technology*, October 1991, 31(10), pp. 23–28.

Juell, P. and Wasson, J. "A Comparison of Input and Output for a Knowledge-Based System for Educational Diagnosis." *Educational Technology*, March 1988, pp. 28(3), 19–23.

Kearsley, G. (Ed.). *Artificial Intelligence and Instruction*. Reading, MA: Addison-Wesley, 1987.

Kestelyn, J. "Volvo's Neural Nets (Application Watch)." *AI Expert*, September 1992, 7(9), p. 56.

Kestelyn, J. "Bull's Eye. (Application Watch)." *AI Expert*, July 1992, 7(7), p. 56.

Knezek, G. A. "Intelligent Tutoring Systems and ICAI." *The Computing Teacher*, March 1988, pp. 11–13.

Knox-Quinn, C. "A Simple Application and a Powerful Idea: Using Expert System Shells in the Classroom." *The Computing Teacher*, November 1988, pp. 12–15.

Larkin, J. H., and Chabay, R. (Eds.). *Computer Assisted Instruction and Intelligent Tutoring Systems. Shared Goals and Complementary Approaches*. Hillsdale, NJ: Lawrence Erlbaum Associates, 1991.

Lawler, R. W., and Yazdani, M. (Eds.). *Artificial Intelligence and Education*, Volume One. Norwood, NJ: Ablex, 1987.

Levinson, P. *Intelligent Writing. The Electronic Liberation of Text*. Hillsdale, NJ: Lawrence Erlbaum Associates, 1991.

Lianjing, H., and Taotao, H. "A Uniform Student Model for Intelligent Tutoring Systems: Declarative and Procedural Aspects." *Educational Technology*, November 1991, 31(11), pp. 44–48.

Lockard, J., and McHugh, B. "CBT and Expert Systems for Training University Residence Hall Staff." *Proceedings of the Seventh Conference on Interactive Instruction Delivery*. Warrenton, VA: Society for Applied Learning Technology, 1989.

MacKenzie, I. S. "Courseware Evaluation: Where's the Intelligence?" *Journal of Computer-Assisted Learning*, December 1990, 6(4), pp. 273–285.

Maddux, C. D., Johnson, D. L., and Willis, J. W. *Educational Computing. Learning with Tomorrow's Technologies*. Boston, Allyn and Bacon, 1992.

Martindale, E. S., and Hofmeister, A. M. "An Expert System for On-Site Instructional Advice." *Educational Technology*, July 1988, pp. 18–20.

McArthur, D., and Stasz, C. "An Intelligent Tutor for Basic Algebra." Santa Monica, CA: The Rand Corp., 1990. ERIC Document ED 334 069.

McEneaney, J. E. "A Prototype Expert System with Applications in Teacher Training and the Diagnosis and Remediation of Reading Problems." *Computers in the Schools*, 1991, 8(1/2/3), pp. 315–318.

McFarland, T., and Parker, R. *Expert Systems in Education and Training*. Englewood Cliffs, NJ: Educational Technology Publications, 1990.

Merrill, M. D. "An Expert System for Instructional Design." *IEEE Expert*, Summer 1987.

Merrill, M. D., Li, Z., and Jones, M. K. "Limitations of First Generation Instructional Design." *Educational Technology*, January 1990, *30*(1), pp. 7–11.

Merrill, M. D., Li, Z., and Jones, M. K. "Second Generation Instructional Design (ID2)." *Educational Technology*, January 1990, (*30*)(1), pp. 7–14.

Muir, M. *Fantastic Journey Through Minds and Machines*. Eugene, OR: ISTE, 1990.

Newquist, H. P., III. "Apple and AI? No Way! Way!" *AI Expert*, July 1992, *7*(7), pp. 49–51.

Orey, M. A., and Nelson, W. A. "Using Intelligent Tutoring Design Principles to Integrate Cognitive Theory into Computer-Based Instruction." Paper presented at the Annual Convention of the Association for Educational Communications and Technology, Orlando, FL, February 13–17, 1991. ERIC Document ED 335 003.

Park, O., and Seidel, R. J. "Conventional CBI Versus Intelligent CAI: Suggestions for the Development of Future Systems. *Educational Technology*, May 1987, *27*(5), pp. 15–21.

Parsaye, K., and Chignell, M. "Information Made Visual Using Hyperdata." *AI Expert*, September 1992, *7*(9), pp. 22–29.

Poirot, J. L., and Norris, C. A. "Artificial Intelligence Applications in Education." *The Computing Teacher*, August/September 1987, pp. 8–10.

Polson, M. C., and Richardson, J. (Eds.). *Foundations of Intelligent Tutoring Systems*. Hillsdale, NJ: Lawrence Erlbaum Associates, 1988.

Psotka, J., Massey, L. D., and Mutter, S. A. (Eds.). *Intelligent Tutoring Systems. Lessons Learned*. Hillsdale, NJ: Lawrence Erlbaum Associates, 1988.

Ragan, S. W., and McFarland, T. D. "Applications of Expert Systems in Education: A Technology for Decision-Makers." *Educational Technology*, May 1987, pp. 33–36.

Rambally, G. K. "The AI Approach to CAI." *The Computing Teacher*, April 1986, pp. 39–42.

Rasmus, D. W. "Playing the Shell Game. Expert System Shells for the Macintosh." *PC AI*, September/October 1988, pp. 36–43.

Rogers, Y., Rutherford, A., and Bibby, P. A. *Models in the Mind. Theory, Perspective, and Application*. New York: Academic Press, 1992.

Romiszowski, A. J. "Expert Systems in Education and Training. Automated Job Aids or Sophisticated Instructional Media?" *Educational Technology*, October 1987, *27*(10), pp. 22–29.

Steele, J., and Raab, M. M. "Monarch: An Expert System for Classifying Learning Disabled Students." *TechTrends*, 1991, *36*(2), pp. 38–42.

Trollip, S., and Lippert, R. C. "Constructing Knowledge Bases: A Promising Instructional Tool." *Journal of Computer-Based Instruction*, Spring 1987, *14*(2), pp. 44–48.

Valley, K. "Explanation, Exploration, and Learning: The Use of Expert System Shells in Education." *Journal of Artificial Intelligence in Education*, 1992, *3*(3), pp. 255–274.

Van Horn, R. *Advanced Technology in Education*. Pacific Grove, CA: Brooks/Cole, 1991.

Vitale, M. R., and Romance, N. R. "Expert Systems Technology in Teacher Education: Applications and Implications." *Computers in the Schools*, 1991, *8*(1/2/3), pp. 319–322.

Wehrs, W. E. "Using an Expert System to Support Academic Advising." *Journal of Research on Computing in Education*, Summer 1992, *24*(4), pp. 545–562.

Weizenbaum, J., *Computer Power and Human Reason*. San Francisco: W. H. Freeman, 1987.

Wenger, E. *Artificial Intelligence and Tutoring Systems: Computational and Cognitive Approaches to the Communication of Knowledge*. Los Altos, CA: Morgan Kaufmann Publishers, Inc., 1987.

Wetzel, K. "Speech Technology II: Future Software and Hardware Predictions." *The Computing Teacher*, October 1991, *19*(2), pp. 19–21.

Wideman, H. H., and Owston, R. D. "Student Development of an Expert System: A Case Study." *Journal of Computer-Based Instruction*, 1988, *15*(3), pp. 88–94.

Wilson, D. L. "Approaching Artificial Life on a Computer." *Chronicle of Higher Education*, 4 December 1991, pp. A30-A31, A36.

Yang, J. "Individualizing Instruction Through Intelligent Computer-Assisted Instruction: A Perspective." *Educational Technology*, March 1987, 27(3), 7–15,

Objectives

After completing this chapter, you will be able to:

Give your own example of directing a person to do some task.

Fxplain what a computer program is.

Discuss the importance of planning in developing a computer program.

Explain the three major elements of problem analysis.

Describe what a flowchart is and why flowcharts are valuable.

Identify the four basic flowcharting symbols.

Discuss the concepts of structured programming.

Differentiate coding from programming.

Differentiate low-level from high-level languages.

Explain the difference between machine language and assembler language.

Explain the difference between an interpreter and a compiler.

Chapter 14

The Concepts of Programming

This book introduced the computer as a tool in everyday life. We then turned to the computer as a personal tutor that provides direct instruction in a variety of ways. In this chapter and the remainder of this section, you will look at the final major aspect of microcomputer usage: the computer as learner or "tutee."

Previous sections have focused on making use of available programs. This is the most common way that microcomputers are used in schools today. But it is not the only way. Someone had to write the programs that we use. An understanding of programming concepts provides users with an appreciation of how computers are actually controlled, how they are "taught" to perform their tasks.

Lest we create an erroneous initial impression, we do not want to teach you to program. The time and effort required to develop programs from scratch are seldom available within an introductory computer education course. Rather, you will learn the fundamental concepts of computer programming in this chapter. In succeeding chapters, you will explore common implementation tools. This is a sufficient introduction to programming to enable you to make an informed decision regarding further study of programming.

Our conceptual overview begins with a rationale for the study of programming. Next, we present the fundamental concepts of programming: control, planning, structure, coding, and testing and revision. In the final section of this chapter, you will learn about the various levels of programming languages and the different modes of language execution.

A Rationale for Programming

Programming is perhaps the most controversial element of computer education today. Some view it as the key ingredient in "computer literacy." For others, tool and tutoring uses are vastly more important, even to the extent of ignoring programming entirely. The organization of this book indicates our position. We believe educators should be cognizant of programming, but we prioritize it behind tool and direct instructional applications.

Programming and Teachers

There are several possible reasons for a teacher to be exposed to computer programming. While many teachers are afraid to learn to program, others are genuinely curious about it and welcome the challenge that it provides. Some teachers have all but been forced to learn something about programming to be able to handle student inquiries.

In some schools, teachers have been drafted into a computer program that focuses on programming. They actually teach some minimal level of programming to their students. Programming classes or parts of classes can be found at all grade levels. This is often a result of schools acquiring computers but little or no software suitable for other purposes, leaving programming as the primary use for the computers. The higher the grade level, the more knowledge is usually required of the programming teacher.

In addition, understanding programming concepts provides teachers with a starting point for possibly writing their own programs. This may be a necessity in the absence of ready-to-use programs in a school. It may also stem from a teacher's desire to use computers in areas or applications for which either no programs are commercially available or where available programs do not meet specific teacher needs.

Programming and Students

Several reasons are expressed commonly for teaching students to program. One is that it is the best way to show students that computers are under human control, not vice versa. In addition, computer programs seldom have only one correct solution. Thus, programming offers a rare opportunity for students to experience success other than in a right/wrong context.

Many students want to learn programming to satisfy their curiosity about the computer. They have seen many intriguing examples of what the machine can do and want to know how it does them. This has often led to pressure on schools to teach programming, even as an after-school activity. In some schools, the computer whiz may acquire stature comparable to that enjoyed by athletes.

Some educators support programming as a viable approach to teaching problem solving. Clearly, one cannot plan and develop a computer program without application of logical thinking, problem analysis, organization, and other higher-order thought processes. However, research seeking to link development of problem-solving skills and programming instruction has produced mixed findings (e.g., Burton and Magliaro, 1987–1988; Mayer, 1988; McCoy and Orey, 1987–1988; Norris, Jackson, and Poirot, 1992; Wiebe, 1991; Zirkler and Brownell, 1991).

For some, programming is an excellent means of fostering meaningful communication among students. When a group of students is working on a programming problem, there are many opportunities for mutual assistance and cooperation. This may be an antidote to the perception that computer activities tend to isolate students. Programming may lead to student collegiality.

Numerous students today have access to a computer at home and have begun to learn programming on their own with the help of books or parents. They have found it to be fun, something many teachers find hard to comprehend. Perhaps it is appropriate that the school provide opportunities for development of these skills, giving form to what has been self-taught and taking students to a higher level of understanding.

Finally, the extensive programming curricula of some secondary schools suggests that programming is taught either as preparation for postsecondary data processing study or some other prevocational purpose.

Each teacher and school will respond to these justifications for programming in their own way. The most critical factor is that a school have a well-developed rationale for what it does with programming and then assure that its activities support that goal. Several chapter bibliography entries offer guidance.

Fundamental Programming Concepts

Most books purporting to teach programming actually concentrate on specific languages. Yet learning a language is quite different from learning to program. To learn a language, you must master the *statements* that are the vocabulary of the language and all that the computer can understand. You must also learn the *syntax* of the statements; that is, exactly how they are written to be intelligible to the machine.

Programming can be separated conceptually from any language. Most critical is the ability to develop the *logic* needed to solve a programming problem. This is far more difficult to master than the mechanics of a language. An understanding of the concept of control and skills in the process of planning a solution are required. Further, you should apply the best contemporary approaches in programming methodology to the solution. We turn now to these fundamental concepts.

Control
In and of themselves, computers are mazes of electronics awaiting direction. The goal of using a computer is to perform some task. To do so, the machine must be directed in its work, that is, controlled.

In order to understand how a computer is controlled, it may be instructive to consider first how a person could be directed to do something and then to apply the same reasoning to a microcomputer. Control is fundamental to a conceptual understanding of programming and critical to eventually learning how to program.

Individual Control

When an individual does something, that "something" is usually a series of steps, although they may not be conscious ones. When you get up in the morning, your series of steps might well include the following:

1. Open eyes.
2. Look for clock.
3. Shut off alarm.
4. Read time.
5. Decide on forty more winks.
6. Close eyes.
7. Open eyes again.
8. Throw off covers.
9. Swing body around.
10. Hunt for slippers.
11. Stand up.
12. Stretch.

Another example of functioning in steps might be completion of a homework assignment in mathematics to calculate the squares of twenty-five numbers on a list. The answers must be written and will be collected the next day. Most students will go home, work the problem for each number, and write down the answers. However, suppose one of the students in the class is lazy, but has a little brother who is good at numbers and even knows how to square them. Little Brother is cooperative, but unfortunately has no ability to organize and, what is worse, forgets what he has done as soon as he has done it.

Lazy Student decides there must be some way of getting Little Brother to do the assignment, since he has other plans for the evening. It occurs to him that if he breaks the assignment into many simple steps, writes these steps down, and gives them to Little Brother, then Little Brother might complete the assignment. Lazy Student then would be free to go out.

Even though the preparation might be time consuming, Lazy Student decides that it is worth the trouble. To begin with, he must thoroughly understand the problem, after which he may outline the solution, and finally write the individual steps to achieve the solution. Each step must be one operation. When Little Brother has completed one step, he will go on to the next. In addition, the numbers to be squared must be provided as part of the step-by-step procedure.

Now Lazy Student can turn his attention to writing the steps necessary to do the homework assignment.

STEP 1. Read a number on the sheet from the teacher.

STEP 2. Square the number just read.

(This presents no problem since Little Brother does know how to find the square of a number. How he does it is not important.)

STEP 3. Write the answer down.

(It would not help Lazy Student if Little Brother did not record the obtained square of the number.)

STEP 4. See if there are more numbers on the list.

(This is a simple step, but crucial if the entire assignment is to be finished. The answer to this is either YES or NO. If the answer is YES, then Little Brother can be instructed to go to STEP 5. If the answer is NO, then Little Brother can be instructed to skip STEP 5 and go directly to STEP 6.)

STEP 5. If there are more numbers, go back and start again with STEP 1.

(Little Brother would do this if the answer to STEP 4 was YES. The squaring procedure would then continue with the next number on the list.)

STEP 6. Stop. The assignment is complete. Put the work away and do whatever you want.

(Little Brother would do this if the answer to STEP 4 was NO—when he has squared all the numbers on the list.)

Although he does not know the terminology, Lazy Student has developed an *algorithm*, a carefully planned series of steps that define a solution to a problem. Algorithm development is fundamental to problem solving.

This series of six steps directs Little Brother to complete the assignment, but Lazy Student must *verify* that this is the desired procedure. Little Brother is not able to figure out what to do if there are any errors in the steps, nor can he do any steps that are not on the instruction list. If Lazy Student forgets to tell Little Brother to write down the answer, Lazy Student will return home to find the task "completed," but no answers on the sheet. Thus, it is important to reexamine the steps to the solution carefully to determine completeness and accuracy. For a simple problem such as this, Lazy Student might even work through the steps with a list of, say, just two numbers to verify his algorithm.

Later that evening, Lazy Student calls Little Brother, gives him the instruction list and the list of numbers to be squared, and leaves. If all goes well, when he returns, his homework will be finished.

Computer Control

Three factors were involved in the homework problem: Lazy Student, the directions he wrote, and Little Brother. This example parallels computer control, which also has three factors: 1) the programmer (Lazy Student), 2) the program (the directions), and 3) the computer system (Little Brother). The computer system and Little Brother are problem solvers with particular characteristics that cannot be changed; they must be accommodated as they are. The programmer, or Lazy Student, has to develop a program or set of instructions for the computer system to do a desired job. This means describing in the program each individual step that the computer must do *in a way the computer can understand.* These instructions must be accurate and complete to get the job done.

Through an input device, the programmer gives the instructions (program) to the computer, which stores them in memory. Next, the system executes the steps sequentially, one at a time, until the program directs it to stop. If the steps were written correctly, the desired result is obtained. If not, the program must be re-examined and "debugged."

A series of instructions that direct the computer is called a *program*, which is written by a *programmer* to accomplish a specific task. The whole procedure is called *programming.*

As long as the instructions are correct and complete, there is no limitation to the jobs a computer can do. Any number of programs can be written, each to do a different job. Programs may be short or long, simple or complicated, depending upon the task to be performed. There is no necessity for continuity across job runs. One job might be to calculate the squares of a series of numbers, whereas the next might be to add groups of numbers together and compute averages. The program for each job is written to do just that job, and the computer executes each program individually.

In the "program" written by Lazy Student for Little Brother, only six steps were needed to direct Little Brother to do the assignment. Little Brother's list of numbers might contain ten or eighty items, and the same six steps would still accomplish the job of squaring them all. Further, the same six steps could be used over and over again, with new sets of numbers.

The directions allowed Little Brother to make some limited decisions. He was told to see if there were more numbers on the list, and the answer to the question resulted in one of two alternatives. If the answer was yes, he was told to go back to the beginning of the procedure and do it again. If the answer was no, he was told to stop.

Just like Little Brother, the computer is capable of handling its own program. The programmer loads instructions into the computer's memory, and, upon command, the computer executes them one instruction at a time. Most programs are written to process whatever volume of data is available and are capable of processing any other comparable sets of data. Based upon decisions, the program directs the system to go back and repeat some of the earlier instructions or to proceed to another set of instructions entirely.

Planning

Now that you understand the control concept, we turn to the most critical factor in programming: planning. The more carefully, thoroughly, and accurately one plans a program, the less time the remaining steps in the program development cycle will require. The total time spent creating a program will also be minimized. We will look at planning as two major steps: problem analysis and algorithm development.

Problem Analysis

Applying sound principles of problem analysis is a complex task that varies from one problem to another, one programmer to another, and one problem-solving situation to another. Skills in problem analysis develop slowly from experience. Do not expect to have everything fall into place quickly and easily. However, a few basic points will serve as a start.

First, as a programmer, you must understand the problem. What *exactly* is the program to do? Never attempt to solve a problem until you are certain that you understand the problem completely. You will avoid much frustration and many failures just by following this advice.

Second, you must know what the input data will be. If you are also in charge of preparing the data, you must have control over the accuracy of data preparation. If data are already prepared, you must be familiar with exactly what is available, what form it is in, and whether more information may be required.

Third, you must know what is required as output from the computer and what its form must be.

A programmer must determine precisely what has to be done to the input to produce the desired output. (In our example, input numbers had to be squared to produce the desired output.) It is the programmer's responsibility to analyze the requirements of a specific problem, to determine how these requirements can be met by the computer, and then to proceed with planning and writing a program that will produce the required result.

The importance of problem analysis cannot be overemphasized. Incomplete understanding of information and poor or faulty planning will only result in having to alter constantly what has been done already as additional facts become available. Even worse, you may never really get off the ground with a solution. It is both easier and more efficient to begin program planning with the initial understanding gained from problem analysis, then proceed to algorithm development.

Algorithm Development (Flowcharting)

Flowcharting is one of several techniques that allow a programmer to graphically represent proposed solutions to a problem. We believe it is the simplest technique for the beginner. A flowchart is a *visual* algorithm, which can be extremely helpful in locating errors in your planning. Flowcharting is a very useful and powerful procedure. It is strongly recommended as a vital step in the programming cycle, prior to any attempt to write the instructions in a specific language.

Flowcharting Symbols. After careful problem analysis, the steps required to solve the problem are diagrammed using standardized symbols. Specific symbols represent each function of processing. Although there are many such symbols, our needs can be met with the use of just four: PROCESS, INPUT/OUTPUT, DECISION, and TERMINAL. Figure 14.1 illustrates these symbols.

For each step in an algorithm, the developer selects the correct symbol and places it on the chart. Within the symbol, a concise statement of the function is written. The symbols are connected by arrows to show the flow of execution.

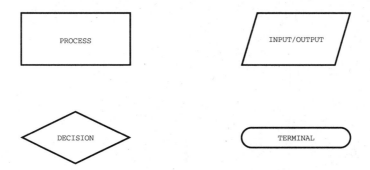

Figure 14.1. Common flowchart symbols.

An Example Flowchart. Our previous example will serve to illustrate flow-charting. The original problem was to square all the numbers on a provided list. Problem analysis yields these steps: obtain a number from the list, square that number, write down the answer, and repeat the process until all the numbers on the list have been squared. A flowchart of these steps is presented in Figure 14.2.

A TERMINAL symbol shows where the flowchart begins and contains the word "Start." "Get a Number" is an INPUT operation and is written in an INPUT/OUT-PUT (I/O) symbol. The PROCESS rectangle is used for "Calculate Square." "Write Answer" is an OUTPUT operation and is also represented by an INPUT/OUTPUT symbol. The determination of whether there are more numbers is a YES/NO deci-sion and the question "More Numbers?" is written inside a diamond-shaped DECISION symbol. Decisions always lead to one of two actions. Here, if the an-swer is YES, processing resumes at the "Get a Number" I/O symbol, and the cycle is repeated. If the answer is NO, processing continues with the next sequential step, a TERMINAL symbol that directs the system to halt. This outlines the entire pro-gram and gives, in graphic or schematic form, the general steps necessary to ac-complish the task.

The writer of this flowchart can now examine it in detail to see if it will accom-plish the desired task. The programmer may discover that additional processing might be necessary under certain conditions, that steps have been omitted, or that there may be ways to simplify the entire procedure. Experienced programmers know that time spent at this stage will greatly facilitate and speed up the more me-chanical steps of coding and debugging.

Discussion of Flowcharting. After you analyze a problem, you may construct several flowcharts, each illustrating a somewhat different approach to the same problem. Beyond the simplest problems, there is seldom only *one* correct solution. As a flowchart is being drawn, you must consider various alternatives that may be encountered during the course of problem solution. A flowchart provides an efficient way to see if any steps have been omitted and if the overall logic of the solution appears to be correct. If errors are discovered later or modifications must be made to achieve the goal, you can return to the flowchart to find and correct them.

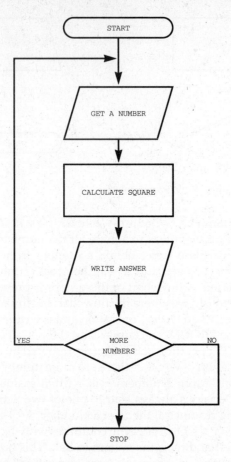

Figure 14.2. A sample flowchart.

Beginning programmers are often more interested in actually writing the computer instructions (coding) than in problem analysis and flowcharting. It seems more useful to be writing instructions than to be drawing diagrams. However, the importance of problem analysis and flowcharting quickly becomes apparent to a programmer working on full-scale problems. To analyze the method of attack on any problem is at least as important as writing the actual instructions. If the structure of the solution is not fully and accurately understood, no combination of instructions will produce useful output.

In fairness, it should be noted that some programmers rarely flowchart their problems and still write sound and efficient programs. The ability to do so is a direct result of extensive programming experience. Flowcharting is a step you might eventually abandon or, more likely, replace with other techniques not presented here. However, we doubt that anyone other than a professional programmer will reach that level and strongly recommend flowcharting as the easiest approach for the beginner.

Structured Programming

"The art of programming is the art of organizing complexity, of mastering multitude and avoiding its bastard chaos as effectively as possible," according to Dahl, Dijkstra, and Hoare (1972, p. 6). The most widely accepted approach to meeting this challenge is called *structured programming.*

Origin and Nature

In the early days of computers, getting the machine to produce the desired output was difficult. Any means of doing so was considered acceptable. Programmers were virtually a priesthood of miracle workers who individually developed ways of achieving results. There were no general standards for how programs should be written.

As the field of data processing evolved, it became necessary to develop common approaches so that programs written by one person would be easily understood by others. Early programs truly demonstrated a level of "operational chaos" in that they worked, but how and why was difficult to tell. Even programmers often were unable to comprehend their own programs shortly after completing them. As computers became more common and the number of programs in existence exploded, the old ways no longer sufficed.

Today, a standard for programming exists and is almost universally accepted in the data processing industry: structured programming. According to Schnake (1985, p. 357), structured programming "is a set of techniques designed to improve the organization of the program, to facilitate solving a problem, and to make the code easier to write and read. . . . "

For our purposes, we will consider four basic components of structured programming: top-down design, modularity, use of a well-defined set of logical constructs, and documentation.

Top-Down Design

Early programmers approached their problems in a manner similar to putting together a jigsaw puzzle with no guarantee that all of the pieces are for the same puzzle and without an illustration of what the completed picture should be. The method has been called *bottom-up design.* The smallest details of a program were attacked first. If they could be solved, then work progressed up a level, putting more pieces together, in the ultimate hope that the total product would still work.

It seems that this approach developed because of the newness of programming and the inexperience of many practitioners. They had little confidence in their ability to solve the entire problem and wished to begin with what they thought would be the most difficult parts. Major problems in making all the pieces work together were common.

Top-down design, in contrast, seems intuitively correct to most people today. It begins with the big picture, not the minutiae. From an overall understanding of the problem, the major components are identified at a relatively abstract level. Each major component is then refined into subtasks required for it to work. The process is carried on through as many levels of refinement as required to reach multiple points, each of which is a relatively trivial programming task. This technique, also referred to as "step-wise refinement," is illustrated in Figure 14.3.

Modularity

Modularity is a logical extension of top-down design. When a programming problem has been refined into minor steps that together meet the requirements, it is only reasonable to prepare the instructions to the computer as a series of *modules*. Each module fulfills one of the well-defined tasks described in the design and therefore has a limited function.

Because planning began at the top, there is little likelihood that the parts will not fit together and work properly as a whole. In fact, each module will have a high degree of independence from others. This makes it possible to reuse modules from one program to the next, so long as the processing need is the same and only the specific data vary. Over many programming projects, this adds greatly to programming efficiency.

Limited Constructs

Within modules, structured programming makes the work of one programmer readily understandable to others by limiting the techniques used to achieve the desired result. These techniques are known as *logical constructs*. They lend a distinctive style to programs, which is known to be efficient and effective, and which reduces the chaos of idiosyncratic programming to a widely accepted standard. One might say that structured constructs produce "educated, literate programming."

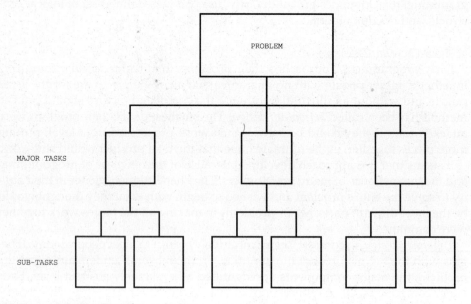

Figure 14.3. Top-down design.

Boehm and Jacopini (1966) proved mathematically that all programming requirements can be met by only three logical constructs. They are sequence, selection, and iteration or repetition. Figure 14.4 shows minimal flowcharts for these constructs.

Sequence entails one or more instructions carried out by the computer in the exact order written. This is the most fundamental of the constructs. Only process and I/O symbols are needed to flowchart a sequence. In fact, every program can begin as a sequence of one process box, as shown in Figure 14.4. This one box is then replaced with a series of symbols in a longer sequence and/or other constructs as the overall program is refined into subtasks.

The *selection* construct involves a question, the answer to which determines what happens next. Only two answers are possible for each question, yes or no. Either answer may cause specific processing to occur, or one may produce no result at all, simply bypassing the processing required in the other case.

The final allowable construct is *iteration*, or repetition. This entails repeating a series of processing operations until some specified condition is met. Another common term for this construct is *looping*.

An iteration construct also involves a *decision symbol*. Rather than leading to two alternate forward paths as selection does, one path of an iteration continues, the other cycles to repeat steps. If the decision is made before any processing, the loop is referred to as a "Do While." If processing occurs first and then the need for repetition is determined, it is known as a "Repeat Until."

Code Documentation

The goal of code documentation is to enable a programmer to read a printed listing of the instructions comprising a program and to understand *what* it does and *how*. This is essential where several programmers work jointly on one program. It is also helpful in program maintenance and modification at a later date. Even the creator of a program easily can forget how it works over time. In fact, if the documentation is thorough, a nonprogrammer may be able at least to understand the essence of the program.

Each language has its own means for placing documentation within a program, but the need for documentation is universal in programming.

Coding

We have now described the programming process in terms of procedures and principles. There has been no reference to a specific programming language, because all of the earlier steps are language independent. This means you can and should plan the attack, devise an algorithm, and express that algorithm as a flowchart using structured constructs apart from any concern over which language will be used.

While most beginning programmers justifiably are concerned over details of a specific language, its vocabulary and syntax, these concerns become important only after the preceding steps are completed. Writing the actual instructions in

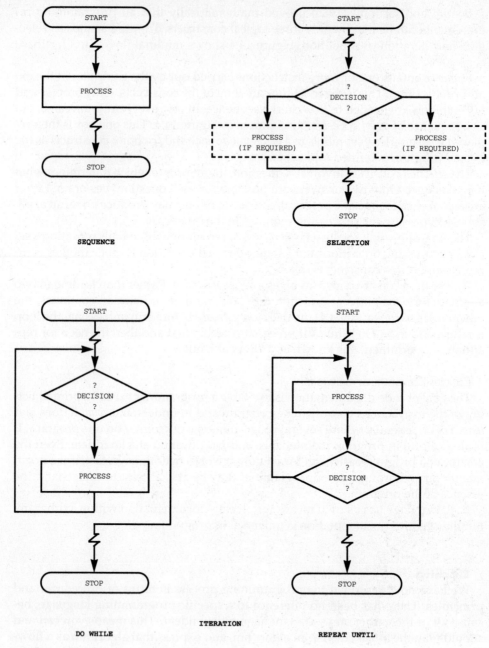

Figure 14.4. Structured programming constructs.

some language is known as *coding*. It is possible to become technically proficient at coding in one or more languages without ever developing the far more critical analytical skills we have described.

Learning to code in any language tends to be a time-consuming task. It may reasonably be likened to learning a foreign language. For some it is far more difficult than for others. You will see examples of code in several languages in the chapters that follow.

For now, it should be clear to you that programming is *not* synonymous with coding. Coding is only one part of the entire process. Our point is that in many school settings, emphasis is placed on teaching students a language, that is, coding. We agree with Luehrmann (1983) who wrote, "the powerful ideas of computing . . . are vastly more important than the details of the programming language used." For a more detailed discussion of what should be taught in a school programming curriculum, see Davidson, Savenye, and Orr (1992), McAllister and Brock (1990), Anderson, Bennett, and Walling (1987), and Lockard (1985–1986).

Testing and Revision

The last phase of the program development cycle is *testing* and *revision*. Following the principles of structured programming, the product under development will be modular in design. In turn, it is both possible and desirable to code the program module by module. Each can be tested for proper operation upon completion.

Especially in the early stages of learning to program, it is only reasonable to expect errors in both logic and coding when you begin to test a module. Errors must be corrected before further work is undertaken, a process known as *debugging*. Debugging is the bane of the programmer and can be a very time-consuming task.

While there is little likelihood of ever becoming so skilled as to have only flawless initial test runs, the time spent on debugging generally decreases significantly with experience. Errors in logic are more difficult to resolve than errors in coding. Meticulous attention to the precoding stages can dramatically reduce logical errors. That is a major reason for structured programming. Coding errors will diminish as fluency in the language increases.

Programming and Languages

When you write instructions for a computer, they cannot be the instructions you would give to another person. Computers have limited capacity to understand, with none of the human ability to compensate for poor communication. Essentially, we humans must conform to the limits of the machine; it cannot adjust to us. Computer languages are the means for human-machine communication.

Computer languages comprise a vast field that is beyond the scope of this book. Let's focus on categorical distinctions, looking at two levels of computer languages as well as two methods of implementation.

Low-Level Languages

Shelly and Cashman (1980) defined low-level languages as languages closely related to a particular computer type. There are two basic categories of such languages, *machine* and *assembler*. Actual implementations of either vary drastically from one computer type to another.

Machine Language

The most fundamental instructions that a computer can understand are referred to as *machine language*. When a computer is designed and built, a specific functional language is provided in its processing circuits. Instructions in machine language can be understood directly and executed by the computer system. In fact, a computer system always executes machine language instructions because they are all that it actually understands.

Machine language is a very intricate and complicated language that would be difficult to use for writing programs. Since a computer is just a massive set of electrical switches, which can be set to either on or off, its native language consists exclusively of binary digits. It is patterns of 0's and 1's that cause the computer to function. If the only language available to a user to control a computer system were binary machine language, computers would be far less popular than they are today.

Assembler Language

The very first stored program computers could be programmed only in machine language. It quickly became apparent that a language more suited to humans was needed. An assembler language is machine-oriented, structured closely around the actual machine language. However, instead of programming in binary digits, machine language instructions are represented by symbolic instructions. For instance, the programmer uses mnemonic instructions such as LDA (LoaD Accumulator) or CLI (Compare Logical Immediate), which an assembler program translates into the corresponding binary representation.

Assembler language represent an attempt to make writing programs easier. They are the lowest level at which you can program most computers today. However, assembler languages remain close enough to machine language to be comparatively difficult to use. We would probably not be teaching programming in schools today if only assembler languages were available. The computer had to come closer to accommodating human needs.

High-Level Languages

High-level programming languages have been designed to meet human needs rather than to accommodate the computer. They are not languages to which a computer can directly respond, and they are *not* closely linked to the internal characteristics of the computer. In fact, most common high-level languages are available for nearly any computer.

In order for a computer to understand and execute high-level language instructions, they must first be translated into equivalent machine language by a "translator" program. Each high-level instruction typically becomes multiple machine language instructions. Most high-level language instructions are common words, such as PRINT or WRITE, which are much easier for humans to learn to use correctly.

High-level language execution can be thought of as a two-step process. In Step 1, the translator program converts high-level instructions into machine code. In Step 2, the system executes the machine language instructions. In this manner, the program in the higher-level language actually is executed by the computer in machine language.

High-level languages make computer language learning and programming accessible to most interested persons, the vast majority of whom would never attempt to learn a machine or assembler language. Such languages require less time to master and make programming far easier. Programmers tend to make fewer coding mistakes, and errors are easier to find and correct.

The two most common high-level languages used in education are Logo and BASIC. Brief illustrations of these and several other languages are provided in Chapters 15 and 16.

Interpreters and Compilers

Within high-level languages, there are two differing approaches to implementation. Both interpreters and compilers translate instructions into machine code.

An *interpreter* is a program that reads another program in some high-level language, one statement at a time. The interpreter translates this "source statement" into the corresponding machine code, which executes immediately. A language interpreter may be a program on a disk, which is loaded into RAM memory for use. In some microcomputers a BASIC language interpreter is provided on a ROM chip.

When the interpreter finds an error in the coding, it cannot translate the statement, so the program halts at that point. This makes it relatively easy to identify the problem and correct it. In fact, an interpreted language is interactive, meaning that you enter the instructions, run the program, and are told of errors as they are found. You can correct the error and rerun the program immediately. This makes interpreted languages ideal for beginners. Logo and many microcomputer versions of BASIC are interpreted languages.

Compilers add another step to the process of moving from code in a high-level language to execution of the code. The programmer creates an entire program in the source language, say, FORTRAN. The compiler program attempts to translate the entire source program into machine instructions, noting errors as it goes, but generally not stopping until the end. The machine instructions are called *object code*.

If errors were found, the programmer must correct them and compile the program again. When there are no language errors, the object code is executed. Logic errors may be revealed that then must be corrected.

Thus, an interpreter translates source code instructions into machine instructions one by one and executes them. A compiler translates the entire source program into object code and executes it only when no coding errors remain. This is a somewhat more cumbersome process altogether, but has the advantage of faster execution of the program. Languages such as FORTRAN, COBOL, and Pascal are usually implemented as compiled languages. Because the process is somewhat more complicated, compiled languages are less suitable to young and beginning programmers.

Summary

A program is a set of instructions to a computer that cause it to carry out some clearly defined task. Programming is essentially a matter of controlling the computer, a process that parallels telling another person how to do something. The most important aspects of programming are understanding the problem and planning a logical approach to solving it, not the actual writing of specific language instructions to do the job.

Structured programming is a set of guidelines for writing programs in an efficient and effective manner. Following the principles of top-down design, modularity, use of only a limited number of logical constructs, and program documentation, a programmer can create programs that are easy to read and modify. Structured programming provides a widely understood and accepted approach to programming with proven benefits.

Programming should not be confused with coding, which is merely the conversion of careful plans into corresponding instructions in a chosen language. Beginning programmers must guard against moving too quickly into the coding phase. Careful planning can prevent many errors. Regardless of one's skill as a programmer, all programs require extensive testing to be certain that they perform as specified under all conditions. Errors are likely, either in coding or in logic. Correcting such errors is called debugging.

Programming languages are divided into low-level languages (machine and assembler languages) and high-level languages, such as BASIC or Logo. Most programmers today use one of the numerous high-level languages that exist to make programming easier and less error-prone. Low-level languages are very closely linked to specific computers and therefore differ widely. High-level languages exist for most computers in forms that are similar regardless of the specific computer.

High-level languages may be implemented as interpreters or compilers. An interpreter is a program that converts high-level languge instructions into their corresponding machine instructions one at a time and executes them immediately. A compiler translates an entire program into machine or object code, which executes only when no language errors remain. Interpreted languages are better suited to any beginning programmer, especially children.

Bibliography

Anderson, R., Bennett, H., and Walling, D. "Structured Programming Constructs in BASIC: Tried and Tested." *Computers in the Schools*, Summer 1987, pp. 135–139.

Boehm, C., and Jacopini, G. "Flow Diagrams, Turing Machines, and Languages with Only Two Formulation Rules." *Communications of the Association for Computing Machinery*, May 1966, pp. 366–371.

Burton, J. K., and Magliaro, S. "Computer Programming and Generalized Problem-Solving Skills: In Search of Direction." *Computers in the Schools*, Fall/Winter 1987/1988, pp. 63–90.

Dahl, O., Dijkstra, E., and Hoare, C. *Structured Programming*. New York: Academic Press, 1972.

Davidson, G. V., Savenye, W. C., and Orr, K. B. "How Do Learning Styles Relate to Performance in a Computer Applications Course?" *Journal of Research on Computing in Education*, Spring 1992, 24(3), pp. 348–358.

Hooper, E. J., and Thomas, R. A. "Investigating the Effects of a Manipulative Model of Computer Memory Operations on the Learning of Programming." *Journal of Research on Computing in Education*, Summer 1990, 22(4), pp. 442–457.

Lockard, J. "Programming in the Schools: What Should Be Taught?" *Computers in the Schools*, Winter 1985–1986, pp. 105–114.

Luehrmann, A. "Slicing through Spaghetti Code." *The Computing Teacher*, April 1983, pp. 9–15.

Mayer, R. E. (Ed.). *Teaching and Learning Computer Programming. Multiple Research Perspectives*. Hillsdale, NJ: Lawrence Erlbaum Associates, 1988.

Mayer, R. E., Dyck, J. L., and Vilberg, W. "Learning to Program and Learning to Think: What's the Connection?" *Communications of the ACM, 1986, 29*(7), pp. 605–610.

McAllister, D. W., and Brock, F. J., Jr. "Using the Logic Diagram in Teaching Programming: An Overview and Preliminary Test Results." *Journal of Research on Computing in Education*, Spring 1990, 22(3), pp. 348–363.

McCoy, L. P., and Orey, M. A., III. "Computer Programming and General Problem Solving by Secondary Students." *Computers in the Schools*, Fall/Winter 1987–1988, pp. 151–158.

Norris, C., Jackson, L., and Poirot, J. "The Effects of Computer Science Instruction on Critical Thinking Skills and Mental Alertness." *Journal of Research on Computing in Education*, Spring 1992, 24(3), pp. 329–337.

Ohler, J. "The Many Myths of Programming." *The Computing Teacher*, May 1987, pp. 22–23.

Reed, W. M. "A Philosophical Case for Teaching Programming Languages." *Computers in the Schools*, Fall/Winter 1987–1988, pp. 55–58.

Schnake, M. *The World of Computers and Data Processing*. St. Paul: West Publishing, 1985.

Shelly, G., and Cashman, T. *Introduction to Computers and Data Processing*. Brea, CA: Anaheim Publishing, 1980.

Soloway, E., and Spohrer, J. C. (Eds.). *Studying the Novice Programmer*. Hillsdale, NJ: Lawrence Erlbaum Associates, 1988.

Taylor, H. G., and Mounfield, L. "An Analysis of Success Factors in College Computer Science: High School Methodology Is a Key Element." *Journal of Research on Computing in Education*, Winter 1991, 24(2), pp. 240–245.

van Merriënboer, J. J. G. "Instructional Strategies for Teaching Computer Programming: Interactions with the Cognitive Style Reflection-Impulsivity." *Journal of Research on Computing in Education*, Fall 1990, 23(1), pp. 45–54.

Walton, R. E., and Balestri, D. "Writing as a Design Discipline: Exploring the Relationship between Composition and Programming." *Machine-Mediated Learning, 2*(1&2), 1987, pp. 47–65.

Wiburg, K. M. "Does Programming Deserve a Place in the School Curriculum?" *The Computing Teacher*, October 1989, 17(2), pp. 8–11.

Wiebe, J. H. "At-Computer Programming Success of Third-Grade Students." *Journal of Research on Computing in Education,* Winter 1991, 24(2), pp. 214–229.

Zirkler, D., and Brownell, G. "Analogical Reasoning: A Cognitive Consequence of Programming?" *Computers in the Schools,* 1991, 8(4), pp. 135–145.

Objectives

After completing this chapter, you will be able to:

Briefly describe the origins of Logo.

Describe the philosophical and psychological bases of Logo.

Define the terms primitive, procedure, *and* recursion.

List the essential characteristics of Logo and its derivatives.

Discuss reasons why Logo is taught.

Present appropriate strategies for teaching Logo.

Discuss Logo research findings.

Assess the potential of Logo for your teaching circumstances.

Chapter 15

Logo

Computer languages enable us to control our computers. Without languages, computer use could never have developed as it has. Almost from the beginning, however, users have longed for an easier way to control computers. In the future, we will control computers by speaking to them, but until that technology is perfected, other means remain essential.

Logo is a means of controlling a computer that has drawn considerable attention in education, especially in the elementary grades. Created in the late 1960s at the Massachusetts Institute of Technology (MIT), Logo is based on a philosophy of learning guided by important learning principles. This chapter introduces Logo and its underlying concepts.

What is Logo?

Logo is unquestionably a programming language, but it is viewed by its developers as much more than that.

> Logo is the name for a philosophy of education and for a continually evolving family of computer languages that aid its realization. Its learning environments articulate the principle that giving people personal control over powerful computational resources can enable them to establish intimate contact with profound ideas from science, from mathematics, and from the art of intellectual model building. Its computer languages are designed to transform computers into flexible tools to aid in learning, in playing, and in exploring (Abelson, 1982, p. ix).

Logo is a unique blend of a programming language, learning theory, and educational philosophy. It is intended to be both powerful and simple to use. Indeed, it is this simplicity and power that have made Logo so appealing.

Philosophical and Psychological Foundations

Logo was developed by a team headed by Seymour Papert, a mathematician at MIT's Artificial Intelligence Laboratory. Papert's thinking was influenced strongly by the 5 years he spent with the Swiss developmental psychologist Jean Piaget, studying how children think and learn.

Piaget's Influence

Piaget believed that all organisms tend to seek or impose structure on all that they encounter. Our basic mental structure results from the interaction of our natural tendencies with our environment. A child's intellectual development systematically proceeds through hierarchical stages that become more complex and integrated as the child matures. Children truly build their own intellectual structures.

Intellectual development is facilitated less by teaching than by allowing children a great deal of activity on their own, time to explore with materials that enhance the cognitive benefit of the activities. Piaget contended that children gain real understanding only from that which they themselves invent. Furthermore, when we try to teach children something for which they are not ready, we prevent them from learning it for themselves. To try to accelerate learning too much is, therefore, largely a waste of time.

Papert's Contributions

Papert presents his views in his book *Mindstorms: Children, Computers, and Powerful Ideas* (1980), which all teachers should read. While largely agreeing with Piaget, especially regarding the need to build one's own intellectual structures, Papert saw hope for accelerating the developmental process. To Papert, the key is an environment that encourages free exploration and provides an abundance of materials that facilitate children's exploration. Given enough access to enough of the right kinds of "tools," children's intellectual development would be stimulated and accelerated.

To counteract the intellectual poverty of our culture, Papert turned to computers and programming to create a totally new type of learning environment for children: Logo. Logo emphasizes discovery, exploration, manipulation, and serendipitous learning. The goal is to provide that rich environment, termed a *microworld,* in which a child uses the computer in ways that best facilitate meaningful learning and intellectual growth.

Implementation

If the computer was the key to intellectual development, the problem was how to provide children with easy access to its power. Mainframe computers were hardly easy to use. Papert envisioned a computer that provided immediate, visual reinforcement of what the child had directed it to do. The solution was Logo, a mainframe language that caused a small robot to move about on the floor in response to commands such as FORWARD and LEFT. The robot, which the team dubbed a "turtle," had pens that it could raise or lower in response to other commands to leave trails on paper of its movements. This led to the term *turtlegraphics.*

The impact of Logo was minimal until microcomputers made it widely accessible. The robotic turtle became a graphic figure that moved about the monitor screen, and the pens were replaced by visible trails, often in different colors. Aside from costs, we speculate that far fewer teachers would have been willing to try Logo if they had needed to contend with a physical robot as well. In the early years, dealing with the new microcomputers alone was enough of a challenge. Low-cost robots are available today, but most Logo users work solely with graphic turtles.

Characteristics of Logo

Papert and his colleagues developed a unique computer environment that offers considerable problem-solving potential, yet it is appropriate for children as well as adults. The uniqueness of Logo stems from its major characteristics, which are described and illustrated next.

Many Primitives

A *primitive* is a basic word that the computer is able to understand. Since Logo was written initially for mainframe computers, its vocabulary required large amounts of RAM. Languages developed for early microcomputers with limited RAM had to be kept small. Logo was not implemented on microcomputers until substantial RAM became widely available. As a consequence, Logo retains a large primitive vocabulary, affording the user simpler yet greater communication potential. Is it not easier to speak effectively with a large vocabulary than a more limited one? While it is beyond our scope to present all of Logo's primitives, an example will suffice.

Logo's graphic primitives are used to cause the turtle to draw on the screen. Beginning with an empty screen, the turtle is located at the center, heading up. All moves are relative to the turtle's heading. To draw a box, use the primitives FORWARD (FD) and RIGHT (RT). The turtle must be told how many "steps" forward to move and how much to turn. The following sequence of instructions illustrates these points:

```
FD 50 RT 90 FD 50 RT 90 FD 50 RT 90 FD 50 RT 90
```

The image left on the screen by the turtle is shown below, with labels added to clarify the movements. The turtle moved from point A to B, turned right 90 degrees, moved to C, and so on back to point A. The final RT 90 returns the turtle to its original heading.

A second box can be added to the first using the primitives BACK (BK) and LEFT (LT).

```
BK 50 LT 90 BK 50 LT 90 BK 50 LT 90 BK 50 LT 90
```

This produces the figure below as the turtle moves backward from A to E to F to D to A, again facing up at the end. You may want to trace these movements yourself using some small object to visualize the outcome. There are many other combinations of moves and turns that would provide the same image.

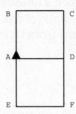

Procedural Base

Logo commands are grouped together into *procedures*. Each procedure must have a unique name. Once you define a procedure, it works like a primitive. You merely type its name to execute its set of commands. Users "teach" the computer to do new things by defining procedures, in effect creating their own programming language by extending Logo's primitive vocabulary. Here's an example.

Your goal is to get the turtle to draw a rectangle. To create your procedure, give it a name using the word TO, that is, TO RECTANGLE. Next, type the required instructions, and conclude with the word END. Complete the definition, and the turtle will respond to your types command RECTANGLE just like FORWARD. Figure 15.1 gives one solution to this problem, along with its output.

A procedural language encourages the user first to look at the overall problem and then to break this large problem into smaller subsets. A procedure is then written for each smaller piece. This is a direct application of the concepts of top-down design and modularity presented in the previous chapter. Students learning Logo come to use these concepts naturally without formal definitions or instruction concerning them. In other words, they can "do" top-down design and modular program building without knowing the terms or being able to define the concepts. This is Papert's key idea of appropriating knowledge. It demonstrates how the Logo environment can give children access to concepts too abstract for their level of cognitive development. Here is another illustration.

Suppose you want the turtle to draw the outline of a house. Can you envision the house as two components, a triangle (the roof) on a box? Now write a procedure called HOUSE.

```
TO HOUSE
  BOX
  ROOF
END
```

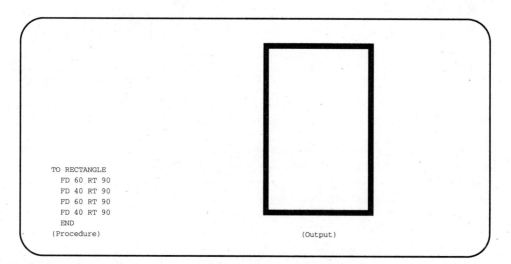

Figure 15.1 Drawing a rectangle in Logo.

Of course, this procedure would not yet work, because Logo does not have a definition for BOX or ROOF. You must create procedures with those names that HOUSE will then use as primitives. You also can test your procedures one by one to determine if they do what they are supposed to. In this way, you can be sure the HOUSE procedure will work correctly.

The box procedure could be just like the earlier example of Logo primitives. However, if you make the height and width the same number of steps, you can simplify the procedure by using the REPEAT command to make the same move and turn four times.

```
TO BOX
  REPEAT 4 [FD 60 RT 90]
  END
```

This is one way to achieve iteration or looping in Logo, although the concept would not be described to children. Any sequence of instructions may be given in square brackets and repeated as many times as required in this manner.

When you test this procedure by typing BOX, a problem appears. It leaves the turtle at the lower-left corner of the box, when it needs to be at the upper left to add the roof. How could you move the turtle to the desired location after drawing the box? How about this approach?

```
BOX
FD 60
```

To create the roof, you need to draw a triangle. This is conceptually more difficult and requires a good deal of trial and error for most beginners. There are many possible approaches, of course. We settled on this one:

```
TO ROOF
  RT 45 FD 43 RT 90 FD 43 RT 135 FD 60
  END
```

For this example, the final RT 135 FD 60 are not critical, as they merely retrace the top line of the box. We included them so that ROOF alone indeed does produce a complete triangle.

Now you can draw a house by typing only the word HOUSE. HOUSE will in turn execute BOX and ROOF to produce the completed drawing. The three procedures and the turtle's drawing are shown in Figure 15.2. You could develop other procedures to add windows, a chimney, and so on.

Recursion

Among the most powerful and least understood of Logo's features is *recursion*. When working with a procedural language, one procedure can use another as a

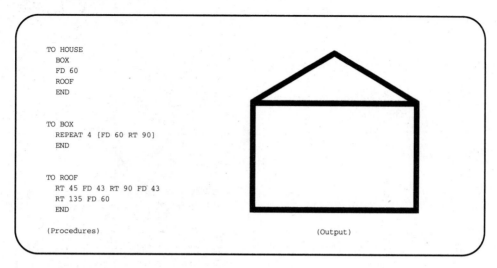

```
TO HOUSE
  BOX
  FD 60
  ROOF
  END


TO BOX
  REPEAT 4 [FD 60 RT 90]
  END


TO ROOF
  RT 45 FD 43 RT 90 FD 43
  RT 135 FD 60
  END

(Procedures)                    (Output)
```

Figure 15.2 Drawing a house in Logo.

subprocedure. In our HOUSE example, the definition of HOUSE uses BOX and ROOF as subprocedures. The next step beyond this concept is recursion.

Recursion occurs when a procedure calls *itself* as a subprocedure. Thus, recursion is nothing more than the ability to use a procedure as part of its own definition. As Harvey (1982) suggested, recursion allows a rather complex problem to be described in terms of simpler versions of itself. Because Logo is recursive, it is possible to build more complex programs by using simpler subprocedures and structurally adding to them.

Perhaps an example at this point will help. An appropriate procedure for drawing a box would be:

```
TO BOX
 REPEAT 4 [FD 40 RT 90]
 END
```

To illustrate recursion, let's use the box just defined to create a "spinning" box design. The procedure for this will be SPINBOX.

```
TO SPINBOX
 BOX
 RT 45
 SPINBOX
 END
```

When you type SPINBOX, one box is drawn, then the turtle turns 45 degrees to the right. The procedure "calls" itself, and the cycle repeats endlessly, eventually

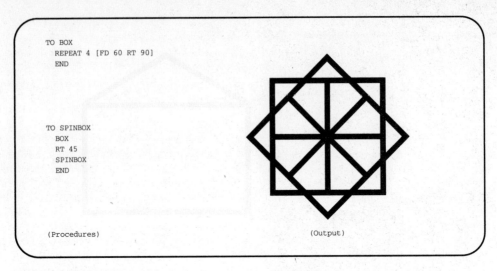

```
TO BOX
  REPEAT 4 [FD 60 RT 90]
  END




TO SPINBOX
  BOX
  RT 45
  SPINBOX
  END
```

(Procedures)   (Output)

Figure 15.3 Drawing a complex pattern with recursion.

drawing over itself. (This procedure must be stopped by the user.) The output is shown in Figure 15.3.

Interactivity

When you type a command (FD 40) or a procedure name (SQUARE), you see the result immediately. With Logo, the user and the computer communicate visually and actively with one another. This interactivity provides students immediate feedback as to their progress, which is a desirable element of learning.

An interactive language makes writing programs relatively fast. You have the opportunity to make corrections ("debug") at the point of the error, which makes it easier to find and fix mistakes. You no doubt realized that what Logo enthusiasts call interactive means Logo is *interpreted*.

Use of Familiar Vocabulary

Another desirable feature of Logo is its use of common words, such as LEFT and BACK. This contributes to its usability with children, who can relate bodily movement directly to the turtle. In addition, students can create procedures with names that are meaningful to them. To develop a face as a procedure, a child can name the top-level procedure FACE. FACE itself may require procedures called EYES, NOSE, and MOUTH, all appropriate and easily understood names.

In addition to allowing the user to develop new procedures from common, easily understood words, Logo also provides easily understood error messages. For example, two error messages in Terrapin Logo are FORWARD NEEDS MORE INPUTS (e.g., you typed just FD, not FD 50) and THERE IS NO PROCEDURE NAMED *whatever* (e.g., you haven't yet written the procedure *whatever*).

Ease of Use

One of the most compelling characteristics of Logo is its initial simplicity. Once you master a few basic concepts such as left and right, forward and back, meaningful, interesting, sometimes unexpected, and always rewarding results begin to appear on the screen. A learner actually can *do* something in just minutes after being introduced to Logo. The basic Logo commands give simple, visual results, affording children a wide range of creative activities and possibilities.

Logo is also easy to use because you control the computer by building new functions in small manageable blocks using primitives, rather than by creating a long, complex set of sequential instructions. Furthermore, when you make changes in a procedure, you see the results immediately. This provides vital reinforcement. If the results are not what you want, simply change the procedure again and again.

Beyond Turtlegraphics

Because Logo has been used largely with younger students, our purposes for this chapter are served by only graphics examples. However, do not assume that this is the extent of Logo's capabilities. Logo is a full-featured programming environment, with mathematics, sound, and extensive text-manipulation features. Text manipulation is termed *list processing* and is much more demanding conceptually than turtlegraphics. However, it offers powerful capabilities that easily can extend the use of Logo to junior high and high school students. As familiarity with Logo has increased, articles in the literature have turned somewhat from graphics to the more demanding list-processing applications (e.g., Muir, 1990; Harris, November 1991; Harris and Lickteig, 1992). A variety of books and articles on Logo are listed in the bibliography at the end of this chapter.

Extended Versions of Logo

Several producers have extended the essential functionality of Logo with other versions, which we only can highlight here.

Logo Plus

Logo Plus is an enhanced version of basic Logo that adds over forty new commands. Users can enhance graphics screens with text in varied colors, fonts and styles. They can create new turtle shapes with the built-in shape editor. Several other features increase ease of use and versatility. The producer also offers *Logo Probability*, *Logo Innovations*, and *Kinderlogo*, which serve specific needs.

LogoWriter / LogoEnsemble

LogoWriter extends turtlegraphics with four separate turtles and multiple turtle shapes. These turtles can be used to create intriguing animations. *LogoWriter's* name stems from added features of word processing, including the ability to copy, search, replace, cut, and paste text. It integrates text and graphics on screen and in printouts, and supports animation and music. New procedures can customize and extend the available text editing features and can be assigned to specific control keys, just like the basic features.

LogoEnsemble goes a step further to mimic integrated software with word-processing, graphics, database, and communications functions.

LEGO TC logo

Students gain opportunities to build, invent, and create when Logo joins forces with the familiar Lego building blocks. *LEGO TC logo* lets students control machines they build from Lego pieces, gears, motors, and sensors. In some ways, this is a return to the days of the physical turtle. *LogoWriter Robotics* is another product along this same line.

One advantage of *LEGO TC logo* is that learners must employ the scientific method as they invent (Rosen, 1988). As they encounter problems with a machine, students must develop strategies to determine the cause. They generate and test hypotheses, gather, record, and assess data. The emphasis is on hands-on experiences with real scientific and mathematical problems.

Why Teach Logo?

Now that you are familiar with some of Logo's features and program enhancements, let's consider why Logo is taught in schools. Many of the general reasons given in the previous chapter for teaching programming also are used to justify teaching Logo. However, because Logo is so different in its origins and nature from other computer languages, some reasons for using it also differ.

A Unique Cognitive Experience

Logo is not just a language, but also a philosophical approach to learning. While you may wish to read *Mindstorms* (Papert, 1980) for an in-depth presentation, the following represent major points taken from an interview with Papert (Reinhold, 1986).

Logo exists to allow students to appropriate other knowledge; that is, to make it their own. This implies a use of knowledge that goes beyond our typical educational emphasis on content. Of greater concern is how children relate to their knowledge. This is an outgrowth of Piaget's constructivism, which emphasizes the importance of the individual as an active learner. The role of the teacher changes from conveyor of knowledge to facilitator of a positive learning environment. Papert stated, "If students could learn topics in a way they could enjoy, they would learn them like anyone else; they wouldn't need remediation" (p. 36).

The computer becomes an "object to think with" when learners can readily interact with it. Logo affords such an opportunity to even the youngest schoolchildren. The computer is a vehicle for important conceptual learning, not the focus of interest itself. Further, the key outcome is not a working program, as is true with most languages. Logo is not taught from the programming frame of reference provided in the last chapter. Rather, the emphasis in Logo is upon process in a learning environment that safely provides opportunity for exploration. Free exploration produces not errors, but unexpected outcomes and serendipitous learning.

Problem Solving Potential

From Logo's process emphasis, it follows that the primary reason for teaching Logo is not programming itself, but to enable learners to use the computer as a problem-solving tool. Many educators are paying increased attention to the need to teach students higher-order thought processes. Paul (1984) suggested that our schools are lacking in those types of learning activities that require children to think in a serious, logical, and analytical way. Logo offers one such activity.

It should be stressed that teaching effective problem solving requires more than one activity, however. Other opportunities for the application of problem-solving skills must be provided in all areas of the curriculum. Teachers may be sadly disappointed in the development of these skills in their students if they rely only on Logo or any other single approach. Effective transfer of learning will require a teaching strategy that calls upon the use of skills in other contexts.

Higher-Level Intellectual Activity

Critics of education often complain that schools focus largely on lower-level intellectual activities. Dale (1986) suggested that Logo has the rare potential to involve students on each of Benjamin Bloom's six levels of activity. For children to use Logo, they must have knowledge (level 1) of direction and distance and must comprehend (level 2) or understand this knowledge. Because Logo uses familiar knowledge and comprehension in a meaningful way, it is not difficult for students to apply them (level 3) to learn simple programming skills quickly. Analysis (level 4) is the recognition of elements, relationships, and organizational structure of selected information or a problem. It is inherent in constructing procedures to solve a problem. When children reorganize or combine existing procedures into new ones, such as our HOUSE example, they are achieving synthesis (level 5). The most obvious incident of evaluation (level 6) comes in debugging, the effort to find and fix errors or to revise procedures to improve a program.

Establishing the Logo Environment

Papert (1980, p. 129) described microworlds as "explorable and manipulable environments." Logo is itself such a microworld and can be used to create further microworlds. In a microworld, subject matter and how you approach it are interwoven in a living laboratory. The Logo environment is obviously intended to be different from the traditional classroom. Papert (1980, p. 6) described the contrast between learning a foreign language artificially in the classroom and learning it naturally by living where it is spoken. Logo is meant to offer such natural learning opportunities.

To establish the type of learning environment espoused by Piaget and Papert requires significant changes in the way teachers interact with students.

Role of the Teacher

At the heart of the Logo environment for Papert is discovery learning. Students are expected to learn through their own investigations rather than being "taught" as most teachers presently teach. The role of the teacher changes drastically from disseminator of knowledge to learning facilitator. The teacher is not expected to know the answer to all questions posed by the students but rather to know the *process* of investigation, or how to go about finding the answers. Appropriate questioning skills are vital.

The teacher becomes essential in establishing an environment where children are comfortable in posing their own problems and working toward solutions. Right or wrong responses are not the end goal; the goal is, rather, reflective thinking and analysis of what has happened and what might happen under certain circumstances. Dale (1984) described the teacher's role with Logo:

> You are not meant to direct learning from a podium and the security of a carefully mapped curriculum. Instead, you are meant to be in the thick of things, sometimes taking an active part in the learning process, sometimes suggesting new ideas, sometimes stepping back and letting explorations continue under student control (p. 183).

Adapting to the Role

Many teachers find it difficult to adapt to the facilitative role. It is contrary to how they were taught and even how they were taught to teach. It is hard not to provide answers to student questions. It may be much more time-consuming to "discover" what a teacher could show or teach students easily. This is a genuine dilemma for teachers who want to work with Logo but who find the facilitator role foreign and uncomfortable.

Some of the concern may stem from an erroneous assumption. Just because the teacher's role changes does not leave the teacher with nothing to do but let the children "do their own thing." Rather, Logo teachers are active participants in the learning. They question and guide; they work *with* learners to solve problems, which requires much knowledge of the learning process. When should you intervene? When should you hold back? How much help is enough? Learning this different active role takes time. Don't be discouraged if it does not happen naturally. One key to success is knowing Logo well enough yourself to be comfortable in an open environment where student needs and questions are unpredictable and you can't specifically prepare for a lesson.

Teaching Strategies

According to Papert (1980), there is no "right way" to use Logo:

> But by definition, there isn't any one way of "using it right." That implies that some particular correct way exists—and *that* would be against the spirit of what Logo is all about. It's like asking, "Did Shakespeare and Hemingway 'use English right?'"

Nonetheless, some strategies are commonly used to help learners acquire important Logo skills and to encourage learning.

Discovery Learning or Structure?

For students to reach maximum achievement levels, a balance between open-ended and more structured "discovery" methods is essential (Maddux, Johnson, and Willis, 1992, p. 278). Pure discovery is inefficient and insufficient for mastery of Logo.

Role-Play the Turtle

Directionality is fundamental to working with turtlegraphics. To move the turtle and develop a design, students must know in which direction the turtle is heading and what direction to move it to achieve their plan.

Younger children may not have developed solid directionality concepts. Older students, even adults, may not translate directions into correct instructions to the turtle. Learners often learn quickly by playing turtle, that is, walking through a design just as the turtle must move. This exercise gives a concrete sense of direction and distance. Have students work in pairs or small groups. One student should record the movements of another to establish the pattern (and commands) needed for the turtle to produce the design. Record all movements to review which moves worked and which didn't.

Navigate through Transparency Mazes

To help students master control over the turtle's movements, produce mazes on transparency plastic. Attach them to the computer monitor with masking tape. One maze might show streets students might take to walk to school. Challenge students to move the turtle from the starting point to school in as few moves as possible. For older students, try a maze of a golf course. The challenge is to "play" the course in the fewest movements or "strokes."

Display Student Work

Just as it is important (and common) to display student achievement in math, science, or language arts, Logo learning deserves the same. Print and display students' graphic designs along with the procedures that created them. This will motivate students to develop new images as they share ideas. Also, send printouts home as you would any other classwork.

Emphasize Peer Questioning

Papert (1985) recounted a classroom in Pittsburgh where the teacher established the rule, "Ask three before you ask me." In other words, it was her expectation that children would ask each other when they encountered questions. The students became teachers and learned from one another. Furthermore, this freed the classroom teacher from responding to often-trivial questions and provided time to deal with more substantive matters.

Hold Contests

The Fall 1991 issue of *Terrapin Times* spotlighted a Delaware teacher whose students love contests. After students clear their screens, teacher Karen Massado allows them 15 minutes to develop a specified image, such as a forest. She uses food, bookmarks, and award certificates as prizes.

Teach for Transfer

If your interest in Logo stems from its potential to teach transferable problem-solving skills, you are apt to be disappointed unless you take steps to assure the transfer (Maddux, et al., 1992, p. 279). Routinely point out how Logo problems and solutions parallel other similar problems relevant to your students. Be sure your students truly master Logo, or there is little base for transfer. Further, graphics alone seem to be insufficient. You'll need to master arithmetic functions and list processing yourself to be able to teach them. Finally, contrary to much practice, wait until the upper-elementary level to teach Logo.

Logo and Structured Programming

We did not present Logo in the context of the programming concepts described in Chapter 14 because Logo is most often used with children. It would be inappropriate and antithetical to the intentions of Logo's creators to "teach" programming. Many programming concepts are abstract and beyond the developmental readiness of children. However, just as children "learn" geometry concepts such as angles and degrees by *using* Logo, even though they may be unable to articulate them, so will they also learn programming concepts, entirely naturally. You need only help them along.

The procedural nature of Logo leads directly to top-down design. Planning will occur, but there will be much trial and error. The sequence construct is inherent in any procedure; iteration is learned with the REPEAT command. The selection construct exists but it is less likely to be needed in exploring graphics. Any student of Logo should grasp programming concepts easily in a more formal context at an appropriate age.

What the Research Shows

Logo is in its third decade of use and remains controversial. According to Maddux et al. (1992, p. 268), "(A)nyone who is uncomfortable with controversy should avoid education . . . especially educational computing in general and Logo in particular." Despite widespread praise of its virtues, much of the literature relies on anecdotal evidence. There is surprisingly little hard research on Logo's effects on students to support what critics see as wildly exaggerated claims. What, then, do we know about Logo?

Cognitive and Metacognitive Development
Singh (1992) provides a detailed review of research on cognitive effects of learning Logo, which we recommend beyond our limited selections here.

Clements and Battista (1990) investigated changes in children's geometry knowledge based on turtlegraphics programming. They found that the Logo environment "enriched" the children's geometric conceptualizations and the sophistication of their geometric thinking.

Clements (1985) investigated the effects of learning to program in Logo on a small group of first-grade students. Students were assigned to either a Logo group or a CAI group. The Logo group showed significant gains from pre- to post-test scores in fluency, originality, and overall creativity based on the Torrance Test of Creative Thinking. Several other metacognitive measures also favored the Logo group. However, Clements found no significant differences between the groups in cognitive development, logical thinking or other aspects measured by the McCarthy Screening Test. He concluded that 12 weeks of Logo programming did not affect cognitive development compared to use of CAI, but that it did appear to affect how children *used* their cognitive abilities.

Horton and Ryba (1986) attempted to examine systematically the effects of Logo on the thinking skills of junior high students. A group of Logo volunteers were taught after school over a 7-week period; the control group had no treatment. The Logo group outperformed the non-Logo group on measures of exploration, analysis and design, and prediction and creativity. Unexpectedly, the non-Logo group excelled in debugging!

Problem Solving and Transfer
Numerous studies by Pea and Kurland seem to demonstrate that students who have Logo instruction show no transfer to planning and other problem-solving tasks, as summarized by Kinzer, Littlefield, Delclos, and Bransford (1985). However, the authors note that most such studies failed to measure the actual extent of Logo learning or have found it to be far less than expected. Clearly, there can be no transfer from what was never learned. For that very reason, Maddux et al. (1992, p. 277) dismiss the Pea and Kurland research as "so flawed that it cannot be interpreted."

According to a study by Simmons and Cope (1990), children adjusted their concepts of angle to accommodate their Logo experiences, even though their experiences lead to erroneous conclusions.

Keller (1990) reviewed published research to determine which strategies appeared best to facilitate transfer of learning from Logo to other contexts. She noted common concerns over problems with the studies themselves: too short a treatment time, too small a sample, and inappropriate teacher/student ratios. Nonetheless, she concluded that research supports the need for a structured Logo learning environment. Discovery learning is ineffective, as is an excessively structured situation. Evidence supports teacher directiveness, but aimed at helping students think about their own thinking, not at giving the answers. Effective use of peer tutoring can also contribute to the goal. The stress should be on the process, not the product, of Logo sessions.

In a study examining the effects of instruction in BASIC and Logo at the university level, Reed, Palumbo, and Stolar (1987–1988) found that both resulted in statistically significant gains in problem-solving skills. Neither was shown to be superior to the other.

An uncommonly carefully designed study by Black, Swan, and Schwartz (1988) found transfer of problem-solving skills among students in grades 4 through 8. In the study, the Logo instruction was well-structured to avoid the failures of many other studies that relied on pure discovery. Other measures also were taken to help students directly apply their skills beyond Logo. The efforts appear to have worked.

De Corte et al. (1990) conducted a systematic experiment in three sixth-grade classes, using a pretest-posttest design with a nontreatment control group. In two experimental groups, the study sought to teach sufficient knowledge of Logo and specific thinking skills related to programming. In one Logo class, they specifically taught transfer skills. Students did acquire the desired knowledge in both Logo classes. In addition, data analysis revealed that transfer was obtained in both experimental groups. This finding implies that transfer of thinking skills is possible without explicit instruction, provided that sufficient Logo learning occurs.

Based on a metaanalysis involving thirty-eight studies and forty-four dissertations, Roblyer, Castine, and King (1988) concluded that Logo showed promise as a means of improving various cognitive skills and appeared particularly promising when compared to learning outcomes from unstructured, discovery-learning approaches.

Reasoning Ability

Another higher-order thought process is reasoning ability. To investigate the relationship between Logo instruction and reasoning ability, Many, Lockard, Abrams, and Friker (1988) used the New Jersey Test of Reasoning Skills as the dependent measure. Scores obtained by seventh- and eighth-grade students who had received 9 weeks of Logo instruction were compared to those of similar students who had received no such instruction. Significant differences were found in favor of the Logo students. In addition, "collapsing" across grades, males in the Logo group outperformed their counterparts significantly, but females did not. Thus, the benefit of Logo appeared to accrue mostly to males.

Zirkler and Brownell (1992) studied undergraduates to see if Logo programming instruction was related to development of general analogical reasoning skills. Their findings suggest that programming does lead to gains in general analogical reasoning and that the gains are related to specific uses of analogical reasoning on programming tasks. One implication is that reasoning skills develop first in a specific context, from which they then can be transferred. Thus, programming should be learned thoroughly before attempting to effect transfer.

Social-Emotional Development

Using first- and third-graders, Clements and Nastasi (1985) compared the effects of Logo programming to those of CAI on the childrens' social-emotional development. Results supported previous research showing that the children played less and worked cooperatively more in the computer groups than in the control group. More conflicts arose among those working at computers, but Logo students also resolved conflicts more successfully than those in the CAI groups. Any computer situations appeared to encourage helping behaviors in grade 3, but Logo groups did not differ significantly from CAI groups.

Research Summary

In discussing the state of Logo research, Ginther and Williamson (1985) concluded that some 20 years of experience remained just that—experience, with precious little hard evidence of value. The years since their review have not changed the situation markedly. Anecdotal evidence demonstrates the enthusiasm of Logo supporters, but solid, well-designed research remains scarce. Thus, the controversy continues to simmer (see Walker, 1987).

The summary statements offered by Clements (1985) appear to remain valid today.

1. It appears that Logo can encourage social interaction, positive self-concepts, positive attitudes toward learning, and independent work habits.
2. Working in pairs while programming in Logo appears to be most advantageous.
3. Only selected areas of achievement may be affected by Logo. Research findings appear conflicting, and even those that support Logo tend to be somewhat unimpressive.
4. Programming in Logo does appear to promote specific problem-solving behaviors.
5. It appears that Logo may enhance certain metacognitive abilities and enhance creativity.

6. Such skills as classifying, seriating, and conserving may be positively affected by the use of Logo.
7. The issue of transfer of learning resulting from the use of Logo is still largely unresolved.

Logo is no panacea for education's ills and no miraculous tool for developing higher-order thinking skills. However, used carefully in a well-conceived curriculum with clearly defined goals and an implementation plan that speaks directly to them, Logo has potential to be yet another Type II learning tool that goes beyond traditional education (Watt and Watt, 1992). Over time, the slowly growing body of empirical evidence may provide a clearer picture of exactly what to expect from Logo and how best to achieve the gains.

Although most aspects of educational computing have suffered from exaggerated, unsupported claims, Logo has suffered perhaps disproportionately. Educators need to look beyond the hype and base their decisions about Logo on students' needs. Further, newer tools such as *HyperCard* may provide similar benefits along with their unique own advantages (see Yoder, 1992). You'll learn about some of them in Chapter 17.

Summary

Logo is a programming language, but it is more than that. It represents the application to computers of Piaget's theories of learning as they relate to cognitive development. Emphasis is placed upon the establishment of an appropriate learning environment, rich with materials, and freedom to explore, using the computer as the explorative tool. Logo is easily learned, yet powerful. It is flexible and affords children a quickly learned vehicle for problem-solving activities. The use of "turtle-graphics" allows the child to apply familiar direction and distance concepts to build procedures. These procedures are modular and, when combined, can be used to develop sophisticated programs.

The teacher's role is one of facilitator or guide in the learning process. This role may be a difficult one for teachers to assume, for it rather drastically changes the traditional role of information disseminator. It must be emphasized that the changed role does *not* suggest that teachers have no responsibility in the learning process. They must have good questioning skills, be able to identify difficulties when encountered by the student, and be able to provide cooperative assistance in working toward a solution of these difficulties.

While there is no one *best* way to teach Logo, using appropriate questioning skills and providing an environment that encourages "freedom to try" without evaluation are important to successful program implementation.

Research studies have increased in number but remain largely inconclusive. The research that exists does afford encouragement that the intended outcomes of Logo are plausible and attainable. There is, however, a continuing need for additional research to provide further evidence as to the justification for many of the claims made by Logo proponents.

Chapter 15 Activities

1. Briefly discuss the philosophical and psychological bases upon which Logo is founded.
2. Do you agree with Papert that cognitive development can be accelerated with the establishment of a proper cultural environment? Discuss your response in terms of learning implications.
3. What do you see as the crucial factors necessary for the establishment of a learning environment appropriate for the teaching of Logo?
4. How would you feel about assuming the role suggested for the teaching of Logo? What would be your biggest concern about assuming such a role? What type of training do you see as essential for the Logo teacher?
5. Several activities were presented in the chapter as appropriate for the teaching of Logo. See if you can suggest at least three other activities that you believe would contribute to learning Logo.
6. Learn Logo using any available version.
7. Develop an original Logo graphics procedure. When done, review in your mind the types of cognitive decisions you made in the preparation of your procedure. What did you learn during the process?
8. "Logo was not meant to be taught and, furthermore, that the type of learning achieved was not intended to be evaluated like other school learning." What is your reaction to this statement?
9. Teaming two students on a computer while working with Logo appears to have several advantages. Discuss what you see as potential benefits derived from such a practice.
10. The suggestion has been made that it is possible for educators to teach programming when they themselves don't know how. What is your reaction to this statement? How does it relate to your potential use of Logo?

Bibliography

Abelson, H. *Apple Logo*. Peterborough, NH: Byte/McGraw Hill. 1982.

Black, J. B., Swan, K., and Schwartz, D. L. "Developing Thinking Skills with Computers." *Teachers College Record*, 1988, *89*(3), pp. 384–407.

Brinkley, V. M., and Watson, J. A. "Logo and Young Children: Are Quadrant Effects Part of Initial Logo Mastery?" *Journal of Educational Technology Systems*, 1990–1991, *19*(1), pp. 75–86.

Clements, D. "Logo Programming: Can It Change How Children Think?" *Electronic Learning*, January 1985, pp. 28, 74.

Clements, D. "Research on Logo in Education: Is the Turtle Slow But Steady, or Not Even in the Race?" *Computers in the Schools*, Summer/Fall 1985, 2(2/3), pp. 55–71.

Clements, D. H., and Battista, M. T. "The Effects of LOGO on Children's Conceptualizations of Angle and Polygons." *Journal for Research in Mathematics Education*, November 1990, 21(5), pp. 356–371.

Clements, D., and Nastasi, B. "Effects of Computer Environments on Social-Emotional Development: Logo and Computer-Assisted Instruction." *Computers in the Schools*, Summer/Fall 1985, 2(2/3), pp. 11–31.

Cohen, R. S. "Computerized Learner Supports in Pre-Logo Programming Environments." *Journal of Research on Computing in Education*, Spring 1990, 22(3), pp. 310–335.

Crume, C. E., and Maddux, C. D. "LogoWriter: An Introduction and Critique." *Computers in the Schools*, 1990, 7(3), pp. 21–34.

Dale, E. "Logo Builds Thinking Skills." In D. O. Harper and J. H. Stewart, Eds. *Run: Computer Education*. 2nd ed. Monterey, CA: Brooks/Cole, 1986, pp. 173–176.

DeCorte, E., et al. "Construction and Evaluation of a Powerful LOGO Learning Environment for the Acquisition and Transfer of Thinking Skills." Paper presented at the Annual Meeting of the American Educational Research Association (Boston, MA, April 16–20, 1990).

Friendly, M. *Advanced Logo. A Language for Learning*. Hillsdale, NJ: Lawrence Erlbaum Associates, 1988.

Ginther, D., and Williamson, J. "Learning Logo: What is Really Learned?" *Computers in the Schools*, Summer/Fall 1985, 2(2/3), pp. 45–54.

Harper, D. *Logo Theory & Practice*. Pacific Grove, CA: Brooks/Cole, 1989.

Harris, J. "Turtle Archetypes." *The Computing Teacher*, April 1992, 19(7), pp. 54–55.

Harris, J. "Parlez-Vous Multiplication?" *The Computing Teacher*, November 1991, 19(3), pp. 37–39.

Harris, J. "Who Says There's No Knocking Logo?" *The Computing Teacher*, October 1991, 19(2), pp. 41–44.

Harris, J., and Lickteig, M. J. "Variations of a Text Pattern: Story Structures and Logo Provide Beginning Steps in Writing." *The Computing Teacher*, May 1992, 19(8), pp. 29–33.

Horton, J., and Ryba, K. "Assessing Learning with Logo: A Pilot Study." *The Computing Teacher*, October 1986, 14(2), pp. 24–28.

Keller, J. K. "Characteristics of Logo Instruction Promoting Transfer of Learning: A Research Review." *Journal of Research on Computing in Education*, Fall 1990, 23(1), pp. 55–71.

Kinzer, C., Littlefield, J., Delclos, V., and Bransford, J. "Different Logo Learning Environments and Mastery: Relationships Between Engagement and Learning." *Computers in the Schools*, Summer/Fall 1985, 2(2/3), pp. 33–43.

Lehrer, R., Littlefield, J., and Wottreng, B. *Seeding Mindstorms with LOGOWriter*, 2nd ed. Fontana, WI: Interactive Education Technologies, 1992.

Lukas, G., and Lukas, J. *Logo: Principles, Programming, and Projects*. Monterey, CA: Brooks/Cole, 1986.

Maddux, C. D., Johnson, D. L., and Willis, J. W. *Educational Computing. Learning with Tomorrow's Technologies*. Boston: Allyn & Bacon, 1992.

Many, W., Lockard, J., Abrams, P., and Friker, W. "The Effects of Learning to Program in Logo on Reasoning Skills of Junior High School Students." *Journal of Educational Computing Research*, 1988, 4(2), pp. 203–213.

Martin, P. B. *Developing Problem Solving Skills of Primary Age Children within a Logo Environment*. M. S. Practicum, Nova University (FL), 1990.

Muir, M. *Fantastic Journey through Minds and Machines*. Eugene, OR: ISTE, 1990.

Neufeld, R. V. *Learning Math with LogoWriter.* London, Ontario: Logo Publications, 1992.

Papert, S. *Mindstorms: Children, Computers, and Powerful Ideas.* New York: Basic Books, 1980.

Piaget, J. *The Science of Education and the Psychology of the Child.* New York: Viking, 1971.

Polin, L. "Research Windows: Subvert the Dominant Paradigm." *The Computing Teacher,* May 1992, *19*(8), pp. 6–7.

Reed, W., Palumbo, D., and Stolar, A. "The Comparative Effects of BASIC and Logo Instruction on Problem-Solving Skills." *Computers in the Schools,* Fall/Winter 1987/1988, *4*(3/4), pp. 105–117.

Rieber, L. P. "Computer-Based Microworlds: A Bridge between Constructivism and Direct Instruction." *Educational Technology Research & Development,* 1992, *40*(1), pp. 93–106.

Robyler, M. D., Castine, W., and King, F. "Assessing the Impact of Computer Based Instruction." *Computers in the Schools,* 1988, *5*(3/4), pp. 1–149.

Rosen, M. "Lego Meets Logo." *Classroom Computer Learning,* April 1988, pp. 50–58.

Shimibukuro, G. "A Class Act: Junior High Students, LEGO, and Logo." *The Computing Teacher,* February 1989, pp. 37–39.

Simmons, M., and Cope, P. "Fragile Knowledge of Angle in Turtle Geometry." *Educational Studies in Mathematics,* August 1990, *21*(4), pp. 375–382.

Singh, J. K. "Cognitive Effects of Programming in Logo: A Review of Literature and Synthesis of Strategies for Research." *Journal of Research on Computing in Education,* Fall 1992, *25*(1), pp. 88–104.

Walker, D. F. "Logo Needs Research: A Response to Papert's Paper." *Educational Researcher,* June–July 1987, *16*(5), pp. 9–11.

Watt, M. L., and Watt, D. L. "Classroom Research on Logo Learning: Creating Collaborative Partnerships." *The Computing Teacher,* April 1992, *19*(7), pp. 5–7.

Wiebe, J. H. "At-Computer Programming Success of Third-Grade Students." *Journal of Research on Computing in Education,* Winter 1991, *24*(2), pp. 214–229.

Yoder, S. B. *Introduction to Programming in Logo Using Logo PLUS.* Eugene, OR: ISTE, 1989. *LogoWriter* version also available.

Yoder, S. B. "Mousing Around with Your Turtle . . . Or Turtling Around with Your Mouse?" *The Computing Teacher,* August/September 1991, *19*(1), pp. 41–43.

Yoder, S. B., "The Turtle and the Mouse . . . A Tale." *The Computing Teacher,* August/September 1992, *20*(1), pp. 41–43.

Zirkler, D., and Brownell, G. "Analogical Reasoning: A Cognitive Consequence of Programming?" *Computers in the Schools,* 1991 *8*(4), pp. 135–145.

After completing this chapter, you will be able to:

List the primary applications of each language presented.

Discuss advantages and disadvantages of each language.

Explain why BASIC is unique among common programming languages.

Assess the potential significance to teachers of the languages presented.

Identify any languages that you may wish to study further and explain why.

Chapter 16

Common Programming Languages

This chapter provides an overview of some of the most common microcomputer languages in use today. Within an introduction to microcomputers in education course, programming proficiency is unlikely to be a major issue. Rather, computer-literate educators should have basic familiarity with the concepts of programming and their implementation in the languages most common in schools.

First this chapter introduces BASIC which is one of the most widely available and used languages for teaching programming on microcomputers. Next comes a brief look at Pascal, the remaining language most likely to be of interest to educators, and C, a language used to develop many application software packages. Finally, because so many people have at least heard of them, we include a glimpse of FORTRAN and COBOL, which are taught in some secondary data-processing curricula.

BASIC

Although computer availability in education developed slowly at first, by the early 1960s educators were looking for ways to make computers accessible to students. In the absence of software of the types covered in the first parts of this book, educational computing had to focus on programming. However, programming requires a computer language, and existing languages had been developed to meet the needs of science and business. For students, a different approach was required.

BASIC (*B*eginners *A*ll-purpose *S*ymbolic *I*nstruction *C*ode) was developed in 1965 at Dartmouth College expressly for education. The language and its operating environment were designed with ease of *learning* as the primary concern, not to serve the needs of professionals in data processing. In contrast to Logo, BASIC was not designed to implement a particular educational philosophy or psychology.

From its beginning at Dartmouth, BASIC became popular as a student programming language in higher education. However, it might well have touched very limited numbers of persons even then, were it not for the development of microcomputers. BASIC became the primary language of early microcomputers because it was easy enough for anyone to learn and required minimal memory. It could be supplied on a ROM chip built into the machine, thereby creating a computer system that was ready to go at a touch of the power switch. Today, many different dialects of BASIC exist. Because of microcomputers, there are undoubtedly more people today who "know" BASIC than any other computer language. The spread of microcomputers brought BASIC to all levels of education.

In order to illustrate BASIC and other languages in this chapter, let's take a simple task and present a program solution for it in each language. The program will calculate the mean (or average) of a set of numbers and display the result. To obtain the data, it will ask the user how many numbers are in the set, then request them one by one. Figure 16.1 presents a solution to this problem in BASIC. Lines starting with REM document what the program does.

Discussion of BASIC

In the world of computing, 1965 is ancient history. Developments since BASIC have occurred at an incredible rate. New computer languages have been created; it is estimated that over 200 now exist. It should be no great surprise that continued widespread teaching of an "old" language would spark debate. BASIC has indeed come under a lot of fire. Now that you have some familiarity with the language, let's look at the controversy surrounding BASIC and try to put into perspective the question: Why BASIC?

It is important to note that the significance of the debate depends on one's purpose for teaching BASIC. Many aspects of the controversy seem relevant primarily to secondary schools that teach programming as college preparation or for some

```
200 REM This program calculates the mean of a set of numbers
210 REM First set counters to initial value of zero
220 LET SUM = 0: LET COUNT = 0: LET MEAN = 0
230 REM Get the number of items from the user
240 PRINT "Enter the numbers of items to average."
250 PRINT
260 INPUT NUM
270 REM Set up a loop for that number of items
280 PRINT
290 PRINT "Enter one of your values."
300 PRINT
310 INPUT VALUE
320 REM Add newest value to SUM and count the item
330 LET SUM = SUM + VALUE
340 LET COUNT = COUNT + 1
350 IF COUNT < NUM THEN GOTO 280
360 REM Calculate and display the result
370 MEAN = SUM / NUM
380 PRINT "The mean is "; MEAN
390 END
```

Figure 16.1 Problem solution in BASIC.

vocational purpose. The arguments presented must be viewed in the context of one's goals and grade level.

Advantages of BASIC

Proponents of BASIC are quick to point out its advantages *within its intended sphere,* that is, for students.

First, BASIC remains one of the easier languages to learn, although the learning curve is broad between enough knowledge to program the computer to perform some small task like our example and actual mastery of the language.

Second, BASIC already exists in the majority of computers in use in schools today. It is on a chip in the microcomputers most schools have purchased or is available on disk free with the system or at very low cost. Thus, schools wishing to teach programming to students have little or no additional investment.

Third, BASIC will run on any microcomputer without additional hardware. Many other languages require more than minimal RAM.

Fourth, the versions of BASIC found on most school computers have been enhanced beyond Dartmouth's original in ways significant to educators. For instance, most have had graphics added, usually with color capabilities. Many can also produce sound. Text-display capabilities are generally as good as any other language.

Fifth, BASIC is already well-entrenched in the schools. Teachers are now available to provide programming instruction, and more are learning the language at all times. No other language has such a ready-to-go cadre of teachers.

Sixth, BASIC has practical carryover value as the basis of macro languages in many tool applications. For example, versions of Microsoft *Word* use a macro language that is actually called Word BASIC.

Disadvantages of BASIC

Vocal groups of computer educators routinely condemn BASIC for a variety of reasons. Such concerns usually center on perceived advantages of Pascal or C and, to a lesser extent, Logo.

First, although BASIC is relatively easy to learn, it may not be well-suited to younger students. An introduction to programming often focuses on graphics, which many young children find too complex in BASIC. Logo is superior for this purpose.

Some argue that Logo can be and is taught as preparation for later exposure to BASIC. Although problem-solving skills developed through learning Logo may help a student to program in another language, there is little similarity between Logo and BASIC. Thus, a change to BASIC at a later age will be essentially a fresh start. Furthermore, if one waits until an appropriate age, say, junior high level, to introduce BASIC, students should be able to learn a "better" language such as Pascal just as readily.

Second, commonly available versions of BASIC are based on early implementations of the language. Dartmouth's creation predates the development of structured programming principles, which are now all but universally accepted as the basis for proper programming. Many believe that BASIC serves only to develop bad programming habits and styles, which a student seriously pursuing programming later in life will have to unlearn. They argue that it is better to begin with proper techniques because old habits are often very difficult to change.

Third, while BASIC can be used in a manner compatible with modern programming theory and style, few books on the market adequately present BASIC in this fashion. Even those purporting to teach "structured" BASIC generally begin with a traditional approach and introduce structure only much later. In effect, they first present "bad" BASIC, and then try to undo their own damage.

Fourth, the existence of BASIC in current computers is no more a justification for its use than the presence of a cigarette lighter in most automobiles requires the driver to smoke. Pascal is readily available for school computers today, it has become easier to use (especially in interpreted versions), and cost is no longer prohibitive. Not all versions of Pascal support graphics, but that is also irrelevant because Logo provides all the graphics experience a student will likely need.

Fifth, the existing pool of BASIC teachers is not a valuable resource, but a problem. For all the reasons cited above, BASIC is not worth teaching, so the pool is irrelevant. Further, the majority of current teachers are self-taught from materials that make no attempt to treat BASIC in a modern fashion. If they at least knew and presented BASIC from a structured perspective, their skills would have more value. Since this may involve substantial relearning, why not just learn a better language instead?

Sixth, the addition of graphics, sound, and other extensions to BASIC has led to many differing versions or dialects in wide use. Even dialects produced for different computers by one company (such as Microsoft) vary considerably. Thus, a program written for an IBM-PC will require modification to run on an Apple II, even though both use a version of Microsoft BASIC. This needlessly complicates the inevitable move from one machine to another and may be avoided with other languages.

Our Response to the BASIC Debate

We stated previously that this language debate is most relevant when the goal is teaching programming as a specific skill. For other goals, such as creating a problem-solving environment, the critical issue is which language best serves the goal. In our view, Logo has far more to offer than BASIC for problem solving, especially for younger pupils. Still, many teachers have developed interesting uses of BASIC to teach content: for instance, in science (Albrecht and Firedrake, 1992) and mathematics (Albrecht and Firedrake, 1993). The continued appearance of such articles in prominent computer publications is evidence of BASIC's staying power.

When programming is taught for its own sake, the arguments over BASIC extend into vociferous disagreements on language choice in general. However, the debate has quieted in recent years. This is due in part to decreased emphasis on programming as the heart of computer literacy. Fewer students are being taught programming solely because it is the only possible computer activity. Furthermore, newer versions of BASIC such as *True BASIC, Visual BASIC,* and *Turbo BASIC* have been enhanced in ways that meet many of the objections. For applications of superior structured BASIC programming using newer versions of the language for the Apple II, see Abernathy (1989) and Albrecht and Firedrake (1992).

In the end, we believe the issue reduces to simply good programming and bad programming, essentially structured versus unstructured style. To that end, we are comfortable with BASIC taught as a structured language, a structured version of the language such as True BASIC, or some other structured language such as Pascal (McIntyre, 1991). We do not expect BASIC to disappear and believe that teachers can profit from some rudimentary familiarity with it, provided it is properly structured.

Pascal

Pascal has been the source of a great deal of interest in the educational world, as well as considerable confusion and misunderstanding. Like BASIC, Pascal was developed to be a teaching language. Its originator was Niklaus Wirth, a Swiss computer scientist, who sought to implement the structured programming concepts of Dijkstra in a new language for beginners. He named his creation after the seventeenth century mathematician Blaise Pascal. Working versions of Pascal became available in the early 1970s.

Pascal quickly became popular with postsecondary computer science departments because it solved the problem of trying to teach structured programming with unstructured languages. The idea was to introduce programming to students via Pascal, so that sound programming habits would develop naturally through the language. These habits should extend quite readily to other languages.

Figure 16.2 provides a Pascal solution to the problem we stated and may give some feel for the nature of the language. Notice particularly that variables are identified at the very beginning and that segments of Pascal code are blocked with BEGIN and END statements, allowing considerable flexibility compared with BASIC.

Discussion of Pascal

Interest in Pascal stems largely from its strict adherence to the principles of structured programming. While it is still possible to write a "poor" program in Pascal, it almost requires an effort to do so. The requirement that variables be clearly specified and identified by data type before they can be used is considered a related advantage. It fosters clear thinking about the needs of your program.

Some versions of Pascal have been enhanced to include turtlegraphics, which can help provide a smooth transition from Logo. Other sophisticated graphics enhancements may also be included.

As a final advantage, study of Pascal at the high school level is more likely to be directly relevant to later college study in computer science than is study of BASIC.

Several disadvantages of Pascal are often noted. Pascal has been available primarily as a compiled language. Thus, students are faced not only with the task of mastering the language, but also must master an editor to enter and alter their programs. The program development process may be slower as explained previously regarding compiled versus interpreted languages. Interpreted versions such as *Instant Pascal* for the Apple IIe and *MacPascal* for the Macintosh address this concern.

Another concern is that far fewer teachers are prepared to teach Pascal than either Logo or BASIC. While the latter have often been learned independently,

```
PROGRAM MEAN;
{DOCUMENTATION IS GIVEN IN CURLY BRACES }
{FIRST, IDENTIFY ALL VARIABLES BY NAME AND TYPE }
VAR
        NUMITEMS, CYCLE : INTEGER;
        ITEM, MEAN, SUM : REAL;
BEGIN
        {GET THE NUMBER OF ITEMS FROM THE USER}
        WRITELN ('ENTER NUMBER OF ITEMS TO AVERAGE');
        READ (NUMITEMS);
        {SET UP A LOOP FOR THAT NUMBER OF ITEMS}
        SUM := 0.0
        FOR CYCLE = 1 TO NUMITEMS DO
                BEGIN
                        {GET ONE VALUE AND ADD IT TO SUM}
                        READ (ITEM);
                        SUM := SUM + ITEM;
                END; {THIS FINISHES THE LOOP}
        {CALCULATE AND DISPLAY THE MEAN}
        MEAN := SUM / NUMITEMS;
        WRITELN ('THE MEAN IS',MEAN);
END.
```

Figure 16.2 Problem solution in Pascal.

Pascal is a more difficult language to learn, and comparatively few self-teaching materials have appeared. Generally, teachers have had to seek opportunities at a college or university to learn Pascal.

As a final concern, although Pascal was intended to be a student's first language, the student envisioned by Wirth was of college age. Some question the suitability of Pascal for younger students. Where it is taught, the audience tends to be the very best students, whereas a broader audience is being served by Logo and BASIC.

In considering possible teaching of Pascal, do not forget that it will rarely be the first language a student learns, which was Wirth's intention. By the time a student reaches the level where Pascal is taught, prior experience with Logo or BASIC is likely. Thus, some of the rationale for Pascal is negated by common practice. Schools need to look carefully at the entire sequence of language instruction and analyze the potential and pitfalls of what has become a fairly common pattern: Logo, followed by BASIC in junior high, then Pascal in high school. The ramifications of this progression have yet to be thoroughly explored.

The C Language

Much commercial application software for microcomputers is written in C (Computer language), which was developed in the 1970s at Bell Labs. C is referred to as a *middle-level language;* that is, in concept it lies between assembler languages and high-level languages such as BASIC, PASCAL, FORTRAN, and COBOL. As a middle-level language, C allows the manipulation of bits, bytes, and addresses, thus making control over processing very direct and fast (similar to the advantages of assembler languages). On the other hand, its program code is *portable;* that is, C can be run on a wide variety of computers, such as different microcomputer families, minicomputers, and even mainframe computers (similar to the advantages of compiled languages). Thus, C incorporates many of the advantages of assembler languages and of high-level languages without their limitations. It is easy to understand why the C language is finding widespread use. See Figure 16.3 for our problem solution in C.

In addition, C has other important characteristics. First, C is *modular.* Each specific implementation includes files for definitions and functions that enable the basic C language to take full advantage of the specific features of a particular computer. This increases its power. A specific C version may be used to control drop-down menus, windows, and sophisticated help screens on the monitor, as well as to make better use of various RAM memory configurations that contribute to optimal program execution.

Second, C is *extensible.* This means the programmer can write "library" routines to meet a particular need and then reuse them in other programs, thus increasing programming efficiency over time.

Third, C is *structured,* which also makes programming easier and more efficient. Finally, C is *concise.* This makes the actual physical inputting of code

```
/* C Documentation is given between slash-star pairs */
/*
/* program mean */
main ( )
{
/* IDENTIFY ALL VARIABLES BY TYPE AND NAME */
int   numitems, cycle;
float item,mean,sum;

/* GET NUMBER OF ITEMS FROM USER */
printf ("ENTER NUMBER OF ITEMS TO AVERAGE", \n);
scanf ("%d", &numitems);

/* INITIALIZE VALUE OF SUM */
sum = 0.0;

/* SET UP A LOOP FOR THAT NUMBER OF ITEMS */
for (cycle = 1; cycle <= numitems; cycle++)
  /* GET ONE VALUE AND ADD TO SUM */
  {
  scanf ("%f", &item);
  sum = sum + item;
  }   /* THIS FINISHES THE LOOP */

/* CALCULATE THE MEAN AND DISPLAY IT */
mean = sum / numitems;
printf ("THE MEAN IS %4.2f \n", mean);
}
```

Figure 16.3 Problem solution in C.

quicker, easier, and more accurate. It is easy to understand why programmers like this language.

For all of these reasons, the C language will continue to find considerable use as the language of choice for professional developers of general applications programs (as discussed in Part 2 of this book), as well as an all-purpose programming language for more specific applications.

FORTRAN

FORTRAN is one of the oldest of the high-level languages. It was developed by IBM and released in 1957. The essence of FORTRAN is revealed in its name, *FOR*mula *TRAN*slator. IBM designed this language for use by persons with need for complex mathematical calculations requiring great precision, notably engineers, scientists, and mathematicians. FORTRAN spread quickly among computer manufacturers and came into very wide usage. There were few options at the time.

While FORTRAN was developed for mainframe computers, its lingering familiarity has brought microcomputer versions into existence. Although there are still many FORTRAN users in the world, the language has primarily vocational applicability. In today's schools there may be little reason to teach it.

A possible FORTRAN solution to our problem is given in Figure 16.4.

```
C        FORTRAN EXAMPLE PROGRAM
C        LINES BEGINNING WITH C ARE DOCUMENTATION COMMENTS.
C        FIRST IDENTIFY ALL VARIABLES BY TYPE AND NAME.
         INTEGER N
         REAL VAL,SUM,MEAN
C        SET THE SUM VARIABLE TO ZERO.
         SUM=0.0
C        PROMPT USER FOR NUMBER OF ITEMS USING FORMAT, STATEMENT 101.
C        DISPLAY STATEMENT ON SCREEN.
         WRITE (1,101)
C        GET USER INPUT IN VARIABLE N USING FORMAT STATEMENT 102
         READ (1,102)N
C        SET UP A LOOP TO INPUT ALL N VALUES.
         DO 10 I=1,N
C        GET ONE ITEM AT A TIME AND ADD IT TO SUM.
         READ (1,103)VAL
         SUM=SUM+VAL
10       CONTINUE
C        CALCULATE MEAN AND DISPLAY RESULT USING FORMAT 104.
         MEAN=SUM/N
         WRITE (1,104)MEAN
         STOP
101      FORMAT ('ENTER NUMBER OF ITEMS TO AVERAGE:')
102      FORMAT(I2)
103      FORMAT (F2.0)
104      FORMAT ('THE MEAN IS',F5.2)
         END
```

Figure 16.4 Problem solution in FORTRAN.

Discussion of FORTRAN

The primary advantages of FORTRAN lie in the characteristics around which it was designed. It remains popular in heavy mathematical applications settings. The language allows easy formulation of complex functions and produces results with decimal place accuracy beyond many other languages, at least in mainframe versions.

A second advantage of FORTRAN is that standards have been set for those features that should exist in all versions of the language. These standards are widely adhered to, enabling a high degree of "transportability" of programs from one computer to another. Differences among computers are accounted for in their respective compilers, while to the user, the language remains constant.

On the negative side, FORTRAN was created to be a "number cruncher." As a result, only limited capacity to process nonnumeric data was provided, precisely the data of most interest in education. FORTRAN also lacks sophisticated file-processing capabilities and is limited in its controls over the format of output, a major concern in both education and business applications.

FORTRAN predates modern concepts of structured programming. As with BASIC, many FORTRAN programmers now attempt to apply structured principles to their programs, but it is something akin to putting the proverbial square peg in a round hole. FORTRAN programs must be heavily documented to be read easily by other than the original programmer; the language does not promote clarity of expression.

COBOL

COBOL is among the most widely used languages in data processing. It is slightly newer than FORTRAN, having appeared in 1960. COBOL was developed by committee, rather than by a single manufacturer, specifically for the needs of the business community. This is apparent in the name, *COmmon Business Oriented Language*. COBOL was carefully designed to provide the kinds of numeric processing required in business applications, as well as extensive, flexible control over output formatting. The vocabulary of COBOL is much like English, providing a degree of self-documentation in a program. The language was also designed to be transportable across computers.

COBOL owes its broad acceptance to two factors. First, it had no peers for business applications when it was released. Second, the federal government was very interested in a standard language for business applications. The COBOL development team was, in fact, led by a naval officer, Grace Hopper, one of the major figures in modern computing (see Mace, 1984). When the government specified that COBOL had to be available for all computers it purchased, many manufacturers quickly released versions of COBOL for their machines.

COBOL is most commonly used on mainframes, although microcomputer versions are available. These are somewhat scaled-down implementations because full COBOL requires very large memory. Like FORTRAN, COBOL is of interest primarily for vocational reasons.

There are many syntactical requirements in COBOL, such as dividing the program into divisions. The Identification Division provides for some rudimentary documentation. The Environment Division contributes to transportability across machines and may be the only part of the program requiring changes if the program is moved. In the Data Division, explicit provision must be made for the types of data to be processed. Finally, the actual "working code" is gathered in the Procedure Division. A solution to our problem is given in Figure 16.5. Notice the English base of COBOL and its heavy reliance on verbs to specify functions to be executed.

Discussion of COBOL

Despite being more than 30 years old, COBOL is still common in the data processing world. It is a very practical language for persons interested in data processing careers and has some notable strengths.

On a rudimentary level, the syntax of COBOL is easy to learn. The ability to go fairly directly from an English verbal explanation of what is to be done to COBOL syntax is appealing.

```
        IDENTIFICATION DIVISION.
        PROGRAM-ID.MEANCALC.
        DATE-WRITTEN.2-NOV-1993.
        DATE-COMPILED.2-NOV-1993.

        ENVIRONMENT DIVISION.

        CONFIGURATION SECTION.
        SOURCE-COMPUTER. CPM-80.
        OBJECT-COMPUTER. CPM-80.

        DATA DIVISION.

        FILE SECTION.
        * NONE USED

        WORKING-STORAGE SECTION.

            01 NUMBER-OF-ITEMS        PIC S9(1) COMP.
            01 ITEM-COUNT             PIC S9(2) COMP.
            01 ONE-ITEM               PIC S9(4) COMP.
            01 SUM                    PIC S9(4) COMP VALUE 0.
            01 MEAN                   PIC S9(4) COMP.
            01 SHOW-MEAN              PIC S9(3).

        PROCEDURE DIVISION.

        100-MAIN PROGRAM.

            PERFORM 200-INPUT-MODULE THROUGH 200-INPUT-END.
            PERFORM 300-OUTPUT-MODULE THROUGH 300-OUTPUT-END.
            STOP. RUN.

        200-INPUT-MODULE.

            DISPLAY "ENTER NUMBER OF ITEMS TO AVERAGE" UPON TERMINAL.
            ACCEPT NUMBER-OF-ITEMS FROM TERMINAL.
            DISPLAY "ENTER YOUR ITEMS ONE AT A TIME." UPON TERMINAL.
            DISPLAY "PRESS RETURN AFTER EACH." UPON TERMINAL.

            MOVE 1 TO ITEM-COUNT.
            PERFORM 250-GET-ITEMS THROUGH 250-GET-END UNTIL ITEM-COUNT >
                NUMBER-OF-ITEMS.
        200-INPUT-END.

        250-GET-ITEMS.
            DISPLAY "ENTER A NUMBER" UPON TERMINAL.
            ACCEPT ONE-ITEM FROM TERMINAL
            ADD ONE-ITEM TO SUM.
            ADD 1 TO ITEM-COUNT.
        250-GET-END.

        300-OUTPUT-MODULE.

            DIVIDE SUM BY NUMBER-OF-ITEMS GIVING MEAN.
            MOVE MEAN TO SHOW-MEAN.
            DISPLAY "THE MEAN OF YOUR" NUMBER-OF-ITEMS "ENTRIES IS"
                SHOW-MEAN"." UPON TERMINAL.
        300-OUTPUT-END.
```

Figure 16.5 Problem solution in COBOL.

COBOL contains many special features to ease data processing tasks in business, including a special Report Writer option. It is especially strong in file-handling capabilities so vital to business. Studying COBOL can be an experience in business data processing.

The formal structure of a COBOL program into the four required divisions illustrated in our example is a strength of the language. Programmers are required to give thought to many aspects of their task as they approach it.

There are also several disadvantages to COBOL. For the school world, it is not as widely available on microcomputers as many other languages. Typical COBOL applications require greater power and storage capacity than microcomputers have had, so there has been little demand for COBOL on micros.

If you looked carefully at the COBOL example, you may have noticed a certain "verbosity" to the language. While it is easy to understand DIVIDE FIRST BY SECOND GIVING THIRD, persons familiar with other languages tend to prefer the more concise $Z = X/Y$ format.

Finally, COBOL also predates concepts of structured programming and must be forced into the mold by the programmer. However, this is less difficult to achieve in COBOL than in most other unstructured languages.

Summary

Learning any programming language is a major undertaking. Within the context of an introductory computer education experience, it is appropriate for teachers and future teachers to gain some exposure to the more common microcomputer languages available today.

This chapter provided brief background information about five programming languages: BASIC, Pascal, C, FORTRAN, and COBOL. Each was used to implement a solution to the problem of creating a simple program. The strengths and weaknesses of each language were also presented.

The need for an instructional language led to the creation of BASIC at Dartmouth College. Because BASIC is now an "old" language, it has many adherents as well as vocal critics. We suggest that the language itself is not the real issue, but rather whether one adheres to structured programming principles in using it. There no doubt are "better" languages available, but properly used, BASIC remains a viable language in education.

For educators, Pascal is clearly an important language. It has found popularity in secondary schools as well as among computer science departments. Pascal is a modern, structured language, which was designed for educational use. However, it is not a particularly easy language to learn. We believe Pascal is an excellent language to teach and learn, but only if it fits the curriculum goals of the school. Somewhat similar to Pascal, C is a popular language for developing commercial applications.

FORTRAN and COBOL were presented here because they are so well known. Neither is commonly taught on microcomputers, and both are "serious" data processing languages with no particular qualities to recommend them for general study. They merit brief attention only as part of the evolution of computing.

Chapter 16 Activities

1. Check other sources for comparisons of programming languages. How do others rate the relevance of each to schools?
2. Define and defend a position on appropriate languages for teaching in schools.
3. Locate additional resources on any language of particular interest to you.
4. Select one of the languages discussed to which you have access. Using available documentation, modify our example program to run on your system.

Bibliography

Abernathy, J. "Launching into BASIC." *CALL-A.P.P.L.E.*, March 1989, pp. 27–30.

Albrecht, B., and Firedrake, G. "Summer Challenge (Power Tools for Math and Science.)" *The Computing Teacher*, May 1993, *20*(8), pp. 50–52.

Albrecht, B., and Firedrake, G. "Power Tools for Math and Science." *The Computing Teacher*, August/September 1992, *20*(1), pp. 34–35.

Castek, J. E. *Structured BASIC Programming on IBM Personal Computers*. New York: John Wiley and Sons, 1988.

Chen, N. M. "High School Computing: The Inside Story." *The Computing Teacher, May 1992, 19*(8), pp. 51–52.

Coffee, P. "Marriage of Windows, BASIC a Boon to Pro, Novice Developers." *PC Week*, May 20, 1991, p. 5.

Crull, J. L. "The Speed of Sound." *The Computing Teacher*. March 1987, pp. 29–32, 56.

Crume, C. "The TrueBASIC Computer Language: An Introduction and Critique." *Computers in the Schools*, 1990, *7*(4), pp. 125–134.

Duncan, R. (August, 1991). "Visual BASIC: A Major Programming Breakthrough." *PC Magazine, 10*(14), pp. 35–37.

Gassee, J. L. "Going BASIC with HyperCard Development." *MacWEEK*, 4 June 1991. p. 44.

Johnson, J., and Gilda, B. "The Chocolate Chip Cookie Caper—Part I." *The Computing Teacher*, March 1987, pp. 33–35.

Mace, S. "Mother of COBOL—Still Thinkin', Still Workin'." In Craighead, D., and Bitter, G. G., Eds. *The Best of the Proceedings 1982–1984 Microcomputers in Education Conference*. Rockville, MD: Computer Science Press, 1984.

Maddux, C., and Cummings, R. "BASIC, Logo, and PILOT: A Comparison of Three Computer Languages." *Computers in the Schools*, Summer/Fall 1985, pp. 139–164.

McIntyre, P. *Teaching Structured Programming in the Secondary Schools*. Melbourne, F. L. Krieger Publishing Company, 1991.

Moser, D., and Dodge, J. "Back-to-BASIC Approach to Ease Windows Design." *PC Week*, 25 February 1991, p. 1.

Patton, C. "Microsoft is Getting Back to Its BASIC Roots." *PC Week*, 27 May 1991, p. 73.

Poirot, J. L., and Adams, R. C. *40 Easy Steps to Programming in BASIC and LOGO.* Austin, TX: Sterling Swift Publishing Co., 1983.

Ricks, J. "Fourth-Generation Computer Languages: An Overview." *T.H.E. Journal,* October 1988, pp. 101–104.

Righi, C. "Using Advance Organizers to Teach BASIC Programming to Primary-grade Children." *Educational Technology Research & Development,* 1991, *39*(4), pp. 79–90.

Rohm, C. E. T., Jr., and Stewart, W. T., Jr. *Essentials of Information Systems.* Santa Cruz, CA: Mitchell 1988.

Ross, S. M. *BASIC Programming for Educators.* Englewood Cliffs, NJ: Prentice-Hall, 1986.

Stern, N., and Stern, R. A. *Computing in the Information Age.* New York: John Wiley & Sons, 1993

Wagner, P. "The Vas Savant Challenge." *The Computing Teacher,* February 1992, *19*(5), pp. 12–14.

Yoder, S. "On Grading: From BASIC to Logo to HyperTalk." *The Computing Teacher,* August/September 1992, *20*(1), pp. 23–26.

Yoder, S. and Moursund, D. "Programming or Applications: How Best to Empower Students?" *The Computing Teacher,* November 1991, *19*(3), pp. 18–21.

Zachmann, W. F. "Trying to Choose a Programming Language? Climb Aboard the C Train." *InfoWorld,* 28 September 1987, p. 82.

Objectives

After completing this chapter, you will be able to:

Explain several reasons why some teachers develop their own software.

Evaluate your own interest in learning more about software development.

Critique the rationale for students creating software products in light of your own views of what education is all about.

Differentiate authoring systems from authoring languages.

Explain the basic operation of a generic authoring system.

Discuss expert system shells as a software development tool.

Describe concepts underlying hypermedia authoring tools.

Explain the role of programming (scripting) in hypermedia tools.

Chapter 17

Authoring and Hypermedia Tools

To conclude our consideration of the computer as learner, let's consider software development using authoring tools. In this chapter, you will learn reasons why many teachers become software developers, as well as a rationale for students to create software products. Next you will compare the fundamental characteristics of authoring tools to programming languages. There are many different types of authoring tools. We'll look briefly only at authoring languages, authoring systems, expert system shells, and the latest hit: hypermedia tools, which are sometimes termed *software erector sets*.

Why Teachers Develop Software

With thousands of courseware products on the market, and more appearing each week, teachers wishing to use the computer as a classroom tutor might expect to have access to anything they could desire in the way of CAI. You should only need to follow sound processes for software evaluation (see Chapter 11) to locate, select, evaluate, test, and implement CAI. Regrettably, the situation is not so simple.

The first problem is that you may be unable to identify software to fit your specific needs. You may find nothing at all that appears to address the topics of interest, or you may go all the way through field testing, and then conclude that what you found is *not* better than nothing. Of course, that conclusion is preferable to wasting student time (and school funds) on software that is marginal (or worse).

Finding CAI to fit your own curriculum needs can be a serious problem. Not every instructional need necessarily can be addressed by commercial software. Production costs for CAI are high, and producers rightfully expect to earn a profit. A modest retail price, usually well under $100, is critical for most educational software. Therefore, producers must count on sales in volume to succeed. Only those aspects of curriculum that are common to most schools are even candidates for commercial software development. Many topics of interest to individual teachers will never become commercial products because their sales potential is too limited. In turn, many commercial products are so generic that they are not well suited to specific needs. Always remember, the software should fit the curriculum, not drive it, unless the software is somehow truly extraordinary.

A second problem is the school budget. Assume that you are able to identify software that appears to suit your need exactly. Can you proceed to a preview and perhaps eventual student field testing? There may be no cost in arranging to do one or both, but the school may have to submit a purchase order for you to obtain the software at all, even if you can cancel the order or request a refund later. Still, few schools today have the kind of materials budget teachers desire. No matter what the budget amount is, it is rarely, if ever, enough. Consider what a $60 program costs in total for enough copies (or a site license) for a school lab, or even just the classrooms for a single grade. Furthermore, many schools allocate so much of the available budget for hardware that little or nothing remains for software. Even in the best situations, it is common for the software budget to decline over the years, because many schools fail to recognize that software purchases are a recurring expense, like other supplies.

A third reason for home-made software is personal preference. Teacher education programs generally prepare teachers to create many of their own teaching materials, partly in recognition of the first two problems just discussed! If you develop your own worksheets, produce overhead transparencies, or create slide sets, you may want to develop your own software, too. Some teachers all but reach a point of feeling that materials they did not develop are not up to their own standards. Some of those who learn to develop software find it an enjoyable experience as well. You can get hooked on creating software!

Problems with Software Development

Before setting off to develop your own software, you should ask at least two major questions. First, do you have any training in the design of computer-based learning materials? Most teachers do not. Without an understanding of underlying principles, amateurs tend to produce an electronic version of some other approach to meeting the learning need, rather than good CAI. Think again about some of the issues you studied in the context of courseware evaluation. Being able to critique courseware is not tantamount to the ability to design better products yourself. Get specific training in software design before you undertake projects. As in medicine, your "patients" deserve skilled treatment.

Second, if you have the design skills, do you then have the time required to design and develop a software product? A common rule of thumb among experienced software developers is that 1 hour of student CAI will require as many as 200 hours of design and development! Can even the most energetic teacher realistically expect to develop software for the classroom? Even with newer tools that speed the process, in a broad sense, the answer is clearly no. However, you may well contemplate developing some very specific software needs that can't be met as well in any other way. Just don't set out to do the whole curriculum! Many teachers create software on a limited basis.

Students as Software Developers

Throughout this book, we have tried to attend to the fact that education involves both teachers and learners. Whatever the application, we sought to present uses appropriate to both. Software development requires no less.

Until the late 1980s, the only opportunity students in K–12 classes typically had to develop software was in "programming" classes. There was seldom a connection between the software being developed and anything else in the student's studies. Programming was a subject unto itself.

Today, teachers at all levels in schools across the continent have broadened the range of activities available to students within their regular content courses. Much of the impetus for this is attributable to hypermedia tools, which have made it possible for even kindergartners to demonstrate their learning by creating a computer program. Not that all of these "programmers" necessarily know they are programming! Students of all ages have a natural affinity for computers. The ease with which anyone can create certain limited types of software products today has opened up possibilities undreamed of before.

Creative teachers are looking at their course goals and objectives in light of what authoring tools enable students to construct. The emphasis is not on the act of creating a piece of software, but on the final product itself. In fact, students can be a resource to help develop the software you'd like to have for your other students! As you learn more about these tools throughout this chapter, try to imagine student projects suitable to each tool type.

Authoring Tools

Programming languages are the basis for the algorithmic approach to software development. To work with them, you must devise most or all of a program's logic and control structures yourself, using the often-complex command set of the language you have chosen. Unless you invest the time required to become proficient with a language, the language itself will always intrude on your real concern: a viable instructional strategy to convey educational content. Programming languages are purposely general and usable for developing nearly any type of software. Consequently, only the most general and commonly used features are built in. These languages lack precisely the kinds of features of greatest concern in instructional software.

In sharp contrast, authoring tools have been developed, not to be all-purpose, but rather to support and ease the task of developing instructional software. With the exception of authoring languages, which are rapidly becoming obsolete, most of today's authoring tools are based on screens rather than lines of code. Screens are built from objects, the number and nature of which vary greatly among the tools. Programs are collections of interrelated and connected screens, each with elements that permit, encourage, or require interaction with the user.

Let's look at authoring tools in three groups: authoring languages, authoring systems, and expert system shells.

Authoring Languages

Early in the computer's history, some educators recognized its learning potential. They also realized that software was the key, but that the available languages were much too difficult for anyone but a specialist to use. The quest for tools to simplify instructional software development began early.

The BASIC language, which you encountered in Chapter 16, was created in part to permit "ordinary" individuals to develop CAI. How well it was suited to that task has been debated for many years. In its early days, BASIC was the tool of choice. However, its popularity with teachers and students has justifiably waned.

After BASIC came a variety of authoring languages based on the belief that a simplified language was the solution. Languages such as BASIC had too many different commands, and their syntax (or structure for using the commands) was too complex. Countless hours might go into locating a misplaced comma or something equally trivial.

Authoring languages generally have relatively few commands and a simple syntax. Specialized commands provide functions such as answer judging that are essential and frequently needed in CAI. Ignoring design issues and product quality, it is possible to create a lesson quickly with an authoring language.

To gain a sense of an authoring language, look at Figure 17.1, a segment of a program written in PILOT. PILOT is one of the oldest, simplest, and most common authoring languages. You probably can guess most of what this program will do just by reading the code, but here are explanations of each command, just in case.

PILOT commands consist of one or two letters followed by a colon. Labels can appear in the left margin to indicate segments of the code. Here are the critical commands and their functions:

T: (display the text that follows)
A: (accept what the user types as an answer)
M: (match the user's answer to the listed alternatives)
C: (calculate—used for math operations)
J: (jump to the specified label)
E: (end)

Following a match, single-letter commands may have a second letter (either Y or N) to indicate that the command is to be executed only if the student's answer matched (Y) or did not match (N). This is called *conditional* execution. In a series of lines that all have either the Y or N suffix, only all the Y or all the N lines actually will execute.

Look particularly at the two M: lines in Figure 17.1. The Match command and any following conditional commands are the most important feature of PILOT for our purposes. To achieve the same exact result in, say, BASIC, would be much more difficult and would involve far more complex logic.

```
        T: IN THIS PROGRAM YOU WILL BE SHOWN A SERIES OF WORDS.
        T: YOU ARE TO GIVE A SYNONYM FOR EACH ONE.
        T:
        T: PRESS 'RETURN' WHEN YOU ARE READY TO BEGIN.
        A:
*A      T:
        T: GIVE ME A SYNONYM FOR SMALL.
        A:
        M: TINY, LITTLE, PETITE
        TY: VERY GOOD. THAT IS A CORRECT ANSWER
        CY: C=C+1
        TN: SORRY, THAT IS NOT ONE OF MY SYNONYMS. TRY AGAIN.
        JN: *A
        T:
*B      T:
        T: GIVE ME A SYNONYM FOR BIG.
        A:
        M: LARGE, HUGE, ENORMOUS
        TY: EXCELLENT. A GOOD CHOICE.
        CY: C=C+1
        TN: PLEASE TRY AGAIN. I HAD OTHER WORDS IN MIND.
        JN: *B
           [REMAINDER OF PROGRAM]
        E:
```

Figure 17.1. A program segment in PILOT.

Authoring Systems

Authoring systems are tools that purport to eliminate entirely the programming aspects of software development. They provide a framework within which a lesson is developed. Traditional authoring systems are rapidly giving way to much more flexible contemporary systems.

Traditional Systems

Early authoring systems severely limited the range of features that a lesson contained as well as an author's ability to create varying types of lessons. The developer only needed to have the content organized to begin. The system prompted for the information needed, and then "wrote" the program based on it. Beyond an easy to use software "shell," many systems also dictated or restricted instructional strategies and limited screen design. Here's a short, generic "session" with an authoring system.

1. Load the software and select New Lesson from its menu. Name the lesson.
2. Select Tutorial or Drill for the lesson type (the only choices).
3. Assuming Tutorial, the system prompts for text, which the student will read. You only have to enter it. The system makes all decisions about screen layout.
4. The system prompts for a graphic to accompany the text. You may be able to create one with a built-in graphics editor, or you may simply enter the name of a file you previously created with a separate editor.
5. The system prompts for the type of question you want to ask the student about the text and/or graphic. Available options are multiple-choice, true-false, or single (typed) word. The type you select determines how many and which further prompts you receive, assuring that the system has all the parts it needs to create the item and analyze the eventual student response to it.
6. Hopefully, the system then prompts for feedback, at least for right versus wrong answer, possibly for each alternative in multiple choice format.

Beyond those basic elements, authoring systems may offer such capabilities as:

- Providing a hint on request or after a specified number of incorrect responses to an item.
- Varying the number of tries allowed per item.
- Branching to remedial segments.
- Tracking student performance.
- Setting a time limit for each response.

Contemporary Systems

As developers searched for ways to create software quickly and relatively easily, the desire for greater flexibility led to the type of authoring environments common today. Contemporary authoring systems are generally *frame-based*. This means the developer works screen by screen, building each from a variety of components called objects. In some cases, screen prompts initially offer options at each point in the authoring process, as shown in Figure 17.2. Each choice may lead to further options or to step-by-step prompts to enter the information the system requires at that point to achieve the chosen result or feature. The process is essentially the same, whether you are simply linking one screen to another, getting and evaluating student input, or creating an animation.

A somewhat-different approach is the icon-based authoring system, in which actions and the structure of the program are created by visual placement of icons that represent objects and actions. An icon-based system appears to the user to combine program logic and product development into a single entity. You structure the program visually, creating the frames as needed. As you test the product, you make changes simply by rearranging or modifying the diagram (see Figure 17.3). Although a far cry from traditional language-based programming, icon-based systems may require more of an understanding of logic, akin to flowcharting, than prompted systems, for which you need a more global view of program flow.

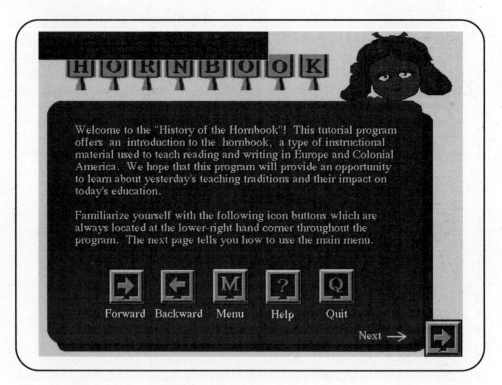

Figure 17.2. A prompted authoring system.

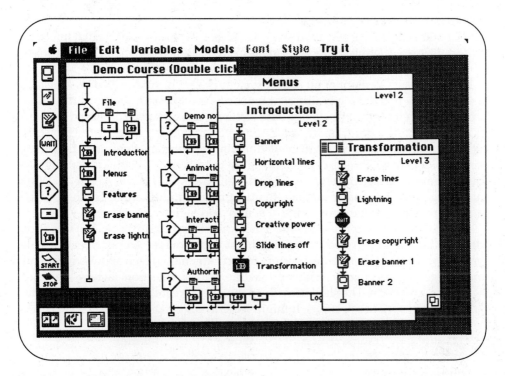

Figure 17.3. An icon-based authoring system.

Advantages and Disadvantages of Authoring Systems

The primary advantage of any authoring system is the step-by-step approach it provides. Organize your content on paper, create some graphics (if not an internal feature), and follow the prompts or arrange the icons. You don't need to learn a language or too much about programming logic, so you focus on content, not mechanics. Answer judging and recordkeeping, graphics and animation, even control over external devices may be much more sophisticated than the same author would attempt with a programming language.

Conversely, the simple and fast "follow the prompts" approach also can be limiting. You sacrifice flexibility for ease of use. You may conceptualize aspects of your program that you simply cannot implement with the software, or that would force you to leave the comfort of the system for the underlying language that most such systems still have. Even an authoring system may not remove all need for fundamental programming understanding and skill.

In addition, authoring systems can be very expensive. The more the system allows or can do for you, the higher its likely price. Prices in excess of $1000 per copy are common, far beyond the reach of many K–12 educators. Prices over $5000 are not unknown. For further information about authoring software, see Krejci (1992), Lo et al. (1992), and Locatis et al. (1992).

Expert System Shells

In Chapter 13 you learned about expert systems, including the fact that many educators are encouraging students to create class projects using them. We purposely left discussion of how expert system shells work for this chapter.

The most basic element of an expert system is a set of rules called its *knowledge base.* There are two distinctly different types of expert system shells. With a *deductive* shell, you create the knowledge base using a word processor or text editor, very much like writing a program in, say, BASIC. You first must complete the *knowledge engineering,* the analysis of the problem domain, to determine the factors that an expert considers in reaching a conclusion. From these, you write the rules using typical programming structures: IF A AND B AND C OR D THEN X AND . . . . While this "language" is usually simpler than a programming language, the process requires much the same knowledge of syntax and logic.

An *inductive* shell requires the same basic knowledge engineering, but it induces (derives) the rules from a set of examples that you provide. Suppose, for example, that you were creating an expert system to recommend or teach about wines. Your knowledge engineering determines that the critical selection factors are color, sweetness, and body. The shell provides a means to create a table of examples that illustrate appropriate selections. It might look, in part, like this:

Color	Sweetness	Body	Result
red	dry	full	burgundy
red	dry	medium	chianti
red	dry	light	gamay
red	sweet	full	cold duck

From your examples, the shell software then would induce a decision tree (a set of rules), such as the one shown in Figure 17.4.

Inductive shells are easy to use. They place the primary focus on the knowledge engineering, which is the source of the cognitive benefit that students may derive from creating an expert system. Details of creating the user interface are not included here, but suffice it to say, this is also simple with an inductive shell and somewhat more complex with a deductive shell. Either offers students a Type II learning experience, something not previously practical in education.

Hypermedia Tools

Chapter 10 introduced the concepts of hyper-environments. At its simplest, the term *hyper* refers to interactive, nonsequential software. From some starting point, the learner/user may freely move about within the environment, sampling, probing, choosing to skim past an element or pursue it and its related elements in great depth. *Hypermedia* is the term for interactive environments that include, even feature, multimedia elements such as sound, still pictures, animations, and video clips.

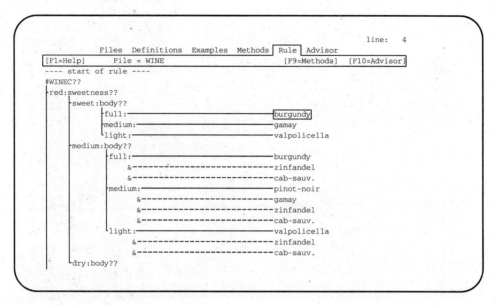

```
                                                    line:    4

        Files  Definitions   Examples   Methods │ Rule │ Advisor
    [F1=Help]       File = WINE                   [F9=Methods]  [F10=Advisor]
    ---- start of rule ----
    #WINEC??
   ┌red:sweetness??
   │   ┌sweet:body??
   │   │      ┌full:─────────────────────────────┌burgundy ┐
   │   │      ├medium:───────────────────────────gamay
   │   │      └light:───────────────────────────valpolicella
   │   ┌medium:body??
   │   │      ┌full:─────────────────────────────burgundy
   │   │      │   &----------------------------zinfandel
   │   │      │   &----------------------------cab-sauv.
   │   │      ┌medium:───────────────────────────pinot-noir
   │   │      │   &----------------------------gamay
   │   │      │   &----------------------------zinfandel
   │   │      │   &----------------------------cab-sauv.
   │   │      └light:───────────────────────────valpolicella
   │   │          &----------------------------zinfandel
   │   │          &----------------------------cab-sauv.
   └dry:body??
```

Figure 17.4. Part of an expert system rule from an inductive shell.

While Chapter 10 dealt with the nature and uses of hypermedia as an instructional tool, this chapter's focus is on creating hypermedia products, an exemplary Type II computer application. Like the authoring systems previously discussed, hypermedia tools are frame- or screen-based. Hypermedia development products have adopted similar metaphors for their structure. Apple's *HyperCard*, the first such tool, set the trend by calling each screen a *card*, symbolic of an index card, a place to store a limited amount of information. *Linkway Live!* and *ToolBook*, the major DOS and Windows counterparts to *HyperCard*, both term each screen a *page*. *HyperCard* groups its cards together into *stacks*. *Linkway* pages together constitute *folders*, while *ToolBook* pages make up *books*. In each case, a potentially strange new software concept becomes more approachable through a familiar analogy.

Also similar to authoring systems, with hypermedia tools you build screens out of objects. While each product has its own specific terms and components, in essence all have objects for text areas (often called *fields*), for images (called *graphics* or *pictures*), and for initiating actions (called *buttons*). Figure 17.5 illustrates the available objects in *Linkway Live!* Hypermedia tools also provide two or more operating modes, each of which permits a different set of operations to be executed. Figure 17.6 summarizes these modes for three common software packages.

Regardless of which hypermedia software you choose, creating text fields and placing images onto a screen are relatively trivial tasks (although producing those images initially may be far from simple). In fact, a novice can create a series of screens in a short time after minimal instruction. (Does that sound a bit like Logo?) But what happens once you have two or more screens completed? As an author, you would know how to move among them, but the authoring mode of any of

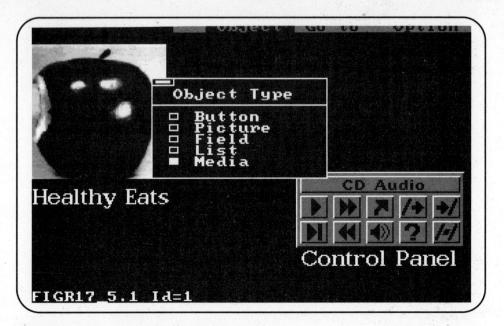

Figure 17.5. Objects available in *Linkway Live!*

these software packages is unacceptable as a user interface. How, then, does the user gain access to the "hyper" aspects of your product? It is the button objects that make things happen.

Again, although each is unique, hypermedia products generally share a similar approach to buttons. A button is a graphic image in some location on a screen to which the user can point with the mouse cursor and then click. The click causes some action to occur. How does this work? The basic software tool has the capability to recognize the current position of the mouse cursor on the screen and to recognize a mouse click. But what, exactly, happens when the software recognizes a click on a particular button? It all depends on the *script* associated with that button.

Each of the three tools we are highlighting has a programming language associated with it. *HyperCard*'s is called *HyperTalk*, and *Toolbook*'s is called *OpenScript*, while *Linkway* just refers to scripting. As with other languages presented in this part of the book, we have no intention of trying to teach you language here. Rather, you should realize that although you can do a lot with these tools without venturing into programming, even a hypermedia tool still relies on a language for its behind-the-scenes actions. In Chapter 14 you learned about the nature of programming. Now it is important to understand that programming also has a place in hypermedia, despite much promotion of these tools as suitable for non-programmers. If you want to create a hypermedia program that does anything more than or different from what someone else has already done in another prod-

Tool	Mode	Operations Allowed
Toolbook		
	Author	Create lessons
	Reader	Take lessons
HyperCard		
	Browse	Go through cards in a stack
	Type	Add or change text in a card's field
	Paint	Use graphics tools
	Author	Create cards, buttons, fields
	Script	Use the *HyperTalk* language
Linkway Live!		
	Read	Go through pages in a folder
	Update	Add text to a field on a page
	Insert	Update fields, add pages
	Delete	Update fields, add or delete pages
	Format	All authoring functions

Figure 17.6.   Comparison of common hypermedia tools.

uct, you have no real choice but to deal with the programming language yourself (Ragan, 1988; Camp and Cogan, 1988).

Figure 17.7 shows the script for one fairly simple button in a *HyperCard* stack. While the exact words used differ among languages, there is a strong and obvious similarity among them. This script contains the instructions the computer will carry out when the mouse cursor is over the button to which the script belongs and the user clicks. It will not execute until the button has been pushed down and then released (on mouseUp). Exactly what the script does is not important, but you should recognize the use of IF . . . THEN to define conditional actions, those that occur only under specified conditions. The point is simply that hypermedia tools have not altered the basic need to understand the concepts and logic of programming, which have changed little over many years.

If you are interested in using a hypermedia tool for Type II learning experiences, there are many practitioner reports available to provide food for thought. The bibliography at the end of this chapter will guide you to these: Braswell, 1991; Holden et al., 1992; McGrath, 1992; Mühlhäuser, 1992; Muir, 1991; Padilla, 1990; Trumbull et al., 1992; and Yoder, 1992.

It is still relatively early in the era of hypermedia tools. Exactly what their impact will be remains to be seen. However, it seems clear at this point that they have enabled a vastly greater segment of computer users to develop their own software products than ever before. We know of very successful Type II applications using *Linkway* with kindergartners, for instance, at the same time that hypermedia is having a major impact on computer-based training products for

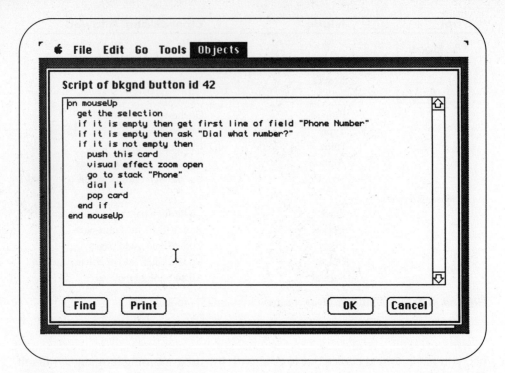

Figure 17.7. *HyperTalk* script for a button.

adults. The future of hypermedia looks very bright indeed. Sparks (1989, p. 10) put it this way:

> Our society will spend the next ten years learning how to produce and distribute high-quality hypermedia. Whole careers and new companies will emerge around it. But it will not be confined to computer professionals. This will be to the 1990s what hobbyist programming was to the late 70s, what word processing and spreadsheets were to the 80s. The difference will be that hypermedia will attract many, many more people who need to get their thoughts and ideas into better circulation.

Summary

This chapter considered some of the reasons why teachers create software themselves, rather than relying on what they can purchase. Our intent was to make you aware of common views on the topic, not to persuade you. Next, the increasingly popular use of simplified software development tools to enable students to pursue Type II experiences was considered.

Authoring tools can be categorized as authoring languages, authoring systems, and expert system shells. Hypermedia tools were treated separately because of their greater popularity in schools. Each tool was presented in minimal depth to provide a basic understanding of their characteristics, how they work, and some of their advantages and disadvantages. Although hypermedia dominates educators' interest at this time, we also believe that excellent experiences can result from the use of expert system shells. Teachers should develop modest familiarity with both to be able to make informed decisions about learning either well enough personally to be able to use it with students.

All of the tools presented in this chapter have been promoted as ideal for nonprogrammers. While they are inarguably simpler to use than common programming languages, we cannot agree that they remove all need for knowledge of programming. As Mandala (1990) wrote: "One of the main mistakes I have seen made on projects is lack of design when using an authoring system. Because these systems are touted as not requiring any experience with or aptitude in programming, many people sit down with no design and little thought about how the project should work." The result is certain to be much less effective than it could be, if approached with something of the programmer's mind-set in addition to sound design principles. We have yet to reach the stage where need for the concepts of programming fades into history.

Chapter 17 Activities

1. Reflect on your own teaching situation as it now is or as you anticipate it will be. Write a position paper giving your view on why teachers should or should not develop their own software.
2. Which of the software development tools presented in this chapter appeals most to you? Justify your position.
3. Most authoring software includes step-by-step instructions for its use. Some even have online tutorials. Develop a small lesson using any available authoring tool.
4. Explore *HyperCard, Linkway Live!,* and/or any other hypermedia tools to which you have access. Execute any finished products that are available. If possible, try your hand at modifying existing screens. Also create a new product of just a few screens that you link together as flexibly as is reasonable.
5. Consult any available expert system. Identify and read several current articles on education and artificial intelligence.
6. If you have access to an expert system shell, develop a simple application just to see how the software operates.
7. What is your position on student use of authoring tools for Type II applications? Defend or refute this increasingly popular use of software development as an alternative to traditional tests and term papers, considering student age among your arguments.
8. Create a lesson plan that includes a Type II computer application of an authoring tool.

Bibliography

Albin, M. "CBT Authoring System Selection: Features and Benefits." *CBT Directions*, June 1991, pp. 20–26.

Barefield, S. L. *Learning to Use IBM Linkway.* Berrien Springs, MI: Clicker Publishing, 1993.

Braswell, R. "The Use of *HyperCard* and *Hypersound* to Design Interactive Videodisc Instructional Materials." *Computers in the Schools*, 1991, *8*(1/2/3), pp. 251–254.

Burrowes, S. K., Chen, V. D., and Burrowes, D. J. *HyperTalk for Educators—An Introduction.* Eugene, OR: International Society for Technology in Education, 1992.

Camp, J., and Cogan, M. "HyperCard: A Milestone in Educational Computing." *Electronic Learning*, March 1988, pp. 46–51.

Collins, M. A. J. "Selecting Authoring Tools for Use in Authoring Biology Courseware." *American Biology Teacher*, May 1991, *53*(5), pp. 310–313.

Gayeski, D. "Software Tools for Interactive Media Developers." *TechTrends*, 1991, *36*(2), pp. 18–21.

Goodman, D. *The Complete HyperCard 2.0 Handbook.* New York: Bantam Books, 1990.

Holden, M. C., Holcomb, C. M., and Wedman, J. F. "Designing *HyperCard* Stacks for Cooperative Learning." *The Computing Teacher*, February 1992, *19*(5), pp. 20–22.

Howell, G. T. *Building Hypermedia Applications. A Software Development Guide.* New York: McGraw-Hill, 1992.

Krejci, B. "The Evolution of the Authoring System." *Instruction Delivery Systems*, March/April 1992, *6*(4), pp. 11–14.

Lamb, A. *IBM Linkway. Authoring Tool.* Orange, CA: Career Publishing, 1993.

Li, Z., and Merrill, M. D. "Transaction Shells: A New Approach to Courseware Authoring." *Journal of Research on Computing in Education*, Fall 1990, *23*(1), pp. 72–86.

Lo, R., Locatis, C., Ullmer, E., Carr, V., Banvard, R., Le, Q., Williamson, M., and Ackerman, M. "Developing a Database of Authoring System Software." *Educational Technology Research & Development*, 1992, *40*(2), pp. 69–76.

Locatis, C., Ullmer, E., Carr, V., Banvard, R., Le, Q., Lo, R., and Williamson, M. "Authoring Systems Reassessed." *Educational Technology Research & Development*, 1992, *40*(2), pp. 77–82.

Mandala, D. "Tech Talk." *Instruction Delivery Systems*, September/October 1990, p. 27.

McGrath, D. "Hypertext, CAI, Paper, or Program Control: Do Learners Benefit from Choices?" *Journal of Research on Computing in Education*, Summer 1992, *24*(4), pp. 513–532.

Mühlhäuser, M. "Hypermedia and Navigation as a Basis for Authoring/Learning Environments." *Journal of Educational Multimedia and Hypermedia*, 1992, *1*(1), pp. 51–64.

Muir, M. R. "Building Houses and Learning HyperCard: An Introductory Lesson." *The Computing Teacher*, November 1991, *19*(3), p. 8–12.

Myers, D., and Lamb, A. *HyperCard. Authoring Tool.* Orange, CA: Career Publishers, 1990.

O'Connor, R. J. "Facilitating CAI Development Via an Authoring Template." *Computers in the Schools*, 1991, *8*(1/2/3), pp. 249–250.

Padilla, R. "HyperCard: A Tool for Dual Language Instruction." *Computers in the Schools*, 1990, *7* (1/2), pp. 211–226.

Ragan, L. C. "HyperCard—A User's Description." *TechTrends*, September 1988, pp. 38–39.

Sparks, D. G. "HyperStudio." *Call-A.P.P.L.E.*, March 1989, pp. 8–10.

Trumbull, D., Gay, G., and Mazur, J. "Students' Actual and Perceived Use of Navigational and Guidance Tools in a Hypermedia Program." *Journal of Research on Computing in Education*, Spring 1992, *24*(3), pp. 315–328.

Yoder, S. "On Grading: From BASIC to Logo to HyperTalk." *The Computing Teacher*, August/September 1992, *20*(1), pp. 23–26.

Yoder, S., Bull, G. L., and Harris, J. *Linkway for Educators. An Introduction.* Eugene, OR: ISTE, 1991.

Ventura, F., and Grover, M. *HyperCard Projects for Teachers.* Newbury Park, CA: Ventura Educational Systems, 1991.

Zellner, R. D. "Development of Interactive Videodisc Modules for Limited English Proficient Students: Techniques, Issues, and Products for Vocational Education." *Computers in the Schools*, 1990, *7*(1/2), pp. 191–210.

Part 5
Microcomputers in Education

Objectives

After completing this chapter, you will be able to:

Briefly trace common computer literacy models.
Differentiate infusion from integration.
Discuss computer integration concepts.
Assess issues involved in considering significant curricular changes.
Persuasively argue you own view concerning the proper model for computers in education.

Chapter 18

Beyond Computer Literacy: Curriculum Integration and Transformation

The growth and acceptance of microcomputers in education has been little short of spectacular. It is both a cause and an effect; a result of new ideas for application, and in many cases, a stimulus for new ideas, as well as a prod to educators to find ways to use these devices. This is the Information Age, where computer technology pervades our lives, and the schools alone may be responsible for preventing generations of "technopeasants" (Collis, 1988).

You have learned about major uses of computers in earlier chapters. Now you will focus on the question, How can we actually deal with microcomputers in our schools? Roblyer, Castine, and King (1988) stated, "[Research] findings have also made it clear that computer applications have an undeniable value and an important instructional role to play in classrooms in the future. Defining that role is the task of the next decade." We place efforts at definition in two categories: *computer literacy* and *curriculum integration*. Let's see what they mean.

Computer Literacy

Computer literacy became a buzzword in computer education around 1980, and has been a topic of controversy. Inherent in the idea is that there exists some body of fundamental knowledge and skill regarding computers that *all* members of society should possess. A literate citizenry has long been an unquestioned goal; the computer is merely a new component. As Luehrmann (1983) stated, "The ability to use computers is as basic and necessary to a person's formal education as reading, writing, and arithmetic." Disagreement about the meaning of "use" is the major concern, not whether there is a need for such literacy.

Central to the arguments is the issue of computer programming. At one end of a continuum are those who have argued strongly that some programming skill is essential if an individual is to be considered computer literate. At the other end are those who view programming as completely unnecessary. Rather, one must be able to *use* computers and application software. In between come various compromises, and some definitions are all-encompassing. Regardless of position on the continuum, we classify as computer literacy those approaches that focus on the computer rather than the curriculum.

The Programming Model

When the first microcomputers entered the schools, there was practically no software available for them. Usually a science or math teacher was the first to attempt to use the new device, probably because those teachers were the most likely to have had some contact with computers during their teacher preparation. That contact nearly always meant programming. With such a background and no software, naturally the microcomputer was used for programming instruction.

Arthur Luehrmann, often regarded as the father of computer literacy, was a vocal advocate of programming as the heart of computer literacy. Luehrmann (1982, p. 20) wrote, "To tell a computer what you want to do, you must be able to communicate with it. To do that, you will need to learn a language for writing your ideas down so that you can review them, show them to others, and improve them." He stressed that computer literacy meant the ability to do something constructive with a computer, not just possess a general awareness gleaned from what one is told about computers. Luehrmann suggested that a computer-literate person can write and interpret a computer program, can select and operate software written by others, and knows from personal experience what a computer is and is not capable of doing. For many educators, literacy and programming became synonymous, which probably contributed to much teacher technophobia.

The Literacy Curriculum Model

Based on various authors (Bitter and Camuse, 1984; Hunter, 1983; Jones et al., 1983; Riedesel and Clements, 1985), a curriculum for computer literacy instruction includes four areas. Let's consider each one briefly.

Survival skills are skills that students must gain if they are to work effectively on a computer. They include knowing how to: boot a computer, handle diskettes, start up software packages, and use the keyboard and mouse. Such low-level skills are important for *all* students who use a computer. Perhaps they are analogous to such basic driving skills as inserting the key into the ignition, turning the key, checking mirrors, and so on.

Computer awareness pertains to knowledge and skills that help us better understand what a computer can and cannot do. Awareness of how computers are used in our society, the misuses of the computer, and computer ethics are topics that would receive attention. Future trends and developments in computer technology could also be dealt with under this category.

Application skills include word processing, the use of database management programs, and spreadsheets. This category emphasizes the use of *existing* programs that enable students to accomplish some desired task and provides considerable carry-over value into later life needs.

Within the context of computer literacy, *programming* experience does not aim to prepare future programmers. Rather, it is a skill that may enhance the student's ability to function as a problem solver. As you learned in Chapter 15, Logo is used widely to introduce students to problem solving through programming. Other languages may follow in higher grades.

Implementing a Literacy Curriculum

A computer-literacy curriculum might be implemented across the existing curriculum or as new, separate courses at various grade levels.

Scope and sequence advocates recommended diffusing computer instruction throughout the K–12 curriculum. Teachers at all levels and in all fields should become "computer teachers," teaching the literacy units for that grade level. This approach requires a strong district commitment. It is appealing because the computer is encountered within the regular curriculum throughout the school years. However, there are also problems. Will all teachers participate? Since that seems unlikely, what about the holes in the K–12 sequence that are apt to occur? Are teachers prepared to handle computer units? Given the demands of a crowded curriculum, will teachers find the time (or inclination) to squeeze in new units on computers?

Luehrmann (1984) strongly advocated separate literacy courses. He suggested a junior-high-level class for all students, based on selected computer literacy goals. Such a class offers potential for careful monitoring of outcomes and may better assure that a well-trained teacher is responsible for computer instruction. Of course, survival skills, including keyboarding would be taught as needed in earlier grades so that students would be able to use the computer for appropriate activities.

Separate courses, then, offer the prospect of well-trained, specialist teachers delivering carefully constructed and sequenced content. Accountability should be greatly enhanced over a diffused approach. Still, separate courses have been criticized for creating a new content area apart from the rest of the curriculum. The computer becomes yet another subject to be learned and then forgotten as the student moves on to other unrelated subjects. Further, teachers may view the computer as "the other person's problem" because it is removed from their domains, a "special subject" such as art, music, or physical education in lower grades. In addition, a separate course usually necessitates a lab facility, which may increase costs or preclude access to computers in individual classrooms.

The Problem-Solving Model

Norton (1988) identified problem solving as another model of computer literacy. Development of problem-solving ability is a universally accepted objective. Concerns parallel those discussed for the literacy curriculum. Software aimed at problem solving tends to be general, making it difficult to link to the curriculum. Although Logo is firmly rooted in mathematics, it is frequently used as a change of pace, as a way to make pretty patterns, as something separate and unto itself. In either case, time for these activities comes at the expense of something else. Unless a teacher is firmly convinced of the value of the activity *and* comfortable in presenting it, there is little likelihood that the teacher will voluntarily do so. If coerced, however gently, effectiveness of use is almost certain to be lessened.

The Tools/Applications Model

By the mid-1980s, even though computers were still new to many educators, the tide had begun to turn against programming as literacy. Literacy curricula proved more difficult to implement than anticipated, Logo's impact was suspect, and the question of whether to find time for problem-solving software was not fully answered. Educators were still seeking ways for computers to make an impact. They turned in many cases to the applications software we discussed in Chapters 2 through 7. In 1988 Collis declared that applications had replaced programming as the most common definition of computer literacy (1988, August/September).

The reasoning was sound. Computers are a part of our lives that will not go away. Schools prepare children for productive lives in society. The "real world" has embraced computer applications wholeheartedly. Therefore, students need to learn to use these tools in school.

In many cases, the approach was to revamp existing computer-literacy courses. Out went programming, computer history, noncritical terminology, and other marginal topics. Survival skills became the precursors of word processing, databases, spreadsheets, and more. Students got excited as did many teachers. The computer had become relevant.

Norton (1988) criticized the tool approach from two perspectives. First, tool courses tend to emphasize mechanics. Assignments are contrived to meet the needs of a stand-alone course. "Tool applications are worthwhile only when students are prepared to use them to solve problems which have meaning and applicability to their needs." Second, tools are typically treated as neutral, which they never are. Students must study the *effects* of the computer on themselves and society, not just how to use them efficiently.

Conclusion

A major problem in dealing with computer literacy is that it is not a single concept. Rather, there have been and still are distinct definitions and approaches to it. They may even represent a developmental hierarchy stretching from the programming model through applications. Each model has had its proponents and defenders, and all have their critics. The common thread through the criticism is that these models all basically treat the computer as subject matter, an end in itself (Hill et al., 1988).

Where do we turn next to capitalize on what experience has taught us? The following section offers one response.

Curriculum Integration

Curriculum integration moves beyond the "sterility" of computer literacy (Johnson, Maddux, and O'Hair, 1988) to make the computer an integral part of the learning process at all levels. *Integration* replaces literacy as a buzzword.

First, we must distinguish between infusion and integration. *Infusion* means simply that computers are physically present in our schools. Collis (1988, p. 3) points out that hardware proliferation is not a sign of the "computer revolution." Statistics about the number of computers in schools and the ratio of computers to students or teachers are evidence of growing infusion. Once the hardware is there, how can it become a vital tool for learning?

Integration means "the process of totally integrating the use of computers into the existing curriculum through learning activities that address the subject-area objectives (Staff, 1988). "(T)he true pioneers . . . are dealing systemically with all aspects of the curriculum in order to create well integrated systems designed (1) to meet the needs of the students and (2) to be improved on the basis of feedback from those students" (Komoski, 1987, p. 22). Data on the extent of computer integration are much more difficult to identify.

What is the Scope?

Integration places the computer in the service of the curriculum. It capitalizes on the best from educational computing that preceded it but starts with the curriculum, not the computer. It seeks to identify those places where the computer can increase learning effectiveness, enable learners to do what they otherwise could not, or teach significant life skills. Integration is all-inclusive, but more importantly, all-pervasive. Let's consider the computer-literacy models in the context of integration.

Within curriculum integration, programming is appropriate whenever it reflects a specific need, such as in a data processing curriculum. In other subjects, programming can be an appropriate technique for mastering particular components (Norton, 1988).

As for a literacy curriculum, it would be difficult to imagine any scope and sequence being more than a rough guide, since curriculum is determined locally in the United States. However, such a model could well contain elements that clearly support curriculum objectives and should be kept in the new plan.

From the beginning, the problem solving model has suffered from lack of a curricular home. Everyone wants the result, but no one claims responsibility, nor wants to give up class time for it. The issue is not an integration model but how to handle problem solving at all. Research suggests that past views of learning problem solving have been too simplistic. Dudley-Marling and Owston (1988) reviewed a vast range of research and concluded that "while problem-solving skills within any particular domain can be taught, . . . transfer . . . across domains is difficult to achieve. . . . Therefore, it is likely that no single problem-solving program, Logo or CAI, will develop the wide range of problem-solving skills students need to survive in and out of school." However, they did not suggest giving up the quest. Rather, they advise starting with the curriculum and then examining carefully the potential of any problem-solving approach to effect curricular goals. And, don't expect unattainable results.

Finally, there is the application software model, which has been our bias throughout this book. We believe the potential of software tools is practical to begin with and that tools offer powerful ways to improve learning with Type II activities. Curriculum integration simply means using software tools throughout the curriculum *wherever appropriate*, rather than relegating them to a specific course. The Wellesley (MA) public schools dropped their middle-school applications course "to the shock and dismay of staff who taught the course, but to the benefit of all students, who now learn to use word processors in their English courses and spreadsheets in their math courses" (November, 1989). Banas (1991) describes the integration in a Downers Grove (IL) junior high school that is possible because students have used computers since first grade. A typical seventh-grader creates graphs for social studies, uses paint software in art, word processes compositions, illustrates science concepts with drawing software, composes music with software, and uses CAD in industrial arts. Such integration has been our ideal throughout this book.

Advantages Over Literacy

Why is such an approach "better" than its predecessors? First, integration puts the emphasis squarely where it belongs: on the curriculum, not on the computer. Second, there is no need to add new objectives to the school's curriculum to deal with computers. Instead, existing objectives are enhanced with computer applications. This minimizes, but may not totally dispel, the problem of, "How do we make room for it?" Third, the computer becomes a partner, not a competitor. Any lingering fears that teachers may be displaced by computers can be vanquished. Fourth, integration treats the computer in a natural way, as one fundamental tool for learning and living. Was there ever a course in pencil? Perhaps for those who aspire to manufacture them. Does there need to be a course in computer? Outside of data processing, we think not. Fifth, integration fosters invisibility. Someone once said that technology *essential* to a process becomes invisible; technology is visible *inversely* to its necessity. Computer technology is here for the duration and will, one day, be as invisible as pencil or calculator technology. By *not* separating it from current routine, educators can help computers become invisible.

Beyond Integration: Transformation

For some educators, curriculum integration is a step in the right direction, but not enough in and of itself. Norton (1988) saw significant gains in the integration approach but found it insufficient nonetheless. "(I)ntegration carries with it a set of unspoken assumptions which fail to recognize the unique potentials of the computer. . . (It) defines learning and education as content specific and content oriented and presupposes an existing curriculum that is best left unchallenged" (p. 10). Norton argues that it is not enough to bolster a curriculum that needs to be changed.

The report of the National Assessment of Educational Progress (NAEP) released in early 1989 noted that "most students' school experiences are dominated by memorization of content presented by teacher or textbook, and by the practicing of skills in workbook or ditto exercises. . . Students are given limited opportunities to apply knowledge and procedures for new purposes" (Banas, 1989). The report urged educators to find ways to make students more active learners and to move away from traditional authoritarian roles. The recommended approaches include computers.

Johnson (1991) offered a provocative view of curriculum (see Figure 18.1), which we present here without limiting it to any specific content area. The relative sizes of the areas in the diagram do not represent corresponding amounts of content.

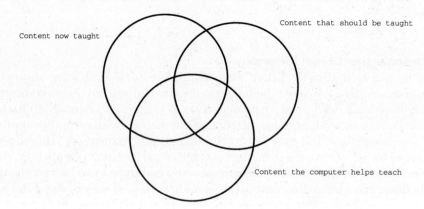

Figure 18.1. A model of curriculum (Adapted from Johnson, 1991).

Rather, the diagram simply presents relationships. Johnson suggests that part of what is now taught should not be (although it may once have had value) and that the computer can help teach some things that we do not now teach. However, computers also add possibilities that exceed the bounds of what should be taught, while leaving untouched other areas of the content field. What does this suggest concerning whether integration is an end or merely a step toward a larger goal? Johnson's views remind us that the computer is no panacea.

The issues involved in significant curricular transformation are numerous and complex. Moursund (1992) notes that both teachers and students resist change. Johnson (1991) suggests educators should examine the role of the computer in their field(s) based on its ability to help *teach, learn,* and *do* what is appropriate to the field. Polin (1992) addresses the issues from the viewpoint of emerging constructivist theory. Norton (1988) maintains that society expects students to develop higher-order thinking skills, adaptability to change, and creativity. Educators must identify the unique potentials of the computer. "Using computers in education . . . permits curriculum designers to expand their concepts of the curriculum—to emphasize processes for acquiring experiences and applying knowledge (doing) as well as content to be mastered" (p. 11). In short, she views content as a reason to teach process, not as an end unto itself.

Views such as these deserve careful consideration. Rather than being radical, they appear to offer a rational approach to deliberate change in a profession that is more accustomed to glacial movement than upheaval. (Who once said that changing education is the only task more difficult than moving a cemetery?) We accept that change will come slowly. In this last decade of the twentieth century, some educators are still at the programming-as-literacy stage, many have adopted the applications model, and others are well along the road to integration. Some are even exploring more dramatic transformations of curriculum. All deserve recognition for their efforts and encouragement and assistance as they evolve. We also accept Norton's challenge to make more of the computer than integration necessarily does but believe transformation is a long-term goal that requires intermediate steps toward its attainment.

Summary

There is widespread agreement that knowledge and understanding of computers and those skills essential to computer use are legitimate educational goals. Computer literacy sought to meet such goals by treating the computer as something unique and special. The four common models of computer literacy are programming, a literacy curriculum, problem solving, and application software or tools. All added new content to the curriculum.

Curriculum integration, in contrast, can incorporate all the literacy content, but does so in direct support of the curriculum. Problems of finding time for computers largely vanish because there are no new curriculum objectives. Rather, the computer is the teacher's colleague and on the way to becoming as invisible as the pencil. Students learn what they need to know when and in the context in which they need it—much like real word computer use.

Still, some educators contend that while integration is a step in the right direction, it does not go far enough. The curriculum should not be static but, rather, must change to capitalize on the unique potential of the computer, to move into more Type II applications, experiences seldom before possible. Merely to support what already is may retard the inevitable transformation of education that must occur to keep pace with societal changes.

Chapter 18 Activities

1. Which model of computer literacy appears to be most acceptable? Justify your position.
2. In your opinion, is programming skill essential for an individual to be truly computer literate? Why or why not?
3. Discuss the respective merits of the separate class and the K–12 scope and sequence approaches to the literacy curriculum. Which is preferable? Why?
4. Is *computer literacy* a meaningful term? How can it assist or hinder the implementation of computers in our schools?
5. Define computer integration in contrast to computer literacy and infusion. Outline its essential characteristics.
6. Analyze literacy versus integration, setting forth strengths and weaknesses of each.
7. Determine the position of your state education authority on computers in education, both for K–12 students and for teachers. How has this changed? What further changes would you support, if any?
8. Evaluate the view that integration is itself insufficient unless curriculum change also occurs.
9. What is the legitimate role of the schools relative to computers? What are the historical, philosophical, and/or sociological bases for this role?

Bibliography

Banas, C. "Study: Students Not Using Knowledge." *Chicago Tribune,* 15 February 1989, Section 1, p. 5.

Banas, C. "Computer-Savvy Students Beginning to Come of Age." *Chicago Tribune,* 20 February 1992, Section 2, pp. 1, 4.

Bitter, G., and Camuse, R. *Using a Microcomputer in the Classroom.* Reston, VA: Reston Publishing Co., 1984.

Brock, F. J., Thomsen, W. E., and Kohl, J. P. "The Effects of Demographics on Computer Literacy of University Freshmen." *Journal of Research on Computing in Education,* Summer 1992, 24(4), pp. 563–570.

Brownell, G. *Computers and Teaching,* 2nd ed. St. Paul: West Publishing, 1992.

Collis, B. *Computers, Curriculum, and Whole-Class Instruction.* Belmont, CA: Wadsworth, 1988.

Collis, B. "Research Windows." *The Computing Teacher,* August/September 1988, *16*(1), pp. 6–7.

Dudley-Marling, C., and Owston, R. D. "Using Microcomputers to Teach Problem Solving: A Critical Review." *Educational Technology,* July 1988, pp. 27–33.

Franklin, S., and Strudler, N., (Eds.). *Effective Inservice for Integrating Computer-as-Tool into the Curriculum.* Eugene, OR: International Society for Technology in Education, 1989.

Galloway, J. P. "Teaching Educational Computing with Analogies: A Strategy to Enhance Concept Development." *Journal of Research on Computing in Education,* Summer 1992, 24 (4), pp. 499–512.

Graves, W. H., (Ed). *Computing across the Curriculum: Academic Perspectives.* McKinney, TX: Academic Computing Publications, 1990.

Hignite, M. A., and Echternacht, L. J. "Assessment of the Relationships Between the Computer Attitudes and Computer Literacy Levels of Prospective Educators." *Journal of Research on Computing in Education,* Spring 1992, 24(3), pp. 381–391.

Hill, M., Manzo, F., Liberman, D., York, J., Nichols, C., and Morgan, P. "A Plea for Computer Integration: Let's Bring Computers into the Classroom." *Educational Technology,* May 1988, pp. 46–48.

Hunter, B. *My Students Use Computers.* Reston, VA: Reston Publishing Co., 1983.

Johnson, J. "Are Paradigms Worth More Than a Pair of Dimes?" *The Computing Teacher,* October 1991, *19*(2), pp. 38–40.

Johnson, D. L., Maddux, C. D., and O'Hair, M. M. "Are We Making Progress? An Interview with Judah L. Schwartz of ETC." *Computers in the Schools,* 1988, 5(1/2), pp. 5–22.

Jones, W., Jones, B., Bowyer, K., and Ray, M. *Computer Literacy: Programming, Problem Solving, Projects on the Apple.* Reston, VA: Reston Publishing, 1983.

Kay, R. "Bringing Computer Literacy into Perspective." *Journal of Research on Computing in Education,* Fall 1989, *21*(1), pp. 35–47.

Kay, R. H. "The Computer Literacy Potpourri: A Review of the Literature, or McLuhan Revisited." *Journal of Research on Computing in Education,* Summer 1992, 24(4), pp. 446–456.

Kay, R. H. "The Relation between Locus of Control and Computer Literacy." *Journal of Research on Computing in Education,* Summer 1990, 22(4), pp. 464–474.

Komoski, P. K. "Beyond Innovation: The Systemic Integration of Technology into the Curriculum." *Educational Technology,* September 1987, pp. 21–25.

Langhorne, M. J., Donham, J. O., Gross, J. F., and Rehmke, D. *Teaching with Computers. A New Menu for the '90s.* Phoenix: Oryx Press, 1989.

Luehrmann, A. "Computer Literacy: What It Is, Why It Is Important." *Electronic Learning,* May/June 1982, pp. 20, 22.

Luehrmann, A. "Computer Illiteracy—A National Crisis and a Solution for It." In D. O. Harper and J. H. Stewart, (Eds.). *Run: Computer Education.* Monterey, CA: Brooks/Cole, 1983, pp. 29–32.

Luehrmann, A. "The Best Way to Teach Computer Literacy." *Electronic Learning,* April 1984, pp. 37–44.

Maddux, C. D., Johnson, D. L., and Willis, J. W. *Educational Computing. Learning with Tomorrow's Technologies.* Boston: Allyn & Bacon, 1992.

Moursund, D. "Restructuring Education Part 6: A New Definition of Computer Literacy." *The Computing Teacher,* March 1992, *19*(6), p. 4.

Moursund, D. "Restructuring Education for the Information Age. Part 7: Competition." *The Computing Teacher,* April 1992, *19*(7), p. 4.

Mueller, R. O., Husband, T. H., Christou, C., and Sun, A. "Preservice Teacher Attitudes towards Computer Technology: A Log-Linear Analysis." *Mid-Western Educational Researcher,* Spring 1991, 4(2), pp. 23–27.

Norton, P. "In Search of a Computer Curriculum." *Educational Technology,* March 1988, pp. 7–14.

November, A. "Pioneers and Settlers." *ISTE Update,* February 1989, pp. 1–2.

Polin, L. "Research Windows: Subvert the Dominant Paradigm." *The Computing Teacher,* May 1992, *19*(8), pp. 6–7.

Riedesel, C. A., and Clements, D. H. *Coping with Computers in the Elementary and Middle Schools.* Englewood Cliffs, NJ: Prentice-Hall, 1985.

Roblyer, M. D., Castine, W. H., and King, F. J. "Assessing the Impact of Computer-Based Instruction." *Computers in the Schools,* 1988, 5(3/4), entire special issue.

Simonson, M. R., and Thompson, A. *Educational Computing Foundations.* Columbus, OH: Merrill, 1990.

Staff, "One Hundred and One Things You Want to Know about Educational Technology." *Electronic Learning,* May/June 1988, pp. 32–48.

Staff, "Ninth Annual Survey of the States." *Electronic Learning,* October 1989, 9(2), pp. 22, 24–28.

Objectives

After completing this chapter, you will be able to:

Outline the implementation goals and methods of the early 1980s.

Analyze reasons why the so-called computer revolution has had limited impact.

Discuss the concept of computer competence as it relates to computer literacy and curriculum integration.

Compare the fundamental concepts of integration, reform, and restructuring.

Assess reasons commonly given for why teachers do not employ technology.

Explain the importance of a plan for technology in education.

Describe and assess the role of a technology coordinator and the need for teacher involvement in technology planning and implementation.

Discuss issues and ideals for staff development and articulation.

Argue an appropriate position regarding hardware purchases for your specific situation, including needed peripherals.

Analyze the merits of a lab, computers in classrooms, and mobile computers, based on your position on cooperative learning strategies.

Outline potential applications in a one-computer classroom.

Briefly discuss technology as it relates to special-needs populations.

Propose and justify distribution of budget funds across categories of necessary expenditures.

Outline approaches to stretching a limited budget.

Chapter 19

Technology Implementation

It took education more than 300 years to fully take advantage of the technological revolution in movable type. And it was almost 100 years between the invention of the pencil and its wide use in schools. This is not so with microcomputers. Change has come quickly. Our challenge is to manage that change, and to put the new technology into the service of quality education (Lengel, 1983, p. 18).

Scarcely 10 years later, former Secretary of Education Terrel Bell wrote:

The technological revolution that has greatly enhanced the efficiency of industry, business, and publishing has had little impact on the classrooms of America. . . . Teachers desperately need the advantages that today's technology offers to address the many diverse needs of students. . . . Neither educators nor students are trained or equipped to do their work; we send them to a 1950's model classroom and expect them to deliver a product ready to face the 21st Century. . . . American education truly is wobbling down the electronic avenue in an ox-cart (Bell, 1992).

The contrast between these two statements is stark. The pace of change—at least in the sense of computer infusion—has been rapid, as Lengel noted, and there are outstanding examples of technology-enriched learning environments (see McCarthy, 1993). However, looking at education broadly, the impact now appears to be far less than Lengel envisioned (Borrell, 1992; Kinnaman, 1992). Why have we not "put the new technology into the service of quality education?" One possible explanation is that "revolutions have a way of mandating change while glossing over logistical details" (Roblyer, Castine, and King, 1988). The dream is alive, but we must learn from the experiences that have contributed to Bell's indictment and move forward based on those experiences that have succeeded.

Chapter 18 presented a theoretical consideration of the proper goal for computers in education—namely invisible integration into the curriculum. This chapter considers a short history of the first 15 years of educational computing, including some of the problems encountered by computing pioneers and reasons why a different approach may be required. Some of the critical logistical issues that require attention by any teacher committed to twenty-first century education using computer technology are then surveyed. True progress must come through *you!*

One View of Implementation History

From its initial availability, schools have embraced microcomputer technology at a rate unprecedented for educational innovations. In no other case in the history of American education has so much money been spent with so few questions asked, so little known about the implications, so little thought given to implementation, and, ultimately, so little expected in return. Computers flooded schools with less consideration than was given to ordering the year's supply of paper towels for the washrooms. Schools competed with one another to acquire greater *numbers* of computers, with little thought given to their actual use. There were exceptions, of course, but far too often the approach was just hopping on a bus, destination unknown.

The Early 1980s: Getting Started

Idealists arose in the early eighties and proclaimed the need for *planning* (e.g., Fisher, 1983; Klein and Strothers, 1983–1984; Lengel, 1983). The process could be neat and tidy. First, establish a planning committee to draft a school (district, state) philosophy concerning computers and get the appropriate authorities to endorse it. Extend the philosophy into policy statements. Develop a curriculum plan, even a scope and sequence, with clear objectives for all grade levels. Establish a computer budget, determine hardware and software to purchase, and plan staff development activities. Draw up a facilities plan for placement of the computers, and order hardware and software. Implement staff development. All teachers will be inspired and will eagerly use computers throughout the schools. Learning magically will flower.

As with many generalizations, there is a thread of truth running through the preceding synopsis, however inaccurate it may be for specific cases. The longed-for magic has not occurred broadly. Concerns arose within the first decade of educational computing (Komoski, 1987): Bell's comments that opened this chapter reiterate McCarthy's (1988) and the Federal Office of Technology Assessment (U.S. Congress, 1988). What we *thought* would happen did not.

The Late 1980s: Assessment and Reflection

One significant explanation for lack of greater change is that we put all our faith in the technology and gave, at best, lip service to the critical need for teacher training (Preskill, 1988; McCarthy, 1988; Knupfer, 1988). A federal study found that only one-third of K–12 teachers had even 10 hours of computer in-service training (U.S. Congress, 1988, p. 18). Knupfer reported a median of 3 hours of in-service for sixth-grade teachers in Wisconsin, with the large majority having none at all!

The issue is greater, however, than just training opportunity. Friedman (1985) maintained that teacher resistance to computers was much greater than most experts believed and needed to be addressed directly. Stieglitz and Costa (1988) found that an overwhelming majority of Rhode Island teachers opted *not* to continue beyond an introductory computer workshop, although six coordinated sessions were readily available. These researchers also reported that, despite positive attitudes, less than half the teachers reported any actual classroom computer use. Balajthy (1988) concluded that it would take significant effort to increase teacher motivation to incorporate computers into classroom instruction.

Some teachers felt they had too little hardware available to attempt anything of consequence. Others were discouraged by the physical placement of computers in their schools (Knupfer, 1988) or found computers too difficult to incorporate into their teaching (Preskill, 1988). These may be training issues, but frankly, teaching with computers takes more time than before (Collis, 1988). The Ontario Ministry of Education concluded that most technology advocates "vastly underestimate how difficult it will be for teachers to implement the changes they (new educational technologies) will require in practices, materials, beliefs, and skills" (Fullan, Miles, and Anderson, 1987, p. 141).

Mathinos and Woodward (1987) studied an "exemplary" school with plenty of hardware and software, a computer coordinator and aide, extensive in-service programs, and a 5-year district plan in its final year. Over 13 weeks, sixty percent of the students never used a computer; half of those who did had only one experience. Typically, computer use was a reward for completing work early rather than an integrated experience for all. Plomp, Steerneman, and Pelgrum (1988) observed similar patterns in Holland.

According to Collis (1988), computer implementation has had minimal impact because it has not been integrated tightly into the curriculum. In addition, many efforts to evoke change failed to take present reality into account, notably that computers run counter to long-established teaching styles. Teachers generally lack role models during their own training of strategies for implementing and managing computers in the classroom (Collis, August/September 1988).

We also believe that more patience is required. The potential of computers to revolutionize education has been overstated, expectations have been raised to unreasonable levels, and the time to achieve such goals has been greatly underestimated. We need a more realistic view. In general, implementation succeeds or fails on the level of the individual teacher. The only thing you can count on in your school is what you are yourself ready and willing to do. This book attempts to provide you with the motivation and knowledge to implement computers productively so that their educational potential may more nearly be attained.

Implementation for the 1990s and Beyond

The history of education is littered with the artifacts of innovations that failed to deliver on their promises. Perhaps the preceding discussion suggests that the computer is only the most recent such fad. If you have come this far with us and accept that view, then we have failed completely. By now, we hope you are so convinced of the potential of educational computing that you will let nothing stand in your way! Read on as we sketch some directions and offer resources for additional help.

The Goal: Computer Competence

The preceding chapter stressed that the overall goal for computers in education is curriculum integration in which the computer plays an essential, invisible role in daily classroom activity. Your students must become not computer literate, but *computer competent*—that is, able to use a computer productively and effectively whenever appropriate. *You* must achieve computer competence as well, although what is appropriate for you as a teacher is different from what your students should achieve. Still, personal competence will determine the extent to which you integrate technology into your teaching.

The very content and structure of this book supports Kelman's (1993) view that the most promising uses of computers in education are:

- As tools of personal and professional productivity.
- As facilitators of higher-order thinking skills.
- As vehicles for creative expression.
- As facilitators of cooperative learning.
- As multiple modality learning environments.
- As a means of empowerment.

Of course, each of these points is a fundamental goal of education per se. When computers are invisibly integrated into the curriculum, students will develop computer competence as they work to attain these broad goals. That is twenty-first century education, and it stands in marked contrast to simply adding the computer to the curriculum as a special object of instruction.

Integration, Reform, Restructuring?

It is popular today to proclaim that today's schools are in such bad shape that modest change is no longer viable. The concern leads to the contention that schools must be reformed, even totally restructured, to reclaim their significance. Restructuring is not necessarily physical change, but more critically, a fundamental change in the way students are taught and learn. In turn, many voices strongly contend that successful restructuring requires technology to play a central role in the "new" schools (Brady, 1992; Bruder, 1990, 1992; DeLoughry, 1992; *Computers in the Schools*, 1991, 8(1/2/3); *Educational Technology*, November 1992; *Electronic Learning*, April 1993).

Although we certainly do not disagree with the ideals of the reform and restructuring movements, their potential to go beyond rhetoric into widespread adoption is not yet clear. The history of education suggests that such radical change is uncommon on a wide scale. If technology integration is linked to total school restructuring, then educators in schools not yet committed to such change would appear to be helpless. We cannot accept such an all-or-nothing position.

In school districts where teachers are committed to radical change, we support fully the rapid move to technology-rich learning environments. Bruder (1990) provides an exciting look at a school undergoing such restructuring. For others, significant technology integration is still possible, and it must begin with recognition of existing reality. Start where teachers and the curriculum currently are (Collis, 1988). Identify places where the computer has the potential to make a difference. Implement at those points in ways that are compatible with the "existing rhythms of school life" (Knupfer, 1988). Provide appropriate conditions, and the curriculum itself will evolve. Bracey (1993) reported results of an extensive study showing that technology first strengthens the existing curriculum, which gradually yields to "far more dynamic learning experiences for students."

Technology Planning

To work toward curriculum integration, a carefully developed plan is vital for many reasons. "If you fail to plan, you plan to fail" (Robert Schuller, quoted in Collis, 1988, p. 302). Developing that plan requires strategic planning to articulate the vision of the school district in a concrete way and also sets a tone for budgets. "It must be directly connected to the educational aims of the school district, and it needs community-wide support and ownership" (Kinnaman, 1992). A district plan commands support at the building level and signals broad commitment. Regardless of position on the reform/restructuring scale, a plan should have three key elements: a long-term view, system-wide applications, and major involvement of teachers. Detailed planning resources are listed in the bibliography at the end of this chapter.

The Technology Coordinator

Early in the planning process, schools should address the issue of a *technology coordinator*. Successful change in education requires effective leadership. Computers represent a qualitatively different change from the influx of videocassette recorders (VCRs), for instance. Integrating computers throughout the curriculum for effective learning is an enormous task. There are many issues to face, many decisions to make, and someone has to be in charge. An excellent resource is *The Technology Coordinator* (Moursund, 1992).

Questions to address about coordination include the range of responsibilities (district, building, both), extent of commitment (full- or part-time), and position type (administrator, teacher, or both). Principals must assume a vital leadership role in technology implementation (Bruder, 1990), but district and building-level coordinators are also needed (Collis, 1988; Becker, undated). Another possibility is a building computer liaison, a full-time teacher or media specialist who takes on extra responsibilities, including serving on the planning committee, providing building leadership in technology applications, and conducting staff-development sessions (Kinnaman, 1993). This could well become *your* role, one you should promote and then be prepared to accept.

Short of total restructuring of a school and major infusions of new hardware and software, technology integration is certain to be achieved only over some years. A shotgun approach to integration throughout the curriculum tends to spread the effort too thin for real effect. The maximum benefit is more likely to accrue from focusing resources on specific areas (Pogrow, May/June 1988; McCarthy, 1988). Most of these will be identified by those teachers who are ready to move forward with technology. The coordinator can help empower these teachers to achieve their goals.

Teacher Involvement

The real success of technology integration depends ultimately on the classroom teachers who develop and implement actual plans on the curriculum, class, and unit level. Teachers like you have already self-selected themselves to participate in the exciting new possibilities of technology. Most of the resources should be focused on this group of teachers.

Teachers who have not yet decided to adopt technology personally should continue to be exposed to the possibilities, gently encouraged, and offered support, but their participation cannot be forced. More will result from supporting the willing than from cajoling the reluctant. To try to interest reluctant colleagues, inquire as to the areas of their teaching that cause them the most difficulty. Consider the potential for technology intervention. If there is an acknowledged problem, that teacher may be more willing to consider a new approach. If not, try again next year.

Years of mandatory in-service for all teachers have failed to persuade many teachers to join the technology movement. It is time to concentrate on those of you who are convinced and to hope that the excitement generated in your classes will pique the interests of less adventuresome colleagues. Eventually, perhaps the vast majority of teachers in a school will use technology broadly and effectively, but that is a long-term goal.

Staff Development

The level of support that a school invests in training teachers to use technology is directly proportional to the extent of its educational impact (Komoski, 1987). Schools that invest in hardware and software, but not teacher training, make a serious mistake. Kinnaman (1993) maintains that teachers like technology and want to use it but need help to do so. What, then, should characterize staff development?

One-shot institute days with guest speakers are hardly the answer. Rather, the identified needs of the teachers committed to technology must be addressed, needs that will vary greatly from one school to the next. Training should be "personalized, customized, informal, school-based, small group, flexibly scheduled, and need-based" (Kinnaman, 1993). Teachers now vary greatly in existing knowledge and interest in technology, making large-group sessions less likely than ever to be useful. The ever-increasing range of subject-specific materials also limits large-group potential. As skills and interest grow, technology users become ideal resources for miniconferences and institute days, in which they share their experiences with their colleagues and thus stimulate further interests among them.

Generic staff-development ideas include computer support groups (teachers sharing their experience and knowledge), some form of incentives for the time and effort invested, and setting annual school targets to work toward (McCarthy, 1993; Collis, 1988). Increased technical support has proven effective in enhancing computer use, as have increased salaries for "master teachers" who use technology, summer curriculum development assignments, extra preparation time in the daily schedule, and computer access at home and school (McCarthy, 1993; U.S. Congress, 1988).

In Washington, one district *gave* computers to teachers willing to take in-service training. Classroom usage increased dramatically, labs overflowed, and in one week requests for software equalled those for the entire previous year (McCarthy, 1988). This supports the view that classroom use springs from personal commitment to computer use, which develops from exposure to the technology over time. Some schools assist teachers to purchase their own computers (McCarthy, 1993). The number of computers in teachers' homes may be more significant for what happens in a school than the number of computers in the school itself!

A no-cost approach is to send computers home with teachers on weekends, breaks, and over the summer, as other writers have advocated with only limited acceptance (Moursund, August/September 1988; Collis, 1988). Obviously, a computer sitting unused in a school achieves nothing. That same computer with appropriate software sitting in a teacher's home might enlist a new technology recruit or support further advances by an existing trooper. We recommend that schools announce the availability of loaner computers but keep requests for them confidential. Some potential borrowers may prefer not to let their peers know of their explorations until they feel ready. In the early stages, anything that increases privacy and avoids the potential embarrassment of group in-service is useful.

Whatever the staff-development program, we urge schools to demand computer skills of all candidates for teaching positions. This alone will reduce the need for lower-level staff development and permit redirection of funds and time to more sophisticated uses.

Articulation

Regardless of exact implementation details, coordination across grade levels is vital. All teachers need to know what skills students have learned previously to plan effectively for their own grade level. Just as curriculum is articulated across grade levels, so must be computer utilization to assure appropriateness. This is further justification for a technology coordinator. Inadequate attention to articulation has been a common, serious flaw in technology planning (Moursund, April 1987).

Choosing Hardware: Mac or MS-DOS?

While detailed discussion of selecting specific microcomputer models and peripheral hardware is beyond our scope, the issue of the major competing hardware platforms, Apple versus MS-DOS, warrants comment.

Although there were many incompatible microcomputers from which schools could choose even in the late 1970s, Apple Computer quickly came to dominate the educational market with its Apple II series. The early Apple IIs offered features important to educators, such as relative ease of setup and use, color, graphics, and even limited sound. Software developers embraced the Apple II immediately, and as the range of compatible educational software leaped far ahead of competiters, this computer's popularity continued to soar. Software availability drove the market. Apple II remained the most common machine in schools into the 1990s.

Inevitably, the fundamental technology of the Apple II became outdated. Apple (and third-party companies) made many efforts to patch up the Apple II and extend its useful life with memory increases, speed-up chips, and new peripherals, but such efforts could not succeed in the long run. Technological obsolescence is a fact of life with computer technology. The Apple II will always hold a place of distinction in the history of educational computing. Existing systems remain usable, especially at the elementary level and will continue to be a significant percentage of school computers for some years to come.

Apple recognized the need for a different technology base and created the Macintosh, which abandoned the popular color feature. IBM entered the field rather late with its IBM-PC, but its dominance in large systems in business virtually assured the success of the PC. Further, the decision of IBM to make its system specifications open to all stimulated not only third-party peripheral developers (as Apple had always done) but also direct competition with the microcomputer itself, the so-called MS-DOS clones. This spurred rapid advances in MS-DOS computers and drove prices steadily down. In contrast, Apple held to its traditional proprietary base, prevented the development of clones, and kept prices artificially inflated.

As purchasers started to turn away from the Apple II, software developers began to convert existing programs to run on other platforms, as well as to create more complex software that never could have run on an Apple II. Initially, developers assumed that schools would stick with Apple and migrate from the Apple II to Macintosh. Educational software for MS-DOS was more limited. However, a combination of marketing tactics and significant price advantages led more and more schools into MS-DOS computers, and software developers have followed. Today's MS-DOS and Macintosh software offerings are comparable.

While sound advice in the early 1980s was to identify the software that met your needs and then buy the computer that could run it, today there is very little software that is unique to one hardware platform. The trend is clearly toward software for both major platforms that is as identical in look, feel, operation, and capability as the very different underlying system electronics permit. Today, schools can buy the computers they prefer and then get the software they desire, at least in major application tools and popular CAI and utility packages. There will probably always be niche products that are unique to one platform or the other.

Where does this leave schools in the 1990s? What hardware platform should they purchase? The decision is more the personal preference of the decision maker than objective. Both Macintosh and MS-DOS computers are highly desirable systems, and neither is clearly better than the other. Macintosh continues to hold a slight edge in ease of setup and use, whereas MS-DOS systems tend to provide greater power and versatility at lower cost. As we write, MS-DOS computers are much more common than Macintosh in K–12 schools ("Update," 1993). We believe this is largely for financial reasons. Although Apple continues to cut its prices aggressively, Macintosh clones may drive prices further toward parity with MS-DOS systems.

In short, we find no compelling arguments for either Macintosh or MS-DOS systems. In this era of budgetary crises, price may well be the most important factor. Beyond that, intended use or instructional goals play a role. Schools will be well served to move existing Apple IIs down to the elementary level as quickly as possible, where their usefulness remains greatest. At any grade level, for art and graphics work, the Macintosh offers some advantages. For high school business education, MS-DOS with *Windows* makes the most sense since businesses favor that platform overwhelming compared to Macintosh. Students and teachers should learn to use both, however. After all, a microcomputer today is essentially just another household, school, or office appliance. Flexibility in using computers is important.

Regardless of platform, consider several points about wise purchasing (Kinnaman, March 1993b). First, do not insist on machines that are "backward compatible" with older hardware. Don't try to salvage old software. Second, the issue is value, not cost. Fewer well-equipped computers are preferable to more marginal ones. Third, look to the future when networks will deliver multimedia learning materials. Begin to prepare now by including CD-ROM, interactive video, and multimedia projection hardware in purchase plans.

Peripherals

Beyond basic hardware platform, the trend toward tool applications makes printers more important than in a primarily CAI environment. Schools should purchase fewer computers, if necessary, to get enough printers. To enhance group and cooperative learning experiences, projection is valuable, if not essential (Kinnaman, March 1993a). Liquid crystal display (LCD) panels and projectors have become economical. Every school should have at least one, even if it means cutting a computer or two from the purchase list.

Facilities

Is there an ideal physical arrangement for computers in a school? To start, every classroom teacher should have a telephone and computer on the desk (McCarthy, 1993). For student computers, Collis (1988) provided detailed pros and cons of computers as mobile stations, in classrooms, in labs, in libraries, and in "learning assistance centers." Each possibility has merit, and many schools have multiple arrangements. Figure 19.1 presents selected points for the three most common patterns.

Physical arrangement should support the goal of integrating computers into instruction. In many cases, that suggests one or more computers in each classroom.

Factors	Permanent Lab	Mobile Workstations	In Classrooms
Usage Patterns and Potential	Individual or group	Individual or group	Individual without video projection
	Requires scheduling, decreasing flexibility	Same as lab	Always available for maximum flexibility
	Curricular integration only if readily accessable, e.g., daily	May promote integration within the class if easily available	Constant availability supports integration
	Supports tool, tutor, learner functions	Roles supported depend on number of units	Tutor for enrichment and remediation; group work
	Can provide special hardware/interfacing		
Personnel	Needs supervisory/ operating staff	User responsibility	User responsibility
	May necessitate a computer specialist to help student users	Regular teacher with knowledge of content and students	Same as mobile
	Teachers need mostly software skills	Teachers need software and hardware skills	Same as mobile
Cost	Based on number of systems/peripherals	Number of systems plus mobile carts, etc	Number of systems may be more or less
	Potential economies of networking	Moving may increase repairs	May require most copies of software
	Highest security	Moderate security outside school hours	Lowest security
Most Common Grade:	Junior high or above	All levels	Elementary schools

Figure 19.1 Characteristics of three common computer placement patterns.

Where better to integrate them into everyday activity? Consider the probable use of other media, including books, if they were available *only* in a lab or library versus on demand in a classroom (Bitter, 1985). Classroom computers should be provided to those teachers who want them, rather than being placed automatically in every classroom, which may threaten and further turn off some teachers.

Labs are particularly important for vocational skills classes, word processing, and programming instruction. Database research, tutorials, and drill and practice all benefit from more machines but often can be managed on a rotating basis, just like other forms of group work.

Since a lab is just many computers in a single location, any classroom with more than a few computers becomes a lab. The ideal is a computer for every student, which if ever realized, would turn every room into a lab. Perhaps someday notebook computers will be available to students as books are today, rendering the issue of physical arrangement moot.

Cooperative versus Individual Learning

In the early 1970s, educational visionaries longed for the day of electronic calculators for every student. Skeptics scoffed, but the dream became reality rather quickly. Today's dream is of one student, one computer. This dream also seems far-fetched to many observers. While we believe it is the ultimate goal, even when it becomes true, educators must not lose sight of the value of cooperative learning.

In two studies, competitive environments revealed gender differences disadvantageous to females that did not exist in cooperative arrangements (Bracey, 1988). U.S. and British studies found superior gains from group work compared to individual work (Collis, December/January 1988–1989). Glasser (1989) found that students usually said they felt important only in extracurricular activities, which he attributed to the group or team nature of the activity.

Cooperative learning means much more than just putting students together at a computer. One will often get or take more than a fair share of the time. For maximum effectiveness with pairs, for instance, always prepare two sets of activities and designate group members as A and B. Have each complete one exercise. As appropriate to skill levels and the nature of the activity, have students give each other challenges or tasks to perform. This can increase the practicality of their work. Consider designating clusters of two or three computers as mutual help groups. Students should seek answers within their help group before asking you or an aide.

The One-Computer Classroom

A single computer in a classroom is a common situation, even in schools with lab facilities or mobile systems. What can you do with just one computer? Clearly, the answer is not to require word-processed assignments from all students, if there is no other computer facility. However, teachers do not expect more than one overhead projector or VCR. How is a computer different?

Visibility has been one problem. Most computer monitors are too small for more than a few students to see, especially given the tiny text that is often displayed.

However, large-screen data projection is no longer a luxury for schools, given today's prices for LCD projection panels. The issue is more creativity in using software with a student group than how the students can all see.

Much software was designed with a single user in mind, but other uses are possible. Typically, drill and practice, tutorials, and games are hard to use with groups. However, simulations and problem-solving software can be adapted easily to small-group or whole-class instruction. Some software producers, such as Tom Snyder Productions, emphasize group applications for their products. Snyder even produced a videotape on the one-computer classroom which is available free on loan.

Don't overlook the computer as a demonstration tool. Database searching can be a group activity, applying strategies developed by the class, which then sees the result immediately. With spreadsheet software, a group easily can observe the effects of changes in data or how it is manipulated. The ideal in biology may be real dissection, but if that is not possible, or as preparation for the lab, you could project *Operation: Frog* for the group. How many students can actually see a live demonstration?

Finally, presentation graphics software was designed for a single computer and a group. It is an electronic overhead or slide projector without the physical media. You can teach with such software, and students can make their own presentations using it. The real key to effective use of one computer in a classroom is a creative teacher.

Special-Needs Populations

Computers can empower students with special needs. In a New York City junior high school for deaf students, the graphics arts teacher developed Fingerprints Press, a student-run business that uses computers to produce sign-language products. Staff members are severely hearing impaired, and some have other disabilities as well. Through this venture, these students achieve success, overcome communication limitations, work cooperatively, and gain valuable life experiences (Holzberg, 1993). In Michigan, students with severe emotional problems are developing multimedia autobiographies. For some, this is their first-ever success in school. Completed projects are videotaped to send home for parents to see. In Illinois, learning disabled and emotionally disturbed children have become turned on to desktop video production using microcomputers. Holzberg describes several other "special education" success stories that are worth reading about.

Bunescu (1990) termed *adaptive technology* the great equalizer for individuals with physical disabilities. She described software to modify the layout or functioning of the keyboard; software to simplify input by expanding abbreviations into full text or predicting the next words to come; alternative keyboards; devices that substitute for the keyboard's functions; voice input; and hardware cards that provide adaptations. Sources for various products are given. Other significant adaptive devices include speech synthesizers, special input devices (from simple touch screens to complex apparatus to overcome motor impairments), software to enlarge images on the screen, Braille printers, and so on.

The role of computers for individuals with special needs is a subject large enough for entire books and courses. We have only highlighted a few possibilities. For more information, consult the chapter bibliography. The appendix lists suppliers of adaptive resources.

Budgetary Potpourri

The subject of money rears its ugly head. Of course, there is never enough of it. So what can a school do?

Funding

In describing schools that had made extensive commitments to technology, McCarthy (1993) noted the following funding sources: the local school board, bank loans, and converting regular classes into lab classes to obtain increased state funding. Although far from plentiful, outside funding is sometimes possible as well. Companies often donate equipment, rather than cash, for innovative, creative applications. Among the oldest programs are:

Tandy Educational Grants Program, One Tandy Center, Fort Worth, TX 76102.
Apple Education Grants, Apple Computer Inc., 20525 Mariani Avenue, Cupertino, CA 95014.

Local businesses, parent-teacher organizations, area foundations, and district foundations have all assisted schools to acquire educational technology. You'll never know what could be unless you ask.

Allocating Available Funds

The budget should be driven by the technology plan in a given school. It is important to avoid common errors of the past. In the absence of a sound plan, the computer budget has often been like personal savings—consisting of what, if any, funds are "left over." This is an inadequate approach even for the short term and, clearly, contrary to any long-term vision. Kinnaman (1992) proposed that schools allocate at least five percent of the total budget to technology support for the classroom. As he commented, "(F)ive percent is an awfully small price to pay for guaranteed school improvement."

However the budget is set, many schools have spent virtually all of their money on hardware. This is a serious error that ignores the essential need for software, staff development, maintenance, supplies, and even support materials such as computer books and relevant journals. Even a first-year budget should allocate *no more than fifty percent to hardware*, perhaps *twenty percent to software*, and *at least twenty percent for staff development*. The remaining ten percent may cover supplies and other items, excluding salaries. If major hardware purchases are made one year, other budget categories could well increase in the next. These figures are not absolutes, of course, just guidelines to emphasize the significance of nonhardware components, which are often overlooked.

Another common error has been to view the computer budget as a one-time or short-term allocation. In fact, computers in the curriculum mean serious financial commitments every year. Proportions may change, but there will be ongoing needs for hardware repair and replacement, software updating and replacement, new peripherals, and so on (Finkel, 1993). To ignore these needs can doom the technology implementation effort (Moursund, April 1987).

Stretching the Hardware Budget

Since all budgets are inadequate by definition, how can you get the most out of what you have? Shop smart! Always look for educational discounts. Even in the highly competitive price market today, schools should still be able to buy computers at lower prices than the general public does. Teachers often can get school prices for personal purchases, too.

The widespread availability of MS-DOS compatible computers called *clones* has forced major producers from Compaq to IBM to Zenith to introduce low-cost lines and even to sell by direct mail. Desire for a low price need not preclude purchasing a name brand, although top-of-the-line equipment is rarely necessary in schools. Look for bargain clones, and then compare their features to low-end products from the large firms. Brand name quality may be worth the difference. Watch for the arrival of Macintosh clones. While not a certainty, if this occurs, it is likely to lead to cost savings, just as happened with MS-DOS systems.

Since hardware purchases are part of a long-term plan, don't be shortsighted. It often costs relatively little more to purchase computers with more RAM and larger capacity hard disks than you think you need. Next year, you'll be glad you did, since upgrades later tend to cost more than initial enhancements. Finally, many vendors offer system bundles, adding peripherals or software at less than normal cost, which can be excellent buys for schools.

Stretching the Software Budget

Competition is fierce for software sales as well as hardware. Unless a product is sold only by its producer, you should be able to buy it for twenty to forty percent less than "list price." Educational pricing exists for software as well as hardware. Some companies such as WordPerfect, Claris, and IBM offer their own educational prices, either directly or through dealers. A few companies specialize in heavy discounts to educators on major software products. The appendix has addresses for Campus Technology Products, Chambers International, and Diskovery Educational Systems.

Does your need warrant heavy-duty, "professional" software such as Microsoft *Word*, or Aldus *PageMaker*? Full products can get very costly when you need many copies for a school. Some producers, such as Lotus, have special educational packaging or somewhat downgraded versions at far below the full-product price. Consider also the suitability of modestly priced integrated packages such as Microsoft *Works* or *ClarisWorks*. Try out low-end desktop publishing products such as Microsoft *Publisher*. The expensive products often contain many features that you'll never use, making them needlessly complicated for use in a school. Why pay for what you don't need?

Shareware is software that its creator distributes on a "try it and pay me if you like it" basis. It is widely available from user groups, through computer bulletin boards and services such as CompuServe and by mail from specialized companies. The latter charge a service fee for copying and mailing the diskettes. Sometimes you get the full version, and sometimes only a limited trial version. The developer requests a registration fee, often less than $50, which gets you the latest full version, printed documentation, perhaps the next upgrade, and/or other benefits. There is a lot of good shareware that could meet some school needs at very low cost. Shareware sources may also offer *public domain* software that you are free to use without further payment or registration.

Additional Implementation Resources

There are many resources available to help educators plan and implement computers in their schools. We suggest Batey (1988), Collis (1988), and Solomon (1988) as good reading. The International Society for Technology in Education publishes the series *Computer Integrated Instruction: Effective Inservice*. Five volumes cover integration, elementary schools, and secondary math, science, and social studies. Each includes a disk with files of inservice materials that you can modify. ISTE also offers a complete *Restructuring Toolkit*.

A truly unique resource for curriculum integration is EPIE's Integrated Instructional Information Resource (IIIR). IIIR is a database of detailed information about textbooks, software, instructional TV programs, and tests, along with specific strategies for integrating these resources into your teaching. In EPIE's terms, the goal is curriculum alignment, bringing all possible resources to bear on educational needs. Contact EPIE (see appendix) for more information.

Summary

This chapter considered one view of computer implementation history through the 1980s. The initial goal of mass participation by teachers in the computer revolution now appears naive. The impact of computers in schools has been less than anticipated for several reasons that you read. The 1990s demand a new direction to re-target the educational benefits of computers.

The goal remains invisible integration of computers into the curriculum, leading to student competence to apply the computer to whatever tasks may be appropriate. Only some teachers are now prepared to implement computers, and others may join them only slowly. Within that context, you considered issues and ideas for staff development, hardware, physical facilities, budgets, and the need for articulation.

A more thorough consideration of implementation issues exceeds the scope of this book. It is also beyond the immediate need of someone relatively new to educational computing. As your involvement matures, perhaps this initial exposure to some of the issues will come to mind again and lead you into more extensive resources as needed.

Chapter 19 Activities

1. Interview teachers and/or administrators who were involved early in their school's implementation of computers. How do their experiences compare to our "history?"
2. Contact local school districts to learn about their technology plans. Request copies of written plans and other documents (such as the district mission statement) that refer to computers. Contact the National Center for Technology Planning (College of Education Dean's Office, Mississippi State University, Box 5365, Mississippi State, MS 39762) if you lack local resources. Analyze what you obtain.
3. State and defend a position on the question of whether *all* teachers should be involved in computer implementation.
4. Based on your knowledge and views, articulate the most compelling reasons why teachers do not use computers. Try to interview several nonusers to explore their reasons.
5. Propose a staff-development plan congruent with activities 3 and 4 above.
6. Interview persons experienced with computer labs and mobile or room-based computers. Synthesize our commentary and their experiences.
7. Outline a plan for computer usage in a one-computer classroom.

Bibliography

Balajthy, E. "Evaluation of a Pre-Service Training Module in Microcomputer Applications for the Teaching of Reading." *Computers in the Schools*, 1988, 5(1/2), pp. 113–128.

Batey, A., (Ed). *Planning for Computers in Education*. Portland, OR: Northwest Regional Educational Laboratory, 1988.

Becker, H. *Microcomputers in the Classroom. Dreams and Realities*. Eugene, OR: International Council for Computers in Education, undated.

Bell, T. H. "Teaching and Technology. (On Education.)" *School and College*, November 1992, 31(11), p. 6.

Bitter, G. "Computer Labs—Fads?" *Electronic Education*, May/June 1985, pp. 17, 35.

Borrell, J. "America's Shame: How We've Abandoned Our Children's Future." *MacWorld*, September 1992, pp. 25–30.

Bracey, G. "New Pathways. Technology's Empowering Influence on Teaching. (Research)." *Electronic Learning*, April 1993 (Special Edition), 12(7), pp. 8–9.

Bracey, G. W. "Two Studies Show Students Gain When Teaming Up." *Electronic Learning*, January 1988, p. 19.

Brady, H. "Who Will Rebuild America's Schools?" *Technology & Learning*, September 1992, 13(1), pp. 52–57.

Bruder, I. "Future Teachers: Are They Prepared?" *Electronic Learning,* January/February 1989, *8*(4), pp. 32–39.

Bruder, I. "Restructuring: The Central Kitsap Experience." *Electronic Learning,* October 1990, *10*(2), pp. 16–19.

Bruder, I. "School Reform: Why You Need Technology." *Electronic Learning,* May/June 1992, *11*(8), pp. 22–28.

Bunescu, M. "Adaptive Technology." *Electronic Learning,* October 1990, *10*(2), pp. 20–22.

Collis, B. *Computers, Curriculum, and Whole-Class Instruction.* Belmont, CA: Wadsworth, 1988.

Collis, B. "Research Windows." *The Computing Teacher,* August/September 1988, pp. 6–7.

Collis, B. "Research Windows." *The Computing Teacher,* December/January 1988–1989, p. 7.

Computer Applications Planning. Chelmsford, MA: Merrimack Education Center, 1984.

DeLoughry, T. J. "Crucial Role Seen for Technology in Meeting Higher Education's Challenges." *Chronicle of Higher Education,* 23 September 1992, pp. A21–A22.

Finkel, L. "Planning for Obsolescence." *Electronic Learning,* April 1993, *12*(7), pp. 18–19.

Fisher, G. "Developing a District-Wide Computer-Use Plan." *The Computing Teacher,* January 1983, pp. 52–59.

Friedman, D. "I Like Computers But They Don't Like Me." *Electronic Education,* September 1985, pp. 14–15.

Fullan, M. G., Miles, M. G., and Anderson, S. E. *Strategies for Implementing Microcomputers in Schools: The Ontario Case.* Toronto: Ontario Ministry of Education, 1987.

Glasser, W. "Quality: The Key to the Disciplines." *National Forum,* Winter 1989, pp. 36–38.

Holzberg, C. S. "Special Education Success Stories." *Technology & Learning.* January 1993, *13*(4), pp. 53–56.

Kearsley, G., and Lynch, W. "Educational Leadership in the Age of Technology: The New Skills." *Journal of Research on Computing in Education,* Fall 1992, *25*(1), pp. 50–60.

Kelman, P. "Alternatives to Integrated Instructional Systems." In Cannings, T. R. and Finkel, L., (Eds.), *The Technology Age Classroom.* Wilsonville, OR: Franklin, Beedle & Associates, 1993.

Kephart, D. A., and Friedman, J. E. "Integrating Technology for At-Risk Students." *Computers in the Schools,* 1991, *8*(1/2/3), pp. 215–218.

Kinnaman, D. E. "LCD Panels: The Next Generation." *Technology & Learning,* March 1993a, *13*(6), pp. 44–50.

Kinnaman, D. E. "Buying Hardware: How to Avoid Mistakes. (The Leadership Role)." *Technology & Learning,* March 1993b, *13*(6), pp. 59–60.

Kinnaman, D. E. "Making Professional Development Pay Off." *Technology & Learning,* January 1993, *13*(4), pp. 51–52.

Kinnaman, D. E. "A Clear Vision and a Five-Percent Commitment." *School and College,* October 1992, *31*(10), pp. 19–20.

Klein, K., and Strothers, D., (Eds.). *Planning for Microcomputers in the Curriculum.* Bloomington, IN: Phi Delta Kappa, Hot Topics Series 1983–1984.

Komoski, P. K. *Educational Technology: The Closing-In or the Opening-Out of Curriculum and Instruction.* Syracuse, NY: ERIC/IR, Syracuse University, 1987. Document IR-77.

Komoski, P. K. "Beyond Innovation: The Systemic Integration of Technology into the Curriculum." *Educational Technology,* September 1987, pp. 21–25.

Knupfer, N. N. "Teachers' Beliefs about Instructional Computing: Implications for Instructional Designers." *Journal of Instructional Development,* 1988, *11*(4), pp. 29–38.

Lengel, J. G. *Computer Considerations for Vermont Schools.* Burlington, VT: Vermont Department of Education, 1983.

Mathinos, D. A., and Woodward, A. "The Status of Instructional Computing in an Elementary Schools: Removing Those Rose-Colored Glasses." In Collis, B., (Ed.), "Research Windows." *The Computing Teacher*, December/January 1988–1989, p. 8.

McCarthy, R. "A Computer on Every Teacher's Desk." *Electronic Learning*, April 1993 (Special Edition), *12*(7), pp. 10–14.

McCarthy, R. "Making the Future Work." Electronic Learning, September 1988, pp. 42–46.

Morton, L. L., and Thibodeau, B. D. "Lab-Based Word Processing for the Learning-Disabled." *Computers in the Schools*, 1991, *8*(1/2/3), pp. 225–228.

Moursund, D. *The Technology Coordinator*. Eugene, OR: ISTE, 1992.

Moursund, D. "Long-Range Planning." *The Computing Teacher*, April 1987, pp.4–5.

Plomp, T., Steerneman, A., and Pelgrum, W. J. "Curriculum Changes as a Consequence of Computer Use." In Collis, B., (Ed.), "Research Windows." *The Computing Teacher*, December/January 1988–1989, p. 8.

Pogrow, S. "How To Use Computers to Truly Enhance Learning." *Electronic Learning*, May/June 1988, pp. 6–8.

Preskill, H. "Teachers and Computers: A Staff Development Challenge." *Educational Technology*, March 1988, pp. 24–26.

Reigeluth, C. M. "The Imperative for Systemic Change." *Educational Technology*, November 1992, *32*(11), pp. 9–12.

Roblyer, M. D., Castine, W. H., and King, F. J. "Assessing the Impact of Computer-Based Instruction." *Computers in the Schools*, 1988, *5*(3/4).

Solomon, C. *Computer Environments for Children*. Cambridge, MA: MIT Press, 1988.

Staff. "Two at a Terminal? Cooperative Learning and Computers." *The ASSIST Journal*, 1988, Issue 1, p. 7.

Stieglitz, E. L., and Costa, C. H. "A Statewide Teacher Training Program's Impact on Computer Usage in the Schools." *Computers in the Schools* 1988, *5*(1/2), pp. 91–98.

"Update: The Latest Technology Trends in the Schools." *Technology & Learning*, February 1993, 13(5), pp. 28–32.

U.S. Congress, Office of Technology Assessment. *Power On! New Tools for Teaching and Learning*. OTA-SET-379. Washington, DC: Government Printing Office, September 1988.

Objectives

After completing this chapter, you will be able to:

Discuss several ways in which computers are affecting the world of work.

Synthesize several issues related to computers and personal privacy.

Explain four areas of concern related to ethics.

Evaluate the issues of gender and socioeconomic equity in computer access and propose responses to them.

Explain and assess changes occurring in the traditional educational roles of teachers, students, and parents because of computer technology.

Chapter 20

Issues and Implications

Too often, considerations of computers in education are so totally positive as to appear naive. Many educators seem content to accept blindly whatever fate technology brings to them, never questioning, never wondering. The bandwagon continues to move and pick up riders.

The computer does not deserve such blind devotion. Rather, the entire course of computerization of our society should be closely scrutinized. It is difficult to argue against the claim that society is already so computerized that there is no turning back. By now it should be obvious that we have no wish to turn back. However, greater attention to the impact of computers on our lives may serve to better guide the course of future progress.

This chapter, then, is devoted to considering some of the major issues and implications raised by computers in society and, within it, education. It is critical that computer education programs not neglect these issues. We do not claim to provide answers but, rather, seek to alert you to the issues and the need to consider them personally and with students.

Social Issues

Within the broad category of social issues, we will look at the impact of computers on the world of work and on personal privacy. The underlying concern is what computers are doing to individuals and thus to society.

Impact on Work

Major works such as *Megatrends* and *Powershift* have popularized the concept that society has moved past the Industrial Age. The most common terms applied to the present are the Information Age or the Information Society. Some believe the transformation has occurred; others see it as under way, but far from complete. These are mostly semantic differences. A major "product" of today's workforce is indeed information.

The Work Force

Bozeman (1985, p. 173) pointed out some of the changes that have occurred in the workforce. Farmers have dwindled from some thirty-five percent of the work force in 1900 to less than three percent. From over fifty percent in the 1930s to 1950s, the percentage of persons involved in production of goods has fallen to ten percent. Of some twenty million new jobs created in the 1970s, nearly ninety percent were information- or service-related. What are some of the ramifications of these changes that should be considered?

The labor movement developed from concerns over working conditions in industry. Traditional union strongholds, such as the automobile industry and mining, employ far fewer persons than at the peak of union strength. Membership is down accordingly; robots in factories are not potential union members.

What is the future of labor unions? What will be the rallying cries among information workers, if they become unionized? What are the new labor issues in the Information Age? What will become of persons displaced by technology? Technology may create more jobs than it destroys, but not for the same people, or at comparable wage levels.

Perhaps retraining of workers is the answer. Some question whether the present work force can be retrained for new responsibilities. Is there any incentive for industry to retrain older workers if younger people are available with the needed skills? Is it possible that we are approaching an era when blue-collar workers in their 40s and 50s will become permanently unemployable?

Where One Works

Particularly in urban areas, it has become common for people to spend a great amount of time just getting to and from work. Expressway systems become parking lots at 7 A.M. and 5 P.M.; mass transit, where it exists, is crowded. For some years now, this waste of potentially productive human time has been of concern. It was clear in the age of factories that the worker had to go to the factory. Is this still true in information industries?

Technologically, we have long had the potential for employees in certain kinds of jobs to work from their homes via telecommunications. A computer and a modem can link a home office to the "physical" job site. What would it mean if large numbers of workers were no longer required to be physically "on the job?" What would this mean for family life at home? What would it mean for the real estate industry if huge office complexes were no longer needed? How would you like to work alone at home rather than with other people? Past experiments with working from home have tended to founder on the lack of socialization with others. Is this likely to change?

Health/Safety Issues

Concerns over possible physical side-effects of prolonged exposure to computers, particularly monitors, have been raised many times since the early days of computers. Eye fatigue, for instance, can be caused by poorly located monitors, inappropriate eyeglass prescriptions, and other factors. Radiation produced by electronic equipment may also have health implications that are as yet unclear (Stern and Stern, 1993). In the face of inconclusive medical evidence, the Swedish government has imposed on computer monitors standards for emissions, for instance, that are far stricter than most other nations'. Related are concerns over posture-induced back problems brought on by long hours seated at a computer.

Other issues include the toxicity of chemicals used in chip manufacturing, the problems of proper disposal of old equipment, even the trade-offs between the environmental impacts of, say, paper production and those of using computers to reduce or eliminate paper flow in businesses (Nichols and Welliver, 1991). Students should be challenged to investigate and consider all sides of such concerns.

Personal Privacy

Computers have permitted corporations, government, and other groups to create data banks on a scale previously undreamed of. How wonderful it may be to be able to make a purchase anywhere in the world by credit card, which the merchant can instantly verify. How nice to be able to write a personal check in a distant city because the store can quickly determine if the check will clear. For all the convenience, these things are possible only because somewhere a computer has a lot of information on file concerning you and your finances. How willingly would you share such information with strangers, if they simply asked you for it?

Law-enforcement officials in many areas can learn a great deal about you almost instantly by entering your automobile license number or driver's license number into a computer terminal, even a portable one in a squad car. The benefits of such a system are enormous in crime prevention, but what are the less benign possibilities?

Westin (cited in Bozeman, 1985, p. 169) defined the essence of personal privacy as "the claim of an individual to determine what information about himself or herself should be known to others. This also involves when such information will be communicated or obtained, and what uses will be made of it by others." Have we already passed the point where personal privacy can be maintained?

Do you consider the ramifications of filling out a credit card application? Of responding to information requested for a city directory? Of applying for a job? Of subscribing to a magazine or completing a "marketing survey" that comes in the mail? All of these things provide data about you to others.

Data banks have been around for a long time, first on paper, then as computer files. The remote access potential of the latter is a major source of concern. Even if you are not concerned about improper use of personal data by those who gathered it, what about use by persons who obtain access to data banks without authority? The newspapers regularly report on the latest cases of "computer invasion." Is there such a thing as a secure computer system, where only those duly authorized and strictly supervised can gain access to your information? Evidence suggests there is not.

Other electronic wonders are creating trails of information on individuals as never before. Consider the use of automatic teller machines and other systems for electronically transferring funds. All transactions must be fully documented, which means a paper trail possibly open to misuse, though its intent is the opposite. As electronic mail becomes more common, there may be a concern for the privacy of one's written communication. Or is this really any more of a problem than the possibility of someone opening and reading your letters now?

It is not our desire to cause outbreaks of paranoia over the privacy issue. We have yet to see evidence of problems so severe as to bring the entire system into question. However, the issue is one that requires continual scrutiny. Students must become aware of the situation and become part of a monitoring system to insist that necessary laws, standards, or policies are implemented to protect personal rights. (See Mandell and Mandell, 1989; and Stern and Stern, 1993.)

Ethics

According to Hamilton (cited in Bitter, 1984, p. 293), "Today's computer is intellectually a moron, and morally permissive. Provided it is instructed in a language it understands and is programmed to receive the instructions, it will do as it is told whether this be right or wrong."

With the widespread availability of computers have come significant problems in ethical, and even legal, behavior. It is interesting to speculate on what permits individuals who otherwise might never cross the legal line beyond overtime parking to alter their behavior with computers. Is it somehow another effect of computers on individuals? What makes the situation sufficiently different from others to affect moral behavior? Let's consider four areas: software piracy, hacking, viruses, and computer crime.

Software Piracy

The cost of software development is enormous for high-quality, complex products. Copyright law seeks to protect the rights of software producers to profit from sales of their products. Few individuals seem inclined to violate copyright law by making copies of whole books or films, yet many think nothing of "pirating" copies of software for themselves or friends in violation of the law and the license agreement that was part of the software purchase.

While there can be some confusion because of differences in software licenses, in general, you are entitled to use only a single copy of the software you purchase, while storing a backup copy for use in case the working copy is damaged (Maddux, Johnson, and Willis, 1992). Any other use is illegal unless explicitly permitted by the license agreement. Salpeter (1992) and Talab (1992) provide more extensive discussions of copyright and schools.

Software piracy exists among very young computer users as well as adults. To some extent, it falls to teachers to deal with the issue, preferably as a matter of ethics and practical ramifications rather than as a major legal concern. The fact is that few casual pirates are apt to be prosecuted; apprehension is simply too difficult. However, corporations and even schools have been targeted for prosecution. For example, in 1991 the University of Oregon was charged with copying software illegally (Wilson, 1991). Many companies have paid substantial fines for not controlling software usage (see Todd, 1991).

In 1992, the Software Publishers Association released a short video for educators to use with their students. Entitled "Don't Copy That Floppy," the video uses a rap music format to present its message of both the legal and practical aspects of software piracy. Every school should have a copy of this video and show it to all students with computer access. Weller et al. (1992) offer other sound suggestions for dealing with this issue.

We believe that potential software pirates first must understand that their actions are in fact as much larceny as is shoplifting. Many now attach no such stigma to copying a diskette. As soon as children are old enough to learn to duplicate a diskette, they should be taught the legal issues of piracy.

Second, computer users also must become aware of the magnitude of the piracy problem. Stern and Stern (1993, p. 527) report estimates that there may be ten pirated copies of a program for every copy sold! Mandell and Mandell (1989) reported speculation that as much as fifty percent of software *in schools* may be pirated copies. Aldus Corporation estimated its own losses at $47 million per year (Blake, 1991), while the Software Publishers Association put the annual loss total at $535 million for Macintosh software and $1.9 billion for MS-DOS software (Gerstein, 1991). Small wonder the level of concern runs so high.

Third, educators must consider the by-products of piracy. Teachers have long had a less than pristine image among publishers because they have always been "borrowers" of materials. Perceptions of "fair use" have been extended to cover copying virtually anything. Software may appear to be just the latest source of "free" materials. Yet recall that it is economic gain, not altruism, that drives the software industry. Piracy could reduce the choices we all have in educational materials if companies do not succeed financially.

Obviously, school budgets are limited, while the potential demand for software grows daily. Limited school budgets cannot justify piracy. Producers must help find ways to meet legitimate concerns of educators over the cost of the multiple software copies required to remain within the law. In turn, educators *must be role models* for their students. There is no place for pirated software in a school. Budgets must allocate appropriate amounts for software as well as hardware.

The International Society for Technology in Education has published a statement on copyright ("1987 Statement on Software Copyright", 1987) and a code of ethics ("Code of Ethical Conduct," 1987). Educators who use computers should be thoroughly familiar with both documents. They are reproducible for distribution or for use with students. Another guide to ethical and legal software use is available from ERIC ("Using Software," 1987).

Hackers

A somewhat peculiar offspring of the computer age is the hacker. A hacker is usually a young person who is totally caught up in working with a computer, often to the exclusion of other activities. Such people are typically very skilled programmers. With telecommunication access to computers around the world, hackers delight in finding ways around the security checks of systems so that they can just "browse" through a computer's files. Many also use illegal means to avoid long distance telephone charges.

Some hacking can almost be understood as youthful exuberance, a sense of power over mechanical objects. At least at the start, hackers are rarely malicious. However, hacking has led to unauthorized access to government and corporate computers and the changing or destruction of data in them. Cases have been publicly reported of records being altered in hospital files, which could mean harm to patients. Thus, what may have begun as "play" can become deadly serious. Initially, hackers were treated as curiosities and generally escaped punishment, often because of their youth (Seymour, 1990). However, prison sentences are possible ("Computer Hacker," 1989).

Just as schools must bear some responsibility for educating youngsters about software piracy, so, too, they must address the issue of unauthorized entry into a computer system. Elliott (1990) and Markoff and Hafner (1991) offer fascinating looks into the subculture of hackers and other "cyberpunks."

Viruses

Physicians often diagnose an illness as a virus—a submicroscopic agent that causes disease. Today a different virus is receiving attention: the computer virus. A *computer virus* is typically a small program planned and written specifically to cause mischief or damage to computer systems. A virus enters a computer's software where it remains undetected and inactive until a specific date or particular set of conditions occur. At that point it becomes activated and begins its malicious task: perhaps denying access to users, deleting or altering files, or possibly reformatting disks. Some viruses reproduce themselves, taking up more and more memory and/or disk space until they cause the system to crash (Stern and Stern, 1993, p. 526).

In 1989, new viruses were appearing at a rate of four per year. By mid-1991, a new virus was detected every day ("A Virus Epidemic," 1991). Even major newspaper columnists such as Jack Anderson now report outbreaks of viruses (see Anderson and Van Atta, 1991). Viruses often travel with software downloaded from bulletin boards. They then pass from individual to individual as that software is shared. Bulletin board operators are increasingly likely to screen their files. Commercial vendors occasionally have distributed infected software, and the producers of antivirus software are themselves not immune (McCormick, 1991). The best defense against viruses is to be cautious about the source of your software and to obtain and use antivirus software, some of which is available free. Given the rate of appearance of new viruses, the latter cannot be perfect, even though many such products are updated at least monthly. Still, they seem to provide protection against the viruses most common in schools and among typical home computer users.

Computer Crime

Although piracy and hacking are crimes, they are often viewed as less serious than other computer crimes. There is no realm of our existence that is totally free from the potential for crime within it. The computer has merely presented new avenues for criminal conduct, what Scrogan (1988) referred to as the "online underground."

One type of computer crime is fraud, such as improper transfer of funds among accounts or electronic creation of phony assets (Stern and Stern, 1993). Thefts include both computer time (using your employer's computer for personal purposes) and actual theft of data, possibly to sell or hold for ransom. Disgruntled employees and former employees have been known to tamper with a company's computer system. This has led to the seemingly harsh practice of having security staff *immediately* accompany from the premises any employee who has been fired, thereby eliminating further access to the computer.

It is unfortunate that the computer age has spawned its own contributions to criminality, but hardly surprising. As more individuals come into regular contact with computer systems, the potential for such abuses seems to grow naturally. In addition, the frailties of computer security are major contributors to the problem, as well as intriguing challenges to the dishonest. Students must confront the potential for computer crime and, as with piracy, be helped to see that there are no modern-day Robin Hoods in the computer world. Theft is theft, regardless of the method.

Concern for computer ethics is not new. The August/September 1984 issue of *The Computer Teacher* focused on ethics. More recently, the Summer 1991 issue of *National Forum* includes several articles related to the themes of this chapter. There is no shortage of resources if you wish to investigate these issues in greater depth.

Equity

Although you have just considered some of the darker sides of computing, on balance computers have been highly beneficial. However, equity of access to their benefits is an issue of grave concern. In 1984, Pantiel and Petersen (p. 170) wrote, "Probably the most critical question of the decade is whether computers are going to be available to everyone." That question remains unanswered a decade later. According to McGrath et al. (1992, p. 468), inequities in computer access have two implications. "First, the students affected will be educationally handicapped by the lack of powerful learning tools. . . . Second, these students may find themselves at a disadvantage in their preparation for their future academic careers or jobs. . . . " Let's consider two aspects of equity: gender and socioeconomics.

Gender

Many studies have documented that girls are not involved in computing to an appropriate extent given the importance of computers to their futures. Girls are far less likely to participate in elective computer activities than boys, whether in courses or at camps. Female interest begins to lag in middle school and continues from there. Girls exhibit greater anxiety about computers and less confidence. Yet when they do participate, girls perform as well as boys. (See McGrath et al., 1992, for greater detail.)

There are many possible explanations for this gender gap. Computer advertising may be directed more toward males, unless a secretary is shown (Demetrulias and Rosenthal, 1985). Girls are less attracted to shoot-'em-up video games than boys are (Linn, 1985; Hess and Miura, 1985). Computers tend to be identified with math and science, both of which have been male dominated rather than throughout the curriculum (Rosenthal and Demetrulias, 1988; Swadener and Hannafin, 1987). If computers are introduced in elementary grades, interest is comparable between boys and girls, but if the introduction is in the middle school, girls become more passive (Flake, McClintock, and Turner, 1985). According to Collis (1988), females may be less confident with computers because of male dominance of computer labs, perceived irrelevance of school computer offerings to girls' interests, preference for cooperative rather than competitive work, and teachers who accept assumptions that girls are less interested and less capable than boys.

Having reviewed many other studies along these lines, McGrath et al. (1992) attempted to intervene among rural girls before they reached the age of choosing not to participate in computing. The researchers trained rural middle school teachers in both computer education and strategies for gender equity. Back in the classroom, the teachers demonstrated increased computer competence and equity awareness and strategies. However, any ultimate impact will be apparent only among the students in later years.

Educators clearly must guard against gender inequities. Perhaps the best approach is awareness of the issue along with full curriculum integration at all grade levels.

Socioeconomics

The economic side of equity has nothing to do with computers per se and everything to do with the way American schools are organized and funded. Computers only call further attention to the fact that schools in the United States are anything but equal. Inequities affect everything from basic supplies such as paper and pencils to library resources and even the quality of teachers. The computer era may focus attention on the problems; it did not create them.

Student access to computers in school is likely to be linked to the economics of the community or attendance district, which, in turn, is often linked to racial balance. In 1984 the computer usage rate for white children in the elementary through secondary grades was about double that of black and Hispanic children, but it evened out by 1989, according to the Census Bureau, because of massive spending on technology (Piller, 1992). However, when the researcher visited schools, he concluded that poor schools had neither the skills nor funds to maintain their computers and lacked training and support to use them effectively. Affluent schools were more likely to hire teaches who are comfortable with their new role in a computer classroom as a collaborator "negotiating the technological labyrinth." The situation is illustrated by a very poor district in Miami that has many computers but does little with them, while the far wealthier Coral Gables schools have fewer computers, but use them extensively and creatively.

Beyond school, children and teachers in impoverished districts are less likely to have a computer at home (Piller, 1992; Stone, 1987). The potential for home reinforcement of learning is, therefore, absent. Piller also noted that poor schools tend to focus computer use on basic skills and as a reward for good behavior, while affluent schools are more likely to create richly inventive, discovery environments.

The concern reduces to the potential to add to the economic disparities of the country a further gulf between the technological haves and have-nots (Dutton, Sweet, and Rogers, 1989). Given the power and benefit of computers in education, how can equitable access be achieved? Or will computers only increase the separation of those who are adequately prepared to compete in the employment marketplace from those who are not? What does this do to the significance of public education?

Equity is a major social issue, not just an educational issue. A solution is far beyond the local teacher and school, but Stone (1986, 1986–1987) has offered many practical suggestions worthy of consideration. The equity issue must concern educators, however small their individual contribution toward a solution may be. The chapter bibliography includes additional readings on this topic.

Changing Roles

Teachers

Chapter 19 considered some of the issues related to staff development. Teacher training is surely the single greatest obstacle to integration of computers into education. Teachers need to acquire new content knowledge and computing skills. How can this be achieved?

Eventually, computer education will be part of teacher-preparation curricula. New teachers will enter the profession with the needed skills. For the far larger number of teachers whose preparation did not include computer skills training, the only familiar option is continuing education. Neither of these solutions comes close to the level of implementation that could make a profound difference. Further advances will take time, but there is already resistance from those who are unfamiliar with the educational potential of microcomputers.

But what of the teacher's classroom role? This goes beyond knowledge and skills to altered behavior. As computers enable the individualization of instruction that educators have longed for, the role of the teacher must change from dispenser of knowledge to facilitator and guide through the learning process. Teachers must help students learn how to learn and how to use their electronic tools effectively. They need to become guides to the vast resources available to their students.

For the foreseeable future, many teachers will have to accept the fact that some of their students know far more about computers than they do. This is difficult for many teachers to accept, yet the problem is almost solely the teacher's. Few students are bothered if asked to help the teacher with something on the computer. Rather, it can be an interesting contribution to the student's emerging self-image to be able to do things that an adult can't.

In addition, teachers must recognize the time demands that arise from using computers. The time involved in selecting appropriate courseware was discussed in Chapter 11. Examining materials and planning group lessons that utilize them takes more time than skimming a text book chapter. Teachers may have to develop support materials, as well as ways to monitor and assess student progress. Such familiar activities will require teachers to spend time at the computer, rather than being able to mull them over at lunch or while driving. Teaching with computers is more demanding than traditional teaching. Are you ready to accept the challenge?

For an extensive, thought-provoking discussion of the role of the teacher in the computer era, see Ragsdale (1988).

Students

The role of the student is also changing in the Information Age. The exponential growth of knowledge and information makes it impossible for students to "learn" everything they will need in their lives. Rather, they must learn how to obtain, manipulate, and assess the relevance of information from the multitude of resources at their disposal.

Today's younger students are growing up with computers as a natural part of their lives. They do not view them as something unusual, but simply as a normal tool for daily living. The promise of computers for students is that they are being "acted upon" less by the educational process and becoming more active shapers of their own growth and development. This is well illustrated by the experiences of students with hypermedia and databases, to single out just two examples. Students are confronting their world differently than their parents did. They are becoming more sophisticated problem solvers and have new opportunities to develop thinking skills. These are essential life skills of the Information Age.

At the same time, educators dare not lose sight of the fact that living is more than just information management. However sophisticated students become in using computers for the "mechanical" side of life, they must still develop interpersonal and social skills to cope with "human" concerns. The educational system may be able to devote far less time to traditional instructional concerns, but it dare not abdicate responsibility for assisting in the development of the complete human being. It is in this area that the personal touch will never be lost (Ragsdale, 1988, pp. 159–186).

Parents

The traditional role of parents in educating children is also changing. This has been nearly the total responsibility of the schools in the past, with parents providing encouragement and perhaps some help with homework. Computers are altering this role (Ragsdale, 1988, pp. 209–224).

To really allow the microcomputer to become an effective partner in the educational process, not only must the teacher become familiar with its effective use, but parents similarly should become familiar with microcomputer educational usage. This need for parent education may be a considerably more difficult problem than present or future teacher preparation, but it is nonetheless important if the microcomputer is to reach its full potential in our educational system.

Many families have already brought a computer into the home, opening up new possibilities for learning. More will follow in coming years. In those homes where parents are themselves computer-competent, they will be able to assist their children in new ways. They may, however, be unprepared for the task of selecting computer learning materials for home use, as material selection has long been a school responsibility. Educators should consider establishing ways of assisting parents in this task.

Even greater problems loom for parents who perceive a need for a computer at home but are strangers to the technology themselves. Just as the new math caused many difficulties for parents seeking to help their children, so too may computers, probably to an even greater extent. Again, we see a role for the schools to play in developing computer competence in parents through adult education programs.

Computers in the home raise new fears of educational equity, an issue touched upon previously. Just as differences in school budgets are contributing to a potential widening of the gap between the haves and have nots, so too may technology in the home (Stone, 1987). Some districts have addressed this issue by providing parents the opportunity to borrow computers for home use. This is a concept worthy of serious consideration.

Summary

In this chapter we have sought to identify and provide perspective on issues arising from the spread of computers throughout society. Consideration of such issues is a critical component of any computer education program, however difficult it is to address.

The social impact of computers requires careful attention, lest we awaken too late to changes that profoundly affect our lives. Educators must guide their students in thinking about all aspects of the computer's impact on where and how we work, and our personal privacy. Computers have come to pervade society today with little thought given to their effects on individuals. It is not too late to develop a critical stance.

Schools must take a leading role in developing understanding of ethics related to computers. The earliest and most obvious area of concern is software piracy. By example and by teaching, computer users must learn that software is property, which is protected both legally and ethically. Attention to this matter should begin in the early grades. Somewhat later, students should be exposed to concerns over abuse of computer systems, ranging from seemingly innocent "hacking" to full-scale computer crime and the release of computer viruses.

Major concerns for education and society arise from the issues of equity. While the computer as an educational tool offers genuine potential to benefit all students, economic reality suggests that not all will have access to it. How should this problem be approached? In addition, where computers are readily available, concerns exist over use of them by both sexes. To the extent that computers are now more of a "male" experience, what should and can be done to correct the imbalance?

Computer educators also must guard against the danger that students will come to see the computer as the answer to all concerns. We must learn *when* and *when not* to use the computer, and *how* to use it wisely. Thoughtless acceptance of computer output could be enormously harmful.

Finally, the computer is having a significant effect on the educational roles of teachers, students, and parents. To produce the most positive outcome, these changes need to be confronted directly. Both teachers and parents require special help in adapting to their new roles, so that students gain maximum benefit from the technology at hand.

Chapter 20 Activities

1. What do you see as the major areas of computer impact on work? Are there concerns with any of these that should be addressed?
2. Ask acquaintances in different kinds of jobs how computers have changed their work in the past few years.
3. If possible, talk with someone who works from home through telecommunications to gain direct insight into the benefits and the problems involved.

4. Identify several aspects of the effects of computers on personal privacy. How might privacy be better protected? Interview local police, credit bureaus, or banks about the kinds of information available in their databases, the importance of computers to them, and their perceptions of privacy issues.

5. What is your position on software duplication that goes beyond the copyright law? Is there such a thing as "fair use" of software? How should schools present this issue to students?

6. What, if anything, should be done if a student were to bring an illegal copy of a software product to school for personal use?

7. Should such ethical issues as hacking and white collar crime be considered in the curriculum? If so, where? How?

8. What do you see as the major equity issues of computing? How can schools contribute to solving these issues? Interview a school superintendent, board member, and community activist for their views.

9. Describe your perceptions of the changing roles of teachers, students, and parents. How can this change be managed? Talk with teachers who use computers to obtain their experiences.

Bibliography

"1987 Statement on Software Copyright." *The Computing Teacher*, March 1987, pp. 52–53.

Anderson, J., and Van Atta, D. "Bulgarian Computer Hackers Making Waves." *Daily Chronicle* (DeKalb, IL), 9 September 1991, p. 4.

Anderson, J., and Van Atta, D. "Computer Viruses Are Becoming Even More Lethal." *Daily Chronicle* (DeKalb, IL), 12 August 1991, p. 4.

Arias, M. B. "Computer Access for Hispanic Secondary Students." *Computers in the Schools*, 1990, 7(1/2), pp. 243–256.

Arias, A., Jr., and Bellman, B. "Computer-Mediated Classrooms for Culturally and Linguistically Diverse Learners." *Computers in the Schools*, 1990, 7(1/2), pp. 227–242.

Arthur, W., Jr., and Hart, D. "Empirical Relationships between Cognitive Ability and Computer Familiarity." *Journal of Research on Computing in Education*, Summer 1990, 22(4), pp. 457–463.

Bitter, G. *Computers in Today's World*. New York: Wiley, 1984.

Blake, C. "Piracy: Everyone loses." *Aldus Magazine*, July/August 1991, p. 10.

Bozeman, W. *Computers and Computing in Education*. Scottsdale, AZ: Gorsuch Scarisbrick, 1985.

"Code of Ethical Conduct for Computer-Using Educators." *The Computing Teacher*, February 1987, pp. 51–53.

Collis, B. *Computers, Curriculum, and Whole-Class Instruction*. Belmont, CA: Wadsworth, 1988.

"Computer Hacker, 18, Gets Prison for Fraud." *Chicago Tribune*, 15 February 1989, Section 2, p. 3.

Demetrulias, D. M., and Rosenthal, N. R. "Discrimination against Females and Minorities in Microcomputer Advertising." *Computers and the Social Sciences*, April/June 1985, pp. 91–95.

Dutton, W. H., Sweet, P. L., and Rogers, E. M. "Socioeconomic Status and the Early Diffusion of Personal Computing in the United States." *Social Sciences Computer Review*, 1989, 7, pp. 259–271.

Elliott, L. "Hunt for the Hacker Spy." *Readers Digest*, April 1990, pp. 185–232.

Flake, J., McClintock, C., and Turner, S. *Fundamentals of Computer Education*. Belmont, CA: Wadsworth, 1985.

Gerstein, D. "Piracy Stifles Mac Market." *Computer Reseller News*, 26 August 1991, p. 66.

Hess, R. D., and Miura, I. T. "Gender Differences in Enrollment in Computer Camps and Classes." *Sex Roles*, August 1985, pp. 193–203.

Kozol, J. "Rich Child, Poor Child." *Electronic Learning, Special Edition*, February 1991, 10(5), p. 56.

Linn, M. C. "Gender Equity Computer Learning Environments." *Computers and the Social Sciences*, April/June 1985, pp. 19–27.

Liu, M., Reed, W. M., and Phillips, P. D. "Teacher Education Students and Computers: Gender, Major, Prior Computer Experience, Occurrence, and Anxiety." *Journal of Research on Computing in Education*, Summer 1992, 24(4), pp. 457–467.

Maddux, C. D., Johnson, D. L., and Willis, J. W. *Educational Computing. Learning with Tomorrow's Technologies*. Boston: Allyn and Bacon, 1992.

Mandell, C. J., and Mandell, S. L. *Computers in Education Today*. St. Paul, MN: West Publishing, 1989.

Markoff, J., and Hafner, K. *CyberPunk. Hackers and Outlaws on the Computer Frontier*. New York: Simon & Schuster, 1991.

Maxwell, J. R., and Lamon, W. E. "Computer Viruses: Pathology and Detection. *The Computing Teacher*. August/September 1992, 20(1), pp. 12–15.

McCormick, J. "Live Virus Found in Anti-Virus Forum." *Reseller World*, December 1991, p. 32.

McGrath, D., Thurston, L. P., McLellan, H., Stone, D., and Tischhauser, M. "Sex Differences in Computer Attitudes and Beliefs among Rural Middle School Children after a Teacher Training Intervention." *Journal of Research on Computing in Education*, Summer 1992, 24(4), pp. 468–485.

Morton, R. "Tightening Copyright Coverage." *School and College*, March 1991, pp. 11–12.

Nichols, R. G., and Welliver, P. W. "Computers: Issues of Health and Safety." *Tech Trends*, 1991, 36(3), p. 52.

Nolan, P. C. J., McKinnon, D. H., and Soler, J. "Computers in Education: Achieving Equitable Access and Use." *Journal of Research on Computing in Education*, Spring 1992, 24(3), pp. 299–314.

Olson, B., and Krendl, K. A. "At-Risk Students and Microcomputers: What Do We Know and How Do We Know It?" *Journal of Educational Technology Systems*, 1990–1991, 19(2), pp. 167–175.

Pantiel, M., and Petersen, B. *Kids, Teachers, and Computers*. Englewood Cliffs, NJ: Prentice-Hall, 1984.

Piller, C. "Separate Realities." *MacWorld*, September 1992, pp. 218–230.

Questions and Answers on Copyright for the Campus Community. Oberlin, OH: National Association of College Stores, Inc., and The Association of American Publishers, Inc., 1991.

Ragsdale, R. G. *Permissible Computing in Education. Values, Assumptions, and Needs*. New York: Praeger, 1988.

Rosenthal, N. R., and Demetrulias, D. M. "Assessing Gender Bias in Computer Software." *Computers in the Schools*, 1988, 5(1/2), pp. 153–163.

Salpeter, J. "Are You Obeying Copyright Law?" *Technology & Learning*, May/June 1992, 12(8), pp. 14–23.

Sanders, J. S., and Stone, A. *The Neuter Computer: Computers for Girls and Boys.* New York: Neal-Schuman Publishers, 1986.

Scrogan, L. "The On-Line Underworld." *Classroom Computer Learning,* February 1988, p. 58.

Semrau, P., and Boyer, B. A. "Using Interactive Video to Examine Cultural Issues in Art." *The Computing Teacher,* December/January 1991–1992, *19*(42), pp. 24–26.

Seymour, J. "Wheels of Justice Grind to a Halt in 'Worm' Case." *PC Week,* 14 May 1990, p. 16.

Sian, G., Durndell, A., Macleod, H., and Glissov, P. "Stereotyping in Relation to the Gender Gap in Participation in Computing." *Educational Research,* 1988, *30*(2), pp. 98–103.

Soloman, G. "Technology and the Balance of Power." *The Computing Teacher,* May 1992, *19*(8), pp. 10–11.

Spruill, K. L., and Spain, R. V. "Extensive Use of Computers in a Rural, Economically Deprived High School." *Computers in the Schools,* 1991, *8*(1/2/3), pp. 349–352.

Stern, N., and Stern, R. A. *Computing in the Information Age.* New York: Wiley, 1993.

Stone, A. "Action for Equity." *The Computing Teacher,* November 1986, pp. 54–55.

Stone, A. "Action for Equity—II." *The Computing Teacher,* December/January 1986–1987, pp. 54–56.

Stone, A. "Computers in the Home—A Learning Advantage for the Affluent?" *The Computing Teacher,* June 1987, pp. 54–55.

Swadener, M., and Hannafin, M. "Gender Similarities and Differences in Sixth Graders' Attitudes toward Computers: An Exploratory Study." *Educational Technology,* January 1987, pp. 37–42.

Talab, R. "Copyright Scenarios for Media Center Directors." *TechTrends,* 1992, *37*(4), pp. 10–13.

"Technology and the At-Risk Student." *Electronic Learning,* November/December 1988, pp. 35–49.

Todd, D. "In Pursuit of Pirates. The SPA is Putting out the Word: Illegal Software Copying Will Bring Trouble." *Information Week,* 8 March 1991, p. 37.

Using Software. A Guide to the Ethical and Legal Use of Software for Members of the Academic Community. Arlington, VA: Information Technology Association of America, 1992. Available from ERIC Document Reproduction Services ED 352011.

"A Virus Epidemic?" *Data Training,* June 1991, pp. 8–9.

Weller, H. G., Repman, J., Rooze, G. E., and Parker, R. D. "Students and Computer Ethics: An Alternative to Preaching." *The Computing Teacher,* August/September 1992, *20*(1), pp. 20–22.

Wilson, D. L. "Suit against U. of Oregon Alleging Copying of Software Is Likely To Be Settled out of Court, Both Sides Say." *Chronicle of Higher Education,* 29 May 1991, pp. A9, A14.

Part 6
Looking Ahead

Objectives

After completing this chapter, you will be able to:

List and briefly describe at least three trends in computer hardware that seem likely to continue.

Discuss some possible future directions in software, including multimedia.

Describe the concept and potential application of virtual reality (VR).

Synthesize your knowledge and experiences into your own scenario for the future of computers in education.

Define and critically evaluate the role you foresee for yourself as an educator in the twenty-first century.

Chapter 21

Today and Tomorrow: What May Lie Ahead

This chapter provides a brief recap of what you have accomplished thus far. Then it considers what the future may hold for technology and its applications in education. The future of hardware is considered in terms of microprocessor chips, memory, physical size, mass storage, ease of use and versatility, telecommunications and networking, cost, and compatibility. Considerations for the future of software include selection, complexity, cost, software for learning, multimedia, and virtual reality. The future of computers in education is related to the potential for computers to empower teachers and learners in the twenty-first century. The chapter concludes with reflections on your journey toward integration of computers into education.

Looking Back

By this point, you've journeyed through an extensive survey of educational computer applications. Let's summarize the journey before pondering what the future may hold.

Getting Started

Your journey began with our effort to provide a context for the remainder of this book. The first chapter gave an overview of the gradual development of early computing equipment, starting with the abacus. Greater attention focused on the past hundred years, from early census tools to the first modern mainframe computers and the evolution of the personal computer.

From this brief history, the basic terminology and operating concepts of microcomputers were explored. The fundamentals of hardware and how a computer system is controlled were covered next.

The Computer as Tool

Most microcomputer users depend on software that they purchase—the focus of Part 2 of this text. The largest and most popular category of software consists of tool applications, which are those programs that help teachers and students (or any computer user) to perform common tasks more efficiently and effectively.

Tool software is often grouped by function. First, you learned about word processing and related programs that support writing through computers. Word processing alone accounts for the majority of microcomputer usage in many cases. Next, you studied information management through databases, followed by numeric manipulation and presentation with spreadsheets. Graphics and support-tool software enable computer users to communicate more effectively. Integrated software combines most or all of the foregoing functions into a unified package, which can be more cost-effective and easier to learn than separate tools.

Among the newer tools to make an impact in education is desktop publishing, which gives users the ability to manipulate text and images with nearly the precision of a commercial printing shop. Networks and telecommunications have major potential educational applications to bring together individuals and resources in ways never before possible.

The Computer as Tutor

Even before most tool software had been imagined, educators began to experiment with the potential of computers as learning tools. In Part 3 you first studied the traditional forms of computer-assisted instruction (CAI) and some of the research that supports the educational potential of CAI. Today's interactive multimedia brings the entire range of media materials to the personal computer, turning the text- and graphics-based CAI of the past into far more exciting materials that can compete for learner attention in the media age.

Of course, all instructional materials require evaluation before they are purchased and used. We presented a framework for evaluating educational software that is practical and can be tailored to varying needs. We also examined the principles and potential of computer assistance in organizing and administering educational programs, which is often called computer-managed instruction (CMI).

Part 3 concluded with an introduction to the possible future of instructional software: artificial intelligence (AI). AI has the potential to enhance the power of CAI far beyond its current level, though the attainment of these lofty goals is far from assured.

The Computer as Learner

In Part 4, we turned from software prepared by others to the actual development of software. First, you learned the fundamental concepts of programming a computer. Next, you met Logo, a graphics-oriented microworld often used with children. Logo was based on the developmental psychology of Piaget and is unique among computer languages.

Because these languages remain so common, your introduction to instructional computing would have been incomplete without a short overview of programming languages such as BASIC and Pascal. However, we believe you will be better served in any software development you may undertake by environments designed to facilitate your tasks. Authoring languages and systems have existed for many years. Recently, most attention has focused on hypermedia tools such as *HyperCard* and *LinkWay*. We urge you to explore these tools, in part for your own use, but more importantly, for the empowerment they may offer your students.

Microcomputers in Education

After such extensive treatment of the individual aspects of computers in education, we considered, in Part 5, how they might fit together into a school context. We suggested that the concept of computer literacy has become an artifact, replaced by the far more important effort to integrate computers throughout the curriculum. Integration recognizes that the computer has become just another tool for both teachers and students, no different in principle than a pencil or chalk. We stated that we all need to develop a high level of competence in computer use, so that we benefit fully from the technology without being limited or hindered by our lack of knowledge about and skills to use it.

However lofty the goal, there will always be details concerning how to actually achieve it. We attempted to suggest some critical factors in implementation, ranging from the issues of school reform and restructuring to the practical considerations of budget and benefits for individuals with special needs. The section concluded with a chapter devoted to some major concerns and social issues that arise from the spread of computers in society.

Looking Ahead

This final chapter offers some speculation about the future. The discussion is divided into sections on hardware, software, and computers in education. Predicting the future is both difficult and risky, and we claim to have no crystal ball. As Naisbitt (1982) wrote in *Megatrends*, "The gee-whiz futurists are always wrong because they believe technological innovation travels in a straight line. It doesn't. It weaves and bobs and lurches and sputters" (p. 41). Further, we agree with Naisbitt (p. 2) that "The most reliable way to anticipate the future is by understanding the present." Let's look at current trends.

The Future of Microcomputer Hardware

All indications are that the directions of hardware development over the last 10 years will continue and, in some cases, accelerate.

Microprocessors

The processing speeds of microcomputers will continue to increase. From the Apple II operating at 1 MHz (megahertz), microcomputers have advanced to the point where the most basic systems operate at 20 MHz, while 33 MHz to 66 MHz systems are common, and still faster speeds are just around the corner. Speed is most significant as it permits a microcomputer to execute more complex software than ever before. This, in turn, makes defining the differences among computers based on factors other than physical size increasingly difficult. Today's microcomputer is yesterday's mainframe, enhanced and placed on the desktop. Desktop supercomputers aren't far off.

Memory

Faster microcomputers also require more and more memory (RAM). The Apple II eventually reached 128K of RAM. A typical Macintosh or MS-DOS computer now has 4MB to 8MB of RAM, which already is inadequate for some applications. As the capacity of memory chips continues to increase, more memory becomes possible in microcomputers. Just as work expands to fill all available time, software developers continue to expand programs to use (and even demand) more and more memory. The rule today must be: Buy as much memory as you possibly can because tomorrow you'll need more.

Physical Size

As electrical engineers find new ways to achieve the same goals in ever-smaller packages, the physical size and weight of computers has fallen. From the desktop computer evolved the portable, then the battery-powered laptop, and finally the notebook computer (and printer!) small enough to fit inside a standard briefcase. Regardless of miniaturization potential, today's notebooks are about as small as seems feasible without creating unusable keyboards and marginal viewing screens. Attention now shifts to packing still more power into the current-size packages, enhancing the displays from monochrome to excellent color, and adding networking and other support. The best notebook computers today rival solid desktop systems in most every way.

Apart from refinements, there is also a strong move toward still-smaller devices that serve more specific purposes. One type is the pen computer, which requires no keyboard. The user just writes on the "screen," and the computer recognizes the handwriting. As we write this text, pen computers remain somewhat esoteric with a lot of potential but without a totally clear future in education. However, the director of the Media Lab at MIT has suggested that the computer of the future will be worn like a watch (Bane, 1990).

Somewhat along the same lines is substantial interest, especially by Apple Computer, in a product termed a Personal Digital Assistant (PDA). PDAs became available commercially in mid-1993. There is no clear definition of a PDA, other than what its name implies. Early models were limited in function, but the goal was articulated by Apple in the late 1980s in its *Knowledge Navigator* video (Scully, 1989). Though not called anything in the video, the central feature was a digital device that responded to voice instructions, had "intelligence," could retrieve data from virtually anywhere automatically upon command, answered the phone, maintained appointment calendars without overt user action, and so on. For some, the vision was frightening and for others exciting. Whether there will ever be a commercial Knowledge Navigator is unclear, but some firms are working on major aspects of it (Barr and Neubarth, 1993; Coates, 1993).

Mass Storage

As programs and multimedia files grow ever larger, so must the storage devices that hold them. The original 5.25" magnetic diskette holding about 100K of data has largely been replaced by high-density diskettes that hold 1.2MB (in 5.25" size) or 1.44MB (for 3.5" size). Although not widely used a 2.88MB floppy is available, as is a unique "floptical" drive that handles ordinary 3.5" diskettes as well as special magneto-optical diskettes that hold 21 MB. Removable hard disk systems such as the Bernoulli have steadily increased in capacity to a current top of 150MB per cartridge. Nonremovable hard disks under 100MB are becoming justifiably rare as still-larger units become the norm. Magnetic drives holding 1 gigabyte (1000MB)and more are on the market. The limits of storage appear to be well beyond current levels, so the trend toward larger capacity drives will continue.

Looming on the horizon is flash memory (Reid and Hume, 1992), which replaces hard disk drives with far-faster memory chips. The technology offers far-greater reliability by eliminating all mechanical components and also reduced size. The latter will benefit portable computers as well as increase the capacity of desktop computers without increasing size.

Optical discs also have become popular in the form of CD-ROM and laserdiscs because of their large storage capacity. Although these are most common in read-only form and are fine for general storage, online encyclopedias and stable databases, read-write formats have begun to appear and are likely to become more affordable in the near future. While optical discs are the current champions in storage capacity for a given space, their data-retrieval speeds are slow compared to hard disks, including the removable type. Whether optical or magnetic removable versions come to dominate may depend on which storage technology is able to match the advantage of the other most quickly.

It seems likely that some variant of the CD will eventually replace the laserdisc. One reason is simply the difference in the physical size of the medium and its hardware. Another is that digital technology is critical to distribution of data over networks, a phenomenon certain to grow in importance. Until digital images can equal analog laserdiscs in realism, the latter will have a certain, if limited, place. However, digital distribution and the potential to install a CD-size drive in most any computer case, even portables, are powerful incentives for users and developers to accept CD technology.

Ease of Use/Versatility

The phenomenal popularity of *Microsoft Windows* for MS-DOS computers is clear evidence that Apple Computer's vision of how a computer should operate has gained the upper hand. Typing arcane commands at a blinking cursor prompt simply is not satisfactory to many current and potential computer users. This is less a battle between the two hardware platforms than evidence of the significance of ergonomics. Ease of use is important to consumers. But is a graphical user interface enough?

The underlying issue is simply how much the user must conform to the limits of the machine and how much the machine should be able to accommodate the user. AI researchers are working toward the next widespread level of adaptation of computers to users. Keyboard use, already reduced by the mouse, should decline further. Touch screens are one possibility, but not the most likely, in our view. *Pointing devices* (the generic term for a mouse or any related device) and scanning may improve and become still easier or more effective.

However, the real leap will be into voice technologies (Wetzel, 1991). Computers that respond to voice commands became available in mid-1993. Voice-synthesized output can also reduce some of the current dependence on monitors. At the same time, flat-screen monitors with ever-higher resolution and supported by video adapters capable of vast numbers of different colors will make the screen more appealing and richer in information than currently.

Schools will increasingly provide access to laser printers as prices fall to the levels of dot-matrix printers a few years earlier. This will enable students and teachers to take fuller advantage of the capabilities of advanced software for desktop publishing, image manipulation, and artistic work. Color laser printing gradually will become affordable as well.

Telecommunications and Networking

The classroom of the near future will be "wired." Although rare today, classrooms will gain that most fundamental telecommunications tool—the telephone—at long last. What other professional in the 1990s lacks access to a telephone at virtually all times? Network connections will link computers within the school to one another to share data and peripherals and to other computer systems around the world. The fast, efficient, and inexpensive exchange of information with other sites will become easy, common, and cost-effective. Educators will gain access to large-scale data repositories, perhaps analogous to those already serving the medical and legal professions.

We can envision a day not far off when students of all ages routinely will communicate with peers, adults, and field specialists by E-mail without regard to geographic location or time zones. The broadest possible range of information will be available in a "virtual library," in which access to information has no direct connection to physical ownership of items. The problem of obsolete data will be replaced by the more enormous challenge of identifying in volumes of data never before known those items of greatest relevance and importance to the need at hand.

While the benefits of telecommunications and networking accrue to all, they have particular significance in rural areas, where they are likely to be the most cost-effective solution to distance education problems.

Cost

From the beginning, electronic hardware costs have gone downward routinely despite general trends toward higher prices for most goods in our economy. Some of this is due to manufacturing efficiencies and economies of scale from growing demand. Much is due to intense competition in the marketplace. Even without direct competitors, Macintosh prices have been forced downward to acknowledge that brand loyalty is limited by economic reality. While would-be owners will pay more to get just what they want, many will not pay much more.

Obviously, prices cannot fall indefinitely, since there must be a minimal price level at which the product will be improved for the same price rather than sold for less. It appears that this plateau is at about $1000 per computer system. For several years, it has been possible to purchase a complete entry level microcomputer system for that price. Over the years, what you get for the investment has evolved from an Apple II or basic PC-XT clone to a basic Macintosh or a 486-based MS-DOS machine—either one a far more powerful and desirable computer than its predecessors. We expect this trend to continue. New chips such as the Pentium and PowerPC and other developments will cause current top-of-the-line models (or features) to become the entry-level product of tomorrow.

Similarly, desirable peripherals also continue to decline in price. Laser printers are now affordable. Internal CD-ROM drives are available as options for less than $200, the price of a floppy drive not long ago. Monitors are significantly better today, if not cheaper. Computer hardware offers genuine value.

Given the apparent stability of the $1000 price level, there is less justification than ever for schools to delay purchasing computer hardware. Each term or year of delay carries with it significant "opportunity cost," that is, lost opportunity to enhance education.

Compatibility

We can only hope that over time the problems caused by two hardware camps based on operating system (MAC-OS and MS-DOS) will be overcome. It may be encouraging that Apple and IBM jointly created a company (Kaleida) to work toward applying the best that each has to offer to products that neither could produce alone. We remain skeptical that two such competitors can ever effectively cooperate, but we resoundingly support their attempts. Education would benefit greatly from no longer having to choose between Macintosh and MS-DOS. There have been early reports of computers with both a 68030 (Macintosh) and an 80486 (MS-DOS) chip that can run either type of software (Swartz, 1993; Quinlan, 1993). Better still, systems based on the PowerPC chip feature emulators that run existing software, making them the future systems of choice (Corcoran, 1993; Norr, 1993).

Compatibility could lead to an eventual triumph of Digital Video Interactive (DVI) hardware as the basis of multimedia, since DVI images already require no conversion to be used on either current platform. Producers can save significant development costs.

The Future of Software

Historically, advances in hardware have far outpaced progress in software development. The high-performance hardware readily available in the mid-1990s has little software that truly capitalizes on its power. Software such as *Windows* and *QuickTime* demands a high-powered system, but more for its brute strength than its sophistication. Software will continue to evolve, but is unlikely to catch up with hardware.

Selection

The vast market of microcomputer users has created a demand for software, and the market responds to profit potential. New products for personal productivity flood the market. Developers are producing high-quality products in currently popular market segments such as word processing, while constantly searching for additional applications for which little, if any, software now exists. This is consistent with the view of microcomputers as a Swiss army knife, an all-in-one tool. No one knows what the next *VisiCalc* will be, but you can be confident there will be one.

Complexity

Recent refinements in word processors, databases, and spreadsheets are vivid testimony to market economics and increased computer power. These packages do far more with less user effort than ever before. Programs are becoming increasingly comprehensive in scope. Freed from the constraints of small, underpowered hardware, developers can produce a new generation of software.

Perhaps more important to educators than increased power is increased ease of use, often through enhanced human-machine interfaces. Some gain comes from the strong emphasis on GUI (*graphical user interface*) and WIMP (*windows, icons, mouse, pointer)* interfaces first created by Xerox researchers and popularized by the Macintosh. Still more may come from advances in AI research. For instance, *neural networks* seek to model the human mind. Rather than "programming" a neural network, one "teaches" it by example to recognize patterns and reach decisions. Neural nets actually learn from their experiences. When technology such as this becomes part of software applications, programs will be able to customize themselves to the user's usage patterns and needs. This will represent a whole new generation of "intelligent" software, perhaps similar in some ways to the Knowledge Navigator mentioned earlier.

Cost

Significant reductions in prices for educational software seem unlikely. The market is already sensitive to school budgets, with most CAI and utility products priced under $100 per copy. Heavily discounted multidisk lab packs and network versions leave little room for further reductions. Although major applications software tends to carry list prices in the $500-per-copy range, "street prices" are much lower, making such noneducational products more affordable than might appear initially. Also, features pioneered in leading products tend over time to filter down into less expensive ones as well. We foresee little likelihood of further major declines in prices.

Software for Learning

As both the theory and application of microcomputer teaching and learning evolve, a new generation of educational software should appear. This software will take greater advantage of the hardware's capabilities to interact with learners in more sophisticated ways. It will focus greater impact on learning, while offering greater ease of use and more assistance to teachers.

As traditional publishers move more heavily into the software industry, expect more and more software as part of a complete set of teaching materials to accompany text series and individual books. Books with diskettes are becoming increasingly common. In some cases, textbook adopters are provided master diskettes to duplicate locally for students. Perhaps the day will come when every textbook sold to schools will come with correlated software, including CDs for multimedia. All it will take is one successful experiment by a publisher, and others will follow quickly.

Home use of educational software may increase to supplement the schools' educational programs. Education will be more fluid, with both home and school contributing significantly to the overall result. This is especially significant in what it does to integrate these two realms for the common good.

Interactive Multimedia/Hypermedia

The scope and realism of computer courseware will grow with further developments in interactive video technologies, including the likely integration of DVI into future CPU chips. This is the software side of the current rapid merging of traditional computer, television, and telephone technologies (Van, 1992). Using still and motion sequences, simulations will take on new levels of sophistication. Dual stereo sound tracks will serve many purposes, including bilingual and foreign languages instruction. Multimedia courseware on optical discs unites the potential of all media into truly interactive instruction. The impact will be greatest when CD drives become as common as floppy drives and the range of courseware on CD expands to meet the demand for it.

While books are unlikely to disappear, we anticipate further gains for multimedia products as co-equals with textbooks, such as the success that Optical Data has had positioning its products on state textbook purchase lists. Given the choice between traditional texts and multimedia, many educators will opt for the latter, further pressuring publishers to augment their traditional books. However, the real age of multimedia may only arrive when there has been a major multimedia "hit" to produce an effect such as Pacman did for electronic games (Silverstone, 1992).

Virtual Reality

Seymour Papert and Logo are largely responsible for the concept of a microworld in which children can explore and experiment on their own terms. Another form of microworld is *virtual reality (VR)*, the "ultimate multimedia interface" (Brandt, 1992). Typically, the VR user blocks out the physical world by donning a helmet with small monitors before the eyes and speakers over the ears. A computer generates a virtual, that is, simulated, environment through the monitors and speakers. The user interacts with that environment through some set of controls, often a special high-tech glove (Hamilton, 1992). It is possible to walk around in the environment, touch and examine elements of it. (We've seen one VR environment in which the user could wander through a house, pause and raise a hand to a bookshelf and remove a "book," plunge into a swimming pool and move among the fish, etc.)

Among the current public applications, entertainment dominates, such as Battletech Center in Chicago, which bills itself as the world's first multiplayer, interactive, real-time simulator. Battletech offers a war game in which contestants compete against each other within a VR world that changes for every game.

No doubt you can see from this brief narrative that VR offers potential to become the ultimate simulation (Wilson, 1992). Medical educators are excited by the possibilities for learning. Most fields of study offer intriguing possibilities to immerse students in active simulations of events, principles, or whatever (Ferrington and Loge, 1992; Wilson, 1992). We do not foresee K-12 applications in the next few years and share Roblyer's concerns (1993) that VR is more likely fantasy than practical for schools at the moment. Still, the potential of VR is such that educators should remain alert to developments. Resources include Meckler's monthly *Virtual Reality Report* and quarterly *Virtual Reality Review*. For an outstanding history of VR, see Rheingold, 1991.

Computers in Education

Whatever exciting developments occur in hardware and software, their ultimate significance to educators lies in their application in schools. Just as software advances trail hardware, similarly education's ability to use what is available trails business and other sectors. One popular computer publication termed education "the final frontier" and proclaimed that "computers will ultimately have their greatest impact on education" (Zachmann, 1991, p. 97). Education has made progress in computer use since the late 1970s, yet it is painfully apparent that far less has happened than computer advocates expected. The obstacles to widespread, effective computer use in schools have been more nearly intractable than most "experts" imagined.

A major concern is the vast amount of overzealous evangelism that has accompanied the computer education movement. Predictions were made that computers would transform and save education, reflecting Naisbitt's "danger of the technofix mentality" (1982, p. 52). Realists do not see computer technology as the answer to all of education's ills. We can think of few more certain ways to undermine a dream than to oversell it. That happened with many other educational innovations; and it could happen to computers, as well. Perhaps the greatest single factor that should prevent failure of the computer movement is that much of its support comes from outside the schools. Unlike, say, the new math, about which few people outside of schools cared, advocates of computers in the schools are found everywhere. Too many people have a stake in this to let it fail.

In most cases, the glowing scenarios from the early 1980s of an education revolution have yet to be achieved. Will they ever be? In many cases, we believe the answer is no. In fact, Dede (1987) argued that we really have no idea yet how best to use computers in education. His points largely remain valid today. There is still much need for experimentation to determine how to maximize the value of computers in education, but we think we are on the right road. The trend toward developing computer competence through integration of computers into the curriculum is encouraging. It will indeed make the computer a tool of empowerment for students and teachers—its ultimate value.

Empowerment for the Twenty-First Century

For the computer to empower teachers and students, computers in education must attain a level of *invisible integration*. They must become such an essential part of education that no one notices them or thinks about them as something more remarkable than a book or chalk is considered now. A computer has unique power and capabilities, but it is fundamentally just a tool in the service of learning and living. Children now are expected to learn to read, write, calculate, spell, and behave in school. They will come to experience the computer as a tool, a resource, not something as uncommon as a field trip.

However, it would be unfortunate if computer integration meant only support of the existing school curriculum and structure, however beneficial that might be. Teachers empowered by computer technology will see the nature of teaching differently. The "sage on the stage" will yield to the "guide on the side." There will be little need for a dispenser of information. Teaching will focus on individuals and their development, on motivation, thinking, creativity, and not on bodies of content to present or absorb. Students will become investigators, builders of their own knowledge stores, and not just recipients of information. Teachers will pose problems, help learners identify problems, and assist learners to find solutions to them. Information resources will be explored and used as needed and will not be divided into small components to be committed to memory. The ultimate test will be whether students can locate, assess, and synthesize information to create personal knowledge. This demonstrates the skills of a lifetime, not just the short-term memory that gets you through the next test. Life skills are inherently empowering.

Reflections

The vision of computers as tools of empowerment is filled with possibility, not certainty. To the extent that empowerment occurs, teachers and students will be richly rewarded. However appealing the vision, we do not believe it represents the dominant direction today. The computer competence required to become empowered as a teacher is far greater than most teachers today possess. We see no viable means of changing that situation quickly or widely, as a true revolution in education would require. Rather, we foresee an evolution in that direction that will take much more time.

Is there an alternative to patience? We cannot be certain. Private initiatives such as Whittle Communication's Edison Project may offer one. But we are not overly optimistic. Instead, we hope that those teachers who have experienced the power of computers in their teaching will become catalysts for change among their peers.

This makes you, a teacher on the way to computer competence, critical to the future. You have a vision of what computers can mean in education, and you have at least begun to develop your skills to pursue that vision. With even one computer in your classroom, you can accomplish more than many schools have with quantities of unused computers. Your example and enthusiasm can encourage others to explore the possibilities. Your willingness to share your knowledge and skills can ease the transformation of a reluctant, skeptical, or technophobic colleague into a hesitant, then comfortable computer educator. *You* are the key to the future of computers in education.

Charge to Readers

This book has attempted to present an overview of the expanding field of educational microcomputing. This field has quickly become important to us all as educators concerned about the future of our children. Computers cannot be ignored; they will become increasingly important in the educational process. You already have made a commitment to become both a more knowledgeable user of microcomputers and a better teacher by empowering students to use them. In this way, you will contribute to the evolution of education from a nineteenth century model to one worthy of the twenty-first century. Accept the challenge, and help transform education!

Chapter 21 Activities

1. Which of the trends in hardware development do you believe will be most significant for education? Why?
2. What developments in software would you most like to see? What, if any, evidence offers promise that these may occur?
3. Develop and justify your own vision of the future. What contributions do you foresee making personally to that vision?

Bibliography

Amthor, G. R. "DVI Technology: The Digital Future of Multimedia." *AV Video*, April 1992, *14*(4), pp. S-18–S-24.

Asch, T. "Designing Virtual Worlds." *AI Expert*, August 1992, *7*(8), pp. 22–25.

"Apple Computer and Education: An Interview with Burt Cummings." *The Computing Teacher*, April 1992, *19*(7), p. 27.

Bane, M. "Lippman Says, Try This Computer on for Size." *Chicago Tribune*, November 18, 1990, Section 19, pp. 11, 24.

Barr, C., and Neubarth, M. "Pen Pals." *PC Magazine*, 12 October 1993, pp. 116–182.

Coates, J. "Lombard Firm Says 1st of New Wave of Minuscule PCs Is Finally Near." *Chicago Tribune*, 12 February 1993, Section 3, pp. 1–2.

Corcoran, C. "First PowerPC System Finally Hits the Street." *InfoWorld*, 27 September 1993, pp. 1, 12.

Dede, C. "Empowering Environments, Hypermedia, and Microworlds." *The Computing Teacher*, November 1987, pp. 20–24, 61.

Ferrington, G. and Loge, K. "Virtual Reality: A New Learning Environment." *The Computing Teacher*, April 1992, *19*(7), pp. 16–19.

Geisert, P., and Futrell, M. *Teachers, Computers, and Curriculum*. Boston: Allyn and Bacon, 1990.

Hamilton, J. O'C. "Virtual Reality. How a Computer-Generated World Could Change the Real World." *Business Week*, 5 October 1992, pp. 96–104.

"IBM and Education: An Interview with Jim Dezell." *The Computing Teacher*, April 1992, *19*(7), p. 26.

Kerr, T. J. "Mastering Instructional Technology." *School and College*, March 1993, *32*(3), pp. 15–19.

Kurz, P. "Disenfranchising Technology? (Up Front)." *AV Video*, July 1992, *14*(7), pp. 6–7.

Moursund, D. "Restructuring Education Part 2: Now and 10 Years Ago." *The Computing Teacher*, October 1991, *19*(2), p. 4.

Naisbitt, J. *Megatrends*. New York: Warner, 1982.

Norr, H. "Apple Aims for Mainstream with PowerPC Licensing Plans." *MacWeek*, 27 September 1993, pp. 1, 91.

Norr, H. "IBM's Workplace OS May Run MAC Apps." *MacWeek*, 27 September 1993, pp. 1, 91.

Quinlan, T. "Apple Set to Unveil Revolutionary Hybrid." *Infoworld*, 15 November 1993, pp. 1, 175.

Rebello, K. "Your Digital Future." *Business Week*, 7 September 1992, pp. 56–64.

Reid, T. R., and Hume, B. "New Chips Will Be Here in a Flash." *Chicago Tribune*, 24 May 1992, Section 7, p. 6.

Rheingold, H. *Virtual Reality*. New York: Summit Books, Simon & Schuster, 1991.

Roblyer, M. D. "Virtual Reality, Visions, and Nightmares. (Technology in Our Time.)" *Educational Technology*, February 1993, *33*(2), pp. 33–35.

Scully, J. "The Knowledge Navigator." *PC AI*, January/February 1989, p. 31.

Silverstone, S. "Robert Abel Discovers a New World." *Publish*, March 1992, p. 108.

Swartz, J. "NuTek Mac-Compatible CPU Doubles as 486 CPU." *MacWeek*, 15 March 1993, *7*(11), pp. 1, 124.

Van, J. "Schools a New Frontier for Phone Industry." *Chicago Tribune*, 16 June 1992, Section 3, pp. 1, 6.

Wetzel, K. "Speaking to Read and Write: A Report on the Status of Speech Recognition." *The Computing Teacher*, August/September 1991, *19*(1), pp. 6–12.

Wetzel, K. "Speech Technology II: Future Software and Hardware Predictions." *The Computing Teacher*, October 1991, *19*(2), pp. 19–21.

Wilson, D. L. Researchers Hope to Lead Students into 'Virtual Reality.' " *The Chronicle of Higher Education*, 22 April 1992, pp. A23–A25.

Zachmann, W. F. "Education: The Final Frontier." *PC Magazine*, August 1991, *10*(14), pp. 97–98.

Software Mentioned in the Text (with Producers)

All software titles are the trademarks or registered trademarks of their respective owners.

1st Class (AI Corp.)
ABC News Interactive (Optical Data)
Action! (Macromedia)
Activitymakers (Teacher's Aide, Inc.)
Address Book & Label Maker (Spinnaker)
The Adventures of Jasper Woodbury (Optical Data)
All Star Drill (Tom Snyder)
Animator (AutoDesk)
Applause (Borland)
AppleWorks (Claris)
Atlas of U.S. Presidents (Applied Optical Media Corp.)
Authorware Professional (Macromedia)
Bank Street Filer (Sunburst)
Bank Street Writer (Scholastic)
Bibliography (PRO/TEM)
Blockers and Finders (Sunburst)
Bluegrass Bluff (MECC)
Building Perspective (Sunburst)
Bookshelf (Microsoft)
Calendar Creator (Power Up)
Calendar Maker (CE Software)
Carmen Sandiego series (Brøderbund)
"Cell"ebration (Software for Kids)
Certificate Maker (Spinnaker)
Certificates and More (Mindscape)
Chart (Microsoft)
Children's Reference Plus (R. R. Bowker)
Children's Writing and Publishing Center (Learning Company)
ClarisWorks (Claris)
College Application Essay Writer (Scholastic)
Columbus: Encounter, Discover, and Beyond (EduQuest)

Compel (Asymetrix)
Compton's Interactive Encyclopedia (Compton's NewMedia)
Corel Draw (Corel)
Crosscountry Canada (Didatech)
Crossword Magic (Mindscape)
Dataquest (MECC)
Dazzle Draw (Brøderbund)
dBase (Borland)
Decisions, Decisions series (Tom Snyder)
Delta Drawing Today (Power Industries)
Delta Drawing Today Version Español (Power Industries)
DeluxePaint (Electronic Arts)
DeluxePaint Animation (Electronic Arts)
Designer (Micrografix)
Designer Puzzles (MECC)
Director (Macromedia)
Discis Books (Discis)
The Election of 1988 (ABC News Interactive)
Electronic Mailbag ((Exsym)
Electronic Village (Exsym)
Encarta (Microsoft)
Exam in a Can (IPS Publishing)
Excel (Microsoft)
Explore-a-Classic (William K. Bradford)
Explore-a-Story PLUS (William K. Bradford)
The Explorer Series (Wings for Learning)
Facts on File News Digest CD-ROM 1980–1991 (Facts on File)
Fields of Learning: Life Science (K-12 MicroMedia)
Fifty States (MECC)
FileMaker Pro (Claris)
Formtool (BLOC Publishing Corp.)

Framework (Ashton-Tate)
FrEdBase (CUE Softswap)
FrEdWriter (CUE Softswap)
Freehand (Aldus)
Function Analyzer (Sunburst)
Function Supposer (Sunburst)
Genie (Microsystems)
GeoGraph (MECC)
The Geometer's Sketchpad (Key Curriculum Press)
Geometric Supposers (Sunburst)
Geoworld (Tom Snyder)
Grade Machine (Misty City Software)
Gradebook Plus (Mindscape)
Graph-in-the-Box Executive (New England Software)
A Graphic Approach to Calculus (Sunburst)
Graphical Analysis (Vernier)
Grammatik (Reference Software)
Graph Wiz (William K. Bradford)
Green Globs and Graphing Equations (Sunburst)
GTV (National Geographic)
Guide (Owl)
Harvard Graphics (Software Publishing)
History in Motion: Milestones of the 20th Century (Scholastic)
Hollywood (Claris)
Home Town: Local Area Studies (Active Learning Systems)
Hurricane Hugo (Turner Educational Services)
HyperCard (Claris)
HyperStudio (Roger Wagner)
IconAuthor 4.0 (AimTech)
Illuminated Books and Manuscripts (EduQuest)
Illustrator (Adobe)
Imaginator 3-D (Hearlihy)
Immigrant (CUE Softswap)
Incredible Lab (Sunburst)
Interactive NOVA: Race to Save the Planet (Scholastic)
Interactive Physics (Knowledge Revolution)
Interleaf (IBM)
J&S Gradebook (J&S)
Just Grandma and Me (Brøderbund)
Kalamazoo Teacher's Record Book (Successful Software)

KidCAD (Davidson)
KidMail (CUE Softswap)
KidPix (Brøderbund)
KidWriter (Spinnaker)
The King's Rule (Wings for Learning)
LEGO TC logo (LCSI)
Let's Write! (Realtime Learning Systems)
Library of the Future (World Library Inc.)
Linkway (IBM)
Linkway Live! (IBM)
LogoEnsemble (LCSI)
LogoPlus (Terrapin)
LogoWriter (LCSI)
LogoWriter Robotics (LCSI)
Lotus 1-2-3 (Lotus)
MacWrite II (Claris)
MacDraw II and Pro (Claris)
MacProof (Claris)
Magic MacSearch (Hirschfelt)
Magic Slate II (Wings for Learning)
MagnaCharta (Third Wave Technologies)
Make-a-Flash (Teacher Support Software)
Mammals (National Geographic)
MapView3D (Philosoft)
Martin Luther King, Jr. (ABC News Interactive)
Math Connections: Algebra II (Wings for Learning)
Math Shop series (Scholastic)
Mavis Beacon Teaches Typing (Software Toolworks)
MediaText (Wings for Learning/Sunburst)
Mental Math Games (Waterford Institute/Brøderbund)
Microsoft Works (Microsoft)
Modemless CMS (CUE Softswap)
Multimedia Toolbook (Asymetrix)
Mystat (SYSTAT)
The New Grolier Multimedia Encyclopedia (Grolier)
NewsBank CD News (Pioneer)
NewsMaster (Unison World)
NewsRoom (Spinnaker)
Nigel's World (Lawrence Productions)
Notebook II (PRO/TEM)
One World (Active Learning Systems)
Operation Frog (Scholastic)
Oregon Trail (MECC)
Our Environment (Optilearn)

Our Town (Sunburst)
PageMaker (Aldus)
PaintBrush (ZSoft)
Paradox (Borland)
Persuasion (Aldus)
PFS: First Choice (Software Publishing)
PhotoFinish (ZSoft)
Photoshop (Aldus)
PhotoStyler (Adobe)
Picture Publisher (Astral Development Corp.)
The Play Room (Brøderbund)
PLUS (Spinnaker)
The Poet's Journal (Hartley)
Point of View (Scholastic)
PowerPoint (Microsoft)
Power of Nation States (ISTE)
Premier (Adobe)
The Presidents: It All Started with George (National Graphic)
Print Magic (Epyx)
Print Master (Unison World)
Print Shop (Brøderbund)
Print Shop Companion (Brøderbund)
Publisher (Microsoft)
Publish-It! (Timeworks)
Quark Express (Quark)
Quattro (Borland)
Quiz Writer Plus (Midwest Agribusiness Systems)
Readability (Scandinavian PC Systems)
Readability Machine (Prentice-Hall)
Reader Rabbit (Learning Company)
Reading Strategy series (Prentice-Hall)
RightWriter (Que)
Safari Search (Wings for Learning)
SAS (SAS Institute)
Science 2000 (Decision Development Corp.)
Science Literacy: The Lio Project (Encyclopedia Brittanica)
Search series (McGraw-Hill)
The Second Voyage of the Mimi (Wings for Learning)
SemCalc (Sunburst)
Sensible Grammar (Sensible Software)
SimAnt (Maxis)
SimCity (Maxis)
SimEarth (Maxis)
SimuComm (CUE Softswap)
Slide Shop (Scholastic)

Solve It! American History Mysteries 1492-1865 (Wings for Learning)
SPSS (SPSS Inc.)
Storyboard Live! (IBM)
SuperPrint (Scholastic)
Star Plus IV (Hartley)
Stickybear (Optimum Resource)
Story Tailor series (Humanities Software)
SuperCalc (Sorcim)
SuperCard (Silicon Beach)
Symphony (Lotus)
Systat (Systat)
Tale of Benjamin Bunny (Discis)
TenCore (Computer Teaching Corp.)
Terrapin Logo (Terrapin)
TestBank 4.0 (Microsystems)
Teacher's Assistant (Microsystems)
Test and Tutor (Microsystems)
Test Quest (Snowflake)
Testmaker (Testmaker)
Toolbook (Asymetrix)
The Tree House (Brøderbund)
Turbo Basic (Borland)
True BASIC (True BASIC)
TutorTech (Techware)
Understanding Multiplication (Hartley)
The United States: A Geographic Overview (Society for Visual Education)
Ventura Publisher (Xerox)
Verb Usage (Hartley)
Video Encyclopedia of the 20th Century (CEL Educational Resources)
VideoSpigot (SuperMac Technology)
VisiCalc (Visicorp)
Visual BASIC (Microsoft)
Visualizing Algebra: The Function Analyzer (Sunburst)
Voyage of the Mimi series (Sunburst)
VP-Expert (WordTech)
Wagon Train 1848 (MECC)
Weather and Science Lab (Scholastic)
Windows (Microsoft)
Windows for Workgroups (Microsoft)
Windows on Telecommunications (Exsym)
Wizard of Words (Advanced Ideas)
Word (Microsoft)
WordPerfect (WordPerfect Corp.)
WordStar (Wordstar International)
Works (Microsoft)

World Community (MECC)
Writer's Helper (Conduit)
The Writing Center (Learning Company)

Writing to Read (IBM)
Writing to Write (IBM)

Selected Software Producers/Distributors

ABC News Interactive, 7 West 66th St., New York, NY 10023; 212-887-4060

Active Learning Systems, 5365 Avenida Encinas, Ste. J, Carlsbad, CA 92008; 619-931-7784, 800-423-0818

Adobe Systems, Inc., 1585 Charleston Rd., Box 7900, Mountain View, CA 94039-7900; 415-961-4400, 800-833-6687

Advanced Ideas Inc., 2902 San Pablo Ave., Berkeley, CA 94702

AI Corp., 138 Technology Dr., P.O. Box 9156, Waltham, MA 02254-9748; 800-677-2400

AimTech Corp., 20 Trafalgar Square, Nashua, NH 03063; 800-289-2884

Aldus Corp., 411 First Ave. S., Seattle, WA 98104; 206-628-2320

Apple Computer, Inc., 20525 Mariani Ave., Cupertino, CA 95014-6299; 408-996-1010

Applied Optical Media Corp., 1450 Boot Rd., Bldg. 400, West Chester, PA 19380; 800-321-7259

Ashton-Tate, 20101 Hamilton Ave., Torrance, CA 90502-1341; 800-437-4329, 213-329-8000

Astral Development Corp., Londonderry Sq., Ste. 112, Londonderry, NH 03053; 613-432-6800

Asymetrix Corporation, 110 110th Ave. N.E., Ste. 717, Bellevue, WA 98004-0419; 800-448-6543, 206-637-1500

AutoDesk, Inc., 2320 Marinship Way, Sausalito, CA 94965; 415-332-2344

Baudville Software, 5380 52nd St. S.E., Grand Rapids, MI 49508

Borland International, 1800 Green Hills Rd., Scotts Valley, CA 95066; 800-437-4329, 408-438-8400

BLOC Publishing Corp., 800 Southwest 37th Ave., Ste. 765, Miami, FL 33134

Brøderbund, 500 Redwood Blvd., Box 6125, Novato, CA 94948-6125; 800-521-6263

CE Software, 1854 Fuller Rd., Box 65580, West Des Moines, IA 50265; 800-523-7638

Claris Software, 5201 Patrick Henry Dr., Box 58168, Santa Clara, CA 95052-8168 800-747-7483, 408-987-8169

Compton's NewMedia, 2320 Camino Vida Roble, Carlsbad, CA 92009; 800-862-2206

Computer Teaching Corp., 1713 S. State St., Champaign, IL 61820; 217-352-6363

Conduit, University of Iowa, Oakdale Campus, Iowa City, IA 52242; 800-365-9774, 319-335-4100

Corel Systems Corp., 1600 Carling Ave., Ottawa, Ontario K1Z 8R2, Canada; 613-728-8200

CUE Softswap, Box 271704, Concord, CA 94527-1704; 415-685-7265

Davidson & Associates, Box 2961, Torrance, CA 90503; 800-545-7677, 800-556-6141

Decision Development Corp., 2680 Bishop Dr., Ste. 122, San Ramon, CA 94583; 800-800-4332, 510-830-8896

Developmental Learning Materials (DLM), Box 4000, Allen, TX 75002; 214-248-6300

Didatech Software, 3812 William St., Burnaby, British Columbia V5C 3H9, Canada; 800-665-0667, 604-299-4435

Discis Knowledge Research Inc., 45 Sheppard Ave. E., Ste. 410, Toronto, Ontario M2N 5W9, Canada; 800-567-4321, 416-250-6537

Eastgate Systems, Box 1307, Cambridge, MA 02238; 617-924-9044

EduQuest, The IBM Educational Systems Company, One Culver Rd., Dayton, NJ 08810-9998; 800-426-3327

ElectronicArts, 1820 Gateway Dr., San Mateo, CA 94404; 415-572-2787

Encyclopedia Brittanica Educational Corp., 425 N. Michigan Ave., Chicago, IL 60611

Epyx, 600 Galveston Dr., Redwood City, CA 94063

Exsym, 301 North Harrison St., Bldg. B, Ste. 435, Princeton, NJ 08540; 609-737-2312

Facts on File, Inc., 460 Park Ave. S., New York, NY 10016-7382; 212-683-2244

Gessler Publishing Co., Inc., 55 W. 13th St., New York, NY 10011; 212-627-0099

Grolier Electronic Publishing, Sherman Tpk., Danbury, CT 06816; 800-356-5590

Hartley Courseware Inc., 133 Bridge St., Dimondale, MI 48821; 800-247-1380, 517-646-6458

Hearlihy & Co., 714 W. Columbia St., Box 869, Springfield, OH 45501

Hirschfelt Software, Box 215, Sheridan, NY 14135

Humanities Software, Box 950, 408 Columbia, Ste. 222, Hood River, OR 97031; 800-245-6737

IBM (general), contact your local IBM representative

IBM (multimedia), 1133 Westchester Ave., White Plains, NY 10604; 800-426-9402

Intellimation, 130 Cremona Dr., Box 1922, Santa Barbara, CA 93116-1922; 800-346-8355, 800-443-6633

ISTE (International Society for Technology in Education), 1878 Agate St., Eugene, OR 97403-1923; 800-336-5191, 503-346-4414

IPS Publishing, Inc., 31316 Via Colinas, Ste. 110, Westlake Village, CA 91362

J&S Software, Box 1276, Port Washington, NY 11050; 516-767-0393

K-12 MicroMedia Publishing, 6 Arrow Rd., Ramsey, NJ 07446; 800-292-1997

Key Curriculum Press, 2512 Martin Luther King Jr. Way, Box 2304, Berkeley, CA 94702; 510-548-2304

Knowledge Revolution, 497 Vermont St., San Francisco, CA 94107; 800-766-6615

Lawrence Productions, Inc., 1800 South 35th, Galesburg, MI 49053; 800-421-4157, 616-665-7075

Learning Company, 6493 Kaiser Dr., Fremont, CA 94555; 800-852-2255

LCSI (Logo Computer Systems Inc.), P.O. Box 162, Highgate Springs, VT 05460; 800-321-LOGO

Lotus Development Corp., 55 Cambridge Pkwy., Cambridge, MA 02142; 800-343-5414, 617-577-8500

Macromedia, 600 Townsend, Ste. 310W, San Francisco, CA 94103; 800-248-4477, 415-442-0200

Maxis, 2 Theater Sq., Ste. 230, Orinda, CA 94563-3346; 510-254-9700

McGraw-Hill, 1221 Avenue of the Americas, New York, NY 10020; 212-512-2000

MECC (Minnesota Educational Computing Corp.), 6160 Summit Dr. N., Minneapolis, MN 55430-4003; 800-685-6322, 612-569-1500

Micro Power & Light Co., 8814 Sanshire Ave., Dallas, TX 75231; 214-553-0105

Micrografix, Inc., 1303 Arapaho Rd., Richardson, TX 75081; 800-733-3729, 214-234-1769

Microsoft Corp., One Microsoft Way, Redmond, WA 98052-6399; 800-426-9400, 206-882-8080

Microsystems Software, 1834 E. Baseline Rd., Ste. 102, Tempe, AZ 85283; 800-767-3552, 602-820-8585

Midwest Agribusiness Services Inc., 4565 Highway 33 West, West Bend, WI 53095; 800-523-3475

Mindscape Software, 1345 Diversey Parkway, Chicago, IL 60614-1299; 800-829-1900

Misty City Software, 10921 129th Place N.E., Kirkland, WA 98033; 206-828-3107

National Geographic Society, Educational Services, Box 96892, Washington, DC 20090; 800-368-2728

New England Software, Greenwich Office Park 3, Greenwich, CT 06831; 203-625-0062

Optical Data Corp., 30 Technology Dr., Warren, NJ 07060; 800-248-8478

Optimage Interactive Services Co. LP, 1501 50th St., Ste. 100, West Des Moines, IA 50265; 800-234-5484, 515-225-7000

Optilearn, Box 997, Stevens Point, WI 54481; 715-34-6060

Optimum Resource Inc., 36 Bow Circle, Hilton Head, SC 29928; 800-327-1473, 803-785-7441

Owl International, Inc., 2800 156th Ave. S.E., Ste. 205, Bellevue, WA 98007-9949; 800-344-9737, 206-747-3203

Philosoft Inc., World Trade Centre, 10 Yonge St., Ste. 2809, Toronto, Ontario M5E 1R4 Canada

Pioneer Communications of America, Inc., 600 East Crescent Ave., Upper Saddle River, NJ 07458-1827; 201-327-6400

Power Industries, 37 Walnut St., Wellesley Hills, MA 02181; 800-395-5009

Power Up Software, 2929 Campus Dr., San Mateo, CA 94403; 414-345-5900

Prentice-Hall, Education Publishing Group, Englewood Cliffs, NJ 07632; 201-757-9277

PRO/TEM Software, 814 Tolman Dr., Stanford, CA 94305-9965; 415-947-1024

Quark, Inc., 1800 Grant St., Denver, CO 80203; 800-476-4575, 303-894-8888

Que Software, 11711 N. College Ave., Ste. 140, Carmel, IN 46032

Realtime Learning Systems, 2700 Connecticut Ave. N.W., Washington, DC 20008; 800-832-2472, 202-483-1510

Reference Software International, 330 Townsend St., Ste. 123, San Francisco, CA 94107-9883; 415-541-0222

R. R. Bowker, 121 Chanlon Rd., New Province, NJ 07974; 800-323-3288

Roger Wagner Publishing, 1050 Pioneer Way, Suite P, El Cajun, CA 92020; 619-442-0522

SAS Institute, Box 8000, Cary, NC 27512-8000

Scandinavian PC Systems, 51 Monroe St., Ste. 1101, Rockville, MD 20850

Scholastic, Inc., Box 7502, 2931 E. McCarthy St., Jefferson City, MO 65102-9968; 800-541-5513

Sensible Software, 335 E. Big Beaver, Ste. 207, Troy, MI 48083; 313-528-1950

Sierra On-Line, Box 485, Coarsegold, CA 93614; 800-326-6654

Silicon Beach Software, Inc., 9770 Carroll Center Rd., Ste. J, San Diego, CA 92126; 619-695-6956

Snowflake Software, 8 Cedar Heights Rd., Rhinebeck, NY 12572; 914-876-3328

Society for Visual Education, Inc., 1345 Diversey Pkwy., Chicago, IL 60614-1299; 312-525-1500

Software for Kids, 9950 Concord Church Rd., Lewisville, NC 27023; 919-945-9000

Software Publishing Corp., 3165 Kifer Rd., Santa Clara, CA 95951; 408-986-8000

Software Toolworks, 60 Leveroni Ct., Novato, CA 94949; 415-883-3000

Sorcim Corp., 2195 Fortune Dr., San Jose, CA 95131; 408-942-1727

Spinnaker Software Corp., 201 Broadway, Cambridge, MA 02139; 800-323-8088, 617-494-1219

SPSS Inc., 444 N. Michigan Ave., Chicago, IL 60611

Successful Software Inc., 2232 Crosswind Dr., Kalamazoo, MI 49008; 616-381-1691

Sunburst Middle and High School Division, 101 Castleton St., Box 870, Pleasantville, NY 10570; 800-338-3457

SuperMac Technology, 485 Potrero Ave., Sunnyvale, CA 94086; 800-334-3005, 408-245-2202

Symantec Corp., 10201 Torre Ave., Cupertino, CA 95014; 800-441-7234, 408-253-9600

Teacher Support Software, Box 7130, Gainesville, FL 32605

Teacher's Aide, Inc., Box 1666, Highland Park, IL 60035

Techware Inc., Box 151085, Altamonte Springs, FL 32715; 407-695-9000

Terrapin Software Inc., 400 Riverside St., Portland, ME 04103; 207-878-8200

Testmaker, 912 Kingsley Dr., Colorado Springs, CO 80909

Third Wave Technologies, 11934 Lorain Ave., Cleveland, OH 44111

Timeworks, 444 Lake Cook Rd., Deerfield, IL 60015; 708-948-9200

Tom Snyder Productions, 90 Sherman Street, Cambridge, MA 02140; 800-342-0236, 617-876-4433

True BASIC, 12 Commerce Ave., West Lebanon, NH 03784-9758; 800-872-2742

Turner Educational Services Inc., One CNN Center N. W., Box 105366, Atlanta, GA 30348-5366; 800-344-6219

Unison World, Kyocera Unison Inc., Box 3056, Berkeley, CA 94703; 800-443-0100

Visicorp, 2895 Zanker Rd., San Jose, CA 95134

Vernier Software, 2920 S.W. 89th St., Portland, OR 97225; 503-297-5317

The Waterford Institute, 1480 E. 9400 South, Sandy, UT 84092; 800-767-9976

William K. Bradford Publishing, 310 School St., Acton, MA 01720; 800-421-2009

Wings for Learning/Sunburst Communications, 1600 Green Hills Rd., Box 660002, Scotts Valley, CA 95067-0002; 800-321-7511, 408-438-5502

WordPerfect Corp., 1555 N. Technology Way, Orem, UT 84057; 800-451-5151, 801-225-5000, 800-321-4566

WordStar International, Box 9000, San Fernando, CA 91341-9978

WordTech Systems, Inc., 21 Altarinda Rd., Orinda, CA 94563; 800-228-3295; 510-254-0900

World Library Inc., 12894 Haster St., Garden Grove, CA 92640; 800-443-0238, 714-748-7197

Xerox Corp., 360 N. Sepulveda Blvd., El Segundo, CA 90245; 800-445-5554

ZSoft Corp., 450 Franklin Rd., Ste. 100, Marietta, GA 30067; 800-444-4780, 404-428-0008

Selected CD-ROM and Laserdisc Producers/Suppliers

ABC News Interactive, 7 West 66th St., New York, NY 10023; 212-887-4060

Applied Optical Media Corp., 1450 Boot Rd., Bldg. 400, West Chester, PA 19380; 800-321-7259

Belser Knowledge Services, 54 W. 21st St., Ste. 309, New York, NY 10010; 212-727-3888

Bowker Electronic Publishing, 121 Chanlon Rd., New Providence, NJ 07974; 800-323-3288

Brøderbund, 500 Redwood Blvd., Box 6125, Novato, CA 94948-6125; 800-521-6263

Bureau of Electronic Publishing, Inc., 141 New Road, Parsipanny, NJ 07054; 800-828-4766, 201-808-2700

CEL Educational Resources, 477 Madison Ave., New York, NY 10022; 800-235-3339, 212-421-5000

Compton's NewMedia, 2320 Camino Vida Roble, Carlsbad, CA 92009; 800-862-2206

Compuwest, 300 Boblett St., Box 3379, Blaine, WA 98230; 800-663-0001

Coronet/MTI Film & Video, 108 Wilmot Rd., Deerfield, IL 60015; 800-777-8100

Discis Knowledge Research Inc., 45 Sheppard Ave. E., Ste. 410, Toronto, Ontario M2N 5W9, Canada; 800-567-4321, 416-250-6537

EDUCORP, 7434 Trade St., San Diego, CA 92121-2410

Emerging Technology Consultants, Box 120444, St. Paul, MN 55112; 612-639-3973

Interaction: CD-ROM & Optical Storage, 24705 US 19 N., Ste. 308, Clearwater, FL 34623; 800-783-3ROM, 813-799-6007

Microsoft Corp., One Microsoft Way, Redmond, WA 98052-6399; 800-426-9400, 206-882-8080

Multimedia Nuts and Bolts, 115 Bloomingdale Lane, Woodbridge, Ontario L4L 6X8, Canada; 800-363-3227

National Geographic Society, Educational Services, Box 96892, Washington, DC 20090

Optical Data Corp., 30 Technology Dr., Warren, NJ 07060; 800-248-8478

Optimage Interactive Services Co. LP, 1501 50th St., Ste. 100, West Des Moines, IA 50265; 800-234-5484, 515-225-7000

Optilearn, Box 997, Stevens Point, WI 54481; 715-34-6060

Pioneer Communications of America, Inc., 600 E. Crescent Ave., Upper Saddle River, NJ 07458-1827; 201-327-6400

Scholastic, Inc., Box 7502, 2931 E. McCarthy St., Jefferson City, MO 65102-9968; 800-541-5513

Sierra On-Line, Box 485, Coarsegold, CA 93614; 800-326-6654

Society for Visual Education, Inc., 1345 Diversey Pkwy., Chicago, IL 60614-1299; 312-525-1500

Software for Kids, 9950 Concord Church Rd., Lewisville, NC 27023; 919-945-9000

Software Toolworks, 60 Leveroni Ct., Novato, CA 94949; 415-883-3000

Turner Educational Services Inc., One CNN Center N. W., Box 105366, Atlanta, GA 30348-5366; 800-344-6219

Updata, 1736 Westware Blvd., Los Angeles, CA 90024; 800-882-2844

Videodiscovery, 1700 Westlake Ave. N., Ste. 600, Seattle, WA 98109; 800-548-3472, 206-285-5400

The Voyager Company, 1351 Pacific Coast Hwy., Santa Monica, CA 90401; 310-451-1383

Walnut Creek CDROM, 4041 Pike Lane, Ste. E, Concord, CA 94520; 800-786-9907

Wisconsin Foundation for Vocational, Technical and Adult Education, Inc., 2564 Branch St., Middleton, WI 53562-9965; 608-831-6313

Selected Telecommunications/ Information Services

Accu-Weather, 619 College Ave., State College, PA 16801; 814-237-0309

America Online, 8619 Westwood Center Dr., Vienna, VA 22182-9806; 800-227-6364

Applelink-Personal Edition, 8619 Westwood Center Drive, Vienna, VA 22180; 800-227-6364

ARPANET, Stanford Research Institute, Menlo Park, CA 94025; 800-235-3155

AT&T Long-Distance Learning Network, 295 North Maple Ave., Rm. 6234S3, Basking Ridge, NJ 07201; 201-221-8544

BRS (Bibliographic Retrieval Service), 1200 Route 7, Latham, NY 12110; 800-468-0908

CompuServe, 5000 Arlington Center Blvd., Columbus, OH 43220; 800-848-8990, 614-457-8600

Delphi, 3 Blackstone St., Cambridge, MA 02139; 800-695-4005

Dialog Information Services, Inc., Classroom Instructional Program Administrator, 1901 N. Moore St., Ste. 500, Arlington, VA 22209; 800-334-2564

Dow Jones News/Retrieval Service, Box 300, Princeton, NJ 08543-0300; 800-522-3567, 609-520-8349

EDUCOM (Bitnet), Box 364, Princeton, NJ 08540; 603-520-3377

FrEdMail Foundation, Box 243, Bonita, CA 91908-0243; 619-475-4852

GEnie (The General Electric Information Service), 410 N. Washington St., Rockville, MD 20850; 800-638-9636

GTE Education Services Inc., 8505 N. Freeport Pkwy., Ste. 600, Irving, TX 75063-9931

Mead Data Central, 9443 Springboro Pike, Box 933, Dayton, OH 45401; 800-227-4908

NASA Spacelink, 202-895-0028 (modem up to 2400 baud, 8N1)

National Geographic Society KidsNet, Educational Services, Box 96892, Washington DC 20090

NSFNET, National Science Foundation, 1800 G Street N.W., Washington, DC 20550; 202-357-9717

OCLC (Online Computer Library Center), 6565 Frantz Rd., Dublin, OH 43017-0702; 800-848-5878

Prodigy Services Company, 445 Hamilton Ave., White Plains, NY 10601; 800-776-0836

SpecialNet, c/o Colorado Department of Education, 201 E. Colfax, Denver, CO 80203; 303-866-6722 (special education)

Major Educational Software Discounters

Campus Technology Products, Box 2909, Leesburg, VA 22075

Chambers International Corp., 5499 N. Federal Highway, Ste. A, Boca Raton, FL 33487

Diskovery Educational Systems, 1860 Old Okeechobee Rd., Ste. 105, West Palm Beach, FL 33409

Selected Shareware/Public Domain Software Sources

BizComp Services, Box 345, Moorpark, CA 93021

Chariot Software Group, 3659 India St., San Diego, CA 92103 (Mac)

Computer Budget Shopper, 2203 Park Ave., Cheyenne, WY 82007

Hypermedia and Instructional Software Clearinghouse, University of Colorado at Denver, Campus Box 106, Box 173364, Denver, CO 80217-3364

PC-SIG, 1030-D E. Duane Ave., Sunnyvale, CA 94086 (Total collection available on CD)

Profit Press, 824 E. Ft. Lowell Rd., Tucson, AZ 85719; 602-770-0000

RB Shareware, Box 4382, Mankato, MN 56002-4382

Reasonable Solutions, 1221 Disk Dr., Medford, OR 97501-6639; 800-876-3475

Shareware Express, 1908-D Ashland Ave., Ashland OR 97520; 800-346-2842

Software Labs, 100 Corporate Pointe, Ste. 195, Culver City, CA 90231; 800-569-7900

Walnut Creek CDROM, 4041 Pike Lane, Ste. E, Concord, CA 94520; 800-786-9907

Windows Discount Shareware (BBS), Box 1912, Binghamton, NY 13902-1912; 607-722-0177 (modem up to 16.8K baud, 8N1)

The Computer Shopper, widely available on magazine stands, prints directories of bulletin boards and lists of user groups.

Selected Integrated Learning Systems Sources

Computer Curriculum Corporation, Box 3711, Sunnyvale, CA 94088-3711

Computer Networking Specialists, Inc., Rt. 1, Box 286-C, Walla Walla, WA 99362; 800-372-3277, 509-529-3070

Control Data Corporation, PLATO Educational Services, 8800 Queen Ave. S., Bloomington, MN 55431; 800-328-1109

DEGEM Ltd., Two Park Ave., New York, NY 10016-5635; 212-561-7200

Houghton Mifflin Company, Mount Support Rd., Lebanon, NH 03766; 603-448-3838

Ideal Learning Inc., 5005 Royal Lane, Irving, TX 75063; 214-929-4201

Jostens Learning Corp., 7878 N. 16th St., Ste. 100, Phoenix, AZ 85020-4402; 800-442-4339, 602-678-7272

Skills Bank, 15 Governor's Court, Baltimore, MD 21207-2791; 800-847-5455

Unisys Corporation, Box 500, MS B330, Blue Bell, PA 19424; 215-542-4583

Wasatch Education Systems, 5250 S. 300 W., Ste. 350, Salt Lake City, UT 84100-0007; 801-261-1001

WICAT Systems, Box 539, Orem, UT 84057; 801-224-6400

Special Needs Resources/ Adaptive Devices

Access Unlimited—Speech Enterprises, Box 7986, Houston, TX 77024; 713-461-1666

ARTS Computer Products, Inc., 145 Tremont St., Ste. 407, Boston, MA 02111; 617-482-8248

COMPUPLAY Resource Centers, National Lekotek Center, 2100 Ridge Ave., Evanston, IL 60204; 708-328-0001

Computer Aids Corp., 124 W. Washington, Ste. 220, Fort Wayne, IN 46802; 800-647-8255

Computer Options for the Exceptional, 85 Market St., Poughkeepsie, NY 12601; 914-471-2765

Health Resource Center (Higher Education and Adult Training for People with Handicaps), One DuPont Circle N.W., Ste. 800, Washington, DC 20036-1193; 800-544-3284, 202-939-9320 (voice/TDD)

Glen Brown & Associates, 8 Tami Court, Bloomington, IL 61701; 309-827-5450

Kurzweil Applied Intelligence, Inc., 411 Waverley Oaks Rd., Waltham, MA 02154; 617-893-5151

Laureate Learning Systems, 110 E. Spring St., Winoski, VT 05404

LINC Resources Inc., Publications Division, 91 Vine St., Pawtucket, RI 02861; 401-725-3973

Microsystems Software Inc., 600 Worcester Rd., Framingham, MA 01701; 800-828-2600

Personal Touch Corp., 4320 Stevens Creek Blvd., San Jose, CA 95129; 408-246-8822

SpecialNet, c/o Colorado Department of Education, 201 E. Colfax, Denver, CO 80203; 303-866-6722

Trace Center, Waisman Center, University of Wisconsin-Madison, 1500 Highland Ave., Madison, WI 53705; 608-263-5408

Xerox Imaging Systems, Inc., 9 Centennial Dr., Peabody, MA 01960; 800-248-6550

Professional Organizations of Special Interest

American Educational Research Association (AERA)

This organization of educational researchers has a special interest group for members interested in computer-based learning. The annual meeting includes many computer-related research reports. Publisher of *Educational Researcher, American Educational Research Journal,* and *Review of Educational Research,* among others.

Address: 1230 17th St. N.W., Washington, DC 20036

Association for the Advancement of Computing in Education

Publisher of *ED-TECH Review, Journal of Artificial Intelligence in Education, Journal of Computers in Mathematics and Science Teaching, Journal of Computing in Childhood Education, Journal of Educational Multimedia and Hypermedia,* and *Journal of Technology and Teacher Education.* Sponsor of ED-MEDIA (world conference on educational multimedia and hypermedia) and AI-ED (world conference on artificial intelligence in education).

Address: Box 2966, Charlottesville, VA 22902-2966

Association for Computing Machinery (ACM)

This professional association has local chapters and supports various special interest groups (SIGs), including SIGCUE for computer users in education. Publisher of *Communications of the ACM* and *SIGCUE Bulletin.*

Address: 1133 Avenue of the Americas, New York, NY 10036

Association for the Development of Computer-Based Instructional Systems (ADCIS)

This group seeks to promote computer-based learning by stimulating and fostering communication among educational institutions at all levels, government agencies, and the private sector. Publisher of *Journal of Computer-Based Instruction.*

Address: ADCIS Headquarters, Ste. 111, 1601 W. 5th Ave. Columbus, OH 43212

Association for Educational Communications and Technology (AECT)

Devoted to applications of all technologies to the learning process, AECT members come from all levels of education and from business and industry. The Division of Information Systems and Computers (DISC) is a special interest group for computer educators and users. Publisher of *Tech Trends* and *Educational Technology Research & Development.*

Address: 1025 Vermont Ave. N.W., Ste. 820, Washington, DC 20005

Computer Using Educators, Inc. (CUE)

CUE is a nonprofit corporation founded by teachers in 1978 to promote development and growth in the use of computer and other technologies in education and to contribute to development of information, materials, and software for all interested educators. As an organization, it serves California educators with statewide conferences. Others benefit from Softswap, its distribution system for low-priced, freely copiable educational software.

Address: Box 2087, Menlo Park, CA 94026

Educational Products Information Exchange (EPIE) Institute

The "Consumer's Union" of educational computing, responsible for very stringent testing of courseware. See Chapter 11 for further information.

Address: P.O. Box 839, Water Mill, NY 11976

International Society for Technology in Education (ISTE)

The flagship organization for computer educators. ISTE is the successor to the International Council for Computers in Education (ICCE) which merged in 1989 with the International Association for Computing in Education (IACE, formerly the Association for Educational Data Systems or AEDS). The organization focuses on computer technology applications at all levels, especially K-12. ISTE publishes many excellent periodicals, including *The Computing Teacher* and *Journal of Research on Computing in Education*. See the publications section of the appendix for others.

Address: 1787 Agate St., Eugene, OR 97403-1923

The Logo Foundation

A source for varied materials related to Logo, including research reports and software.

Address: 250 W. 57th St., Ste. 2603, New York, NY 10107-2603

Microcomputer Software and Information for Teachers (MicroSIFT)

MicroSIFT has been a leader in developing software evaluation practices and itself collects and assesses educational software.

Address: Northwest Regional Educational Laboratory, 100 S.W. Main, Ste. 500, Portland, OR 97204

National Council of Teachers of Mathematics (NCTM)

Professional organization for mathematics teachers at all levels, with a strong commitment to applications of computer technology in math education. Publisher of *Mathematics Teacher*, a source of many reviews of mathematics software.

Address: 1906 Association Dr., Reston, VA 22091

National Science Teachers Association (NSTA)

Similar to NCTM, but aimed at science teachers. Publisher of *The Science Teacher*.
Address: 1742 Connecticut Ave. N.W., Washington, DC 20009

Society for Applied Learning Technology (SALT)

An organization concerned with technological innovation. Geared largely to higher education, business, and the military. Sponsors seminars and workshops on interactive video and other emerging technologies. Publisher of *Journal of Educational Technology Systems*.
Address: 50 Culpepper St., Warrenton, VA 22186

Technical Educational Research Center (TERC)

TERC is an educational computing research and development center, with special interest in science applications including interface of laboratory instruments to microcomputers. Publisher of *Hands On!*
Address: 2067 Massachusetts Ave. Cambridge, MA 02140

Publications of Special Interest

Journals and Magazines

AI Expert, Miller Freeman Publications, 500 Howard St., San Francisco, CA 94105

BYTE, McGraw-Hill, Inc., 70 Main St., Peterborough, NH 03458

CD-ROM Today, GP Publications Inc., 23-00 Rte. 208, Fair Lawn, NJ 07410

Computer Assisted English Language Learning (CÆLL) Journal, International Society for Technology in Education (ISTE), 1787 Agate St., Eugene, OR 97403-1923

Computer Science Education, Ablex Publishing Corp., 355 Chestnut St., Norwood, NJ 07648

Computer Science Syllabus, P.O. Box 2716, Sunnyvale, CA 94087-0716

Computers and Composition, Michigan Technological University, Department of Humanities, Houghton, MI 49931

Computers and Education, Pergamon Press, 600 White Plains Rd., Tarrytown, NY 10591-5153

Computers in Human Behavior, Pergamon Press, 600 White Plains Rd., Tarrytown, NY 10591

Computers in the Schools, Haworth Press, Inc., 10 Alice St., Binghamton, NY 13904-1580

Computers, Reading and Language Arts, Modern Learning Publishers, Inc., 1308 E. 38th Street, Oakland, CA 94602

The Computing Teacher, ISTE, 1787 Agate Street, Eugene, OR 97403-1923

Curriculum Product News, Educational Media Inc., 992 High Ridge Rd., Stamford, CT 06905

ED-TECH Review, Association for the Advancement of Computing in Education (AACE), Box 2966, Charlottesville, VA 22902

Educational IRM Quarterly, ISTE, 1787 Agate St., Eugene, OR 97403-1923

Educational Technology, 720 Palisade Ave., Englewood Cliffs, NJ 07632

Educational Technology Research and Development, Association for Educational Communications and Technology (AECT), 1025 Vermont Ave., N.W., Ste. 820, Washington, DC 20005

Electronic Learning, Scholastic, Inc., 730 Broadway, New York, NY 10003

Future Generations Computer Systems, Elsevier Science Publishers, 52 Vanderbilt Avenue, New York, NY 10017

Hands-On! Technical Education Research Center, 2067 Massachusetts Ave., Cambridge, MA 02140

HyperNEXUS: Journal of Hypermedia and Multimedia Studies, ISTE, 1787 Agate St., Eugene, OR 97403-1923

IAT Briefings, Institute for Academic Technology, Box 12017, Research Triangle Park, NC 27709

InCider/A+, IDG Communications, 80 Elm St., Peterborough, NH 03458

InfoWorld, InfoWorld Publishing Co., 155 Bovet Rd., Ste. 800, San Mateo, CA 94402

Instruction Delivery Systems, Communicative Technology Corporation, 50 Culpepper St., Warrenton, VA 22186

Interact, International Interactive Communications Society, 2120 Steiner St., San Francisco, CA 94115

Interactive Learning Environments, Ablex Publishing Corp., 355 Chestnut St., Norwood, NJ 07648

Journal of Artificial Intelligence in Education, AACE, Box 2966, Charlottesville, VA 22902

Journal of Computer-Based Instruction, Association for the Development of Computer-based Instructional Systems, (ADCIS), 1601 W. 5th Ave. Ste. 111, Columbus, OH 43212

Journal of Computer Science Education, ISTE, 1787 Agate St., Eugene, OR 97403-1923

Journal of Computers in Mathematics and Science Teaching, AACE, Box 2966, Charlottesville, VA 22902

Journal of Computing in Childhood Education, AACE, Box 2966, Charlottesville, VA 22902

Journal of Computing in Teacher Education, ISTE, 1787 Agate St., Eugene, OR 97403-1923

Journal of Educational Computing Research, Baywood Publishing Company, Inc., 26 Austin Ave., Box 337, Amityville, NY 11701

Journal of Educational Multimedia and Hypermedia, AACE, Box 2966, Charlottesville, VA 22902

Journal of Educational Technology Systems, Baywood Publishing Company, Inc., 26 Austin Ave., Box 337, Amityville, NY 11701

Journal of Interactive Instruction Development, Society for Applied Learning Technology (SALT), 50 Culpepper Street, Warrenton, VA 22186

Journal of Research on Computing in Education, ISTE, 1787 Agate St., Eugene, OR 97403-1923

Journal of Science Education and Technology, Plenum Publishing Corp., 233 Spring St., New York, NY 10013-1578

Journal of Technology and Teacher Education, AACE, Box 2966, Charlottesville, VA 22902

Learning, P.O. Box 2580, Boulder, CO 80322

Logo Exchange, ISTE, 1787 Agate St., Eugene, OR 97403-1923

Machine-Mediated Learning, Taylor & Francis Inc., 242 Cherry St., Philadelphia, PA 19106-1906

MacUser, P.O. Box 56972, Boulder, CO 80321-6972

MacWEEK, Ziff-Davis Publishing Co., One Park Avenue, New York, NY 10016

MacWorld, MacWorld Communications Inc., 501 2nd St., San Francisco, CA 94107

Media and Methods, American Society of Educators, 1429 Walnut St., Philadelphia, PA 19102

Media in Education and Development, Taylor & Francis Inc., 242 Cherry St., Philadelphia, PA 19106-1906

Microcomputers in Education, Two Sequan Rd., Watch Hill, RI 02891

Microsoft Works in Education, ISTE, 1787 Agate St., Eugene, OR 97403-1923

MIPS-the Magazine of Intelligent Personal Systems, 400 Amherst St., Nashua, NH 03063

NewMedia, HyperMedia Communications Inc., 901 Mariner's Island Blvd., Ste. 365, San Mateo, CA 94404

PC AI, Knowledge Technology, Inc., 3310 West Bell Rd., Ste. 119, Phoenix, AZ 85023

PC Computing, Ziff-Davis Publishing Company, One Park Avenue, New York, NY 10016

PC Magazine, Ziff-Davis Publishing Company, One Park Avenue, New York, NY 10016

PC Week, Ziff-Davis Publishing Company, One Park Avenue, New York, NY 10016

PC World, Box 78270, San Francisco, CA 94107-9991

Personal Computing, Hayden Publishing Co., Inc., 10 Mulholland Dr., Hasbrouck Heights, NJ 07604

Personal Publishing, Hitchcock Publishing Company, 191 S. Gary Ave., Carol Stream, IL 60188

Presentation Products, Pacific Magazine Group, 513 Wilshire Blvd., Ste. 344, Santa Monica, CA 90401

SIGTC Connections, ISTE, 1787 Agate St., Eugene, OR 97403-1923

Syllabus, P.O. Box 2716, Sunnyvale, CA 94087-0716

T.H.E. Journal—Technological Horizons in Education, 150 El Camino Real, Tustin, CA 92680

Teaching and Computers, Scholastic, Inc., Box 2040, Mahopac, NY 10541-9963

Technology & Learning, Peter Li Inc., 330 Progress Rd., Dayton, OH 45499

Tech Trends, AECT, 1025 Vermont Ave. N.W., Ste. 820, Washington, DC 20005

Telecommunications in Education (T.I.E.) News, ISTE, 1787 Agate St., Eugene, OR 97403-1923

Windows Magazine, CMP Publications, 600 Community Dr., Manhasset, NY 11030

Windows User, Wandsworth Publishing Inc., 831 Federal Rd., Brookfield CT 06804

The Writing Notebook, Creative Word Processing in the Classroom, Box 1268, Eugene, OR 97440-1268

Newsletters

Apple Education News, Apple Computer Inc., 20525 Mariani Ave., Cupertino, CA 95014

Education Technology News, Business Publishers Inc., 951 Pershing Dr., Silver Spring, MD 20910-4464

Interface (The national newsletter of the IBM Teacher Preparation Grant schools), Curry School of Education, University of Virginia, 405 Emmet St., Charlottesville, VA 22903

ISTE Update, ISTE, 1787 Agate St., Eugene, OR 97403-1923

LCSI Logo Link, Logo Computer Systems Inc., Box 162, Highgate Springs, VT 05460

Logo Update, The Logo Foundation, 250 West 57th St., Ste. 2603, New York, NY 10107-2603

Online Searcher, 14 Haddon Rd., Scarsdale, NY 10583

The Sloane Report, P.O. Box 561689, Miami, FL 33256

Telecommunications in Education News, ISTE, 1787 Agate St., Eugene, OR 97403-1923

Terrapin Times, Terrapin Software Inc., 400 Riverside St., Portland, ME 04103

Glossary

Abacus. An ancient computing device consisting of several rows of rods that represent columns, and small beads that move on these columns to represent digits.

Ada. Computer language named for Lady Ada Augusta Lovelace, colleague of Babbage and daughter of Lord Byron.

Adaptive technologies. Hardware and/or software designed to compensate to some degree for user handicaps.

Algorithm. Step-by-step procedure for obtaining a specific result.

ALU. Arithmetic Logic Unit. That part of the CPU that performs calculations and logical functions. See also *CPU.*

Analog. Electronic signals that vary continuously over a range in the form of wave patterns (Cf. *digital.*)

Analog computer. A computer that represents values by a continuously changing physical variable, such as amount of electrical current. (Cf. *digital computer.*)

Applications software. Computer programs designed and written to perform certain major tasks, especially spreadsheets, data bases, or word processors.

Arithmetic Logic Unit. See *ALU.*

Articulation. Agreement as to what is taught at each grade level and therefore can be assumed at succeeding levels.

Artificial intelligence. A specialty area of computer science concerned with the development of machines and programs capable of functions that, in humans, appear to require consciousness or intelligence.

ASCII. *American Standards Code for Information Interchange.* A standardized format for representing numbers, letters, and special characters.

Assembler language. Low-level language that uses mnemonics to represent machine-language instructions. Assembler language source code must be translated into executable machine code by an appropriate assembler program.

Authoring language. A specialized high-level language that allows the user to write limited types of CAI without extensive programming knowledge or experience.

Authoring system. Software designed to allow non-programmers to create computer-based learning materials by responding to prompts or completing simple forms.

Automatic recalculation. Changes in the value in a worksheet cell resulting from a change in the value in another cell, e.g., changes in a total when a single entry is modified. Also called *automatic updating.*

Backup.   To make a copy of a data file to guard against loss of the original.

Bandwidth.   The relative ability of cables to carry information. Fiber optic cables have much greater bandwidth than traditional copper wires.

BASIC.   *Beginners All-purpose Symbolic Instruction Code.* A comparatively easy to learn and use high-level programming language. After falling from favor in the 1980s, BASIC is gaining popularity in the 1990s, including new versions such as macro languages in applications software.

Baud rate.   The number of bits per second transmitted between computers over communications lines. Roughly ten times the number of characters being transmitted; e.g., 2,400 baud is about 240 characters per second.

BBS (Bulletin board).   Computer system set up for posting and exchange of messages and software. See *RBBS.*

Binary.   Any system composed of only two alternate states, such as zero and one or on and off.

Bit.   *Binary Digit.* The smallest unit of information meaningful to a computer, usually represented as zero or one. (Cf. *byte.*)

Bitmap.   A graphic image saved as a pattern of dots, or a computer file containing such an image.

Boot/Boot up.   To start up a computer so that it is ready for normal operations.

Branching tutorial.   Tutorial CAI in which learners follow alternative paths through the lesson based upon their responses to questions.

Bug.   An error within a computer program.

Button.   An area on a computer screen that causes some action to occur when the user points to it with the mouse cursor and clicks a button.

Byte.   A series of bits, usually seven or eight, that together represent an individual letter, number, or other character. See also *K, Mega*

C.   A highly structured computer language developed by Bell Labs originally for the Unix operating system. Widely used to develop applications software.

CAI.   *Computer-Assisted Instruction.* Interaction of a learner with a computer that is playing a direct instructional role. Also the instructional software itself.

Card.   A single screen in a hypermedia product such as *HyperCard.* Called a page in *Linkway* and *Toolbook.* Similar to a database record.

CAV.   *Constant Angular Velocity.* Laserdisc format that provides up to 54,000 individually viewable images (or 30 minutes of motion video) per side.

Cell.   The space that is the intersection of one row and one column in a worksheet.

CD-I.   *Compact Disc-Interactive.* See *CD-ROM.*

CD-ROM.   *Compact Disc- Read Only Memory.* An optical disc technology with massive storage capability. Derivatives include CD-I (Compact Disc-Interactive) and DVI (Digital Video Interactive).

Chip.   A small piece of semiconducting material such as silicon upon which electrical circuits are etched.

Classroom publishing.   Use of inexpensive software to approximate desktop publishing.

Clip art. Professionally drawn graphics purchased specifically for use in one's own products, such as computer screens or desktop-publishing materials, in lieu of costly original artwork.

Clone. A computer functionally equivalent to another that is itself a standard, e.g., all MS-DOS computers not made by IBM.

CLV. *Constant Linear Velocity.* Laserdisc format for extended play. Provides up to 60 minutes of full-motion video per side, but without individual frames that can be viewed independently.

CMC. *Computer-Mediated Communication.* A form of electronic distance education in which communication among learners, who may never meet as a group, occurs through computers. Essentially similar to e-mail.

CMI. *Computer-Managed Instruction.* Use of a computer in the organization and management of instructional and classroom activities. (Cf. *CAI.*)

COBOL. *COmmon Business Oriented Language.* A high-level language for business applications that uses common English words and phrases.

Code. Instructions to a computer. Usually modified to indicate the nature of the code, e.g., machine code, source code, COBOL code. Also, the act of converting an algorithm into the specific statements and syntax of the programming language being used to develop software.

Command. An instruction to a computer system to perform a specified input, processing, or output task.

Commercial network. See *information service.*

Communication. The process of one computer transferring data to and from another computer through channels such as telephone lines.

Compiler. Program that translates an entire program in a high-level language into machine code prior to execution. (Cf. *interpreter.*)

Computer awareness. Intellectual knowledge of computers with no implication of any specific usage skills.

Computer competence. Sufficient knowledge to recognize when computer use would be advantageous, combined with necessary skills to use a computer effectively and efficiently for such identified tasks.

Computer literacy. The knowledge and skills required to function in an environment that utilizes computer and information technologies. Less knowledge and skill than computer competence.

Computer network. Any of several distinct ways in which groups of computers (and users) are connected together to share information and peripheral devices. (Cf. *workgroup, LAN, WAN.*)

Computer-assisted instruction. See *CAI.*

Computer-managed instruction. See *CMI.*

Computer-mediated communication. See *CMC.*

Conferencing. Real-time communication between two or more parties via computer. Requires participants to be on-line simultaneously, in contrast to e-mail.

Connect time. In telecommunications, the time spent on-line from signing on to signing off the host system.

Control unit. That part of the CPU that directs and manages all system components.

Courseware. Instructional computer programs and related support materials designed to enhance the teaching potential of the product.

CPU. *Central Processing Unit.* A microprocessor chip that is the ``brain'' of a computer system. Consists of the control, arithmetic, logic, and primary memory circuits where processing is actually performed.

Cursor. A movable spot of light that indicates current location on a computer monitor; often an underscore, lighted box, or arrowhead.

Data. Pieces of information, especially information used by a computer.

Data manager. See *filing system.*

Data processing. Manipulating pieces of information to produce a desired result.

Data redundancy. Data duplicated in multiple files for the purpose of identifying related records across the files.

Database. Information stored in an organized system of electronically accessible files, e.g., information on all students in a school.

Database management system (DBMS). Application software for creating and manipulating databases.

Debug. Identify and correct errors in a program.

Deductive shell. An expert system shell that requires the system developer to write the rules that constitute the system's knowledge base.

Desktop presentations. Electronic presentations created and delivered on-screen using presentation graphics software.

Desktop publishing. Use of sophisticated (and sometimes costly) software to compose text and graphics into near-typeset-quality pages.

Digital. Electronic signals consisting solely of on and off. (Cf. *analog*.)

Digital computer. Computer in which all data are represented digitally as on or off states. (Cf. *analog computer*.)

Digital Video Interactive. See *DVI, RTV, PLV*.

Disc. A data storage medium from which the computer can read, but to which it normally cannot write, e.g., compact disc, laser disc. (Cf. *disk*.)

Disk. A data storage medium with both read and write capability, e.g., hard disk. (Cf. *disc*.)

Diskette. A small, flexible disk with limited storage capacity that is inserted into a drive and removed as needed, e.g., a floppy disk.

Distance learning. Any instructional situation in which some or all learners are physically separated from one another during class time. Includes audio conferencing and computer-mediated communication (CMC).

Documentation. The manuals and accompanying materials that explain the functioning, use, and possible applications of computer hardware and software.

DOS. Any *Disk Operating System.* See *operating system*. Also part of the name of specific systems, such as MS-DOS & PC-DOS (used by IBM-PCs and compatibles) and DOS 3.3 & ProDos (used by Apple II computers).

Dot matrix printer. A printed whose characters are patterns of dots formed by small pins striking an inked ribbon.

Download. To transfer data from a remote computer to one's own computer. (Cf. *upload.*)

Drill and practice. A form of CAI that provides repetitive opportunities for a student to respond to questions concerning already-learned content and to receive feedback from the computer (Cf. *tutorial.*)

DVI. *Digital Video Interactive.* A multimedia encoding/decoding system for digitizing video and sound onto a hard disk drive and for playback of such digital files.

Electronic mail. See *e-mail.*

E-mail. Transmission and receipt of files, typically messages, among users of a computer network.

Ethernet. A standard specification for high-speed *LAN* connections. Also the most common type of *LAN* connection.

Expert system. Computer program which performs some task at the level of an expert. Consists minimally of a knowledge base, an inference engine to manipulate it, and a user interface.

Expert system shell. An expert system development tool consisting of user interfaces, an inference engine, and a structure for handling the knowledge base, but which is empty. Analogous to spreadsheet software.

Export. Save a file in a format other than that which is normal for the application software, thus requiring format translation.

Field. In data management, the smallest meaningful unit of information, such as ZIP code or last name. See also *file, record.* In hypermedia, an area on a screen that can contain text.

File. A group of related database records, such as an inventory. Also, any digital data saved onto a *hard disk* or *diskette.* See also *field, record.*

File server. The "master" computer of a *LAN* on which a common copy of application software as well as shared data files reside. Peripherals are attached to the server for the use of all work stations on the *LAN.*

Filing system. Data management software suitable for simple, single-file applications, but lacking many features of database software. Also termed *data manager.*

Floppy disk. See *diskette.*

Flowchart. A graphic representation of an algorithm or program; a visual algorithm.

Formula. An expression of calculations to be performed or relationships among cells in a worksheet.

FORTRAN. *FORmula TRANslator.* A high-level language particularly suited to mathematical and scientific applications.

Forum. A discussion group on an information service, e.g., CompuServe. Similar to a conference or a list on Internet, but charges apply.

FPU (Floating Point Unit). See *math coprocessor.*

Frames. In desktop publishing, areas of varied size and shape on a page, each designated for text, a graphic image, a photo, or other content.

Useful in creating a specific look in a product, independent of the actual frame contents.

Freeware. Software distributed at no more than diskette duplication cost, such as *FrEdWriter*.

Function. A previously defined formula.

Fuzzy logic. The basis of decision making in an expert system, using confidence levels to indicate the strength of a judgment that is hoped to be "usable" rather than the only correct outcome.

GUI. See *Graphical User Interface*.

Graphical User Interface (GUI). Popularized by Apple's Macintosh computer, a GUI enables users to perform many computer operations by pointing to icons (graphics) with a mouse cursor and clicking its button(s). See also *WIMP*.

Graphics. Computer output in the form of images, pictures, charts, graphs, etc. as opposed to alphanumeric characters.

Graphics pad/tablet. An input device on which the user can draw with a stylus or other device to create images on the computer screen.

Hacker. An individual who accesses and uses a computer system without authorization.

Hard copy. Printed computer output.

Hard disk. A large-capacity, high-speed data storage device with multiple magnetic disks that are generally not removable. (Cf. *diskette*.)

Hardware. The physical components of a computer system.

High-level language. A programming language whose instructions resemble English statements more than computer codes. These statements must be converted into machine code by an *interpreter* or *compiler* before the computer can execute them. (Cf. *low-level language*.)

Host. The computer which controls a telecommunications network, to which you log in or sign on after calling from your computer. A server on a *WAN*.

Hyper. As used in hypertext or hypermedia, non-linear or non-sequential.

HyperCard. Software for the Apple Macintosh that implements hypertext and hypermedia concepts.

Hypermedia. Software that interconnects nodes containing differing data formats in a nonlinear fashion. Text, graphics, sound, animation, and laser or compact disc segments can all be interrelated in a web or network of information.

Hypertext. Text with cross-reference links among words that allow for non-sequential reading. Ted Nelson is credited with coining the term.

Icon. Graphics used to represent actions, functions, or components of a computer system. See *graphical user interface*.

Import. Load a file in a format other than that which is normal application software, e.g. load a *MacWrite* file into *Word*. Often necessitates translation of file formats.

Individualized instruction. Instruction tailored to the specific needs of each student, in contrast to group instruction.

Inductive shell. An expert system shell that derives its rules from examples provided by the system developer, requiring little or no programming.

Inference engine. The logic or reasoning component of an expert system.

Information service. National or international network offering access to a vast and diverse array of resources. Examples include CompuServe and America Online. Also called *information utility* or *commercial network*.

Information utility. See *information service*.

Infusion. The physical presence of significant numbers of computers in a school or district, apart from their actual use.

Ink jet printer. Printer whose characters are formed by spraying tiny droplets of ink onto the paper.

Input. Data received by a computer system. Also the process of entering data.

Input device. Any device that transmits data to a computer. Examples include keyboard, mouse, disk drive, and modem.

I/O. Input/Output. See *input, output*.

Instructional game. CAI that integrates content into a game format.

Integrated circuit (IC). A complete, complex electronic circuit etched onto a single piece of semiconducting material, usually silicon.

Integrated learning systems (ILS). Hardware and software systems, usually provided by a single vendor, that combine CMI and CAI for most or all of the curriculum.

Integrated software. A single computer program that can perform the functions of more than one major application and is capable of transferring data easily among its applications.

Integration. Use of computers to support and enhance curriculum goals and objectives in all content areas and in any appropriate manner so that the computer is no longer viewed as something special or unusual.

Intelligent CAI (ICAI). Any form of CAI in which branching decisions are made by program components based on artificial intelligence.

Intelligent tutoring system (ITS). Complex CAI that attempts to replicate a Socratic tutorial. The system teaches, then queries the learner, seeks to identify misconceptions, and remedies appropriately.

Interactive multimedia. Software which incorporates media beyond the computer, such as digitized video, still photos, sound, and text in a nonlinear environment. Also called *hypermedia*.

Interactive Video Instruction (IVI). Multimedia CAI in which a computer controls a videodisc player to show graphics and/or motion segments.

Interface. Circuits that connect separate parts of a computer system, such as a disk drive or printer controller, or even separate computers. Also, the means whereby humans and machines interact. See *graphical user interface*.

Interpreter. A program that translates and executes, one instruction at a time, another program written in a high-level language. (Cf. *compiler*.)

ISDN. *Integrated Services Digital Network*. An international communications-network architecture through which any two digital devices can communicate directly without need for a modem. ISDN also has sufficient *bandwidth* to carry digital video and other high volume data types.

Iteration.   Repeated execution of one or more statements in a program. See *loop.*

Joystick.   An input device that moves the screen cursor in correspondence with the user's movement of a vertical stick or lever. Used primarily for games.

K (Kilo).   A prefix used to represent 1000. Technically, in computing K means 2^{10} or 1024. Used to measure memory or disk capacity in bytes.

Keyboard.   The most common input device, consisting of an arrangement of keys resembling those of a typewriter with the addition of function and cursor-movement keys.

Keyboarding.   Use of a computer keyboard efficiently, without need to look at one's hand movements. Differs from touch-typing in that keyboarding does not involve page layout concerns.

Knowledge base.   A set of rules that contain the subject matter content and interrelationships in an *expert system.*

Knowledge engineering.   The analysis of a problem domain to determine the factors, procedures, and information that an expert considers in reaching a conclusion as the basis for an *expert system.*

Labels.   Alphanumeric or alphabetic data entered into a *worksheet* cell.

LAN.   *Local Area Network.* An interconnected group of computers that share applications, data files, and peripherals through a centralized *file server. Bus, ring,* and *star* configurations are common.

Language.   A set of words, syntax, and rules that allows humans to communicate with, and direct, a computer.

Laser disc.   Optical disc containing digital data that is read by a laser beam. Includes, digital compact discs (CDs) and analog videodiscs.

Laser printer.   Printer whose characters are formed using technology similar to photocopiers. Produces the highest-quality output among printers.

LCD panel.   *Liquid Crystal Display* device that connects to video output of a computer and lies on an overhead projector to project computer images onto a large screen for group viewing.

Light pen.   Input device resembling a ballpoint pen that is used to select from choices on a screen by touching it to the screen.

Linear tutorial.   Tutorial software with only a single path through the lesson for all students.

Links.   Connections among nodes in a hyper environment.

LISP.   *LISt Processor.* The dominant logic language used in artificial intelligence applications in the U.S. (Cf. *Prolog.*)

List.   On the Internet or Bitnet, an e-mail discussion group. Participants must subscribe, but there is rarely any subscription charge.

List processing.   Text manipulation in *Logo;* manipulation of symbols rather than numbers in logic programming such as using *LISP.*

Local area network.   See *LAN.*

Logical constructs. Structural elements of a computer program, such as *sequence, selection,* and *iteration.*

Logo. A high-level language and computer environment based on the theories of Swiss psychologist Jean Piaget and derived from the artificial intelligence language LISP. Created by an MIT team headed by Seymour Papert. Emphasizes learning by discovery in a computer-based microworld.

Loop. A sequence of operations repeated within a program. See *iteration.*

Low-level language. Computer language closely related to a specific computer type; e.g., machine language, assembler language.

Machine language. Binary coded instructions that a computer can process without any form of translation.

Mainframe computer. A large computer system capable of operating at extremely fast speeds, handling large volumes of data, and servicing many users simultaneously.

Marginalia. Those elements of a publication that appear in the margins of a page, e.g., marginal glosses, headers, page numbering.

Mark sense scanner. An input device that "reads" data into a computer by scanning specially prepared sheets marked with pencil in designated areas, such as test answer sheets.

Mastery learning. The educational premise that all students can achieve to a high level under the right conditions.

Math coprocessor. A chip that enhances the processing power of a microcomputer through its advanced mathematical capabilities. Also called an *FPU.*

Mega. Prefix that represents one million. Hard disk capacities are given in megabytes (MB).

Memex. Vannevar Bush's hypothetical "memory extender" that was the conceptual forefather of interactive multimedia systems.

Memory. A computer's capacity to store data as patterns of ones and zeros. Also the chips and storage devices that contain the data.

Microcomputer. A small computer system usually containing only a single microprocessor and intended for individual use.

Microelectronics. Miniaturized electronic components, such as the chips used in computers.

Microprocessor. See *CPU.*

Middle-level language. A language such as C that offers the advantages of both low- and high-level languages while minimizing their disadvantages.

Modem. Computer peripheral that *MO*dulates/ *DEM*odulates information, enabling digital computers to communicate over analog telephone lines.

Monitor. Output device that displays text and graphics on a screen, similar to a high-quality TV.

Mouse. A hand-held input device that is moved on a flat surface to position the screen cursor and to select what is beneath the cursor with a button click.

MPC. *Multimedia Personal Computer.* Designation accorded MS-DOS computers that meet specifications that include a CD-ROM drive, sound circuitry, graphics capability, and so forth to accommodate interactive multimedia software.

Multimedia. Any system that combines two or more media into a single product or presentation, e.g., sound filmstrips, videos, motion pictures, TV. There is no inherent computer component.

Multimedia CAI. See *interactive multimedia*.

Network. See *computer network*.

Neural Network. A type of artificial intelligence program that is patterned after the human brain and "learns" from its experiences, rather than requiring programming of its knowledge base.

Node. Basic organizational unit of hyper environments. In typical interactive multimedia/hypermedia, equivalent to a single screen.

Nonvolatile. Term applied to memory chips that are permanently programmed and thus do not lose their contents when the system is turned off.

Object code. Machine-language output of a compiler.

Object-oriented software. Software in which each screen consists of discrete objects, such as areas of text and graphics, that can be created and edited independently of one another, e.g., most hypermedia software.

On-line. Ability of a user to gain immediate access to data through a computer system; the act of being connected to a remote computer system such as through an information service.

OCR. *Optical Character Recognition.* The process by which specialized software attempts to convert the graphic image of text created by a scanner into a true text file or word processor document for manipulation.

Operating system. Software that controls and manages a computer system and its various peripheral devices.

Optical disc. Any disc format from which the data are read by laser beam, e.g., CDs, CD-ROM, laser video discs, photo CDs.

Optical character recognition. See *OCR*.

Optical scanner. An input device that "reads" pages of text and graphics and converts them into computer files.

Output. Information sent from the CPU after processing to any peripheral device.

Output device. Any peripheral capable of receiving output from a computer, e.g., monitor, printer, disk drive, modem.

Overlay card. Computer circuit boards that can display full-motion digital video on a computer monitor simultaneously with normal text and graphics.

Parallel. Mode of data transmission in which multiple bits are transmitted simultaneously through sets of lines, such as from computer to printer. (Cf. *serial*.)

Pascal. A high-level language known for features that promote structured programming. Popular in computer science instruction. Named for 17th-century French mathematician Blaise Pascal.

Peripheral. Any piece of auxiliary hardware, such as a printer, modem, or scanner.

Performance support system. A combination of an expert system and other software applications to assist a human on the job, when and where aid is needed, in the most useful form possible. Also called electronic performance support system.

PILOT. A CAI authoring language designed to be very easy to learn and use.

Piracy. Making and/or using copies of software beyond those that the specific software license agreement permits.

PLATO. A computer-based educational system and related software developed at the University of Illinois for delivering CAI to multiple remote learners.

Plotter. Output device that uses pens to create high-resolution graphic images and text, in multiple colors if desired.

PLV. Production *Level Video*. Highest quality DVI format, which only labs can produce. Comparable to VCR image quality. (Cf. *RTV*.)

Points. Unit of measure for the height of typeface characters, one point being approximately 1/72 of an inch.

Port. Connecting point on a computer or peripheral, e.g., serial port, modem port, monitor port.

Presentation graphics. Software for production of graphics screens combining text and images which may then be printed or, more commonly, displayed on screen as an alternative to traditional overhead transparencies.

Prewriting. Activities that precede the actual start of composition that are intended to stimulate the writer's creativity.

Primitive. Any word that the Logo language understands under all circumstances, such as FORWARD; the fundamental Logo vocabulary.

Print graphics. Software for production of hard copy graphics, e.g., *Print Shop.*

Printer. Output device that produces hard copy on paper or transparency plastic.

Problem solving software. CAI intended to help learners to develop their critical thinking skills in hopes of transfer to other contexts.

Procedure. Commands in a programming language, such as Logo primitives, that are grouped together and given a name. Together they cause a complete action to occur, such as drawing a box, when the name is used as a command.

Process approach. A method of teaching writing which focuses on the total act of writing, from prewriting through completion, rather than only on the final document.

Program. A series of instructions that direct and control a computer to perform a desired task.

Programmer. Person who writes computer programs.

Programming. Planning and creating a new computer program using some language or software development tool.

Programming language. The words, structure, and syntax used to communicate intelligible instructions to a computer.

PROLOG. *PRO*gramming in *LOG*ic. A language popular in Europe and Japan for work in artificial intelligence. (Cf. *LISP*.)

Prompt. A symbol on the monitor screen that informs the user that the computer is ready for further input.

Prompt area. That location within a spreadsheet's display where the user's current typing is displayed.

Public Domain. Not copyrighted. Software legally copiable by anyone.

RAM. *Random Access Memory.* Memory chips in a computer system that accept and retain data temporarily, but lose it when the system is shut off. See *volatile.* (Cf. *ROM.*)

RBBS. *Remote Bulletin Board System.* Computer system set up for posting and exchanging of messages and software among its users.

Real time. Processing of data instantly as it is available, as in digitizing video at full running speed. In telecommunications, connection to other users who are themselves currently on-line on the network, as opposed to e-mail, which does not require an active recipient.

Rebus. A story in which some words are replaced by images of the item, e.g. replace "cow" with a graphic of a cow.

Record. A group of related fields containing information that is a logical unit, e.g. all data on Jane Doe. See also *field, file.*

Recursion. The ability to use a procedure as part of its own definition.

Relational. Database software that can link multiple files together based on a common "key."

Research network. National or international network linking researchers and other users, such as Internet, Bitnet, and ARPANET.

Restructuring. Reorganizing schools at a deeper, more fundamental level than just typical curriculum changes, so that the organization better serves the needs of learners. More involved than "school reform."

ROM. *Read Only Memory.* Nonvolatile memory chips that are programmed by the manufacturer. The computer system can read their contents, but cannot write to them. (Cf. *RAM.*)

RTV. *Real-Time Video.* Type of DVI files that can be produced with appropriate boards in a PC, without services of a lab. Approaches VCR quality. (Cf. *PLV.*)

Sans serif. A plain typeface lacking ornamentation at the ends of the lines of the characters, e.g. Univers. (Cf. *serif.*)

Scanner An input device that "reads" existing materials such as pages of text or pictures and creates computer files from them. Also called *optical scanner.*

Script. Instructions that determine the action of a hypermedia button.

Serial. Mode of data transmission in which data are transferred one bit at a time in sequence. (Cf. *parallel.*)

Serif. A typeface with extra lines or curves at the end of the essential lines of each character, e.g., Times Roman. (Cf. *sans serif.*)

Shareware. Software distributed on a pay-if-you-like-it basis.

Simulation. Form of CAI in which the learner assumes a role to play within a structured environment that is an interactive model of some "reality."

Software. The programs that cause a computer system to perform desired tasks.

Source code. Computer instructions written in some language.

Special characters. Characters on a keyboard that are neither numbers nor letters, e.g., punctuation marks.

Spreadsheet. An electronic tabular workspace that is used to enter and manipulate data, especially numeric data.

SQL. *Structured Query Language*. An interface in advanced database software that permits access to data on differing computer types with common commands. (Cf. *worksheet*.)

Stack. Collection of related screens ("cards") in *HyperCard* among which the user can move about in a non-linear manner. Called a *book* in *Toolbook* and a *folder* in *Linkway*. Similar to a database file.

Statements. The basic vocabulary items of a programming language.

Storage devices. Floppy, optical, and hard disk drives that provide large amounts of data storage external to the CPU, RAM, and ROM.

Stored program control. The concept that a computer should be general-purpose and that a program, not its wiring pattern, should control it.

Streamer. A high-speed tape drive with large capacity; used for hard disk backup.

Structured programming. Programming using a limited set of logical constructs, minimal branching, modularity, and thorough documentation.

Style. In desktop publishing, variations in the appearance of a character without changing typeface or points, e.g., bold, italic.

Support tools. Special-purpose software that assists the user to do some task more efficiently than by traditional means, e.g., puzzle and test generators.

Survival skills. Those basic computer skills that students must gain to begin to use a computer, such as booting, diskette formatting, mouse movement.

Syntax. The required form or structure for the statements of a computer language; the rules governing use of a language.

Sysop. The *sys*tem *op*erator of a remote bulletin board system (RBBS).

Tape drive. An external storage device that writes to and reads from magnetic tape similar to audio tape. Used for backup of large volumes of data.

Technology coordinator. Individual in an organization designated as responsible for overseeing technology usage and assisting current and potential users to meet their own needs.

Telecommunications. Communication by telephone lines that does not necessarily involve computers and modems.

Telecomputing. Telecommunications specifically connecting computers over telephone lines, including all exchanges between them.

Template. A reusable master plan for a word-processor document, worksheet, presentation graphics screen, or desktop-published material.

Text editor. Computer program for editing of text, but with much more limited functions than a word processor. Included within some publishing software and within MS-DOS.

Tool software. See *applications software*.

Top-down design. Development of a program starting with the overall goal and refining it into subparts until each part at the lowest level is trivial to program.

Touch screen. A special monitor that allows the user to input information by touching designated areas on the screen.

Turtlegraphics. Graphics created by a robotic or cybernetic turtle, as implemented in the Logo environment.

Tutorial. A form of CAI in which the computer initiates and carries on a dialogue with the learner, presenting information, posing questions, and providing feedback. (Cf. *drill and practice.*)

Typeface. In typography and desktop publishing, the unique shape of the letters that comprise any given character set, e.g., `Courier`, Times Roman.

Typeface family. See *style.*

Unit record. Data specific to one instance, such as the census data for an individual. Also the cards developed by Hollerith to record such data in the early days of automated data processing.

Unix. Operating system originally for minicomputers, now available on micros, noted for ability to execute multiple tasks simultaneously.

Upload. To transfer information from one's own computer to a remote computer. (Cf. *download.*)

Values. Numbers entered into a worksheet cell; numeric data.

Video disc. See *laser disc.*

Virtual reality (VR). An computer-generated microworld with which a user may interact as if it were real. Often requires special viewing helmets and controls such as a wired glove.

Virus. A program planned and written to cause mischief or damage to a computer system. Can spread through computer networks, bulletin board systems, and from infected diskettes.

Visual cueing. Using design elements (such as lines) in desktop publishing to help the reader locate and distinguish elements of the page.

Voice recognition. Ability of a computer to respond to spoken commands.

Voice synthesizer. Output device that converts computer output into intelligible speech, especially useful for the visually impaired.

Volatile. Term applied to memory chips that retain data only so long as the system is turned on, e.g., RAM.

VR. See *virtual reality.*

WAN. *Wide Area Network.* A network that spans a large area, necessitating connections through dedicated telephone lines rather than direct cabling. (Cf. *LAN.*)

Wandering. Meandering aimlessly through a hyper environment. Often raised as a potential weakness of hypermedia as a learning tool.

WIMP. Term sometimes applied to graphical user interfaces, denoting the major components of a GUI, namely *W*indows, *I*cons, *M*ouse, and *P*ointer.

Window. A portion of the computer screen, used for a different purpose than the rest of the screen, such as a help window or a space in which to work in a different application within integrated software.

Workgroup. A type of computer network in which each computer is connected to the group by cable, but is also fully functional as an independent work station. Files are not stored centrally on a file server. (Cf. *LAN.*)

Word processing. The act of using a word processor to generate written materials.

Word processor. Software for writing, editing, revising, formatting, and printing text. Also a computer running such software, or a skilled user of such a system.

Word wrap. In word processing, the automatic arrangement of text to fit within the margins established for the document, such as moving words that are too long for the line on which they began to a new line.

Worksheet. A specific application of a spreadsheet, such as the student records for one class or one specific budget. Often used as a synonym for spreadsheet.

WORM. (*Write Once Read Many*) A type of optical drive that can both read and write files. The files cannot be erased and the disc cannot be reused.

Writing aids. Software such as spelling checkers, thesauruses, and grammar or style analysts, which extend the composition assistance provided by a word processor.

Index

Page numbers followed by f denote figures.

Engelbart, Douglas, 216
Enhancement tools, for desktop publishing, 145–146
ENIAC, 9–10
Environment
  hyper, 217, 217f
  interactive multimedia, 216–219
  Logo, establishment of, 331–335
  teaching/learning, and word processing, 42–43
The Environment, 195
EPIE, 252, 445
  Integrated Instructional Information Resource (I.I.I.R), 65, 399
EPIEgram, 252
Equity issues, and computer technology, 410–411
Erase, 22
Erase function
  spreadsheet, 89
  word processor, 32, 32f
ERIC, 74, 171
Ethernet, 160
  definition of, 453
Ethics, and computer technology, 406–409
Evaluation. *See* Courseware evaluation
Excel, 130
Expert systems, 289–292, 290f
  controversies over, 291
  definition of, 453
  in education, 291–292
Expert system shell, 292, 364, 365f
  definition of, 453
Exploration Models, 230–231
Export, 129
  definition of, 453

Facilities, and technology implementation, 394f, 394–396
Facts on File News Digest CD-ROM 1980–1991, 233
Fast food comparisons, spreadsheets for, 100
Feedback, providing, 259
FIDOnet, 173
Field, 59, 60f
  definition of, 453
Fields of Learning, 232
Fifty States database, 72, 74
File, 8, 59, 60f, 61
  concepts of, 59–61
  creation of, 63–65
  definition of, 453
File server, 159
  definition of, 453

File sharing, 129
File transfer protocols, for telecommunications, 166–167
File transformation, 129
Filing system, 61. *See also* Databases; Data manager(s)
  definition of, 453
First generation, of computers, 10–11
First National Item Bank & Test Development System, 75
Flatbed scanners, 111
Floppy disk, 18
  definition of, 452
Floppy disk drives, 18
Florida Department of Education, @Micro evaluation project, 252
Florida-England Connection Project, 175
Florida Information Resources Network, 252
Florida State University, CAI research, 186
Flowchart
  definition of, 453
  example of, 209, 210f
  symbols, 308, 309f
Flowcharting, 308–311
  discussion of, 309–310
Flyers, produced with desktop publishing program, 148–150, 149f
FOL. *See Fields of Learning*
Foreign Policy, 195
Formal logic, 10
Format function, 22
  spreadsheet, 89
FormTool, 124
Form tools, 124
Formula, in spreadsheets, 86, 88–89
  definition of, 453
FORTRAN, 349–351
  definition of, 453
  problem solution in, 349, 350f
Forum, in telecommunications, 169
  definition of, 453
Fourth generation, 11–12
FPU (floating point unit). *See* Math coprocessor
Frames, definition of, 453–454
Framework, 130
FrEdBase, 62, 73
FrEdMail, 173
FrEdWriter, 46
Free Educational Electronic Mail Network (FrEdMail), 173
Freehand, 109
Freeware, definition of, 454

Function(s)
definition of, 454
spreadsheet, 89
word processor, 31–33, 32f–34f
The Function Analyzer, 201
The Function Supposer, 201
Fund(s), allocation of, 397–398
Funding, 397
Fundraisers, spreadsheets for, 99
Fuzzy logic, 290
definition of, 454

Games. *See* Instructional games
Game theory, 288
Gender inequities, and computer technology, 410
The Geometric Supposer, 201
George Washington University, computer applications skills project, 232–233
GeoWorld, 74
Gigabyte, 18
Grade book, 122–123
spreadsheet, 96–98
Gradebook Plus 6.0, 122
Grade Machine, 122
Grammar checkers, 36–37, 37f
Grammatik, 36, 121
Graphical Analysis, 114
Graphical user interface, 21, 21f, 86–87, 87f, 105, 427–428
definition of, 454
A Graphic Approach to Calculus, 201
Graphic design skills, for desktop publishing, 147–148
Graphic primitives, 323–324
Graphics, 104–116
definition of, 454
drawing programs, 109–111
presentation, 108–109
definition of, 459
print, 105–108
definition of, 459
Graphics control, for desktop publishing, 144–145
Graphics pad/tablet, 14, 15f
definition of, 454
Graphing, 94, 94f
in desktop publishing, 144
software, 113–116, 114f–115f
Graph-in-the-Box Executive, 114
Graph Wiz, 114
Graves, Donald, 38
Green Blobs and Graphing Equations, 201
Group projects, word processors for, 47–48

GTV: A Geographic Perspective on American History, 231, 235
GUI. *See* Graphical user interface

Hacker, 408
definition of, 454
Hand scanners, 111, 112f
Hands-On AppleWorks, 137
Hands-On ClarisWorks, 137
Hands-on evaluation, of courseware, 253–254
Hard copy, 16
definition of, 454
Hard disk, definition of, 454
Hard disk drives, 18
removable, 19
Hardware, 13f, 13–19. *See also specific component*
budget, allocation of, 398
choice of, 392–394
definition of, 20, 454
for desktop publishing, 147
digitizing, 223–224
future of, 423–427
interactive multimedia, 219–224
telecommunications, 165–166, 166f
Harvard Educational Technology Center, 137
Harvard University, Department of Classics, *Perseus* project, 232
Health issues, with computer technology, 405
High density (HD) floppy disk, 18
High-level language, 316–318, 348
definition of, 454
High-Performance Computing Act of 1991, 163
High school mathematics, spreadsheets for, 98
History in Motion: Milestones of the 20th Century, 232
Hollerith, Hermann, 8
Hollerith Tabulating Machine Company, 8
Hometown: Local Area Studies, 74
Host, 160
definition of, 454
Human intelligence, 287
Hyper, definition of, 454
HyperCard, 62, 74, 109–110, 169, 225–226, 231–232, 236, 266, 365–367, 367f, 454
Hyper environment, 217, 217f
Hypermedia, 65. *See also* Interactive multimedia